The Complete Manager

THE COMPLETE MANAGER

Edited by
Dennis Lock and Nigel Farrow

Wildwood House

First published as *The Gower Handbook of Management* 1983

Abridged paperback edition with revisions published in 1986 by
Wildwood House Limited
Gower House, Croft Road
Aldershot, Hants GU11 3HR
England

The Complete Manager
1. Management
I. Lock, Dennis II. Farrow, Nigel III. The Gower handbook of management
658 HD31

ISBN 0-7045-0518-5

Printed in Great Britain at the Alden Press, Oxford

Contents

Illustrations xiii
The Complete Manager, by *Nigel Farrow* xvii

INTRODUCTION

1 **Principles of Management** 3
Philip Sadler
The Beginnings of Management Thought — The Pre-War Management Writers — Management Theory in the Post-War Era — Modern Management Principles — Further Reading

PART 1 FINANCIAL MANAGEMENT

2 **Sources of Finance** 17
Stephen Badger
Why Capital may be Required — Type of Capital Required — Sources of Long-Term Finance for Unlisted Companies — Going Public — Sources of Long-Term Finance for Listed Companies — Methods of Issue with a Listing — Other Methods of Supplementing Cash Flow — Looking at the Overall Capital Structure — Further Reading

3 **The Annual Accounts** 32
W P Ridley
Accounting Requirements of the Companies Acts — Standard Presentation — The Directors' Report — Organisation of Information —

Judging a Company from its Accounts — Profit and Loss Account for Pangloss PLC — Return to Shareholders — Trading Prospects — Balance Sheet for Pangloss PLC — Inflation Accounting — Further Reading

4 **Budgetary Control** 52
Alan R Leaper
What is a Budget? — Budget Centres — Compiling a Budget — Controlling the Plan — Flexible Budgets — Use of Computers — Zero-base Budgeting — Installing the System — Conclusions — Further Reading

5 **Managing Working Capital** 69
Leon Simons
Liquidity — Profitability — Solvency — Further Reading

6 **Cost Accounting** 82
R M S Wilson
The Nature of Cost Accounting — Collection of Cost Data — Absorption Costing — Apportionment of Overheads — Absorption of Overheads — Over and Under Recovery — Fixed and Variable Overhead Rates — Why Absorb Overheads? — Marginal Costing — Absorption Costing versus Direct Costing — Standing Costing — Checklist on Cost Accounting — Summary — Further Reading

PART 2 MARKETING AND SALES MANAGEMENT

7 **Marketing Planning** 111
John Stapleton
Standards for Measuring Performance — The New Product Development Programme — Determining Company Objectives — Profit is the First Operating Expense — Developing the Market Plan — Bias Towards One's Own Company — Contingency Planning — Definition of the Total Market — Control of Distribution — Monitoring the Market Plan — Investment in Company Resources — Communicating Profit Responsibility

8 **Market Research** 124
Colin McDonald
The Growth of Market Research — The Occasions for Market Research — Why Research at All? — Research Methods — Analysis, Interpretation and Use

9 Advertising 142

John Hobson

Advertising as a Marketing Activity — Advertising Objectives and Techniques — Tactics — Advertising and Market Research — Developing Image and Subjective Values — Techniques of Advertising — The Unique Selling Proposition — The Advertising Campaign — The Strategic Framework of Advertising — Media Planning — The Agency Relationship — Ethics — Further Reading

10 Sales Promotion 155

Christian Petersen

What is Sales Promotion? — Sales Promotion Media — Special Targets — International Sales Promotion — Researching and Evaluating Sales Promotions — Summing Up — Further Reading

11 Pricing 167

Bryan Atkin

Economic Theory and the Practical Businessman — Pricing Policy, Strategy and Tactics — Pricing Policies and Techniques — Aids to Pricing — Devising Pricing Strategy and Tactics — Discounts and Discounting — Pricing and New Product Planning — Pricing and Product Lines — Summary — References and Further Reading

12 Distribution Channels 199

Jack Wheatley

Planning for Distribution — The Wholesaler — The Retail Trades — The Commodity Market — Agents, Brokers and Merchants — Exporting — Industrial Distribution — Conclusion — Further Reading

13 Managing a Sales Force 209

M T Wilson

How to Plan the Sales Operation — How to Organise the Sales Force — Training the Sales Team — How to Motivate the Sales Force — How to Control the Sales Operation — Further Reading

PART 3 PURCHASING AND INVENTORY MANAGEMENT

14 Procurement Policy 225

Peter Baily

Procurement Strategies — Input Management — Materials Management — Purchasing and Quality Assurance — References and Further Reading

15 Purchasing Procedures **233**
Peter Baily
Initiation — Supplier Selection — The Contract Stage — Small Order Procedures — The Completion Stage — References and Further Reading

PART 4 PRODUCTION MANAGEMENT

16 Planning for Production **247**
J Mapes and C C New
The Production Management Task — The Planning of Production — Strategic Planning — Forecasting Demand — The Make or Buy Decision — Preparing an Operating Plan — Further Reading

17 Production Control **260**
Peter Jackson
Differences Between Systems — Loading and Scheduling Work — Loading Methods — Provisioning — Monitoring and Progressing — Management Control Information — Paperwork — Computers — Further Reading

18 Quality Control **276**
David Desmond
Principles — Organisation — Requirements — Using Control Charts — The Quality Standard — A Procedure for Estimating the Quality Standard — Further Reading

19 Maintenance **289**
E N White
Terotechnology — Maintenance Planning and Control — Computer-controlled Systems — Condition-based Maintenance — Capital Project Management — Further Reading

PART 5 ADMINISTRATION

20 Company Law **311**
F W Rose
Formation of a Public Limited Company — Capital and Shares — Membership — Meetings — Directors — Provision for Employees — Dividends — Insider Dealing — Further Reading

21 **Office Services** 325
R S Henderson
Organisation of Office Services — Office Layouts — Reprographics — Microfilming — Telephones — Security and Safety — Building Maintenance — Centralised Services — Further Reading

22 **Managing Information** 339
R E Wiggins
Information and the Organisation — Information: its Acquisition and Value — Sources of Information — Information Resource Management — Information and Library Services — Technological Aids — Further Reading

23 **Managing the Electronic Office** 364
Ted Bennett and Garfield Collins
Word Processing — Communications — Document Storage and Data Retrieval — A Look Ahead — Implementing the Changes — Three Case Studies — Further Reading

24 **Warehouse Operation and Management** 378
Ken Firth
Modern Warehousing — Load Unitisation — Utilisation of the Warehouse Cube — Minimising Movement — Paperwork Reduction — Receiving and Dispatch — Conclusion — Further Reading

PART 6 HUMAN RESOURCE MANAGEMENT

25 **Recruitment and Selection** 399
P T Humphrey
Basic Planning and Procedure — Stage One: The Run Up — Stage Two: Face-to-Face: The Employment Interview — Stage Three: The Follow-Through — Further Reading — Appendix: The IPM Recruitment Code

26 **Salary Management** 425
Irene Innes
Example of a Salary Policy Statement — Job Descriptions — Job Evaluation — Salary Bands/Grades — Salary Surveys — Use of Graphs — Deciding How Much to Pay — Rate for Age — Salary Anomalies — Employee Benefits — Departmental Budgets — Performance — Salary Reviews — Management Salaries — Further Reading

27 **Wage Management** 442
Irene Innes
Changing a Wage Structure — Job Evaluation — Legislation — Costing — Financing the Wage Structure — Designing the Wage Structure — Incentive Element — Added Value — Productivity Agreements — Single Status — Communication — Supervisory Structure — Example of a Wage Policy Statement — Checklist: Changing a Wage Structure — Further Reading

28 **Working Conditions** 465
Patricia George
Health and Safety at Work Act 1974 — The Factories Act — Offices, Shops and Railways Premises Act — Regulations — Codes of Practice — Employers' Liability — Fire Precautions Act 1971 — Checklist of Notices to be Posted — Checklist of Notices to be Sent to Factory Inspector or Other Authority — Checklist of Registers to be Kept — Advice and Further Information — Further Reading

29 **Industrial Training** 480
Derek Torrington
The Need for Training in Companies — Administering the Training Function — Training for Different Categories of Employee — Training Methods — Further Reading

30 **Employee Relations** 492
Derek Torrington and J L Cookson
Trade Union Recognition — Arrangements with Trade Unions — State Agencies — Further Reading

31 **Redundancy and Redeployment** 504
Peter Mumford and Tom Carew
Redundancy Policy — Tribunals — Rebates from the Redundancy Fund — Standard Procedures — Employment Services and Agencies — Redeployment — Further Reading

PART 7 THE SKILLS OF MANAGEMENT

32 **Management Self-Development** 527
Michael Williams
Self-Development in Theory and Practice — Self-Development: Disclosure and Feedback — The 'Fly-on-the-Wall' — Self-Development:

Case Study in Activity Analysis — Achievement Objectives as a Means for Self-Development — Some Vehicles for Self-Development — Sources and Resources — Further Reading

33 Career Planning **548**
Michael Williams
Identifying the 'Plus-Me' and 'Plus-Job' — Career Transitions — What Can the Individual Manager Do About Career Progression? — Further Reading

34 Personal Organisation **562**
A N Welsh
The Need for Personal Organisation — Creating a List — The Constraint of Time — Wasted Time — Delegation — Subordinates' Time — Improvements — Further Reading

35 Negotiating **572**
Bill Scott
Negotiating Towards Agreement — Negotiating To Independent Advantage — Fighting — Summary — Further Reading

36 Effective Communication **588**
Gordon Bell
Speaking — Report Writing — Meetings — Further Reading

Index **613**

Illustrations

Figures

2.1 Uses of funds by individuals and institutions 21
2.2 Selected sources of capital funds for industrial and commercial companies 22
3.1 Profit and loss account of a limited company as presented to its management 33
3.2 The accounts shown in Figure 3.1 in the form to be filed with the Registrar 34
3.3 Format of the statutory profit and loss account 36
3.4 Presentation of taxation details 37
3.5 Format of the statutory balance sheet 38–9
3.6 Abbreviated profit and loss account of Pangloss PLC 43
3.7 Earnings, dividends and retentions of Pangloss PLC 44
3.8 Performance ratios for Pangloss PLC 45
3.9 Abbreviated 1982 balance sheet for Pangloss PLC 46
3.10 The impact of current cost accounting adjustments 48–9
3.11 Profit and loss account after current cost adjustments 51
4.1 Example of a profit and loss statement with provision for budgets and standards 59
4.2 Example of fixed budgeting 62
4.3 Example of flexible budgeting 63
5.1 Group balance sheet for ABC PLC 71
5.2 Profit and loss account for ABC PLC 72
6.1 Overhead apportionment and absorption 93
6.2 Over- and under-recovered overheads 95
6.3 Monthly and annual overhead rates 96
6.4 Flexible overhead budget 97
6.5 Combined flexible overhead budget 97
6.6 Cost-plus pricing 99
6.7 Contributed margin 100
6.8 Cost, profit and sales revenue summary 101
6.9 Revised cost, profit and revenue summary - 1 101

6.10	Revised cost, profit and sales revenue summary - 2	102
6.11	Contribution margin statement	102
8.1	Market research appropriate to different purposes	131
11.1	Simple breakeven chart	168
11.2	Evaluation of entry price strategy	187
11.3	Types of discount	192–3
14.1	Materials management reorganisation	229
15.1	Outline of standard purchase procedure	234
15.2	Purchase requisition	235
15.3	Travelling requisition	236
15.4	Request for quotations (enquiry)	238
15.5	Follow-up copy of purchase order	244
16.1	Time-scale for planning decisions	248
16.2	Requirements for market success	251
16.3	Forecast based on a 5-period moving average	253
16.4	Forecast based on exponential smoothing	254
16.5	Production stage chart for pigment manufacture	256
17.1	A job sequence loading chart	263
17.2	Works order	271
17.3	Requisition, job ticket and stores receipt note	272
17.4	Production control and documentation package	273
18.1	Quality management checklist	279
18.2	Quality control flow diagram	281
18.3	Number defective control chart	283
18.4	Control limits for number defective charts	284
19.1	A terotechnology system	290
19.2	Terotechnology considerations in a life cycle	292
19.3	Components of a planned maintenance system	294
19.4	Typical maintenance control system	295
19.5	Maintenance control with trigger system	297
19.6	Record of downtime	299
19.7	Effect on maintenance investments	305
19.8	Factors affecting maintenance efficiency adversely	307
19.9	A maintenance consultant in a project team	308
21.1	The scope of office services	327
21.2	An office services departmental organisation	328
22.1	Information types	340
22.2	Information systems for different activities	341
22.3	Sources of information - a general outline	343
22.4	Traditional repositories for information	344
22.5	Item entry edge-punched card	352
22.6	Terminal digit term entry cards	353
22.7	Optical coincidence (Peek-a-boo) term entry cards	354
22.8	Integrated service network	359
23.1	Productivity improvements from word processing	374
23.2	Example of an evolutionary approach to a combined word processing, data processing and microfilm system	375

23.3	Combined text and voice communications	377
24.1	Cartons stacked on pallets	380
24.2	Simple flow diagram for palletised bulk storage design	383
24.3	Simple block stack	384
24.4	Drive-in racking	386
24.5	Very narrow aisle racking and truck	388
24.6	High-bay warehouse	389
24.7	Second level order-picker	391
24.8	Base location order-picking system	392
24.9	Horizontal carousel order-picking machine	394
24.10	General view of a modern loading bay	395
25.1	Processing of applications	409
25.2	Interview notes	416
25.3	Initial assessment and interview summary	417
26.1	Job questionnaire	430–31
26.2	Ranking chart	433
26.3	Job evaluation matrix	434
26.4	Salary structure	435
26.5	Comparison of old and new salary structures	437
26.6	Salary review form	440
27.1	Scattergram of earnings (excluding overtime)	448
27.2	Example of a wage structure of the Philips Premium Pay Plan type	452
31.1	Formal notice required	511
31.2	Redundancy pay	512
31.3	Scale of pension damage	514
31.4	Factors affecting the time taken to find a new job	521
32.1	Personal growth	530
32.2	Hierarchical support needed for change to be implemented	532
23.3	Format for activity log	536
32.4	Activity log compiled for John Walton, Transport Manager	539–40
32.5	The extent to which objective setting between superiors and subordinates may be mandatory or discretionary	541
32.6	Scope for self-development within managerial jobs	544
33.1	The influence of personal ambition and organisation needs on career development	549
33.2	Typical managerial career progression	550
33.3	Impact of 'middlescence' on career path	551
33.4	Influence of technological or major organisation developments upon career path	552
33.5	Shift in the nature of primary work	553
33.6	Changing patterns of skills required to match primary work shift	554
33.7	Evolving needs for different skills in 'linear' career progression	555
33.8	The 'plus-me' exercise	556–7

33.9	The 'plus-job'	558
33.10	The crucial career move	559
34.1	Checklist for reviewing your function	564
34.2	Specimen manager's diary sheet	566
34.3	Manager's work distribution chart	567
36.1	Axes for graph of value and interest against time	595
36.2	Graph of value and interest against time	596
36.3	Four ways of displaying a set of numerical results	603–5

The complete manager

Nigel Farrow

Merlin, wizard and medieval management consultant, is sitting in his study. He is wrestling with one of his most difficult assignments: the tuition of the future King Arthur in the arts of management.

The course is full of practical work. Using his magical powers and the experience of already having lived in the future, Merlin often projects himself and King Arthur into the twentieth century in order to work on real business problems. Together they have designed a small car for British Leyland, which has taken 60 per cent of the Japanese domestic market. They have negotiated one-man-one-job agreements in the British newspaper industry and modernised French agriculture. They have found an uncontested site for the third London airport and re-financed Poland. In 1933 they bought IBM and in 1965 they sold Rolls Royce. Merlin believes in the case study method.

But Arthur notices that whenever a particularly difficult issue arises, Merlin consults a big book which lies on his desk, along with his portable crucible, philosopher's stone, and bottled bat's blood.

Arthur *Merlin, please tell me what's in that big paperback you keep referring to? Is it a book of spells?*

Merlin No, it's *The Complete Manager*, which I acquired on a quick trip to 1986. ... There's no wizardry in it, just sound advice on almost every aspect of management.

Arthur *But was it written by a wizard?*

Merlin Not by a wizard, but by many experts. Over 35 of them.

Arthur *(after some thought) – Merlin, there's something that's been troubling me. If there are going to be so many management experts in those days-*

yet-to-come and so much written and published on management and so many people tutored in the arts of management, why will they have so much trouble with their businesses?

Merlin Because they will attempt so much. It will be an heroic age. Ordinary managers, without the weapons of social privilege or personal wealth, will be required to ride out as champions of the whole kingdom to defeat poverty, ignorance and sloth.

Arthur *You make these managers sound like a new order of chivalry. I thought that they would be arriving as bag-men and the servants of bag-men. People who will be out to line their own pockets.*

Merlin It may well start like that, but it will have become something very different by the time *The Complete Manager* is written. I see that a little yet-to-be-history lesson is required.

First, I will let you into a secret about the system of free business enterprise, which by some will be called 'capitalism'. Contrary to reports, mostly put about by its own practitioners, it will be a tremendous success. By the twentieth century, it will provide the material means of feeding, housing and clothing huge populations. It will sustain individuals and groups of individuals regardless of their origins and promote their fortunes largely on the basis of their usefulness to society. It will transmit wealth and knowledge around the world. It will finance science and encourage the arts. In fact, it will be far too successful for its own good.

Arthur *What do you mean?*

Merlin Because of its success, governments and individuals will link their hopes and programmes for social development to its economic performance. By the middle of the twentieth century, business will be the main source of income in work and in retirement for most men and many women. Through taxation, business will contribute massively to the welfare services of the community, as well as developing many health, educational and housing schemes of its own. Through legislation, business will be obliged to advance racial and sexual equality, protect the natural world and train the young. Not content with the controls of taxation and legislation, governments will force themselves into partnership with business so as to be able to direct its resources to the achievement of their social goals.

Arthur *But will this be a bad thing? If, as you tell me, the Age of Chivalry cannot last forever, then the Age of Business Enterprise sounds as though it will provide a better life for most people than many of the ages that will come between now and then.*

Merlin Indeed it will. And that's the point. Having – as another old wizard will say – never had it so good, people and their popularly elected governments will seek to extract from business enterprise ever better conditions of living. You only have to look at the contents of this book (*he taps The Complete Manager*) to see that by the late twentieth century the manager will have taken over many of the functions performed in previous ages by the feudal lord, the priest, the teacher, the money-lender, the physician, the lawyer, the watchman and even (*he glances with suspicion at the section on market research*) the astrologer.

Arthur *Are you saying that the decline of some businesses in the late twentieth century is therefore not the responsibility of the managers but the fault of society?*

Merlin Not entirely, of course not. Management incompetence, fraud and idleness will contribute their share of failures, as in all other occupations. But the feeling of weakness that you have observed in some areas of business and government during our visits to the mid-to-late twentieth century is in large part a reflection of managers' frustration with their social roles and people's disappointment at the failure to fulfil their expectations. Indeed, some businesses will fail just because the original purposes and skills of business management – buying, making, selling – will be lost in a mass of unproductive administration. For a while, this trend will be encouraged by the very people who should stand out against it – the Business Schoolmen. They will be teaching high finance to those who need low cunning; planning to those who should be doing; organisational theory to those who need personal skills. It will take a great recession in business to bring some of them back to teaching the basic arts.

Arthur *Merlin, you said that the system of free business enterprise will be a success. And that to cope with this success and the expectations that it will create, the arts of business management will be developed. However, in spite of this development, the managers will not always be able to deliver all the benefits that the people expect. Does that mean that in the end management and managers will be rejected as the means of controlling business? On our study tours, we have never been beyond 1985. What happens after that?*

Merlin Ah . . . I'm not going to tell you the answers before you have done the practical research. You will have to wait and see. But you should have already observed that towards the end of the 1970s there will be significant changes in the context of management.

Small businesses, whether owned by their managers or by large corporations, will come back into favour. Governments will notice that small businesses employ the majority of people. Large corporations will realise that smaller operating units have smaller costs of administration. The costs of basic resources - manpower, energy, materials - will all rise dramatically as the owners of these resources realise that they can fix a market price for them - and that society is no longer prepared to risk wars or revolutions in order to hold down the cost of such resources. More people and nations will acquire the means of production and the skills of management, so that competition will increase faster than custom. As a function, management will be invaded by machines, which will take over the task of assembling and analysing information, and by working people, who will seek to participate in the process of decision making.

Arthur *So, what will this mean for the manager?*

Merlin That he needs to go back to the basics of business - and with the consent and encouragement of a society which has a better appreciation of the true role of business. Increased competition will mean getting closer to the customer and involving the whole workforce in the satisfaction of his needs. The scarcity and expense of resources will mean developing better ways of making things and generating less waste. With more machine-produced information and analysis, there will be a greater need for human judgement. Smaller business units employing better educated people will require more effective styles of leadership.

These are all reasons why *The Complete Manager* will be such a good guide for businesses in the latter part of the twentieth century. It is concerned with the basic practicalities of managing a business and it also contains a section on personal skills, such as negotiation, communication, and self-development.

Arthur *If it is so full of wisdom and management is so important to the future, I think I should have the copy of this book. After all, as the 'once and future king', it is I that must be the complete manager.*

Merlin contemplates this suggestion. For Arthur to study the book himself would save a lot of time in tutorials. Time in which he could be earning fees from other consultancy assignments, like the plan to start a quality circle for knights called the Round Table. But Merlin considers that to let *The Complete Manager* out of his possession could be dangerous for his own business. It is the Middle Ages: wizards are two a penny, but good management consultants are few and far between. Better not risk spoiling the market.

Merlin No, thank you, Arthur. I think it would be most appropriate if I kept the book – just for the next few hundred years.

With apologies to T. H. White, author of *The Sword in the Stone.*

INTRODUCTION

1 Principles of management

Philip Sadler

When practising managers are faced with difficult and complex problems – for example, designing an organisation structure for a new manufacturing plant, or attempting to motivate a workforce characterised by apathy and low productivity – they quite naturally feel the need for a set of principles to turn to, in order to help them reach the right decisions.

This is sensible when it involves a willingness to learn from the experience of others as opposed to a stubborn determination to learn only from one's own mistakes. There is also the risk that so called 'principles' which carry all the authority of tablets of stone, but which are frequently based on limited experience, may be accepted uncritically as if they were eternal truths and used by managers as substitutes for their own thought processes.

The principles of management are, of course, quite unlike the principles of mathematics or the laws of the natural sciences. In the management field there is no universal agreement as to what the principles are, nor can it be said that the principles of management are valid for all situations. (There is little point in adding the qualification 'other things being equal' since in the human context in which management is set the 'other things' are rarely if ever 'equal'.)

It would, perhaps, be better not to use the term 'principles' at all, but to refer instead to 'guidelines'. They are, quite simply, sets of potentially useful generalisations about the factors which make for success in management. People have been making such general statements for thousands of years, usually as a result of thinking deeply about their own experiences in organisations. In modern times the wide-ranging types of experience gained by successful management consultants has been a particularly fertile source of such ideas.

In this chapter the historical development of management principles will be traced briefly in order to set the scene for a more detailed examination of some of the more recent and contemporary writings on the subject. The chapter will conclude with a statement of some management principles which have emerged from experience and research in recent years.

THE BEGINNINGS OF MANAGEMENT THOUGHT

The search for 'principles of management' – rules or 'laws' which, if observed, will result in effective managerial performance in all situations – has been going on for thousands of years (George, 1968). Early Egyptian writings show that the builders of the pyramids recognised certain basic principles such as authority, responsibility and specialisation. The Babylonian Code of Hammurabi set out principles of control and responsibility and Moses developed principles of organisation when leading the tribes of Israel on the flight from Egypt. Mencius, writing in China in 500 BC emphasised the importance of the systematic application of principles of management: 'Whoever pursues a business in this world must have a system. A business which has attained success without a system does not exist.' Plato, in the *Republic*, argued the merits of the principle of specialisation, and Socrates stressed the universal nature of management: 'I say that over whatever a man may preside he will, if he knows what he needs, and is able to provide it, be a good president, whether he have the direction of a chorus, a family, a city or an army.'

Many instances of early management thought come from the writings of great military strategists, for example, the staff principle, probably first used during the reign of Alexander the Great (336–323 BC). Machiavelli, in the sixteenth century, developed four principles – reliance on mass consent; cohesiveness; leadership; and the will to survive. Although he was writing about government in his time, the same principles might be applied to the management of companies today.

Modern industrial management theory dates from the introduction of the factory system. Techniques for financial control, incentive payment schemes, planning systems and investment appraisal methods were rapidly developed and applied. A rational approach to management was developed in the nineteenth century, and became known as 'scientific management'. Typical of pioneering work of this kind was the development of techniques such as product forecasting, production planning and work study at the Boulton, Watt Co. Engineering Works in England in the early years of the century. At the same time, in the United States, Eli Whitney was developing cost accounting, quality control and the concept of interchangeable parts. In Scotland, Robert Owen laid the foundations of modern personnel management at the New Lanark Mill, demonstrating that concern for employee welfare and the provision of good working conditions were compatible with a profitable and thriving business.

In 1881 the first business school (the Wharton School at the University of Pennsylvania) was established – some eighty or more years before the decision to establish business schools in London and Manchester.

Thirty years later Frederick Winslow Taylor published the work which has possibly had more influence on management practice than anything published since, his famous *Principles of Scientific Management* (Taylor, 1911). He advocated that managers should gather together all the traditional knowledge possessed by workmen and then classify it and reduce it to laws, rules and formulae. They should then develop a 'science' for each element of a man's work to replace old rule-of-thumb methods and 'scientifically' select and train workmen in the new methods. Finally, managers should take over certain tasks, such as planning and scheduling of work, which were previously left to the workmen to cope with as well as they could.

THE PRE-WAR MANAGEMENT WRITERS

Taylor's work had a profound and far-reaching influence on works management and much workshop practice today still reflects this. In the field of general management, however, a number of writers, in the years up to the Second World War, exercised a similarly powerful influence - most notably Henri Fayol, a French mining engineer; Elton Mayo, a Harvard professor; Mary Parker Follett, an American educationalist trained in philosophy, law and political science; Chester Barnard, president of the New Jersey Bell Telephone Company; and Lyndall F. Urwick, a British army officer who became a management consultant.

Fayol's work was first published in France in 1916 under the title *Administration Industrielle et Générale* and failed to be noticed in Britain and North America until translated and published by Pitman in 1949 as *General and Industrial Management* (Fayol, 1949). He analysed management activity into five elements - planning, organising, commanding (or directing), co-ordinating and controlling - an analytical framework which has been borrowed and built upon by countless writers since. He also argued that, to be effective, management should be founded upon fourteen principles as follows:

1 Division of work and specialisation
2 Authority must match responsibility
3 Discipline
4 Unity of command (one man, one boss)
5 Unity of direction
6 Subordination of individual interest to the general interest
7 Remuneration must be fair in relation to effort
8 Centralisation
9 The scalar or hierarchical principle of line authority
10 The principle of order (a place for everyone and everyone in his place)
11 Equity
12 Stability of tenure of personnel
13 Importance of initiative
14 Importance of *esprit de corps*.

This represented the first attempt at a complete theory of management. The fact that it received widespread recognition and acclaim when published in the English language more than thirty years after it was originally written is an indication of the extent to which Fayol was regarded as an authority on management matters.

Elton Mayo's distinction lies in the fact that his contribution was based on research rather than on direct personal experience, and in the way he shifted attention away from the more mechanistic issues of structure and control on to the human factors affecting industrial performance. The now famous studies he conducted at the Hawthorne Works of the Western Electric Company (Mayo, 1933) led to the conclusion that questions of human motivation and the emotional response elicited by the work situation were more important than logical and rational arrangements in determining output. Mayo also held that social relationships in working groups were the most important factor influencing the satisfaction the workers derived from their work.

Mary Parker Follett (Follett, 1949), reached similar conclusions, but on philosophical grounds rather than as a result of applied research. She emphasised the importance of group processes in decision making and had much to say that is relevant today on the question of resolving conflict.

Chester Barnard was a practising manager, but his analysis of the managerial role and the nature of organisations in *The Functions of the Executive* (Barnard, 1937), constitutes an important part of our sociological literature. His analysis linked together hitherto unrelated ideas about the factors affecting individual performance, the nature of organisations and the role of the manager.

The final figure in this group of people writing in the 1930s and '40s is Lyndall F. Urwick, whose most influential work was *The Elements of Administration* (Urwick, 1949). He produced a new synthesis based on the work of such people as Taylor, Fayol and Follett.

The principles which Urwick gathered together in this way have come to be known as the 'classical' principles of management. They are based on a combination of experience and philosophy rather than rigorous research and have been widely criticised for this. They have attracted criticism on other grounds also. First, the underlying assumption of their work – that there exists a common set of principles applicable to management in all types of situation – has been frequently challenged. Second, their work is criticised (perhaps unfairly) on the grounds that the world in which they had their experience no longer exists and that the principles they derived from that experience have little or no validity for the contemporary organisation operating in the modern business environment. (An example of the way ideas have changed in recent years in the widespread loss of confidence in the so-called economies of scale; another is the extent to which the principle of specialisation has been challenged as a result both of new ideas and much research and experimentation in the field of job design.)

Thus, changes in our ideas about management have conspired with the march of events to destroy the credibility of the classical management principles. The main changes which have affected the managerial role and altered it beyond recognition in the last quarter of a century include:

1 The impact of the computer, and more recently the microprocessor, on information processing tasks in production and administration
2 The increase in the pace of technological change generally, with consequences for the speed with which manufacturing processes and products themselves become obsolete

3 The growth of international trade and the associated intensification of competition, together with the growth of the multinational corporation and the impact on business of unstable exchange rates
4 The much greater impact of legislation on business activity – in such fields as employment protection, consumer protection, environmental care, health and safety, etc.
5 Changes in social climate leading to demands for employee participation in decision making
6 High rates of inflation

These and other factors have brought about a geometric increase in the complexity of the management task such that decisions can not easily be taken in the light of a few clearly formulated principles or guidelines of the classical kind.

MANAGEMENT THEORY IN THE POST-WAR ERA

The post-war era has seen great expansion in the volume of literature on management. The range and variety of approaches is so great as to defy any simple grouping or system of classification into schools of thought, but some commonalities can be detected.

First, the tradition of the consultant or practitioner theorising on the basis of his experience has continued, primarily because this approach genuinely meets the needs of many practising managers seeking to bring a greater degree of system and order into their own thinking. Often the most successful writers in this category have been those who can most clearly communicate, and elaborate into a system of thought, what practising managers already believe to be the case on the basis of their own experience. The best-known writers in this category in the English language have been such eminently successful consultants as Brech, Louis Allen and, above all, Peter Drucker.

Drucker in particular has taken account of changes in the nature of business environment and the managerial task, and has been successful precisely because he speaks to the contemporary manager and deals with the issues that currently concern him (Drucker, 1971).

Second, and closely related to the first group, is a smaller number of highly influential writers who have illuminated management thought with shafts of humour or satire. The most outstanding in this respect are C. Northcote Parkinson's *Parkinson's Law* (Parkinson, 1957); Robert Townsend's *Up the Organisation* (Townsend, 1970) and Antony Jay's *Management and Machiavelli* (Jay, 1967).

The ideas of these writers are well known outside management circles and indeed Parkinson's work has a place of its own in the literature of post-war society.

Third, there are the propounders of functional principles or of principles concerned with part rather than the whole of the management task. We have already seen that the classical principles of management were developed by people such as Fayol and Urwick on the basis of earlier work in production management by Taylor and others. In the post-war period we have seen considerable elaboration of theory in such areas as principles of marketing (Levitt, 1969, and Kotler, 1976), principles of personnel management (Pigors and Myers, 1969) and corporate strategy and planning (Ansoff, 1965).

This third group differs from the previous two in that it is dominated by academics as distinct from practitioners or consultants, reflecting the growth of management studies as an academic subject in the universities and the growing influence of the business school - initially in the US but more recently in Britain and other European countries. This group, in consequence, overlaps to some extent with the fourth and perhaps most important group - the management researchers. Primarily industrial psychologists and sociologists, their work builds on the tradition pioneered by Elton Mayo of detached, empirical and comparative studies of behaviour in industrial organisations. In turn they can be subdivided according to the main focus of their research. Looked at in this way the field breaks down quite logically into studies of the individual industrial worker and his motivation; studies of the behaviour of industrial work groups; studies of the factors influencing organisation effectiveness and researches into managerial and leadership behaviour.

Under the first heading three American psychologists, Herzberg, McClelland and Maslow, have had a strong and enduring influence on management theory and practice.

Herzberg is best known for his distinction between 'motivators' such as the work itself, achievement, responsibility and recognition, and what he describes as 'hygiene' factors, which do not provide motivation but merely act so as to prevent workers from being dissatisfied. These factors include pay, working conditions and relations with supervisors. Herzberg's work has led to important experiments in job enrichment as well as casting doubt on the effectiveness of many financial incentive schemes (Herzberg, 1959).

McClelland's researches emphasised the importance of the motivation to achieve in relation to the performance of work (McClelland, 1969), while Maslow's most important contribution was to draw attention to the way in which human needs are ordered into a hierarchical system, with basic needs such as survival and security as the foundation of motivation but with higher-order needs such as belonging, esteem, achievement and self-actualisation acting as the more important day-to-day motivators in advanced societies where survival and security can reasonably be taken for granted (Maslow, 1954).

Insight into the behaviour of industrial work groups has been provided by researchers on both sides of the Atlantic. Outstanding examples include Gouldner's study of gypsum mineworkers (Gouldner, 1954), and Walker and Guest's work on assembly line workers in the US (Walker and Guest, 1952), while in Britain there have been equally illuminating studies such as Lupton's participant observation of shop floor behaviour (Lupton, 1963).

The functioning of whole organisations and relationships between different forms of organisation structure and effectiveness have been the focus of a great deal of research on both sides of the Atlantic. This work in particular has had a powerful influence both in demolishing the credibility of the simple classical principles and in establishing new but more complex guidelines for management decisions.

In Britain, the work of members of the Tavistock Institute of Relations has demonstrated the importance of taking account both of the constraints imposed by technology and the needs of human beings for satisfying social relationships when designing organisation structures. From their work emerged the principles of 'joint optimisation of the social and technical systems', which stresses the need to search for forms of organisation in which technical requirements and human aspirations are simultaneously fulfilled (Rice, 1963, and Trist *et al*, 1963).

Joan Woodward (in her studies of organisation structures and levels of technology) conclusively showed that there is no one best way to organise a business and that the form of organisation advocated in the classical principles, with its emphasis on unity of command, hierarchy and clarity of structure, was far from universally adopted by successful firms (Woodward, 1965).

In a similar vein Burns and Stalker were able to demonstrate that the classical principles worked well in firms with highly stable technologies and markets but failed to be associated with successful performance in firms faced with the need for rapid adjustment to changing conditions (Burns and Stalker, 1961).

Organisation studies in the US that have contributed to the theory and practice of management include the work of Rensis Likert and in particular his concept of the organisation as a series of interlocking groups (Likert, 1961). These US studies also include the analysis by Lawrence and Lorsch of the problems faced by firms which need on the one hand to differentiate their activities to be able to relate to different markets, but which must simultaneously integrate these activities into a coherent and cohesive organisation for purposes of control and co-ordination (Lawrence & Lorsch, 1967).

Among the many studies of managerial behaviour, those of Mintzberg in the US (Mintzberg, 1973), and Rosemary Stewart in Britain (Stewart, 1967) have thrown much needed light on what managers actually do, and how the job content of managers with different roles in the organisation varies. The relationship between leadership style and management effectiveness has also proved to be a fruitful area of research, with outstanding contributions to our knowledge of leadership processes emerging from the work of Bass (Bass, 1960), and Fiedler (Fiedler, 1971) in the US.

The fourth and final group of contributors to modern management theory can be traced in its origins to two main sources: first, the application of scientific methods and mathematical problem-solving techniques to the solution of operational problems in wartime and second, to the subsequent development of computers and related mathematical approaches to solving complex problems. This fourth group is variously known as operational research or management scientists. It has included a number of eminent thinkers who have moved beyond the development and application of techniques to develop whole theories of management and organisation based on concepts derived from systems theory or information theory. In the US the outstanding personalities are March and Simon of the Massachusetts Institute of Technology (March and Simon, 1958); Diebold, the 'father of automation' (Diebold, 1965) and Norbert Weiner (Weiner, 1948), the man who first developed ideas in the field of cybernetics and related them to management.

In Britain, Stafford Beer clearly falls into this category. Beer exemplifies the approach of this group of writers in several ways. He is enthusiastic about prospects of management becoming more 'scientific'. He regards the computer as a potential tool for revolutionary changes in the practice of management. He conceptualises management as an information-processing activity and management's task as primarily one of *control.* Given that cybernetics is the science of control systems, it follows that the principles of cybernetics are also the key principles of management (Beer, 1972).

The management world described by Beer and others writing in the same vein is one with a strange language of its own – familiar perhaps to specialists in control engineering or to consultant neurologists, but foreign to generalists, and marketing and personnel specialists to whom terms such as 'heuristic', 'negentropy' and 'reticulum' convey little or nothing. At the same time it is a world in which problems of labour relations, emotions, attitudes, irrational conflicts and organisational politics have no place.

The main influence of this school of writers has been in the design, development and application of mathematically based operational research techniques to the solution of certain types of business problem.

MODERN MANAGEMENT PRINCIPLES

To what extent is it possible to draw from these various approaches a body of knowledge which, when summarised and distilled down to its essentials, could be said to represent the principles of modern management as distinct from the 'classical' ones? The task is a daunting one, not only because of the sheer volume of literature that now exists, but also because the principle trends have been towards divergence of theory, specialisation of topic and fragmentation of knowledge rather than reflecting convergence, integration and synthesis.

It is possible, however, to identify a number of recurring ideas or themes which, albeit given different treatment by different authorities and accorded differing degrees of importance in different conceptual schemes, would, nevertheless, command widespread acceptance. What follows is an attempt to state these.

The main propositions, 'principles' or guidelines about management which command widespread agreement today are:

The organisation as a complex system

The achievement of the purposes of a human organisation will involve a wide range of activities which are interconnected so as to form a system, such that changes to the pattern of activities in one part of the system will trigger related changes in other parts of it.

The technical and social sub-systems

The organisation as a system is made up of two princpal sub-systems - the technical and the social. The former is made up of such elements as the plant and machinery in use, the work flow between the different production stations and the system of production adopted (batch, mass production, continuous flow, etc.). The social system consists of the pattern of relations between the people who work in the organisation. In designing organisations regard must be given both to the need to adapt the structure to the technical system and to provide a structure which makes for a satisfying pattern of human relationships.

The organisation as an open system

The existence of any organisation depends on some process of exchange of goods or services with other organisations, social units or individuals in its environment. From this it follows that in the long run, organisations cannot survive if they are managed exclusively in ways which meet the needs of their members. Management is, therefore, partly the process of achieving a delicate balance between the expectations and needs of such internal 'stakeholders' as shareholders, managers, employees and pensioners on the one hand, and the demands and constraints imposed upon the organisation by its markets, its customers, its suppliers, trades unions, government departments, pressure groups of various kinds and, not least, by the strategies and tactics of competitors. To create and preserve such a balance calls for the continuous monitoring of the organisation's environment and the will to bring about appropriate responses on the part of the organisation.

The key resource of the modern business organisation in advanced industrial societies is knowledge

The key workers are the 'knowledge workers'; management, therefore, is more to do with the profitable exploitation of knowledge than with the productivity of labour or the utilisation of physical capacity. 'Knowledge' in this context may mean product knowledge, process 'know-how' or knowledge of the market. It is the task of management to ensure that the organisation's level of investment in the acquisition of new knowledge is sufficient to give it the competitive strength it requires to achieve profitable growth.

Management's key task is to secure the future survival of the organisation by means of appropriate and timely innovation

The classical principles of management tend to conjure up a vision of some mythical factory for producing 'widgets' which has always produced widgets and always will, using the same technology for the purpose and selling them in a stable market to loyal customers and without any Japanese competition! In the modern organisation, by contrast, successful innovation in both products and processes is indispensable to survival. Effective management, therefore, involves the ability to develop an innovative, creative climate, to establish an efficient system of market intelligence so as to discover needs for new products and to generate the funds needed for R & D and investment in new plant and equipment.

Management is the process of getting things done by other people

From this proposition it follows that the achievements of an organisation will reflect the degree of motivation and commitment of employees. Motivation is an extremely complex aspect of human behaviour about which we still have much to learn. We have, however, advanced beyond the naïve belief that it is a simple response to reward (in the form of financial incentives, for example) or punishment (fear of 'the sack'). Other factors such as job satisfaction, leadership and recognition clearly play an important part.

Management as an activity is universal but does not take the same form in all situations

Managers in all organisations and at all levels have to get things done by others, have to ensure that decisions are taken and cannot escape the need to exercise leadership. At the same time the qualities and skills required in the chief executive of a large organisation are very different from those required in a first-line manager, while the qualities needed to be effective as manager of a building site differ from those required in the successful manager of an R & D group in the electronics industry.

There is no one best way to organise a business

The most successful systems of organisation differ markedly from one kind of business to another. Any one business must continuously adapt its organisation to meet the demands of changing circumstances.

Small is beautiful

Entrepreneurial drive, creativity, adaptability and innovation alike are stifled by the bureaucratic systems of administration and control which characterise large, monolithic organisations. Effective management structures therefore involve autonomous profit centres, served rather than directed by small head-office teams.

Management is a process involving a mix of rational, logical decision-making and problem solving activities and intuitive, judgemental activities

In this sense it is both science and art. An important skill is to be able to recognise which problems and decisions fall into which category and to treat them accordingly.

None of the foregoing statements, whether they are described as generalisations, precepts, principles, or guidelines, has necessarily any enduring validity. There is no point in smashing one set of tablets of stone in order to create another. Given the high level of uncertainty and, indeed, turbulence in today's business environment, coupled with the values system of our modern society, and the stage of development of our economic institutions, these statements provide some indication of the likely paths to success. Should further radical changes take place in the nature of the environment, new guiding principles will inevitably be needed.

FURTHER READING

Ansoff, H.I., *Corporate Strategy*, McGraw-Hill, New York, 1965

Barnard, C., *The Functions of the Executive*, Harvard University Press, Cambridge, Mass, 1938

Bass, B., *Leadership, Psychology and Organisational Behaviour*, Harper, New York, 1960

Beer, S., *Brain of the Firm*, Allen Lane, The Penguin Press, London, 1972

Burns, T. and Stalker, G. M., *The Management of Innovation*, Tavistock, London, 1961

Diebold, J., *Focus on Automation*, British Institute of Management, London, 1965

Drucker, P., *Drucker on Management*, Management Publications Ltd, for the British Institute of Management, London, 1971

Fayol, H. *General and Industrial Administration*, Pitman, London, 1949

Fiedler, F., *Leadership*, General Learning Press, New York, 1971

Follett, Mary P., *Freedom and Coordination*, Management Publications Trust, London, 1949

George, C.S., *The History of Management Thought*, Prentice-Hall, Englewood Cliffs, NJ, 1968

Gouldner, A. W., *Patterns of Industrial Bureaucracy*, The Free Press, Glencoe, Ill, 1954

Herzberg, F. J., *The Motivation to Work*, Wiley, New York, 1959

Jay, A., *Management and Machiavelli*, Hodder & Stoughton, London, 1967

Kotler, P., *Marketing Mangement*, Prentice-Hall, Englewood Cliffs, NJ, 1976

Lawrence, P. R. and Lorsch, J. W., *Organisation and Environment*, Harvard Business School, Cambridge, Mass, 1967

Levitt, T., *The Marketing Mode*, McGraw Hill, New York, 1969

Likert, R., *New Patterns of Management*, McGraw Hill, New York, 1961

Lupton, T., *On the Shop Floor*, Pergamon Press, Oxford, 1963

McClelland, D. C. and Winter, D. G., *Motivating Economic Achievement*, Free Press, New York, 1969

March, J. G. and Simon, H. A., *Organisations*, Wiley, New York, 1958

Maslow, A., *Motivation and Personality*, Harper & Row, New York, 1954

Mayo, G. E., *The Human Problems of an Industrial Civilization*, Harvard

Business School, Boston, Mass, 1933
Mintzberg, H., *The Nature of Managerial Work*, Harper & Row, New York, 1973
Parkinson, C. Northcote, *Parkinson's Law*, John Murray, London, 1957
Pigors, P. and Myers, C. A., *Personnel Administration*, McGraw-Hill, New York, 1969
Rice, A. K., *The Enterprise and its Environment*, Tavistock, London, 1963
Stewart, R., *Managers and their Jobs*, Macmillan, London, 1967
Taylor, F. W., *Principles of Scientific Management*, Harper and Brothers, New York, 1911
Townsend, R., *Up The Organisation*, Michael Joseph, London, 1970
Trist, E. L., Higgin, G. W., Murray, H. and Pollock, A. B., *Organisational Choice*, Tavistock, London, 1963
Urwick, L., *The Elements of Administration*, Harper & Brothers, New York, 1944
Walker, C. R. and Guest, R. H., *The Man on The Assembly Line*, Harvard University Press, Cambridge, Mass, 1952
Weiner, N., *Cybernetics*, Wiley, New York, 1948
Woodward, J., *Industrial Organisation: Theory and Practice*, Oxford University Press, Oxford, 1965

PART ONE

FINANCIAL MANAGEMENT

2 Sources of finance

Stephen Badger

In theory three sources of wealth are available to a company – land, labour and capital. These are not wholly interchangeable, but to some extent the balance in any given company can be changed by the entrepreneur; land can be turned into capital by sale and leaseback (see Long-term facilities, below) or a given process can be made more capital-intensive and so generally require less labour (or vice versa). These decisions are within the scope of management, one of whose functions is to optimise the balance between the different factors of production. The first step before raising capital is therefore to ensure that it is really financial capital that is required.

WHY CAPITAL MAY BE REQUIRED

Capital is required to finance the conduct of the business. When a manufacturing business is first established, for instance, factory and office premises will be needed and plant and machinery and transport vehicles. These can either be bought outright or hired; in the first case the expenditure represents capital permanently invested in the business (for the second, see Medium-term facilities, below). In addition funds will be required to finance production from the initial purchase of raw materials until the sale of the finished product to an external purchaser, to pay wages and to meet overheads: these funds are known as working or revolving capital. As the business expands, fresh injections of both permanent and working capital will be required. If on the contrary it contracts (or is merely run more efficiently) capital will be freed for alternative uses. When the original fixed assets need replacing, more expenditure will be needed. This should have been adequately provided out of profits by depreciation provisions over the life of the assets, but in times of inflation there may well be a shortfall which will need an injection of new capital.

Capital may also be required for acquisitions.

TYPE OF CAPITAL REQUIRED

Capital is conventionally described as short-term, medium-term or long-term. The distinctions are not rigid, but short-term capital may be regarded as any liability repayable within one year; medium-term as being repayable between one and ten years in the future; and everything else as being long-term capital (this covers both the proprietors' ordinary risk capital, or equity, and long-term borrowings, or debt capital). In general, working capital requirements should be financed by short-term capital and capital permanently invested in the business should be long-term. Medium-term capital is useful to give added flexibility and balance to the overall financial structure: if a project is expected to generate sufficient cash flow to repay the initial investment within, say, seven years, medium-term financing may be appropriate.

This chapter deals primarily with sources of long-term finance (both debt and equity) but sources of short- and medium-term finance are considered in outline.

SOURCES OF LONG-TERM FINANCE FOR UNLISTED COMPANIES

The types of finance available to a company that is not listed on a stock exchange are much the same as those for one that is. The difference in the two situations is that the unlisted company is restricted to a much narrower range of sources, since many potential lenders or shareholders will be unwilling to put up funds if their investment is unlisted and so not marketable. In addition, if the company is private in the legal sense it is not permitted to make any invitation to the public to subscribe for shares or debentures.

In the first place an unlisted company will rely on the permanent capital put up by its promoter and his friends and relations, supplemented by bank borrowings. But in due course, if the company expands faster than retained earnings by themselves allow, there will come a time when these individuals are unable to find all the funds required; or they may wish to realise part of their investment. If the company has not yet reached a stage where a public flotation is appropriate, it should be possible to find one or more institutions to put up more capital (consisting either of ordinary shares or a mixture of ordinary and loan capital) on the basis that a flotation will take place within a few years so that the institutions will then be able to realise their investment if they wish. This type of investment is referred to as venture capital and there are a number of specialist institutions providing this kind of finance, such as Industrial and Commerical Finance Corporation, a subsidiary of Finance for Industry which is owned by the Bank of England and the clearing banks. The merchant banks are also active in this field, and insurance companies, pension funds and investment trusts may participate in a placing if the company is large enough.

In recent years considerable attention has been focused on the financial needs of the smaller company and this has led to the proliferation of bodies prepared to make money available. These include a number of consortia specially set up by banks and investment institutions. There has also been increasing interest in arrangements to effect greater marketability without a formal listing, such as the over-the-counter market sponsored by M. J. H. Nightingale and the Unlisted Securities Market instituted by the Stock Exchange.

GOING PUBLIC

Obtaining a listing on the Stock Exchange is a most important step in any company's development. But at the end of 1979 there were a total of more than 677 000 companies registered in the UK of which about 660 000 were private companies (in the legal sense) and only 3000 were listed on the Stock Exchange, including nearly 400 overseas companies. Many companies will therefore never reach a stage at which a listing is appropriate, or their proprietors may for various reasons not wish to seek a listing; taking in new shareholders provides an additional source of capital but at the same time involves added responsibilities towards those shareholders typified by the Stock Exchange's requirements on disclosure. The interests of 'outside' shareholders may at times differ from those of 'family' shareholders and the future management of the company must reflect the new spread of interests represented.

The reasons for going public are usually among the following:

1 To make the shares marketable and hence more valuable
2 To diversify the family investment and so to reduce the degree of risk
3 To provide funds to meet capital transfer tax liabilities when necessary
4 To make acquisitions of other companies for shares practicable
5 To raise new funds once the resources of the existing shareholders cease to be adequate.

This chapter is concerned with the last of these, but it is important to realise that going public does not necessarily involve raising money for the company – the shares sold to the public are often existing shares being sold on behalf of existing shareholders.

Where money is being raised for the company the procedure is normally to use an offer for sale made by a merchant bank or a firm of issuing brokers. The offer will be underwritten so that the money will be available even if sufficient public subscriptions are not forthcoming. But it is most important for the company's future capital-raising ability that the issue should be successful, which means that it should be fully subscribed, that the shares should open at a premium and that a free after-market should be maintained. To achieve this it is essential that the company should have the continuity of good management and attractive prospects and that large shareholders should not continue selling frequent blocks of shares once the offer for sale is complete. The amount of money that can be raised initially will depend primarily on the present and future profit levels of the company and hence on its ability to pay reasonable dividends on the increased capital. The Stock Exchange will not grant a listing unless the company as a whole is expected to have a market value of at least £500 000 (which probably involves after-tax profits of at least £75 000), but in practice it is probably not worth a company going public until it is several times this size since the amount of money raised will otherwise be relatively small, the proportion of it consumed by the expenses of the issue will be unduly high and an adequate after-market is unlikely to result. To cater for companies which want marketability for their shares without a full listing, the Stock Exchange has recently instituted the United Securities Market.

SOURCES OF LONG-TERM FINANCE FOR LISTED COMPANIES

Once a company has taken the important step of going public it can seek to raise funds from the whole range of investors, both private and institutional, without restriction.

In recent years private investors have tended to an increasing extent to channel their saving through life assurance policies, pension schemes and unit trust purchases rather than making direct investments in securities themselves. Figure 2.1 illustrates this by showing, for recent years, selected uses of funds by the personal sector and by financial institutions (other than the banking sector). This shows that there has been a steady net divestment of corporate securities by individuals, whereas financial institutions have been substantial net purchasers. They have also increased their rate of investment in property significantly. Any company wishing to raise funds therefore has to try to issue the sort of security that will appeal to this type of investor – primarily insurance companies, pension funds and unit and investment trusts.

Figure 2.2 shows some of the ways in which companies have in fact raised finance over the same period. It can be seen from this that bank lending plays a very important role, since banks are the first (and often the cheapest) source of finance to which all companies turn. Even more important in the overall picture are internally generated funds: the figures in Figure 2.2 must be viewed in the perspective of a total figure for undistributed income (before providing for depreciation or stock appreciation) of £14 824 million in 1980.

Types of security

The types of security usually issued are the following:

1 Ordinary shares
2 Preference shares
3 Debentures, secured either by a floating charge or a specific mortgage
4 Unsecured loan stocks
5 Unsecured loan stocks with conversion rights or warrant attached
6 Foreign-currency bonds

Ordinary shares

Ordinary shares represent the equity or risk capital in a business. They entitle their holders to a share of the profits by way of dividend only to the extent that the directors think fit. Thus if the business prospers its ordinary shares may become very valuable but if it declines they may become valueless. Ordinary

YEAR	PERSONAL USES OF FUND		USES OF FUNDS BY FINANCIAL INSTITUTIONS		
	Investment in company securities	Life assurance and super-annuation funds	Corporate loan capital	Ordinary shares	Land, property and ground rents
1971	-1213	2004	214	937	333
1972	- 997	2455	237	1843	323
1973	-1872	3354	111	544	664
1974	-1041	3493	-10	-283	788
1975	- 897	4450	57	1552	817
1976	-1511	5568	7	1135	1111
1977	-1817	6138	-117	1815	1084
1978	-1152	7333	-33	1430	1313
1979	-2105	9320	-68	1825	1328
1980	-2026	10688	-31	2017	1909

***Figure 2.1** Uses of funds by individuals and institutions (CSO Financial Statistics)*

YEAR	BANK BORROWING	OTHER LOANS AND MORTGAGES	UK CORPORATE ISSUES		ISSUES OVERSEAS
			Ordinary Shares	Fixed Interest (net)	
1971	732	286	152	215	75
1972	2988	139	317	289	119
1973	4504	875	143	51	113
1974	4411	245	126	-56	20
1975	482	491	1003	202	-9
1976	2398	439	785	42	6
1977	2966	38	730	-67	102
1978	2890	386	829	-71	-32
1979	4903	616	906	-22	-15
1980	6640	667	897	423	5

***Figure 2.2** Selected sources of capital funds for industrial and commercial companies (CSO Financial Statistics)*

shareholders are also usually entitled to control the company's activities by voting at general meetings.

Preference shares

Preference shares carry the right to receive a fixed dividend in every year that the company makes a sufficient profit, but to no further participation unless they are specifically participating preference shares. They may in some cases be redeemable at a fixed future time or at the company's option and they can also be issued on the basis that they are convertible in a specified ratio into ordinary shares of the company, but they will normally only carry full voting rights in special circumstances. Preference shares became relatively unpopular after the tax changes introduced by the Finance Act 1965 but more recently they have been used as a way of increasing the capital base without diluting the interests of ordinary shareholders.

Debentures and loan stocks

The other types of capital are generically referred to as loan capital, which may be either secured or unsecured. It can be seen from Figure 2.2 that the use of these instruments has declined substantially in recent years.

A debenture, according to *s*455 of the Companies Act 1948, includes debenture stock, bonds and any other securities of a company whether constituting a charge on the assets of the company or not; but in stock exchange parlance the expression debenture normally means a secured stock while unsecured loan stock is used to refer to a stock which is not secured. This is the terminology used here.

Unlike shareholders, holders of a debenture or unsecured loan stock are not members of a company, simply its creditors. They are therefore entitled merely to receive the agreed rate of interest (which is normally paid semi-annually) and to receive repayment of capital on final maturity. Their rights will be incorporated in the trust deed constituting the stock which will be made between the company and (usually) a trustee on behalf of the stockholders. It is a requirement of the Stock Exchange that there must be such a trustee if the stock is to be listed; the trustee will normally be one of the insurance companies or investment trusts which specialise in this type of work.

Investors in fixed-interest stocks have historically required a long life to final maturity. In fact most stocks issued in the London market have a term of twenty to twenty-five years, although some medium-term issues have been seen. There is usually a period of five years before final maturity when the company can repay the stock without penalty and the average life of the stock may be reduced by the operation of a sinking fund. Since the creditworthiness of a company, and even the nature of its business, can change materially over an interval of this length the trust deed constituting the stock will impose certain restrictions on the company. These will vary from case to case, but they may include limitations on such things as disposing of more than a certain proportion of the business, changing the nature of the business and giving security. An unsecured loan stock deed will also probably contain a permanent limit on the overall borrowings of the company and its subsidiaries and a separate limit on secured borrowings and the borrowings of UK subsidiaries. A debenture deed will not impose a continuing limit but will require the presence of a certain level of cover in terms both of income and of assets before any further issue of another tranche of the stock can be made. In general, debenture stock holders, since their claims are supported by security, will require rather less in terms of restrictions than the holders of an unsecured loan stock who merely rank alongside trade and other unsecured creditors. But in either case the trustee will have the power to declare the stock immediately repayable if interest is not paid or if the company defaults on certain other obligations.

Convertible and warrant stocks

These are a compromise between borrowing and equity. A convertible is an unsecured loan stock which initially merely carried a fixed rate of interest but which, on specified dates or within a specified period, may be converted, at the option of the holder, into ordinary shares of the company at a fixed ratio. Warrant stocks are stocks which are not convertible but which are issued together with warrants which entitle the holder to subscribe for ordinary shares of the company at specified times and at a specified price. Convertible stocks have been popular for a long time, but warrant stocks have never really become familiar in the UK.

The advantage to a company of issuing convertible stock is that for the initial period it can service the stock at a lower rate of interest than would be necessary for a stock that was not convertible, that when it is finally converted the effective price of issuing the resultant shares will be higher than it could have been initially, and that in the interval the interest payments (unlike ordinary dividends) will have been an allowable expense for tax purposes. A warrant stock gives the company a long-term borrowing (at a lower rate of interest than a simple borrowing), and when the warrants are exercised there is a further inflow of cash into the company. Both kinds of stock will impose the same sort of restriction on the company as an ordinary unsecured loan stock with additional provisions to protect the holders' rights to convert or exercise their warrant rights.

Foreign-currency bond

Only the very largest companies will want long-term loans in foreign currencies. In the great majority of cases, the UK market will be amply sufficient as a source of capital and in general it is unwise to incur a foreign-currency liability unless one has corresponding assets in that currency. Moreover only the largest companies would be well enough known to attract the interest of foreign lenders. However, in the 1960s a substantial international capital market developed in eurodollars (US dollars deposited outside the USA, but not necessarily in Europe, and so not subject to any national restrictions on capital flows). A large number of US, and a smaller number of European companies have taken advantage of this to raise the quoted eurodollar loans (both fixed interest and convertible) and there have also been issues in Deutschemarks, French and Swiss francs, eurosterling and artificial units such as the European unit of account. Unlike domestic issues, eurobond issues usually have a life to final maturity of not more than fifteen – and in some cases as little as five – years. With the abolition of exchange control in the UK the dividing line between the domestic and Euro issues in sterling has become blurred.

METHODS OF ISSUE WITH A LISTING

The four chief methods of making an issue for cash on the Stock Exchange are:

1 Offer for sale
2 Rights issue
3 Open offer
4 Placing

Offer for sale

In this case all members of the public are invited to subscribe for the issue by advertisements inserted in the press. The offer is usually made at a fixed price Sometimes an offer for sale by tender is used where only a minimum price is fixed and applicants themselves decide how much they are willing to pay; a striking price is then fixed at a level at which the issues will be fully subscribed and the shares fixed at that price to all applicants who applied at that price or above. In either case, only a fixed number of shares are available for issue and, if a greater number of applications are received, each applicant is scaled down proportionately. Priority is sometimes given to existing shareholders or employees who are sent special application forms.

An offer for sale is normally used when a company goes public for the first time, as described earlier. It may also be used in an issue of loan capital where the amount of capital required is very large or where it is necessary to appeal to a particularly wide circle of investors for some other reason. In most cases, however, a placing is preferred because of its speed and simplicity (see overleaf). By comparison an offer for sale involves significantly larger advertising and administrative costs.

Rights issue

In a rights issue new ordinary shares or other securities are offered to existing shareholders of the company *pro rata* to their holdings. Shareholders can then choose between taking up their entitlement (their rights) by subscribing the set amount per share, or they can sell some or all of their rights in the market if these are quoted at a premium. If they choose to sell they of course receive money rather than paying it out, but their percentage holding in the company is reduced so that in theory the effect is the same as if they had sold some of their existing shares. From the company's point of view the subscription money will still be received from the purchaser of the rights.

It is a requirement of a listing on the Stock Exchange that new equity shares (or other securities involving an element of equity) should only be issued for cash to existing shareholders of the company in proportion to their holdings (unless they consent otherwise in general meeting), and this has now been given wider application by the Companies Act 1980. As a result, issues of ordinary shares or convertible stocks are normally made by way of rights so that shareholders have the opportunity of maintaining their proportionate stake in the company.

Open offer

An open offer is an offer of loan capital restricted to shareholders (and possibly the holders of loan capital) of the company making the issue. However, the offer is not made *pro rata* to their holdings. Each shareholder can apply for as much stock as he wishes or for none; if more applications are received than stock is being issued, each application will be scaled down proportionately. This method of issue is relatively infrequent, but it may be used if it is thought that the stock being issued may attract a large premium and the benefit of this should accrue to shareholders. It is appropriate only where the company has a large number of shareholders, but in that case the effect is very similar to an offer for sale but without the attendant advertising costs.

Placing

In a placing, stock is offered direct to a relatively small number of large institutional investors who are the principle holders of fixed interest stock; it is therefore a quick and effective method of issue which allows the most precise pricing. Placing for an unlisted company was considered under Sources of Long-term Finance. Stock Exchange permission must be obtained for a placing with a listing and it is a condition of such permission that a proportion of the stock should be available publicly in the market. As already noted, a placing of new equity issued for cash is only possible with shareholders' consent but, because of its simplicity, placing has become the most usual method of raising loan capital for UK companies.

Underwriting and expenses of an issue

Once a company has decided that it needs money, it will clearly wish to be assured of that money as soon as possible, come what may. Rather than making an issue itself it will therefore go to a merchant bank or issuing broker who, in addition to advising on the documentation and terms of the issue, will arrange for it to be underwritten; that is, the issuing house will undertake to subscribe or find subscribers for the issue on the terms fixed in so far as it is not fully subscribed by the public or shareholders as the case may be. In return for accepting this risk and for its overall co-ordinating work on the issue, the issuing house normally charges a total commission of 2 per cent, $1\frac{1}{4}$ per cent of which is passed on to the subunderwriters, that is the institutions who agree to take up different amounts of the issue *pro rata* to the extent that it is not fully subscribed. In the case of a placing, however, the stock is placed directly with a number of the same institutions. Accordingly, no subunderwriting commission is required and only a placing commission of perhaps ¾ per cent (varying with the size of the issue) is payable; however, the issue terms will be slightly worse so that the net proceeds receivable by the company will be much the same. The other major expense of an issue of share capital duty levied at a rate of 1 per cent on the value of the shares being issued. Duty is no longer payable on the issue of loan capital but, in the case of a convertible stock, capital duty arises on conversion. By comparison the administrative costs of an issue, especially in a placing, are small.

OTHER METHODS OF SUPPLEMENTING CASH FLOW

The main methods of raising long-term capital with a listing have now been outlined. It remains to consider briefly the various other possible methods of supplementing cash flow, which are of course open to quoted and unquoted companies alike. Some of these can provide relatively long-term finance, but the majority are short-term.

Long-term facilities

These include mortgages, sale and leaseback transactions and public authority and specialist institution lending. The main sources of mortgage and sale and leaseback finance are the insurance companies and pension funds. In the case of a mortgage loan, a single lender will advance up to two-thirds of the value of a building for a specified term on the specific security of that building – the borrower retains the ownership of the building but his rights are subject to a mortgage charge for the term of the loan. In a sale and leaseback transaction he will actually sell the building (and so forfeit any appreciation in value) in return for a capital sum and at the same time lease the building back for his own use from the purchasing institution for a long period at a specified rent. Other sources of relatively long-term facilities include the Department of Industry (for specified purposes in development areas and in accordance with such schemes as may be in effect from time to time), local authorities where employment is being created in their areas, and various specialist semi-official organisations such as Finance for Industry, Agricultural Mortgage Corporation, Commonwealth Development Finance Company and National Research Development Corporation, all of which exist to lend for certain purposes. Similarly, Equity Capital for Industry has been formed as a vehicle through which insurance companies and other institutions can subscribe new share capital in certain circumstances.

Medium-term facilities

These include leasing, hire-purchase, project finance and term loans.

Leasing and hire-purchase are most appropriate for items such as vehicles, plant, machinery and office equipment. In leasing, the ownership of the item remains with the lessor, but the lessee is entitled to the use of it for a specified term in return for regular payments under the lease. This is not strictly a borrowing at all and it is often referred to as off-balance-sheet finance since it need not as yet be shown on the face of the company's balance sheet. A tax-based lease may also be particularly attractive to a company with no immediate liability to taxation. In a hire-purchase transaction the purchase price of the item and interest thereon is paid in instalments over a set period, at the end of which ownership of the item does pass to the hirer. There are a large number of finance houses which specialise in these activities.

Similarly, merchant and other banks may undertake to arrange finance for a specific project. This will involve tapping a number of different sources of finance in accordance with the cash flow requirements of the individual project and is a particularly flexible form of financing.

Finally, banks sometimes engage in term lending for periods up to five or even ten years. A term loan could come from a single bank or it might be syndicated among a number of different banks. It might be at a fixed rate of interest but it will more usually be on a roll-over basis; that is, with interest fixed periodically at the prevailing rate. In the latter case it is also possible to arrange for drawings to be made in different currencies at different times.

Export finance

Particularly to assist exporters in financing their contracts with overseas buyers the UK Government, in common with other major industrialised countries, runs an export credit programme which has two purposes; firstly, to provide UK exporters with insurance against political, transfer and commercial risks in respect of export contracts; and secondly, to assist in the provision of attractive credit to overseas buyers of UK capital goods and related services. The UK export credit authority is the Export Credits Guarantee Department (ECGD), which operates as an autonomous unit within the overall responsibility of the Secretary of State for Trade.

With the support of ECGD, finance can be made available in several different forms. For short-term transactions, the supplier can insure his receivables with ECGD and assign the insurance policy to the bank, thereby obtaining commercial finance from his bank on more attractive terms than may otherwise be available to him; alternatively, the supplier can secure from the buyer bills of exchange or promissory notes and discount or sell them to his bank at commercial rates, again using his ECGD insurance policy as security. In such cases the transaction can be done without recourse to the supplier.

For transactions with a credit period of more than two years, the available export finance is not on a commercial basis, but has a fixed and subsidised rate of interest. The applicable fixed rate is established with reference to the total term of the credit, to the credit rating of the borrower's country in the eyes of the ECGD, and to the general consensus on export credit terms arrived at by OECD member countries. Broadly speaking the fixed interest rates vary between 7.5 per cent for the poorest countries through to 8.75 per cent for the richest countries.

For smaller supply of goods transactions the most appropriate finance structure is a supplier credit. Under such a structure the supplier receives bills or notes from the buyer and insures those receivables with ECGD. The supplier then sells those bills or notes to his bank who is guaranteed as to 100 per cent by ECGD under a Specific Bank Guarantee. Legally, the ECGD then has rights of recourse against the supplier for 100 per cent of any amount paid out to the bank, but this is set off against the supplier's insurance cover which is normally for 90 per cent of commercial risk and 95 per cent for political risk in respect of contract receivables. It will be seen, therefore, that under a supplier credit the supplier carries a continuing financial risk on the buyer throughout the credit period. The second appropriate credit structure for medium-term transactions is a buyer credit, under which the supplier essentially enters into a cash contract. He does not take out specific insurance cover in respect of such a contract, but instead is paid a loan made available by a bank explicitly and solely to the foreign buyer. Advances by the bank are guaranteed by ECGD as to 100 per cent of principal and interest at the appropriate fixed rate of interest. ECGD is entitled to take recourse on the supplier in the event of a claim by the bank on ECGD only in the circumstances where the UK supplier is in default under his contract. There is thus no continuing financial risk throughout the credit period on the UK supplier, and it is worth noting that ECGD has never to date exercised its right of recourse against a supplier under a buyer credit. Buyer credits are more normally used for major or turnkey contracts.

Because the rate of interest payable under a medium-term contract is on the above mentioned fixed rates, ECGD agrees with the banks who provide the funds that they will receive make-up to give them a commercial return on their lending. The cost of this subsidy to the UK government is causing concern to the UK authorities - in the fiscal year 1980-81 it amounted to over £500 million. The greatest providers of export credit finance are the UK clearing banks. A large proportion of the major projects are, however, arranged by the UK merchant banks with the clearing banks and certain active non-UK banks (for example the large American banks) providing a substantial proportion of the funding. If finance for an export order is required it is advisable to contact ECGD or a merchant/clearing bank sooner rather than later, since ECGD is not allowed by Act of Parliament to support export orders which have already been secured.

Short-term facilities

These include bank overdrafts and loans, bank acceptance credits, bills of exchange, trade credit, invoice discounting and factoring. Of these, bank overdrafts and loans are the most common and are used universally by companies, as Figure 3.2 shows. They may be supplemented by acceptance credits, where a bank undertakes to accept approved bills of exchange up to a certain limit so that the bills can be discounted at the finest rates. Alternatively, bills of exchange can be used as a form of trade credit, whether or not discounted with a bank or discount house, or various arrangements may be made between buyers and suppliers as to the length of credit given in payment for goods. Finally, invoice discounting and factoring are undertaken by various specialist institutions. Invoice discounting means financing the collection of specific invoices (at the risk of the selling company). Factoring involves making immediate payment against invoiced debts which are then normally collected at the factor's own risk for an appropriate charge. All these methods have in common the fact that they finance relatively small revolving trade transactions, but in aggregate they provide the finance of a vast amount of business on a continuing basis.

Current trends

The willingness of lenders to lend for long periods will depend on their being able to foresee a reasonable rate of return in real terms. In times of high inflation there is therefore a reluctance to tie up funds in this way except at rates so high as to be unacceptable to many borrowers. Equally, companies may prefer to borrow for relatively short periods in the hope of being able to refinance their obligations later at a lower rate. For these reasons, there has been a considerable shift in recent years away from long-term issues to more flexible short-term borrowing. This has been encouraged by the greater availability of bank credit following the new monetary policy adopted by the Bank of England from 1971 onwards in its new approach to competition and credit control.

LOOKING AT THE OVERALL CAPITAL STRUCTURE

We have outlined the chief avenues open to a company wishing to raise new capital. Before raising any new capital a company should consider what the capital is needed for, whether it is permanent or likely to be repaid out of cash flow within a period and what rate of return it is likely to earn. One can then go on to decide how it can best be supplied. For instance in the case of an investment with a high degree of risk the best source of finance is likely to be equity (or risk) capital; but, if it is a relatively risk-free long-term investment, loan capital may be more appropriate. If it is a specific project of medium-term duration, project finance should be considered, while if it is a working capital requirement, bank overdraft facilities are likely to be the answer. In all cases the various methods of supplementing cash flow in other ways must be borne in mind so as to minimise the amount of new capital actually required. Finally, the rate of return must be set against the cost of capital to ensure than an adequate margin exists to justify the investment.

One of the most important considerations is to preserve a proper balance between debt and equity in the company's financial structure. This relationship is described as the company's financial gearing; if the company's source of income is reasonably stable and assured (such as the rental income of a property company) it is safe for it to be highly geared, but if it is operating in a cyclical industry (such as machine tools) it is prudent to keep the gearing (that is, the element of borrowing) at a low level, for interest on borrowings has to be paid in adverse as well as favourable times and if a temporary set-back combined with high interest charges results in the company making a loss, its overall status will suffer. The degree of gearing will depend both on the absolute amount of borrowing and the extent to which any of this borrowing is at fluctuating interest rates which may rise faster than the company's income. In inflationary times, borrowing at a fixed cost can be most advantageous to a company. But the closer the company gets to what is thought to be an unduly high level of borrowings, the more reluctant lenders will be to provide new funds and the more the equity interest of existing shareholders will be endangered.

The object of company financial management should be to see that the company has adequate funds at the lowest cost consonant with all these factors and so to seek to maximise its earnings for ordinary shareholders.

FURTHER READING

Admission of Securities to Listing, Stock Exchange, London, revised 1973, with subsequent amendments

Brearley, R. A., and Pyle, C., *Bibliography of Finance and Investment*, Elek Books, London, 1973

'Competition and Credit Control', Bank of England, reprinted in *Bank of England Quarterly Bulletin*, June 1971

Leach, J. H. C., 'The Role of the Institutions in the UK Ordinary Share Market', *Investment Analyst, December, 1971*

Leach, J. H. C., 'The Weight of New Money – Once Again', *Investment Analyst*, September, 1975

Merrett, Howe and Newbould, *Equity Issues and the London Capital Market*, Longmans, London, 1967

'New Capital Issues Statistics', *Midland Bank Review*,, commentary published annually in Spring edition

Royal Commission on the Distribution of Income and Wealth (Diamond Report), Report No. 2 (Cmnd. 6172), HMSO, London, July, 1975

'The UK Corporate Bond Market', *Bank of England Quarterly Bulletin*, March, 1981

The various volumes of evidence given to the Committee to Review the Functioning of Financial Institutions (the Wilson Committee) and published by HMSO may also be of interest.

3 The annual accounts

W P Ridley

Anyone interested in the management of a company, whether taking an active part or merely investing capital, needs to have financial information of two kinds concerning the company:

1 Where the capital is invested (shown in the balance sheet)
2 The return earned from the investment (shown in the profit and loss account).

Those in active management can call for financial reports and accounts to be designed according to their own requirements. But, for investors and others, forms of balance sheet and profit and loss account have been laid down by Acts of Parliament. This chapter starts by describing the formal requirements, and then proceeds to discuss other aspects of the accounts, including the interpretation of accounts in order to judge a company's financial performance.

ACCOUNTING REQUIREMENTS OF THE COMPANIES ACTS

The form of the published accounts and the directors' report is set by the Companies Act 1985, but this Act must be read in conjunction with the previous major Acts on the subject dated 1948, 1967, 1973, 1976, 1980 and 1981. These documents must be sent to each member of the company, debenture holder and certain other interested parties at prescribed intervals.

The final accounts in the prescribed form, together with the directors' report, must also be filed with the Registrar of Companies.

Note that filing of accounts does not imply an inspection of such accounts by the Registrar or the Department of Trade. It means exactly what it says–the documents are filed. Such filing, however, involves laying the documents open to public inspection at Companies House. A search fee is payable before the accounts and report can be inspected. These accounts, however, are likely to be markedly different from management accounts, particularly the profit and loss account. The contrast between typical management accounts and accounts prescribed for shareholders is shown in Figures 3.1 and 3.2.

	£'000	£'000
SALES		5000
less		
Purchases of raw materials	2000	
Manufacturing wages	1500	
Foremen's wages	50	
Factory expenses	150	
Depreciation of plant and machinery	60	3760
GROSS PROFIT ON SALES		1240
add		
Investment income from:		
quoted investments	10	
unquoted investments	45	
Rents	300	
		355
		1595
less		
Distribution costs	80	
Directors' fees	10	
Directors' remuneration	80	
Salaries	600	
Rent	10	
Rates	12	
Insurance	20	
Property repairs	100	
Provision for renewal of office building	5	
Depreciation of office equipment	2	
Telephone and postage	6	
Provision for doubtful debts	11	
Bad debts	25	
Interest on bank loans	6	
Interest on debentures	8	
Plant hire	2	
Auditors' remuneration	1	
		978
NET PROFIT BEFORE TAXATION		617

***Figure 3.1** Profit and loss account of a limited company as presented to its management*

	£'000	£'000	£'000
TURNOVER			5000
Cost of sales			3760
Gross profit			1240
Distribution costs		80	
Administrative costs		884	964
			276
Rents receivable (net)			300
			576
Income from shares in companies outside the group	55		
less interest payable outside the group	14		41
NET PROFIT BEFORE TAXATION			617

Note depreciation in fixed assets of £62,000 charged in above figures

Figure 3.2 ***The accounts shown in Figure 3.1 in the form to be filed with the Registrar***

The Companies Acts do not limit the information to be presented, but they set out what must be included in the final accounts and directors' report, including any notes which may be required for clarification. Such information is termed the minimum legal requirements. In fact, the Companies Acts select the information that needs to be filed. The full final accounts must therefore be adapted to meet the needs of the Acts. The balance sheet and profit and loss account of a company based on this selected information are termed the statutory accounts.

Growth of information required

The information required for the statutory accounts has grown enormously during the past sixty years, owing to pressure from investors, the government and the general public. The pressure from investors for more information has grown with their increasing separation from management in industry and commerce. This separation has led to a need of investors to learn as much as possible of the state of the companies, in order to assess the security of their investment. The general public, which in this connection includes creditors and potential investors, are concerned to know how companies are being managed, and whether they are financially sound. (This demand for information becomes especially apparent when public confidence in company administration has been shaken by a well-publicised fraud.) Successive governments have responded to these two pressures in their legislation.

The government itself may wish to have more information made public if it feels that this will have a beneficial effect upon industry or commerce as a whole. Thus the publication of export figures by each company, for example, can have the effect of increasing emphasis on overseas sales and thereby stimulating trade. As a result, the successive Companies Acts tend to set increasingly stringent requirements for company disclosure while accounting standards are continually being tightened to achieve uniformity in reporting.

STANDARD PRESENTATION

Figures 3.1 and 3.2 highlighted typical differences between management and shareholder information. However, the accounts shown were not comprehensive since they took company information only to the stage of profit before taxation and did not cover all the possible items that can be included. After this point there is no difference between the information required by the Companies Acts and that normally presented to the management. The balance sheet designed for management is also broadly similar (in most cases) to that which is required by the Companies Acts to be presented to the investors and filed with the Registrar.

Full details of a stand profit and loss account are given in Figure 3.3 indicating information that has to be published, if not in the face of the accounts by way of note.

Directors' emoluments

In addition to the information shown in Figure 3.3, certain information concerning directors' emoluments must be given, either in the accounts or in a statement attached to the accounts. All directors' remuneration and past directors' pensions, paid by the company or by any other person, either for their services as directors or for services in other capacities, must be shown. Likewise the statements or accounts must show any compensation paid by the company or any other person to past or present directors for loss of office. In addition the statement must show the number of directors who have waived their rights to emoluments and the aggregate amount that has been waived. The chairman's emoluments must be shown, and also those of the highest paid director if these are in excess of the chairman's emoluments.

The number of directors must be shown, broken down into income groups; that is, the number of directors whose emoluments do not exceed £2500; the number whose emoluments exceed £2500 but do not exceed £5000; and so on for each successive integral multiple of £2500. For each of these items, the term

	1982 £m.	1981 £m.
Sales outside the group (directors' report to give split by major activities and show exports)	=	=
Trading profit (cost of items inset in Figure 3.2 to be noted)	+	+
Interest paid less dividends and interest receivable (The amount of interest payable on overdraft bank loans and loans repayable within five years to be distinguished from other interest payable; and income from investments listed on a recognised stock exchange to be distinguished from income on unlisted companies)	+	+
Profit before tax	+	+
Taxation (see below)	+	+
Minority interests	+	+
Profit after tax and minority interest	+	+
Extraordinary items (to be noted separately)	+	+
Profits after extraordinary items	+	+
Dividends (cost of dividends net of tax to be shown split between amounts paid and amounts proposed to be paid)	+	+
Retained profits for the year		
Profit & loss brought forward		
Profit and loss A/c at end of year		
Earnings per share (based on profit after tax and minority interest and average shares issued during year)		

Figure 3.3 Format of the statutory profit and loss account

'emoluments' does not include contributions paid by the company for the benefit of directors under any pension scheme.

Taxation items

The more detailed requirements about disclosure of taxation items are covered by the layout shown in Figure 3.4.

Taxation based on profits for the year:		
Corporation tax at 52% (including £xx (previous year £) transferred to deferred taxation) on profits excluding those of associates	x	x
Less relief for overseas taxation	x	x
	x	x
Overseas taxation	x	x
Prior-year adjustments	x	x
Tax on share of profits of associates	x	x
Total tax charge		

Note: Taxation charged against profit for the year has been reduced by £xx due to deferment of tax liabilities for which provision has not been made.

Figure 3.4 Presentation of taxation details

The balance sheet

Figure 3.5 provides a format for a company's balance sheet, together with the notes which relate to the corresponding figures shown in the table. The principles of valuation are also set out.

1 Fixed assets: the amount to be included in respect of a firm's fixed assets is the amount of its purchase price or production cost less provisions for depreciation. Similar principles shall be applied where goodwill or development costs (only rarely to be treated as an asset) are given balance sheet values.

For fixed assets shown at valuations, the year in which the valuations were made must be disclosed. For fixed assets valued during the last financial year, the names or qualifications of the valuers and the bases of valuation they used must be given.

Freehold land must be shown separately from leasehold land, and land held on a long lease (one having not less than fifty years to run) must be distinguished from that held on a short lease (having less than fifty years to run).

There must also be shown (i) the aggregate amount of fixed assets acquired during the year; and (ii) the book value at the date of the last balance sheet of fixed assets disposed of during the year.

If the detail to be disclosed is considerable it might best be given on a statement attached to the accounts, reference thereto being made in the balance sheet.

2 As with other fixed assets, for long-term investments it is necessary to show the cost of valuation and the aggregate amount written off, except in the case of:
(*a*) Shares in subsidiaries which may be shown as a single figure – but it is necessary to state the basis on which the amount was arrived at, as illustrated in the balance sheet;
(*b*) Quoted investments and unquoted investments, provided the value as estimated by the directors is shown either as the amount of the investment or by way of note.

For any investments in the form of unquoted equity shares in respect of

LIABILITIES	£	£	£
SHARE CAPITAL			
Authorised and issued for each class of share			x
(Give notes of: 1 Earliest and latest dates of redemption of any redeemable preference shares: 2 Whether the shares must be redeemed in any event or are liable to be redeemed at the option of the company; 3 Whether any, and if so what, premium payable on redemption; 4 Any capital on which, and the rate at which, any interest has been paid out of capital during the year under *s*65 of the 1948 Act.)			
RESERVES			
Capital redemption reserve fund	x		
Share premium account	x	x	
Other reserves	x		
Balance carried forward from profit and loss account	x	x	x
SHAREHOLDERS' FUNDS			
Deferred taxation			x
DEBT FINANCE			
Loans not repayable within five years of the balance sheet date (with a note of the terms of repayment and the rate of interest)		x	
Loans or other amounts due to subsidiaries (under current liabilities of short term)		x	
Debentures and other (long-term) loans		x	x
TOTAL LIABILITIES			*T*

Figure 3.5 Format of the statutory balance sheet

ASSETS

FIXED ASSETS (Other than investment) (**1**)	AT COST	AT VALUATION	DEPRECIATION	£	£	£
	£	£	£			
Freehold land and buildings					x	
Leasehold property:						
long lease					x	
short lease					x	
Plant and machinery					x	
Other					x	x
Goodwill, patents and trade-marks; at cost less amounts written off					x	x
INVESTMENTS (any short-term items should be shown under current assets) (**2**)						
Quoted investments					x	
Unquoted investments					x	x
CURRENT ASSETS (**3**)						
Stocks and work in progress (if the amount is material a note must be given of the manner in which these items were computed)				x		
Debtors (after deducting any provision)				x		
Balances at bank, and cash				x		x
less						
CURRENT LIABILITIES AND PROVISIONS						
				£	£	£
Bank loans				x		
Bank overdrafts				x		
Taxation currently due				x		
Creditors				x		
Dividends proposed				x	x	
WORKING CAPITAL					x	x
TOTAL ASSETS						*T*

The figures in parentheses refer to the notes in the main text.

Figure 3.5 (continued)

which the estimated value is not given, there must be disclosed:
(*a*) The year's gross income from those investments;
(*b*) The company's share of the profits (or losses) both before and after taxation, for the last accounting period of the bodies in which the investments are held;
(*c*) The company's share of the undistributed profits (or losses) accumulated by those bodies since the investments were acquired;
(*d*) The manner in which any losses incurred by those bodies have been dealt within the company's accounts.

3 Current assets shall normally be valued at production costs or purchase price (which may be calculated on a last in first out or first in first out price or average weighted price). However, where the net realisable value is estimated to be lower than this cost, this lower value will be substituted.

Items requiring disclosure

Other matters to be disclosed in the published accounts (by notes if not otherwise shown) include:
(*a*) The corresponding figures for the preceding year:
(*b*) The nature and amount, or estimated amount, of any contingent liabilities not provided for;
(*c*) The amount or estimated amount of any contracts for capital expenditure, so far as not provided for, and of any capital expenditure authorised by the directors but not yet contracted for;
(*d*) The bases on which foreign currencies have been converted into sterling;
(*e*) Any special circumstances affecting the company's taxation liability for the current or succeeding financial years;
(*f*) The number of employees (other than directors of the company) whose emoluments for the year (from the company, its subsidiaries or any other person in respect of services to the company or its subsidiaries):

exceeded £10 000 but did not exceed £12 500
exceeded £12 500 but did not exceed £15 000
exceeded £15 000 but did not exceed £17 500

and so on in successive integral multiples of £2500;
(*g*) The information required by *s*3 of the 1976 Act concerning each of the company's subsidiaries;
(*h*) The information required by *s*4 of the 1967 Act:
(i) where the company holds equity shares in another company (other than a subsidiary) exceeding one-tenth of the nominal value of the issued equity of that other company, or
(ii) where the company holds shares in another company (other than a subsidiary) which, in the investing company's balance sheet, are shown at an amount exceeding one-tenth of the investing company's assets (as stated in its balance sheet).
(*j*) Under *s*5, a subsidiary has to give the name and country of incorporation of its ultimate holding company.

THE DIRECTORS' REPORT

The directors' report must accompany the balance sheet and profit and loss account filed with the Registrar of Companies, and must be sent to all members of the company, debenture holders and other interested parties.

The report, which is presented by the board of directors, contains much relevant information concerning a company's activities, and its minimum contents, summarised below, were considerably extended by the Companies Act 1967. It should be especially noted that these minimum contents are required by legislation and are not subject to directors' choice any more than the information contained in the statutory account.

Minimum contents of directors' report

Review

A review of the company's affairs during the period covered by the accounts: particulars of important events that have occurred since the year end; likely future developments; an indication of research and development activities.

Dividends

The amount(s) recommended to be paid by way of dividend.

Reserves

The amount(s) proposed to be transferred to reserves.

Activities

The principal activities of the company and significant changes in these activities.

Directors

The names of all directors who acted in such a capacity at any time during the period under review.

Changes in fixed assets

Significant changes in the company's fixed assets. If the market value of land is substantially different from the value shown in the balance sheet, an indication of the difference in value.

Share and debenture issue

The reason(s) for making any issue of shares or debentures during the period under review, and details of classes issued and amounts received in each class. Particulars of dealings by a company in its own shares.

Contracts

Contracts with the company (except service contracts) in which a director of the company has an interest; the parties to the contract, the director involved, the nature of the contract and the nature of the director's interest must be specified.

Arrangements between company and directors

Any arrangement whereby the directors are able to obtain benefits by the acquisition of shares or debentures in the company or any other body corporate.

Directors' interests

Directors' interests (at the beginning and end of each year) in shares or debentures of the company. This requirement is extended to include the directors' spouses and infant children (the directors' 'family interests').

Matters showing the state of the company's affairs

Particulars of any matter required for an appreciation by its members of the state of the company's affairs, so long as in the opinion of the directors the publication of such information would not be harmful to the company.

Relative profitability of different activities

Turnover and profit or loss of each class of business carried on by the company, if such classes differ substantially.

Persons employed

The average number of persons employed in the UK by the company (on a weekly basis) during the year, and the aggregate remuneration paid or payable to such persons in respect of that year. This information is not required where a company has fewer than one hundred employees.

Political and charitable contributions

The amount of contributions, if exceeding £50, given for political or charitable purposes, and the identity of the political party concerned.

Exports

The turnover from exports when the value exceeds £50 000, and a note where no goods are exported.

Previous year

The corresponding amounts in each section for the immediately preceding year.

ORGANISATION OF INFORMATION

It is clear that the company's book-keeping systems must be designed to ensure that this statutory information can be easily obtained. This requires an analysis for each category of data that has to be published under the relevant Acts of Parliament. Careful organisation on these lines can avoid a great deal of end-of-year panic, which so often delays preparation of final accounts. It will also give the directors of the company a better opportunity of reviewing their progress, thus facilitating a more meaningful review of their activities and management of the funds under their control.

JUDGING A COMPANY FROM ITS ACCOUNTS

Reports by a company to its shareholders are regulated in detail by law. As a result, outside assessments of the financial standing of a company are almost inevitably based on the information given in these reports (normally issued annually) rather than on other publications of the company or on its trade reputation. Increasingly it is being realised that this outside assessment is important to the company – in raising finance, whether by loan or equity, in merger discussions with other companies, or in trading negotiations. It is therefore advisable for senior company executives to consider in detail the standards against which their company's financial performance – as set out in the fully audited report to shareholders – will be judged.

PROFIT AND LOSS ACCOUNT FOR PANGLOSS PLC

This chapter takes the abridged accounts of a company called Pangloss PLC to highlight information on which a financial examination is based (see Figure 3.6).

In the year to 31 March 1981, Pangloss earned £1.4m, before a charge of £0.4m for depreciation; depreciation is singled out because it does not represent a direct cash outflow but an accounting adjustment to the value of fixed assets – some of which are likely to have been bought many years before. Therefore when considering the cash resources available to the company both the level of depreciation and retained profits will be taken into account. The trading surplus net of depreciation gives pre-interest profits – an important indicator of company trading performance – of £1.0m (see Figure 3.8).

YEAR TO 31 MARCH 1982	£m
Trading surplus (before depreciation)	1.4
Less: Depreciation	0.4
Pre-interest profits	1.0
Less: Interest	0.3
Pre-tax profits	0.7
Less: Tax	0.3
Available to shareholders	0.4

Figure 3.6 Abbreviated profit and loss account of Pangloss PLC

Interest charge

The interest charge depends on the amount of loans and overdrafts outstanding, which is an integral part of the financing of the company's assets, rather than of current trading. It is therefore of prime significance to those providing finance, whether as lenders or investors. From the point of view of a potential lender, the relation of the interest charge to the level of pre-interest profits give some indication of the security for loans; in this case with interest at £0.3m he is likely to be deterred by the relatively high ratio of 30 per cent of pre-interest profits (of £1m) already absorbed by interest. From the point of view of the equity investor, this ratio represents the gearing given to the amounts available to ordinary shareholders. Thus if pre-interest profits increase by 70 per cent to £1.7m with interest remaining at £0.3m, pre-tax profits will double to £1.4m, while if they fall by 70 per cent pre-tax profits will be reduced to nil. So the element of gearing offers both opportunity for increasing the return to shareholders where the company is successful and additional risk if trading returns fall. The degree of gearing that investors are prepared to accept varies according to the industrial risk and this must be borne in mind by the company executive when negotiating loans, overdraft facilities or equity finance.

Tax charge

The tax charge depends not only on the rates of tax ruling in the countries where profits are earned, but also on any special allowances or grants offered. Where the charge appears abnormal it will be analysed to ascertain whether this is due to temporary or permanent factors. The tax charge shown for Pangloss, however, of £0.3m on £0.7m represents a tax rate of 43 per cent which is unexceptional. This leaves £0.4m available for distribution to shareholders which will be evaluated by investors with reference to the number of shares issued.

RETURN TO SHAREHOLDERS

Earnings of £0.4m on 2 million shares (see Figure 3.7) are equivalent to 20p per share in Pangloss. The value of the share is normally directly related to this figure; thus, if the share price is £2, an investor will consider whether it is reasonable to buy or sell the share, given that £2 is equivalent to ten times the earnings attributable to that share (that is a p/e ratio of 5). The dividend must also be considered – for long term investors, this represents the direct return. At a price of £2, the dividend of £0.1 per share represents a 5 per cent net return on the investment; because tax is already deducted, the dividend is free of tax up to the standard rate in the hands of the recipient. The 5 per cent return is therefore worth 7.5 per cent in gross terms to the standard taxpayer at current rates of tax. Better returns are offered by an investment in gilts. The investor has therefore to judge whether the trading prospects of Pangloss offer scope for this dividend to be steadily increased.

YEAR ENDED 31 MARCH 1982	
Earning for the year to 31.3.82	= £0.4m or 20p per share*
Recommended dividend	= £0.2m or 10p per share*
Retained profits	= £0.2m

*Issued capital 2 million ordinary shares of £1

Figure 3.7 Earnings, dividends and retentions of Pangloss PLC

TRADING PROSPECTS

The record of Pangloss will first be examined to assess the management's abilities to secure satisfactory returns. Figure 3.8 shows the ratios normally applied to the results published in the accounts to judge the management's ability in running the trading of the business.

INDUSTRIAL AVERAGE		YEAR ENDED 31 MARCH 1980	1981	1982
	Pre-interest profit (£m) a	0.8	0.9	1.0
	Turnover (£m) b	8.0	8.0	9.0
11%	Margin on sales a/b	10%	11%	11%
	Capital employed (£m) c	10.0	11.0	11.0
11%	Return on capital a/c	8%	8%	9%

Figure 3.8 Performance ratios for Pangloss PLC

Performance

Figure 3.8 shows Pangloss's performance measured against sales and capital employed. These criteria are used as a guide to management efficiency, as they allow comparison with other companies in the same industry, as well as to the underlying viability of the company. In this table, pre-interest profit (taken because it excludes interest which depends on the method of funding of the capital employed) has advanced by a quarter from £0.8m in 1980 to £1.0m in 1982; with turnover (up from £8m to £9m) and capital employed (up from £10m to £11m) both rising less fast, margins on sales and returns on capital have increased over the period. Margins at 11 per cent in 1982 are the same as for the industry as a whole, which therefore indicates normal trading returns and one without volatile fluctuations; return on capital, however, at 9 per cent, is well below the industry level of 11 per cent indicating that the amount of capital employed is high compared with other companies in the industry. Moreover, since the return of 9 per cent falls below the general level of interest rates, it is insufficient to justify the use of new capital in the business; indeed disposal of the existing assets or a change of management - whether through merger or staff recruitment - could be justified in these conditions. For the business cannot justify to its shareholders the employment of funds which could be better invested elsewhere. Thus return on capital forms a key element in the financial assessment of a company; capital in this context however has to be carefully defined and this is considered in detail with reference to the Pangloss balance sheet.

BALANCE SHEET FOR PANGLOSS PLC

Pangloss's balance sheet is given in abbreviated form in Figure 3.9.

		£M
Sources of Finance		
Share capital 2 million ordinary shares of £1		2
Retained profits		4
Shareholders' funds		6
Debt finance		
4% Debenture 1982	3	
Bank overdraft	2	5
Total funds		11
Assets Employed		
Fixed assets		
Property	5	
Machinery	1	
Vehicles	1	7
Net current assets		4
Total assets		11

Figure 3.9 Abbreviated 1982 balance sheet for Pangloss PLC

Values of shares

The first point of interest raised by the balance sheet is the book value of the shares. Of the £11m capital employed in Pangloss at the end of the 1981-2 year, £6 m is shown to be financed by shareholders' funds giving a book value of £3 each for the 2 m shares. (This allows for the assets of the company fetching the £11 m shown and thus providing £6 m surplus after paying off the debt finance of £5m.)

Scope for raising funds

Secondly the balance sheet gives an indication of the scope for raising further finance. In this case with borrowing at £5 m against £11 m capital employed, it is unlikely that lenders would be interested in advancing further funds to Pangloss. In addition to checking the company's ability to service the interest charge out of current profits, lenders are concerned with the asset backing for loans. It is rare for a company to obtain half its funds from borrowing. Within the £5 m debt the £3 m 4 per cent debenture explains the relatively low interest charge given in the profit and loss account. However, since it falls to be redeemed in 1982 it can be considered, with the bank overdraft, as short-term finance; the refinancing of the debenture could well be at a rate of interest of 15 per cent instead of 4 per cent, increasing the interest charge by £420 000 from £120 000 to £540 000. Thus the funding problems of the Pangloss Company are clearly likely to discourage investors, for shareholders will expect to be asked to contribute further equity finance.

Assets employed

However, close attention must also be paid to the assets shown in the balance sheet, for the value attributed to these assets is critical to measuring the efficiency of the company through the rate of return on capital and the potential debt finance that they can secure. In particular the value given to the property must be considered; for if the book figure represents cost or an out-of-date valuation, the current value may be considerably higher provided the property is freehold or on a long lease. The annual report must therefore be examined for details of the basis of valuation of the property; if the up-to-date value of the Pangloss property was, for instance, £8m against £5m shown, the total assets employed come to £14m; and with pre-interest profits of £1m, return on capital is little over 7 per cent, indicating that higher rewards could be gained by investing the money in gilt-edged stocks. (This assumes that the machinery, vehicles and current assets, which include stocks and debtors net of creditors, raise their book value of £6 m.) On the other hand the prospect of raising debt finance is clearly less forbidding; not only does property tend to appreciate but legal rights to it can be granted to lenders. As a result up to two-thirds of the value of the property can commonly be raised by debt finance and, provided it is invested at a rate of return that exceeds the interest charge, this offers opportunities for expansion. Property may make Pangloss attractive as a takeover prospect whether on a break-up basis or on the prospect of improving the present returns.

Assets other than land have to be treated more cautiously; the value of the plant may be minimal on a break-up basis, while current assets, such as debtors and stock, may not fully realise their book values – particularly if the company does not impose sufficient financial control. The trend of these assets to turnover will therefore be examined closely to see whether normal business standards are being achieved. On a forced realisation, these assets may recover much less than their book value if standards have not been maintained.

Other information

There is much other information that can be taken from the report, for instance on the extent of capital commitments, or the subsidiaries and associated companies of the group. These do not affect the key standards applied to the balance sheet and profit and loss account that have been examined here. These standards are used for assessing the company from several standpoints. For the shareholder the attraction of the company may be measured by the trend in

Depreciation	To adjust the depreciation charge to take account of the current value of fixed assets rather than historical cost.	Assuming: (a) depreciation charge of 10% – on fixed assets. (b) the current value of fixed assets is £1,000 but the book value is £600. A further charge of 10% on £400 (£1,000 less £600) would be made against profits.
Gearing	Offsets the impact of the previous adjustments by taking into account the proportion of funding secured by borrowings (partly reflected in the profit and loss account through the interest charge.)	Borrowings typically comprise loan capital (say) £800 deferred tax £300 other current liabilities £200 £1300 Net operating assets include: fixed assets 1,000 stocks 4,000 monetary working capital 200 5,200 The gearing adjustment is therefore $\frac{1300}{5200}$ or 25%

Adjustment	*Effect*	*Example*
Cost of Sales	To charge against profits the current cost of stocks. This ensures profits made from holding stocks are excluded since they do not form part of operating profits.	Assuming: (a) opening stocks were valued at £100 per ton. (b) all opening stocks (say 20 tons) were used during the year. (c) the value of stocks doubled to £200 per ton during the year. (d) profits would be reduced by the difference between the replacement value of opening stocks and the opening value – i.e. £100 × 20 tons =£2,000.
Monetary Working Capital	To take account of the change in working capital required to finance the net creditor/debtor position.	Assuming: (see table below) On the basis that the net increase in funding is entirely due to inflation within the business, a charge of £100 (£300 less £200) would be made against profits.

	1 Jan	31 Dec
creditors	£300	£400
debtors	£500	£700
net increase in funding	£200	£300

Figure 3.10 The impact of current cost accounting adjustments

earnings per share. Potential lenders will look at the cover for the interest charge, the proportion of capital funded by loans and the type of security offered. Management will be gauged by the margin on sales and return on capital secured. The significance of the information given in the annual report is therefore of fundamentl importance to a company in any assessment of its financial standing and the efficiency of its management.

INFLATION ACCOUNTING

As inflation is becoming more and more an accepted part of the economic environment, considerable attention has been paid to adjust company results to take this factor into account. A simple approach is to charge to the profit and loss account with the amount that is required to maintain the real value of the equity base.

However, after much debate the official approach adopted is to apply adjustments to the profit and loss account that reflect the rate of change of prices experienced by each company in its existing business, rather than the general rate of inflation – as represented, for instance, in the changes in the retail price index. The purpose of this approach is to check the success of the company in maintaining its interests rather than providing for the equity base to be maintained.

From 1 January, 1981, quoted companies with few exceptions (such as property companies, investment trusts, and insurance companies) were required to include current cost statements in their annual reports.

To judge the company's effectiveness in coping with inflation the following adjustments are made to conventional profits:

1 A cost of sales adjustment
2 An adjustment to the depreciation provision to take account of replacement value (rather than historic value) of fixed assets
3 An adjustment to allow for the consequential change in the net working capital required
4 The impact of gearing.

The impact of these adjustments is shown in Figure 3.10, and the amended profit and loss account would normally be as illustrated in Figure 3.11.

The figures can be carried down to show current cost earnings per share; current cost retentions and reserves which take account of supluses on assets valued on a current cost basis, and an amended balance sheet reconciling the liabilities (as amended by the current cost reserve) with assets on a current value basis. The major advantage of current cost accounts (CCA) is that they concentrate attention on the impact of inflation on the cash flow of a business. While accounts provided on an historical cost convention still provide the prime analysis of a company's past performance, CCA figures indicate the ability of a company to finance its operations in the future.

		Comment
Operating profit on the historical cost basis (after depreciation but before interest).	£4,000	
Current cost adjustments (see note 1)	£2,140	
Current cost operating profit	£1,860	
Gearing adjustment	465	25% of £1860
	£1,395	
Interest	395	as in 'historical accounts'
Pre-tax profits on current cost basis	£1,000	

Note 1
The current cost adjustments comprise:

Cost of sales adjustment	£2000
Monetary working capital	100
Depreciation adjustment	40
	£2140

Figure 3.11 ***Profit and loss account after current cost adjustments***
This relates to the examples in Figure 3.10

FURTHER READING

How to Read a Balance Sheet, ILO, Geneva, 1975

Merrett, A. J. and Sykes, A., *Finance and Analysis of Capital Projects*, Longman, London, 1973.

Reid, W., and Myddelton, D. R., *The Meaning of Company Accounts*, Gower, 3rd edition, 1982

Rockley, L. E., *The Meaning of Balance Sheets and Company Reports*, Business Books, London, 1975

4 Budgetary control

Alan R Leaper

All businesses have some form of budgetary control in existence whether or not they recognise it or call it by that name. Someone in the organisation co-ordinates the resources of the business in some degree to achieve some sort of plan, but whether they examine alternative plans, ideal criterion and harmony of objectives is possibly another question.

There are many benefits to be derived from the introduction of a formalised budgetary control system among which are:

1 It defines the objectives of an organisation as a whole and in financial terms
2 It provides yardsticks by which to measure efficiency for various parts of the organisation
3 It reveals the extent by which actual results have varied from the defined objective
4 It provides a guide for corrective action
5 It facilitates centralised control with delegated responsibility.

The disadvantages of a formalised procedure are by no means so readily identifiable; in general terms they usually concern the following:

1 The additional costs/personnel necessary to perform the function
2 The suspicions aroused by its introduction that it is merely another vehicle to implement cost reduction programmes
3 The complacency of paper work becoming routine with the eventual possibility that little notice or action is taken.

Immediate benefits should not be expected from the introduction of a budget procedure. It may take a year or two to educate those concerned in the proper compilation of the data required and in the proper application of the data subsequently made available.

WHAT IS A BUDGET?

A budget, in business planning, is the expression in financial (and rather summarised) terms of a comprehensive short-term operational plan for a business entity. The financial numbers relate to specific action programmes, which give rise to asset acquisitions and disposals, the earning of revenues and the incurring of expenditure. A budget in which these financial numbers have been 'pulled out of the air' is worse than useless.

Many alternative plans may be considered before the final one showing the most practical profit is chosen. Executives and other responsible officials from all functions of the company must contribute towards the plan. Data in the unit terms of each of the functions concerned must be collected and translated into monetary terms. For example, the sales manager is primarily concerned with units of the finished article or service and he would therefore contribute the volume and models to be included in the plan. The production manager talks in standard hours and efficiencies. The personnel manager will be responsible for the levels of wage rates, absenteeism factors, welfare schemes, etc. The chief executive must be fully convinced of the benefits to be derived from the plan and really believe in it.

Budgetary control is the process of managing these facets - planning and co-ordinating all functions so that they work in harmony and control performances and costs. It establishes the responsibility, throughout the corporate structure, of all managers for achieving the company's budgeted objectives. It entails measuring at suitable intervals how the plan is actually progressing and, if divergencies are occurring, taking the necessary corrective action to ensure that the company gets back on course again.

By having a budget built up in this manner it is possible to fix responsibility at every level of the organisation - and this is important.

Most managements have found that it is not sufficient to face the problems of a business on a day-to-day basis or even on a year-to-year basis; medium-term operational (or programme) planning is therefore carried out over a time-horizon of three to five years ahead. Generally, such planning involves a projection of the total market for the company's products and an assessment of what the company's share of that market should be, based on historical performance and management objectives. Obviously the degree of accuracy of the projections and plans varies with the period covered. As a matter of fact, in view of the many uncertainties involved in projecting activities over, say, a three-year period, the usual procedure is to prepare plans for the first year in considerable detail, i.e., the Budget, and then to resort to summary projections for the remaining two years. As each year's plan is done, refinements are made on the basis of recent experience and a new third year is added.

BUDGET CENTRES

Efficient control requires acceptance that costs are best controlled at the point where they are incurred. The transport manager should therefore control the transport department's cost. But the control span of any one person should not be unduly large. The area controlled by an individual is known as a *budget centre*, defined by the Institute of Cost and Management Accountants as 'A section of the organisation of the undertaking defined for the purposes of budgetary control.'

Budgets prepared at a given level of budget centre are then consolidated at the next level up (profit centre, division or company, as the case may be). A substantial business organisation will generally comprise a number of operating units, each with primary responsibility for its own profits and cash flow (profit centres) as well, perhaps, as its own capital investment (investment centres). Thus a business may include several profit centres which, in larger organisations, may be grouped into investment centres or divisions. Every division will normally have its own financial controller, responsible for preparing the divisional master budget (see the following section of this chapter). Larger profit centres may also employ their own management accountants, who prepare draft profit and loss and cash budgets. Within each budget centre there may be other smaller areas to which costs are attributable: for example, it may be desirable to identify and control groups of trucks in a transport department. Such a smaller area of control is defined as a *cost centre*, which the Institute of Cost and Management Accountants describes as 'A location, person or item of equipment, or a group of these, in or connected with an undertaking in relation to which costs may be ascertained and used for purposes of cost control.'

Within each budget centre, only one person should be responsible for incurring costs. Ultimate responsibility for budgetary control lies with the chief executive.

COMPILING A BUDGET

There is really no established order in which budgets should be prepared provided all parts are geared into a common factor. This is generally the principal limiting or bottleneck factor which varies for each individual company.

Most companies tend to establish a sales target determined on market potential and their share of the market as the basis of their budgets. Many others prefer to establish their production capacity and plan a budget to ensure the full utilisation of available equipment. The ideal, of course, is to achieve a harmony of both of these important items. However, there are many other factors which may determine the level of activity to be budgeted, amongst which are insufficient cash to finance expansion, a scarce raw material, and, possibly, the non-availability of skilled labour.

Having established the basis for compiling the budget all known external factors which could have a bearing on its fulfilment must be examined – national wage awards, sales taxes, credit squeezes, the movement of purchase prices, etc.

In larger organisations a budget committee is usually formed to review these items and determine, as best it can, the likely effect they will have on business during the period to be used in the budget. Having determined these external factors, the budget accountant/committee would advise functional and departmental managers of their effects and provide guidelines for the compilation of the subsidiary departmental budgets, the main examples of which are considered below.

Sales budget

The sales budget should show total sales, expressed both by value and quantity. It may be further analysed by product, by area, by customer and, of course, by seasonal pattern of expected sales. The main problems arise in determining quantities and in the calculation of standard prices. Constraints such as competitive activity have to be borne in mind (new products and aggressive pricing policies).

The budget should be compiled by the sales manager. He will seek the opinions of his salesmen and use any statistical forecasting techniques arising from market research. Other considerations include general business and economic conditions, company advertising policy, new products, supplies, product demand and plant capacity. A special pricing study is usually helpful at this stage, and this should show the complete product range, the relevant market sector, competitive models or products (taking into account both the pricing and the features available), introduction dates, discount structures and advertising strategy. In some cases, when jobbing production is involved, budgets must be made in terms of the expected sales value only.

Production budget

The production budget is a statement of the output by product, and is generally expressed in standard hours. It should take into consideration the sales budget, plant capacity, whether stocks are to be increased or decreased and outside purchases. The form the production budget would take depends on circumstances. Usually, the quantities are shown for each department (budget centres) and information is taken from machine loading charts, material specifications, time schedules and other production or time-study records.

When computing labour cost, the average labour rate used depends on the wage plan in effect. For hourly rated employees not on incentive bonuses, an overall plant rate may be sufficient. In other cases, departmental or labour grade rates may be used. When a straight piece rate plan is in force, the labour cost is the amount paid per unit produced. When other incentive plans are used, labour rates have to be computed to include estimated amounts for bonus payments. In companies using standard costs, cost accounting records can be very useful in determining budget requirements for non-productive direct labour. Many cost accounting systems are sophisticated enough to indicate the breakdown of non-productive direct labour into down time, waiting time, changeover or set-up time and so on.

The plant manager will prepare the production budget in close collaboration with accountants, production engineers, work study engineers and other key personnel. Adequate lead times for the delivery of new equipment and the development of new processes must be considered.

At this stage, the sales and production budgets should be compared to ensure maximum utilisation of capacity aligned to satisfactory sales growth. If the sales budget exceeds production capacity, then decisions on capital expenditure and new plant may be required before proceeding further. If, on the other hand, significant under-utilisation of capacity is denoted, decisions on how best to use this spare capacity must be taken (to determine, for example, if sub-contract work would be profitable, if a revised pricing structure could increase the volume of sales, or if plant should be declared surplus and sold off or scrapped, etc.).

Production costs budget

This supplementary budget should determine the 'cost of sales' allied to the required production.

Generally, by far the largest element in cost terms is direct material. This part should be compiled by the chief buyer in conjunction with the production manager. Using the sales and production budgets, it will determine the requirements of raw material and piece-parts, period by period, to meet the output, and will be evaluated in cash cost terms. Considerations should take into account bulk buying, delivery periods, stock holding, suppliers credit terms and trade discounts, as well as recognising any changes in material specifications, new model introductions, etc. In timing the purchase of raw materials, piece-parts etc., consideration must be given to the necessity to keep inventory levels to the very minimum and thereby not tie up valuable capital. Special competitive pricing exercises should be undertaken from potential suppliers to ensure that costs are strictly controlled and keen.

Direct labour is another most important element of production costs. The work study department should be called upon to establish standard times for individual units. These may then be evaluated by the required volumes and converted into direct labour requirements. The degree of labour efficiency must be determined, as must the type of employee necessary, that is, male/female; skilled/semi-skilled/unskilled.

Direct expense budgets covering warehousing, transportation, warranty and special tools should be determined by the appropriate managers responsible for incurring or approving the respective expenses.

Factory overhead costs (burden) should be established by departmental foremen and consolidated by the production manager. Expenses of all types should be considered and some assistance may be necessary from the finance department in determining depreciation, insurance and other expenses possibly beyond the control of the local foremen.

Personnel budget

This is a headcount schedule of the total labour requirements necessary to carry out the sales and production budgets and, in fact, run the whole business from managing director to office boy and production worker to office cleaner. It should be prepared by the personnel department in conjunction with all other functional departmental heads.

The schedule will show the number of personnel required, the hours to be worked, wage rates, salaries etc., and should be built up by departments. The respective costs should, of course, be incorporated in the applicable departmental budgets. The recruitment and training policies of the company will be incorporated in the budget and cognisance should be taken of all labour-related costs - for example, national insurance, and pension schemes.

Operating and service department budgets

The type of department falling into this category may be administration, finance, selling, advertising and service, and might also include warehousing and shipping. The departmental head of each of these functions will be responsible for compiling his individual budget. The data included will cover personnel requirements by number and grade and be cost-determined in conjunction with the personnel manager; and departmental running costs detailed by account, namely utilities, operating expenses, depreciation, insurance, rates, etc.

Special note should be taken of competitors' activity in determining the size and use of the advertising budget.

If raw material or bulk purchases are necessary, the usage and cost of these will be planned with the purchasing agent or chief buyer.

The basis of determining costs included in these budgets invariably depends on the actual trend in previous years adjusted, of course, for known changes. It should also be remembered that historical costs will include inefficiencies and these must be identified and determined if likely to continue. The considered effects of volume and activity should also be borne in mind.

Capital expenditure budget

This supplementary budget is usually compiled by senior management in conjunction with engineering and technical services.

The budget will show details of the capital expenditure proposals in the period of the master budget and will probably be prepared for a number of years because of its longer-term implications. Items included will be distinguished by the various types of asset - land, buildings, equipment, furniture, etc., and should also state the reasons for proposals - replacement, new methods, capacity, etc.

Back-up data should also accompany the proposals to justify the expenditures, and will take the usual forms of capital evaluations, such as return on investment and discounted cash flow analysis. The strain on cash resources should also be considered when compiling this budget.

Profit and loss account

The first component of the master budget is the budgeted profit and loss account. This budget will summarise the effects of all the relevant data contained in the supplementary operating and service budgets, sales, purchasing, personnel and capital expenditure (depreciation, salvage receipts) budgets. It will be prepared in months or other chosen periods and be compiled by the financial controller. A sample profit and loss statement incorporating provisions for budget and standards is shown in Figure 4.1.

Cash budget

The second component of the master budget is the cash budget, which is critical in view of the possible constraints that an unsatisfactory cash availability position may have on the required expansion of a business and hence on the acceptability of the master budget as a whole.

The financial controller, with the assistance of all other management, should determine the timing by period, usually monthly, of production, sales, fixed asset purchases etc., and then prepare the effects on the cash balance. The reason for this budget is to determine by period where additional cash may be required or where surplus cash may be available for short-term investments.

The income side is built up from the sales and debtors budget plus any other miscellaneous receipts, such as loans, new capital, sale of assets, grants, interest, etc. On the expenditure side will be the incurred expenses of the production and service department budgets, purchasing and capital expenditure budgets plus other payments relating to the distribution of profits, such as dividends and income taxes.

Balance sheet

The third component of the master budget is the projected balance sheet which will show the net effect of the budgets on the financial position of the company. Again, being compiled by the financial controller, it will consider information contained in the budgeted profit and loss account, capital expenditures and cash and the related movement of the working capital and financing.

Management must examine these results of the profit and loss, cash and balance sheet master budgets that result from the consolidation of the subsidiary budgets and determine if they are acceptable. Do they show the most practical overall profit to be accepted as a plan for the ensuing year or period to be budgeted? If the answer is negative then the problem areas should be determined and the departments concerned advised specifically of their shortcomings. As all the budgets are mainly interrelated, such a change generally means the re-submission of all the subsidiary budgets. Whilst this exercise may appear to be rather long-winded and even time-wasting, it is one of the real values of preparing budgets in this manner in that the consideration, discussion and communication of the short-term profit objective of the company is involving all levels of management in its achievement, and by this process is most likely to reveal the maximum practical profit objective for the company.

In practice, a lot of companies tend to take either sales or production in

	Budget	%	Standard	%	Actual	%	Variance
Current Month							
Gross Sales							
Less: Deductions from sales							
Total Net Sales							
Manufacturing Standard Costs							
Material							
Labour							
Burden							
Direct expense							
Total Standard Costs							
Standard Manufacturing Gross Profit							
Budget and Volume Variances							
Actual Manufacturing Gross Profit							
Expenses							
Selling							
Advertising							
Administrative							
Engineering							
Total Expenses							
Operating Profit							
Net Profit Before Taxes							
Income Tax Provision							
Net Profit							

Figure 4.1 Example of a profit and loss statement with provision for budgets and standards

isolation and agree independently what the level of activity should be in these fields; once decided on, they proceed to build all the other budgets around them. If the resultant profit is in excess of the outlook for the current year, they are happy to leave it as such. However, assuming that the job is to be tackled properly, it is at this stage of review that any attempts at over-budgeting or, worse still, conservative budgeting, should be weeded out. The level of responsibility for performance of the plan from each manager should be agreed upon, so that he fully commits himself to its attainment.

When the master budgets have been finally agreed upon and accepted, they should be adopted formally by management as its policy and plan for the forthcoming year or period and thereby provide a budget against which performance or achievement will be measured.

CONTROLLING THE PLAN

As indicated, budgets are built up by responsibility. It follows, therefore, that operating statements will be prepared for each budget centre involved. These operating statements should form part of the management information system used to control actual performance against the budget plan.

Good budgetary control follows the theory of 'management by exception'. Whilst management is provided with full details of expenditure, sales, production, etc., under its functional control, reports and information should be focused on matters that are adverse, or that show an unusual favourable variance, so that its energy is concentrated in the right direction and its effort is not being diluted with a lot of information which merely indicates that things are going as planned.

There are differing schools of thought on the amount of detail that should be provided to management. Some management accountants prefer to provide only data over which managers have some degree of control. For instance, if depreciation policy is decided by the board, there is no point in giving an operational manager a depreciation charge for say, the machine shop. He has no control over what that charge will be; according to this theory, this information is unnecessary and does not help him to perform his part of the plan under normal conditions. This theory does not give management the full picture and lacks the important benefit of enabling management to see the overall effect and contribution of its department to the business as a whole. The statement may be broken down into two sections labelled 'controllable' and 'uncontrollable'. Just what is controllable or uncontrollable can be surprising. For example, a shop foreman shown a list of fixed assets in his area on which there is a depreciation charge may well indicate items of equipment which are surplus to his requirements but for which he has not bothered to raise a disposal request. These items can then be removed from the department, sold with good salvage values being obtained, valuable floor space being released, routine maintenance checks ceasing and administration time and effort being saved in searching for and identifying equipment at physical inventory time.

Timing of feedback

Timing is of great importance. When should the measurement of control be effected, and over what period? Having decided what period the budget is to cover (usually annual) the budget itself will be divided into sub-periods: possibly months and quarters, or perhaps into thirteen four-weekly intervals, depending on the type of business. In addition to the detailed annual budget, most companies have some form of long-range planning for a number of years ahead covering, for instance, the profit and loss account, balance sheet, cash flow and capital expenditure.

This longer-term planning concerns itself primarily with determining whether or not the internal fund flow of the business will cover its commitments and capital expenditure programme, etc., but of course the longer-term plans will not be prepared in anything like the same detail as the yearly short-term operating budget. It is a matter of individual company requirements to determine which data is best controlled on a quarterly, monthly, weekly or even daily basis.

An organisation must generally have a fairly sophisticated accounting system to generate and disseminate information on a daily basis and this type of data is generally confined to production data. Standard hours produced, finished units, efficiencies, absenteeism, etc., all lend themselves to daily control. Billings in terms of unit sales and value would best be reviewed on a weekly basis, although for local consumption this, again, may be preferred on a rough daily basis.

All other profit and loss and cash flow data would be embodied in monthly financial statements. A balance sheet could be prepared on a quarterly basis.

Whatever is right for a business must be determined by the constraints within which it works and what is needed to control the situation. Normally, data of a daily and weekly nature are restricted to middle management to facilitate operational control and are not fed through the pyramid of top management unless a special situation demands such close control. As a general rule, the lower down the management line one goes, the sooner information should be in management's hands. The foreman should have his output in standard hours measured against budget and his material usage for his batch of machines during the following morning so that he can take the necessary corrective action to correct any deviation from his target.

Thus it has been said that this first-line information is the life blood of the business, and the accounting results which follow at the end of the month confirm and quantify an already known situation.

FLEXIBLE BUDGETS

One criticism sometimes levelled at budgetary control is its rigidity. In practice, actual results may be the outcome of circumstances which have changed from those existing when the budget was first prepared. Budgets, when set and agreed upon, can only be based on one set of circumstances. As actual conditions seldom equate with budgeted conditions, the difference between actual costs and budgeted costs must be demonstrated. Information should therefore be available to suggest the appropriate level of expenses, generally known as budget standards, which fluctuate at varying levels of production activity or sales volume.

Flexible budgetary control (as opposed to fixed budgeting) was introduced to control this situation. Flexible budgeting is applied in businesses where it is impossible to make a firm forecast of future conditions. Although fixed budgeting should be satisfactory for the more stable industries, these are very few and far between. Flexible budgeting is more widely applicable.

Flexible budgeting is designed to provide a more realistic picture of the variance between actual expenses and budgeted expenses. One expects to be able to distinguish that part of the variance which is due to volume and for which a manager will not have control, and that part of the variance over which the manager should have control. To achieve this, one must be in a position to calculate budget standards at varying levels of activity.

The application of this calculation is demonstrated below by considering first a report on the basis of fixed budgeting and then showing a similar report calculated on a flexible budgeting basis. Before looking at these reports, it must be clear that costs are classified for flexible budgeting purposes. This in itself is a most difficult task and one that may be tackled in many ways which cannot be amplified in this chapter. However, for the purpose of this exercise, the following broad categories are used:

1 Fixed costs – costs which do not vary in the short term with volume
2 Variable costs – costs which do so vary
3 Semi-variable costs – costs which will vary with volume but not in direct relationship.

The later chapter on cost accounting gives more details of these types of costs: of course, if standard costing is already applied in the company, the setting of a flexible budget is rendered considerably easier. If standard costs are not available, the technique of marginal costing will need to be applied in dealing with individual costs to determine the degree of variability. Scatter graphs or

Expense type	Budget (£)	Actual (£)	Variance (£)
Material	10 000	12 500	+ 2500
Labour	5 000	5 900	+ 900
Rent	3 000	3 000	—
Salaries	1 000	1 100	+ 100
	19 000	22 500	+3500

Figure 4.2 Example of fixed budgeting

the regression theory may be used. Figure 4.2 is based on fixed budgeting and demonstrates how much the actual is off target. This type of measurement is an improvement on, say, measuring against last year's performance when circumstances may have been different. The report provides some conception of the amount by which actual experience varies from budgeted plans.

However, if one is to adhere to one of the basic principles of budgetary control, that people should only be responsible for cost over which they have control, this report may not provide the solution.

Figure 4.3 applies similar information but is calculated on the basis of flexible budgeting. Thus, clearly, the advantages of flexible budgeting are demonstrated by the second report. It shows in reality that instead of the manager being responsible for an adverse variance of £3500 as he was in the first report, he is, in fact, only responsible for the adverse variance of £500, the

	Budget			Actual	Variance Analysis	
	Standard per unit	Fixed budget	Flexed budget		Control-able	Volume
Output in units		10 000	12 000	12 000	—	+ 2 000
% of original budget		100%	120%	120%	—	+ 20%
		£	£	£	£	£
Variable Costs						
Material	£1.00	10 000	12 000	12 500	+ 500	+ 2 000
Labour	£0.50	5 000	6 000	5 900	- 100	+ 1 000
Fixed Costs						
Rent		3 000	3 000	3 000	—	—
Salaries		1 000	1 000	1 100	+ 100	—
TOTAL		19 000	22 000	22 500	+ 500	+ 3 000

Figure 4.3 Example of flexible budgeting

remaining £3000 being due to increased volume in production which may be the result of conservative sales forecasting, or some other factor which must be taken up with some other department in the organisation.

Flexible budgeting is thus extremely useful for getting behind the causes of variances, particularly if quantities, as well as costs, have been budgeted. With sales variances, for example, one can determine whether the variance is due to prices, volume, outlet mixture, product mixture, or a combination of these.

USE OF COMPUTERS

Generally, manual methods of making the planning computations are time-consuming, with the result that only a few alternative plans of operation can be fully evaluated when setting a budget and analysis of variances may be limited by time constraints. Computerised financial models have been developed to assist in simulating what the results would be under many different assumptions as to volume, products and plans of operation. Most steps in budgeting usually involve some alternative assumptions or decisions, and the final outcome of the budget process can vary greatly in terms of the profits and resources which will result from each assumption or decision. As a practical matter, the burden of making the planning and budgeting computations, under even one set of assumptions, is generally considered to be all that a company can expect its people to carry in addition to their current operating responsibilities. Very often the work is such that deadlines are missed and budgets for the new year are not available on time. The computerised financial model takes the drudgery out of the computations, once the computer programs are prepared, by applying the given relationships to different sets of assumptions and conditions. This process of simulating different methods of operations is a big help in exploring the alternatives available in the planning process.

ZERO-BASE BUDGETING

Zero-base budgeting is a technique for short-term operational planning, whereby existing levels of expenditure on ongoing activities are systematically questioned. This is in contrast to the more common 'incremental' approach. In incremental budgeting, the benchmark tends to be the level of activity and expenditure in the immediate past, budget proposals being related to this in terms of 'more' or 'less'. In zero-base budgeting, the benchmark is the 'minimum survival' level of activity and expenditure as seen by the manager of the activity in question. If the budget proposal is only to maintain the existing level of activity, assuming this to be above the 'minimum survival' level, the proposal must explain why the additional expenditure involved over and above the 'minimum survival' level is justified. A manager in charge of several activities will be required to state which level of expenditure on each of these activities he would choose if he could only spend, say, 80 per cent of his budget. The point of this approach is to squeeze out 'budget slack' at the lower levels of decision-making and to allow the senior levels to decide how, if at all, the balance of the budget will be spent.

INSTALLING THE SYSTEM

The organisational chart should be examined with a view to determining where the responsibility for sales, costs and profits really lies. Revisions where appropriate, may be considered at this time. The organisation structure should be so developed as to fix responsibility right down the line. There must be an organisation chart which clearly defines the levels of responsibility and the chain of command, setting out who is responsible for what and to whom. It is desirable to support each functional position with a job description defining the function, duty and responsibility. Tradition must be ignored, responsibility and control being given to those who are responsible for taking the decisions, but care must be taken to preserve the 'business flair' of an organisation, and those given the responsibility should be placed where their individual resources can be best used.

The key factors should then be determined before designing the system most suitable to the company's needs. The system design should cover flow diagrams of the information generated, collection data necessary for budget preparation and control reports to be subsequently prepared. During this period consideration should be given to the level of sophistication of the existing information system, whether the proposed system will provide an improvement and also the level of human resources with which one has to work the new system.

Having obtained a positive reaction to these considerations, the next step is to test the initial design with various personnel at all levels in order to determine its suitability to meet their requirements for management information.

Once initial design is finalised, the next step is to prepare a series of seminars and teach-ins to explain the thinking behind the purpose and operation of the system. Questions, constructive criticisms and improvements should be invited so that all are involved and communicate at all levels.

A timetable for installation of the programme should be established. A critical path analysis is the ideal basis for identifying the order in which the budget data should be collected and which information is to be cross-referred to two or more departments.

Now is the time for the collection of information for the 'first budget'. Considerable time, assistance and guidance should be made available to staff at this stage, and perseverance on behalf of those taking responsibility for the installation of the system will be required. It is vital that all levels of management go through the discipline of thinking through and preparing their portion of the budgets. Miracles should not be expected from the first results. It is not unusual for a company to take two or three years to get a control system of this nature fully operational. However, at each stage one should expect to produce some results which are usable even in the first year. What these results will be may differ from company to company but initially they usually provide a good insight to sales and cash flow data. An important by-product is management eduction and awareness of what the business is all about.

Budget period

There is no general rule governing the selection of a period of time for a budget. This will be decided by the particular circumstances of the business. For instance the fashion industry must, of necessity, have a very short budget period, sometimes of three or four months duration, whereas in the shipbuilding industry a budget may range over three or four years. For most businesses, however, the calendar year is normally the accepted period: it is broken down into twelve monthly periods and the information is complementary to the published accounts.

However, if there is a strong seasonal influence affecting sales, it is sometimes prudent to have a 'model year' upon which to base the budget and this usually starts just ahead of the main selling period. Businesses which rely mainly on the summer or Christmas trade may well justify a model year. Model years, as the name implies, usually commence with the introduction of new models. A car manufacturer, for example, may run its model year from September to the following August in order to have a good start to the year following the autumn motor shows and new year car registrations. The motive behind this is that if business has not gone as well as expected there is still sufficient time before the end of the model year to curtail activity, restrict costs and reconsider expansion programmes or introduce special promotions in order to keep profits in line with, or better than, budget.

Budget manual

It is helpful to have such a document available within the company so that there is no ambiguity about what is required of each individual in relation to budgets. The type of information one might expect the budget manual to contain is a brief explanation of the purposes of budgetary control as practiced within the company and organisation charts and job descriptions showing quite specifically the budget responsibilities for each function; routing of budgetary control forms for collection and control documentation; timetables or programmes for completion of budgets and control data feedback; budget periods; samples of reports and statements to be employed and accounts classification and coding data.

Budget committees

The question of who should control the preparation of budgets and who should review these controls is one that each organisation arrives at during some stage of the budget preparation.

It is desirable that top and middle management contribute to and agree levels of activity to be budgeted, although it must be recognised that the human factor involved makes this difficult to achieve. A keen manager, anxious to please at a budget review meeting, will possibly incorporate a stretch element to his plan. Another manager setting his own targets against which his performance is to be measured may be inclined to be over cautious (particularly if an achievement bonus is paid). Investigations have been made in this area and the results carry important lessons for the business man interested in making the most of his budget system. One conclusion is that the budgets studied were used as pressure devices for constantly increasing efficiency, but because of the effects on people, the budgets tended to generate a long-run result of decreased efficiency. Naturally enough, this is attributed to the lack of participation in the budget preparation phase by those being budgeted and to the lack of sales ability on the part of accounting personnel. Another study concludes that successful budgeting is more concerned with human relationships than with accounting techniques and that if good principles of human relationships are applied, successful budget practices become inevitable. Yet another appraisal of current business budgeting indicates that important weaknesses in practice are the result of superficial appreciation of budget concepts by management, inadequate techniques, and the absence of a disciplined environment in many organisations. Upon reflection, it becomes apparent that the requirements for a successful budget operation are not restricted to accounting or finance planning techniques but that successful managers are those who keep such considerations in mind while executing the more mechanical aspects of the budget process.

There are various views held on this point. If operating managements are made responsible for profits, then one of the objectives of budgetary control, that is, the proper co-ordination of the organisation, is achieved.

The same processes should be involved as with the control aspect. What an organisation should attempt to achieve is the total commitment of all levels of management to the plan. Each level of management should review its plans and performances through the usual management committees, be they formal or informal groupings, right up to the chief executive, and the overall objective should be clear and unambiguous at each stage.

However, one person will be responsible for pulling together the various parts of the master budget. This job usually falls on the chief accountant or financial controller or his department. Larger companies employ a budget manager and, of course, this co-ordinating exercise naturally falls into his lap. He may be called upon to undertake a number of exercises to determine what the various results thrown up mean within the overall company objectives, but it must be emphasised that his role is one of support. The responsibility is fixed upon the persons committing and accepting stewardship over resources.

The budget organisation can be regarded as analogous to a telephone company operating an important communications system; it is responsible for the speed, accuracy and clarity with which the messages flow through the system, but not for the content of the messages themselves.

Information codes

Budgetary control has extended control information beyond the more traditional accounting information to broader aspects of control, setting out data in terms of hours worked, output of production in standard hours, information on market share, quality of product, etc. This is all necessary for the achievement of the plan. However, looking at the pure accounting contribution to budgetary control, a suitable system of accounts coding should be designed so that the information is collected and analysed within the budget and cost centres.

The accounting code should be what is commonly called a subjective/objective system. The subjective part of the code should qualify information into its primary or traditional classification, that is, the nature of the expenses, for example, wages, fuel, rent, etc. The objective part of the code will be used to analyse the expenditure to the cost and burden centres, that is machine X in the machine shop.

It is important to give considerable thought to the design of the coding system, as it should not only be able to cope with existing needs for information, but also have the flexibility to be expanded to meet future demands. A system of this sort should enable a company, using the subjective code, to produce information necessary for the preparation of the traditional statutory accounts. And by going through the objective section of the code, the information required for budgetary control and management accounting can be produced which should be made available to those drawing up the budgets as appropriate.

CONCLUSIONS

Budgetary control often strikes apprehension or fear into non-financial people. People tend to be sceptical or untrusting of having their performances measured against a standard. This is a human and understandable response. Most people, at some time during their careers, have had budgetary control used against them as a cost reduction tool.

It is up to finance managers to clarify and emphasise that budget flexing and control is an essential and deliberate need of modern-day management. It is a management tool designed as a *fair* basis upon which to measure performance against a predetermined plan, and conduct business in the most efficient manner possible, thereby improving profitability.

FURTHER READING

Cave, S. R., *Budgetary Control and Standard Costing*, 3rd edition, Gee, London, 1973

Willsmore, A. W., *Business Budgets in Practice*, 5th edition, Pitman, London, 1973

5 Managing working capital

Leon Simons

LIQUIDITY

Working capital is normally taken to mean the excess of current assets over current liabilities, this amount being the net current assets. If the balance sheet for ABC PLC is examined (Figure 5.1) the working capital for that company is seen to be £3 065 539 minus £2 505 132, which amounts to £560 407.

The working capital indicates the liquidity of the company, and there are two commonly used ratios to express the degree of liquidity. One is the current ratio which is simply the current assets divided by the current liabilities. ABC's current ratio is $\frac{3065}{2505}$ = approximately 1.2.

Some accountants consider that it is more useful to ignore inventories when looking at liquidity, since they could take considerably longer to turn into cash than debtors or creditors. They feel that it is more pertinent to compare the quick assets (current assets minus inventories) with the current liabilities. This is known as the quick ratio or acid test ratio and is

$\frac{\text{quick assets}}{\text{current liabilities}}$ which in ABC's case is $\frac{2190}{2505}$ or 0.88.

There is no generally ideal current ratio since companies differ so greatly from each other. 1.2 may be appropriate for a light engineering company like ABC PLC with a short production cycle. The same ratio, however, may be too low for a company with a longer cycle and a proportionately bigger stock investment. On the other hand, a supermarket with no work in progress (because it does not manufacturer) and no debtors (because its business is purely cash) would very likely have a current ratio of less than 1; that is, an excess of current liabilities over current assets.

One should try neither to maximise nor minimise the liquidity ratios; one should try to optimise them in relation to the objective, which in the case of a commercial company is probably the maximisation of profit on capital employed. The lower the liquidity ratios are, the more vulnerable the company is to pressure from creditors which it is unable to meet. The higher the liquidity ratios, the more the capital which is not being fully exploited in terms of the return earned on it. Therefore, one should seek to have as little working capital as is consistent with not being unduly vulnerable to pressure from creditors. This ideal level of liquidity would not only vary from company to company but would vary through time in one company as conditions changed.

Stock

Excess stockholding has an adverse effect on liquidity. The ratio normally used for assessing stock level is the stock/turnover ratio. ABC's ratio is

$\frac{875}{6364} = 13\frac{3}{4}\%$, which expressed as a percentage of a year is about 7 weeks.

(The denominator is the turnover stated in Figure 5.2.)

This figure on its own has little absolute significance but, like most other management ratios, can be used to monitor changes through time. We do not know if 7 weeks' average stock is too high or too low or how great a deviation there is around the average. Like liquidity, stockholding has to be balanced; it should be neither maximised nor minimised but optimised in terms of profit. Too much stock means that there is money tied up in it which is costing more than it is contributing. Too little stock means that the cost of lost sales due to being out of stock exceeds the savings made in not holding the additional stock.

However, there are other factors to be considered in deciding the optimum stock level: for example, whether there are additional costs in holding increased stock rather than just the interest on the capital. If the stock level were to be reduced by a given amount, would the company be able to vacate a warehouse with consequent savings in rates, rent, insurance, heating etc? How many storemen could be dismissed or redeployed?

Stock appreciation should also be brought into account. If the company uses volatile commodities, it might save a great deal of money in holding more than its immediate requirements of a material whose market price is expected to rise during the period covered by the holding: this saving may far outweigh the extra stocking costs and throw in as a bonus freedom from the danger of being caught out of stock.

The stock ratio is not ideal in a number of respects. Firstly, the turnover is at selling prices, while the stock is at cost. Secondly, the turnover covers a period, while the stock is at a point of time which may not be typical of the period. Thirdly, the cost of the stock is not factual but is a function of the company's costing system which includes arbitrary assumptions and subjective judgements.

Debtors

Apart from inventories, a major development of working capital is in the credit

ABC PLC

BALANCE SHEET

as at 28 February 1982

		1982		1981	
		£	£	£	£
Share capital and reserves					
Share capital					
5 500 000 ordinary shares of 10p each (authorised 7 400 000)			550 000		550 000
Reserves					
Share premium		182 727			
Other reserves		734 412			
Ordinary shareholders'			917 139		814 543
funds			1467 139		1364 543
Minority shareholders' interest			154 620		82 050
Secured loans			360 957		—
Current liabilities					
Creditors		938 009		545 552	
Taxation		394 246	356 311	356 311	
Bank overdraft (secured)		936 927		634 619	
Proposed dividends		235 950		206 250	
			2 505 132		1 742 732
			4 487 848		3 189 325
Fixed assets	Cost or valuation	Aggregate Depreciation	Written down value		Written down value
Freehold land and buildings	585 818	7 044	578 774		400 346
Plant and motor vehicles	1 191 729	348 194	843 535		453 603
	1 777 547	355 238	1 422 309		853 949
Interest in subsidiary not consolidated			—		88 765
Current Assets					
Stocks and work-in-progress		875 196		594 628	
Debtors		1 906 981		1 621 063	
Cash at bank and in hand		283 362		30 920	
			3 065 539		2 246 611
			4 487 848		3 189 325

Figure 5.1 Group balance sheet for ABC PLC

Group balance sheet of a manufacturing light engineering company and its subsidiaries as at 28 February 1982 with the corresponding figures (as required by law) as at 28 February 1981

ABC PLC

PROFIT AND LOSS ACCOUNT

For the year ended 28 February 1982

	1982	1981
	£	£
Turnover	6 364 014	5 088 579
Profit before taxation (see note 1)	613 883	922 022
Deduct: taxation	262 108	370 691
	351 775	551 331
Deduct: exceptional item	—	12 500
Profit after taxation	351 775	538 831
Add: proportion of losses attributable to minority shareholders	6 648	2 500
	358 423	541 331
Dividends	235 950	288 750
Balance retained and added to reserves	122 473	252 581
Earnings per 10p ordinary share	6.5p	9.8p
Note 1		
After deducting:		
Depreciation	133 808	90 780
Emoluments of directors	61 573	42 480
Auditors' remuneration	12 723	9 500
Interest on bank overdraft	32 330	14 772
Interest on secured loans	25 573	—
Hire of equipment	10 321	5 004

Figure 5.2 Profit and loss account for ABC PLC
The profit and loss account summarises receipts and costs of a company over a given period. This example covers the year ended 28 February 1982 and complements the balance sheet for ABC PLC shown in Figure 5.1.

taken by customers. This does not of course apply to those retailers and others who do not conduct a credit trade. The debtors/sales ratio is the measure, and this again is usually expressed in weeks. ABC's ratio is

$\frac{1907}{6364}$ = 30% or about 15½ weeks. This ratio has the same disadvantage as that

mentioned concerning the stock ratio, namely that the point of time at which the debtors are taken may not be typical of the period to which the turnover relates. Alternatively, there may be a strong seasonal bias within the year's total sales figure. For example, if two-thirds of the year's turnover was sold in the second six months, then the ratio is $\frac{1907}{4242} \times 26$ weeks, which is just under 12 weeks. However, this is a problem for the external readers of the balance sheet, since managers with access to the management accounts could take the seasonal bias into consideration in calculating the ratio.

Creditors

These are the opposite side of the coin to the debtors. They are a source of funds to the company, and the more capital the company can borrow from this source, the less it requires from others, or alternatively the more it can deploy in various assets and build up the activity (and possibly the return) on the same net capital.

The creditors, being money owing in respect of purchases, will be compared with the purchases in the recent period and expressed in weeks. The purchases are not a figure which is required to be shown separately in the published accounts, but once again it will be available to managers. They should use it in the same way as the debtors' ratio by allowing for the seasonal bias.

Readers of the published accounts can make the assumption that purchases are roughly the same proportion of sales in the recent year as they were in the previous year. Then they can compare the movement of creditors with that of debtors, ABC's debtors increased from £1 621 063 to £1 906 981 by 17½ per cent. The creditors rose from £545 552 to £938 009 which is over 73 per cent and a considerable relative improvement. Indeed, in absolute terms the increase in creditors exceeds the increase in debtors, so that the net cost of credit to the company may have fallen despite the increase in turnover.

However, the average length of credit taken by the company from its suppliers is still not known. Suppose for the sake of argument that the £938 000 represents two months credit, that is, average monthly purchases have been running at half that level. Then, an increase of one month to three months will, other things being equal, raise borrowing from this source by about £469 000 and at the same time reduce the bank overdraft by the same amount. The total current liabilities will remain the same but the company will have substituted additional borrowing from suppliers for part of what it previously borrowed from the bank. The effect on profit of the change, assuming overdraft interest at, say, 15 per cent pa, is a gain of about £70 000 pa. This is not a once and for all gain but will continue at that rate for as long as the additional credit is taken. This assumes that *(a)* purchases continue at the current level, *(b)* interest rates continue at 15 per cent pa and *(c)* relations with suppliers remain unaltered.

If there are changes in either *(a)* or *(b)* the effects can be easily ascertained, but assumption *(c)* requires careful consideration. If we take more credit from a supplier, will that supplier react and if so how will his reaction affect us?

There are a number of things the supplier can do, from writing a letter (which costs the customer nothing) to withholding supplies (which may cost the customer a great deal). Between these extremes, he may reduce quality, increase prices, cut down deliveries and so on. However, there is doubt about the validity of these intermediate reactions.

He may reduce the quality of the product or the frequency of delivery or after-sales service, but this may not be acceptable to the customer who may then withdraw his custom. Before taking any of these steps, the supplier would have to be prepared for this eventuality, the effect of which would be the same as if he himself withheld supplies.

Similarly, if the supplier increases his prices, the higher prices may or may not be acceptable to the customer. If they are, why did the supplier not increase them previously? If they are not, he once again risks losing the business. Therefore, the question facing the supplier is whether or not he can risk losing the business.

From the customer's point of view, he must decide whether he can tolerate loss of supplies from this source because, even though it may not be in the supplier's best interest to stop supplies, he may act irrationally and the customer must be prepared for this. The summary of this discussion is that the customer's ability to take longer credit from a particular supplier depends on the balance of power between them.

Since this varies with different suppliers it follows that an individual credit policy with at least the major suppliers is necessary if optimum credit is to be taken. If a blanket credit policy is adopted to cover all suppliers, this assumes that they are all equally powerful, which is most unlikely to be the case. The consequence of this would be to take from some less credit than one could take with impunity, and to take from others more than is wise.

These arguments apply with equal force to debtor control, and since sales exceed purchases tight debtor control is even more important.

It is often suggested that if a company takes longer credit from its suppliers, its own customers will in turn extend their credit and the move will be self-defeating. This is woolly thinking.

Customers cannot know how a company behaves to its suppliers, save in the exceptional case where customer and supplier are the same and a two-way trade is conducted. In the normal case, the customer will take whatever credit he thinks he can get away with – with impunity. This consideration is based on the same assessment of relative power as already discussed concerning creditors.

However, many companies recognise the importance of intelligent debtor control and designate is as a specific management function, whilst attention is paid to prompt invoicing and follow-up procedures. It is the treatment of credit obtainable from suppliers that is relatively neglected.

Cash discount

So far we have not considered the effect on one's credit policy if one is offered a discount for prompt payment. For example, a supplier may offer a discount of $2\frac{1}{2}$ per cent on invoice for payment within 30 days.

If one pays two months from date of invoice and forgoes the discount, one has in fact borrowed for one extra month (since the first 30 days would be taken in any event) at a cost of $2\frac{1}{2}$ per cent which is equivalent to a straight annual cost of $12 \times 2\frac{1}{2}$ per cent = 30 per cent. The discounted annual rate would be even higher than this. Since one is borrowing at say 15 per cent from the bank, 30 per cent is far too dear to contemplate. Break-even point would occur with 3 months' credit; ie 2 extra months at a cost of $2\frac{1}{2}$ per cent = $\frac{12 \times 2\frac{1}{2}}{2}$ per cent or 15 per cent pa. Therefore, it is only worthwhile losing the discount if one can take at least 3 months' credit. However, if bank facilities are scarce it will pay to borrow at more than 15 per cent from suppliers if the benefit derived from the utilisation of the extra credit exceeds the cost.

So far in this chapter the various factors concerning liquidity have been discussed. We have seen that suboptimal utilisation of working capital is expensive. At least, it costs the interest on the unnecessary money used, but it also prevents that money from being properly employed in the company and could inhibit the company's growth through lack of cash.

Cash flow

Liquidity is the life-blood of the company and lack of cash is the only thing which could force the company out of business. Cash flows into the company by direct cash sales and the collection of debts from customers, and also, though less regularly, from the sale of assets. Cash flows out in direct purchases and payments to creditors, in payment of wages and other costs, and in the purchase of capital equipment. It also flows out in payment of taxes and interest on borrowed money and dividends to shareholders.

These flows have to be predicted and controlled. This is done by forecasting and budgeting (see Chapter 5). Cash has always to be available to meet committed expenditure. If not, the company can be forced into liquidation by its creditors even though it has an overall excess of assets over liabilities. The company can also obtain additional transfusions of cash from time to time by means of additional bank facilities, which are likely to be relatively short-term, by raising fresh loans which are likely to be long-term and by rights issues of further ordinary shares which are permanent funds.

PROFITABILITY

We shall assume, since there is not the space here to argue it, that the objective of a public commercial company is the maximisation of profit on capital employed. This objective covers the total future and, of course, does not apply to any single year. Almost every company could make a bigger profit this year if in so doing it was prepared to jeopardise the future. The cessation of advertising and research, for example, would often increase this year's profit but might cripple the business in the following year.

Profit on capital employed, on its own, does not mean very much. Are we talking about profit before tax or profit after tax, shareholders' capital or total capital, for example? In fact, different definitions of profit are appropriate at different levels in a company because of varying degrees of authority to control resources and make decisions.

At parent company board level, the directors are directly accountable to ordinary shareholders, and therefore the capital for which the directors are accountable is the ordinary shareholders' funds (OSF) which consists of the ordinary share capital plus reserves. Similarly, the profit which the directors are seeking to maximise is the profit attributable to the ordinary shareholders. This profit is often referred to as the company's earnings, and the earnings divided by the number of ordinary shares in issue is the earnings per share (EPS). The earnings are the trading profit less all interest charges, taxation, minority shareholders' interest and preference dividend, since these are all the deductions which must be made before the ordinary shareholders are entitled to the remainder.

Thus the profitability ratio relevant in assessing the performace of the directors is $\frac{\text{earnings}}{\text{OSF}}$ which, in the case of ABC PLC, is $\frac{358\,423}{1\,467\,139}$, ie about 24½ per cent. Notice that the earnings figure is struck before deducting ordinary dividends. The earnings can be used by the directors either in paying a dividend to the ordinary shareholders or by being retained in the company as an addition to the OSF. How the directors dispose of the earnings is entirely within their discretion.

Let us now look at the position of the chief executive. He is directly accountable to the board of directors and is sometimes called the managing director (if he also sits on the board) or the general manager (if he does not). The chief executive is accountable for profit since he controls both sides of the profit equation - income and expenditure. However, he does not control dividends, since he does not raise capital, and for the same reason he does not control loan interest. On the other hand, he does control the level of bank borrowing by his credit policies, etc, and so he is accountable for bank interest.

Taxation is affected within the company by board decisions, particularly those regarding capital expenditure and the raising of capital. Capital expenditure gives rise to government capital allowances. New capital may be raised by a rights issue of shares (on which dividends are paid) or by the issue of loan stock (on which interest is paid). However, interest (being a cost) is allowable for corporation tax. Dividends, which are distributions of profit, are paid after corporation tax has been charged, but are paid net of income tax. With corporation tax at 52 per cent and the basic rate of income tax at 30 per cent, every £1 of gross interest actually costs the company 48p and a £1 of gross equivalent dividend costs 70p.

Minority interests are no concern of the chief executive since the decision of whether to own subsidiaries partly or wholly is a board decision. The chief executive is therefore accountable for $\frac{\text{trading profit}}{\text{total investment}}$. Trading profit is defined as profit after bank interest but before deducting loan interest, taxation, minority interests and dividends. Total investment is the total long-term capital made available by the board to the chief executive. It consists of the ordinary shareholders' funds, plus preference capital, plus loan capital, plus minority interests.

$$\frac{\text{ABC PLC's trading profit}}{\text{total investment}} \quad \text{is} \quad \frac{639456^{\star}}{1521759} \text{ or about 32 per cent.}$$

* The 639456 comprises the profit before tax (613883) plus the interest on secured loans (25573).

The chief executive's ratio is different from the board's, but contributes towards it: the better the trading profit, the better the earnings (other things being equal). The chief executive's profitability is almost always higher than the board's because his is before tax and theirs is after.

These profitability ratios have little absolute significance, since both profit and capital employed are worked out in an arbitrary manner, and within a given factual context there is a wide range of possibilities for both.

The elements which make annual profit arbitrary are depreciation, stock valuation and the capitalising or writing off of expenditure. Capital employed is arbitrary because assets are often included at cost, or at cost less depreciation, or at valuation. It is not uncommon to find a balance sheet with some assets at cost less depreciation, some assets at 1965 valuation, and other assets at 1982 valuation all added together as if they were the same currency.

The main use of ratios is in monitoring trends. It might be thought that a given ratio at one time can be compared with the equivalent ratio at another time if, although they have certain arbitrary elements, they are calculated consistently.

This would only be partly true. Suppose, for example, that assets are entered in the balance sheet at cost, or at cost less depreciation, and not at value. At a time of inflation, profit will reflect the effects as prices and costs rise, except for depreciation which is usually based on historical cost instead of replacement cost. However, capital employed, in being consistently 'valued' at cost, will depart more and more from reality and so, therefore, will return on capital employed. The ratio will tend to rise, simply because the conventions used are holding back the denominator to a far greater extent than the numerator.

Furthermore, the ratios are determined by judgements as well as by conventions. Whilst the same conventions can be used in the calculation of ratios through time, there will inevitably be changes caused by different judgements being used, even by the same people. Thus, ratios can be no more than broad indicators.

Whereas the shareholders have to accept the accounts as they are published, and make the best of what is too often a bad job, fortunately more can be done by management, in this case the board of directors. They can ensure that the accounts (at least the management accounts if not the published ones) are prepared with maximum reality in order that they can provide a basis for management decision-making.

In the calculation of profit, stocks should be based on net realisable value instead of cost which is irrelevant. Depreciation should be the reduction in the market value of the assets between the beginning and end of the year plus the increase in the replacement cost of these assets during the year.

The reduction in the market value of the assets should be deducted from the asset value in the balance sheet at the end of the previous year to arrive at the balance sheet value at the end of the current year. In this way the assets will always be included at market value, which is the only treatment of relevance to the readers of the balance sheet.

The increase in the replacement cost of the asset will not be deducted from the balance sheet value as this could eventually cause a negative value of the asset which is of course impossible. Instead, it is taken to an asset replacement provision on the sources side of the balance sheet. Thus when as asset is sold, a figure similar to the balance-sheet value should be obtained, in addition to which depreciation has been provided between the historical cost and realisable value of the asset, and between the replacement cost and the historical cost, so that the company will have provided sufficient funds for the replacement of the asset. Conventional historical cost depreciation does not achieve this, as a result of which profit is overstated, non-existent profit may be distributed as a dividend, and the company may leave itself short of the capital necessary to continue the business at the same level as before.

Gearing

The principle of gearing is a very important one in any decision to raise new capital and it is also one of the differences between the board's profitability ratio of $\frac{\text{earnings}}{\text{OSF}}$ and the chief executive's ratio of $\frac{\text{trading profit}}{\text{total investment}}$. The measure of gearing is the gearing ratio, which is $\frac{\text{total investment}}{\text{OSF}}$. Total investment has already been described as the total long-term capital, including OSF, preference and loan capital. OSF (ordinary shareholders' funds) is the ordinary share capital and reserves. ABC PLC (Figure 5.1) has no long-term capital other than OSF and is, therefore, ungeared. The ratio of an ungeared company is 1.

Now suppose that an ungeared company has OSF of £10m and makes a trading profit of £2m. The profitability ratios can be set out thus:

Trading profit		£2.0m
Loan interest		nil
Profit before tax		2.0m
total investment	10m	
Corporation tax (at 40%)		
Earnings		

Chief executive's ratio =

$$\frac{\text{trading profit}}{\text{total investment}} = \frac{2\text{m}}{10\text{m}} = 20 \text{ per cent}$$

Board's ratio = $\frac{0.8\text{m}}{1.2\text{m}}$ $\frac{\text{earnings}}{\text{OSF}}$

$$= \frac{1.2\text{m}}{10\text{m}} = 12 \text{ per cent}$$

Now suppose that the chief executive makes an application to the board for £4m additional capital, the additional funds being required for a long-term project on which the chief executive is confident of making his present 20 per cent return. The board, after examining his proposals, and comparing them with alternatives, decide to go ahead with the project and raise the necessary capital. Basically, the choice facing them is a rights issue to increase the equity (owners' capital or OSF) or an issue of 10 per cent loan stock. We shall look at both possibilities on the assumption that the chief executive (CE) meets his forecast of 20 per cent return. Here are the figures:

	Case 1 (rights issue)	*Case 2 (loan stock issue)*
OSF	£14m	£10m
10% loan capital	nil	4m
Total investment	14m	14m
Trading profit	2.8m (CE's ratio = 20%)	2.8m (CE's ratio = 20%)
Loan interest	nil	0.4m
Profit before tax	2.8m	2.4m
Corporation tax at 40%	1.12m	0.96m
Earnings	1.68m (board's ratio = 12%)	1.44m (board's ratio = 14.4%)

In case 1, the board's ratio is $\frac{1.68\text{m}}{14\text{m (OSF)}}$ and in case 2 it is $\frac{1.44\text{m}}{10\text{m (OSF)}}$

Case 2 is preferable because money has been borrowed at 10 per cent pre-tax, and invested at 20 per cent pre-tax, the difference going to the benefit of the ordinary shareholders with no further investment on their part. The gearing ratio in case 1 is 1 and in case 2 is 1.4.

Gearing, however, is a two-edged weapon. It will magnify the effect of a change in trading profit on the earnings. Suppose that in the following year (year 2) trading profit doubles and in year 3 it falls to half of the year 1 level. Then, assuming the capital structure in case 2, the positions would be as follows:

	Year 2	Year 3
Trading profit	£5.6m (CE's ratio = 40%)	£1.4m (CE's ratio = 10%)
Loan interest	0.4m	0.4m
Pre-tax profit	5.2m	1.0m
Corporation tax at 40%	2.08m	0.4m
Earnings	3.12m (board's ratio = 31.2%)	0.6m (board's ratio = 6%)

Notice that in the year 2 the $\frac{\text{earnings}}{\text{OSF}}$ has more than doubled from 14.4 per to 31.2 per cent and from year 1 to year 3 it has more than halved from 14.4 per cent to 6 per cent.

A simple and dramatic example of the effect of gearing is to be seen in the case of the private house. A man buys a house in 1964 for £5000 and finances it by a deposit of £1000 and a 25-year endowment-linked building society mortgage of £4000. In 1974 he sells the house for £15 000 and repays the mortgage. The gearing ratio is $\frac{\text{total investment}}{\text{OSF}}$ which is $\frac{5000}{1000} = 5$.

		1964		1974
Deposit	(equity)	£1 000	+1 000%	£11 000
Mortgage	(loan capital)	4 000		4 000
House	(total investment)	5 000	+200%	15 000

Although the house has appreciated by only 200 per cent, the owner's equity has increased by five times that proportion (since the gearing ratio is 5), namely, 1000 per cent. Equally, of course, if the house had fallen in value by £1000, which is 20%, the fall in the equity would have been 5 × 20 per cent = 100 per cent. In other words, the owner would have lost his entire capital since the remaining £4000 in the value of the house would have been just sufficient to repay the mortgage.

There is no generally ideal gearing ratio. It can be seen that gearing adds a speculative element to a company in the method of financing it, but the degree of speculation tolerated in the financial structure of the company depends on how basically speculative the company is. A nice steady company which is relatively unaffected by seasonal and cyclical variations in profit can stand a considerable degree of gearing whereas a company whose profit fluctuates a great deal is perhaps better left ungeared.

SOLVENCY

Finally, we come to the concept of solvency. Just as liquidity is concerned with a company's ability to meet its current liabilities out of its current assets, solvency is concerned with the ability of the company to meet its total liabilities out of its total assets. The solvency ratio is $\frac{\text{OSF}}{\text{total assets}} \times 100$ per cent which in ABC's case is $\frac{1467}{4488} \times 100$ per cent which is approximately 32.7 per cent.

This means that 32.7 per cent of all ABC's assets are financed by the owners and therefore borrowed money is the source of the remaining 67.3 per cent of the assets. In other words, even if 32.7 per of the assets are lost, the company is still solvent since there is enough value remaining just to repay all the borrowing and no more.

Once again, optimum solvency is a question of balance. A company financing too high a proportion of its total assets by equity is not maximising its profitability (since the denominator of the profitability ratio is unneccesarily high) even though it is extremely safe. The art is in judging how much external financing an individual company can stand.

The true degree of solvency, like the true degree of liquidity and gearing, can only be ascertained if the values of the assets in the balance sheet are realistic.

Book values based on cost are of little help in making these assessments.

FURTHER READING

Simons, L., *The Basic Arts of Financial Management*, 2nd edition, London, Business Books, 1978

6 Cost accounting

R M S Wilson

Cost accounting has traditionally been associated with product costing. This is concerned with determining the amount of cost to be assigned to each unit of output as a basis for valuing stocks of goods (as shown in a balance sheet) and as a basis for computing the cost of goods sold (which is deducted from sales revenue to show profit). Apart from aiding in these ways in inventory valuation and income determination, product costing is employed in the cost-plus approach to product pricing (e.g., in the contracting and printing industries).

THE NATURE OF COST ACCOUNTING

Cost is synonymous with sacrifice, but its precise definition must depend on the situation in which a measure of sacrifice is required. Different cost concepts apply to different sets of circumstances. There are only three elements of cost:

1 Materials
2 Labour
3 Expenses

Any of these can be directly related to a cost unit (*direct cost*) or indirectly related (*indirect cost*). Costs that change in accordance with the level of activity or output are termed *variable costs* and have a different behaviour pattern from *fixed costs,* which only vary with the passage of time. Some costs are partly fixed and partly variable, but it is possible to separate the two types by statistical means. Break-even analysis and other techniques relevant in cost control are based on these important distinctions between variable costs and fixed costs, and between direct costs and indirect costs.

The approach to product costing is generally to assign to each unit of output a 'fair share' of the total cost of operations. This is quite straightforward in a single product (or single service) company, but complexity tends to increase in proportion to the number of product lines manufactured and/or marketed. In a single product company all costs can be seen to be incurred to support that product (e.g., an output of 1 000 000 units at a cost of £5 000 000 gives a unit cost of £5.00). If there are two product lines – or 2000 product lines – the problem is much more difficult and the cost of any one item from a multiproduct line is impossible to measure accurately.

In addition to product costing, cost accounting is also concerned with deriving costs for other units of activity. The products produced by a company are not the only cost units; one can be interested in the cost of operating particular departments; in the cost of operating in certain sales territories; in the cost of serving various industries and customer groups; in the cost of using different channels of distribution; in the cost of servicing orders below a given value; in the cost of hiring new salesmen; and so forth.

Whatever cost unit (i.e., product, department, etc.) is selected as the focus of attention, some costs will be direct (e.g., direct labour and direct materials for a unit of manufactured output, a salesman's salary and expenses for a sales territory) while the other costs will be indirect (i.e., overheads). Much of this chapter will be concerned with the treatment accorded by cost analysts to overheads.

Overhead costs are those that cannot be traced directly to units of output. An increasing proportion of costs are of this indirect nature for various reasons (mainly relating to technological developments). While the classification of overhead costs according to their behaviour patterns (with time in the case of fixed costs, against the level of activity in the case of variable costs, and in relation to both time and activity in the case of mixed costs) is of fundamental significance, another important way of categorising these costs is under natural and functional headings. A *natural expense* is an outlay that is classified by its nature (e.g., salary, rent, etc.) rather than by the purpose for which it was incurred. On the other hand a *functional expense* is one incurred either within a particular section (or function) of an organisation – such as the marketing or manufacturing function – or to carry out a specific function (e.g., typing a letter). In a cost control context the latter category (functional classification) is more useful than the former (natural classification).

By definition, overhead costs cannot be traced directly to cost units, so any procedure whereby overheads are assigned to cost units means that the resulting *absorbed cost* is inaccurate to an unknown degree. The assigning of a fair share of cost (made up of direct costs plus a portion of overhead costs the magnitude of which depends upon the costing techniques used) to cost units is at the heart of product costing, but cost accounting exists for other reasons. In particular these are:

1 Control purposes, the aim of which is to assign controllable costs to responsibility centres
2 Planning purposes, the aim being to collect cost information that can help to indicate the cost implications of alternative courses of action. These decision-making purposes require cost information to answer such questions as:
   (*a*) What would be the effect on the company's net profit of discontinuing

product A and re-allocating the resources to product B?

(b) If an order/contract is accepted at a given price, will that price be sufficient to enable the company to earn a profit on the job?

(c) Why was last year's profit low despite a major increase in output?

(d) What will be the effect of a given wage increase on product costs and hence on profits?

(e) What effect will replacing specified equipment have on costs?

In some discussions cost accounting is defined to include management accounting, budgeting, investment appraisal, and other areas, but it is seen in the present context as being narrower in scope than this and complementary to, for instance, budgeting. Cost accounting, therefore, is seen to be an essential part of a company's total accounting and control system, but not synonymous with that system.

The orthodox financial accounting system found in every company has a major objective of recording all income and expenditure to permit a measure of profit to be derived which can then be reconciled with the increase or decrease in net worth as shown in the company's balance sheet. Income determination (i.e., the measurement of profit) is certainly the central problem of financial accounting, but the scope of financial accounting extends beyond purely recording financial transactions to include the summarising, analysing, and reporting of financial information. Its purposes can then be seen to include:

1 The provision of a working basis for the annual distribution of profits to shareholders, along with details of retained earnings, contributed capital, and other measures relating to net worth
2 The classifying of liabilities on the basis of, for example, maturity, with other information on security, and the division and grouping of assets according to significant characteristics
3 The provision of a basis on which tax assessments can be made
4 An indication to shareholders and creditors of the future prospects of the company, and of the relative success of the directors and the effectiveness of broad managerial policies and stewardship
5 To indicate to shareholders the remuneration that has been enjoyed by the directors.

The first, third and fourth purposes relate directly to the income measurement problem, illustrating how pervasive this problem is. Nevertheless, solutions must be found within the conventions on which financial accounts are drawn up. Apart from the conventional accounting principles that are prescribed by the professional authorities, the content of financial accounts is prescribed to a large extent by law. This permits the satisfying of shareholders and tax authorities, and good practice in this sphere is largely a matter of learning and applying the relevant law. An outcome of this restriction, from a management control viewpoint, is that financial accounting deals with financial flows classified by natural expense headings, whereas other types of accounting consider functional flows. This accords with the financial accounting imperative to record and interpret financial facts in as objective a manner as possible, but it does not aid in controlling costs or the activities that give rise to costs. Accounting is an expensive activity that in itself has no value: its value is derived from the importance of its objectives and its success in attaining these objectives. In so far as financial accounting has managerial objectives, these can be thought of as the provision of data to enable management to plan and control operations, but it has been shown that financial accounting is not successful in this endeavour.

The effectiveness of traditional financial accounting lies in its authoritative character rather than in the nature of the information that it produces. The existence of internal controls relating to the financial accounting system acts in a disciplining way on employees and enables the company's financial structure to be depicted in a simple and crude, but overall model that constitutes a huge barrier to chaos. But it can go further.

The intelligent presentation and classification of financial accounts; the provision of comparative figures, percentages and notes; the accompanying of the accounts with tables, graphs, diagrams, and other interpretative devices; and the supplying of supplementary information, such as funds statements and trend tables, enables the financial accountant to make his statements more informative to those who must study and use them. In this way it is possible for financial accounts to be of some limited value in cost control by giving a wide view of events in the recent past, but their value in controlling day-to-day operations is even less, and their relevance to the future is almost nil. Generally, financial accounts are too incomplete, compiled too infrequently, and too late to be of prime value in cost control.

In contrast to the reliance of financial accounting on standard accounting conventions and legal requirements, cost accounting is governed by the particular characteristics (in the form of products, structure, personalities, processes, policies, etc.) of the organisation within which is operates. Furthermore, cost accounting is concerned with internal matters whereas financial accounting is largely concerned with dealings between the company and third parties (such as creditors, shareholders, inland revenue, customers, etc.)

Needless to say, the distinguishing feature between cost accounting and financial accounting is not just that the former deals with costs. Cost accounting is concerned with the composition and control of costs, whereas financial accounting deals mainly with income determination. Once financial accountants have (in what purports to be an objective manner) ascertained income, cost accountants (in what they admit to being a subjective approach) proceed to analyse it. The analysis performed by cost accountants enables them to show not only whether a profit has been made on the working of the business as a whole, but whether a profit has been made for each process, job, product, or whatever. Such an analysis aids management in determining the output level and products that should lead to the most desirable level of operations.

The cost accounting function is therefore concerned with:

1 Cost findings (from measurement and estimation)
2 Cost analysis (covering relationships and behaviour)

3 Cost recording (including classification)
4 Reporting.

In overall terms cost accounting's objective is related to the company's profit goals, but accounting (as a service function) is a charge against profits. In relation to its contribution to managerial cost control, therefore, the cost of financial accounting should be minimised and the overhead constituted by cost accounting should be rendered as efficient as possible.

Although the cost accountant must be familiar with managerial problems if he is to perform his duties adequately, he must always be aware of the fact that the actual controlling of costs is a management function rather than an accounting one (i.e., line rather than staff). Control requires both data and action, with the accountant endeavouring to supply the former and with management providing the latter if the control process is to be effective.

COLLECTION OF COST DATA

The type of data that are to be gathered together for costing purposes will depend on the type of costing system in force and this will tend to depend on the nature of the type of production being undertaken by the company. Essentially there are three types of production. These are:

1 Job production. This involves the manufacturing of a single complete unit. The building of bridges and ships are good examples of the one-off nature of job production. 'Jobbing' is a term used to describe work carried out against a customer's order rather than for stock.
2 Batch production. This is employed when the number of units to be manufactured of a given production increases. It involves the work being divided into operations, and each operation will be carried out on the whole batch before the next operation is undertaken. Batch production permits the specialisation of labour, although the organisation and planning required to ensure freedom from idle time are considerable.

   In principle there is little difference between job and batch production.
3 Flow production. Since the various operations in batch production will inevitably take up different amounts of time, programming the work flow to avoid wasted time is almost impossible. As the scale of operations increases it often becomes possible to establish continuous flow production where there is no wasted time between operations. Such an arrangement requires balancing the times of every operation (including inspection) so that bottlenecks or surplus capacity do not render the line inefficient. Clearly a fault at any stage will have effects on all other stages of the production line.

The distinction between process costing and job/batch costing is that the former deals with broad averages and large numbers of like units whilst the latter attempts to apply costs to specific jobs.

Attention can now be turned to considering the costing treatment of overheads.

ABSORPTION COSTING

Both process costing and job costing can be carried out in accordance with overhead absorption principles. The aim of overhead aborption is to ultimately spread the total cost of the company's operations over the jobs, batches, contracts, units, etc., that pass through the company's manufacturing facilities. Dangers abound in attempting to do this: overhead is applied as an average to products that are not average, and this is only partly resolved by subdividing the factory into cost centres.

The basic procedure for applying overhead to manufactured throughput involves developing overhead rates along the following lines:

1 Analyse and classify all costs into their direct and indirect categories. (This can be done as a retrospective exercise using actual costs, or as a predictive exercise using estimated costs.)
2 Relate direct costs to the particular jobs, processes, etc., for which they were/are to be specifically incurred.
3 Of the indirect costs, some will relate to particular production departments through which products pass in the course of the manufacturing cycle, and others will relate (on a responsibility basis) to service or ancillary departments (i.e., non-production departments such as maintenance, production control, stores, costing, etc.). The cost of these service departments is then apportioned to the production departments on some 'fair' basis relating to the benefits enjoyed by different production departments.

   The whole question of apportioning service department costs to production departments is complicated by the fact that some service departments render services in a reciprocal manner to each other – the boiler-house supplies heating to the stores which in turn supply stores to the boiler-house, and the canteen supplies meals for personnel department employees who in turn help in administering the canteen. This problem can be dealt with in various ways:

   (*a*) It may be thought best to disregard the cost of any service rendered by one service department to another, and to apportion the total expenses of each service department directly to the manufacturing departments
   (*b*) It may be felt to be most appropriate to first apportion the expenses of that service department that renders services to the greatest number of other service departments but which receives in return the least service from these other departments. The expenses of the next most important provider of services can then be apportioned over the remaining service departments, and so on until all the expenses have been distributed to manufacturing departments
   (*c*) Perhaps the most accurate – and also the most complex – method is to proceed as in item *(b)* above, but with the difference that when the expenses of the second service department are apportioned, some of these expenses may be carried back to the first department, provided that it has benefited from the services rendered by the second depart-

ment. The whole cycle of apportioning service department expenses in this way will have to be repeated on account of the re-apportionments until the remaining balances are so small that they can be charged directly to manufacturing

4 An overhead rate can be established for each production department or cost centre, determined by the formula

$$\frac{\text{departmental overhead} + \text{apportioned service overheads}}{\text{level of activity}}$$

and applied to each job, process, or whatever. This is termed the *recovery of overheads*. (A simpler alternative of obvious applicability in a single product company, but also applicable in other circumstances, is to have a single company-wide overhead rate. However, even in the single product company it will often be desirable to know the cost of each operation through which the work passes, and also to know the cumulative cost of the product as it passes through the various stages of manufacture.)

Overhead rates in practice are generally determined once a year - and preferably in advance rather than retrospectively, but in changing circumstances it will be advisable to revise them as necessary. The level of activity at which a department is expected to operate is of crucial importance and whenever overhead rates are determined in advance very careful attention must be paid to estimating this dimension.

Items 3 and 4 in the above list will now be considered in a little more detail.

APPORTIONMENT OF OVERHEADS

Initially, management must specify the cost centres that are to be used - the company itself as one all-embracing cost centre; major service and production departments; sub-departments; responsibility centres; or some variation of these.

Overhead costs that are directly attributable to the selected centres should be allocated to them. Once this has been done, the objective is to apportion service centre costs to production cost centres on a 'reasonable' basis, which means some basis that seems to reflect the benefits received by each production centre (and service centre if the approach suggested in item 3 (*c*) above is adopted), or which is seen to represent a 'fair share' of service centre costs.

It will be seen, of course, that this procedure contradicts the criterion of responsibility (that is, a responsible individual - such as a departmental manager - cannot control apportioned costs, and there is a strong argument against apportionments of overhead costs for this reason. However, a certain amount of influence may be brought to bear on such apportioned costs as heating, cleaning, and so forth). It follows, therefore, that the methods generally employed for apportioning and reapportioning overhead costs among departments for product costing purposes do not give rise to meaningful data for cost control purposes: an individual cannot be made accountable for cost apportionments from a cost centre over which he has no control. A clear distinction must always be made between cost control (be responsibility accounting for instance) and product costing (by overhead apportionment and absorption).

Possible bases for apportioning service department costs are generally related to physical identification (e.g., in items 9, 10 and 11 below), facilities provided (e.g., in items 4, 5 and 6 below), or the ease of apportionment itself (e.g., in item 3 below). Before apportioning costs it will usually be necessary to make a survey of the factory to ascertain the floor space per department, the number of employees and their distribution throughout the organisation, the investment in plant and equipment per department, the horse-power hours worked by each department, and similar matters. Suggested bases of apportionment for service department costs are:

1 Direct wages paid to production employees
2 Direct material costs incurred by production departments
3 Number of employees per department. (This is especially useful for personnel, canteen, welfare, supervision, and costing overheads. But its efficacy is affected by differences in the skilled/unskilled ratio, the rate of labour turnover, the variations in attention given by different services to different production departments irrespective of the number of employees – as when the people using a subsidised factory canteen do not represent a proportional cross section of employees.)
4 Floor area occupied (in square metres). (This is frequently used for apportioning rents, rates, building costs, insurances, and depreciation. However, it presupposes that each square metre of space is of equal value to the organisation, and it is complicated by having to find ways of dealing with corridors, stairways, washrooms, etc.)
5 Cubic space occupied. (This modification of 4 can be used for the same purposes, but is more useful for heating overheads.)
6 Capital employed. (Maintenance, depreciation, rates, and insurance costs can all be apportioned on this basis. Care must be taken in deciding on the values to be put on capital assets: replacement value may be more appropriate than written-down book value.)
7 Direct labour hours worked. (As a measure of productive activity this can be useful for apportioning personnel, medical and production planning/control overheads.)
8 Machine hours worked. (As with 7, this can be a good basis for production planning and similar costs, and it is particularly suitable for dealing with maintenance overheads.)
9 Actual measurement/technical estimates. (Electricity, gas, water, oil, compressed air and steam can either be metered so that the actual consumption per department will be given, or technical estimates can be made with reasonable accuracy.)
10 Units of output. (Materials handling, production control, stores, maintenance, depreciation, etc., can be spread on the basis of physical output.)
11 Number of requisitions received. (Purchasing, stores, tool-room activity

revolves around the processing of requisitions which make the number of requisitions processed a sensible basis for making apportionments. However, it must be borne in mind that differing degrees of attention must be paid to different requisitions – some materials are easy to obtain whilst suppliers must be sought for others, some items can be issued simply from stores whilst others must be cut before being issued.)

The most important criterion in selecting a base is to relate the overhead cost to its most causal factor: machines require maintenance, space involves paying rates, outputs require inputs. Nevertheless, the whole methodology of apportioning service department costs is plagued by the necessity of having to rely on some arbitrary rules (i.e., relating to 'benefit' or 'fair share') that have been developed in order that service departments costs might be rationally spread over production departments. Such apportionments are carried out solely for product costing purposes: the control of individual overhead costs will not be achieved by cost apportionments, and nor will the method of cost apportionment influence cost control.

ABSORPTION OF OVERHEADS

The absorption of recovery of overheads entails computing and applying overhead rates for each production department to products passing through those departments. The absorbed cost of each job or process can be derived by adding the overhead element (calculated on the basis of one of the methods shown below) to the prime cost of the job or process. (Prime cost is the aggregate of direct material cost, direct labour cost and direct expenses.) A more accurate absorbed cost will tend to result from overhead rates developed for each cost centre through which a product passes as opposed to the absorbed cost that results from one company-wide overhead rate. The essential rationale is to consider why one unit of product or particular job should bear more overhead cost than another, and then to select a suitable basis from the seven given below to reflect the answer. The bases on which production overheads (including apportioned service department costs) may be absorbed are:

1 As a percentage of prime cost. This is given by:

$$\frac{\text{Expected overheads}}{\text{Estimated prime cost}} \times 100$$

Its major failing is in not considering the time factor since overheads tend to be incurred over time. Unless a standard product is being manufactured that requires constant material and labour inputs per unit the absorbed cost computed on this basis will be inaccurate (see items 2 and 3 below).

2 As a percentage of direct labour cost, given by the formula:

$$\frac{\text{Expected overheads}}{\text{Estimated direct labour cost}} \times 100$$

This basis gives some consideration to the factor of time since, for a given grade of labour, the higher the cost the greater the time spent. It has the advantage of simplicity and is economical in that it can be developed directly from payroll data, but it fails to allow for different mixes of labour or for overtime or for payment by results.

3 As a percentage of direct material cost, given by:

$$\frac{\text{Expected overheads}}{\text{Estimated direct material cost}} \times 100$$

Only when output is uniform (i.e., when only one kind of product is manufactured, involving a constant material input for each unit of output) is this method fair. Fluctuations in material prices render it unstable, and because an expensive material may be used on one product in a multi-product company, this does not mean that that product should be expected to recover a proportionally higher amount of overhead.

Items 1–3 will only be acceptable if overheads vary in proportion to the cost base selected – prime cost, direct labour cost, or direct material cost. Any variations in wage rates or material prices will require a change in the overhead rate.

4 As a rate per unit of productive output. This method is appropriate for flow production (i.e., process costing) and separate rates can be developed for each process. The rate is derived by applying the formula:

$$\frac{\text{Expected overheads}}{\text{Estimated output (in units)}}$$

and is only suitable when the units being produced are homogeneous and receive identical (or nearly identical) attention.

5 As a rate per direct labour hour, computed as:

$$\frac{\text{Expected overheads}}{\text{Estimated direct labour hours}}$$

The base depends for its accuracy on proper records being kept of the direct labour time being spent on each activity. It is best suited to labour-intensive operations and may not give very satisfactory results when one group of operatives use machines and another group do not.

6 As a rate per machine hour, given by:

$$\frac{\text{Expected overheads}}{\text{Estimated machine hours}}$$

7 This complements 5 above in being suitable for capital intensive situations. As a rate per production hour for situations which are neither suitable for method 5 nor for method 6. The formula is:

$$\frac{\text{Expected overheads}}{\text{Estimated production hours}}$$

Since fixed overhead costs are related in time it is often suggested that time (i.e., methods 5, 6 and 7) is the most important dimension for overhead absorption. There seems to be a very general acceptance that rates based on time or output (i.e., methods 4–7 above) are to be preferred to those based on value (i.e., methods 1–3 above). But whether they are developed in relation to time or output, overhead absorption rates should be based on a consideration of such factors as:

(*a*) The nature of the manufacturing processes – manual versus mechanical
(*b*) The nature of the materials used
(*c*) The constancy (or otherwise) of material prices and quality
(*d*) The differentials in pay rates
(*e*) The seasonality (if any) of production
(*f*) The extent to which available capacity is utilised.

There should be some cause-and-effect link between an overhead cost and the basis of absorption (e.g., if supervisory labour is apportioned to productive cost centres on the basis of direct labour cost, then it should be absorbed into product costs in accordance with direct labour costs).

It is not always necessary to distribute each overhead cost separately: some fixed costs – such as depreciation, rates, insurance premiums and rent – can be spread collectively on the basis of, say, machine hours (since this factor represents the time during which a product 'rents' the machinery and premises).

Other costs – such as maintenance, certain utilities, operating supplies, and so forth, may be distributed on the basis of units of output. However, those costs that are proportional to direct labour (such as indirect labour, supervision, holiday accruals, overtime premiums, welfare services, personnel department, etc.) can be distributed on the basis of labour cost, man-hours, or the number of people employed – whichever seems most appropriate.

Diagrammatically, Figure 6.1 summarises the apportionment/absorption routine. The first step is to separate service centre costs from production department overheads. The service department overheads are then apportioned over the production departments. Finally, the resulting departmentalised overheads are absorbed into units of production.

It should again be emphasised that when a company produces a heterogeneous range of jobs/products, with each receiving an unequal amount of attention as it moves from one cost centre to another, it is essential to develop and apply departmental overhead rates (rather than one total company-wide overhead rate) to each job if the resulting product cost is to bear and relation to the true (but unknown) full product cost.

OVER AND UNDER RECOVERY

The actual overhead costs of a particular period will only be equal to the applied overheads of that period (i.e., predetermined overhead rate × number of units produced) by chance (unless, of course, the period's costs and activities were all rigidly determined in advance, or the forecaster was in the improbable position of having a perfect view of the future).

If more overheads are applied to units of output than are actually incurred, then overheads are said to be over-absorbed (or over-applied or over-

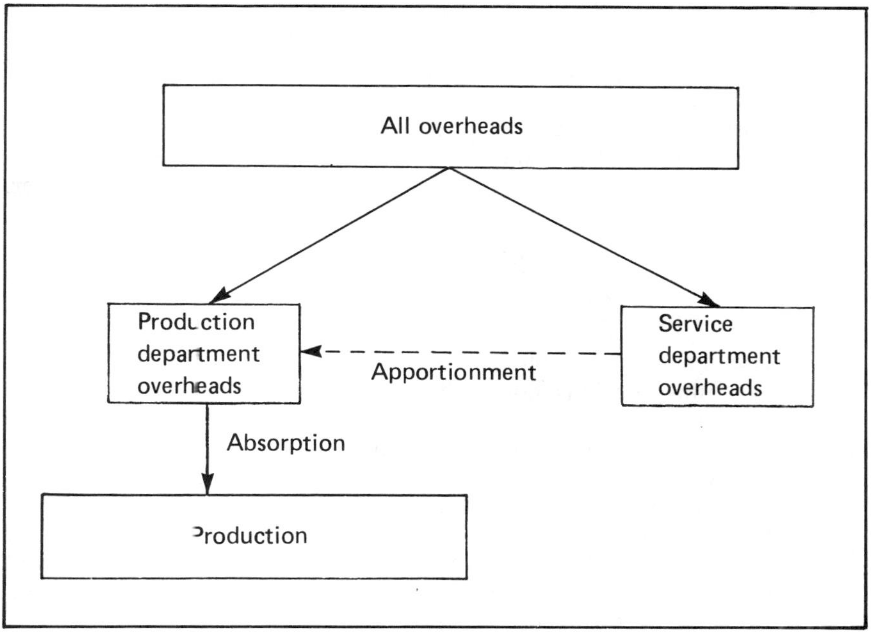

Figure 6.1 Overhead apportionment and absorption

recovered). Conversely, if too little overhead is applied to units of output, then overheads are said to be under-absorbed (under-applied, under-recovered). The degree to which overhead costs are over- or under-absorbed is a useful piece of management information. A record should be kept of the extent to which the overheads of each cost centre are over- or under-absorbed, and this can be a guide that indicates when overhead recovery rates require adjustment. (Because over- and under-absorbed overhead costs are charged directly to the profit and loss account, they are not reflected at all in any product cost. Clearly this is unsatisfactory in an absorption costing system that exists purely for product costing reasons.)

An over- or under-absorption of overheads may arise because the actual level of overhead costs has varied from the amount anticipated, or because the level of activity actually experienced during a period has differed from the level predicted. Either of these causes - or the two of them acting together - can render the predetermined overhead recovery rate inappropriate. (It is also possible for these two causes to act together in such a way that the overhead rate remains appropriate: thus an expected level of activity of 10 000 direct labour hours in conjunction with a predicted level of overhead costs of £20 000 gives an overhead rate per direct labour hour of £2.00. If costs actually amount to £25 000 and the level of activity was 12 500 direct labour hours, the effective overhead recovery rate remains £2.00 per direct labour hour.)

The explanations behind the major causes of over- and under-recovery are price rises, an expanding level of general economic activity, poor marketing, and so on. If plant capacity along with materials are available but sales volume is so low as to create an under-recovery of overheads, then this may be considered to be a marketing responsibility. However, if there is a backlog of orders and under-absorbed overhead costs result from the ineffective use of manufacturing facilities, then it becomes a manufacturing responsibility.

Normalised overhead rates save having to make minor changes every month in attempting to recover precisely 100 per cent of overhead costs during a year. For example, if overhead costs are expected to be £60 000 for a forthcoming year in which a company is expected to produce 120 000 units of output at an uneven rate, then a monthly over- or under-recovery is bound to occur if a normalised rate of $\frac{£60\ 000}{120\ 000}$ = £0.50 per cent unit is chosen. However, over the full year it should even out.

Figure 6.2 illustrates this more fully, with cumulative figures for over- and under-recovered overheads balancing out over the whole period of twelve months. The effect of different monthly production levels of a more extreme nature is shown in Figure 6.3. If a normalised rate (of £3.715) is used, the overhead per unit of product will vary from £51.00 at one extreme to £2.00 at the other, depending on the month in which the product was made (August or April). These extremes are unacceptable because they are not representative of the typical, or normalised, production circumstances which have a horizon beyond the end of the current month.

Apart from highlighting the need to use normalised overhead recovery rates for seasonal products, these examples further illustrate the point that the product costing imperative to absorb all overheads is of no value in controlling costs since cost control cannot operate under a regime that is confined to apportionments and absorption.

FIXED AND VARIABLE OVERHEAD RATES

So far the discussion has focused exclusively on deriving overhead rates that do not distinguish fixed from variable costs, but an important refinement of absorption costing is to derive different rates for both variable overheads and for fixed overheads.

Consider, for instance, a labour-intensive cost centre having estimated fixed overheads of £40 000 for a period, and estimated variable overheads of £30 000 for the same period, with an expectation of working 20 000 direct labour hours. A fixed overhead recovery rate of $\frac{£40\ 000}{20\ 000}$ = £2.00 per direct labour hour, and a variable overhead recovery rate of $\frac{£30\ 000}{20\ 000}$ = £1.50 per direct labour hour can be readily derived. If the actual figures for the period in question are:

Fixed overheads	£41 500
Variable overheads	£31 500
Direct labour hours	19 500

then the fixed overhead will be under-applied by £1000 [i.e., £40 000 – (19 500

Month	Production units	Annual overhead rate (£)	Monthly applied overhead (£)	Monthly actual overhead (£)	Over-applied overhead (£)	Under-applied overhead (£)	Cumulative balance over (under) (£)
January	6 000	0.5	3 000	4 200	—	1 200	(1 200)
February	5 500	0.5	2 750	4 100	—	1 350	(2 500)
March	8 000	0.5	4 000	4 600	—	600	(3 150)
April	11 000	0.5	5 500	5 200	300	—	(2 850)
May	16 000	0.5	8 000	6 200	1 800	—	(1 050)
June	19 000	0.5	9 500	6 800	2 700	—	1 650
July	11 000	0.5	5 500	5 200	300	—	1 950
August	8 000	0.5	4 000	4 600	—	600	1 350
September	10 500	0.5	5 250	5 100	150	—	1 500
October	13 000	0.5	6 500	5 600	900	—	2 400
November	7 000	0.5	3 500	4 400	—	900	1 500
December	5 000	0.5	2 500	4 000	—	1 500	—
Total	120 000	0.5	60 000	60 000	6 150	6 150	0

Figure 6.2 Over- and under-recovered overheads

Month	Total budgeted overhead (£)	Units to be produced	Monthly rate per unit (£)	Annual rate per unit (£)
January	70 000	20 000	3.50	3.715
February	80 000	30 000	2.67	3.715
March	90 000	40 000	2.25	3.715
April	100 000	50 000	2.00	3.715
May	65 000	15 000	4.33	3.715
June	60 000	10 000	6.00	3.715
July	55 000	5 000	11.00	3 715
August	51 000	1 000	51.00	3.715
September	55 000	5 000	11.00	3.715
October	60 000	10 000	6.00	3.715
November	65 000	15 000	4.33	3.715
December	70 000	20 000	3.50	3.715
	821 000	221 000		3.715

Figure 6.3 Monthly and annual overhead rates

× £2.00)] whilst fixed overhead prices have risen by £2500 [i.e., £41 500 – (19 500 × £2.00)]. Variable overheads to the extent of £29 250 (i.e., 19 500 × £1.50) will have been absorbed, but the actual variable overheads incurred (£31 500) is made up of price changes and inefficiencies of £2 250 (i.e., £31 500 – £29 250).

To take a slightly more involved example, Figure 6.4 shows a flexible budget for a machining department of a company for anticipated monthly levels of activity. (A flexible budget is one that recognises the differences in behaviour patterns of fixed and variable costs, and which is designed to change in relation to the level of activity actually attained during a period.) This budget gives a variable overhead rate of £1.70 per direct labour hour. If variable overhead costs have been properly analysed and classified, and if the estimates forming the basis of the flexible budget are accurate, then this rate should be valid over the relevant range.

Fixed overheads cannot be absorbed on the basis of this type of flexible budget, but must be absorbed on the basis of some predetermined estimate of capacity utilisation – such as normal capacity. (Normal capacity is defined as that level of activity – or productive output – that can be expected to be attained over a future period of time covering the ups and down of the business cycle.)

Suppose that normal capacity is 10 000 direct labour hours, and that the combined flexible budget is as shown in Figure 6.5. At normal capacity of 10 000 direct labour hours, the fixed overhead recovery rate is given by $£\frac{10\ 000}{10\ 000}$ = £1.00 per direct labour hour.

Standard direct labour hours	8 000	9 000	10 000	11 000
Variable factory overhead:				
Material handling	£8 000	£9 000	£10 000	£11 000
Idle time	800	900	1 000	1 100
Rework	800	900	1 000	1 100
Overtime premium	400	450	500	550
Supplies	3 600	4 050	4 500	4 950
Total	£13 600	£15 300	£17 000	£18 700
Variable overhead rate = £1.70 per direct labour hour				

Figure 6.4 Flexible overhead budget

			Normal capacity	
Standard direct labour hours	8 000	9 000	10 000	11 000
Variable factory overhead:				
Material handling	£8 000	£9 000	£10 000	£11 000
Idle time	800	900	1 000	1 000
Rework	800	900	1 000	1 100
Overtime premium	400	450	500	550
Supplies	3 600	4 050	4 500	4 950
Total	£13 600	£15 300	£17 000	£18 700
Variable overhead rate = £1.70 per direct labour hour				
Fixed factory overhead:				
Supervision	1 700	1 700	1 700	1 700
Depreciation – plant	2 000	2 000	2 000	2 000
Depreciation – equipment	5 000	5 000	5 000	5 000
Rates	1 000	1 000	1 000	1 000
Insurance	300	300	300	300
Total	£10 000	£10 000	£10 000	£10 000
Fixed overhead rate for normal capacity = £1.00 per direct labour hour				

Figure 6.5 Combined flexible overhead budget

The combined overhead rate (at normal level of output of 10 000 direct labour hours) is thus a variable rate of £1.70 per direct labour hour and a fixed rate of £1.00 per direct labour hour, amounting to £2.70 per direct labour hour.

WHY ABSORB OVERHEADS?

The simple answer to this question is 'product costing'. Overheads are applied to products because management needs to have some idea of the fully absorbed cost of each product as a guide, perhaps, for pricing decisions, as a basis for inventory valuation, and hence as a prerequisite to income measurement (i.e., the determination of profit). *But* flexible budgets require the predetermining of overhead rates also, and the purpose of flexible budgets is to control costs.

If a company has estimated the level of sales for the next operating period, and if the planned overhead costs have been spread over the planned output along with the expected prime costs, then management may tend to feel that as long as the company sells the budgeted level of output of each product at a price that is at least equivalent to the sum of prime cost plus overhead element plus required profit margin, the company will achieve at least its planned level of profit. This way of thinking focuses attention on 'full' cost, but since different expenses are aggregated in overhead recovery rates, it is difficult to see what is implied in a unit overhead cost figure, and hence in a unit 'full' cost figure. The very fact that any one of several bases may be used for both apportioning and absorbing overhead costs, with the resulting full cost differing under each method, demonstrates the lack of accuracy and meaning that may be exhibited. However, when a company must base its prices on cost plus a desired profit margin (as in contracting) then overheads must be allocated to jobs. Yet pricing on the basis of full costs in other circumstances can be distinctly damaging. For instance, the higher the level of activity, the lower will be the unit full cost. That is, direct material cost per unit, direct labour cost per unit, and variable overhead cost per unit are all assumed to be constant within the relevant range (the range of activity within which the company is expected to be operating during a given period of time) but fixed overhead costs are lower per unit the more units over which they are spread. This means that a company using full cost as its basis for pricing will tend to have lower prices the higher level of activity and higher prices the lower the level of activity. Let us assume that a company bases its prices on full cost plus 25 per cent, that fixed overhead costs are £10 000 per period, and that the level of sales may vary from 100 000 units (giving a unit fixed overhead element of £0.10) to 50 000 units (giving a unit fixed overhead element of £0.20).

Assume that direct material cost is £0.25 per unit, direct labour cost is £0.30 per unit and variable overhead cost is £0.15 per unit. Then the price per unit can be calculated as in Figure 6.6.

The outcome of cost-plus pricing may be to depress sales when it is desired to encourage sales because prices rise as demand falls. Cost-plus pricing is unable to respond to market conditions, and for this reason – along with a general dissatisfaction with overhead allocations – marginal costing has been more and more widely adopted in recent years. Whilst absorption costing aims to ascertain the 'full' cost of jobs and processes, marginal costing aims to deal with the effects of changes in either the volume or type of output.

MARGINAL COSTING

Marginal – or direct – costing is concerned with differences in aggregate cost (i.e., direct labour + direct material + direct expense + variable overhead) caused by producing one unit more or one unit less (where a 'unit' will usually – but not always – refer to a unit of manufactured output).

	High sales 100 000	Low sales 50 000 units
Direct material cost	0.25	0.25
Direct labour cost	0.30	0.30
Variable overhead cost	0.15	0.15
Fixed overhead cost	0.10	0.20
Full cost	0.80	0.90
Profit @ 25 per cent	0.20	0.225
Selling price per unit	£1.00	£1.125

Figure 6.6 Cost-plus pricing

Marginal costing is essentially short-run in nature and is concerned with variable costs. In contrast, differential costing (also known as incremental costing or relevant costing) is concerned with longer-run questions (e.g., adding or dropping a product line, make-or-buy decisions, lease-versus-own decisions, etc.), and since these questions involve a consideration of the costs of following one course of action rather than another, fixed costs are important.

In direct costing systems, fixed overheads are viewed as being *period costs* and are changed directly to the profit and loss account as costs of a period of time instead of being spread over processes and units of output as product costs. Fixed costs are thus treated as costs of being in business rather than as operating costs related to manufacturing given product lines. This approach facilitates the analysis of the effects of changes in the volume and type of output by means of the cost-volume-profit (or break-even) technique. The fundamental distinction between variable costs and fixed costs is here seen to be of great significance again in controlling costs – for flexible budgets, in cost-volume-profit analysis, and in marginal costing.

The highlight of marginal costing is the contribution margin (i.e., the excess of sales revenue over variable cost). This margin represents the contribution that the item in question makes to fixed costs and profit. In Figure 6.7 it is the distance between the variable cost curve and the revenue curve.

In simple equation form:

Contribution = sales revenue – variable costs
Since: sales revenue = fixed costs + variable costs + profit
By substitution: contribution = fixed costs + profit

A contribution margin per unit can be easily worked out. If the selling price of a product is £1.00 and its variable cost amounts to £0.60 then the contribution margin will be £0.40. The immediate implication of this is that for every increase in sales, 40 per cent of that increase for this product is the contribution

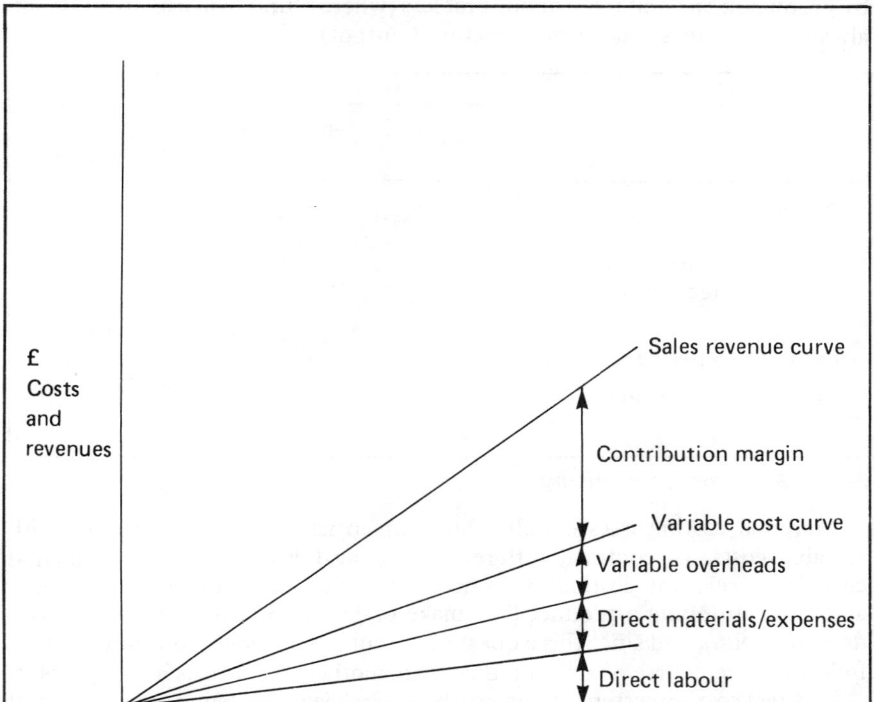

Figure 6.7 Contributed margin

towards fixed costs and profit. If the level of fixed costs is £100 000 and it is sought to make a profit of £50 000, how many units should be sold? The answer can be readily determined by substituting known variables into the basic equation:

Sales revenue = fixed costs + variable costs + profit

Let R = desired sales revenue, and as it is already known that FC = £100 000, P = £50 000, and $VC = 0.60R$

Then $R = 100\,000 + 0.60R + 50\,000$

Therefore $0.40R = 150\,000$

Therefore $R = 375\,000$ at £1.00 . . . . = £375 000

Or more simply

$$\frac{\text{Fixed costs + profit}}{\text{Contribution margin}} = \frac{150\,000}{0.40} = 375\,000$$

Determining total contribution

It is important to determine how much contribution exists for a given product line, and whether the total contribution from all product lines is sufficient to cover fixed costs and leave a satisfactory profit. Let us take the example of a company producing three products – A, B and C – with aggregate cost, profit and sales figures as shown in Figure 6.8.

	Product A (£)	Product B (£)	Product C (£)	Total (£)
Direct materials	20 400	35 600	16 000	72 000
Direct labour	6 000	12 200	1 800	20 000
Overheads	6 600	13 500	1 900	22 000
Total cost	33 000	61 300	19 700	114 000
Profit	2 000	3 700	300	6 000
Sales Revenue	35 000	65 000	20 000	120 000

Figure 6.8 Cost, profit and sales revenue summary

It would seem from Figure 6.8 that product A is making a profit of £2000, and if product A is deleted from the range it may be thought that total profit would fall to £4000 from its current level of £6000. But the allocation of overheads (of £6600) to product A includes various fixed overhead costs amounting to, say, £5500 that would still need to be paid even though product A was no longer in the range. Let us suppose that £5275 of this amount is transferred (i.e., re-allocated) to product B and the balance of £225 is re-allocated to product C. The outcome of deleting product A and transferring the fixed charges is given in Figure 6.9.

	Product B (£)	Product C (£)	Total (£)
Direct material	35 600	16 000	51 600
Direct labour	12 200	1 800	14 000
Overheads	18 775	2 125	20 900
Total cost	66 575	19 925	86 500
Profit or (loss)	(1575)	75	(1 500)
Sales Revenue	65 000	20 000	85 000

Figure 6.9 Revised cost, profit and revenue summary – 1

Figure 6.9 shows that the deletion of product A causes a reduction in profit of £7500 (i.e., from a profit of £6000 to a loss of £1500). To think that the fall in profit would only be £2000 is clearly erroneous because it ignores the fixed costs that must be re-allocated once A is deleted. Mistaken assumptions can be avoided if fixed overheads are separated from variable overheads (in accordance with Figure 6.10) in such a way that the contribution that each product makes to common fixed overheads and profit is evident. The contribution approach is highlighted in Figure 6.11.

If a product is not covering its marginal cost (i.e., it is making a negative contribution), it would be essential to ensure that its selling price is not too low (given its quality in relation to competitive products) and that the production methods and materials are appropriate. In cases where a product's sales revenue is below its marginal cost but prices cannot be increased and production methods cannot be improved, careful consideration should be given before it is deleted lest the picture of Figure 6.8 is found.

	Product A (£)	Product B (£)	Product C (£)	Total (£)
Direct materials	20 400	35 600	16 000	72 000
Direct labour	6 000	12 200	1 800	20 000
Variable overheads	1 100	6 600	1 625	9 325
Marginal cost	27 500	54 400	19 425	101 325
Fixed overheads	5 500	6 900	275	12 675
Total cost	33 000	61 300	19 700	114 000

Figure 6.10 Revised cost, profit and sales revenue summary – 2

	Product A (£)	Product B (£)	Product C (£)	Total (£)
Sales	35 000	65 000	20 000	120 000
Marginal cost	27 500	54 400	19 425	101 325
Contribution	7 500	10 600	575	18 675
Total fixed costs				12 675
Profit				6 000

Figure 6.11 Contribution margin statement

Margin of safety

Within the context of marginal costing and cost-volume-profit analysis, a useful concept is that of the *margin of safety*. This refers to the amount by which sales revenue can fall before a loss is incurred. For instance, if a company can break even at 50 per cent of expected sales, then it has a margin of safety of 50 per cent. The expected sales level may be 1000 units, and the break-even volume may be sales of 500 units, so sales can fall by 500 units or 50 per cent before a loss will be made and the margin of safety is given by the formula:

$$\frac{\text{Actual sales} - \text{break-even sales}}{\text{Actual sales}}$$

$$\text{Margin of safety} = \frac{1000-500}{1000} = 0.5 = 50 \text{ per cent}$$

Summary of the value of marginal costing

The following points summarise the value of the contribution approach of cost-volume-profit analysis and marginal costing to management planning and control:

1 A change in either the selling price of a product or its variable cost rate will alter the break-even point and the contribution margin ratio (i.e., the proportion of sales revenue that is left when variable cost is deducted)
2 When sales are above the break-even point, a high contribution margin ratio will result in greater profits than will a small contribution margin ratio
3 A low contribution margin ratio will require a large increase in sales volume to create a significant increase in profit
4 If other factors stay constant, a change in total fixed costs will alter the break-even point by the same percentage and the net profit will vary by the same amount as the change in total fixed costs
5 A large margin of safety will mean that a major fall in sales can occur before losses are incurred.

ABSORPTION COSTING VERSUS DIRECT COSTING

There are various advantages of using marginal costing, amongst the most important of which are the following:

1 Marginal costing systems are simpler to operate than are absorption costing systems because they do not involve the problems of overhead apportionments and recovery. This makes costs easier to identify and accumulate, and it does not confuse product costing with cost control
2 Marginal costing avoids the difficulties of having to explain the purpose and basis of overhead absorption to management that accompany absorption costing. Fluctuations in profit are easier to explain because they result from cost-volume interactions and not from changes in inventory. In absorption costing systems a varying element of fixed overhead will be contained in the cost of inventories, and fluctuations in inventory levels can affect profit due to the fixed cost element. However, marginal costing introduces a direct relationship between sales volume and marginal income (i.e., the contribution)
3 It is easier to make decisions on the basis of marginal cost presentations. For example, marginal costing shows which products are making a contribution and which are failing to cover their avoidable (i.e., variable) costs. Under absorption costing the relevant information is difficult to gather, and there is the added danger that management may be misled by reliance on unit costs that contain an element of irrelevant fixed costs.

However, on the other side of the coin are various disadvantages of using marginal costing. For example:

1 Economic selling prices over the long run cannot be set without some attention being paid to fixed costs. Each product line/job must not just

cover its marginal costs, but collectively the contributions of all jobs must cover at least all costs if a profit is to be made

2 The importance of time tends to be overlooked in marginal costing: two jobs may have the same marginal cost, but one may take twice as long to complete as the other and hence its 'true' cost will be more. This aspect of capacity-utilisation is not brought out in marginal costing

3 The difficulties and dangers of spreading fixed overhead costs do not mean that they should be ignored: they are just as vital as are direct wage costs, etc. In fact, as production becomes more automated and greater in volume, more costs will tend to be fixed, and hence they should not be overlooked.

The choice between using absorption costing and marginal costing will be determined by such factors as:

1 The system of financial control in use (e.g., responsibility accounting is inconsistent with absorption costing)
2 The production methods in use (e.g., marginal costing is favoured in simple processing situations in which all products receive similar attention; but when different products receive widely differing amounts of attention, then absorption costing may be more realistic)
3 The significance of the prevailing level of fixed overhead costs.

How a cost system is to be used is more important than its form, since a technique *per se* does not achieve anything. From the point of view of cost control, a costing system should be able to show promptly costs that are running out of control, guide corrective action, indicate the effects of alternative decisions, and focus on helping to secure control rather than being the perfect systems design.

STANDARD COSTING

A logical step onwards from either absorption costing or marginal costing, especially in view of the fact that both approaches already involve a considerable amount of future cost level prediction, is to institute a system of standard costs. The principle is to develop a complete specification of all expenditure levels from which standards are derived.

A predetermined standard can be established for each element of cost at each stage of production. For direct materials, the standard cost would indicate the estimated amount of each kind of material and the cost per kilo (or other unit). For labour, the standard would show the number of hours in each department or cost centre; the hourly rate; and the total cost in each department.

The standard cost for overheads in each department would indicate the number of hours of machine time, direct labour hours, or whatever; the standard overhead recovery rate; and the total expense (i.e., hours × rate). When all the cost elements (direct materials, direct labour, direct expenses, fixed and variable overheads) have been accumulated, the standard should indicate the desired cost of all elements of a unit of productive output.

The standard cost of materials shows what the cost *should be* if the correct types of material are used in the right quantities with the minimum of waste. Similarly, the standard labour cost shows what labour *should cost* if the job is performed at a specified level of efficiency by properly trained operatives of the appropriate grade working for agreed rates of pay. The standard overhead cost for a unit of output will be based upon standard fixed overhead rates and standard variable overhead rates developed in relation to particular assumed circumstances.

Standard costing differs from conventional absorption costing because the latter aims to charge units of output with a 'fair' share of the *actual* costs (either predictively or retrospectively) of making the product. In contrast, standard costing is based (either wholly or in part) on the principle that the costs to be charged to units of output are the costs that *should* have been incurred.

Direct or marginal costing systems can be developed along standard costing lines, in which event fixed overhead costs are not standardised but all direct costs, along with variable overheads, are standardised.

When a standard costing system is in operation, it can be operated in an integrated manner with the budgeting system, since both are concerned with what costs ought to be, what they actually are, and the reasons for the differences that arise. In other words, both standard costing and budgeting are concerned with cost control.

CHECKLIST ON COST ACCOUNTING

1 Is the company's costing system tailored to the company's needs?
2 Have cost centres been clearly defined?
3 Are the benefits of the system commensurate with its costs?
4 Are all costs classified into their direct and indirect, fixed and variable, controllable and uncontrollable, and separable and joint categories?
5 Is the behaviour of different costs understood in relation to changes in the level of activity?
6 Are cost reports made available promptly? How often? How quickly?
7 Could statements be presented earlier if more estimates were used? (Are estimating procedures reliable?)
8 Are figures rounded so that results are more easily understood?
9 Can any figures of small value (as shown on the chart of accounts) be grouped?
10 Are the descriptions of reported items clear?
11 Are unusual items adequately explained?
12 Will further (or less) mechanisation affect the overhead of cost accounting?
13 Can the effectiveness of cost accounting procedures be improved?
14 Has sufficient thought been given to the type of costing system to use? (That is, standard costing, absorption costing, or marginal costing.)
15 Has the purpose for which costing is being performed been fully considered? (For example, pricing, product costing, cost control.)
16 Is the costing system adequate in determining the relative efficiencies and profitability of divisions, processes, product lines, jobs, etc?

17 Is the costing system adequate for the needs of EDP and operations research analysts?
18 Are ratios, graphs, etc., used to supplement the figures produced by the costing system?
19 Is a satisfactory procedure being operated to price material issues from stores?
20 Are all withdrawals of stock and ordering of goods from outside suppliers duly authorised by requisitions?
21 Are job allocation numbers recorded against labour time, material usage, etc., in all cases?
22 Do employees understand the importance of recording the allocation of time to jobs? How are they encouraged to do this accurately?
23 What is the basis for the apportionment of each service department's costs? Is the most suitable basis selected in every case?
24 How are overheads absorbed into productive output? Is the most suitable basis used?
25 What action is taken on the basis of over- or under-recovery of overheads?
26 Are normalised overhead recovery rates used? if not, why not? For example, is the level of activity stable from month to month?
27 Have separate overhead rates been developed for fixed overhead costs and variable overhead costs?
28 Why are overheads absorbed (if they are absorbed)?
29 Is the contribution margin concept understood within the company?
30 Is cost-volume-profit analysis undertaken?
31 Is marginal costing undertaken?
32 Has the company's margin of safety ever been worked out?
33 Are the comparative advantages and disadvantages of marginal costing versus absorption costing fully appreciated?
34 Is the costing system closely geared to the type of production processes operated?
35 What role does cost accounting play in relation to special decision-making?

SUMMARY

Cost accounting is principally concerned with product costing (for pricing, inventory valuation, and income determination purposes), and only concerned in a secondary manner with cost control.

Data for product costing (and cost control) is derived from many sources, such as labour summaries, weekly time sheets, job cards, material requisitions, stock cards, and expense summaries. The pricing of material issues from stores is a particularly difficult topic in times of rising prices.

The type of costing system – and hence the nature and source of much costing data – will be determined by the structure of the organisation and its methods of production. Job costing and process costing have been developed to deal with job/batch production and flow production respectively.

Conventional absorption cost accounting requires that all overheads be spread in some way over the productive output of the company. This is achieved by apportioning service department overheads to production departments, and then absorbing these accumulated production + service overheads over units of output. Many different bases exist for both apportioning and absorbing overheads, and the most suitable will be that which characterises a cause-and-effect relationship between the activities and the outputs.

Overhead rates can be developed for fixed and variable overheads, but when the actual level of activity differs from the estimated level, there will be an over- or an under-recovery of overheads. This may signal the need to revise overhead recovery rates.

For various reasons the apportioning/absorbing of overheads is dangerous (or at least gives misleading results) and marginal costing has developed to overcome these problems. Attention centres around the contribution margin, and the interrelationships of cost-volume-profit are a focal point for decision-making. Whilst marginal costing is a short-run function, relevant (or differential) costing is more suited to longer-run decisions in which fixed costs may vary in addition to changes in variable costs.

Standard costing is a normative refinement of either absorption or marginal costing that can be usefully integrated with budgeting in attempting to control costs.

FURTHER READING

Anton, H. R., Firmin, P. A. and Grove, H. D. (eds.), *Contemporary Issues in Cost & Managerial Accounting*, 3rd edition, Houghton Mifflin, Boston, Mass, 1978. A comprehensive selection of articles on aspects of cost and management accounting, with suggestions as to further reading on specialist topics

Benston, G. J. (ed.), *Contemporary Cost Accounting and Control*, 2nd edition, Dickenson, Encino, Calif., 1977. Another valuable collection of articles but less comprehensive than Anton, et al.

Hart, H., *Overhead Costs: Analysis and Control*, Heinemann, London, 1973. This short book looks at the how's and why's of overhead apportionment, etc., with a strong emphasis on linking UK company practices to an evaluative framework.

Hongren, C. T., *Cost Accounting*, 4th edition, Prentice-Hall, Englewood Cliffs, NJ, 1977. This is the standard international textbook on cost accounting.

Shillinglaw, G., *Managerial Cost Accounting*, 4th edition, Irwin, Homewood, Illi., 1977. Another standard textbook that is even more comprehensive than that by Horngren.

Sizer, J., *An Insight into Management Accounting*, 2nd edn., Penguin Books, Harmondsworth, 1979. The most widely used British introductory book: very readable and lucid.

Solomons, D., (Ed.), *Studies in Cost Analysis*, 2nd edition, Associated Business Publishers, London, 1968. An advanced collection of key articles on aspects of cost analysis.

Thomas, W. E., (ed.), *Readings in Cost Accounting, Budgeting & Control*, 5th edition, South-Western, Cincinnati, Ohio, 1978. The longest established compilation of articles in the field – but regularly revised – and one which probably has greatest appeal to the non-specialist.

PART TWO

MARKETING AND SALES MANAGEMENT

7 Marketing planning

John Stapleton

Every marketing activity is an investment in time, energy and money. Few companies would spend thousands of pounds on, say, a purchase of capital equipment without a full investigation into its justification, the alternatives available, and the expected return on expenditure. Yet every year the vast majority of companies allocate a substantial part of their revenue to marketing actions without fully assessing the value or likely return on that investment. By introducing the disciplines arising from marketing planning a company should be able to ensure that the costs of marketing show an equitable return and are subject to measurement in the same way as all other business investments.

Many executives believe that the costs of marketing form an additional expense that has to be borne in order to sell their goods. Whilst it is true that many companies use certain tools of marketing for this purpose, it is true also that the most successful companies accept marketing as an essential and integral part of the company's total commercial operation, for it is an essential cost in just the same way as production or finance.

Companies often avoid marketing planning procedures because of the effort needed to express their forward policy in a written form. Executives commonly consider that their time is too valuable to spend on anything other than pressing operational problems; those that face them from day to day. In fact, the manager who devotes his time to dealing with current administrative detail is almost certain to have ignored proper planning in the past. For if properly prepared the marketing plan will contain sufficient details of the company's policy and operational strategy for the implementation to be undertaken by an assistant. As the many alternative courses of action are programmed it is merely necessary for the assistant to activate the appropriate remedy or decision. Only unusual situations need be dealt with by the manager.

The first step in preparing a marketing plan is that of producing the information necessary for decision making. Usually, a company will have within its own administration and control system the raw material necessary for the plan's foundations. In addition, there is an abundance of published information which is made available by government departments, para-governmental bodies, institutions, associations, and the national, trade, and technical press.

Marketing research is an activity which has yet to be fully exploited by the majority of companies. It has so far only been used by companies that have recognised that their existing information sources are inadequate. Because of the scale of operations that now confront the typical businessman it is essential that investment decisions are based upon relevant information, so reducing the number of variables and, hence, business risk.

STANDARDS FOR MEASURING PERFORMANCE

For a marketing-oriented activity to produce lasting results the entire operation has to be systematically planned. By producing basic information in written form and establishing goals and aims for the future the company is creating standards against which actual performance can be measured. Documentation of detailed policy actions then provide the basis for monitoring and controlling the company's operation. Future trends may be predicted through the investigation of all factors that are likely to influence company results.

It is, however, unusual for future opportunities to be easily isolated or even defined. The possibilities are infinite, but it is essential that the most promising are fully investigated and the potential assessed. It is particularly important that the man responsible for planning be a senior executive, for the full appraisal of market opportunities will enable that executive to gain far more intimate knowledge of the workings and the environment of the business operation than could be achieved from a lifetime of working within the close confines of the limited philosophy and procedure of one company. The executive will be able to learn about the interactive forces that affect the company, the industry and, more important, its markets.

In studying the company's future market the businessman will try to discover basic needs for which there is no satisfaction or possibly where there is an inadequate match. It is by discovering the peculiar needs of each existing and potential customer that the enlightened company starts its marketing-orientation. It is upon such special needs that the foundations are laid. Looking at the market and listing the operational needs of each industry, then measuring the extent of each need and then the value that the market places on overcoming the problem gives an indication of the potential – in volume and in profit opportunity.

THE NEW PRODUCT DEVELOPMENT PROGRAMME

From this stage the company will embark on a new product development programme in an effort to resolve the problems that face the market. Once a satisfactory product has been produced the basis for a promotional campaign is already apparent, as the original market assessment will have shown the prospects either by size, industry or location, and the product feasibility studies will have indicated the most appealing stimulus to demand for advertising and field selling purposes.

It must be apparent from these observations that success in marketing cannot be achieved overnight except by coincidence or good fortune. Often a minimum of three years will be required before the first hopeful signs become apparent. Successful use of certain marketing activities alone does not automatically mean a company is marketing-oriented. This situation frequently presents management with an almost insoluble problem. As the whole company has to become involved with marketing principles for success to be possible, it is unlikely that a new recruit hired for his expertise will be able to win sufficient confidence from colleagues by results in the time span that is normally allowed a new manager.

There is usually only one man in a company who can inspire the confidence and support that is necessary and who will automatically have the authority to implement the total changes that may be justified, and he is the chief executive. Introducing satisfactory marketing-orientation is more likely to be successful if the present chief executive delegates most of his daily activities to an assistant or to senior line managers and devotes his entire energies to planning, than if a manager is appointed with such responsibilities.

DETERMINING COMPANY OBJECTIVES

Few company executives have ever formally determined their company's business activity. If they have it is often specified in terms of the means by which the business activity is achieved, e.g. printing rather than communications; or the end-product, e.g. aero-engines rather than propulsion; or by convention, e.g. insurance rather than security. The only sure means of defining the business activity is by thinking in terms of applications for a product, for whilst products, no matter how successful they are now, are heading for eventual decline, the need will usually remain – to be satisfied by the latest innovation.

Determining the appropriate business activity is the first essential step in the marketing plan. In this first step the executive will establish the parameters within which his efforts should be confined initially, but will also rely upon the know-how, expertise, market reputation, and resources the company has accumulated during its history.

At the preliminary planning stage the company will need to decide upon the course that it wishes to take and the stages that have to be reached during each step in the journey. These objectives have to be achievable and yet sufficiently challenging to enable executives and staff to take pride in their fulfilment. The aims and goals of each company have to be expressed in the marketing plan in a way that is beyond dispute while being capable of measurement and comparison. The only medium that achieves these standards is money – the means by which company prosperity is valued. The prime requirement for the survival and development of any business is profit. Too many managers still regard profit as the amount of money that is left over after all the operating expenses have been met. This view almost has connotations with a death wish, for profit is the prerequisite of all business activity and as such must be the first cost to the business.

PROFIT IS THE FIRST OPERATING EXPENSE

By writing in the profit required as its first operating expense the company recognises its major priority and then gears all its other objectives to ensure the acquisition of that profit. The sales volume needed, the orders to be won, the tenders or quotations to be sent out, the inquiries to be solicited, and all the means by which they are obtained are secondary objectives to be achieved before the prime objective becomes possible – in practice.

Any objectives of this sort must be based upon certain assumptions. It may have to be assumed that raw materials will continue to be available or that the government will not cause a market to dry up following an Act of Parliament. Whatever the objectives they will depend for their satisfaction on certain events happening or not happening. These assumptions are incorporated in the plan with a cross-reference to the strategies that will have to be implemented or the tactics employed should the assumptions become invalid. The strategies a company adopts are the means by which the company approaches its market opportunities and by which it adjusts its resources to exploit those opportunities. Its tactics are the methods it uses to meet short-term situations or more frequently the steps it takes when in immediate contact with customers.

In documenting the preliminary marketing plan it is also necessary to list all the major problems that have faced the company during its immediate history, as well as those that are expected to confront the company in the future. At the same time it is prudent to list all opportunities that have been under consideration with the expected profit return, when they are to be achieved and under what circumstances. Both problems and opportunities are then subjected to the same appraisal as the objectives and assumptions when the company strategies are built into the plan.

Every company struggles to improve its profit performance and any attempts planned for the period of the marketing plan, in detail for one year and in outline for five years, should be included. It is possible that improved productivity at the plant will make it possible for the company to improve its profitability through increased sales volume. Sales may be improved either by additional expenditure on marketing actions or by reducing price in an effort to expand the total market. It is by marketing planning that a company can be sure that whatever action it chooses will be based upon facts and information obtained from the marketplace.

Every action and every decision taken by the company executives will have an effect somewhere in the business. It may be favourable, it might be unfavourable. In formulating a marketing plan the company will be formalising its actions, weighing its alternatives, and deciding the most appropriate route open to it. Unless each marketing decision is made with the full and detailed consideration of the known, likely and possible effects upon the business, the investment that marketing actions require will be unmonitored and the management will have lost effective control of a major asset and the benefits that should accrue from that asset.

DEVELOPING THE MARKET PLAN

Preparing a sales forecast, the basis of the total marketing plan, is not just a matter of looking at past sales and trying to establish trends, but a conscious effort to look into the future and assess potential sales opportunity.

A company has started to be objective about its future when it attempts to evaluate the future and forecast what the market will require in the way of new or improved products. Most companies, in making long-range sales forecasts, choose a period varying between five and twenty years, while more detailed sales targets are usually prepared for the financial year immediately ahead. Many products which will be available in five years' time are already on the market and firmly established in the product range. It is often possible to use such historical sales performance as the basis for projections into the future, but only as the basis, for such projections are dependent upon future events being similar to events which have happened in the past. Allowance must be made for changes due to economic circumstances and changes in competitive forces within the industry under investigation.

Comparison of movements, either short-term fluctuations or medium- to long-term trends, can often be achieved using the published economic data. Sometimes, acceptable degrees of correlation can be traced and these tied indicators will be useful parameters in forecasting.

The sales forecast can be as sophisticated or as simple as is justified by the business. The small- to medium-sized business is usually better placed than its larger competitors for maintaining close contact with its markets and can use elementary methods of forecasting which often produce better results than the methods employed by larger firms, where customer contact has become more remote because of larger lines of communication.

While the larger company will normally handle the research necessary to prepare a sales forecast by using its own personnel, the smaller concern cannot justify the expense of recruiting and retaining specialist staff. Where such forecasts are prepared, outside agencies are usually brought in for the task and, in recent years, multi-client projects have been evolved to cater for this demand. As the cost of research is spread over several sponsors, the research organisation can afford to employ highly skilled staff and carry out projects in some depth across a wide front. In addition, the research organisation is often able to prepare a report confidential to each client concerned.

BIAS TOWARDS ONE'S OWN COMPANY

Any sales forecast is subject to numerous influential factors, each of which must be isolated and measured. Some factors will have more effect than others and the forecaster must attempt to isolate and grade those factors according to their significance in such a way that weightings can be applied and an acceptable forecast determined within tolerable limits. In forecasting there is inevitably some bias towards the forecaster's own company and this must be avoided otherwise operating budgets, based on the forecasts, will be over-estimated, adversely affecting profitability.

It is also necessary to predict trends in related industries which provide indirect competition to the company's own products and which could have a bearing on the growth rate of the industry concerned. It is here that the forecaster can discover opportunities for product innovation or new product development. Since new products are the lifeblood of a company their discovery, development and subsequent production programming are necessary parts of the sales forecasting procedure.

To maintain a constant growth rate it is essential that every company estimates the life cycle of each of its products and introduces new products at the apex, or earlier, of an established product's life cycle in order to continue company growth. New products should not be introduced in a haphazard manner, but properly planned to fit the firm's expansion programme.

Price cutting, the most often observed tactical device in the struggles against competition, is a negative approach unless done from a position of strength with the company anticipating growth in the market and increased consumption achieved as a result of the price stimulus.

New markets are occasionally created following new legislation by government. Such changes can also be the cause of a substantial growth or decline in established markets and are often put forward as attempts to improve the social and/or economic life of the nation. Sudden changes in taste or fashion can cause sudden shifts in demand. Climatic changes can seriously affect sales of products which rely on extremes of temperature for their sales volume. Economic recessions, strikes or industrial disputes often bring in their train changes in purchasing habits.

CONTINGENCY PLANNING

Fortunately, many of these factors are predictable. There will certainly be any amount of published comment indicating possibilities. Research into future events is sometimes sponsored by trade and professional bodies; many thousands of words are produced by numerous authoritative writers in scores of newspapers, magazines, and trade and professional publications. These reports can be very valuable to businessmen seeking an insight into the future.

While one cannot forecast accurately what is going to happen, plans can be laid to cover any eventuality in advance of the event, at different levels of effectiveness. If the consequences of events are quantified in purely monetary terms, the businessman will be able to equate consequences with sales volume and, thus, profitability. Where necessary, contingency plans can be brought into operation.

It is true to say that many manufacturers take their products for granted and rarely investigate the uses to which they are put by customers, or how relevant they are to the customer's applications. Research can establish whether new features introduced by the manufacturer in good faith in the belief that they provide a plus for the buyer are not really required and not used, although paid for by the customer in the original selling price. It is possible, of course, that customers may not have realised the significance or relevance at the time of purchase.

In assessing product performance the businessman needs to relate application to product characteristics. Several companies have developed their share of the market as a direct result of providing a superior finish or excellent design. Buyers are often impressed by tales of long life for some mechanical item and sometimes make buying decisions in favour of such devices because the cost can be amortised over several years' operational life.

In arriving at the final assessment based on established standards relating each factor to every other factor, the researcher can compare the total significance of these in terms of market share and will be able to relate the performance of individual companies according to factors on which they concentrate. Comparison of results is the only certain way of monitoring company performance in a competitive commercial environment. The standards established in the appraisal of competitor profiles provide the foundations for a full analysis of market shares. Companies desiring to break into a completely new market will need to examine the extent to which policies adopted by those already serving this market have been successful.

Having obtained full information on total market size it is necessary to assess the extent to which the market can be penetrated either by winning a share of the existing market or by concentrating on growth and winning the business which would otherwise have gone to present suppliers. Once this work has been done the company can make a full and realistic evaluation of the marketing budget necessary to achieve its objectives.

It may be easier in some industries to take business from established suppliers than to expand the total market. In other projects it may be more feasible to opt for developing the growth market potential than to get involved in a battle with those already active in the market. Only when the business activity of the company has been decided should any attempt be made to measure the total market and to prepare a reasoned definition of the market.

DEFINITION OF THE TOTAL MARKET

Many people are confused about the total market for a particular product. It is the total amount of money spent in satisfying a need, irrespective of the products which satisfy that need. This means that all types of food are in competition with one another, the various forms of transport are competitors, and all aids to business efficiency are locked in combat for the purchaser's money.

The market situation for any given company or industry is continually changing and violent fluctuations can occur in market shares from day to day. Over a period shifts in the pattern of demand will become evident and it is imperative that a check be kept on such trends. Steadily rising sales turnover is not, in itself, a true indicator that a company is making the best use of its potential. It is quite possible for a company to achieve reasonable increases in sales year by year yet find that it has a rapidly diminishing share of the market. It will be losing sales opportunities unless sales volume is rising at least as rapidly as that of the industry as a whole.

A company also needs to keep track of its competitors' market shares and be able to explain any change that becomes apparent. There must be a reason why a competitor is expanding his market share faster than anyone else. If, on the other hand, a competitor with a strong marketing team is seen to be losing out on a market share, it could be that he has decided to diversify because of a forecast over capacity or a decreasing growth rate. It is for these reasons that it is vital to carry out constant analyses of market share at frequent intervals, even if in a simple form, rather than rely on occasional extensive research projects, no matter how sophisticated.

Confusion sometimes arises when referring to marketing research and market research. The former is the activity which examines all the elements which make up marketing practice, including markets, products, channels of distribution, pricing behaviour and opinions. Market research is only one element of marketing research, albeit the most widely known and practised.

When it comes to getting the goods to the customer, different companies use different channels of distribution. While some use stockists or distributors, others deliver direct to the retailer or even direct to the ultimate consumer. Different channels of distribution achieve different levels of success in selling their suppliers' products, and their effectiveness can be critical to the sales volume achieved by any one company. Channels of distribution in the consumer field have undergone considerable change in recent years. The development of supermarkets and self-service stores has progressed very rapidly in some areas of retailing, more slowly in others. Some companies have achieved considerable growth through the provision of mail order facilities, while others have built their share of the market through new selling methods such as party plan or vending machines or through selling direct to the household.

In the industrial field there have not yet been such fundamental changes in the pattern of distribution, although some changes have become apparent, for example leasing of factories and capital equipment, and the use of time sharing for data processing equipment.

CONTROL OF DISTRIBUTION

It is not generally realised that the cost to industry of distributing a product may range between 5 and 60 per cent of the final selling price, depending upon the nature of the product and the method of distribution selected. Active control of distribution can reduce these expenses and allow a substantial increase in profitability. Many related activities could be improved following an improvement in actual distribution.

The marketing executive must endeavour to reconcile the needs of the customer for a full service with his company's requirements for the provision of an economic level of service. If he decides that the most appropriate way to win sales from a competitor is by providing a superior distribution service, then that is a deliberate expense incurred in the marketing budget as an alternative to other marketing activities and expenditure.

Because of the forces of competition, demand for any one product from one source can vary considerably. It is the distributive function to provide a contingency against wide fluctuations in demand, and the businessman's responsibility to develop a distributive pattern to cater for those deviations from the norm. Some are more predictable than others and the product mix from the factory must be adjusted to cope with the demand.

Properly controlled, the distributive system can protect a company against giving customer dissatisfaction and will enable it to achieve a high level of productivity by ensuring economical production runs according to predetermined planning.

MONITORING THE MARKET PLAN

No matter how carefully a management may plan, some objectives will always be more difficult to achieve than others. Marketing planning is not a panacea for all commercial and industrial problems.

Ideally the marketing plan will include any action which may have to be taken to avoid diminution of profits. Even if actual performance exceeds all expectations there should be built-in provisions for the favourable conditions which have become apparent. If proper care has been taken to structure the marketing plan the contingency section should be straightforward, being no more than the detailed consideration of alternative courses of action. The contingency plan should include action which may need to be taken in the short term to minimise or maximise the possible consequences of deviation from the schedule as well as the medium- to long-term action necessary to exploit a changed environment.

To ensure that the right action is taken at the right time - to ensure best results - it is essential that a barometer of company and industry performance be developed. Steps must be taken to monitor actual results against forecast company sales and forecast market shares.

There are several specialist organisations which provide, at reasonable cost, performance comparisons within an industry. If one of these organisations is used, the company needs to develop only an internal early warning system. This can be done by plotting orders received by major product groups against the purchasing industry by standard industrial classification.

In the shorter term, signals can be provided by relating actual inquiries, quotations, orders received, and sales by major product groups against the forecast. Then if the average timelag between inquiry and order is, say, six weeks, and between order and delivery is four to six weeks, the company will have, automatically, nearly three months' notice of an imminent fall-off in sales. Care must be taken to ensure that conversion ratios between each stage do not vary, or that if they do adjustment be made accordingly.

Whilst it would not be wise to institute remedial action as a result of one deviation from plan - for occasional fluctuations *do* happen - once a trend becomes apparent, the cause should be established and appropriate action taken. In addition to showing industrial performance as a whole, some specialist comparison organisations quote the detailed performance of unspecified companies against which the performance of one's own firm can be measured.

Here, the company should be able to judge the extent to which it will be able to exert influence on the market. If the entire industry is suffering the same deteriorating position, it is probably wise to curtail any plans for expansion unless there is a clear indication that the present circumstances can be favourably exploited. The timing and extent of any cutback in this area should be provided for in the contingency plan, which should show detailed profit and loss statements for 70, 80, 90, 110 and 120 per cent actual performance against forecast. Each of the detailed accounts should include the appropriate departmental budgets and head counts. The major driving principles must be to preserve net profit and indemnify future profits. These considerations often prove incompatible in practice and a working compromise may be necessary. Sometimes, profit comes from the last 15 to 20 per cent of sales, after overheads have been covered, and when costs become marginal. Under such circumstances a reduction of 20 per cent in sales volume will warrant, perhaps, a cut of 30 per cent in expenditure in order to maintain net profit at par value.

A company can sometimes avoid the disaster of a temporarily poor market position by acquiring another company. A study of competitive profiles in the marketing plan, followed by detailed investigation of suitable partners, may disclose a competitor which could supplement, or ideally complement, the company's own operations.

Although the possibility of making a takeover bid will almost always be considered first, realistic management must not discount the advantages of soliciting a bid for one's own company, as this may be more prudent.

Detailed consideration of both rationalisation and diversification policies should form a logical part of any contingency plan. There is nearly always conflict between the sales department, anxious to meet individual customer requirements, and the production department needing long production runs and the elimination of time-consuming 'specials'. Some firms reconcile these differences by adopting a market segmentation policy, producing 'specials' for each industry group. They then become so well-established within these industries that they achieve long production runs of these so-called specials. While these firms concentrate their efforts on the part of the market for which they are best suited, others have diversified into other activities in order to absorb their surplus production capacity.

Where there is a possibility that an imminent scientific breakthrough will bring product obsolescence, companies affected should attempt to concentrate future plans on less vulnerable fields of operation. A side-step into a related industry or technology is a natural and logical move for most companies as their technology and management expertise can then be put to profitable use.

INVESTMENT IN COMPANY RESOURCES

Although the need for improved efficiency and productivity has long been accepted by manufacturing processes in industry, and a similar need recognised for some time in the marketing function, it has never been satisfactorily resolved in the latter because of the difficulties of reconciling accounting principles with a business function which is considered part art and part science. While many marketing activities operate under disciplines not widely appreciated – let alone understood – by management, the practice of marketing is still an investment in company resources. If control is to be maintained marketing will be subject to the same accounting appraisal as any other form of investment.

The cost of handling orders of varying sizes must be ascertained if stock levels are to be controlled with great accuracy. It may be found more profitable to refuse orders selling below a price-level considered to be uneconomic. Such selective selling often increases profitability. Location of warehouses, planning of sales territories and routes of salesmen can be organised, using accurate cost statistics rather than intuition. Improving direction and supervision of salesmen through the setting of performance and activity targets can result in increased selling and operating efficiency.

Management in many companies is not always able to recognise that its products or services are mediocre or even inferior to others on the market. Where such blindness exists the company is unlikely to introduce new methods or procedures to assist in rectifying or overcoming the problem. In the same way the firm is unlikely to experiment with new ideas or make a fresh approach in an attempt to improve its future prospects. In these circumstances the only avenue left for that firm is to continue in its own fashion no matter how much the position may deteriorate.

Because of the pace of technological change, a greater demand is manifesting itself for information to be employed in decision making. Investment decisions become more and more complex as businesses grow. The businessman must endeavour to forecast growth potential, and the factors likely to influence his company's penetration of that potential, in an attempt to reduce the risk facing every business enterprise.

Companies should be able to identify the influences on their major activities and show how they are being controlled to the benefit of the entire organisation. The extent to which the information provided is relevant to the company's needs should be assessed. Executives need to eliminate unused material being prepared and to discover additional information previously unknown. Such research into the marketing effort will help to ensure that an economic level of expenditure is being maintained. Appropriate marketing policies should ensure that all products are developed according to the needs of the market and resources are not wasted on products which the market shows are unsatisfactory.

COMMUNICATING PROFIT RESPONSIBILITY

One of the important developments in marketing consumer goods is the change in emphasis to impersonal selling techniques such as advertising and point-of-sale display. Personal selling still has the most important role in industrial marketing. Improvement in the function and performance of industrial sales forces justifies more attention than is now perhaps necessary in consumer goods selling efforts. These salesmen cannot be expected to sell the ideal product mix without guidance and direction nor differentiate between the profitability of various products.

In any organisation the level of profit responsibility must not only be decided but also widely communicated to ensure the satisfactory implementation of the most critical of business activities.

The marketing plan and all its ancillary documents must be used by executives as a day to day control and development manual. The planning process must not be treated as an annual political exercise suffered by busy executives concerned with other tasks. Planning, organisation, direction and control are basic management jobs and, in a successful marketing-oriented company, will fill the management's working days. Each manager needs to understand the interactive nature of the individual tasks which have to be completed during each period of the marketing plan.

The timing of each step, at all levels, and in each function, is critical if the total plan is to be satisfactorily co-ordinated and the anticipated results achieved. A flexible attitude to planning principles needs to be adopted so that management recognises the need for contingencies and their control within corporate strategy.

Unforeseen events create a different scale of priorities, and flexibility in policy interpretation as allowed for in the plan must be recognised if the company's interests are to be best served. The results of monitoring actual performance against forecasts have a definite value in personnel development and in operating efficiency, as does the preparation of forecasts itself.

The chief executive of any marketing-oriented company retains the final responsibility for marketing policies. The marketing manager gives advice in the field of marketing and may well carry a line responsibility. If the marketing concept is to be adopted the entire company and, in particular, the management team must be oriented towards customer satisfaction. And this is the essence of planning in marketing. For the end result – the marketing plan – is not so important as the benefits gained from the input. The effort, study, appraisal, and evaluation of the business environment provides the major bonuses from the preparation of the plan and it all starts from considering customer needs.

In the foreseeable future most companies will become increasingly involved in computerisation. Even if not directly concerned as users, companies will become involved by the extent to which suppliers, competitors and customers become geared to electronic data processing. Every businessman must appreciate how the computer can be applied to marketing problems. He needs some appreciation of the effects of computers on present-day and future marketing decisions. Future growth potential of computer-linked terminals making computerisation possible and economic for many smaller firms will certainly assist in the scientific application of marketing. The day is not far off when a company's entire planning process will be subject to computer storage and processing.

FURTHER READING

Allen, Peter, *Marketing Techniques for Analysis and Control*, Macdonald and Evans, Plymouth, 1977

Kotler, Philip, *Marketing Management: analysis, planning, and control,* 4th edition, Prentice-Hall International, London, 1981

Stapleton, John, *How to Prepare a Marketing Plan*, 3rd edition, Gower, Aldershot, 1982

Wilson, Richard M.S., *Management Controls and Marketing Planning,* Heinemann on behalf of the Institute of Marketing and the CAM Foundation, London, 1979

8 Market research

Colin McDonald

It is a favourite military adage that 'time spent in reconnaissance is seldom wasted'. Market research is the way in which industry does reconnaissance. It seeks to provide knowledge of customers, how they behave and to what they respond and the current and expected state of the market. Without this knowledge it would be very much more difficult and less safe to plan marketing, to decide between options and to evaluate the effect of decisions.

Market research is by no means all the information a marketer needs, but it is a quite specific sector of it. The military analogy is useful here. 'Reconnaissance' is a survey of the ground before a battle, knowledge of the enemy and how his troops are disposed. It cannot itself determine military objectives; other information (for example, about the resources available on one's own side and their state of readiness) is necessary for this. Nor can it decide the political objectives of the war. But it can modify the general's appreciation of his objectives and suggest the best ways of achieving them (provided of course that it is good reconnaissance; misleading information is worse than none, as Napolean doubtless felt after Moscow). In the same way, well-conducted market research provides systematic and accurate knowledge of the market 'out there', the people we are trying to sell to; it can correct false impressions and aid understanding of their needs and responses. It cannot *by itself* determine marketing objectives but, allied to a proper appreciation of the product it helps the resources of a business to be deployed effectively.

Market research does not guarantee success. Even the best-conducted intelligence service may be misinterpreted or misused; Napolean did not fail at Moscow through lack of information, but because he refused to pay attention to the information he had available. Market research costs money, and there are often strong pressures to skimp on it or to think of it too late, instead of integrating it into the marketing plan. Market research provides an important part of the basis for better, more cost-effective marketing, but only if it is well designed and well thought out in accordance with marketing objectives, and if the results are taken seriously and understood.

THE GROWTH OF MARKET RESEARCH

Although the beginnings of market research can be said to date back to the turn of the century, when advertising agencies such as the J. Walter Thompson Company in America began to build successful businesses on the basis that they understood the market, its growth into a substantial industry is entirely post-war. In Britain a few advertising agencies had established market research subsidiaries before the war, and one or two successful entrepreneurs (A. C. Nielsen, Gallup, Mass Observation, for example) had set up their own specialised services. Government work for the Ministry of Food and other departments kept these bodies in operation during the war, but when the Market Research Society was formed in 1947 there were only a dozen market research agencies in the country, six of which still operate today: British Market Research Bureau (the oldest *ad hoc* agency in Britain), Bureau of Commercial Research, Mass Observation, Nielsen, Research Services and Gallup.

Today the market for research in Britian is estimated to be worth over £80 million. During the 1970s the increase in real terms, adjusted for inflation, was more than two-thirds. Some 4000 persons are thought to be employed in market research, three-quarters of whom are members of the Market Research Society, and there are nearly 200 supplying agencies.

It is still the case that the industry depends heavily on consumer goods clients, especially in food and drink. Advertising agencies, the original founders of most market research suppliers, now directly commission less than 10 per cent; the post-war years have seen the development of in-house research departments, staffed by professionals, with an established place in the marketing organisation of their companies, and the decline of the full-service agency. In 1979 the following distribution of research revenue was estimated (based on the returns of members of AMSO, the Association of Market Survey Organisations, adjusted for non-members):

1	Food, drink and tobacco	35	
2	Other manufacturing companies	15	
3	Advertising agencies and media	15	
4	Public sector	10	
5	Service traders	5	
6	Overseas	5	
7	Miscellaneous	15	
		100	per cent

It is now generally felt by commentators that the very rapid growth in the industry during the 1960s and 1970s has probably reached its peak, and that it will settle down to follow more closely the national rate of economic growth.

THE OCCASIONS FOR MARKET RESEARCH

The variety of problems presented for treatment by market research methods, and of sources from which they come, is so great these days that no classification can give its full flavour. However, some sort of intelligible grouping is needed to break up the subject. Let us consider first the occasions when, and the purposes for which, market research is used. Since this book is intended for managers, we shall concentrate on market research for industrial and commercial clients making consumer goods; but much of what follows will apply in the different context of work for government departments, local authorities, nationalised and non-consumer industries or university research projects. All of these use the same tools of the trade in differing degrees.

As a first step, one might distinguish three aspects of business where market research is naturally involved:

1 *Description* of the market
2 *Monitoring* how the market changes
3 *Action* taken by the company, both at the state of *initiation* (choosing which action to take) and *evaluation* of the results of action taken.

Each of these three can be applied at two levels of distribution: the level of the *retailer*, and the level of the eventual *consumer*. Thus we can think of the field divided into a sixfold framework:

	Retailer level	Consumer level
Description		
Monitoring		
Action (initiation and evaluation)		

The way in which research methods fit into the cells of this framework will be discussed later, but first these three aspects of business will be described:

Description

The primary purpose for which research is required. The need is obvious for a company coming new to a market. To work out the overall strategy, to formulate the product correctly and to decide how to market and promote it, it is clearly necessary to learn whatever relevant information is not already known about the brands (if any) already in the market, how they are distributed, their share of market, who the users are, how frequently and how they use the brands, whether they are single- or multiple-brand users, and the reasons why they make their choices. A new entrant would *have* to learn these things but it is equally important, if less obvious, for an established brand that those who market it should keep up to date with the context in which their product is bought.

Yankelovitch, in a paper in 1966, tells the story of the runaway success of Timex watches in the United States, and attributes it to their correct appreciation of the actual demand in their market. The Swiss manufacturers, against whom Timex were competing, discovered (from a survey which they misunderstood) that low-cost Timex watches were being purchased not merely by low-income groups but by high-income groups also. They failed to appreciate that as many as two-thirds of the watch-buying population either wanted a low-cost watch which they could replace if it wore out, or a reliable watch (paying extra for the quality); in both cases a *practical* purchase. They continued to address all their promotion to the remaining third of the market, which saw a watch solely as a gift for a special occasion with an emotional content. The quality watch companies stressed the symbolic aspect in their advertising and concentrated it all around Christmas and graduation day, leaving the rest of the year uncovered. Timex exploited the gap with brilliant effect. It is unusual to find so clear a case history, but there have been other examples quoted publicly, by managers responsible for brands of acknowledged success and prestige, which have stressed the importance they attach to keeping up to date their knowledge of the 'health' of the brand, and the place this takes in their marketing strategy.

Monitoring

By this is meant period checking for *changes*, in the brand's share or distribution, usage or image. There are obvious dangers in formulating plans on out-of-date information when significant changes have occurred since the original picture was taken.

A typical research strategy might involve periodic studies of a market in some depth, taking a cross-section at a certain point in time, linking these together by continuous measurement of a limited number of key variables which are expected to be liable to change.

Action

Whereas 'description' and 'monitoring' refer to obtaining information about the market 'out there', the 'action' heading would include all the ways in which market research can help a company to operate within that situation, both in initiating and deciding between options, and in evaluating action taken. It can include the following areas of activity:

1 New product launches and development
2 Alteration to existing products (i.e., testing for acceptability)
3 Developing and evaluating advertising campaigns, in matching creative treatment and media to target markets
4 Developing and evaluating promotions, sampling drops, mailing shots etc.
5 Promoting the company's image.

Another area of research which really deserves a separate heading, although it is not included in the 'management' scheme above, is *media*. Information on the audiences for different media is needed on a continuous basis to provide the currency in which agency buyers can deal with media sellers. Television viewing, radio listening and newspaper and magazine readership are all regularly measured in surveys paid for by media owners and controlled by joint industry committees representing media, agencies and advertisers. Apart from these, a number of specific surveys are carried out to establish the coverage or effectiveness of particular media.

WHY RESEARCH AT ALL?

As already stated, market research is not the whole of the information needed for marketing, but a special kind of information, obtained by survey methods from the population of potential consumers or from the distribution system. Before moving on to consider how the different purposes outlined above are satisfied by different research methods, it is pertinent to ask why we need market research at all. After all, it costs money to collect and process research data, and it is not so long ago that there was no market research at all. Didn't people manage then, and are there not firms who seem successful enough today without it?

It is tempting, especially in times of financial stringency, to believe that a company's own knowledge of its product and contacts with the trade should be adequate. Nor would it be right to decry the know-how of (for example) a good sales force. But there are several problems in relying solely on reports from salesmen or other departments. One is lack of the coverage we need: salemen's contacts with the trade are not likely to tell us enough about *customers'* attitudes. Second, what salesmen are able to discover is limited by the contacts they make among retailers and will not represent them all. Third, information gathering is not their principal job, and their selection and interpretation of what seems important will inevitably be affected by their primary interest in selling. Although information from salesmen or other sources may have considerable qualitative value, we need to be sure that the information on which decisions are based is as far as possible complete and representative in coverage, and objective.

To ensure representativeness and objectivity, market research makes extensive use of *sampling*.

Sampling in market research

Sampling is not, of course, exclusive to market research; it is a familiar concept in quality control. It is the only practical way of measuring the composition (taking a sounding) of a very large population which it would be impossible, or prohibitively expensive, to measure in a complete census (a 'population', by the way, in statistics means any defined group of people or things which is to be sampled).

If a sample is selected by correct methods, every member of the population will have an equal probability of being selected (or, if not equal, a known and deliberately weighted probability). There is thus no bias in the selection, so that the results remain unknown and uncalculated.

Central to the theory of sampling is the concept of standard error. From a very large population there is a very large number of ways, almost an infinity of ways, of selecting samples. Suppose a very large number of different samples of a given size were selected. What would we expect the variation to be in any estimate derived from samples? To make it concrete, let us suppose we want to find out the proportion of all adults who are men. We happen to know it should be about half, but the same principle applies to any other unknown proportion we want to estimate. The different samples will not give exactly the same estimate, but we would expect *most* of them to give *roughly* the right estimate; otherwise sampling would be of little value. In fact, we know from sampling theory that the estimates given by a very large number of samples fit into a standard pattern, called the *normal distribution*, a bell-shaped curve in which most of the sample estimates bunch together around the centre while some tail off in either direction, above and below the central estimate. It is possible to calculate how sample estimates form themselves into a normal distribution, by calculating the standard error; two-thirds of all the estimates would be within plus or minus one standard error of the average (central) estimate, 95 per cent within two and 99 per cent within three standard erros. Thus we know, by calculation based on sampling theory, the probability that the true proportion for the population (or the average estimate from a number of samples, which approaches closer to the true proportion as the number of samples approach infinity) lies within a certain range of the estimate given by our *one* sample.

A very important point here, and one often not understood by laymen, is that the error probability we can calculate for a sample depends only on the size of the sample itself and *not at all* on the proportion of the population sampled. People are often surprised at the idea that one can estimate a quantity for a population of many millions from 'only' 500 or 1000 people. But if it is a properly selected sample, the error calculation depends only on the sample size and the fact that the sample is only a tiny proportion of the population is irrelevant. If from a sample of 1000 people we estimate that 45 per cent of the population of the country is male we know that there is a 95 per cent chance that the true figure will lie between plus or minus 3 per cent (in other words, there is only one chance in twenty that any similar sample would have produced an estimate lower than 42 per cent or higher than 48 per cent). If the sample size were increased to 4000, the range of error would be reduced to plus or minus 1.5, i.e., between 43.5 per cent and 46.5 per cent. The general rule is that to *halve* the standard error you have to increase the sample size by four times.

The above explains why sampling theory provides a safe and economical a procedure for accurate estimation of large populations. In practice, in market research, the pure theory just described nearly always has to be modified. This is because we sample people, and people living all over a country are expensive to contact and interview; a simple equal probability sample of the population of Britain would involve a great deal of expensive travelling by interviewers to contact isolated individuals.

Basic sampling theory has been developed in many ways sc as to combine statistical validity with practical cost-effective interviewing. The two most important modifications are *clustering* and *stratification*. By clustering is meant that, instead of sampling across the board, we sample in *stages*, selecting first a sample of geographical areas (e.g. wards, polling districts or census enumeration districts) and taking the sample of people within those districts. Clustering slightly increases the standard error of a sample, but this is calculable and is normally a small price to pay for the benefit of cost-effective interviewing, since interviewers can be given assignments with contacts all living reasonably close together and can then achieve a higher rate per day's work. Stratification means that before selecting the geographical areas (normally called sampling points) within which we are to sample, they are arranged in an order which makes sure that we include in correct proportions all relevant local characteristics: north and south, urban and rural areas and so on. There are now in existence very sophisticated methods for classifying geographical areas, based on information from the census, and computer programmes for picking stratified sampling points.

There are many possible ways of sampling individuals but they group essentially into two: random and non-random. In random, or probability, sampling, the interviewer has no choice: he has to try to contact a specific individual pointed out to him. Most samples in the UK are picked from the electoral register, and there are systems for picking either households or individuals from the register and for sampling adults with the correct probability from selected households even if they are themselves not registered. With a probability sample one knows what proportion of the selected sample could not be contacted and therefore has a chance to estimate any bias in the results; the statistical calculations of standard error, etc., all apply. Probability samples are usually demanded for government surveys and for others which are required to be publicly accountable. There is however a cost penalty, since it is more expensive to require interviewers to contact specific individuals, calling a number of times if necessary, than to allow them some latitude in their selection of persons to interview. For this reason, many market research projects use a form of non-random, or quota sampling, in which interviewers are required to deliver certain numbers of interviews with specified types of people whom they must find themselves. Quotas can be set in line with what is known of the population. Strictly, quota sampling does not have the statistical theoretical base of random sampling, although empirical tests of the consistency (stability) of non-random samples are possible. In much sampling practice quota samples are selected multi-stage, with the primary sample of areas (wards etc.) being chosen by strict probability methods after stratification. The interviewers are issued with lists of street numbers and given strict instructions to obtain their interviews within those streets. The only quota controls which then remain necessary are those relating to the probability of someone being at home: typically, interviewers have to find a certain proportion of working women or women with children, and must interview men in the evening so as not to find only unemployed or shift workers. Most of the major research agencies operate a system of this general kind.

The above account of sampling applies (obviously) to consumer research. But the variety of problems which can arise often calls for ingenuity in devising new ways of sampling, often in cases where there does not exist a 'universe' from which the sample can be drawn: industrial firms, people in professions, people with certain minority characteristics, users of certain products etc.

RESEARCH METHODS

We can now consider in broad terms the research approaches which are appropriate for the different levels of information required, classified above as description, monitoring and action. It should not be thought that these are hard-and-fast distinctions. Good research is always designed to fit a specific problem and there are cases, for example, where retailers or manufacturers are properly researched by sample survey (certainly where we are involved in measuring their opinions). Much detail is omitted from the table in Figure 8.1. Nevertheless, it is a convenient way of breaking up the subject so that we can *start* thinking about it.

	For retailers	For consumers
Description of market	Retail audit	Sample surveys
Monitoring changes and trends	Retail audit	Panels or sequential surveys
Action:		
Initiation	Test market	Experimental tests
Evaluation	Area evaluation	Product tests etc.
The media	Not applicable	Sample surveys or panels

Figure 8.1. Market research appropriate to different purposes

Retail audits

The retail audit is one of the earliest known types of research, pioneered by Nielsen in the United States. It stemmed from the realisation that relying on measurements of sales ex-factory was not fast enough or accurate enough to identify areas of weakness in distribution or adverse trends that would need correction. A falling demand could be concealed by stock build-up at the wholesalers; conversely, retailers might be content to tolerate shortages of stock in areas where a little activity could stimulate a healthy demand, etc. It was necessary to go to the front line, so to speak, and observe directly what consumers were taking off the shelves.

Retail audits work in the following way. A panel of stores is recruited to represent the universe (grocery outlets, chemists, off-licences or whatever the definition is) being stratified so that different turnover levels and types of organisation (multiple, independent, voluntary group, cash and carry etc.) are represented. The audits are carried out at regular intervals, usually bi-monthly. At each audit, an interviewer counts the stock of the audited items on display on the shelves and in the storeroom, and all goods invoiced since the previous check. Movement off the shelf between two checks is then calculated by the simple formula:

(Stock at check 1) + (Goods invoice since check 1) – (Stock at check 2)

The key data normally reported for audited product fields are sales brand shares and volume trends, purchase brand shares and volume trends, and distribution. These are broken down by relevant classifications such as area of the country, type of shop or turnover level, and all shown both in unit volume and sterling value terms: where relevant, pack sizes within brands are also broken out separately. Advertising expenditure is usually monitored and fluctuations in this can be set alongside sales and purchase movements, although it may be dangerous to draw simple conclusions about relationships between them. Most retail audit companies will, for a lower charge, supply a distribution check which merely tells one what proportion of stores have the brand in stock and on display. Merchandising material and display advertising can also be monitored.

Setting up a retail audit panel and the facilities to process the data is an expensive investment, and it is crucial to this kind of operation that it should be *syndicable* (that is; sold to a number of clients). Syndication is economically possible because, once the initial investment of recruiting and visiting the panel is made, it is relatively inexpensive to collect the data for a large number of product fields. Following the pattern pioneered and still operated by Nielsen, clients pay agreed subscriptions for packages of selected brands within a defined product field, reported and presented so that the information is tailored to their needs.

Although most retail audit work is thought of in connection with grocery and chemist products, audits are run in hardware stores, tobacconists, garages, off-licences, travel agents, record shops and other specialist outlets. Prescription auditing, in which either chemists' invoices or doctors' prescriptions (from duplicate pads) are counted, is also an established service.

In buying an audit, of course, one always has to be aware of the proportion of trade that passes through outlets *other* than the particular group being measured by the audit.

It is widely expected that the spread of new technology, especially electronic data capture at the checkout, will eventually change the face of auditing. Through scanners, retailers can acquire instant, accurate and continuous knowledge and therefore control to assist them in their day-to-day management. They may not wish to make this information available to competitors; alternatively, they may agree amongst themselves upon the extent to which information for the whole trade (or the few companies responsible for 80 per cent of it) is to be disseminated and shared. The detail available from scanners will make traditional auditing seem very slow and old fashioned; on the other hand part of the market (the smaller outlets) will be relatively slow to adopt scanners. In America (where some 4000 stores now have scanners) there are already a number of research firms who have set up consumer panels in association with scanner stores, so that these people's purchases can be logged automatically over time (without trouble to the respondent) and related to their opportunities for seeing advertising, etc. It will be a few years yet before new-look audit facilities are in being but eventually (we may be confident) scanner-based data will win on cheapness as well as quality and new types of service will compete for the business.

Consumer sample surveys

These are what most people automatically think of as 'market research': the interviewer with a clipboard, the structured questionnaire, the so-called opinion poll. Indeed, these methods are still the backbone of market research, and are likely to remain so. To stop short at the level of the retailer's counter is not enough; marketers must know what consumers do with their products, how they buy them, what they like or dislike, what needs are unsatisfied. New products could not otherwise be optimally designed and launched; existing ones could not be promoted to best effect.

The personal interview, with the interviewer knocking at the door or stopping people in the street, is the popular picture of consumer surveying but not the whole story. Occasionally the necessary data are collected by *observation.* Often *self-completion* questionnaires are used, either in the course of a personal interview, or left with informants to return by post or to be collected later. Self-completion is used for the Target Group Index (a syndicated survey of 25 000 people covering usage of over 2000 brands and services and media). It is also a good procedure for certain kinds of scaled attitude data. Finally, there are the alternatives of *postal* and *telephone* interviewing.

Personal interviewing is the most costly alternative, and this trend is likely to continue. The reason is obvious: it is a highly labour-intensive method. Interviewers are paid some £10–£20 for a roughly six-hour day, depending on their quality and experience. Pay is increased for unsocial hours (evenings or weekends) which are necessary in most surveys these days even when only housewives are being interviewed, since so many of them are out at work during the day. In addition, interviewers have to be paid for their time in travelling to the place where the work has to be carried out, which may be some distance from their home, and their mileage expenses, which must increase in line with petrol prices. The days of interviewing as a relatively low-cost part-time job are over. More importantly, a large section of the time paid for is 'dead' time, travelling to and between contacts, and this lowers the effective daily interviewing rate, which is the principal variable determining the cost of a survey.

Nevertheless, for many survey purposes personal face-to-face interviewing is considered necessary. A good interviewer forms a rapport with respondents which can lead them to focus their minds in a relaxed and concentrated way on the subject under discussion. The interaction between two people plays a part in improving the quality of the response. Stimuli can be shown, ranging from words on a card through photographs to actual products. Also, a questionnaire can be taken in a designed order, with respondents not being alerted to questions due to come later and which could affect the earlier response.

A device commonly used to offset the high cost of face-to-face surveys where the method is judged necessary is *syndication*, in which the data collection costs of the survey are shared between a number of subscribers. The commonest form of such syndication is what has come to be known as the 'omnibus' survey. In this a regular sample is interviewed weekly (so many housewives or adults) and subscribers buy questions on the survey at a standardised fee per question and sample size. Many regularly repeated surveys, advertising tracking studies and so on, have been successfully and economically run on omnibus survey vehicles. The only serious limitation is the length of the interview. No individual can tolerate being interviewed for too long, however fascinating the subject matter, and if a number of topic areas for different subscribers have to be fitted into an interview the amount of time which can be allowed for any one of them is clearly much less than would be the case if the whole interview could be given over to that topic. For this reason, if a subject has to be explored in some depth by a large number of questions, an omnibus is unlikely to be suitable and a tailor-made survey will probably be required. The same is true if there is some special requirement in the sample which cannot be fulfilled by the general purpose sample used for the omnibus. But if only one or two things are required to be known and if a representative sample of the total population will do, an omnibus can offer significant savings. A special advantage of an omnibus is that because relatively large samples are interviewed weekly it can be an excellent way of finding minority samples quickly; for example where questions are to be asked of users of a product which is known to be used by only 2 per cent (say) of the population. With a tailor-made survey the cost of contacting the other 98 per cent to find out that they are not eligible for our survey is considerable, but on the omnibus that cost is almost entirely shared between the other subscribers.

Postal and *telephone surveys* are ways of interviewing which do not incur the cost penalties of sending interviewers out to people's homes to make their contacts.

The postal survey is perhaps neglected a little unfairly in the UK except where a special sample assumed to be highly interested in the subject matter is involved (for example, the members of an organisation being asked their opinions about that organisation). There is an obvious incentive to use postal surveys where we have a population to sample for whom it is easy to obtain names and addresses and where the sample is so scattered as to make the cost of face-to-face interviewing prohibitive (the same applies, of course, to telephone interviewing). There are two main potential disadvantages with postal interviewing. The first is that a respondent can scan the whole questionnaire before he answers it (there is no possibility of leading the respondent through one stage at a time) and he can take as long over answering it as he likes; postal surveys are therefore suitable for 'considered opinions' but not for 'instant reactions'. The second and more serious disadvantage is that it is so easy for people not to reply at all. The normal procedure is to send out the questionnaires with reply-paid return envelopes, to send a reminder (with a spare questionnaire) after (say) ten days, and a second reminder some ten days after the first.

Even so, it is common to get not more than 40–50 per cent of the sample responding, and it has been known to be as low as 20 per cent. There is no simple answer to this difficulty, the important question being whether the non-respondents are *biased* in some way which would affect our interpretation of the survey results. However, this is certainly not a reason for avoiding postal surveys altogether. Postal surveys are suitable for an *interested* population, and much can be done to encourage people to respond by good design, good layout and (occasionally) incentive payment; non-response bias can be checked by telephone calls on a sub-sample.

Telephone interviewing is, in Britain and other industrialised countries, the most likely main development for the future. In the United States, where 95 per cent of the population have telephones, it is now a major data collection method. In the UK the proportion with a telephone at home has passed the 70 per cent mark, which is about the point at which telephone interviewing began to take off in the US. At these levels the question of what bias there may be among non-telephone households assumes less and less importance for most marketing interests.

Telephone interviewing preserves the interviewer–respondent interaction but in a rather different form: the interviewers' *voice* becomes crucial, other aspects of the interviewer's personality much less so. It is acknowledged that telephone interviewing is a different type of operation with its own requirements of questionnaire design and the kind of person suitable to be an interviewer. It can achieve much greater productivity than face-to-face interviewing because it can be centrally organised. No costs are incurred in travel to locate respondents and many more calls (both contact calls and successful interview calls) can be made in a day. Moreover, there is a facility for instant supervision and correction of interviewer error which is lacking in a face-to-face survey. As technology improves, telephone interviewing will make possible the automated questionnaires and immediate data capture and processing by computer which are already in operation to a limited extent in the United States.

There are some obvious limitations. One cannot show stimulus material over the telephone (although it is possible to mail stimulus material to people already recruited to a sample with instructions not to look at it until the interview). There are worries also about the psychological reaction of respondents to the telephone: will they be nervous of a disembodied voice or resentful at the intrusion into their privacy that the telephone may seem to represent? American experience does not suggest that these are serious problems, but only time will tell whether in other countries there is an anti-telephone feeling. That any such problem can be overcome with time and good design, there is little doubt.

Although telephones are not yet used widely in general consumer surveys in Britain, they are extensively used for surveys among respondents at the executive level who can, of course, most easily be contacted by telephone. Frequently, such respondents are recruited by telephone for face-to-face interviews in greater depth.

Panels

If you wish to measure *change* in attitudes or behaviour, an obvious approach is to interview the same set of people twice. Any change observed is subject to the standard error of the one sample only, whereas, if two separate samples are used, there are two standard errors to take into account. One can get a more direct, more accurate picture of change within people, and perhaps that can be related to a stimulus such as a new advertising campaign. The drawback, of course, is that one must be careful not to alert people by questions which in themselves could lead them to notice things or to modify their behaviour and thus distort their answers the second time round.

Any repeat interviewing of the same people could be called a panel. Normally, in research parlance, a panel has a more restricted meaning than that. *Either* it is a sample which agrees, on recruitment, to be available for contact on all sorts of subjects (some firms run telephone panels on this basis) *or* (more commonly in the UK) a panel is recruited to provide *continuous* information over a period, typically information which needs to be recorded day by day otherwise it would not be remembered. Such panels may be run either as continuous syndicated services (requiring an investment too great for a single company to underwrite) or for specific *ad hoc* projects. Examples of operations suitable for panel treatment include:

1 *Retail audits*, where the data are provided from panels of shops
2 *Consumer audits*, where panel members keep records of purchases and interviewers periodically call and check stocks (one method is the so-called 'dustbin check', where special containers are provided for used cans or cartons of the product being measured)
3 *Media*; the television audience measurement required for the industry is provided by a panel of homes with meters showing when the set is switched on and to which channel; diaries record who was watching. The radio audience measurement is based on diary panels
4 *New product launches*; there are well-established techniques for covering the launch period of a new brand with a panel record of purchases and, forecasting from that, the eventual development of penetration and repeat purchasing.

Panels on any scale are expensive to operate. If the panel is continuous, new members have to be continuously recruited to replace those who drop out or have to be dropped because they grow stale or too 'professional'. With diaries or similar records the task is heavier than with a single interview, and panel members may need much more in the way of 'nursing' by frequent calls from interviewers (if not more practical incentives) to make certain they keep at it. And panels generate very large amounts of data, which are seldom analysed in enough detail to get full advantage from the panel's unique capacity to trace changes over time within individuals; better analysis of panel data may be expected to be one of the major benefits of new technology in the next few years.

Experimental design

Hitherto we have been thinking mainly of strategic research, with population descriptions and monitoring of change. But much market research is concerned directly with marketing action, not only planning but evaluating it. Which option to take? What happens if we do that? What has happened as a result of action already taken, and how should it be modified in future?

The key to such questions is *comparison*, and the problem is to control for other possible sources of variation than the one we are trying to measure. Suppose we want to try out, or learn the effect of, a new advertisement. A typical approach would be (assuming the advertisement had not yet appeared on the air) to show the advertisement to a group of people and then ask questions about the brand, their attitudes to it and what the advertisement conveyed to them. The trouble is that from just this one sample it would be difficult to be sure just how far their answers were being determined, not by the new advertisement at all, but by previous experience of the brand, other advertising seen, and other influences triggered off by our questioning. To deal with this difficulty we could take another sample, like the first in all relevant respects (such as social grade, age groups, usage of the brand) and ask them the same questions but *without* showing the advertisement. Comparing the two sets of answers gives one a much better basis for believing that the *differences* between them are due to the advertisement, since that is the only relevant factor we have allowed to vary.

Many research users do not distinguish clearly enough between *survey* and *experiment* in market research, or appreciate the important part that well-designed experiments could play in their decisions.

A survey has description as its main purpose and may range widely in its coverage, but it must be based on a sample which represents the population properly. Experiments may be (and usually are) based on representative samples, but the point is less crucial for them; much more important is the matching of samples to control for extraneous sources of variation. An experiment is set up with a specific objective, usually to establish the relation between two specific variables (for example, seeing advertising and changing one's state of awareness or attitudes) and it achieves that objective by ensuring as far as possible that other sources of the effect are accounted for. The objective of an experiment determines how it is designed and how the results are to be looked at, and as a rule it is not possible to follow more than one such objective at a time.

One of the commonest types of experimental research is *product testing*. When a new version is developed (for example, a new flavour) it needs to be tested out on consumers in natural conditions to establish whether it is a good investment. Alternatively, opportunity of economy may arise by a change in the ingedients, but this must be tested on the consumers to assess whether they notice or object to any difference. There are many approaches to product testing. Members of the sample can compare two or more versions directly, test them one at a time, or the comparison can be made between samples testing one product each. The versions can be tested blind, or in their full dress concept; it may be the package or the label which is to be tested, etc. The correct design should be chosen to obtain, as economically as possible, what is needed for decision: for example, a blind paired comparison would often be appropriate if one was trying to check that a minor alteration in ingredients would remain unnoticed whereas, if two clearly different versions were being tested for overall preference, a good approach would be to take two matched samples and test each version blind on one of the sample against a 'control': since the control is common to both samples, the two sets of differences between test product and control can be compared. Sample sizes should be chosen on the basis of the degree of difference required for decision; for instance, if it is decided that a new ingredient should be adopted *unless* the old one is preferred by a difference of 10 per cent or more, the sample would be set so that a 10 per cent difference would be unlikely to occur in the sample by chance.

In real life, in the market-place, it is usually impossible to set up perfect laboratory-style experiments. Human beings and their environments are so complex that the influences which *could* affect relevant attitudes or behaviour cannot all be controlled. This does not invalidate the experimental approach; it merely means one has to keep one's head. *Advertising evaluation*, for example, is often done by a 'before and after' approach: a survey is done before the new campaign and another done after it has finished (with perhaps others at stages during it) and the differences between them measured. There can often be a problem with timing: the precise point at which the second measurement is taken could affect the result according to how long it is after the end of the campaign. It may therefore be advisable, even if a little more expensive, to run a continuous tracking measurement or, alternatively, to obtain some measure of probable exposure to the advertisement so that one can compare *within* the sample those likely and unlikely to have seen it. There are no general rules; the right tactics have to be worked out according to the case. But common sense and intelligent thought about the research design and the required outcome *before* embarking upon it pay dividends.

Test marketing for new brands, and *area tests* of advertising weights and treatments, are normal management practice for most major consumer goods companies. The reason is that however careful one may be to test the effect of product or promotional variations on a small scale, there are so many influences on consumer behaviour in the market-place which cannot be controlled that the only secure way of predicting what will happen after a major launch decision is to try it out in real life. The basis of all such work is implied experimental comparison, involving an estimate of what sales *would have been* in the test area without the action taken (taking account of all other known special features of the test area which make it different from other areas) and a comparison of that prediction with sales actually achieved.

There are many difficulties with test marketing. Suitable areas for test are difficult to select and isolate in a small country like Britain. Some operators believe that the domination of the retail trade by a few large multiples has now made test marketing in a restricted area much less practical, since they are often unwilling to negotiate the special deals required. Nevertheless, provided the maximum care is taken to understand all the factors which could affect a test, it is usually thought better to subject a plan to the discipline of an area evaluation, depending on the marketing circumstances. Time can be a problem; practitioners of test marketing usually stress the importance of allowing the test market to continue for long enough to allow the product to settle down in a normal sales pattern. With an advertising test, since advertising interacts with many other variables to induce sales, one should beware of generalising too readily that a relationship found in a test would always be reproduced.

Qualitative research

It would be wrong to conclude this brief review of market research methodology without a mention of qualitative research. Qualitative research is a form of research in which small groups of people, not sufficient for *statistical* analysis or for quoting as numbers representing the population, are interviewed in much greater depth and a more free-ranging manner than is possible with a quantitative survey. Typically this is done through group discussions, or by single taped, in-depth interviews; the interviewers or group leaders follow through points raised from a discussion brief, instead of asking fixed-format questions from a questionnaire precoded for instant analysis.

The distribution between qualitative and quantitative is often presented as a rather sterile conflict between opposing research schools. It should not be so. Each method has its benefits, its limitations and its place. Qualitative methods may provide deeper insight into a situation, and are often a necessary preliminary for the selection and correct wording of questions in a quantitative survey which, in turn, is needed to provide sound numerical estimates. The two approaches are thus complementary. Danger can come from ignoring either aspect. Questionnaire design is the most difficult part of research, and a base of qualitative understanding may enable one to avoid stupid mistakes through, for example, not realising the way in which people talk about a subject naturally. On the other hand, reliance on qualitative work only, because it is cheaper, can lead to unwarranted assumptions about what the population believes. This does not mean that qualitative work ignores the need to be representative. Frequently, great care is taken to set quotas, and in major projects as many as thirty or forty groups may be recruited from different strata of society and areas of the country. But the inference that the results represent the population remains an inference, not based on statistical theory.

ANALYSIS, INTERPRETATION AND USE

Even a modest research project may produce very large amounts of data, in the form of cross-tabulations and combinations of variables. The management of this information can pose problems. The development of data handling by computer has made it very easy to produce pages of tabulation; it has not made it easier to draw relevant and useful information from the data in a form which management can appreciate and use. The expensive research report gathering dust on the library shelf is, unfortunately, very often a reality.

The key to the problem is integration. Research will be effective if it is planned as part of a marketing process into which the information produced fits in its proper place. It follows that before going to the expense of collecting information one must have a clear picture of where that information is to fit in the scheme of things, how it is to be used and the actions or consequences which are to follow from different anticipated results. Indiscriminate, undirected information is an expensive luxury. It follows that thought must be given in advance not merely to the content of the information but also to its dissemination: the right people must have it presented to them in a form which they can use.

These considerations should be effective not merely at the analysis and reporting stage of a research project but at the beginning, when it is being planned and designed. This is not to say that there will be no scope for creative ideas once the survey has gone out into the field. It usually happens that the process of analysis itself suggests new ways of looking at the subject which are worth following through. But this does not absolve a researcher from recognising in advance the limitations of any research proposed and designing the project to take advantage of those limitations. If the marketers who commission work are to get full value from their investment, they need themselves to be aware that the research will only answer the questions it is designed to do, and to realise the importance of being clear about their objectives so as to ensure that the design will meet them.

Normally a research project begins with a written brief from a client to one or more agencies. It is sadly true that most briefs from commercial sources are very badly written indeed. It is often impossible for the reader to draw from the brief a clear idea what the research is intended to do or how it will be used: if it is to be descriptive, what measures are relevant; if experimental, what are the criteria for action.

The best results nearly always require that the research designer be taken into his client's confidence. His speciality is to map out the route from A to B, but to do that effectively he must know where B is. Interaction between a researcher and his marketing client can be very fruitful. Research designers do not seek to have everything cut and dried in a brief, but they must obtain somehow a clear, agreed view of the objectives; from this, the design, the choice of methods and the analysis often fall naturally into place. It is relatively easy to choose the best route and means of travel, once one knows where one has to go and how quickly. Research can never be an alternative to clear thinking on the part of the management which commissions it.

The objectives determine the design and the main thrust of the analysis in one go. Analysis in quantitative survey or experimental work is rarely exploratory: it confirms or tests ideas rather than searches for them. Computers have made possible an increasing sophistication in analysis, but it is a mistake on the part of the researcher or his client if this is allowed to get out of control and confuse the reader. It is very tempting to think that, since it is easy to obtain certain tabular breakdowns in the same computer run, we 'might as well have it' because 'it may show something', even if there is no purpose in mind. This temptation has to be resisted firmly. Unnecessary tables adding to thick volumes increase the probability that none of the tables, including the most useful ones, will be read at all.

It is important to pay attention to the way in which results are presented. It is common practice to prepare research reports at least at two levels:

1 A detailed commentary with technical appendices. This gives the specialists a clear account of the basis from which conclusions are drawn
2 A summary of the main findings, with their conclusions and implications. This part of the report is for the benefit of senior management, who need such information as a basis for decisions, but who do not have the time or inclination to absorb all the detail. This summary can be reinforced by visual presentation in person, which gives the opportunity for questions and discussion. The executors of the research should not be too shy to make recommendations where the results justify them.

New technology is making it increasingly possible to access data banks in a flexible way. Random access storage of information on disks and the use of on-line terminals enable a client to buy not merely a set of tabulations on paper but also the right to run off tabulations of his own, piecemeal, at relatively little expense. As these facilities spread, especially with continuous research services, the habits of users will change and they will become accustomed to *interacting* with a data source, asking questions of it to order, and linking data banks together. With the development of on-line data sources, the dusty books on the shelf should become an anachronism.

FURTHER READING

Davies, Anthony H., *The Practice of Marketing Research*, Heinemann, London, 1973

Green, Paul E., and Tull, Donald S., *Research for Marketing Decisions*, Prentice-Hall, Englewood Cliffs, NJ, 1975

Harris, E. Edward, *Marketing Research*, 2nd edition, McGraw-Hill, New York, 1978

Rawnsley, Alan (ed.), *Manual of Industrial Marketing Research*, Wiley, Chichester, 1978

Stacey, N. A. H., and Wilson, A., *Industrial Marketing Research*, Hutchinson, London, 1963

Stapleton, John, *How to Prepare a Marketing Plan*, 3rd edition, Gower, 1982

Wentz, Walter B., *Marketing Research: management and methods*, Harper & Row, New York, 1972

9 Advertising

John Hobson

In a modern industrialised society virtually the whole population has some discretionary spending power, i.e. money to spend on goods which are not necessities, like basic foods, shelter and clothing. It has the capacity to buy improved utilities, extra amenities and modest luxuries. Industry responds by making goods and offering services to suit a wide variety of tastes. No one could want or afford them all. People have to choose.

In order to choose, the consumer needs suggestions and information about what is available, what might suit his personal preferences, what could be new and interesting experiences. Before buying goods or services, he wants to hear about the performance or satisfaction which those goods and services will give him. He may see the products on display in shops or supermarkets; the satisfactions he can be informed about through advertising. If one were to say that the totality of advertising as it appears in print, or on television, or by radio is a kind of supermarket of satisfactions, it would not be an unfair definition of the place of advertising in modern society.

Although advertising owes its existence in this way to the service it gives the consumer, it becomes a vital service also to the producer. To him advertising offers the lowest-cost channel of communication for his messages offering the goods or services he has for sale. As a result of low-cost communication to millions of people with considerable frequency, he can achieve economies of scale which enable him to reduce prices. He can influence demand in such a way as to maintain a steady flow, which in turn enables him to maintain a steady flow of production. He can modify seasonal influences on demand with the same advantage, and can assure himself of the rapid pay-off of investment in new production lines and machinery and in research and development. Although advertising is only one element – the communication element – in the marketing mix, it very often can be the critical factor in a marketing decision because it can control the speed at which vital costs can be reimbursed, and new products or improvements to existing products launched.

As a result, advertising has a vital role to play in the economy of the consumer societies of the West. It is one of the most vital tools of competition and innovation which maintain the dynamics and the initiative of industry. It provides the outlet for the results of sound research and development, without which an industrial nation must go into a decline. Advertising helps to maintain employment and the uses of all resources, at a steady pace, without undue swings in supply or demand. It increases the aspirations of the public so that the desires to work harder and earn more money are increased. It improves the quality of material life for the mass of the public. It may be objected that it puts too much emphasis on material aspiration and well-being, but advertising is only responding to social trends, encouraged by the redistribution of wealth over the last century. Advertising does not govern the shape of society, it only reflects the shape that exists.

Advertising is basically communication. There are many kinds of advertising other than in the marketing context: government propaganda, advertising for churches and charities, financial news, advertising to fill jobs and get jobs, and so on. In the rest of this chapter, the word 'advertising' is used in the context of the commercial functions of advertising.

ADVERTISING AS A MARKETING ACTIVITY

The impression the public has of advertising might be that a vast amount of money and effort is being spent on a lot of bright ideas or momentary inspirations. It is a misunderstanding for which even the less well-informed social observers could be pardoned, but it is curiously prevalent also among many people concerned with industry even in the consumer goods fields.

In fact, good advertising is the result of careful planning and research, which lead in almost every case to each advertisement being given its particular content or form, and its direction to a selected audience of potentially interested consumers. The serious sponsors of advertising have no money to waste; for them it is not an art form, or a display of ego or personal interests. When industry spends nearly £2 000 million a year on consumer goods advertising it not only expects to get, but actually does get, what it regards as a proper return for its outlay.

The basic purpose of advertising, then, is to offer goods and services for sale. Each particular advertising campaign for a particular product at a particular time is part of what one may term a deliberate marketing intention on the part of the sponsors, who base their carefully considered strategy and tactics in the first instance on the properties and utilities, shape, packaging and colour of the product, and calculate the latest trends of public behaviour, recreation or outlook, new factors in retail distribution and effect of competition. The marketing intention takes in the method of transport, trade margins, price merchandising, wholesaling and retailing decisions, the role of the sales force, the after-sales service facilities, and a number of similar considerations. It will comprise a careful identification of the best potential market in terms of people, geography, seasons and spending power; and will duly arrive at the advertising message, and the deployment of budget best calculated to carry it. The choice of advertising is virtually the last element to be decided in the marketing complex, and, although it may represent a very large part of the financial outlay and may in the result determine the success or failure of the whole marketing plan, it is in itself very largely governed by the other elements in the plan. Because the advertisements are the main, and certainly most obvious, outward and visible signs of the plan, many people get the impression that the advertising is the only really important element, that it *is* the plan in its own right.

Next, it is worth remarking that virtually no two marketing plans, or their consequent advertising programmes, have identical intentions. There are, of course, certain broad groups of similar circumstances which call for fairly similar treatments; but with each tactical situation, on which each plan is based, there are differing weights of contributory factors which make every case different from any other. It is not feasible to lay down a kind of blueprint that will fit the needs of a number of marketing or advertising intentions.

ADVERTISING OBJECTIVES AND TECHNIQUES

The two most crucial stages in developing an advertising campaign are (*a*) the strategic decision on objectives and (*b*) the choice of creative treatment. The former is bound up in the total marketing intention; the latter is a matter of advertising techniques.

The considerations leading to decisions of strategy are as wide and various as the field of commerce itself. Nevertheless, it is possible to list five main types of consideration which normally affect the advertising objectives:

1. The range, type and intensity of consumer wants comprising the market for our product, together with estimates of the trends of public outlook or trade development, which may affect those wants in the future
2. The efficacy of the product itself
3. The strength of the sponsor's resources for promoting it
4. The existing disposition of competitor's strength
5. The type of purchasing occasion arising from the character of distribution for this type of product.

One talks of 'the market' for a type of product, but this apparently straightforward concept of the market conceals a wide variety of types and degrees of want varying by age, geography, outlook, habit, price, occasion of usage, availability and so on. By means of a painstaking assembly of facts through market research, retail contacts, and all other methods of fact finding, the size of the potential sale for our product, associated with each degree of necessity can be calculated, thus setting-up a choice of differing objectives for the advertising. It is axiomatic that no product is ever equally perfect for all sectors of the market.

The first consideration in choosing an objective will probably be the special qualities or performance of a product. The addition or adjustment of qualities would be considered in order to create a better advertising proposition. The decision will also be affected by the areas of strength or weakness of the competition. It is no good tackling an objective head-on where strong competition is entrenched.

A vital factor is the resources which our sponsor can put behind his campaign. Only too often, ambitious sponsors with slender resources attempt an objective too big for them.

The strategic advertising decision will also be greatly influenced by the type of purchasing occasion, e.g. an impulse market, a carefully considered purchase, a product limited by distributive conditions to tied outlets, a cut-price supermarket situation etc.

Finally, one must look forward from the market, the competition and the distribution, as they now exist, to possible developments foreseen as a result of trends in public spending, outlook and living patterns, and position of the product in its market accordingly.

An illustration of the strategic advertising decision might be given in the case of the breakfast cereal market. Here are five products which have been deliberately aimed at five sectors of the market. The market leader uses his dominant resources to promote a broad sense of pleasure and wholesomeness, which can apply to everyone. Another brand with a more rugged product and a lower budget concentrates on youngsters through their sporting interests. A third attacks a limited but specific health area. A fourth goes for the children's market with the appeal of a sense of fantasy and fun, while a fifth tackles the same market with the appeal of premium gifts.

It is probable that this strategic decision overrides even the creative decision of importance. The most sparkling and competent creative execution will be wasted if the policy objectives are not correctly chosen. It happens only too often. At the same time, within the right strategic decision there is wide scope for success or failure, brilliance or dullness, competence or incompetence, in the creative execution.

There are three main considerations likely to influence the approach to the creative decision, *(a)* the tactical objective of the particular phase of advertising *(b)* the choice of main and secondary selling arguments, and *(c)* the manner or atmosphere of the presentation of those selling arguments.

TACTICS

There are an infinite variety of tactical situations. To name a few – we may be launching a new product with new utilities which need proclaiming and explaining. A dramatic piece of news like a price reduction or a new model may be announced, or the memory of an estabished brand name may be merely sustained with a fresh rendering of its well-known claim. The virtues and the responsibility of a serious industrial concern may be expounded to an audience of managers, or the objective may be to give a company in the popular consumer goods field a favourable image against which its goods will sell automatically. A race for our brand against a very similar brand of some other firm to gain a larger share of the market may occupy much of our time, or it may be that greater concern is felt for widening the total market for a class of goods because, if the market widens, our brand must automatically gain the lion's share.

There are probably three main elements in the tactical case of advertising – to penetrate, remind and create favourable associations. The relative importance of each element in the plan of the particular campaign will tend to determine which type of media or campaign approach will be used. For example, television and large spaces in the press and magazines are ideal outlets for telling a story in depth, while posters and smaller spaces in the press and short television flashes (little more than moving posters) are good for repetition which, as Dr Kelvin points out in *Advertising and the Human Memory*, not only prevents us forgetting but serves as the means of progressive assimilation of the advertising message.

Then the question of the selling arguments arises. It might seem as if the choice were obvious, determined simply by the properties of the product. This, however, is unlikely to be so in the majority of cases. It will be true at the moment when a product has clear and simply expressed product advantages over its competitors; but this situation will not hold good for long because it will only be a matter of time before the competition is forced to include those same advantages. Look around the whole field of consumer goods and you will find very few markets in which there is not a handful of equally good competitive brands. If one has edged ahead in product quality, the others have caught up. Indeed, this continuous competitive improvement is one of the great merits of the system of which advertising is a part. In this situation advertising has to find some aspect of a brand on which to focus, an aspect on which the competition has not focused. Nor is this limitation of the scope of the product claim to a single aspect a disadvantage; indeed quite the reverse. The consumer finds it far easier to identify, and therefore to remember at time of purchase, a product which has one single claim associated with it. So, however many good points a product may have, it is wise for the purposes of advertising to focus on one only, and allow the other values to emerge in course of use. Naturally, that one point must be an important one capable of influencing a sizeable part of the market.

ADVERTISING AND MARKET RESEARCH

What are the techniques for assessing the best choice of product claim? First, there is the obvious selection of an objective built-in utility superior to that of competition, but this is usually a short-lived advantage. Next, there is the historic flair and inspiration of the salesman for judging what the public wants most in the area of this product, and for concentrating on this aspect of the brand's properties. This competence, whether rational or intuitive, is one of the chief qualities of a great industrialist or a great salesman.

But in the intensive competition of today, and where the stakes are high and the penalties great, the hit-or-miss risks of intuition are not always acceptable. Market research, and especially depth research, are employed more and more to help in defining those areas to which the product's copy claims can best be directed. Market research covers all types of consumer investigation, but is generally associated with research designed to establish a pattern of behaviour. From the patterns of behaviour by people of various descriptions the motives of that behaviour are deduced. Depth research, or motivation study as it is called, consists of interviews directly designed to establish attitudes, motives and feelings about products and their usage, without the risks of deducing them from behaviour patterns.

A lot has been written and spoken about 'hidden persuaders' since Vance Packard's book of that title was written. Certainly, the book overdramatised what is a very natural and sensible process. Let us be clear that in buying, as in many aspects of life, the number of decisions that can be taken on strictly rational grounds is very few; not only because it is seldom possible to assemble all the facts, but also because rational decisions involve a painful and complicated mental process which only a few people are either capable of or willing to undertake. Therefore, the majority of decisions are made out of feelings, habits, instincts and impulses. It is commonsense, therefore, to try to chart those feelings, habits and impulses which surround the purchase of goods being sold.

The purpose of any such research, as indeed of the alternative - flair and intuition - is to establish that aspect of the product's claims which interests a large enough market, which has been neglected by competitors, and with which therefore this particular brand can become associated with major selling effect. Sometimes, of course, the need for being different leads to an exaggerated or partly untenable vision of a claim, even among well-intentioned salesmen. The public's safeguard in this case is that, since the success of any product depends on repeat purchases, not merely on a single purchase, and since nothing makes the public react against a product more than disappointment in an advertised claim, it is bad commercial policy as well as undesirable ethically to fall into the trap of exaggerated or dishonest claims.

DEVELOPING IMAGE AND SUBJECTIVE VALUES

The third main area of consideration in the approach to the creative decision is the associations with which the advertising can endow the product. This is something quite apart from the substance of the claims one makes for the product, yet it is of very real significance in the selling situation. It is the same subjective element which, when applied to corporations, is sometimes called the 'image'. It arises from the fact that when people make a purchase, they do not only buy something having objective values, but they buy satisfaction which includes subjective values also. The most obvious case is a woman buying a hat. She does not only buy a head-covering or a piece of coloured felt, she buys a satisfaction that includes such subjective values as fashionableness, a feeling of style, a sense of daring or renewed youth or whatever. But while this is an obvious case, the same principle applies just as readily to purchases of everyday things. With petrol you buy a sense of power or the feeling of a wise bargain. With beer you may buy a sense of manliness, or a sense of fun or a sense of healthfulness. With chocolate biscuits you may buy a feeling of gaiety, and with a car you certainly do not only buy a means of transport, but also a feel of dashingness, of luxury, of importance, of smartness, or whatever attribute has been added to the machinery by the advertising, the line of the bonnet, or the number of marginal gadgets.

There is plenty of evidence to show that these subjective values represent a very real increase of satisfaction in the purchase and use of the product; and the improved product commands a definite preference, and often a higher price, from the buyer than the same product not so improved. In the advertising aspect of their creation (and it is one of the most potent effects of advertising) the method is usually that of building up certain deliberate associations by the type of verbal or visual treatment, the use of colour and the associated pictures or personalities. It is as if a pattern of subjective associations is integrated with the substance of the product and becomes a real part of it. In an economy where the public could afford to pay for nothing except objective values this situation could hardly arise, but in an affluent society where almost everyone has a spending power in excess of physical needs, scope is widening for following one's whims into the area of subjective satisfactions.

Techniques of advertising presentation are a subject of endless fascination. They embrace all the most intricate aspects of perception, communication and persuasiveness. They cover everything in verbal and visual techniques from journalism to poetry, from realism to impressionism, from the *News of the World* to *Vogue*. One can only hope to touch on a few of the main points.

The first is to recognise the different audiences to whom the advertising must be addressed: top management or the housewife in the Durham back streets; children or the fashion-conscious women of society; bank managers or miners. The tone, the contents and the treatment will vary according to the audience. But certain factors will remain reasonably constant.

The first need for any advertisement is to gain attention. By and large, people do not aim to read advertisements - though in fact the advertisement section of a woman's magazine has a high readership in its own right. However, even here one is wise to start with the assumption that people will not want to read a particular advertisement. In the newspapers advertisements have to capture attention. On television there is much talk of a captive audience, but this can be misleading. The audience may be captive, but its attention is not necessarily so; it may be talking or knitting or reading.

TECHNIQUES OF ADVERTISING

Here is a first axiom for getting attention: that it is the interest of the message that attracts attention - not the size, visual impact or its violence. The eye and mind work so fast that they shrug off instinctively a first impact of size or surprise or violence in an advertisement, before they have even assimilated what it is about, unless subconsciously there is an awakening of genuine interest. Clearly, interest in a product message is not universal; it will always limit itself to some section of the total public. For example, even a little advertisement headed 'Indigestion' will be noticed by the 3 or 4 per cent of people who at that moment are conscious of having a problem of indigestion. One of the reasons why advertising gets a bad name for being excessive or boring is that far more people every year are being exposed to far more messages than can be of interest to them personally. Men particulary become irritated with all the household advertisements which have no interest for them. In newspapers one can select those advertisements on which, because they say something of personal interest, one wants to focus, and ignore the rest. On television it is not so easy to ignore those of no personal interest, and this is why television tends to get a worse name in the context of intrusion that the press does.

Since the attention of an advertisement is gained by the first awakening of interest, it is vital that the attention-getting element should signal the sector of interest the advertisement aims to attract. Otherwise, one may only attract interest that cannot lead to sales. Humour, so beloved of many superficial observers of advertising, is a dangerous weapon for this reason, because (although it can add a certain cheerfulness to the image of the product) it too often attracts the attention of masses of people who are not potential buyers, and it may obscure or even damage the serious appeal to those who are.

The second key factor is the essential need to offer a benefit to those forming the potential market. People neither buy, nor want to think about buying, something that does not promise them a benefit for their money. It may sound a self-evident truth, but it is surprising how often it gets overlooked in the intricate and elaborate process of advertisement creation. Ideally, the benefit should be clearly conveyed in the attention-getting element in the advertisement. Sometimes the sponsors of advertisements, or their creators, are so shy about their whole function of selling they will go to great lengths to avoid seeming to intrude anything so blatant as a selling-point in the advertisement. But really the function of advertising is not to amuse, not to educate; not to decorate the hoardings or enliven the newspapers, but to sell; and only when an assured commitment emerges can it afford to do the other things as well.

The third element worthy of focus as important is that of giving a 'reason why', i.e. the reason why the product can offer such and such a benefit. More is often achieved through an appeal to the emotions than to the mind (because people are lazy about using their minds); but people are both mind and emotion, and their emotions react more easily if they are offered some concession to their logical process as well. It is wiser therefore to say 'X is better because . . . ' than just 'X is better'.

The final element in a good advertisement is a bold display of the brand name. Once again this may seem obvious. After all, the function of an advertisement is to get the public to ask for a product or at least to recall its name in the shops. But there are some people who believe that a prominent display of a brand name will make people pass on from your advertisement because they believe they know what you are going to say about that product. This is a risk which must be taken, and be counteracted by the other elements in your advertisement. There are advertisers who believe that their advertisements are so well-liked and recognised that it is a good idea to leave the name out altogether. This is treating advertising as some kind of parlour game, not the expensive, productive and important process it really is.

THE UNIQUE SELLING PROPOSITION

Ideally the benefit should be one which the product alone can offer: it may be desirable to go back to the product formula and build-in some unique added benefit that its competitors do not comprise. It may only be possible to seek a unique way to express the benefit, or a unique aspect of the benefit to stress.

Most products can offer a whole spectrum of benefits ranging from solid factors such as the price and performance, to elaborate subjective benefits derived from the manner of presenting either the product or the advertising. Somewhere at some point of this spectrum the advertising can be coloured with a unique shade, giving it a separate identity from its competitors. It is vital to end up by leaving in the public's mind a clear identity for your product – a uniqueness in an important selling area; what has been termed by one great American expert, Rosser Reeves, a Unique Selling Proposition.

This positive proposition of a benefit can then be enhanced by any one of a wide range of subjective associations which, providing they are relevant to the purchase of the product, can add to its total attraction. Such associations may be gay or fanciful or fashionable; they may offer a sense of a bargain, youthfulness, or keeping up with the Joneses. These are well-tried examples; there are many others. From these elements the total advertising presentation is built up to do its job of making a potential market interested in trying this product through the promise of a satisfaction which is part objective and part subjective.

THE ADVERTISING CAMPAIGN

A campaign concerns the total effect and sequence of the advertisements for a product. This technique was crystallised by Sir William Crawford, one of the great advertising technicians of the early days, in the three-word precept, 'concentration, domination, repetition'. It is still, and must always be, the clearest reflection of the processes which go to make up mass selling.

Concentration

This is the selection of one shade in the spectrum of possible appeals for the product and the avoidance of diversity of appeal and dispersal of resources. It implies, of course, the careful selection of the appeal best calculated to gain a response from a sector of the market, which in turn is calculated to offer the best sales potential, having regard to the particular attributes of the product, the state of competitive activity and the resources available for promotion. It would be useless to select an area of product appeal which brought head-on collision with a competitor of much greater resources or to comprise a sector of wants to which the available budget was insufficient to do justice. It implies also the virtues of simplicity and single-mindedness in execution.

Domination

Domination is the gathering of the available forces of money and presentation techniques in such a way as to create a dominant impact on the minds of the chosen public. It will comprise an element of size at the initial stages of the campaign so as to gain attention and outweigh competitive claims. It will ensure that in the selected area of consumer needs, the name of the product will come out top of the alternatives in the memory of the potential customers. Given a budget insufficient to cover all areas, classes or segments of the public, domination will necessitate a concentration of effort in terms of geography or choice of media or some other means so that in that area of concentration the product can outweigh all rivals.

Repetition

Repetition is an essential part of the techniques of all advertising. With most consumer goods it is the repeated purchase that makes the selling investment pay off. The product drops only too easily out of mind and memory, and is supplanted by some lively newcomer unless the satisfied customers are reminded. Then it must be remembered that virtually no first impact of advertising reaches everybody; what appears to be repetition is very often merely a continuation of first impact on groups of customers not previously reached with the message. Every week of every year a new group of potential customers grows into the market. The advertising campaign therefore needs to be continued over a period of time, and a disposition of available resources must be made accordingly.

THE STRATEGIC FRAMEWORK OF ADVERTISING

The above are the salient factors which go to the strategic framework of an advertising campaign. There are executive processes which have then to be considered.

First and foremost comes the creative execution. To some people the creative element appears to be the most important, and certainly it is usually the most noticeable. A campaign tends to be judged superficially on its creative impact; in fact, unless the marketing conception is right, the creative impact can increase and intensify the misdirection of the expenditure and effort. Creative execution can only be considered after the strategic conception. It is usually a wise plan to present the strategy as a document for agreement by all concerned before going to the next stage of writing or visualising the actual advertisements.

Clearly, there must be vitality, craftsmanship, humanity and hopefully, a touch of creative inspiration, to turn a campaign plan into warm, sparkling communication. The agreed campaign message can be given vividness and brilliance, but it is wise to remember that vividness and brilliance have their own glamour and can divert the critical instinct from the fact that the basic message may be the wrong one. Both in the creative process and in the initial selection of the creative executive, those concerned must keep their eyes firmly on the ball.

It is of little value to try to define the right ingredients for creative quality. Too many experts would give different answers. Tastes change from year to year. Different media require different treatment. If an advertisement is to be as helpful as possible to the consumer in making a choice, it needs to portray a realistic situation with which that consumer, usually a woman, can identify. In that situation her need is defined, and the usefulness of the product or service in satisfying that need realistically presented. The creative quality will emerge in the vividness, the impression, the humanity, in which the need and its satisfaction are pictured. Television is of course an ideal medium for this kind of treatment, because realism and demonstration are a natural part of it. The essence of creative ability then becomes the capacity to stand in the very shoes of the people you are appealing to, understand their needs, sensitivities and feelings, so that the process of identification comes most cogently to them.

A good deal of advertising creativity concerns itself wrongly with over-emphasis on technique, and the intrusion of the creator's own ego and feelings. A typical case is the use of sex interest or symbols into irrelevant contexts, simply because the creator is interested in these symbols. Many advertisements appealing to women portray sex interests which are clearly male because the creator is a man. A certain amount of advertising also betrays the creator's desire for applause for his own cleverness among his own confrères, rather like the centre forward who has just scored a goal, lifting up his arms and waiting to be embraced by his colleagues. And other advertising betrays a misuse of techniques admired and copied from more relevant contexts, which in a wrong context become just plain silly.

The right creative execution is a vital part of the marketing concept of the campaign because clearly the more effectively and cogently the advertisement can communicate with the maximum number of potential buyers, the quicker the budget cost of the advertising will pay off, to the profit and success of the advertiser.

MEDIA PLANNING

The next step in the executive process will be the choice of media. Indeed, it may need to be considered at an early stage because it may govern both the economics and the creative execution of the whole campaign. The choice of media is a whole subject in its own right. Suffice it to say here that the essence of the choice is to reach the maximum number of the clearly defined target audience, in the right atmosphere for the particular message, at the lowest cost. Since target audiences for a particular product seldom identify themselves, in the consumer goods area, exactly with media readership, the problem very often comes down to choosing the media with the minimum wastage. Again, however, television which may involve maximum wastage may nevertheless be the best choice simply because it offers the best medium for the message. The available media statistics, whether sifted by computer or other techniques can offer extensive guidance to relate coverage of a particular audience to cost, but there still remains an imponderable element of choosing the best media to suit the character of the product or the particular type of message.

The only other aspect of running an advertising campaign that this chapter will cover is the function of the advertising agency in this context. The basic contribution of the agency must be its expertise in particular services – top creative ability, experienced media men for selecting and buying media, good technicians in the printing and blockmaking and other mechanical processes, and competent coordination, at executive level, of all the many details of a campaign. It is possible for an advertiser to buy many of these services from specialists outside the service agency, but, in this country at least, there is no real sign that advertisers prefer to take on the job of coordinating such outside services themselves. The agency package is still the most convenient method.

THE AGENCY RELATIONSHIP

There is, however, one other great value in the agency arrangement. The manufacturer tends to look at his marketing proposition from the boardroom downwards. He relates it to his manufacturing, profits, raw materials, distribution and the like. It is, to many manufacturers, an enormous advantage to have the compensating service of people who look at the same proposition from the market upwards. This is the special competence of the good agency. The manufacturer's personnel, even if they have the ability and training to take a consumer's view may, in certain circumstances, not have the independence to prevail on the board to make essential changes. The agency is an independent body and will be listened to more readily by the board. Finally the manufacturer, being concerned with his own type of business and immersed in it, may not have had the useful experience of outside industries, of successes and failures in other related or unrelated fields, which an agency with many clients can gather together. The manufacturer values someone competent to trade ideas with as a means of measuring his own interests against outside criticism.

ETHICS

Much has been written about the ethics of advertising. Essentially, since advertising is a communication process, the ethics of advertising are the ethics of those who utter the communication. The advertising of bad products or services is bad ethics. Sometimes, also the urgent search for additional sales may lead an advertiser into promoting his product for purposes outside its normal range, for which it is of dubious value. But good marketing, which is offering products which clearly have a true and well calculated market, does not need 'sell at all costs' advertising.

Within the limits of advertising itself there are two aspects of ethics which may be considered. The first is the honesty and truthfulness of the satisfactions offered and the information given. In the UK this requirement is controlled by the combination of the Advertising Standards Authority (operating through the Code of Advertising Practice Committee) in relation to print and other non-broadcast media, and the control committee of the Independent Broadcasting Authority, in relation to television and radio. And the International Chamber of Commerce operates a Code of Advertising Practice that applies throughout the world.

The second is a much more subjective area of advertising, what may be called the helpfulness of the advertisement to the consumer in making his or her choice. Questions of relevance, good taste, sufficient information, and other factors which cannot be controlled by a rule-of-thumb system as easily as truth and honesty can be, are inevitably left to the good sense and sensitivity of those, whether advertisers or agencies, who are practising advertising. At the same time, self-interest works to encourage the advertiser to make his advertisements helpful, because they will improve the long-term goodwill of his business, and the confidence of the public in his advertising. Social sense and business expediency combine, and in the long run the factor of consumer acceptance will be paramount.

FURTHER READING

Jefkins, F., *Advertising Made Simple,* W.H. Allen, London, 1973.

Nicholl, D., *Advertising: its purpose, principles and practice,* Macdonald & Evans, 1973.

White, R., *Advertising: what it is and how to do it,* McGraw-Hill, Maidenhead, 1980.

10 Sales promotion

Christian Petersen

Sales promotion is important. Every day, sales promotion reaches out to the consumer, salesman, and retailer. Promotion techniques are used to market a vast variety of goods and services. In many markets, expenditure on sales promotion equals or exceeds expenditure on advertising.

This importance is recent. Although the techniques involved have been in use for decades, and often for centuries, the spectacular growth of promotion dates only from the mid 1960s. In many markets sales promotion expenditure (discounting inflation) has grown *five times or more* in the last twenty years.

Such dynamism reflects a change in western economies. There has been a change from 'pull' purchasing to 'push' selling. In the 1950s and the 1960s, the growth of consumer spending power, accelerated by easily available credit, meant that people were keen to purchase whatever could be manufactured and retailed.

With the slowing and then flattening of the demand trend, the primary effort has switched to 'push' selling, in order to maintain, as far as possible, the momentum of manufacturing and retailing.

As more inducement is now necessary to get people to purchase, sales promotion techniques have come into full play.

WHAT IS SALES PROMOTION?

Sales promotion covers just about everything you can do to give people a *tangible* incentive to purchase. Everything, that is, on top of the basic sales message.

The variety of promotional techniques is as extensive as our ingenuity can devise, and as disciplined as the laws of different countries allow. New developments and refinements of technique happen every year. And because sales promotion is part of the total marketing mix, and usually co-exists with other forms of marketing, it is often difficult to decide what sales promotion is, and what it is not.

No one has yet produced a wholly satisfactory definition of sales promotion. A definition that attempts to be thorough and precise is usually too limiting for so dynamic a function. Such definitions, if accepted, cut out creative opportunism. Loose definitions hardly help either, since they give no firm idea of promotion, and often could be defining marketing as a whole. Also, the practical dimensions of sales promotion vary from country to country, so definitions adopted from other markets can be misleading and even legally dangerous.

The reader may like to experiment with his own definition of sales promotion. Any valid definition is likely to include the following elements:

1 There must be a *featured offer* (something done as a normal part of trade and not featured in any special way does not count as sales promotion)
2 The offer must be of *tangible* advantage. A message alone is intangible
3 The offer must be designed *to achieve marketing objectives*, which will usually, but not necessarily, mean sales.

These are, of course, rather abstract terms. An easier, though less objective, way of recognising sales promotion is to look for any of these *four key propositions:*

SAVE!
FREE!
WIN!
GIVE!

Just about every known form of sales promotion will include one or more of those propositions.

Save!

People have always loved a bargain. And keen pricing is central to 'push'-selling.

The promotional use of bargains, where featured offers of a price saving are made, can be classified under the following headings:

1 A retailer's price cut
2 A manufacturer's price cut
3 Coupons
4 Rebate schemes
5 Self-liquidating offers

1 A retailer's price cut

The format is usually simple: the retailer cuts the price of a product or service and features the promotional price on store material and perhaps in his advertising.

Many retailers now consistently cut the price of the goods they stock, so that the prices they offer are no longer specially featured bargains of a promotional nature, but an integral, and often *the main*, aspect of their business.

2 A manufacturer's price cut

Again, usually a simple format. The manufacturer cuts the price of his product and features the promotional price on his pack, or on display material, or in advertising.

Most promotions of this kind are straightforward and regular aspects of a brand's existence. Sometimes, however, a price cut can be exploited in spectacular fashion.

For example, the British motorist has become aware that a car costs more to buy in the UK than the identical car bought in most parts of Europe. In March 1982 the Ford Motor Company announced substantial cuts in the UK prices of many of its more expensive models, presenting this as the company's single-handed effort to bring UK prices into line with Europe.

Ford's competitors rushed into print to say that the savings were not all that exceptional, but Ford had scored a major victory in putting its proposition into the front of the consumer's mind, in a believable way.

3 Coupons

A coupon is a promissory note entitling the consumer to a saving on a product or service.

Some coupons are printed on or inserted in a pack, entitling the consumer to money off his or her *next* purchase.

Coupons are a popular method of offering savings, and can be more precisely targeted than price cuts. An audience can be selected by placing a coupon in a newspaper with a particular kind of readership, or an area can be selected by delivering coupons door-to-door there. Increasingly, promoters select a retailer and make a coupon redeemable only in his stores. A development of the technique in the United States is that the manufacturer issues a coupon for, say, 3 cents off his product, and an individual retailer offers to double the value of the coupon if it is redeemed in his stores.

4 Rebate schemes

The rebate scheme offers either cash or a coupon by return if the consumer *mails in* a stated number of proofs of purchase.

An advantage of the rebate technique over coupons is that the promoter receives proof of purchase, whereas ordinary coupons can be wrongly used for other purchases (the two categories of wrong redemption are *malredemption*, where the wrong use is deliberate, and *misredemption*, where the wrong use is accidental. Because coupons are, effectively, currency, malredemption and misredemption are serious dangers).

Rebate schemes are frequently used to retain the loyalty of customers. Effectively, the loyal customer is receiving a volume discount. The proofs of purchase required can be carefully calculated against the regular user's repeat purchase pattern, and the rate can be speeded up (e.g. five packs purchased over the time usually taken to purchase four packs).

A variant of the technique is the *step-sum rebate* where each proof of purchase qualifies for a rebate amount, say 20p per proof of purchase. This variant can be used to attract the occasional purchaser or the non-purchaser sampling for the first time. And, of course, once a customer starts on the scheme, there is an incentive to go on collecting proofs of purchase in order to qualify for more and more money.

5 Self-liquidating offers

The first four 'save' techniques relate to savings on the price of the promoted product. The self-liquidating technique involves the offer of a bargain price on another item, which the consumer usually applies for by mail.

The price the consumer pays for the offer item covers all the costs of making the offer – hence the term 'self-liquidating'. Essentially, the promoter is acting as a direct marketer, buying the item in bulk and cutting out profit margins.

In a class of merchandise where regular retail prices and margins are high, significant success can be achieved with a dramatic bargain offer. But consumers can be suspicious, expecting the offer item to be of inferior quality. Therefore it is usual to seek items which carry well-known brand names and are of that manufacturer's regular quality, or to offer the item on approval.

Of course, as mass retailing spreads to cover most classes of merchandise, and prices and margins fall, it becomes difficult to find known, branded items, which can be liquidated at a price below retail, especially when the increasing costs of postage have to be offset.

There are two ways round that problem. One is to regard the self-liquidating offer as a nil-cost opportunity to develop the character of a brand. A coffee manufacturer, for example, might offer a coffee mug imprinted with the brand name – an item unique to the product. This is a simple and frequent use of the self-liquidating technique.

A more ambitious way of communicating brand values is shown by the case of the Ovaltineys LP. Ovaltine (Ovomaltine in Europe) is a food beverage; its TV campaign recalls the brand's advertising of the 1930s, when it was known to everyone via a Radio Luxembourg show featuring the 'Ovaltineys of the Air': children who sang songs and made jokes. So, in 1980 an LP record was made of the Ovaltineys singing many of their famous songs. This was offered to Ovaltine's customers at a self-liquidating price. But the LP was also put on sale in leading record stores throughout the country (at a price £1 higher than the bargain price available to Ovaltine purchasers), and copies of the record were given to radio disc jockeys for airplay. Also a short television film of the singing Ovaltineys was made and offered to producers of suitable TV shows for inclusion in their programmes.

The overall effect was to create increased awareness of the brand, not only through on-pack promotion but also via free radio and television exposure (the value of this exposure, if it had been purchased at ratecard cost, was around £750 000).

Another creative use of the self-liquidating technique was developed for Marlboro cigarettes: the mail-in element was eliminated. Marlboro retailers were offered cigarette lighters carrying the Marlboro name for resale to their customers at a price of 89p if the customer did not also purchase Marlboro cigarettes, or 69p if he or she did. This simple mechanism produced very big business – Marlboro became the biggest selling brand of cigarette lighter, and the effect on Marlboro cigarette sales was very beneficial too.

Free!

'Free' is a very powerful word. Most people are irresistibly drawn to the prospect of something for nothing.

Of course, for a free offer to be of commercial value, the something will usually be for something. And the power of the promotion will depend on whether the value offered is as good as it appears to be at first sight. It is possible to lose customers by misleading them with the word 'free', and it is also possible to attract the attention of the regulatory authorities.

There are two main types of free offer – the free product and the free item.

1 Free product

Here the promoter gives away some of his product. For example, a *free sample*, distributed door-to-door, or included in a magazine, or handed out in-store, or banded to another product. Or *extra product free*, where, for example, a product usually sold in a 100g size will be sold in, say, a 120g size at the same price. Free product promotions are often an excellent way to get occasional purchasers or trialists to buy your brand. Where the offer is being made on-pack, a devastatingly effective 'sales appearance' is achieved.

2 Free item

Here the promoter gives away an item with his product. It can be fixed on or packed inside the product; or the product can be packed in it – for example, a free storage jar containing coffee.

The free item can be handed out to the customer, and sometimes purchase is not required; the item serves as an advertising device. Such giveaways were legion in the nineteenth century. For example, that great promoter, H J Heinz, drew massive crowds to his stand at the World's Columbian Exposition in Chicago in 1893 by advertising a free badge to all asking for it. The badge showed a pickle with the name Heinz enamelled on it. The crowd was so dense that the floor sagged under their weight. And the pickle badge became the trademark of the Company.

Or the free item can be available by mail. An attractive free item allows the promoter (where permitted by law) to 'charge' a large number of proofs of purchase.

A remarkable free offer was mounted for Chivers Jelly in the UK in the early 1970s. The marketing objective was to persuade consumers to buy the Chivers brand loyally (and to take the opportunity to try out the various flavours). In return for *eighteen* proofs of purchase mailed in, the consumer was offered a free family of goldfish! Five live goldfish were delivered to the consumer's house (in an aerated water-filled container); there was also a self-liquidating offer of a fish tank if the consumer didn't already have one. Considerable planning and management went into the organisation of that promotion, which was a huge success.

The free item offer gave rise to two forms which are almost techniques in their own right. The *free picture card*, inserted in or printed on a pack, was originally developed in the cigarette industry. When cigarettes were sold in paper packets, a piece of card was put in to stiffen the pack. In Canada, in 1879, someone had the idea of printing something on the card and this developed into the 'cigarette card'. Cigarette cards were issued in series, and each series had a theme - famous actors, flowers, warships - to encourage collection (and therefore loyal brand purchasing). Though cards disappeared from cigarettes a long time ago, the picture card is still a widely used free in-pack offer.

The other major development of the free item offer is the *trading stamp promotion.* A retailer issues trading stamps in proportion to the amount you spend in his store; you save the stamps and then redeem them against a wide range of gifts published in a catalogue. The same mechanism applies if you substitute a 'voucher' for a stamp: vouchers related to free gifts in a catalogue have been widely used to motivate retailers and salesmen.

Win!

Promoters did not invent the idea of winning a prize. Gambling and prize contests and games of skill have been part of life in most civilisations. In the UK in 1978, for example, gamblers laid out £7 000 000 000 on stakes (though £6 000 000 000 was returned in the form of prize money). Apart from horse-race betting, we trade fortunes in casinos and bingo halls, on dogs and in amusement machines, doing the football pools, and a host of other activities. Games of skill - crosswords, Monopoly, and now video games - provide hours, even weeks, of amusement.

All this would continue if there were no sales promotion. But sales promotion can harness the appeal of winning to marketing, and can do so very effectively.

The most important quality of a prize promotion is, or should be, *excitement.* This is often ignored. One attraction of a prize promotion is that the value of the prizes, and therefore the main cost of the promotion, is usually fixed. This appeals to promoters who want to mount activity which won't overrun budget. With such pedestrian ambition, these promoters run contests as routine and often poorly executed activities. They attract few entrants, and those few contain a proportion of *professional* contest entrants.

Lose excitement and you have lost the basic value of a prize promotion.

The main types of prize promotion are:

1 *A contest*, in which success depends to a substantial degree upon the exercise of mental or physical skill
2 *A free draw* (also known as a sweepstake), in which success depends on your name being drawn at random
3 *A game*, where you compete but your success does not depend primarily upon skill
4 *A lottery*, where you purchase (or make a contribution of some kind to get) a ticket which entitles you to entry into a prize draw of some kind.

It must be stressed that the laws relating to prize promotions are individual to different countries and are usually vigorously policed. Expert advice is needed when planning a prize promotion.

Some examples of prize promotions

One of the most effective prize promotions ever run in the UK is *free bingo*, tied to the sale of daily newspapers. The promotion format was pioneered by *The Daily Star*, immediately taken up by *The Sun*, and soon copied or adapted by every popular national daily and Sunday newspaper. Taking advantage of highly sophisticated random printing techniques, the promoters deliver cards with assortments of numbers to every home in the UK; you check your numbers against those published in the newspapers and, when you have matched all the numbers on your card, you can claim a large cash prize.

The mechanics of the game are the same as in the traditional game of bingo played in halls and social clubs for generations: the excitement comes from the scale of the exercise and the size of the prizes.

The drawback to the promoters is that since *every* popular newspaper is running its own variant of the scheme, the high expense is not being matched by additional circulation. Only a truce, or fresh creative thinking, can free the promoters from a costly battle.

A quite different kind of excitement was achieved by a British Airways contest. Everyone buying a British Airways ticket to any destination became eligible to enter; the prize was a place on a British Airways' Concorde aircraft making a special flight to the 1982 World Cup venue, Madrid. The beauty of this scheme is that it associates the excitement of the World Cup with British Airways' most exciting product – and the prize is unique. The idea justified British Airways in heavily advertising the scheme.

What is sales promotion and what is not? A remarkable kind of prize contest, demanding extraordinary skill, was the core idea of a book, *Masquerade*; the book contained a series of highly cryptic clues, woven into the storyline; if a reader correctly solved the clues he or she would find a jewel, buried somewhere in England. Finally, after phenomenal world sales of the book, someone did find the jewel. It is very rare indeed for a book to have this kind of built-in *real* dimension.

The use of prize promotions is heavily regulated in many European countries; for example, in France entry to a contest must be open to purchaser and non-purchaser alike. This discipline should make the promoter aim for fresh ideas which create news and interest around his product. One example: a vermouth manufacturer staged an angling contest – an enjoyable day's fishing of the normal kind – but with the added bonus that some of the fish in the river had been specially marked with indelible ink. If you hooked one of the marked fish you won an angling holiday for two in Norway!

Give!

Sales promotion's 'big three' – Save! Free! Win! – have recently been joined by a fourth – Give!

Promotions linked to charitable causes appeared only rarely until the early

1970s. Now charity promotions form a very large and visible part of promotional activity in the United States and in the UK – less so, as yet, in Europe.

The basic charity promotion asks the consumer to collect the promoting brand's proofs of purchase, and then hand them in or mail them to the promoter, who will donate to the chosen charity a specified amount per proof of purchase.

Frequently the charitable aspect is coupled with a free offer, especially where children may be involved. Badges and wallcharts relating to the charity's sphere of action can be very popular.

The Olympic Games gave the first serious impetus to charitable collections – to raise funds to train a country's athletes. Rothman's cigarettes were linked to a major appeal for 1972, and many promoters have since followed the Olympic theme. Association with sporting endeavour, and the achievements of the national team, can be a very effective form of publicity.

The H J Heinz Co has chosen a charitable theme for several of its annual, block-busting, multi-brand promotions. Heinz twice ran an appeal to raise funds to build a new children's home. In 1980 they pursued the charitable theme into a wholly new area – the public were asked to collect labels, against which Heinz would make a donation, to provide the things needed by schools that had registered with the scheme – sports equipment, for example. Since such material had traditionally been financed out of public funds, the promotion raised some eyebrows. And you did have to collect a lot of labels to get anything worthwhile!

The *Sunday Express* commented: 'Three thousand five hundred cans of baked beans for a football? Isn't it a mercy for hundreds of little tummies, not to mention the Clean Air Society, that they hadn't set their sights on a swimming pool?'.

In 1980/81, Golden Wonder, makers of crisps, snacks and nuts, linked with the World Wildlife Fund to celebrate that fund's twentieth anniversary. Against the proofs of purchase received, Golden Wonder financed the cost of six specially equipped Landrovers for use by the WWF in protecting the game parks of East Africa; the scheme was coupled with the offer of a free set of badges showing the various endangered animals helped by the WWF. Thirty million proofs of purchase were sent in to Golden Wonder.

SALES PROMOTION MEDIA

Sales promotion is a combination of content – the various techniques – and *media* – the channels via which the promoter reaches the market. All forms of advertising can be used, and frequently are used, as sales promotion media.

In addition, there are certain media specially associated with sales promotion:

1 The pack
2 Point-of-sale material
3 Field personnel

4 Direct mail
5 The telephone
6 Presentation material

1 The pack

The pack in which a product travels is a fine communication medium. Admittedly, it does not have moving pictures, nor does it talk, but it is umbilically bound to the product; it is there at the point of sale at the time of sale; it goes into the home; often a pack offers space, the advantages of colour printing, and the facility of a proof of purchase. And since the pack is required in any case, the extra cost of having it carry a sales promotion message is minimal.

2 Point-of-sale material

A promotion should not exist in limbo: it should be an integral part of the marketing mix, and in many cases the most significant integration will be between the promotion and the *total effect* created at the point of sale.

The pack is an item of point-of-sale material. So too are window bills, showcards, shelf-strips and many other vehicles for point-of-sale advertising. The trend to mass-retailing through supermarkets and superstores has created many disciplines for, and often against, point-of-sale material of the conventional kind. Such material can be messy, and, in fairness, it has to be admitted that much material was produced with no idea of the real situation in-store. So many retailers have banned display material. The resulting drabness has been fashionable for some time, but is likely to give way to revived point-of-sale advertising if that material is designed with awareness and flair.

3 Field personnel

Field personnel – salespeople, demonstrators, and merchandisers – augment the regular sales teams of their clients. They can be used in many ways – to offer samples, or coupons, to show how a product works, to give information and answer questions, or just to ask people if they'd like to buy the product. And specially hired personnel are often used to sell goods into the trade, reinforcing the regular sales people.

4 Direct mail

Though direct mail can succeed simply through the use of words, most direct mail solicitations include a promotional offer of some kind.

Heavy direct mail promoters, such as magazine publishers, usually offer a price cut to a new subscriber, or a free gift such as an atlas or set of cutlery.

The key to effective direct mail is the quality of the mailing list. Thorough up-dating of the names on a list is vital, especially if the message is to be personally addressed. Changes of status must be meticulously monitored.

Don't send a message 'Dear Mr Smith, You as a captain of industry . . .' to a man who has just been made redundant.

A great amount of thought has gone into the writing and designing of direct mail messages, and into the development and use of successful incentives. Because most direct mail asks the recipient to respond in some way, the responses can be counted and carefully analysed: every ingredient can be thoroughly tested. So direct mail can be an exceptionally accurate promotional medium.

5 The telephone

Few people today write letters as a matter of personal choice. Most people use the telephone. And since many promotional techniques require the public to respond in some way, it is natural to choose the means of response that they normally prefer.

Consumers can be asked to telephone to claim a voucher; or to enter a prize promotion; or to hear further details of an offer. Complications are that the cost of a telephone call varies by distance, and a customer may be loath to call long-distance; a list of local telephone numbers can be presented, but some administration is needed to set that up. And it is difficult to obtain proof of purchase via the telephone.

But the telephone offers considerable scope for immediacy, and creativity in promotion.

6 Presentation material

A manufacturer mounting a promotion will want to tell his salesforce and retailers about it. So printed and audio-visual media are used to communicate the message. Generally speaking, these presentations are accorded low priority by marketing departments and are often poorly executed. This is thoroughly bad business practice: improved presentation must be a major objective for promoters in the 1980s.

SPECIAL TARGETS

Most of this chapter is about consumer promotion. But all the techniques can be used for *industrial promotion*, both to reach new customers (frequently via personal selling, exhibitions, and direct mail), and to maintain business with existing customers. There are many factors specially relevant to industrial promotion which cannot be covered in this chapter. A useful guide to these will be found in *Sales Promotion – Its Place in Marketing Strategy* by Peter Spillard.

Promoting to retailers is an important aspect of manufacturer's marketing, with techniques ranging from special discounts to free gifts to competitions. Such activity is governed by law in many countries, and there can be a fine dividing line between legitimate promotion and bribery.

And, of course, most companies will seek to motivate their own sales teams with incentives ranging from cash bonuses to holiday prizes to free items. If it is true that a salesman loves being sold to, then sales motivation must be particularly effective.

INTERNATIONAL SALES PROMOTION

The opportunity to mount international marketing campaigns will be substantially increased by the development of satellite television. It is therefore possible to conceive of a sales promotion campaign operating simultaneously in many countries.

But different countries have different laws. Even the individual states of the USA have different laws affecting certain kinds of sales promotion.

There has been much talk of a 'harmonisation' of the laws of EEC countries which affect sales promotion. This task, which would make Europe-wide promotion an attractive possibility, has proved to be difficult, if not impossible, to progress. Harmonisation, if it comes at all, is likely to be a long way off in the future.

RESEARCHING AND EVALUATING SALES PROMOTION

Most kinds of sales promotion activity can be easily evaluated; sales performance can be measured, and redemptions and applications can be counted, and compared with track record.

Promotions are rarely researched in advance, largely because the activity is likely to be of short duration, with few strategic implications. There is an important trend, however, towards *strategic sales promotion*, where one technique, or one 'strategy platform' is intended to apply for many years. In this case, researching the technique or platform is as valuable and essential as researching a long-term advertising strategy.

SUMMING UP

A short chapter in a wide-ranging book can touch on only the most important aspects of sales promotion. More comprehensive information is available in the books listed below. And the reader must look carefully at the nature and practice of sales promotion in his or her own market, because the differences are not only interesting, but of crucial practical importance – differences of law, for example.

Moreover, sales promotion is dynamic, and what applies today can have changed dramatically in many respects within a few years.

This very dynamism makes sales promotion a key marketing tool. It is especially relevant to 'push'-selling market conditions, but in tough or prosperous economies modern sales promotion has a major role to play.

FURTHER READING

Petersen, C., *Sales Promotion in Action*, Associated Business Press, London, 1979

Piper, J., (ed.), *Managing Sales Promotion,* Gower, 1980
Spillard, P., *Sales Promotion – Its Place in Marketing Strategy*, Business Books, London, 2nd edition, 1975
Toop, A., *Choosing the Right Sales Promotion,* The Sales Machine, London, revised (paperback) 1978
Toop, A., *'Only £3.95?!' – The Creative Element in Sales Promotion,* The Sales Machine, London, 1978

11 Pricing

Bryan Atkin

Setting and maintaining the right prices for its products is perhaps the most delicate and important of all the problems facing a company. Whatever other things impinge on sales volume and on profitability, the pricing executive can be sure that the consequence of *his* decisions will be reflected in his firm's financial performance. However successful a firm may appear, poor pricing will inevitably result in sacrificed profit either through loss of sales or loss of margin or both. The importance of the pricing decision is, moreover, not diminished by limitations faced by the individual firm in its degree of flexibility in setting prices – even relatively small differences or changes in price can have a dramatic effect on the profitability of a product or service.

It is, however, a reality of business life that there is probably no area of business activity in which practice differs so widely from theory as the area of pricing. The simple – and well attested – truth is that in a great many firms, prices are set in a way which is disorganised, inconsistent and often illogical. The reasons for this are not hard to find. Pricing decisions, even under the best of conditions, are difficult to make and frequently have to be taken against what can often seem overwhelming odds – inadequate information; time pressures; corporate demands; changing and sometimes unpredictable competitive situations; higher than budgeted R and D and other overhead costs; inflationary pressures on labour, material and other production costs. Added to this, those responsible for pricing in the firm are often managing directors, sales or marketing managers or financial managers who face a great many other demands on their time.

The purpose of this chapter is to provide a framework within which the reader can evaluate the opportunities for greater profitability available to his own firm through the development of a more rational pricing policy and implement practical procedures leading to the shaping, introduction and control of this policy.

ECONOMIC THEORY AND THE PRACTICAL BUSINESSMAN

There is a substantial body of economic theory dealing with price and pricing. The practical businessman can, however, expect little direct help from the academic in applying economic theory to the solution of everyday pricing problems. Certainly, theories of price are effective in describing *in general* the way markets behave: demand and to some extent supply volumes do respond to price approximately as predicted by theory and markets do vary in the degree of responsiveness to price changes as provided for by the concept of price elasticity. Technically, price elasticity is measured by dividing the percentage increase or decrease in the volume of demand (or sales) resulting from a change in price by the percentage change in price. 'Elastic' markets are those where the change in demand is more than a proportionate price change. Conversely, 'inelastic' markets are those in which a change in price is greater, proportionately, than the effective change in demand.

The problem is that the theory breaks down when applied in particular cases largely because the assumptions on which theoretical calculations are based turn out to be inappropriate in real life. For one thing firms rarely possess the empirical data required to construct actual demand or revenue curves for their products and are often unable to distinguish costs sufficiently clearly to construct cost curves. Second, the goals which businessmen set themselves and the constraints which surround their achievement are usually far different – and less rational – than the idealised principles and responses of the theoretical firm. Third, markets do not in practice display the assumed characteristics of perfect competition and rational purchasing behaviour on which theory is based.

Nevertheless, since it has long enjoyed a certain popularity, an adaptation of economic theory worth mentioning at this point is the concept of 'breakeven'. The concept, in its simplest form, purports to show the minimum quantity of its product(s) a firm has to sell simply to cover its costs. Figure 11.1 shows the classic breakeven chart in its most widely reproduced form.

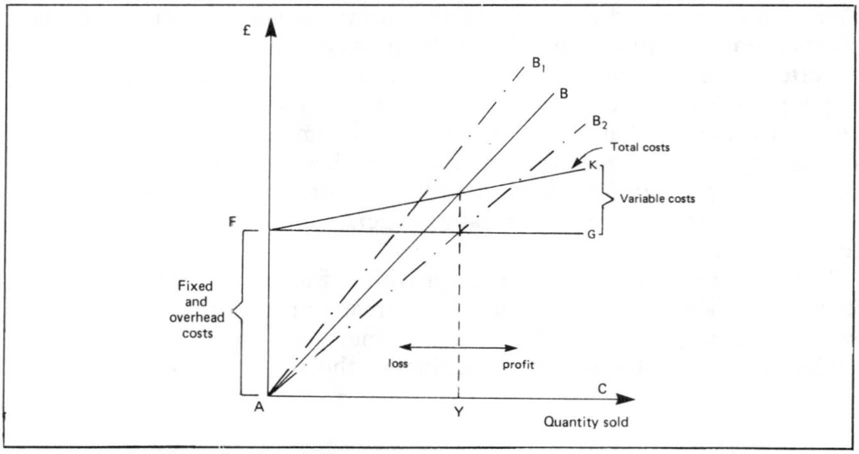

Figure 11.1 Simple breakeven chart

In the chart, the line AB represents gross revenue from unit sales at a specified price, and the line FK denotes the total costs of making those units. These total costs are made up of fixed costs (incurred whether or not the product is made and sold at all) and variable costs (which vary according to the number of units produced). The intersection of lines AB and FK represents breakeven – the point at which gross sales income is exactly equal to the costs involved in producing those units (Y) for sales. At the price set, the firm makes increasing losses with every unit as sales fall short of Y and an increasing profit with every unit in excess of Y. The chart can be developed to show alternative breakeven points at assumed different selling prices (represented by lines AB_1 and AB_2 in Figure 11.1).

The attractiveness of the 'breakeven' idea – which in principle can be applied both to individual products and to the firm as a whole – is obvious in the context of a chart on the managing director's wall dramatising what the firm has to do to stay in business *once selling price has been determined*, by indicating the volume of sales to be achieved to reach breakeven. However, the concept is of little help in actually setting prices because of the crude and unrealistic assumptions which the theory assumes about the level of, and relationship between, price, demand and costs. Thus:

1 The sales income line (AB) takes no account of the price elasticity of demand. The breakeven quantity (Y) is a 'formula' calculation – not a forecast of the actual sales, which would still need to be made to determine the profits likely to be generated at a particular price (or indeed whether breakeven were achievable at all at that price)
2 The assumptions that variable costs increase proportionately with unit output (as represented in line FK) and that fixed costs remain the same irrespective of the level of output are poor representations of business reality.

In Gabor (1977), a more sophisticated variant of the concept is described. This takes account of the relationship between price and quantity in drawing the curve of gross sales returns, but goes on to observe that its practical value is similarly diminished by the lack of information on costs and demand elasticity available to the average firm.

One of the problems in applying the concept of elasticity is that the theory assumes a constant relationship between demand volume and price, when in fact research has shown that consumers (and industrial buyers) respond differently to the *size* of price changes – particularly when these are measured in a competitive (one brand versus another) rather than a global (total market change) context. Depending on the circumstances therefore a market can be both elastic and inelastic in terms of response to the pricing activities of the individual firm – a paradoxical situation requiring sound judgement and market knowledge.

At best the 'breakeven' concept – which is closely associated with cost-based pricing formulae described later – is mostly of value as a simple 'rule of thumb' method for evaluating pricing options in the context of other market-oriented information on (potential) demand and competition.

PRICING POLICY, STRATEGY AND TACTICS

Before looking in more detail at pricing decisions and the way they are arrived at, it is useful to draw a distinction between three terms often used rather interchangeably by businessmen - insofar as they are used at all! These terms are *pricing policy, pricing strategy* and *pricing tactics.*

Pricing policy refers to the framework of rules and constraints within which pricing decisions are taken. The nature and scope of this framework can vary widely from one firm to another, even within the same industry or between firms with apparently similar pricing problems. At one extreme pricing policy can be little more than a rationalisation of rule of thumb judgements or historical practice. At the other end of the scale can be policies devised and spelled out in considerable detail. An example is the policy operated by the Metal Box Company (1978) described by the Price Commission as comprising the following elements:

1 An immediate objective of raising return on capital to 17 per cent
2 Through the discount structure to pass on to large customers the cost savings commensurate with the scale, continuity and stability of their demand
3 For non-standard containers to price these at a level related to the operating costs of the lines while producing these containers
4 To ensure that customers share with the company the benefits arising from productivity improvements and reductions in specification
5 In the case of new business, selling prices are to be set on the basis of (achieving) 70 per cent capacity usage of (production) equipment. (If demand fails to reach target volume, a decision has to be taken whether to increase selling price or to eliminate the product.)
6 To obtain high export prices wherever possible but retain flexibility to use marginal cost techniques for opportunistic business
7 Regular review of standard margins to ensure equity across the range.

Simply having a pricing policy, however formal, does not imply that it is either logical or sensible in the broader arena of the market place. Nor does the existence of a policy guarantee that it will be observed in practice - policies are often more honoured in the breach than the observance. Indeed it is entirely feasible for a firm to trade without a pricing policy at all or for decisions to be justified by reference to a policy which is to all intents and purposes a *post hoc* rationalisation. This is often the case with small companies where pricing, like many other decisions, is in the hands of one forceful personality - a situation in which whim, prejudice and ignorance can easily play a powerful role.

Whereas *pricing policy* is the outcome of largely internalised objective of a financial or other corporate nature, or statements of pricing principles, *pricing strategy* reflects the (longer-term) market-oriented (or externalised) objectives of a firm. In effect *pricing strategy* involves the systematic manipulation or planning of pricing decisions and policies over a period of time in the context of achieving the broader objectives contained in corporate and marketing plans. It implies recognition of the role of price as an active, and important, component of the overall marketing 'mix' rather than a largely intractable obstacle which marketing has to overcome in order to compete successfully. Insofar as pricing policies and strategies are the expression of needs and objectives over different time periods and on different planes it is not unusual for firms to have a pricing *policy* but no pricing *strategy*.

Whereas pricing strategy is concerned with the projection over the long term, without regard to short term fluctuations in market conditions, pricing tactics are concerned with the manipulation of prices themselves, and the way in which prices are presented to achieve optimum response from a targeted customer group against competition. Pricing tactics take as much from interpreting the psychology of the buyer as from more rational 'economic' judgements. Tactics are, by their nature, often short-term. They may be changed several times during the life of the strategy of which they form a part. Such changes are the practical means of responding on a more day-to-day basis to changing market conditions. There are a great many variations of pricing tactics, some of which are described later in this chapter, and in practice they are often mistakenly elevated to the level of pricing strategy.

Oxenfeldt (1960) sees the pricing process involving a series of decisions taken over a period of time, rather than as a single all-embracing solution. The six steps he proposes are:

1 Identification of target markets
2 Choosing an appropriate image
3 Constructing the marketing mix
4 Selecting a pricing policy
5 Determining price strategy (and tactics)
6 Definition of a specific price.

This multi-stage approach has a particular relevance to new product development but can be recycled wholly or in part as a means of reappraising existing products. The approach is particularly interesting in the emphasis it gives to broader issues of market segmentation and planning the marketing mix as the essential framework for pricing decisions.

PRICING POLICIES AND TECHNIQUES

In Wilson (1972), pricing is described as 'an exercise which must be undertaken on two dimensions. First it is necessary to think in terms of establishing the right price and second of using the correct methodology for arriving at it.' In a way this observation neatly encapsulates the practical dilemma facing most firms. At one level the pricing process takes place within a framework which is the product of many influences, inside and outside the firm. These factors, which provide the basis for defining pricing policy, strategy and tactics, include:

Internal	*External*
Corporate objectives and business goals – both generalised and specific	The nature, strength and pricing behaviour of competition (direct and indirect; existing and potential)

Cost structures – direct and indirect	The role and importance of distributors and their attitudes and needs relating to price (including need to create/maintain acceptable margins)
Existing prices (e.g. of other products in the same or other product lines)	
Historical practice and precedent in price setting within the firm	(Pressure from) suppliers of raw materials, components etc. used in the product
Degree of market knowledge (or ignorance) of key executives	The size, structure and perceived price sensitivity of demand
Pressures from feedback of other individuals within the firm, e.g. salesmen	The purchasing procedures and motivations of (potential) customers
Levels of R and D and pace of new product development	Existing and anticipated government policies
	General conditions prevailing in different markets (especially where export markets are concerned).

At the second level pricing should involve a sensible and coherent procedure for actually determining the final price at which the product will sell. That this procedure or methodology needs to be conceived and operated within a broader framework of attitudes and subjective judgements which may not always be logical (and may even be in conflict) is simply a fact of commercial life.

However, pricing policies and strategies do not necessarily define, or even imply, a particular methodology for arriving at the selling price itself. In many cases this is set as much by guesswork, trial and error, historical analogy and simple entrepreneurial judgement as it is by some more formal procedure.

There is no single 'correct' methodology or golden rule for arriving at the right price. For example, the pricing decision process and the degree of flexibility available are heavily conditioned by whether prices are *declared* or *negotiated* (the pricing system). At one extreme the executive responsible for setting catalogue or list prices is in theory at least creating a structure of 'ruling' prices for his products which will remain in force for all or a substantial proportion of sales until a change is notified; at the other extreme the executive involved in contract or tender pricing is faced with a new pricing decision with each new order or customer. The apparent coherence and stability of published prices have to be seen, however, in the context of the discounts, concessions, rebates, differentials and other devices employed by firms to manipulate the prices actually paid by customers. In a substantial number of firms list prices can be said to exist mainly as a basis for discounting with the bulk of turnover being generated from sales at discounted and negotiated prices (see Atkin, 1975). An apparently logical framework of declared prices can, therefore, be rendered meaningless and misleading by the reality of a haphazard system of discounts and/or individual negotiations with strong customers. (See Discounts and discounting later in this chapter).

The 'right' price is not necessarily what theorists would call the 'best selling price' in the sense that it maximises profit for a given product considered by itself. In any meaningful sense what is 'right' can only be assessed in the context of what the firm identifies as its general strategic or operational goals. Because these differ according to the size, product range, historical development, future ambitions, geographical trading pattern, financial resources and management philosophy of individual companies, so the concept of 'right' price will vary.

The precise combination and weighting of factors will depend on the product, the market and other circumstances. The following paragraphs look in more detail at five categories of factor which both shape pricing policy and contribute to the process of actual price setting. To the extent that one of these categories may carry the greatest weight it is possible to talk about pricing which is profit, cost, competition, demand- (customer) or distribution system-oriented.

Profit targets and other corporate objectives

Perhaps the most widely quoted of all business aphorisms is that it is the objective of every firm to maximise its profits. The most cursory examination of this proposition in practice, however, shows it to be one which should not be taken too literally. Firms rarely set out even with the *theoretical* objective of maximising profits (or return on capital employed) and often introduce criteria into pricing strategies and policies the deliberate effect of which is to contain profits at a level below that which otherwise might be achievable.

Few would deny that, in a free market economy, a firm exists to make a profit and, indeed, needs to make a profit to exist. More fundamentally, perhaps, the profits generated by the firm have to be sufficient to satisfy the providers of the capital – shareholders, bankers, etc. – on whom the firm's existence and future ultimately depend. Simply making a profit does not itself guarantee the continued flow of funds required to renew current plant and invest in facilities for producing new products. Equally, given the scarcity and cost of capital, it is nonsense to suggest that a firm would be able, even if it wished, to continue to pour capital into the production of a product until the last drop of profit has been extracted from the market.

Profit is therefore a less meaningful criterion for judging performance in the longer term than return on capital employed or 'return on investment'. Thus the Price Commission commented, with respect to UG Glass Containers Ltd (1978), that 'for (the company's) profit to be adequate it must be sufficient after paying for the cost of capital to fund all expenditure on fixed and working capital necessary to maintain the fabric of the business and to make a contribution towards capital required for expansion'. The Commission went on to state that the company's corporate strategy provided specific targets relating to pre-tax profit and return on investment to be 'achieved and maintained'.

The question of time dimension also needs to be considered. A quick glance at the city pages of any national newspaper shows that profits achieved by even the largest firms fluctuate from year to year for reasons, often connected with the general economic, environmental and trading conditions, over which the firm has no control. Financial objectives can therefore be expressed both as long-term and immediate.

Longer-term financial objectives tend to be set in the context of achieving a targeted average level of return on investment or profit for the whole of the company which is considered to be 'reasonable' taken over a period of years (and across all products). Judgement of what is reasonable is in this context largely a pragmatic affair, owing more to general perceptions within society of what might be considered as 'fair trading profit' or to historical experience or analogy, than to the projection of a mechanistic formula. In the short term, different targets may be set either for return on capital for profit or for margins or contributions (difference between selling price and *direct* costs usually expressed as a percentage) which reflect prevailing economic and market conditions in individual years or even short planning periods.

As indicated earlier, however, financial objectives are not the only determinants of corporate policy and are therefore by no means the only factor underlying pricing decision. Other considerations include:

1 *(Market) growth aspirations.* Targets relating to achievement of an annual percentage rate of growth in revenue and/or volume terms or of an overall target for a period of time (for example, a five-year plan)
2 *Market share* Targets relating to achievement either of some specific share of total industry sales (or consumer uptake) of some or all of the company's products or of some more vaguely defined objective such as 'market leadership'
3 *Corporate stability/expansion.* Development of products and businesses to achieve more broadly conceived goals concerning the longer-term stability and growth of the firm as a whole with implications for balancing investment decisions, R and D expenditure and other aspects. Decisions which appear unattractive from a purely financial standpoint in the short term may have important longer-term implications for the firm's financial health either individually or as part of a framework of such decisions
4 *Corporate image.* Pursuit or rejection of a course of action in the light of judgements – objective and subjective – about the way the company wishes to be seen in the market place. This may be related to protection of an existing image, for example where a manufacturer of a range of products with a reputation for quality rejects the chance of selling a range of popularly priced goods (however profitable potentially) because of the risk of tarnishing a carefully fostered image. Or it may be related to development of a targeted image (e.g. for product reliability, speed of after-sales response, innovative design) which has attendant implications for costs and prices
5 *R and D.* This can be both the lifeblood to and a leech on corporate profit-

ability depending on the extent to which it is controlled and goal-oriented. Where R and D, especially in fast-moving high-technology industries, becomes tied up with the image and reputation of a company it is possible to generate sunk costs which for reasons of competition or strength of demand are difficult to recover through the prices the company is able to command in the market place

6 *Costs and efficiency.* Corporate plans often contain cost reduction and efficiency objectives linked to opportunities that provide for keen competitive pricing and/or greater margins
7 *Customer/public opinion.* Winning and retaining the regard of customers and perhaps of a broader public through performance or specific design, e.g. safety aspects of equipment for which profit may be a secondary consideration, or by being seen to be trading 'responsibly'
8 *Competitive arena.* Implementation of strategies for pre-empting, containing or meeting competition
9 *Capacity.* Gearing of pricing and marketing strategies to achieve acceptable level of use of production capacity.

An example of the way in which various strands of corporate policy combine to affect prices was demonstrated in the Price Commission report on BOC Ltd (1979) which stated:

> The company's central thinking is based on the need to manage a portfolio of businesses. Essentially, this is to invest for market growth and to increase market share on the assumption that scale benefits on costs will be obtained. This gives the investor market dominance based on competitively low cost which in turn provides the power further to secure market position by keen pricing. When the growth slackens off the rate of investment can be reduced to yield a positive cash flow which may be reinvested in another growth market. . .

The role of costs in pricing

It has often been claimed that the pricing of industrial products is based on costs and very little else – a process which Wilson has derided as 'faith, hope and fifty per cent'. The argument runs that the cost accountant and the engineer have dominated the pricing process and that neat formulae based on cost are most easily comprehended by these types of executive whose knowledge of, and exposure to, the market place itself is limited. Research into pricing behaviour has tended to support this view of the pricing process: when asked directly about the pricing of their products firms will indeed claim that they arrive at their prices largely by the application of some formula related to costs.

How rigidly companies stand by such formulae or, indeed, whether they actually have a formula at all, is very much open to doubt. Gabor claims that 'pricing is not in fact carried out by the alleged mechanistic application of cost-based formulae' and goes on to quote Edwards: 'the manufacturer has a "hunch" as to the price at which his article can be sold and makes use of "costing" or "estimating" to justify that price'. In other words a price 'derived from cost' can often be in effect the reverse procedure, with margins and contributions justified *post hoc* by reference to costs when in fact they are subsumed from price. Nevertheless if prices are rarely based exclusively on cost, it is equally rare for costs not in some way to form the starting point either for calculating prices or for evaluating the profit consequences of various prices indicated or set by reference to other factors. Indeed, insofar as goods ultimately have to be sold at a profit for the firm to survive, it is inevitable that costs will enter into the pricing equation in some form.

In order to use costs at all in pricing it is obviously necessary for the firm to have a clear idea of what its costs are and how these should be allocated to individual products. This is all very well for the firm producing only one product since all costs are, by definition, attributable to that product. Where more than one product is concerned, as it is for most firms, cost allocation can be exceedingly complex and the solutions at best arbitrary. The costs of producing and selling a range of products can be classified broadly into three main components:

1 *Variable (including direct) costs* – costs which vary in relation to output, e.g. materials and components, labour, advertising
2 *Fixed costs* – costs which do not vary in relation to output except in the longer term, e.g. buildings, machines, vehicles
3 *Overhead costs* – costs attributable to management.

The problem of allocating management overheads will be obvious but what of variable and fixed costs? *Shared costs* are a common feature with respect, say, to vehicles and buildings but can also occur with respect to materials and labour. Consider, for example, the furniture factory which uses the same labour force, the same machinery and to some extent the same materials to make beds, wardrobes and dining room tables. Add to this a constantly changing balance of production volume between these different product lines – and within each product line between different model ranges – and the problems of allocation assume daunting proportions. The cost accountant might be able to devise an acceptable formula for allocation if each product was always produced in the same proportions but the formula becomes increasingly unworkable and arbitrary where these are constantly changing. Basing a formula on historical experience is equally undesirable as it makes pricing for the future dependent on past and possibly greatly outdated sales levels. The scale of difficulty increases still further where several products are produced by the same process (as in oil refining or dairy processes) and therefore incur, not so much shared costs as *joint costs*, or where a marketable product is a by-product of the production process for another good.

The problems outlined above become highly relevant when costs are used as a means of calculating price. There are two main concepts or procedures for cost-based pricing – *absorption or full cost pricing* and *variable cost or incremental cost pricing*.

Absorption cost pricing, to put it simply, involves the principle of adding a pre-determined mark-up to total unit costs derived from the formula

$$\frac{\text{total of fixed and variable costs attributable to the product}}{\text{total units produced}}$$

By this procedure, sometimes known as 'cost-plus', each product produced by the firm is made, in theory, to cover all of its costs and make a known profit on each unit of sale or order.

Variable cost pricing is based on the principle of relating prices not to total costs but to variable costs only with the mark-up on costs (or the price less variable costs if the price is set by a procedure independent of costs) making a *contribution* to fixed costs and to profit, the scale of which depends on sales objectives being achieved. Gabor distinguishes two variants of variable cost pricing: one is based on average variable costs (for a predicted level of output) and the other, which he calls incremental cost pricing, is based on the incremental or additional cost of producing a particular batch of the product which may be different from the variable costs of total production when considered in unit terms. Incremental cost pricing is a concept particularly appropriate to pricing individual orders, in cases where demand is made up of discrete orders or batches, or in evaluating the relative contribution of alternative possible orders where the price available is fixed by some other means perhaps beyond the firm's direct control.

Absorption cost pricing is a method which has had particular appeal to the firm with a substantial proportion of its total costs in the form of fixed costs and overheads, since it places all products, in theory, on a sound profit footing and eliminates cross-subsidisation and below-cost trading. It is particularly useful in tender or contract pricing as a reference basis for pricing where there are no other useful indicators and in setting some practical limits to prices of new products with no relevant competitors. However, absorption costing has a number of major drawbacks as the basis for pricing. The arguments can be summarised as follows:

1 It is not always easy to isolate the total costs attributable to a particular product where there are several product lines and ranges. Depending on the conventions and assumptions used to apportion costs, the outcome of absorption cost pricing could be sustantially varying price levels for individual products
2 There is, anyway, no compelling reason why any particular segment of the business, individual product, or specific order *should* be made to bear its proportionate or 'fair' share of overheads even where these can be calculated. Looked at in an overall corporate sense, the ability to offer a full product range, stability of production, attraction or retention of a major customer, response to a change in the competitive environment and many other factors may in individual cases and pricing decisions be considered to carry greater weight
3 Absorption costing takes no account of demand. The fact that a price can be computed by this method does not guarantee that consumers will buy the item at that price or at the predicted volumes. Nor are firms willing in reality to implement one of the apparent implications of the method which

is to *raise* prices when demand falls short of expectations or declines from a previous level (since total costs will be spread over a smaller volume of output). The inclination of most firms in this situation would be to *reduce* prices

4 Absorption costing takes no account of competition. No firm can guarantee that its competitors will play by the same rules either by adopting the same method of costing or by allocating its overhead and fixed costs to particular products on the same basis. The firm rigidly applying absorption cost pricing would find its products highly vulnerable to a competitor using direct or incremental cost methods or simply pricing irrationally.

The proponents of incremental cost pricing tend to use arguments which are the obverse of their criticisms of absorption cost pricing emphasising the flexibility of the method as a means of responding to changing demand and competitive conditions. Thus it is pointed out, for example, that since market conditions vary between different industry segments of a given national market and even more, perhaps, between different national markets it is logical to seek (or accept) prices which reflect those conditions. Using a direct or an incremental cost approach enables the firm to operate at different prices in different markets while maintaining overall control over the aggregated contribution derived from sales and provides a means of assigning supply priorities between them in the event of demand outstripping capacity. Similarly the method enables the firm to consider and respond to individual orders in a way appropriate to specific circumstances. Thus, at times of high demand a means is provided of selecting orders or pieces of business which yield the greatest contribution and at times of low demand of indicating how far the firm might reduce its prices before an order ceases to make any contribution at all.

Despite its apparent pragmatism, variable or incremental costing is not without its dangers. In the first place, it has been said with some truth that all costs become variable if the firm is to survive – that is, in the end, the firm depends on making sufficient revenue from its sales to cover all costs incurred whether variable, fixed or overhead. Incremental cost pricing cannot therefore be pursued unchecked. It must be conducted within some framework of required contribution based on profit targets or targets for return on capital invested.

Second, firms using incremental cost pricing to justify accepting an order at reduced contribution may find they have made a rod for their own backs in subsequent dealings with the same customer. However logical the concept of variable pricing might be to the seller, the buyer is given a weapon to use in subsequent negotiations, when general demand conditions have improved and the firm has been able to command higher prices. If the seller gets to the point of refusing an order offered at too low a price there is a danger that the buyer may simply eliminate him from future consideration or allow a competitor to gain entry.

Third, there is always a risk of provoking price retaliation from competitors resulting in reduced margins all round and a steep hill to climb back to acceptable profitability in a market environment which can become accustomed with remarkable rapidity to low prices.

Finally, it must be appreciated that it is not always easy to determine clearly either the variable costs attributable to a particular product or the incremental costs associated with a particular batch or order. Some so-called variable costs are not, in fact, more than marginally variable, at least in the shorter term. Few firms are able or willing, for example, to manipulate the size of their labour forces constantly to reflect changes in the level of orders. Unionisation and a natural desire on the part of firms to keep a trained and effective work force together play an important role here. It is easy for firms to delude themselves therefore as to what the incremental or marginal unit cost of a product actually is. Similarly, taking on an additional order in certain circumstances may have its own 'hidden' incremental costs in the form of overtime working, loss of efficiency in output in machines pushed closer to maximum capacity, extra 'blocks' of production space requiring heating, lighting and maintenance and many other items.

Pricing is not only difficult in practice to base entirely on costs but it renders the firm vulnerable in other respects. In a strictly competitive sense it hardly matters a jot how reasonable a profit mark-up or contribution target a firm sets in relation to its own costs if these costs are higher than those of competitors. Indeed the costs which ultimately matter are those of the lowest-cost producer. Of course, most markets support producers who vary in efficiency, but the greater the disparity in efficiency, the greater is the pressure exerted on the least efficient producers.

More broadly, cost-based pricing formulae often provide little encouragement to company management to consider improving margins by reducing costs as distinct from raising prices. Firms rarely explore as rigorously as they might the various ways in which costs might be cut, from better materials purchasing to tighter control of office costs. This is not, however, the only way costs can be cut and here we return again to the need to be alive to *market* needs and conditions. Research has consistently shown over the years that products and services can quite simply be 'over-engineered' – that is contain features to which the user attaches little economic significance or which are designed to a quality standard which exceeds customer needs. By eliminating these features from the product the firm may well be able to make considerable savings in costs without reducing prices, at least to anything like the same extent.

Competition and pricing

There are few products or services indeed for which there is no effective competition. Even when a firm has no direct competitors – as in the case of an innovative product – it usually has to take into account products capable of acting as alternatives or substitutes in some way, or the prospect of competition developing.

Long-term monopolies are therefore rare outside the realms of state enterprises but it is possible for short-term monopolies to develop on the basis of new products, particularly where high technology is involved. Firms may be able to protect themselves for a time from direct competition by taking out patents, as Xerox Corporation did with plain paper copiers and Polaroid Corporation with instant photography. But in the end competition will come, either through expiry of patents or through a competitor finding a means of entry which does not infringe the patents (as Kodak did with instant photography). The short-term monopolist needs to consider pricing in the context of the breathing space he has to establish himself in the market place before competition develops, rather than in terms of the apparent freedom of action of the true monopolist.

At the most fundamental level, the product competes on the basis of its usefulness or value to the buyer compared with the many other items on which income or resources can be expended.

Price acts as an element in competition therefore at up to three levels: it can help determine whether or not a product is bought at all (or whether the decision to purchase is taken now or at a later date); it can help determine in which of a number of alternative ways a particular need is satisfied; and it can help determine which supplier's product is selected.

It is not surprising then that in most cases prices are set and maintained with some reference to the general level and range of competitive prices. In a more specific sense, however, pricing against competition can become in itself a technique of pricing. This can work in one of two main ways:

1 By establishing the prices being charged by all (or a selected cross-section) of the competitive suppliers active in the market and positioning one's own price to occupy a certain position in the range. This may reflect either 'safety' pricing (pricing in the middle of the range) or 'aggressive' pricing (pricing at either extreme). In the latter case particularly, given that price variations reflect product differentiation, the adoption of competition pricing also tends to imply judgements about demand response and price segmentation in the market (see below)
2 By gearing prices to those charged by a specific competitor on the basis of achieving parity with them or of achieving a designated discount or premium. This approach is often used where one company has achieved a position of such pre-eminence in the market place that both sellers and customers accept its prices as a reference level. An example is the market for open-top containers in relation to which the Price Commission commented that 'where prices are negotiated by individual contract they are set by reference to Metal Box levels'.

In so far as competitors' prices are declared or easily established, competition-orientated pricing is relatively straightforward and has the advantage of placing prices within the known parameters of the market place. The price structure of markets is not, however, always easy to establish. Published price lists often give a highly misleading guide to actual price levels which may be arrived at largely by discounting or special negotiation. Further, buyers are frequently reluctant to indicate even to independent researchers, let alone company salesmen, the terms of a bargain struck with a competitor. There is always a danger therefore that prices may be set on the basis of a competitive price structure which is different in reality from that assumed.

The extent to which firms are willing and able to take a competitively independent line in setting and maintaining prices is partly a reflection of factors such as market share, established reputation, financial strength, distinctiveness of product and relative costs of production, and partly a reflection of competitive psychology. Many writers on pricing have drawn attention to the fact that price competition often tends to be of a muted and controlled nature in which a few (perhaps only one or two) dominant suppliers (price leaders) both set the price levels and pricing systems around which competition is fought, and determine the timing and scale of price changes. Other firms (price followers) are essentially content to respond – raising and lowering prices in line with the price leaders. Markets operating on this basis can become highly conservative and regulated structures in which price competition is to all intents and purposes eliminated. In certain industries, typified by large commodity-type businesses such as cement, animal feeds and tyres, the institutionalisation of competition among a small number of large companies has resulted in prices fixed and maintained at very similar levels with price rises taking place in rounds under the 'leadership' of one company – a situation to all intents analogous to the outlawed 'price ring'.

In theory, price leaders 'undertake' to behave in a responsible manner with respect to price setting and act as 'policemen' for any firm threatening to take a more aggressive and independent pricing line. However, in practice the *status quo* is protected more by mutual compliance than any genuinely effective sanction which the price leaders can bring to bear. As Japanese companies have demonstrated repeatedly in European markets, complacent and conservative competitive environments – which in turn lead to reduced interest in increasing efficiency and cost savings – are highly vulnerable to a bold and determined aggressor.

The attitudes and motivations of the buyer

Price is rarely, if ever, the only factor entering into the purchasing decision and is sometimes only secondary. The success of pricing decisions is therefore highly dependent on the ability of the firm to comprehend and respond to the purchasing environment into which its products are sold. Many ineffective, even disastrous, pricing policies can be traced back to misconceptions about the attitude of buyers to price and the role of price in the purchase decision. These misconceptions are often rooted in a popular industry folklore the credibility of which has been reinforced by constant repetition to a point at which the desire or willingness of firms to go against this conventional wisdom has been almost totally sapped. The philosophy of price cutting as the only effective means of competition which pervades some industries is often due more to uncritical acceptance of this folklore than to a sober analysis of marketing options.

Distinguishing fact from fiction in the market place is therefore the first task of the would-be rational pricing executive. Some of the elements bearing on the role of price in the purchase decision will now be considered. The most important of these is the concept of 'product differentiation'. This relates to the differences in functions, performance, design and other product-related or physical attributes which a manufacturer can introduce to distinguish his products from those of his competitors. The greater the differentiation, it is argued, the more invidious direct price comparisons by the buyer become, thus giving the firm greater flexibility in turn to gear its prices to the value it believes, or can persuade buyers to believe, attaches to the features or benefits it is offering. In many industrial markets this is characterised by the weighting attached by buyers to factors such as 'technical specification' and 'quality'. The range of price competition in such markets reflects the fact that buyers vary in the value they attach to different product features. The principle of segmentation – designing and pricing products to cater to a particular target group of customers within the market as a whole – derives from the concept of differentiation.

Economists usually assume, in theorising on purchasing behaviour, that the buyer, being rational and efficient, will tend to purchase at the lowest price prevailing in the market place, for the product which best fits his needs and requirements. Where there is little or no product differentiation, such as in the case of electrical cable or industrial fasteners, he might be expected to look for the lowest price *per se*. Where there is substantial differentiation, such as in an industrial engine or a conveying system, then the buyer will weigh up all the economic aspects of the alternatives to arrive at the product which offers him the highest cost benefit. As consumer goods companies and advertising agencies have long appreciated, the domestic consumer is neither rational nor efficient but there is a widely held belief that the industrial buyer, being a 'professional', cannot be deceived as easily and will go unerringly to the 'bottom line'. Research into the buying decision has consistently shown this simply not to be true when considered in any detail.

In the first place, economic factors are not the only criteria employed in the purchase decision. Even in the case of non-differentiated products, many other factors can intrude to justify purchases at other than the lowest price available. These include:

1 Delivery (firms are often prepared to pay more for fast delivery or guaranteed delivery or for a delivery particularly convenient to the purchaser)
2 After-sales service/availability of spare parts
3 Previous good experience of the product or other things produced by the same manufacturer
4 Proximity of supplier to the purchaser
5 Security of supply/risk spreading (e.g. by dividing requirements between two or more suppliers)
6 General reputation of supplier/advice and recommendation of own staff and other firms in buyer's industry
7 The volume of other goods purchased from the same supplier
8 Good personal relationship with salesman, technical staff and other aspects of the supplier's organisation.

Second, economic considerations can go far beyond the 'price' of the product. In the case of a capital product such as a commercial vehicle, a forklift truck or a machine tool, the purchase price of the product is only one of several cost-related considerations such as running costs (in terms of fuel and power, cost of spare parts); 'whole life' cost (the estimated total cost of the machine or vehicle over the whole of its expected operational life, reliability in service, running costs and disposal value); facilities for financing the purchase (are credit or deferred payment terms available? Is a leasing or rental facility available as an alternative to purchase?).

Third, industrial buyers are perfectly capable of being irrationally influenced by factors such as a persuasive salesman; clever advertising; cosmetic product features such as design; fashion trends within the industry and simple prejudice. A manufacturer of circular knitting machines for whom the author once carried out a research project found it hard to accept that many customers rejected his technically well-engineered but old-fashioned looking product in favour of a streamlined, push-button import with, by objective standards, an inferior price/performance relationship. Various writers have drawn attention to cases where new products have been unsuccessful initially because they were priced too cheaply, thus creating buyer suspicion, and became successful when the price was brought more into line with what the buyers expected to pay! Differentiation is therefore feasible at a level well short of genuine product differences.

Finally buyers rarely have perfect knowledge of the markets for all the products they have to buy. Thus the buyer for a fabrications firm may have an extensive and systematically compiled knowledge of the suppliers and prices for the steel products which make up a substantial proportion of his firm's costs but has neither time nor the inclination to develop the same knowledge for less significant items he may also be responsible for such as paper clips and toilet rolls.

It has rightly been said that the price the final buyer is prepared to pay for a product is, in the end, the best guide to optimum pricing. Because it is the best guide, however, it is inevitably the most difficult concept to employ as a practical technique in pricing. The attraction of cost-based pricing formulae and using competitors' prices as a yardstick for price setting can be attributed at least in part to the fact that they are simple to understand and employ information which, in theory at least, is readily to hand or easily generated. By contrast it is often exceedingly difficult to establish in a direct way how much customers for a product are prepared to pay for it, or put another way, how many customers would be won at different alternative prices, given the variety of factors which affect the purchase decision of individual buyers. Nevertheless it is within the capacity and resources of most firms to develop sufficient information from their own knowledge and experience of trading in particular market places or by talking to some potential customers, or by some experimentation or by extrapolating the results of market research surveys. Then they can make broad assumptions about the size and structure of demand for a product and responsiveness to price in a competitive context which can be used to narrow the limits within which price should be set and define the strategy and tactics which best fit market conditions.

Distribution structure

Where a product is sold direct from manufacturer to end user, as many industrial products are, the pricing executive has only to consider pricing at a single level. The situation becomes more complex when distributive intermediaries - agents, wholesalers and retailers - are involved, as he then has to consider not just the price at which the product is sold to his immediate customer, say a wholesaler, but also the price at which it ultimately sells to the final consumer after it has passed through one, two or even three sets of hands each of which have added their own mark-up. Wholesalers and retailers tend to price by adding a designated percentage mark-up to the price they buy-in the product in order to cover overhead and sales costs and yield a profit. It is, however, relatively unusual for a single fixed percentage to be applied to all products. Rather the percentage mark-up is manipulated between products according to circumstances or design around some overall average (which may itself reflect long-standing practice or folklore in a particular industry rather than any independent judgement on the part of the distributor).

Since the ending of resale price maintenance the manufacturer is unable to dictate the ultimate selling price of his products (and therefore in effect distributors' margins). Distributors may therefore manipulate margins in a way which favours or disfavours the products of the individual manufacturer and thereby impacts on ultimate sales. Pricing to the *distributor* but with an eye to reselling prices is therefore a special component of the art of pricing.

It should also be recognised that the effect of passing on, say, a reduction (or an increase) in the cost of materials or components is heavily affected by the length of the distribution chain. Not only might the change be much smaller proportionately in respect of the final selling price than it is to the ex-factory price but distributors can choose to pass on the change across a spectrum of options ranging from no price adjustement at all to one in excess of that made by the manufacturer.

AIDS TO PRICING

Models and computer simulations

In the main, however practical or logical the basic technique adopted, pricing decisions tend to involve a great deal of individual judgement by the pricing executive. Because the individual has to apply precise weightings to the many influences bearing in practice or in theory on this decision, the final outcome is at best an approximation of the best selling price and is as good, or as bad, as the quality of judgement applied to it. Various attempts have been made to construct 'models' of a more formal nature designed to help the firm fix the optimum price of its products under actual competitive conditions. These models differ widely in their nature, purpose and origin, but most frequently relate to the pricing of goods for retail sale (particularly fast-moving goods such as baked beans and washing powder) and pricing in a competitive bid or tender situation.

All models work by simulating, in terms of mathematical relationships, the interaction of the variables – company-, competition- and demand-related – which govern the pricing decision. They share therefore inevitable problems in defining and assigning a value to each variable. Their success depends on the quality of research or of the market knowledge or insight the firm is able to feed into the model, and on the manipulation of the variables which normally requires access to a computer. The cost and complexity of model building has tended to make it the preserve of the largest firms only at present, although it is possible with the development of modestly priced small computing systems and more effective pricing research techniques that some elements of modelling may come within the compass of a great many more firms in the future.

Market research

Whether or not a pricing model is being developed, firms still require information on customers and competitors to help them reach sensible pricing decisions. This information is rarely readily available 'off the shelf' and some level of active information gathering is therefore predicated. The most widely employed source of intelligence is the salesman. The reasons for collecting information via the salesman are, naturally, seductive; the salesman is already employed by the firm 'on the road' and he is in constant contact with customers, In theory he ought to be particularly alive both to competitors' prices and to the price sensitivity and purchasing considerations of the buyer. In practice, however, salesmen are a highly unreliable source of pricing intelligence and tactical judgement. Research into the pricing of industrial products has suggested that it is not unusual for salesmen to convince themselves that they have lost orders on the basis of price when in fact other factors were of greater or equal importance in the purchase decision and it seems likely that many buyers use price as an excuse for not placing an order with a particular firm rather than give the real, possibly more contentious, reason.

While it is not suggested that firms should give up monitoring price through feedback from salesmen, it would seem prudent that where key pricing decisions are concerned, such as pricing a new product or a change in pricing strategy, information should be generated where required by means of more systematic market research conducted by a reputable and competent consultancy with experience in asking and interpreting questions about price and setting these in the context of other data on market structure and the purchasing process. Market research can make a valuable contribution to the analysis of pricing situations and the selection of appropriate strategies and tactics, although in view of the difficulties in collecting detailed information on prices actually paid and in measuring likely response to hypothetical price levels, it is not usually a tool for setting actual selling prices.

DEVISING PRICING STRATEGY AND TACTICS

Entry strategies

The concept of pricing strategy as a means of using price as an element in the achievement of specific marketing goals was mentioned earlier. This involves the co-ordination of pricing decisions in the context of their longer-term impact and implications rather than their short-term or tactical benefits and requires the firm to take an extended view of such factors as probable product life; volume and price sensitivity of potential demand; opportunities for segmentation of demand by price and the optimum phasing of segmentation; pace of likely consumer acceptance taking into account competitive, alternative and substitute products; build-up of production capacity and the opportunity for scale economies in unit costs; timescale for recovery of R and D costs.

The most sensitive, and probably the most important, time for strategy formulation is before the launch of a new product – whether or not the product concerned is an innovative or unique one with no direct competitors or is a new brand entrant on an established market place. It is frequently stated that at the stage of market entry the firm has a choice between two basic strategy options known as *skimming* and *penetration.*

Skimming strategies involve the deliberate setting of an initial price which is high in relation to anticipated long-term price levels towards which the price will be progressively lowered as competition and demand conditions change. The benefits of this strategy derive from the high gross margins achieved at the outset against which R and D and other 'sunk' costs and often heavy initial promotional costs can be set and from the flexibility afforded for using subsequent price changes as a means of controlling market expansion (since, setting aside inflation the direction of price changes will be downward) and meeting merging competition by aggressive pricing. Skimming enables the firm to cream off that component of demand prepared to buy the product at its highest price before attacking the broader potential market which may exist for the product at a lower price. In so far as the progressive effective price reductions can be implemented on a 'step-wise' basis, the market may be, in effect, creamed off at different (and progressively larger) levels. The firm employing a skimming entry strategy also gives itself the option of approaching the anticipated longer-term downward adjustment in price by introducing variations of its original product or even a different brand rather than by simple price reduction, thus enabling it to maintain a premium price on its original product. This strategy might be termed progressive segmentation. A further advantage of skimming which should not be overlooked is that it conforms to the well attested dictum that it is easier to correct a pricing mistake in a downward direction than in an upward one.

Penetration strategies are intended to generate the highest possible volume of sales from the outset by keen (low margin) pricing. In practice they can be divided into two categories – demand-oriented and competition-oriented strategies (see Figure 11.2). Demand-oriented penetration strategies are based in the main on a combination of an expected high level of price sensitivity

Skimming	Penetration: demand-oriented	Penetration: competition-oriented
Anticipated short product life (technological changes, fashion) Slow initial consumer acceptance (new applications, new technology) Uncertainty over ultimate scale and elasticity of demand Market segmentation – 'cream' those prepared to pay high price before moving to mass market (perhaps with lower priced variants) Inelastic production costs/capacity constraints Recovery of high R and D costs Generation of funds for mass marketing Competition slow to develop due to patent protection, research lead time, high production entry costs Exploitation of established reputation/differentiation aspects of product	Anticipated long product life Belief in rapid consumer acceptance/high price elasticity Economies of scale in output – threshold sales level before economies can be achieved Expectation of rapid competitive response – establish sound market position/market leadership before competition can develop Exploitation of established reputation/sales, marketing, distribution strengths Create platform for continued sale of related products e.g. labelling machines and labels	Anticipated need to tempt users to try new product rather than continue with existing functional alternatives (gain foothold especially where differentiation not immediately clear to, or valued by, consumers) Pre-emption of competition – exclude prospective competitors by raising entry costs/establishing entrenched position Displacement of entrenched competition by aggressive pricing in directly competitive market (market launch of similar or identical product)

Figure 11.2 Evaluation of entry price strategy

among potential buyers and a need for a high volume of demand to justify plant investment or achieve projected economies of scale in production (i.e. some products have to be produced in volume or not at all). Competitively they have the advantage of potentially creating a strong market position or an image as market leaders before competition emerges (although this will depend on the speed and strength of the competitive response).

One specific variant of demand-orientated penetration strategies is worth mentioning – this might be called the 'razor and razor blades' strategy. Basically it involves pricing a unit of hardware (e.g. razor, labelling gun, copier, abrading machine) at a level which achieves the maximum market penetration or placement so that profits can be achieved on repeated sales of related consumables. If the consumable can be made unique in some way to the hardware, at least initially, a curious combination strategy of penetration for the hardware and what amounts to skimming on the consumable presents itself.

Demand-oriented penetration strategies usually assume a slight under-lying downward trend in prices under the impetus of further economies of scale and competitive pressure. This assumption is not necessarily true of competition-orientated penetration strategies. Penetration pricing in the broadest sense can be regarded as a means of deterring potential competitors by pressuring the margins which can be achieved to offset the costs of entry implicit in product development, investment in production facilities and marketing/promotional efforts. To this extent bold penetration pricing might be employed to pre-empt the (immediate) risk of competition. Even so the strategy may still call for prices to be kept, in relative terms, around the launch level or even drifting lower to keep up the deterrent.

Two situations exist, however, where the strategy may be one of low entry price and an underlying plan for either a sharp or gradual increase in price. First, where a new product is being launched in a market where the competition comprises substitute or alternative products, price has been used as a means of persuading potential users to try the product (about which they may have, for example, technical doubts) on the assumption that when it has proved itself they would be prepared to pay a price equal to, or higher than, the existing alternatives. The second example concerns the use of a low entry price as a means of displacing or forcing out entrenched competition from an established market place or of gaining a substantial market share on the basis of which prices can subsequently be increased to a more profitable level. This highly aggressive strategy is one which has been successfully employed by Japanese companies in European markets for a wide variety of products. An example is marine engines. 'The prime target for the Japanese . . . was the European market and the view in the trade was that their strategy would follow the familiar pattern of gaining a large initial market share at cut prices, forcing the opposition out and then raising prices' (*Marketing*, 1979, Oct., p. 32).

The temptation to use price as an entry wedge becomes increasingly great the more difficult it is for the firm entering a well established existing market to differentiate its product sufficiently clearly from those already available to ensure achievement of a satisfactory foothold on other competitive grounds. It can, however, be a high-risk strategy: if competitors have the resources to fight a rear-guard battle or even to step up the price war or if customers do not respond to the entry price as expected, the firm employing this strategy might find itself blocked, forced even to lower prices with consequent loss of profit margins all round or even faced with a situation in which serious resistance is encountered to the subsequent price rises implied by the strategy.

In general terms the more innovative the product the more the firm is likely to incline towards a skimming rather than a penetration strategy, particularly if R and D costs have been high and production capacity is limited, at least in the short term. However, the right strategy will depend on the firm, the product and the market.

Reviewing strategy after entry

Although pricing strategies are conceived as operating over a period of time, ignoring short-term fluctuations or pressures which may demand a tactical response, this does not mean that the strategy does not need to be kept under regular review. Nor that it is not necessary for strategies to be changed if conditions in the market place become sufficiently different from those that prompted the original plan.

The firm which has adopted a skimming strategy is faced with the need to decide when to implement the price cuts envisaged by the strategy and how large these should be on each occasion. There can be no hard and fast rules to guide these decisions. Depending on the pace at which competition develops – and this may be slowed down by patent protection, high entry costs and other factors – a high initial price might be retained for some considerable time before it needs to be reduced. On the other hand it can be advantageous to make the first cut well ahead of competition as a pre-emptive measure. Equally the timing and size of the cut may be best related to taking advantage of the demand interest opened up by initial entry to boost sales by a substantial cut in price justified by reference to cost savings from increased scale of production and greater efficiency. Similar considerations apply to subsequent cuts.

The firm which has implemented a penetration strategy has less room to manoeuvre in terms of price adjustments in the face of developing competition. The major problem facing pricing executives is maintaining a long-term view of price developments when competitive pressures appear to be forcing the firm into a growing number of reactive or short-term tactical decisions most probably associated with price cuts. In order to maintain its strategic grip the firm must be able to retain a broader view of the development of demand, its sensitivity to price changes and its susceptibility to non-price differentials.

It is probable that for many products, pricing decisions shade from the strategic to the tactical in the longer term whichever entry strategy is adopted as competition develops, as product differentiation becomes increasingly difficult to sustain and as sales approach saturation. Even so it would pay the firm to be alive to the opportunities which exist for using a deliberate change in strategy to revitalise its position in the market place or improve profits. The variations of strategy option are legion but include:

1 Switching from a skimming strategy to a penetration strategy to exploit mass market potential of a product initially pioneered at a high price – perhaps by introducing a simplified and cheaper version rather than by cutting the price of the original product
2 Introduction of replacement or second generation products which can be differentiated sufficiently to command a premium price (return to skimming strategy)
3 'Re-packaging' of products in a way which takes them out of the competitive arena. A good example is the development of 'electronic office' concepts linking more conventional pieces of equipment in a unique total way (return to skimming strategy)
4 Concentration of attention on more profitable market segments even at the cost of volume – diversion of released production resources into other products
5 Improve margins by concentration on cost savings through more efficient production rather than by increasing prices (although the ability of the firm to use this strategy is limited by the long-term tendency of all production methods to ape the most efficient).

Tactical considerations

In theory, strategy precedes tactics in the pricing process, the latter providing the short-term dimension to the implementation of strategy which governs the actual prices charged and the way these are expressed to the customer. In practice it is not always easy to separate the two. Tactics can be considered at two levels. First there are tactical decisions which relate to gearing actual price levels, and the form they take, to what might be termed the 'psychology' of the customer and the nature of the purchasing process. Such tactical considerations, insofar as they hold true over a period of time, in effect form part of strategy.

The semantics of such pricing tactics tend to be those of the consumer market and retail pricing. However, many have a more universal relevance whatever the product or service being sold. Probably the most widespread tactical device is discounting and this is considered in more detail below. However, mention might also be made of such tactics (based on Wilson, 1972) as:

1 Offset – low basic price, 'lost' margin recouped on extras, replacement parts or consumables
2 Diversionary – low basic price on some products (in range or line) developing overall image of low cost
3 Discrete – tailoring of price to bring product within the purchasing competence of a given seniority of buyer (relevant where the location of purchase decision is determined by corporate price ceilings)
4 Price lining – price kept constant but quality of product or extent of service adjusted to reflect changes in costs
5 Financing – alternative options to purchase such as leasing and rental (can be used as a specific means of extracting greater profit by changing the bases

on which 'price' is assessed by the customer); might be coupled with special credit terms, trade-in allowances and special offers.

The above tactics are basically concerned with price. However, these need to be considered alongside what might be termed non-price differentials - ways of competing with command customer loyalty outside the framework of direct price competition, such as delivery services, after-sales support, technical back-up and advice and advertising and promotion effort.

In addition to these 'tactics of strategy' there are tactical questions of a more practical day-to-day level: what is the best way to pass on a price increase forced by rises in costs? Should ways be sought of keeping prices stable by modifying the product? Is it better to make price changes at regular and infrequent intervals (as until recently was mainly the case) or often in line with cost changes (as inflation is increasingly forcing on firms)? Should prices be changed to take into account positions of short-term strengths or weaknesses in the market place? How should the firm react to changes in competitors' pricing - is it necessary to react at all? By how much?

The combination and application of tactics require, if they are to have the desired effect, a detailed knowledge of the customer groups to which they are applied and the way these take purchasing decisions as well as a good appreciation of the likely response from competitors and the tactics which they are using themselves.

DISCOUNTS AND DISCOUNTING

The principle of discounting, whether formal or discretionary, is entrenched in most sectors of manufacturing industry where list prices of some kind or other are employed. The variations in discounting practice in everyday use are numerous. Four main types of discount: quantity discounts, trade discounts, cash discounts and seasonal/load shedding discounts are summarised in Figure 11.3. Other types of discount include those based on geographical factors (e.g. zonal pricing based on delivery distance); delivery method (e.g. discounts for customer collection); trade-in allowances on old equipment; 'free' supply of related consumables (e.g. labels used in price marking equipment). There are various ways also in which discounts are actually effected: they can be based on physical volume or money sales; be a percentage discount or a cash difference from a 'list' price; be shown as a flat sum rebate or a net price; be made 'on-invoice' or 'off invoice'. Finally discount structures can be formal (with details published for customer use) or discretionary (in the form of guidelines within which sales managers can negotiate) or a combination of the two.

Special contract or 'net price' arrangements with key customers are, in effect, an extension of the discounting principle but with the essential difference that the terms of the sales agreement are usually the result of direct negotiation between buyer and seller rather than a development of the existing discount formula. Prices are inevitably keen but how much so will depend in individual cases on the bargaining strength of buyer and seller at the time and can be obscured by the introduction of product modifications, non-standard delivery

	Method of operation	Reasons for use
Quantity or rebates	1 Single order – discount based on physical volume purchased at one particular time	1 Respond to individual purchasing power of customer in a competitive environment
	2 Cumulative – discount based on physical volume purchased over a fixed period of time usually one year)	2 Pass on cost savings involved in servicing larger orders (economies in packaging, transportation, sales, administration)
	3 Guaranteed offtake – version of cumulative discount involving commitment by the buyer to take up either a fixed minimum quantity over the period as a whole or in specified amounts at fixed intervals (e.g. monthly) or both. Sometimes penalties in the form of surcharges are made for exceeding a contract offtake as well as for falling short. In other cases bonuses can be paid for exceeding contract minimum	3 Encourage customers to purchase in larger quantities than they might otherwise do 4 Discourage small orders which are expensive to process or unprofitable 5 Promote repeat purchasing 6 Create stability in demand and foster greater regularity and consistency in supply (benefits in stock-holding, organisation of transportation, operation of product lines, etc.)

Trade discounts	Usually percentage discount from a specified 'list' price, designed to represent the distributors' operating expenses and profit. Alternatively may be be represented as net trade prices available only to recognised 'trade' customers. Where more than one level exists in the distribution chain, discounts may discriminate between levels (e.g. between wholesalers and retailers) Trade discounts may be characterised as a flat rate trade concession (e.g. 25 per cent to trade, list to other buyers) or combined with a quantity discount	1 Aid in controlling or guiding final selling price (subject to legislation) 2 Means of discriminating between different types of distributor, e.g. wholesaler and retailer; general distributor and special distributor who may offer additional or enhanced service 3 Simplicity – easily understood by distributors 4 Economy – reduce need to keep changing catalogues (since discounts, not 'list' prices can be manipulated 5 Protection of distributor against direct buyers
Cash discounts	Deductions offered by the seller if payment of an invoice is made within a specified time period	Encourage immediate or early payment thus saving costs involved in the extension of credit and management of overdue accounts
Seasonal discounts/ load shedding	Differential prices according to season, day of week or time of day, where demand has a cyclical pattern and supply is fixed or intractable – most appropriate in consumer markets	Encourage spreading of demand, diversion of peak loading, boosting of demand at low periods Examples – electricity, coal, hotels, cross channel ferries, public transport, cinemas

Figure 11.3 Types of discount

arrangements and other special conditions. Special terms can come to dominate sales, for example, approximately 80 per cent of the sales of the Metal Box Company (open-top group) in 1977 were covered by special arrangements.

Of course in theory and in practice there are excellent reasons for operating a discount policy, some of which are indicated in Figure 11.3. Carefully operated and controlled, discounting provides firms with a flexible facility for fine-tuning response to (changing) demand and competitive conditions while retaining the overall integrity of catalogue and list price structures. The danger of discounting as general practice is that it can lead to inconsistency and lack of control. Special terms to important customers can individually be defended on the basis of pragmatism and expediency but add up in total to a jungle of prices which inevitably becomes perpetuated in successive deals with the same customers.

Discounts and special details in effect represent the reality of pricing while formal price lists and formulas represent the theory. The greater the flexibility or informality of the discounting procedure, and the more discretion which is granted to individual sales executives in negotiating actual prices, then the more the difficulty the company faces in maintaining a firm grip over the effects of its pricing activities. Anticipating revenues and profit is a basic component of financial budgeting and control. However, the ability to make realistic forecasts and impose meaningful controls is directly related to an appreciation of the way prices are actually arrived at, the extent and 'mix' of sales at discounted prices and the relationship these prices have with formal price structures.

The firm operating discounts should keep asking itself:

1 *Do we need to discount at all?* Tradition and convention often play a major role in the operation of formal discount policies and structures. Yet firms have successfully fought the weight of conventional practice. For example, one major US-owned manufacturer of office furnishing systems has successfully operated a list price only policy for sales of whatever size in a market where discounting is notoriously widespread
2 *What types of discount should we offer?* The types and scales of discount appropriate in individual cases cannot be embodied within a general set of rules. These will depend on the markets concerned, on the cost structures faced by the firm, perceived customer sensitivity to price changes, on the competitive situation and many other factors. What is important is that discounting procedures are subjected to rational evaluation of all the factors involved and kept consistent with changes in cost, sales structure and the market environment. Discount structures have a habit of becoming entrenched so that they remain in force long after they have ceased to be relevant to the firm's business. A manufacturer who has switched from selling through distributors to mainly direct sales does not, for example, need to offer trade discounts pitched at a level which encourages heavy stocking
3 *What proportion of sales will be made at discounted prices?* Company management should be aware of the sensitivity of revenue and profit to the extent and level of discounting. This should include a particular appreciation of

the role of special terms negotiated with large customers and the impact of a wide flexibility or discretion in fixing discount prices.

PRICING AND NEW PRODUCT PLANNING

It can be said that the only time a firm genuinely has complete discretion in pricing is before it has committed itself to developing and marketing a new product at all! Once resources start to be committed to R and D, and even more once production facilities have been invested in, the pricing options available to the firm become progressively narrowed by practical considerations: the costs 'sunk' in bringing the product to market; the fixed costs represented by the scale of plant laid down to produce it; the direct costs of production consequent on choice of production process and scale of production; the constraints imposed by demand and competitive conditions and by the pricing of existing product lines with which the new product might be expected to interact.

New product development has always been a high-risk activity - various studies in the USA have shown failure rates among those actually launched running as high as 60 per cent. Many others are abandoned before they reach the production stage after large sums have been spent on R and D. The risks are moreover tending to become greater as the pace of technological change and competitive pressures force up development costs. The more greedy on resources new product development is, the more careful the firm needs to be that the products selected for development are those standing the best chance of achieving a good rate of return on investment when the product finally goes into production. Many writers on new product planning have emphasised the need for establishing clear frameworks of controls, systems and guidelines for appraising the relative merits of new product ideas so that management time and resources are channelled to those products offering the most attractive investment opportunity.

The process of new product appraisal is one which involves a large number of corporate and marketing considerations. However, anticipation of the price ranges at which the product is likely to sell and the market conditions or assumptions underlying those ranges is something which should normally take place at the earliest stages of product planning and be held under review throughout the development process. In effect it is argued that firms should think far more concretely about gearing new product development to a broad target selling price derived in turn from a realistic valuation of potential demand and the nature of competition than they do at present. This would have several major benefits:

1 It would contain the tendency in R and D to 'over-engineer' products (since the price target will also imply production cost targets which would have to be met if satisfactory profits are to be made)
2 It would prevent the development of products based on unrealistic assumptions about likely sales volumes (which often result from the use of cost plus formulas to project price, at the planning stage)
3 It would provide a framework for 'fine-tuning' the product during the later

stages of development to maximise competitive success within the selected price range.

Admittedly this approach is not easy to apply to the product which is itself a dramatic technological breakthrough or creative innovation for which existing price indications in the market place are inadequate and hypothetical testing of consumer responses at best unreliable. However, the great majority of new products do not fall into this category but relate in some reasonably direct way to established applications and existing products against which price targets can reasonably be set.

PRICING AND PRODUCT LINES

A great many pricing decisions take place in the context of product lines or ranges rather than as entirely independent exercises. Product lines or ranges comprise individual products linked together in some identifiable way - by a common function, by a common design or structure, by a common production process, by a common user group or application area. An office equipment manufacturer may, for example, offer a range of copiers of different print speeds or output capacities; within each model type a choice of features, e.g. automatic or manual operation; ranges of other office products, e.g. typewriters, word processors and facsimile transceivers.

The basis for product-line policies and the justification for offering different models, lines and ranges is a subject in itself. It is sufficient to note here that the existence of product lines raises particularly complex issues of pricing because of the way demand for each individual product interacts. Product lines as a whole may be mutually supportive but individual products within the line can easily be competitive with each other, particularly if encouraged by lack of care in pricing. Simply applying a common mark-up to each individual product is clearly unsatisfactory since it is probable that each product will vary in its production and marketing cost profile and in the opportunities and constraints implied by demand and the competitor environment it is selling into. This argues for a pricing policy which provides for each product in a line to be individually priced according to costs and market conditions subject to certain broad principles of consistency to minimise the risk of anomalies leading to the firm competing with itself.

Even so the firm faces sensitive issues each time a product line is extended, supplemented or modified by introduction of revised models or when a new product line is introduced. An example of the dangers faced, in the author's own experience, is provided by a building board company which tried to launch a new and superior grade of board at a premium price in a market which turned out to place much less value on the higher quality offered by the new product than the company expected. The result was that as the price of the new product was forced down to a level close to that of the firm's existing range of building board, buyers of the original range simply switched allegiance to the new product forcing the price of the original range still lower in order to maintain sales. What started off as an exercise in market segmentation turned out to cause disastrous loss of profit all round.

SUMMARY

This chapter has sought to demonstrate why pricing is perhaps the most complex and demanding – and least clearly understood – of all tasks facing company management. Some conclusions are now drawn which might help the financial executive, in particular, contribute more effectively to pricing policy formulation and price setting.

1 *Pricing is much more of an art than a science.* There is no universal formula or golden rule for arriving at the right price. Those responsible for price setting have to balance and allow for a variety of factors and influences both internal to and external to the firm itself which, far from the ordered and rational world of the theoretical economist, may not always be logical and may even be in conflict. Nevertheless, profitability can significantly be enhanced by injecting greater coherence into the rules and principles, whatever these may be, which govern the way prices are fixed and maintained. The financial executive has an important part to play in the preparation and implementation of pricing policy

2 *Successful pricing decisions cannot be based on costs alone.* Prices are far less often arrived at by the mechanistic application of cost-based formulae than is widely believed. Even so, costs and cost-related profit targets remain a major obsession of many firms in pricing, particularly in the case of industrial products. Financial executives have tended on the whole to encourage and reinforce this essentially inward-looking approach. The success of pricing decisions is, however, highly dependent on the ability of the firm to comprehend and respond to *market* needs and conditions. The contribution of the financial executive to pricing decisions would be substantially enhanced by greater recognition of the role of such factors as competition, buyer attitudes and motivations and the impact of distributive systems in optimum pricing

3 *Price is a much neglected and potentially powerful element in the marketing mix.* Price is widely treated more as a handicap which has to be borne rather than as a positive tool for achieving designated marketing goals. This chapter has looked at the ways pricing can contribute to overall marketing plans both in the longer term (pricing strategy) and in the short term (pricing tactics). The financial executive should be prepared to be sufficiently flexible in his own advice and policies not to inhibit sales and marketing personnel from manipulation of price as a marketing weapon

4 *Pricing considerations are a key element in product planning.* Anticipation of price ranges and market conditions are an essential precondition to effective investment and product planning. The financial executive should seek to ensure that pricing factors are introduced at the beginning and not at the end of the planning cycle for new products.

REFERENCES AND FURTHER READING

Atkin, B. and Skinner, R., *How British Industry Prices*, IMR, 1975.
Price Commission, *Compressed Permanent Gases and Dissolved Acetylene Sold in Cylinders, Cylinder Rentals and Fixed Charges* (BOC Ltd), HC 223, 1979.
Gabor, A., *Pricing, Principles and Practices*, Heinemann, London, 1977.
Price Commission, *Open Top Food and Beverage Cans and Aerosol Cans* (Metal Box Ltd), HC 135, 1978.
Oxenfeldt, A. R., 'Multi-Stage Approach to Pricing', *Harvard Business Review*, July/August 1960.
Price Commission, *Report for the period 1st February to 30th April 1980.*
Price Commission, *Prices of Glass Containers* (UG Glass Containers Ltd) HC 170, 1978.
Wilson, A., *The Marketing of Professional Services*, McGraw-Hill, 1972.

12 Distribution channels

Jack Wheatley

The process of distribution is not merely concerned with physically getting goods from a manufacturer to his eventual customer. Distribution strategy covers the following basic activities: the choice of available channels, whether or not to confine distribution to one channel or several; whether to go direct to the customer or deal through intermediaries; how much expenditure to allocate for distribution and whether to take a complete or partial financial interest in the available channels.

What might seem the best or only channels available at the start of a marketing campaign may prove to be inadequate or too restrictive for subsequent development of sales, so a manufacturer who opts to distribute entirely through wholesalers may regret his lack of contact with retail outlets when he needs extra sales or when he realises that his wholesaler is also promoting a competitor's output, perhaps to the exclusion of his products.

The choice of distribution channels is therefore one requiring careful thought and a full consideration of the available alternatives.

PLANNING FOR DISTRIBUTION

In arriving at a final decision on which channel or combination of channels should be used many points have to be taken into account. The choice depends not only on costs in relation to funds available, but also on the location of the consumer, the places where he is most likely to see the product and the extent to which it is desirable and/or necessary to maintain direct contact with the consumer. It also depends on the bulkiness of the product, anticipated average order value, credit risks involved in the alternative methods available and the risks entailed in placing all distributions in the hands of an outside and independent agent or wholesaler.

With a new product, and particularly if the market is a new one to the manufacturer, it still takes great courage to try and by-pass traditional channels. The patterns of distribution and demand are now changing, however, as the ranges of choice open to consumers widen.

Not so long ago, nobody would have considered garages as an outlet for confectionery and soft drinks, newsagents for pop records, chemists for wines and spirits or food supermarkets for clothing and furniture, but all these changes have taken place to the advantage of the retailing outlets and the manufacturers.

Distribution itself cannot be considered in isolation from other aspects of the marketing plan because it is usually up to the manufacturer to promote his products to the eventual consumer and to stimulate demand that will materialise into a decision to buy at the chosen point of distribution.

New methods of large-scale distribution such as hypermarkets and cash and carries are attractive in that they facilitate bulk distribution to a limited number of outlets but, in opting for this method as a sole means of distribution, the manufacturer is vulnerable in the sense that changes in the buying policies of one or two of the outlets can have a significantly adverse impact on his sales volume. The ultimate decision on which distributive channels to use must depend on the costs involved and the estimated net profit contribution available within the various alternatives.

What might seem the best short-term solutions are not necessarily in the long-term interests of the manufacturer and therefore extreme care must be taken before placing all distribution in the hands of an outside body be it a wholesaler, agent or merchant.

The ideal is to have full control over all aspects of distribution, but this may well involve the manufacturer in direct selling costs that the product could not carry in the light of the anticipated sales forecast.

THE WHOLESALER

Traditionally the wholesaler has been one of the oldest links in the distribution chain but, while still popular, this method is losing some of its appeal with manufacturers beginning to develop their own images to their consumers. Even so, the wholesaler still offers the cheapest form of distribution as he takes responsibility for storing in bulk and delivering in small quantities to the consumer. This relieves the manufacturer of the major part of delivery costs for he is only concerned with making the more economical bulk deliveries to the wholesaler's warehouses. The wholesaler takes all the small credit risks and absorbs direct selling costs, but very rarely will he avoid selling a competitive product.

Because of the nature of their business, wholesalers carry wide brand ranges and their salesmen become initially 'order takers' with no specific selling emphasis on any particular brand. They tend, therefore, to reflect consumer demand rather than create it.

Although wholesalers can handle all distribution it is advisable for a manufacturer to employ at least a small sales force calling on ultimate outlets to persuade them to place orders for his products from the designated local wholesaler. Orders can be taken and passed to the wholesaler as a gesture of good faith but also as a positive encouragement to stock the manufacturer's product.

Some companies have set up their own wholesaling operations. The speedy, prompt, delivery (SPD) organisation set up by Unilever is an example, and in this case the wholesaling/distribution company stores and distributes for other organisations on a proper commercial basis. In the main, it is better to regard wholesaling as a specialist function and to set up an in-company operation only if it can be done properly and expertly. Few organisations have the required range to do that.

A combination of direct distribution and wholesaling is preferable as the sales contacts that the wholesalers have built up over the years are very useful, but if wholesaling is used it is important to remember that the eventual consumer will need to be exposed to product promotion from the manufacturer. The wholesaler cannot be expected to create the demand, for he has too many competing interests.

To avoid conflict with a wholesaler's selling policy a manufacturer can give a different brand name to his product sold through the wholesaler. This technique is used successfully with such products as stationery, clothing and certain foodstuffs.

THE RETAIL TRADES

The structure of the retail trades has altered considerably since Napoleon referred to Britain as 'a nation of shopkeepers'. Many smaller shops have been forced out of business but many that have changed their style of management to compete with the larger, and often impersonal multiples and supermarkets, have survived. Often location has proved to be the prime factor.

Independent retailers

Independent retailers provide an efficient local service at higher prices than the larger chains and multiples and they often provide extended credit and/or free delivery for their customers. As outlets, they tend to sell the products for which there is an established demand, but are often very responsive to good sales promotion of new products and can be more easily persuaded to try new lines than wholesalers.

Voluntary groups

To combat the threat posed by multiple chains and supermarkets, independent retailers have banded together into voluntary groups which started as central buying groups but have now developed into highly efficient retail outlets following common policies extending to product ranges, stock control, accounting, store layout and store promotions. Examples are VG and Mace. Other groups have been formed by large wholesalers to guarantee outlets for the lines they sell and this, in turn, has led wholesalers to develop their own label brands for distribution via the retailers in their group.

Multiple stores

The advantage of using this channel of distribution is that the buying points can be covered by a very small sales force as most items are bought centrally from head office. Store managers work to central promotional and stocking policies and, provided a manufacturer can persuade the central buyer to stock his product, he is assured that the necessary efforts will be made at store level. Because of the need to achieve fast turnover on what are often narrow margins, multiple stores will not persist with slow moving lines and so the manufacturer needs to back up the stores with adequate promotion to consumers. Multiples have developed from being the outlets set up by food manufacturers who wished to extend vertically into retailing, but some have taken the opposite path backwards into manufacturing; this is what has stimulated the growth of 'own label' brands.

Alternatively, some multiples have arranged own label production by outside manufacturers. This is useful to the independent producer as a channel of distribution but he has to be assured of long-term contracts if he uses this channel as a sole outlet for distribution.

Retail chains

Again, store managers follow centrally laid-down policies but there is usually more flexibility allowed according to local conditions. Stores often trade under different names, but the manufacturer is usually offered multiple outlet distribution and, consequently, a wider coverage.

Local chain store managers are usually very responsive to store promotions backed up by press and television advertising. The combination of a television spot naming a particular retail chain as a stockist of a product and a display of that product with a card saying, 'As seen on television' is very successful.

Department stores

Department stores carry a wide variety of merchandise under one roof with specific departments under their own separate buying and selling management. Each department is organised to sell particular product ranges.

The standard of personal service is often very high. Some of the larger stores have almost become institutions to the criterion of good service and are respected as such all over the world. Buyers are usually very skilled professionals who anticipate fashion trends and buy accordingly. Manufacturers using this channel can obtain extremely useful market research information by maintaining contact with store buyers. This channel is also used by companies setting up their own boutiques or 'shops within shops', a method particularly suitable for such products as jewellery, cosmetics and clothing. Exporters would find this a useful means of getting established in a new overseas market. Travel agencies are another example.

Co-operative societies

These are becoming combinations of multiples, department stores and supermarkets with the apparent aim of selling their own manufactured products. This is the complete evolutionary cycle, for the first co-operative societies in the middle of the last century were manufacturers setting up as manufacturers and retailers.

Private brands, however, still account for a significant proportion of total turnover and the use of this channel offers the possibilities of large-scale distribution from a limited number of outlets.

Supermarkets

These are a natural development of multiples and self-service outlets and now account for a significant proportion of total retail trade. Product ranges have extended from food into a wide variety of non-food items operating under very tight control and measuring efficiency in terms of profit per square foot of floor space instead of as a percentage of sales.

Because of their vast buying power, supermarkets are able to extract hard bargains from manufacturers and lay down very strict conditions of delivery times, quantities, packaging, etc. Manufacturers are offered economic distribution in that delivery points are far fewer than for indepedent retailers; buying, however, is in the hands of an equally small number of head offices. A manufacturer who opts for supermarkets as his only outlets is subject to sudden changes of buying policy.

Supermarkets are becoming increasingly concerned with multiple product ranges to such an extent that specialist supermarkets dealing solely in product ranges, such as carpets, radio and television, are appearing to attract the customers who are becoming somewhat disenchanted with the lack of choice in the non-food departments of supermarkets.

Hypermarkets

Regarded as the ultimate in retailing, this type of outlet is now well established in the UK. The principle is to provide 'one-stop shopping' for a wide variety of products in an out-of-town location where space is available at lower rents than in town centres. These outlets are very attractive to manufacturers as access and egress is usually easier because of geographical location.

Cash and carry

These outlets have been developed by wholesalers and voluntary groups whereby retailers select the goods they are going to sell from the wide range displayed and collect, pay and transport them back to the shops. This method tends to be used by the smaller retailers, for example, restaurants, canteens and newsagents. The cash and carry outlets usually maintain regular promotional mailing to their retail customers and run special offer campaigns, but otherwise provide a minimum of service.

As a channel of distribution the manufacturer can make good use of cash and carry outlets to deal with the problems of small deliveries provided he can create a demand by promotion to the eventual outlet and consumer. However, as cash and carries are retailers' supermarkets, good packaging and presentation can be very helpful in persuading retailers to pick products off the shelves and to try selling them in their own stores.

Discount stores

A comparatively recent innovation to the retail scene is the discount store which provides cut-price products with the minimum customer service. This channel is particularly useful for sales of consumer durables and toiletries. Chemists' lines are being increasingly distributed in this manner. Discount trading became increasingly evident following the banning of resale price maintenance.

Mobile retailers

To strengthen the personal service there has been a growth in the number of retailers taking their products direct to the housewife. Grocers, greengrocers, bakers and butchers are using this method and yet dairies who, by tradition have made deliveries of milk direct to the consumer, are trying to cut down on the number of deliveries to reduce costs. Prices charged do not reflect the service provided. Dairies are adding soft drinks and confectionary to the range carried by their milk floats in order to increase sales per journey.

Ready-cooked foods like fish and chips, hamburgers, meat pies and chickens are now sold from mobiles as well as the normal tea, coffee and light refreshments.

Van selling

Van selling is used by manufacturers of perishable foods, particularly bread and meat products, and allows complete control of the distribution operation. Cost per order can be high, particularly in large items where so much time can be lost in finding a suitable parking place or waiting in traffic jams, but total distribution costs can be lower than would be incurred with a separate delivery fleet and a sales force.

Door-to-door selling

This is a very expensive method of distribution. Apart from a few highly successful exceptions, door-to-door selling is not widely practised. Government legislation was formulated to prevent the worst excesses of this type of selling whereby housewives were persuaded by unscrupulous salesmen to buy products that would not work or that they did not need or could not afford. It is often used in combination with a national or local advertising campaign. The regular wider promotion gives an air of respectability to the sales staff who follow up and call from door to door.

Considerable success has been achieved by companies selling cosmetics, but to be effective the use of this channel for such products requires a very large sales force as the average unit of sale is very low in value. Double glazing, central heating and encyclopedias are more applicable to this type of distribution as the average unit of sale tends to be much higher than with the smaller products.

Garages

Apart from selling petrol and oil, garages are now retailing wide ranges of motor accessories and food lines. The appeal is largely geared to impulse buying because consumers do not normally go to garages just to buy ancillary items. As channels of distribution, however, garages are becoming increasingly important.

THE COMMODITY MARKET

Perishables are usually distributed through the commodity markets in the UK, but many of them have become so heavily congested that producers are tending to fix up long-term contracts with outlets and deliver direct. Such contracts can be beneficial to the producer in so far as his selling prices are stabilised, but they have to be fixed in the light of a very accurate assessment of future supply and demand which the commodity markets reflect on a daily basis. Other commodities such as rubber, copper, tin, tea and gold are still bought and sold through the traditional markets in London.

Franchising

This is a method of distribution used mainly to further the sales of an idea or a process rather than a product itself. Successful exploitation of this method has been achieved with a wide variety of products including fried chickens, hamburgers, instant printing, drain cleaning, tyre and exhaust fitting, ice-cream, steaks and Chinese food. Financial assistance is provided to the franchisee to set up his business, with the manufacturer taking a share of the resulting profits and providing training in business management. Common standards and common forms of presentation are very important and are enshrined in agreements between the franchisor and franchisee.

Party plan selling

Under this method a manufacturer appoints agents – usually women – who hold sponsored parties in their homes and invite their friends to see the products. Orders are taken and more agents are recruited and so the operation develops. This channel is useful for selling kitchen and other domestic ware, clothing, jewellery and cosmetics but is difficult to use in conjunction with distribution through traditional retail outlets for these do not take kindly to this type of sponsored competition from their suppliers.

Mail order

This has become a popular channel for a very wide range of products and services. Large department stores and mail order houses are investing large sums in postage, printing and distribution of catalogues direct to the public. At the other end of the scale, rare books, classical records and even collections of specially minted coins and medals are promoted and distributed via direct mail to a specialist public. The big attraction of this method is the direct promotion to the consumer to the complete exclusion of any intermediaries. But perhaps the most spectacular growth in recent years has been direct selling through couponed advertisements in newspapers and magazines – through the Sunday supplements in particular. The method has also spread to television.

Direct selling costs are negligible, but advertising costs are extremely high; however, companies successful in this field continue to use this channel and are clearly satisfied with the returns obtained. Some distributors have extended their operation by setting up their own stores selling nothing but the products advertised by their direct mailing, thus relieving them of small distribution costs. This combination of previously separate channels is typical of what often happens as a marketing operation develops.

AGENTS, BROKERS AND MERCHANTS

The advantage of all of these channels is the personal contact and knowledge they have of a particular market. Agencies are established on an exclusive and semi-exclusive basis and can be very helpful to the supplier entering a completely new market or to one who does not want to employ his own sales force. The agent should act as a member of the manufacturer's sales team as distinct from the wholesaler who is more concerned with the burden of the physical distribution.

Clearly, the granting of a sole agency is a step not to be taken lightly because, if the wrong agent is appointed, considerable harm can be done to the principal's image and development plans before such an agent can be replaced.

Brokers act as intermediaries working on very fine profit margins but, as with agents, they often have very useful contacts. A danger with the broker is that he can depress the market price by selling at cut rates sufficient for him to earn a minimal margin, particularly on volume sales.

Merchants generally operate as a mixture of agents and wholesalers and usually have a good standing in the market place. Care has to be taken in passing them sole selling rights because they tend to carry a wide range of lines and are sometimes unable to put significant emphasis behind any one product.

EXPORTING

Selection of the proper channels of distribution for overseas markets is even more important than in the UK markets where the lines of communication are shorter and mistakes can be more speedily rectified. It is essential that proper account be taken of local customs and practices, attitudes and patterns of demand. For entry into an overseas market the best method of distribution is probably through an export agent. Selection of the agent is clearly very important and the Chamber of Commerce, the Department of Trade and Industry and trade associations can all offer good advice on where to find agents.

Direct representation in large department stores is another successfully used method of distribution because, as in the UK, leading stores are barometers of current demand and can usually place sizeable orders offering economies of scale to distributors.

With some countries, particularly those of the eastern bloc, the distribution has to be through large buying offices in the UK and often there is no direct contact between the manufactuer and his ultimate consumer.

INDUSTRIAL DISTRIBUTION

Techniques of good marketing are being applied increasingly in the industrial field. As far as channels of distribution are concerned the choice is almost as wide as that available for consumer goods.

Industrial products tend to be of a more technical nature so consideration has to be given to after-sales service irrespective of the chosen channel of distribution. Very often a manufacturer will deal with his customer via an agent on all matters of sale and supply, but will deal direct on servicing and maintenance.

Package deals involving products from within a large group of companies can be offered to one common outlet; similarly, a manufacturer may well find many captive outlets within his own group. This opportunity is often missed or just not pursued.

Licensing is a method often used in the engineering industry, for example, with motor cars and aero-engines. Under these arrangements, the licensee undertakes to produce and sell goods to the licensee's specification for a consideration of the resultant profits. This method enables the manufacturer to expand his revenue without a corresponding increase in investment.

Heavy engineering industries make use of consortia to distribute their products. This applies to such projects as off-shore drilling equipment, building and civil engineering contracts, power station supplies, shipbuilding, etc.

CONCLUSION

Inevitably, the final decision on which channels to use must be a compromise, but it is the purpose of this chapter to provide an outline of the range of possibilities, and even if no more than a stimulation of more detailed and rational thinking on this vital aspect of marketing occurs it will have served its purpose.

FURTHER READING

Butcher, M.E., *Elements of Distribution*, Heinemann, London, 1980.
Flipjer, M.T., *Distribution for Exporters*, BIM, 1977.
Guirdham, M., *Management of Distribution Channels*, Pergamon, Oxford, 1972.
Mallen, B., *Principles of Marketing Channel Techniques*, Lexington Books, Lexington, Mass., 1977.

13 Managing a sales force

M T Wilson

The strategy of marketing is concerned with arranging the resources of the company so that the needs of customers can be satisfied by presenting to them a product/price offering which when purchased provides a profit to the firm. This strategy is implemented through a number of tactical tools, some concerned with finding out what the needs are (marketing research), some with ensuring the product/price offering is correct (product development and testing), and some with presenting the offering to the customer. The sales function is a major tactic in this last area, while having a role to play in the first two.

The importance of the sales function cannot be overemphasised in those companies where the bulk of the presentational effort is carried by the sales force. This covers most industrial and speciality markets and many consumer goods industries. In fact, it is not exaggerating far to say that in some markets – for example, office equipment and life insurance – the main difference between competing companies lies in the quality of their sales forces.

Moreover, the sales force can make valuable contributions in the definition of market segments and customer needs, and product development and rationalisation. This is particularly true in industrial markets, where formal market research is less used. Obviously, since salesmen are not usually trained researchers, the information they collect has to be treated with care.

As sales management is a function (often the most important) within the marketing strategy, it is essential for the sales manager at least to be aware of the other tactics of marketing so that he can contribute to and benefit from them. These include:

1 New product development
2 Distribution
3 Sales forecasting
4 Pricing
5 Advertising and sales promotion

6 Public relations
7 Marketing planning and control (particularly the financial aspects).

In some companies the sales manager will directly control some of these; in others, they will be looked after by marketing staff. In every firm, the sales manager must integrate his activities with the rest of the marketing effort if the maximum value is to be gained from marketing expenditure.

The sales manager is the key man in developing a successful sales operation. He must do this by managing his team - not by doing their jobs for them. As a manager he is responsible for working through others to achieve economic objectives, but this process is hindered by the difficulties of dealing with geographically spread subordinates who spend most of their time with people other than their colleagues.

To do his job successfully, the sales manager must possess knowledge and skill in four major areas; selling, management, sales management and marketing. Only then can he claim to be a fully productive member of the executive team.

Sales management comprises five key elements - planning, organisation, training, motivation and control. It is on these that this chapter concentrates.

HOW TO PLAN THE SALES OPERATION

The planning process is only one part of the basic and repetitive management activity necessary in any company seeking to grow. The firm must continuously answer three questions:

1 Where are we going? This is the objective-setting process
2 How shall we get there? This is the planning process
3 How shall we know if we are getting there? This is the control process.

These questions first appear at top management level and the answers constitute the corporate objectives, corporate plans and policies, and corporate control mechanisms. Typically they will result in a statement of the profit objectives of the company (usually expressed in terms of return on capital employed), a description of the business the company is in and its desired position in that industry, its plans and policies for each function of the company, and specific goals and targets to be met within set time-periods.

The whole process will then be repeated for each function of the company. Thus marketing, production, R & D, finance and so on, will each formulate its objectives, plans and controls. Within the marketing framework, the sales manager must specify his answers to the three questions in order to produce a format for his staff to work to. Each salesman may well be required to repeat the process with individual customers.

The sales manager's role in the continuum is obviously critical. If he fails to set clear objectives that are compatible within the hierarchy and does not initiate the appropriate action, the whole firm must suffer.

Setting sales objectives

The sales manager will commence by considering the marketing objectives, policies and strategies and control criteria. He will probably have a forecast of sales by revenue and volume, a forecast of gross profit required, perhaps an expense budget, a description of the product range available with additions and deletions, price structure, promotional support, etc.

Forecasting sales

In many firms the sales manager will be involved as a member of the marketing team in the definition of these items. The process will normally start with forecasting sales for the next period. This is the most critical prediction in the company as it will determine the production schedule, raw materials and finished stocks, promotional expenditure, etc. It is best to approach the forecast in two stages. First, what will sales be, assuming all variables in the situation are the same in the future as they have been in the past? Second, which variables will change and what will the impact be? Some of the variables will be internal factors which management decides to change, others will be external factors which are uncontrollable by the company but whose effect must be predicted.

Developing the sales plan

Having set the sales forecast and targets, the manager must now consider how they can be achieved. Obviously some thought will already have been given to the plan in formulating the objectives. After the plan is written it might well be necessary to reconsider the goals that were previously identified.

The sales manager has to consider five basic questions:

1 What is to be sold?
2 To whom?
3 At what price?
4 By what methods?
5 At what costs?

In some of these areas, notably the product range and pricing structure, he may well have limited influence; they are often controlled by the marketing planning department, through a brand or product management structure. In respect of all five he will certainly have to consider the inputs of other parts of the business. What stocks will be available from production, what money is available from finance, what advertising and sales promotion support is planned, etc.?

Deciding what is to be sold

In determining what the product range should be the sales manager can at least advise his marketing planning colleagues on the saleability of the various items in the range as well as new product requirements.

From a sales management viewpoint he will have to decide whether the full range should be sold to everybody. In some capital equipment markets, for example, where the distributor has to make a heavy investment in stock, it may not be in the interests of the company to supply dealers whose resources may not be adequate to finance the more costly products. Likewise, companies who have to make after-sales service arrangements may well decide not to sell products to customers who are geographically isolated.

To whom are the products to be sold

Next, the sales manager must consider the customers and prospects for his products. First, he will study the existing markets and decide whether business with them is likely to increase, decrease or remain static. This judgement will be based on a study of previous buying records.

By analysing customers in terms of their potential and actual purchasing of the various products he has to offer, he can identify the areas to be attacked. Prospective customers can be analysed in the same way.

Choosing the methods

Having identified from the product/market analysis the segments to be attacked, the sales manager can now consider the methods most likely to achieve the objectives set.

The first question to be answered is – what sort of service should the sales force provide in order to influence the buyer? For example, a crop-protection firm pondering how to increase sales to agricultural merchants will have to consider how the merchant will market the product to farmers. Perhaps the job of the sales force in this case will be to help the merchant develop his skills.

Such an analysis of the kind of sales effort needed will lead to identification of the appropriate sales methods. The complexity of seller/buyer relationships becomes rapidly obvious. It is only by such definition that the sales manager can develop the presentational approach that will enable him to succeed in the face of product/price parity.

Having identified the nature of the sales method he can then consider the scale of effort required. He must calculate how many customers and prospects should be called on how often.

The customers are relatively easy to specify because obviously they are known by name to the company. The level of prospecting is more difficult to calculate, as in many companies potential customers cannot be identified by name. At least, however, the sales manager can indicate the characteristics of likely prospects. Such a profile can then be used by the sales force to select prospects to be called upon. Alternatively, the sales manager can plan simply to allow a certain percentage of time or calls for seeking new business, giving the salesmen the responsibility of using the time or calls wisely.

How often calls should be made is always difficult to assess. Obviously different categories of accounts will require different call frequencies. In some trades where there is an established buying pattern, usually little is gained by calling at a different frequency.

The support of the field force will also be covered by the sales manager's study of the methods required to achieve his objectives. Parts of the supplier/buyer relationship can often be more economically handled by techniques other than personal visiting by representatives. Telephone selling is one method that is successfully used to handle routine ordering, thus freeing the salesmen's costly time for more creative work.

Evaluating the costs of selling

The best approach is to look at the cost-effectiveness of the methods used and particularly to try to analyse the values gained for the costs incurred. For example, if the manager were concerned with the cost of generating prospects he could compare the cost per prospect from advertising, direct mail and cold canvassing. If he were analysing sales force activity, he might question what value was gained from 'courtesy calling' (i.e., routine visiting to check that the customer is satisfied with the products and service supplied). In such a case the manager might experiment by eliminating such calls in a test area and evaluating what, if anything, happened to the sales.

HOW TO ORGANISE THE SALES FORCE

Many sales organisations have developed without objective analysis of their purpose or structure. Today they are out of date and unable to fulfil the purposes for which they were originally designed. This is because the traditional hierarchical structure is based upon conditions which no longer hold true in a great number of firms. Such organisations assume that there is a large number of relatively small, geographically separate and independent buying-points all with similar requirements, and that these can be serviced by a large number of geographically separated salesmen who can perform similar tasks and who represent the major promotional activity of the company.

Changes in buyer/seller relationships

The foregoing suppositions have been made obsolete by two fundamental changes in the buyer/seller relationship.

First, the buying power in many industries is no longer evenly distributed. In a large number of markets, a few big firms control the majority of the purchasing decisions. These oligopolies, developed largely through the processes of merger and acquisition, have resulted in a dramatic reduction in the numbers of independent outlets in the trades concerned. Thus, whilst sales organisations' structures have in many cases changed little, the number and type of customers with whom they deal have altered dramatically.

Second, the development of new marketing techniques has meant that some tasks traditionally performed by the sales force can be more economically or efficiently handled by other methods. The development of advertising and sales promotion in general, as well as the growing use of specific techniques such as telephone selling and contract ordering, have all had an impact on the nature and scale of the sales effort required. Furthermore, the reduction in sales force sizes and improvements in communications have in some cases obviated the need for regionally based management.

The prime objective of all salesmen is to gain business. From an organisational point of view, however, how they are to achieve their goals must be defined in order to identify what kind and quality of skills are required.

Matching the sales effort to customer requirements

Organising the sales effort so that it matches the reality of the market-place can alleviate such problems. First, the level and quantity of customer service must be defined and the personnel concerned identified.

Such an analysis will also begin to identify the work-loads of each level and suggest ways of grouping the various elements so that they can be better managed.

The sales force structure should also be scrutinised. A geographical split may be the most economical in that travel time is minimised. It may not, however, be the most effective. In one glass-container company it was seen that the prime service to be provided to the buyer was a technical knowledge of bottling as applied to the customer's particular industry. Thus the sales force was regrouped on an industry basis, changing the organisation structure. Obviously there was some increase in travel costs because each industry group worked nationally but this was more than offset by the increase in sales.

At sales force level common groupings other than geographical are by industry, by customer size category, by buyer type (for example, purchasers and specifiers), or by service to be provided (for example, order taking and merchandising).

By conducting a customer service requirements analysis the sales manager can identify which organisational approach is appropriate.

The number of salesmen needed

The aim of building an organisation is to give the appropriate level of service to each customer and the appropriate amount of work to each man. The only factor common to all salesmen is the number of working hours and this should be the starting point for a work-load analysis, which is the only really logical way of constructing a sales force. The amount of work per salesman can then be calculated by assessing the elements and the time taken on each. Typically, they include: prospecting, travelling, waiting, selling and report-writing. If the number of actual and potential accounts to be visited and the frequency of visiting can be assessed, it is possible to calculate the number of salesmen needed as follows:

$$\frac{\text{Number of actual and potential customers} \times \text{Call frequency}}{\text{Average daily call rate} \times \text{Number of working days per year}}$$

TRAINING THE SALES TEAM

The art of selling is the presentation of product benefits in such a way that the buyer is persuaded that his needs will be satisfied. If the salesman is to be successful he must not only be knowledgeable about his product and his customer but also skilful in the presentation of this knowledge.

Induction training

When a new salesman joins a company he should be given some form of training. Too often, even when training is given, the whole time is devoted to company and product knowledge in the hope (usually unfulfilled) that the salesman will somehow pick up sales techniques in the field.

This initial training can be critical to the ultimate success of the new man as it will affect both his ability and morale. It must therefore be very carefully planned and skilfully executed.

The programme material will obviously vary from firm to firm, particularly in terms of the company and product knowledge to be taught.

There are, however, some basic areas of the sales job that should be included in most initial training courses, although with specific biases being given by different companies. Ten major elements should be covered.

1 *The marketing concept and the role of the sales force.* The salesman must understand fully the part he plays in the total effort of the company. Otherwise, he will find it difficult to integrate his work with that of other departments
2 *The nature of salesmanship.* It is essential that the salesman has a clear definition of what selling is, its role in society and the basic requirements of the sales job
3 *Communications.* As selling depends on persuasive communication, the salesman must understand the inherent difficulties of interpersonal relationships and be given techniques for overcoming these problems. He must be skilled in other forms of communication, such as reporting and talking on the telephone
4 *Preparation for selling.* This is normally a very weak area of sales skill and yet if a coherent, logical approach to the customer is to be adopted, it has to be structured in advance, and the technique for doing this has to be taught
5 *Prospecting.* Every business depends to some extent on gaining new customers. This is probably the most difficult part of selling and the salesman should be taught a systematic approach to the finding of potential buyers. Having learnt how to look for new business, he will also be better motivated and less likely to avoid prospecting, as so often happens
6 *Opening the sales.* Obtaining interviews with buyers and making the right impression in the early stages of the presentation are areas where skill is required. A casual approach will lead to failure to pass the receptionist or even when that is achieved to curtailed, unsuccessful interviews
7 *Making sales presentations.* To be effective as a persuader, the salesman must

be skilled in oral presentation, visual aid handling and product demonstration. There is a body of techniques that can be learnt which will help the salesman to communicate convincingly

8 *Handling objections.* Every sales interview is likely to produce customer objections on such topics as price, delivery, etc. Some of these can be prevented, others overcome. Certainly most objections can be predicted and the salesman trained in the answers to be given and the methods of expressing them

9 *Closing the sale.* Again, this is normally a very weak area because the salesman fears rejection. He therefore tends to avoid it by never asking for the order. If he never asks the buyer to buy, the buyer never has to refuse. Obviously the whole point of selling is to gain sales and the salesman can be encouraged to request orders more often and more persuasively by thorough training in proven closing techniques

10 *Work organisation.* The main emphasis of initial training is on improving the quality of the salesman's skill. Due regard should also be paid to the quantity of selling so that the man knows how to utilise his very limited time to the maximum. He should be taught techniques of journey planning and day planning.

Concept of customer orientation

Throughout the initial training programme certain themes will have to be constantly emphasised as some of the basic concepts are hard to instil. One of the most fundamental of these is the philosophy of customer orientation. Without this approach, the salesman will find it hard to succeed and yet it is difficult to ensure that it will be practised.

Every salesman must recognise that buyers buy to satisfy needs, both rational and emotional. These needs are fulfilled by benefits of the product and these benefits are derived from product features.

Because of the difficulty of reversing the viewpoint in this way, successful training in this concept can be hard to achieve. It is helped if a product analysis is demonstrated and this technique is inculcated so that the salesmen analyse the needs, benefits and features of a situation before they commence selling.

Field training

The objective of field training is to ensure a continuous improvement in the salesman's performance. To achieve this goal there are five tasks that must be carried out by the manager:

1 Field performance must be assessed systematically against known standards.
2 Deficiencies must be identified and agreed and coaching given in the knowledge and skills necessary to correct the identified faults.
3 Guidance must be given on the self-training that is expected from the salesman.

4 Information should be collected about common faults that can be more economically or effectively corrected on a collective basis.
5 The effectiveness of the initial training should be assessed so that it can be improved in the future.

Sales meetings

The regular gatherings of the sales team create the other major opportunity for developing sales force performance. In all but the smallest sales forces, these are held at local level, where the regional, area or district manager meets with his salesmen. Where there are no intermediate supervisory levels between the national sales manager and the sales force these gatherings have to be held on a national basis. The objectives of such meetings should be:

1 To administer corporate training and development
2 To inform and get feedback from the sales force
3 To stimulate and if necessary rekindle the salesmen's enthusiasm and motivation
4 To provide a meeting place and forum for all the salesmen.

HOW TO MOTIVATE THE SALES FORCE

The motivation of salesmen is probably the most common topic of conversation whenever sales managers meet. Every manager has his own pet theories on how to get the best out of his team. The reason why it is such a popular discussion point is because salesmen can be directly supervised only intermittently. It is therefore vital to success that they are deeply motivated to work on their own. Moreover, the sales job inevitably involves loneliness and certain customer contacts which can depress the morale of any but the most enthusiastic salesmen.

The nature of motivation

Because of the geographical separation and the wearing aspects of the job, it is vital for success that the sales manager possesses or develops the ability to motivate his men. In order to do so he needs a clear understanding of why people work and what they wish to gain from their work. Only then can he create an environment which will cause his men to apply their full abilities to their jobs.

Incentives and disincentives

The basis of motivation is the provision of incentives which encourage salesmen to give of their best and the removal of disincentives which prevent them from devoting their whole energies to their work. Unfortunately, far too often, motivation is equated with incentives only, although it is common to find that the elimination of disincentives – for example, unfair treatment – is the more powerful influence.

It must also be recognised that virtually every incentive brings with it a disincentive, either for the same person or for his colleagues. For example, a competition may be a strong motivation for the winners; but it can be demoralising for the losers, particularly if they believe that because of the poor construction of the contest they never had a real chance of winning.

The task of the manager is therefore to consider the needs of his team, both individually and as a group, and to arrange a balance of motivational influences that will encourage them to achieve the company's objectives. In essence, this is best done by ensuring that the individual's own goals in life are consistent with the aims of the firm. For example, there is little point recruiting people who are highly money-motivated into a company which offers security as its major satisfaction.

Although recognising that everyone has his own individual need pattern, there are five motivational influences that the sales manager must fully understand. These are:

1 Remuneration
2 Direct incentives
3 Job satisfaction
4 Security
5 Status.

Remuneration

First, management should define the salary grades appropriate to the job level. This grade will represent the market value of the position as well as the worth of the job to the company. The bottom of the category will represent the remuneration of a man entering the position exhibiting minimum standards of performance, the upper limit being paid to a man who can achieve completely all the criteria of the job.

Second, the position of any individual within his grade should be determined by his performance against the job standards. An average performer would therefore be paid at the mid-point of the grade. Thus, the salary philosophy will reflect the two main elements of a logical payment structure: the degree of responsibility carried by the position, and the effectiveness with which the man discharges it.

Payment by results system

Such an approach to job grading and appraisal presupposes that the salesman will be remunerated at least in part by salary. Many sales forces are of course paid in addition, to some degree or another, according to results. In a relatively small number of companies the salesmen are paid entirely on commission. The choice of remuneration system – salary only, salary plus some form of commission, or commission only – will depend upon the desired mix of security and incentive.

Direct incentives

This term is used to cover the many systems of payment in cash or in kind other than basic remuneration. It includes fringe benefits, merchandise awards, points schemes and competitions. Apart from fringe benefits, such schemes do not usually make a significant difference to total earnings and their basic intention is motivational. Merchandise awards and competitive schemes are best used to focus short-term attention on particular aspects of the business. They are a tactical rather than a strategic motivational weapon. When employed in this way, they can be very effective to concentrate sales force attention on, for example, gaining new accounts, increasing sales of lower volume products, or even submitting call reports on time!

Job satisfaction

Direct incentives in either cash or kind are important elements in any motivational scheme. The so-called 'psychic wages' of the job however must be given at least equivalent priority. Salesmen spend more than half their waking life working. It is not surprising therefore that they seek fulfilment in the job as well as rewards for the job. It is an essential function of any manager to ensure that such satisfaction can be gained by the sales force from their work.

Security

The need for security is a very common, although seldom admitted, motive. The nature of the remuneration system and the relative importance of salary and commission will obviously affect job security and must be considered from this aspect.

However, the less obvious facets of security should not escape the sales manager's attention. In companies where insecurity is a constant feature of the environment morale tends to be low and, although there is often an appearance of frenetic action, achievement is usually very limited.

Status

The sales manager can help to improve the status of selling within the company and the market by ensuring that the job titles given carry as much prestige as possible. He should ensure, too, that the rest of the company realises the importance of the function so that when a customer telephones and asks for one of the field force by name, the switchboard operator does not reply that as Mr Smith is 'only one of our salesmen (or worse still, "travellers"), he is not in the office'. Likewise when the caller is eventually put through to the sales department, he should be greeted by a girl who says she is Mr Smith's secretary. She can, of course, be 'secretary' to a number of other salesmen as well.

The salesman should be provided with the best possible equipment for his job. Well-printed visiting cards with his name in the middle, a well-made briefcase or sample case and good literature all contribute to his status in the eyes of his customers. His car is perhaps the most significant symbol of all, not only to his buyers but also to his family and friends.

HOW TO CONTROL THE SALES OPERATION

In order to control any activity, there must first be an objective and a plan. Unless it is known what is to be achieved and how, whether it is being achieved cannot be assessed. Conversely, there is little point in setting goals and defining actions unless there is an evaluation procedure.

For example, in one business equipment firm, the sales manager developed a system whereby he could analyse the monthly performance of every salesman under eighteen different categories of activity. Thus he could identify how many hours each man had spent on each facet of his job. He could ascertain for instance that salesman *X* spent seven and a half hours on prospecting, salesman *Y* eight hours on report-writing. He obviously believed that control was constituted by the collection of detailed information. Such attitudes are common among sales management and part of the impact of computerisation is that data suddenly becomes available in vast quantities, thus apparently giving even more minute control.

The concept of control

It must be realised that the collection of information, however accurate, up to date and detailed, in itself in no way constitutes control. This is for the very basic reason that there is little point in knowing what *has* happened unless there is a clear conception of what *should* have happened. Control can then be exercised by comparing actual performance with planned performance and deriving variances. It is on these variances that corrective action should be based. Control can be summarised therefore as:

$$A - S = \pm V$$

where A is the actual performance, S is the pre-set standard and V is the variance between the two.

To know that salesman *X* spent seven and a half hours prospecting is meaningless by itself. However, if the standard for this activity is ten hours then there is a minus variance of two and a half hours and it is this figure which should cause the manager to take corrective action. If, however, the standard were seven and a half hours, as the actual performance is equivalent to the desired standard no managerial action is required. Only by adopting such a concept can management time be economically utilised.

Setting standards of field sales performance

To identify appropriate standards for control, the manager should ask two questions:

1 What constitutes success?
2 What affects the achievement of success?

Descriptive standards

In a sales operation success can usually be defined as the achievement of the sales targets. These serve as the prime standards of control. By themselves, however, they are insufficient. The achievement or otherwise of the annual sales target constitutes a descriptive standard. It measures what has happened but it is then usually far too late to redress the balance. Moreover, it does not indicate *why* the performance has been poor.

Diagnostic standards

Diagnostic standards, which help to identify why performance is varying from target, are defined by asking the second question: 'What affects the achievement of success?'

The manager must consider in the case of a particular salesman failing to achieve target what actions by the salesman himself should lead to the goals being met. Surprisingly, there are only four and these can be identified by the following questions:

1 What kind of people does he call upon?
2 How many does he call upon?
3 How often does he call?
4 What does he do while he is there?

How to set standards

One of the aims of setting standards is to control the sales activity at an early stage to prevent failure to achieve orders. This aspect of control can be further refined by evaluating planned performance against standard before the activity takes place. In fact it is only by assessing the intended action of the sales force that the sales manager can directly prevent failure. Obviously he must check his own plans to ensure that, if achieved, they reach the desired objectives. He can go further by assessing each salesman's activity plans before they are put into action. This is normally done by the submission of weekly calling plans on which each man identifies whom he is intending to visit, for what reason and when he last saw this customer (if applicable).

Variance production and analysis

Variances are produced by comparing actual results against the pre-set standards. However, this simple method may need refining as high variances can result which reflect the forecast error of the standards. For example, if the average daily call rate is set at eight, there is probably no cause for alarm if this varies between six and ten. Because so many of the standards are produced by averaging past performance it may well be necessary to process the actual results before comparing them against standard.

When the actual results are compared with the standards, variances will become apparent. These discrepancies may need more careful analysis before corrective action is taken. For example, in one firm it was known from past experience that most of the selling depended upon seeing the senior management of the customers, which could only be done by appointment. The results of some salesmen, however, were disappointing despite the fact that the percentage of calls by appointment was well up to the pre-set standard. But when performance against other standards was examined it was noted that their call rate was below par. Thus although the appointment to total call ratio was high, this was due to a smaller number of other calls rather than to an over-achievement of appointments. Furthermore, it was discovered that as they increased their number of appointments, their overall call rates decreased markedly.

What in fact was happening was that these men, in their enthusiasm to gain appointments, had not controlled the timing of such meetings. They had placed them in the middle of the mornings and afternoons, thereby limiting their ability to make other calls. The more experienced men systematically made appointments early in the morning, immediately before lunch, immediately after lunch or late afternoon, leaving mid-morning and mid-afternoon free to make cold calls which, although not as important, resulted in enough business to make their results superior. It would have been very easy to jump to the conclusion that the disappointing results of the less experienced men were due to a lack of sales skill. It was only by careful variance analysis that the real problem of appointment timing was identified.

Taking corrective action

Having identified the true nature of the variance, the sales manager has to decide whether it results from faulty standard setting or inadequate salesman performance. If the former, the standards will have to be modified. If the latter, the performance of the man will have to be improved, usually by some form of training or instruction. If the man is to improve he must be given specific targets to achieve within specific time periods, otherwise little or no change will result.

FURTHER READING

Lidstone, J.L., *Motivating Your Sales Force*, Gower, 1978
Lidstone, J.L., *Training Salesmen on the Job*, Gower, 1975
Wilson, M.T., *Managing a Sales Force*, 2nd edition, Gower, 1983

PART THREE

PURCHASING AND INVENTORY MANAGEMENT

14 Procurement policy

Peter Baily

Manufacturing organisations typically spend over half of their total sales revenue on the purchase of materials, components and services from outside organisations. Retailing organisations of course spend an even higher proportion, since what they sell is what they buy. In the case of manufacturing organisations, what they sell is what they make, and most of their purchases constitute the materials and components required for the manufacture of their products.

Although this chapter is mainly about procurement policy for manufacturers, a brief comparison between the situation for manufacturers and that for retailers will be useful to establish the policy variables. Any trading organisation needs to determine, and continually to reconsider, its *market offering*: what products it offers, what prices it charges, how its products are publicised or promoted and how they are distributed to the customer or to places convenient to the customer.

A small independent retailer selects the products offered from those available at the wholesalers, cash and carry outlets, etc. A large chain store on the other hand may develop its own products and seek suitable producers for them. It may also purchase 'own brand' goods which are sometimes nationally available products, bought at a cheaper price without the national brand label. The main trading advantage of the chain store is in fact its ability to buy in bulk and thus both to rationalise its purchases and to get cheaper prices.

A small manufacturing firm will also make much use of wholesalers, and other organisations which specialise in supplying goods and services to manufacturers; but such organisations sell standard products, and even the smaller manufacturer needs to buy special products made to its own design. A large manufacturer may devote the major part of its purchasing effort to finding and trading with suppliers of components and materials which are not nationally available but are specifically called for by the design of the products which it is offering.

Very large manufacturers, and those occupying a *de facto* monopoly position as buyers, are in a position to exert so much leverage on their supply markets that they need to consider, whenever they take a major purchasing decision, the future state of the supply market which will result from it. Such organisations as the National Coal Board, British Telecom, IBM and General Motors constantly need to bear in mind such considerations, and much research and thought may be needed to decide whether a two-supplier market would be better than a three-supplier market, for instance.

The normal purchasing situation for the larger customer is what economists call *bilateral oligopoly*: that is, a small number of powerful suppliers dominate the supply market and a small number of powerful customers dominate the sales market. No formula will determine whether supplier or customer has the whip hand. Negotiation is used to decide the arrangements for supply: the specification, the contract quantity and the delivery quantities, the price and terms of payment, the inspection or quality assurance agreement, etc.

PROCUREMENT STRATEGIES

Corey (1978) classified procurement strategies into three groups:

1 Cost-based negotiation
2 Market-price-based negotiation
3 Competitive bidding.

While these were distinguished from each other basically by pricing mode, they also differed according to Corey in the product scope of the procurement (which could be narrow or broad), in the number and kind of suppliers contacted (ranging from one or very few in the case of cost-based negotiation to many in the second group), in price-quantity determination (including risk-sharing arrangements and the form in which quotations were requested) and in negotiating strategy (which varies considerably between the three groups).

Supplier selection was not just a matter of selecting the type and number of source; it involved the construction of a sourcing system in which different suppliers had different roles, for instance, technical development, price leadership, etc. Long-term supply availability, domestic versus foreign sources, distributors versus manufacturers and the strategy of numbers were some of the factors to be considered. Single sourcing and the stability of vendor relationships were topics of considerable importance, while in certain circumstances it could be quite difficult to persuade a supplier to accept an order. If a manufacturer needs to engage in demarketing its product, the customer needs to engage in marketing its demand, a reversal of the traditional relationship which may become increasingly prominent as material shortages loom larger.

Negotiation has become the subject of an enormous literature and many training courses are available for buyers, sellers, labour union representatives, management representatives, and many others with special interests. Most of this training material stresses the importance of the groundwork which precedes negotiating sessions, in which objectives are set, the relevant facts are assembled and conclusions drawn, and tentative agenda established for the negotiations.

Corey's work is based on research carried out at six very large American corporations during the seventies. Purchasing could be carried out, and in fact in all six cases was carried out, at plant level, divisional level, and corporate level; but a strong trend was noticed to centralise procurement decision-making to corporate level, mainly perhaps because of the increasing importance of the function as perceived by corporate management. Supply shortages and long-term planning of material availability, effective response to a changing business environment, profit improvement by means of purchase cost reduction, and better selection, use and development of purchasing talent were listed as reasons for this trend.

INPUT MANAGEMENT

Similar trends have been reported by Farmer (1981), in his discussion of the management of input to the firm from its supply market. Input in the sense in which it is used here refers to the components and materials used in producing the firm's end products. It is argued that too many firms have confined their strategic planning to output management and the marketing of their end products, regarding the input area as operational rather than strategic. This thinking may indeed have been appropriate to the supply market conditions of the recent past, but it is doubtful if it continues to be appropriate in the present and likely that it will become quite inappropriate to future supply market conditions.

Farmer argues that while input management is one of the variables in a business system, and its importance varies from company to company and from time to time, it is nevertheless hardly ever to be regarded as insignificant. And while the operational aspects of input management are certainly important to the functioning of the business, it has strategic aspects which have often been overlooked in the quest for operational efficiency. The effectiveness of the whole business is not the same thing as the efficiency of the various functions which are elements within it. Co-ordination and balance should be sought betwen the various functions, and between input and output management, at the strategic as well as at the operational levels. To focus solely on cost reduction in the input and conversion stages of a manufacturing system, and to look for profit opportunities solely at the output end, may well, according to Farmer, have been a major contributing factor in the decline and even demise of many manufacturing businesses.

Purchasing policy should thus be seen as part of business policy, purchasing strategy as part of business strategy. Long-term as well as short-term aspects need to be considered, as indeed they have been by successful Japanese manufacturers of motor cars, motor bikes, and TV sets, and by successful retailers such as Marks & Spencer.

Professor Farmer in this paper was looking particularly at the long-term and strategic aspects of supply planning; but the short-term and operational aspects are also important in the determination of procurement policy. Materials requirement planning, greatly facilitated by the more powerful computers and better systems which became available in the early 1980s, brought major improvements to supply and production operations in those companies which implemented it successfully. The insistence that management should devise and authorise a rational, feasible and appropriate master schedule, coupled with the ability to explode this into detailed schedules of what parts, components and materials to make or buy, week by week, over the whole planning horizon, came like a revelation to companies which had previously operated on a chaotic mixture of stock-controlled production and customer priorities.

Materials management was a different but related approach, also intended to improve operational efficiency, but this time by a change in departmental structures.

MATERIALS MANAGEMENT

The term 'materials management' presumably referred originally to the management of the activities within an organisation which had to do with the planning, purchasing, transport, storage and handling of the materials required by the organisation, using materials in the general sense to refer to the whole range of goods and services obtained from outside the organisation in order to provide finished products for sale. However, increasingly materials management has come to refer to the grouping together of these materials-related activities into one department under a materials manager. A typical theoretical approach is shown in Figure 14.1.

In practice, surveys have shown that adoption of some kind of materials management structure has been extremely widespread in the USA, and there has also been considerable interest in the UK; but the kind of organisation adopted has often not conformed to the theoretical approach shown in the diagram. It has been suggested that in seeking the organisation structure which is right for a particular company at a particular time, some key variables should be identified - such as:

1 Purchasing cost reduction leverage
2 Type of production: make for stock or make to customer order
3 Commonality of requirement between different divisions
4 Whether most problems occur between materials-related departments
5 Trade-offs between materials and non-materials departments.

These approaches are discussed more fully in Baily and Farmer (1982), which also quotes evidence to suggest that the adoption of efficient computer systems for materials management appears to have reduced the need to combine the materials-related departments into a single materials management department.

It is obviously not easy to discuss the organisational questions in the abstract because of the great variations in size, complexity and other dimensions which exist between companies. Several large concerns which operate a number of establishments favour some version of the materials management structure at plant level, where purchasing staff are grouped departmentally with stock control, stores, production planning and control, and transport staff, while at corporate level purchasing and contracts staff form a separate planning and negotiating group. Similar developments can be seen in

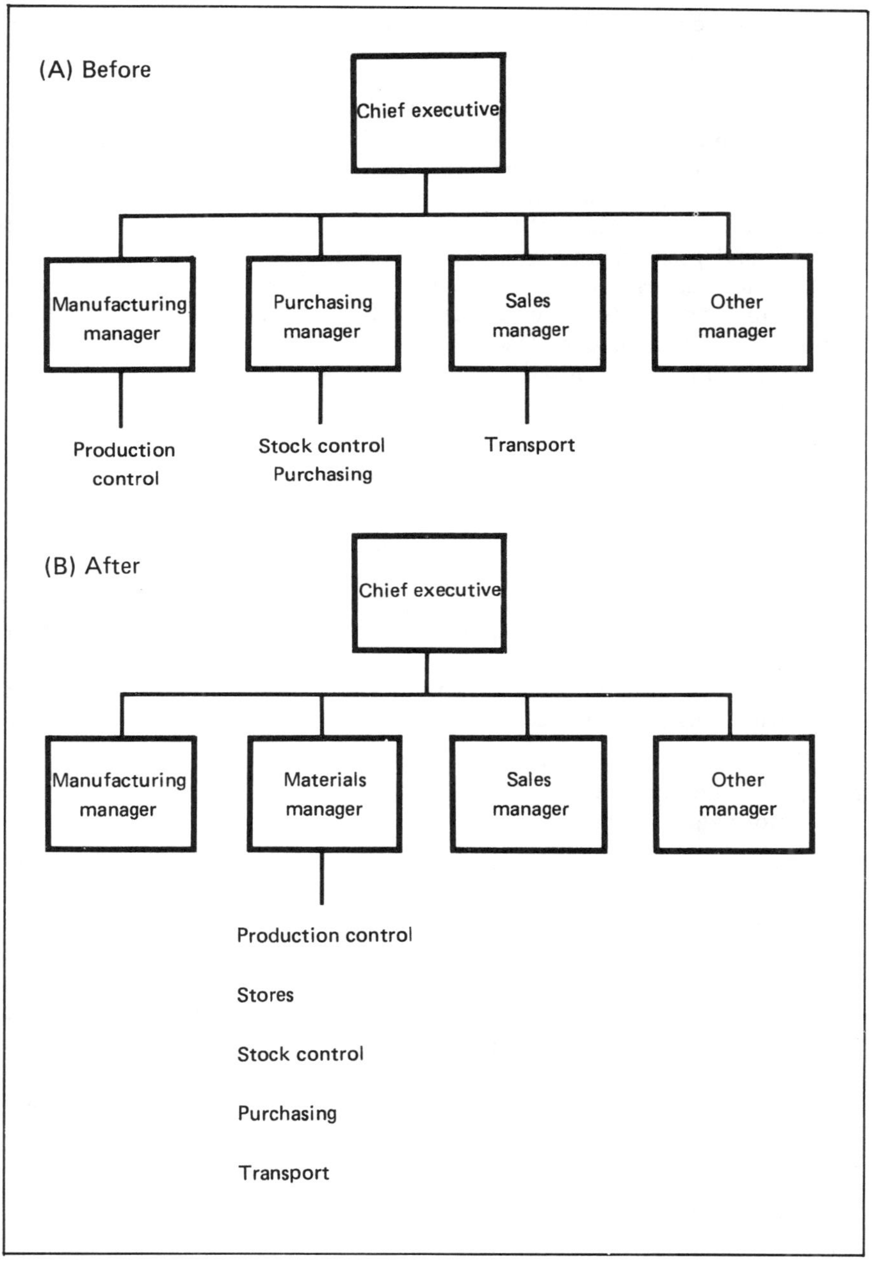

Figure 14.1 Materials management reorganisation

some retailing chains, where ordering and progessing staff are grouped organisationally with stock control, warehousing and transport, while a separate headquarters purchasing unit deals with the merchandising aspects, such as adoption of new lines and negotiation of original prices for first-time buys.

Devising appropriate organisation structures is a difficult process because so many factors affect it. One factor is the calibre and capability of the personnel affected. Purchasing staff who have the ability to contribute to long-term strategy are not necessarily the same people as those who do a sound job of ordering and progressing regular requirements from established suppliers. Another factor arises from the fact that purchasing departments exist to arrange for the supply of goods in accordance with the requirements of other departments, so that inter-departmental co-operation and communication is particularly important. Indeed many problems occur in practice in this area of inter-departmental relationships. An example is the matter of quality assurance, which forms the final topic in this chapter.

PURCHASING AND QUALITY ASSURANCE

Of fundamental importance in purchasing is to make sure that the right quality of goods, materials, etc. is bought. Both technical and commercial considerations are involved. The purchasing department operates jointly with other departments which also have important roles to play in this crucial aspect of arranging for the supply by outside organisations of what is required.

Although a number of different activities or stages occur in the process of purchasing quality assurance, it is convenient to group them under two headings:

1 Specification quality
2 Conformance quality.

The first part of the process is concerned with specifying the quality required. This may consist of a comparison of available merchandise and the selection of suitable brands or standards, or it may involve the preparation of engineering drawings and other forms of internally prepared specifications. Such a specification is a detailed statement of the features or characteristics required in a material, part or product. These features or characteristics may include chemical composition, such physical characteristics as ductility, viscosity, conductivity, weight, colour, surface finish, and physical size or dimensions – to name a few. The tolerance should also be stated: that is, the range of values within which a characteristic may vary without making the product unacceptable.

The second part of the process is concerned with arrangements to ensure that goods received conform with the specification, and that their important features or characteristics are within the allowed tolerances.

Normally in manufacturing industries a specialist department such as design, engineering, standards, etc. is entrusted with the responsibility for specifications. Such a department needs to take account of inputs from marketing (what can be sold) and from purchasing (what can be bought), as well as the production implications. It is difficult to generalise about the role of the purchasing department in this connection beyond saying that it must play some part, and that its concern will naturally be with the commercial rather than with the technical aspects of the product. Commercial aspects include the relative cost and availability of alternative materials or products, and also the feasibility of obtaining the quantity required for bulk production at an acceptable price.

A single instance may illustrate the last point. A certain company manufactures agricultural chemical products, for use mainly by farmers but also by home gardeners. New products are continually being developed by the research and development laboratories. If approved by the new products committee, which is heavily marketing orientated, they are put into a two-year field trial process intended to uncover any unwanted side-effects as well as to provide evidence that the products will in fact produce the effect claimed. During this two-year period, a purchasing research section within the purchasing department investigates the availability on world markets of all the ingredients required by the formulation of each new product under trial. Naturally at the end of the two-year trial it is not possible to change the formulation before going into bulk production. But it would be a mistake for management to authorise bulk production if some of the ingredients could not be supplied in sufficient quantities.

The second part of the process is concerned with the selection of suppliers, the approval of their quality control systems and the inspection of goods received. Inspection is an expensive process, and should not need to be carried out at all if suppliers could be relied on to supply acceptable goods. Increasingly, purchasing organisations are taking steps to ensure that this is so.

Many organisations carry out their own investigations of suppliers, but third-party investigations are also used quite widely: the British Standards Institution, the Crown Agents and a number of other organisations operate in this connection. Most systems for investigating the quality capability of suppliers classify the work into three levels, depending on the extent to which the customer relies on the supplier.

At the simplest level, all that the customer needs to know is whether the supplier has satisfactory instruments, test equipment and inspection procedures for final inspection of his products.

Many intermediate-level products require inspection at a number of successive stages of manufacture, with a reliable system for corrective action if faults occur, so that a more comprehensive system of quality control would need to be certified.

When a supplier is responsible for design as well as for manufacture, the investigation of his quality capability needs to be still more extensive and thorough.

Industries such as aerospace, motor car manufacture, atomic energy and other parts of electrical manufacturing, are already subject to strict official regulation of certain aspects of quality (mainly those which have to do with safety) and this has been one of the factors leading to the development of British Standards such as BS 5179.

At the same time as official regulation of safety and other quality standards has increased, and official guidance as to procedures for ensuring that suppliers are capable of supplying and do in fact supply goods to the standard specified has become more widespread, a parallel development has been occurring within companies. Quality is everybody's business; job security and progression for the individual depends on the organisation's ability to survive and prosper, which in turn to a large extent depends on the quality of its products.

Quality circles are a recent example of many approaches which organisations have adopted to encourage individual and small group initiative in maintaining and improving the quality of the product.

Technical inspection of incoming goods is a costly business which in principle could be dispensed with if suppliers could be relied on to supply acceptable goods. The investigation and selection process described above is intended to ensure that suppliers are in fact to be relied on, and is often used in practice to classify suppliers into three groups:

1 Accept goods on supplier's certificate
2 Accept goods after sample inspection
3 Inspect all goods received; do not order from this supplier if an alternative supplier is available.

If goods received require technical inspection before acceptance, it is often possible to obtain satisfactory results by inspecting a sample rather than every piece submitted. A large body of theory exists which can be applied in this connection to select the size of the sample and to draw conclusions from the results.

REFERENCES AND FURTHER READING

Baily, P.J.H., and Farmer, D.H., *Purchasing Principles & Management*, Pitman Publishing, London, 1981

Baily, P.J.H., and Farmer, D.H., *Materials Management Handbook*, Gower, 1982

Corey, E. Raymond, *Procurement Strategy, Organisation and Decision-Making*, CBI Publishing Company, Boston, Mass., 1978

Farmer, D.H., 'Input Management', *Purchasing & Supply Management*, Institute of Purchasing & Supply, Ascot, Berks., Aug. 1981

15 Purchasing procedures

Peter Baily

Management will naturally wish to adopt or devise purchasing procedures which suit the individual requirements of their own organisations. Retailers do not in general use quite the same systems and procedures as manufacturers, while civil engineering contractors have their own variations: procedures need to be appropriate to the type of operation.

Some of the organisations which employ purchasing staff are quite small, while others are very large and operate on a national or a worldwide scale. Procedures can be affected by the scale of operation.

Procedures are also affected by the type of office technology employed. Communications between buyer and seller can be face to face, by word of mouth, handwritten or typed and sent through the post, or some form of electronic mail can be used. Telex and facsimile have been in use for many years. Communicating word processors, teletext and direct links between customer's computer and supplier's computer are in the early stages of adoption.

The standard operating procedure for purchasing will be affected by the type and scale of operation and by the type of communications and records employed, but in addition to the standard procedure, a number of special procedures may be used. For instance many organisations adopt special procedures for routine low-value purchases, and also for non-routine high-value capital expenditure transactions. Procedures need to be appropriate to the type of purchase, and to enforce a single standard procedure for all purchases, while having the merit of simplicity, is not always the best way to do things.

This chapter outlines a standard purchasing procedure in four successive stages:

1 Initiation
2 Supplier selection
3 Contract stage
4 Completion.

Reference is made in each stage to the special or non-standard variations most commonly encountered, with examples of forms. The process is illustrated in Figure 15.1.

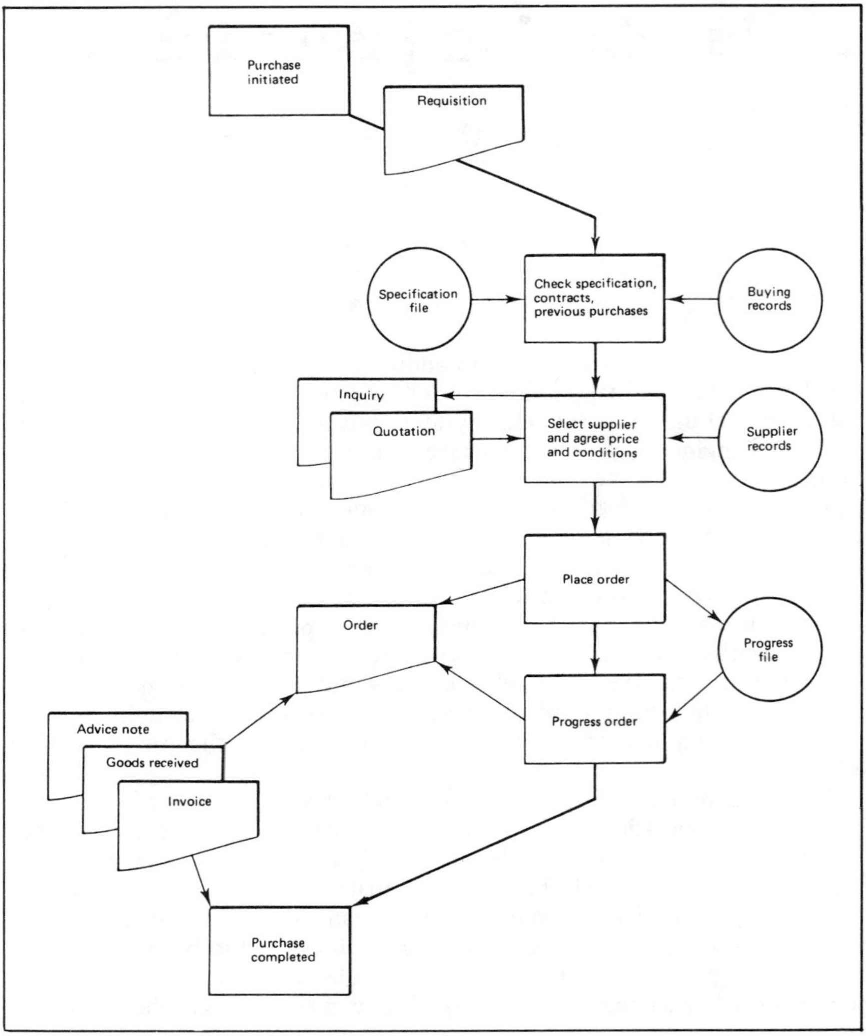

Figure 15.1 Outline of standard purchase procedure

INITIATION

Purchasing for organisations involves arranging for the supply on time and at a suitable price of the goods and materials, equipment and merchandise, services and supplies which are required to meet production programmes, sales plans or operating needs. It is normally the job of the purchase department to make the purchase on behalf of production, sales or operating departments. It is not normally the job of the purchase department to determine what needs to be purchased: most purchases are initiated by *requisitions* from other departments.

A purchase requisition is a request to the purchase department from any other department for something to be purchased. It serves to initiate the purchase, and also for audit purposes to provide evidence of authorisation and action taken. An example is shown in Figure 15.2.

PURCHASE REQUISITION

Department ____________
Date ____________
Number ____________

To purchase department: Please obtain the undermentioned

Suggested supplier	Quantity and description	Price	Required for
	Requisitioned by	Authorised by	

Figure 15.2 Purchase requisition

Such requisitions are date-stamped on receipt by the purchasing section and allocated to an appropriate member of department for action. The buyer may need to check the requisition against specification files, buying records and contract files. Some editing may be required, since requisitioners do not always express their requirements in terms suitable for communications with suppliers. If the item requisitioned is covered by a contract, an order will be placed immediately. Otherwise, a supplier may need to be selected. After the order has been placed, the requisition is filed for a limited period in case of query: two years should be quite adequate.

Many stock items and MRO (maintenance, repair and operating) requirements are ordered several times a year, and for these a *travelling requisition* will save time. This is a card kept in the initiating department on which is entered permanent data (such as description) and variable data (such as quantity required and date). It is sent to the purchasing section to initiate a purchase. After ordering the goods, details are entered on the card which is returned to the initiating department. An example is illustrated in Figure 15.3.

PURCHASE REQUISITION CARD

Card number

Classification ______ Minimum stock ______

Code number ______ Description ______ Average monthly consumption ______

Approved suppliers | Contract | Inquiries issued

Date	Present stock	Quantity required	Unit	Delivery wanted	Required for	Approvals	Date received purchasing department	Purchase order number	Supplier	Price	Carriage	Settlement terms

Figure 15.3 Travelling requisition

Systems for production planning and control used by manufacturers, or for stock planning and control used both by manufacturers and service industries such as retailing, normally generate a large group of purchase requirements periodically. Rather than prepare separate individual requisitions for each item affected, a *blanket requisition* or schedule of requirements is produced.

Materials Requirement Planning (MRP) systems are particuarly suitable for jobbing and batch production. With suitable adaptations they have been used in mass production ever since Henry Ford devised the first assembly line for motor cars. The process starts with the regular production or revision of a master production schedule which states, period by period, what quantities of each end product need to be completed to meet sales commitment or management plans.

For each end product the quantities due in each period are exploded by means of a parts list or bill of materials to determine what parts or materials are required for its completion, and this is offset by lead times to yield a time-phased schedule of gross requirements for parts and materials. Adjustments are then made for uncommitted stock on hand and orders due in to produce a time-phased schedule of net purchase requirements, or blanket requisition.

Stock control systems fall into two main groupings: continuous, and periodic. In continuous systems, each stock item is assigned an order point and an order quantity. Whenever a stock item quantity falls to the order point, an order is triggered for the appropriate order quantity, so that the system produces orders continuously. Travelling requisitions as previously described are often used. In periodic systems, either the whole stock range or a substantial subsection of it is reviewed at regular intervals. Stock on hand is compared with target stock as previously determined, or as calculated dynamically from previously determined rules. A blanket requisition or schedule of stock replenishment requirements is produced.

SUPPLIER SELECTION

Upon receipt of a requisition, the purchasing section checks if the item in question is already covered by a contract. If it is, an order can be placed against the contract without delay. If it is not covered by a contract, the next stage is to select a supplier and agree price and terms.

There is a strong preference for continuing to deal with regular suppliers in the case of regular purchases, so long as they continue to prove satisfactory. Nevertheless it is advisable periodically to check the market, to see what other suppliers have to offer. How often this should be done is a matter for judgement, and will vary with the type and volume of requirement and the structure of the supply market. If the market is dominated by one or two major suppliers it may be greatly to the long-term advantage of purchasers to place their business in such a way as to keep competition alive. Very large purchasers which dominate a market on the customer side often devote a good deal of time and thought to the optimum supply market structure, and sometimes take direct action to support minority suppliers or to develop new suppliers.

It is good practice for purchasing staff to know their regular suppliers well, to be personally acquainted with the people who process and make decisions about their orders, to keep in touch with business plans, product developments and so forth. Suppliers are a major resource without which neither manufacturers nor traders could operate, and the management of supply markets can be a very important matter which calls for advance planning, forethought, and some difficult decisions.

When making a new purchase for which there is no regular supplier, or when checking the market for regular purchases, the usual procedure is to send a *request for quotation* to a short list of possible sources. Names of potential suppliers are obtained from trade associations, commercial directories and buyers' guides, the trade knowledge of the buyers and their colleagues, advertisements and editorial material in the trade press, salesmen and technical representatives who call on the purchaser, and catalogues and other direct mail material which is received. A number of computerised buyers' guides are also available, which can be consulted on-line or by a telephone call; their main advantage is that they can be kept up to date continually, whereas printed directories can only be updated periodically when they are reprinted. As industrialisation spreads to new parts of the world, the search area for potential suppliers continues to widen; particular care should be taken before committing sourcing arrangements for important requirements to an untried overseas source, but major competitive advantage may result.

The request for quotation form (or enquiry as it is sometimes called) is shown in Figure 15.4. The form itself is simply the usual letterhead with, to save typing, a standard preprinted text asking the addressee to quote price, terms and delivery date for supply of the undermentioned goods on the terms and conditions stated overleaf.

Dear Sirs,

PURCHASE INQUIRY

Your quotation is invited not later than .... for the supply and delivery of the goods specified below, carriage paid, to ....

Your tender must clearly state (a) the price which will remain firm, (b) the terms of payment, (c) details of appropriate discounts, and (d) the period required for delivery. It must also incorporate all the conditions (general and special) set out overleaf.

Dear Sirs,

CONTRACT INQUIRY

Your tender is invited for the supply and delivery of the goods specified below to any of the Board's depots listed overleaf.

Your tender must clearly state (a) the price which will remain firm throughout the period of the contract, (b) the terms of payment, (c) details of appropriate discounts, and (d) the period required for delivery. It must also incorporate all the conditions (general and special) set out overleaf.

If your tender is accepted you will then supply and deliver the goods in accordance with draw-off orders issued by the Board's supplies officers and invoices should be submitted for payment in respect of such draw-off orders.

I shall be pleased, therefore, to receive your tender not later than .... in a plain sealed envelope marked "contract inquiry number ...."

Period of contract:
Description of goods:

Yours faithfully,

(Purchasing and Stores Controller)

Figure 15.4 Request for quotations (enquiry)

There is, however, sometimes considerable scope to structure the request for quotation in such a way as to facilitate subsequent negotiation in order to arrive at a mutually satisfactory agreement which gives better value: alternatives may be put forward as to total contract quantity, sub-quantities to be ordered against contract or delivered in particular places at particular times, terms of payment and other aspects of the deal. In some cases suppliers are asked to support their price quotation by a cost breakdown, which will be compared with a price/cost analysis prepared internally by estimating staff attached to purchasing. This latter technique is particularly favoured by mass-production manufacturers, the very scale of whose requirements limits possible suppliers to one or two in a given national economy.

In most cases the information a supplier gives on his tender or quotation needs to be supplemented by information in financial stability, quality capability, performance record, etc., which has to be obtained independently by purchasing staff. Reference was made in the previous chapter to supplier inspection visits in connection with quality assurance. All these matters are of particular importance in sourcing new requirements or considering new suppliers. When considering regular purchases or established suppliers, the track record is of particular importance – although it should not be forgotten that past history is not a sure guide to future behaviour. Management does change, new developments occur, new products are launched, new customers found: nevertheless it would not be prudent to ignore the record of how a particular supplier has behaved in the past. *Vendor rating* is an attempt to systematise this information.

Vendor rating

Vendor rating, or supplier evaluation as it is sometimes called, is the process of systematically accumulating information about a supplier's actual performance and presenting it in numerical form. The usual aspects of performance to be measured are:

1 Quality
2 On-time delivery
3 Service (although this is usually estimated rather than measured)
4 Price.

Quality is delivered or conformance quality: essentially, the proportion of goods delivered by a supplier which are accepted. In practice several rules are used to calculate a figure appropriate to the needs of a particular purchaser: one for instance is:

$$\frac{60\ (\text{number of batches accepted})}{\text{number of batches delivered}} + \frac{40\ (\text{number of parts accepted})}{\text{number of parts delivered}}$$

The delivery measure is again based on goods-received records and is essentially the proportion of goods delivered on time. Since the meaning of 'on time' may not be the same in a large-scale mass producer (within ten minutes of the due hour and date?) and a small-scale batch producer (within two weeks of due date?), rules are specified to suit purchasing needs.

The price rating may be based on a comparison of the price quoted by the supplier in question with that quoted by competitors: the lowest price would score 100, and a price twice as high as the lowest would score 50 in one scheme. Often such a comparison is not feasible, and the price rating is based on a comparison of latest price with standard budget price, or last year's price, or latest target price.

It is not particularly difficult to calculate these ratings manually, since the system will be applied only to a minority of purchases from a relatively small number of suppliers, but computer salesmen have made much of the system as a further argument for extending the application of computers.

In most systems, after calculating individual numerical scores for the supplier characteristics being measured, a further calculation is made by weighting and combining the individual scores to arrive at an overall figure which is regarded as an index of the supplier's total performance – in fact a vendor rating or supplier evaluation figure which can be used in deciding how to allocate business between potential suppliers and also in persuading delinquent suppliers to improve their performance!

Such systems are considered in more detail in purchasing textbooks, and in books about industrial marketing, but it must be admitted that recent accounts in books which have a practical rather than a strictly academic bias are somewhat less than enthusiastic about their use in practice and tend to stress their limitations. See for instance Baily (1978) and Baily and Farmer (1981).

THE CONTRACT STAGE

A contract is a business agreement for the supply of goods or the performance of work in return for a price, and subject usually to a number of terms and conditions. An order on the other hand is an instruction to a trader or manufacturer to supply something.

In most cases both order and contract are incorporated in a single document, the purchase order form. Normal practice is to make it a rule that all purchases, subject to certain clearly defined exceptions, must be made by means of the official purchase order form. This is for practical rather than legal reasons. The purpose of the rule is to prevent sharp practice, whether by some unscrupulous employee or by some shady dealer outside the organisation, and also to establish clearly what the organisation is committed to accept and pay for. Regular suppliers are made aware of the rule by printing it on the order form, or by stipulating that the order number must be quoted on advice notes and invoices. Goods-receiving personnel can then be given instructions not to accept goods which are delivered without an official order number.

Exceptions to this procedure take several forms. The contract, or agreement with the supplier, may cover the supply of aggregated requirements over a considerable period of time, or over a large geographical area as when corporate contracts are signed by headquarters staff for common requirements at a number of divisions or branches. If such a contract is placed on the standard purchase order form it might cause some confusion if the same form is also used for instructions to supply specific quantities of goods against the contract to specific locations.

Three solutions have been observed in practice. First, a special form is used for the contract document, and normal purchase orders are used to order goods against it. Second, the normal purchase order form is used for the contract, and special forms are used for the orders; these may be known as delivery schedules, delivery instructions, contract releases, or call-offs. Third, the same form is used both for order and contract, and care is taken to state on one: 'This is an order against contract', and on the other: 'This is a contract against which goods should not be delivered until orders are placed.'

Most organisations use a preprinted multipart set of forms for purchase orders. Four or five copies are usually provided, and these are distributed to supplier, goods receiving, possibly accounts, possibly originator (department which produced the requisition), to purchase order open file, and possibly to order progress file.

Some large organisations have adopted computer-output order forms, which in the recent past appear to have largely failed to live up to expectations. The clerical work was not reduced, the amount of paper was increased because each order was confined to one item from one supplier, the technology was costly, and so on. But it is likely that such developments as communicating word processors, computer-to-computer links either via telex or telephone connection or several other methods currently being developed, will alter the balance of economics and that the traditional method of typed order forms sent by letter post will gradually become less economic than the newer methods of electronic mail. (A review of the current position, rapidly changing as it is, may be found in the second edition of *Purchasing Systems and Records* mentioned at the end of the chapter under 'Further Reading'.)

Blanket orders or systems contracting methods are often used with considerable commercial advantage where it is possible to group together either numbers of different item requirements from one source, or else a sequence of requirements of one item over a substantial period of time, say, six months or a year. Instead of treating each order, or requisition, as an independent closed transaction, the idea is to look at the flow of requirements over a time and buy the flow. Instead of taking a bucket to the well every day, a waterpipe is laid on.

For example, a small or intermediate value purchase is carbon paper. Instead of placing a series of orders every months or so for the various sizes and grades required, with this technique once a year there is a review of requirements, alternative specifications and sources. Twelve months' requirements are then covered with just one or two orders which specify so many reams of A4 standard weight, so many reams of lightweight, etc., to be delivered each month. If stocks start to build up or fall short during the year, one or two adjustments may be required. Apart from that, supplies come through automatically; and the price, based on a twelve-month contract, is low.

A group one or two production purchase may not seem at first glance amenable to this approach if production programmes are not fixed twelve months in advance. There will usually be a sales forecast going at least a year ahead, and a firm production programme going only one or two months ahead.

The solution then may be to approach management to authorise purchasing to make firm commitments for 50 per cent of the sales estimate for the year, thus getting the benefit of a lower price and also the benefit of a bank stock of finished parts to handle cyclical fluctuations. In one actual case, component X was being bought in lots of 1000 approximately at a price of 26p a piece. It was built into a product with a current sales estimate of 12 000 a year. Contracting for 50 per cent of this, that is 6000 pieces, with delivery called off at 1000 a month, enabled the buyers to bring the price down to 20p, a 23 per cent reduction in invoice cost, with further reductions in administrative costs and paperwork. Both cost and availability are improved, and if sales fall short of forecast, it may well take nine or twelve months instead of six months to clear the components but they would still be used up within the year. This is a useful technique for plastic mouldings, castings, electrical and mechanical parts.

SMALL ORDER PROCEDURES

Wherever possible the small orders should be put through a special procedure. If they are repeating or regular requirements they should be bought once a year in one lot, or perhaps twice a year: it is obviously uneconomic to expend £15 worth of man-hours, cheques, stamps and paperwork in procuring an item with a usage value of only £15 a year, but it happens. Non-repeating small orders are often such things as maintenance requirements, design and development prototypes, laboratory requirements. The requisitioner knows exactly what he wants and where to get it and the price is often a listed price. One solution to this problem is the order/requisition/cheque form devised by Kaiser Aluminium in the United States, and adopted by other organisations, including one in the public service. Through clever forms design, the same document which the requisitioner prepares as a requisition serves as an order, and a blank cheque accompanying it (marked 'not valid above £X') cuts out the invoicing/purchase-ledger/payments procedure.

Other approaches to the small order problem include: local cash purchase – a man with a bag of cash goes round in a van picking up requirements and paying for them as he goes; and laundry list – the local stockholder calls once a week and delivers a wide range of sundry materials against a laundry list type of order: invoices come through once a month and prices are negotiated annually.

THE COMPLETION STAGE

Contracts (or orders) are completed when goods are delivered or work is done in accordance with the agreement and payment is made as provided.

Obtaining delivery on time can be a difficult problem: the sub-contract and component supply section of the engineering industries have got themselves a bad name for late delivery, although large numbers of purchasers throughout industry and commerce have few problems in this connection and would rightly regard late delivery as an exceptional event, to be dealt with by crisis measures when it occurs.

The fundamental step in obtaining delivery on time is to decide accurately and firmly exactly what is wanted at what time, to communicate this decision to those concerned, and to insist that delivery is made at the time specified. All too often firms which complain of late deliveries by suppliers are themselves to blame for inaccurate delivery schedules, continually amended. When both customer and supplier are struggling to operate with production planning and control systems which are defective in practice and misconceived in principle it is astonishing that anything is ever delivered on time, yet this has been the situation in certain sections of the engineering industry. Materials-requirement planning systems, if property designed and operated, have brought great improvements in this connection to manufacturers of complex products.

The next step is to ensure that suppliers know that on-time delivery is a very important element in their marketing mix: in the combination of characteristics which results in their customers doing business with them. If valid due dates are stipulated it becomes easy to measure supplier performance in meeting due dates, and delivery performance tends to improve significantly once it is measured and reported. Customers with accurate, stable and reliable schedules of delivery requirements, who insist on delivery at the time scheduled, and measure and report supplier delivery performance, are on the whole quite satisfied with the results they get. In many cases it has been shown that 99 per cent on-time delivery is normal when suppliers know and are fully aware that the schedule is accurate and that every time they fail to meet the schedule they are going to have to explain it to their customers. Nevertheless, progressing (chasing, expediting or follow-up) of orders remains necessary in many cases. This may be done:

1 At the date when tool or jig designs are to be ready
2 When the items from these designs should be available
3 When materials or components should be marshalled for production
4 When the various stages of production can be achieved
5 When final assembly and testing will be completed.

Often critical areas may be isolated in this progressing for special attention. For example, special castings with long delivery times could be delivered to suppliers and then be rejected because of their porosity. In consequence, some companies extend their progressing activities in such cases to include secondary suppliers.

Methods which can be applied to help ensure that more general orders are controlled – chased when they ought to be – include:

1 Copy orders filed in date-due order, being actioned, say, one week before that due date in general, or as necessary in the particular case.
2 Five divisions made at the top of the copy order numbered one to five (representing weeks in any month). A signal of a different colour is then allocated to each month and one is attached to the relevant square in the particular case. (Thus if January were red and the item were due in week three of that month, a red signal would be placed on square three.) The order copies are then filed in alphabetical order by supplier.
3 A diary system with the serial numbers of orders which are due being entered on the appropriate page of the diary.

It is often useful to provide space on the order form to record the date of progress action, reply, etc., as shown in Figure 15.5.

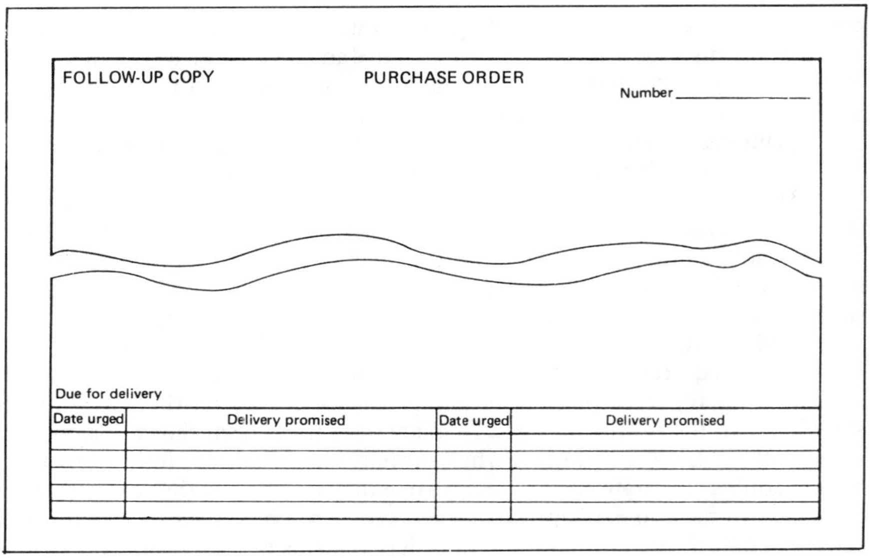
FOLLOW-UP COPY PURCHASE ORDER

Number ____________

Due for delivery

Date urged	Delivery promised	Date urged	Delivery promised

Figure 15.5 Follow-up copy of purchase order

Finally, the supplier dispatches the goods to the customer, usually including a packing note and copy advice note with the goods and also forwarding an advice note by post. The postal copy is passed to the purchasing section to note that goods are in transit and the same morning is passed on to the goods-receiving section. Each day the goods-receiving section check through their file of advice notes and if any goods appear to have been lost or delayed in transit they initiate appropriate action. When goods are actually delivered, a goods-received note is prepared, usually on a multipart form to notify purchasing, accounting, and originating sections of the delivery.

REFERENCES AND FURTHER READING

Baily, P., *Purchasing & Supply Management*, 4th edition, Chapman & Hall, London, 1978

Baily, P., and Farmer, D.H., *Purchasing Principles & Management*, Pitman London, 1981

Baily, P., *Purchasing Systems and Records*, 2nd edition, Gower, 1983

PART FOUR

PRODUCTION MANAGEMENT

16 Planning for production

J Mapes and C C New

Production management is concerned with managing the physical resources necessary to create products in sufficient quantities to meet market requirements. In manufacturing organisations the majority of the workforce and a very high proportion of the total capital investment expenditure will be devoted to the production function. Efficient production management is therefore absolutely critical to the success of such organisations.

Although production management is most closely associated with the manufacturing sector, the techniques of production management are increasingly being applied in service and non-manufacturing organisations. Because of this the modern definition of a production system has been broadened to cover systems for the creation of both manufactured items and services. The problems are very similar for both manufacturing organisations and service organisations. One of the main differences is that the 'product' of service organisations is highly perishable and must be consumed immediately.

While the primary emphasis in this chapter will be on manufacturing organisations, most of the techniques discussed are equally applicable to service organisations like banks, hospitals and public utilities.

THE PRODUCTION MANAGEMENT TASK

The production management task can be divided into two main areas. First, there is the design of the production system. This will involve decisions regarding the performance requirements and desired output levels of the production system. Then decisions will need to be made about the number of production facilities which will be required and their location, the methods of production to be used and the management control procedures to be introduced.

Second, there is the task of operating the production system in order to meet the specified performance requirements. This will include production scheduling and control, inventory management and quality control.

THE PLANNING OF PRODUCTION

The planning of production in an organisation can therefore be considered at two levels, strategic and tactical. Strategic planning is concerned with the design of the production system. Tactical planning is concerned with the running of the operating system. Figure 16.1 shows the kind of planning decisions which have to be taken in production and their relative time horizons.

Strategic	Long-term	2 years +	Introduction of new products Number and location of facilities Type of technology to be used
	Medium-term	1–2 years	Relative mix of products Changes in capacity
Tactical	Medium term	1 year	Size of workforce Subcontracting Overtime working Stockholding policy
	Short-term	3 months	Production schedule Output targets

Figure 16.1 ***Time-scale for planning decisions***

Strategic level decisions

At the strategic level decisions will be required regarding:

The product range

While this is primarily a marketing decision the production capabilities of the organisation together with any limitations on production capacity must also be taken into account.

Product design

By taking into account production implications at the design stage substantial reductions in manufacturing costs and processing time can be achieved.

Selection of processing methods, plant and equipment

Usually there are several alternative methods of manufacturing the product, each being the most appropriate for a particular output range. The choice will depend on the trade-off between capital cost, operating costs and performance requirements.

Plant location

The number of plants, the capacity of each plant and the location of each plant must be decided. This will be influenced by the transport costs for raw materials and finished goods, availability of labour, delivery performance requirements and economics of scale.

Plant layout

Within each plant the number of departments and their relative location must be decided. Within each department the location of machines, storage areas and support facilities must be decided in order to simplify movement and handling of materials between operations.

Planning and control systems

An important part of the design of a production system is the development of procedures for planning and controlling the production process.

Decisions at the tactical level

At the tactical level decisions will need to be taken regarding:

Production control

This covers the detailed scheduling of operations, allocation of jobs to machines and monitoring of actual against planned production. The aim should be to produce a schedule which is practicable and also meets performance objectives in terms of operating costs and delivery.

Stock control

In order to ensure acceptable delivery times nearly all organisations have to carry some stocks of raw materials, sub-assemblies or finished products. For each item held in stock decisions must be made about when to replenish stocks and what the replenishment quantity should be.

Quality control

The quality specification will be set at the design stage. The operational task is to ensure that, as far as possible, all items which leave the factory meet this specification. Decisions must be taken on methods of inspection, on when a batch of items should be rejected or re-worked and on when machines should be reset.

Maintenance

The servicing, repair and replacement of equipment is an essential part of ensuring optimum operating effectiveness. Decisions must be taken regarding the frequency of equipment overhaul, the scheduling of maintenance work and the frequency of equipment replacement.

Labour control

Labour costs are an important part of total production costs. In many industries labour costs are the main component of production costs. In order to exercise effective control the work content of each task must be determined. This enables realistic work scheduling and monitoring of actual against planned performance to be carried out.

While the relative importance of these decision areas will vary for different industries and different companies every organisation will need to give some attention to each of the areas mentioned.

STRATEGIC PLANNING

Clearly strategic planning of production can only take place within the context of the overall corporate planning process. Traditionally the strategic task for the production function has been seen as the design of a production system capable of meeting the requirements of the marketing strategic plan. This is likely to lead to insufficient account being taken of the production implications of alternative strategies at the corporate planning stage. This frequently results in conflicting demands being placed on production which are impossible to resolve. Naturally the marketing department wish to provide as good a service as possible to the customer. As a consequence they may require production to manufacture special products to customer specifications using the same production facilities as standard products with no increase in production lead-times. Alternatively they may ask for immediate availability of all products while insisting that the increased stockholding costs incurred cannot be passed on to the customer.

In order to develop a strategic plan which adequately reflects both market requirements and production capabilities then the production function must play an integral part in the process of strategy formation.

An essential first step must be to gain a clear understanding of the performance measures leading to success in the market-place. Figure 16.2 lists the most common criteria for success. While most organisations would ideally like to meet all of these criteria this is not possible as many of the criteria are in conflict. In order to achieve short lead-times, then increased costs will be incurred leading to increased prices. If quality is an important criterion then it is unlikely that very short lead-times can be achieved.

Of course the key criteria may be different for different product groups provided separate production facilities are used. Problems only arise when the same production facility is required to satisfy different criteria for two product groups at the same time. Setting priorities can be almost impossible if, for example, one group of orders must be completed at minimum cost (implying high levels of machine utilisation) while another group of orders must be completed as rapidly as possible (implying low levels of machine utilisation).

Once the tasks which are vital to corporate success have been identified then a production capability analysis should be carried out. The main purpose of the analysis is to assess whether the organisation is likely to be able to meet the

1 Short lead-times

2 Lead-time reliability

3 Quality

4 Ability to alter specification at short notice

5 Ability to adjust volume at short notice

6 Price

Figure 16.2 Requirements for market success

performance requirements of the market with currently available resources.

If there is a mismatch between the capabilities of the existing production system and market requirements then either the production system must be modified or the strategy must be altered. Otherwise the consequences can be extremely serious. When the Babcock and Wilcox Corporation in the United States tried to enter the nuclear pressure vessel business they encountered very severe problems. They had considerable expertise in the manufacture of steam pressure vessels where the requirement was for a standard product with a short, reliable lead-time, sold at a competitive price. The nuclear power industry required absolute product reliability and reliable delivery but the length of the lead-time and the price were relatively unimportant. Also the large size of nuclear pressure vessels, coupled with the fact that each vessel was a special item fabricated to a very precise customer specification meant that manufacturing methods suited to steam pressure vessels were quite unsuitable for nuclear pressure vessels. Consequently, during the first three years of operation only three pressure vessels were completed instead of the twenty which were scheduled. Eventually the two main contractors transferred fourteen part-completed pressure vessels from Babcock and Wilcox to competing organisations. Between 1967 and 1969 company profits fell from $33m to £5m.

Once the production capability analysis has been completed then decisions will need to be made on the following main components of the manufacturing structure:

Plant and equipment technology

This covers the processing methods to be used, the choice of equipment and the level of automation.

Production systems

These define the procedures for detailed planning and control of production and the performance standards to be met.

Personnel policies

These specify policies on the degree of job specialisation, payment systems to be employed and the type of work group organisation to be adopted.

Product design

This is concerned with those aspects of product design which simplify manufacture and reduce production costs.

Organisation and management

This specifies the organisational structure adopted within the production function and the allocation of responsibilities between staff.

FORECASTING DEMAND

An essential requirement for the planning of production is a forecast of demand for each product. For each forecast an indication of the likely forecasting error should be provided. For forecasts with a high expected error contingency plans can then be made to cope with the occasions when actual demand is much higher or lower than the forecasts.

Forecasting techniques tend to be classified into short-term, medium-term and long-term depending on the underlying assumptions which have been made. In short-term forecasting it is assumed that the underlying trend is linear and stable with changes in external factors having little effect on demand. This enables very simple extrapolative techniques to be used. However, the assumptions are only likely to be valid when forecasting just a few months ahead. The simplest method of short-term forecasting is to use moving averages to identify the underlying trend line and then to project the trend line forward. Figure 16.3 shows the results obtained using a five-period moving average.

Increasingly, however, simple moving averages of this kind are being replaced by weighted moving averages in which the greatest weighting is given to the most recent data. The most popular technique of this kind is called exponential smoothing. This involves updating the moving average each period using the following calculation.

$$\text{new moving average} = a \times \text{sales for this period} + (1-a) \times \text{moving average for previous period}$$

a is called the smoothing constant and is normally given a value between 0.1 and

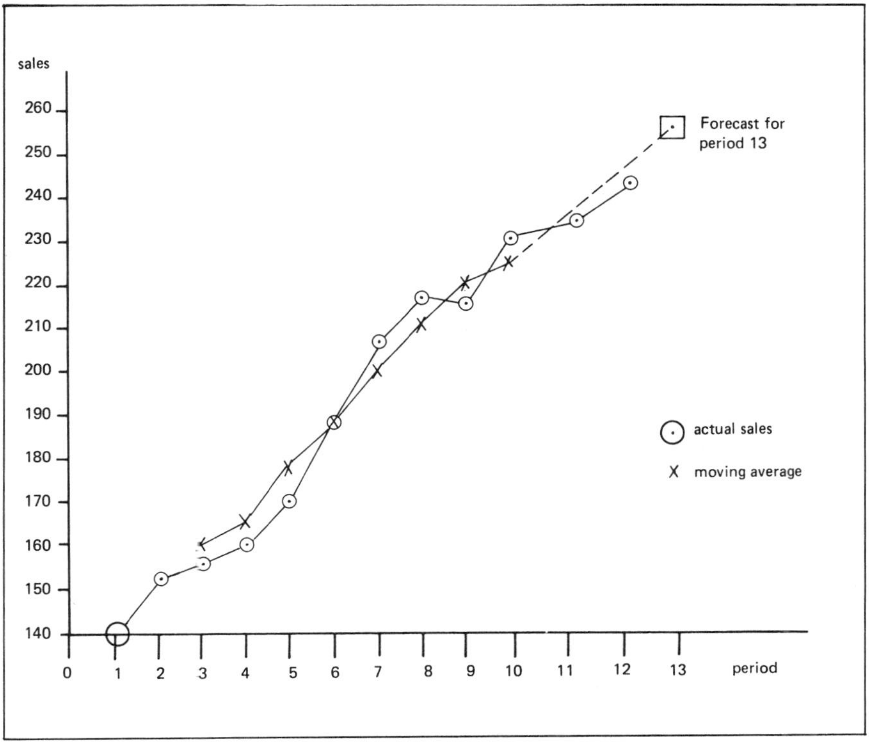

Figure 16.3 Forecast based on a 5-period moving average

0.3. Forecasts based on exponential smoothing tend to be more accurate than forecasts based on a simple moving average, particularly when there are frequent fluctuations in the trend. Figure 16.4 shows the results of using exponential smoothing for short-term forecasting when there are marked short-term fluctuations in sales.

Medium-term forecasting techniques are based on the assumption that the underlying trend follows a regular curve. The most commonly used approach is to fit a curve of the appropriate type to the data and then to project the curve forward to obtain the forecast.

In long-term forecasting it is recognised that external factors will have a considerable effect on the forecast. The emphasis is therefore placed on establishing the quantitative relationship between demand and those factors which influence demand, using the techniques of regression analysis. This enables an equation to be developed which can then be used to forecast demand.

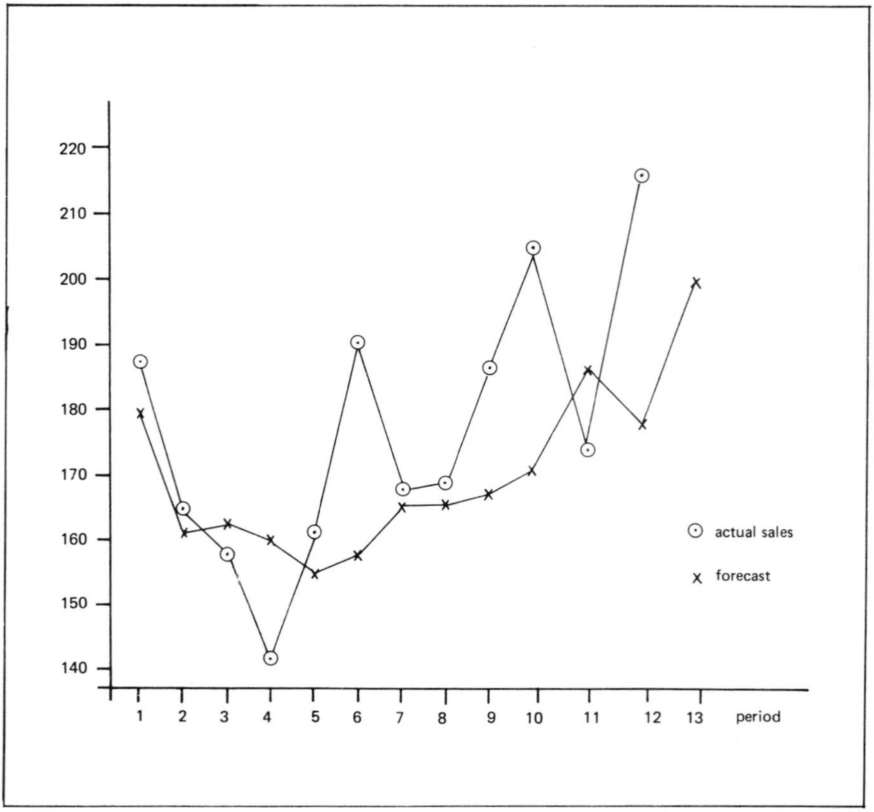

Figure 16.4 Forecast based on exponential smoothing

THE MAKE OR BUY DECISION

One very important part of the strategic planning process is the decision regarding which items are to be manufactured and which items are to be bought in. This decision will be taken primarily on financial grounds but there are other factors which should also be taken into account. Purchase of items gives greater flexibility if large fluctuations in demand occur. It also allows access to specialist skills and economies of scale which may not be available internally. On the other hand manufacture gives greater control over quality and delivery dates.

For most items a change from manufacturing to purchase or vice versa would involve such a major change to the nature of the company that it would not be acceptable on policy grounds. However, there will be a number of items which could either be manufactured or purchased depending on which involves the lowest cost.

When making cost comparisons it is important that only incremental costs are taken into account. Any costs which will be unaltered by a switch between manufacturing and purchasing should be ignored.

In practice the decision is very dependent on current utilisation of internal resources. Manufacturing will nearly always be more attractive if labour and equipment would otherwise be under-utilised. On the other hand buying-in is likely to be preferable if the decision to manufacture the item will involve substantial capital investment and the recruitment of labour. Purchasing will be particularly attractive if there is a possibility of a fall-off in the future level of requirements for the item in the long term.

PREPARING AN OPERATING PLAN

Once demand for each product has been forecast, and it has been decided which items will be manufactured and which will be purchased, then an operating plan must be devised aimed at ensuring that the company's marketing objectives are met.

In order to predict delivery periods and decide on stockholding policy a production stage chart should be constructed. This is a diagrammatic representation of all the stages in the production process including supplier delivery periods, product design and final dispatch to the customer. Estimates of the time to complete each stage are included so that the delivery time can be assessed. An outline of a production stage chart for a pigment is shown in Figure 16.5.

If the delivery time is likely to be acceptable to customers then the organisation can operate as a make-to-order company, only carrying out work on firm customer orders. Usually, however, the delivery time will be unacceptable and it will be necessary to carry out some stages in the chart in advance of customer orders. In some cases it will only be necessary to pre-order raw materials and hold stocks based on forecasts of future usage. In other cases, where customers require very short lead-times, stocks of the finished product will need to be held so that new orders can be met immediately from stock.

The next step should be to decide whether the forecast demand can be satisfied and the desired lead-times met with currently available capacity. In order to estimate capacity requirements then current capacity and forecast demand need to be expressed in the same units, for example, litres of paint or numbers of electric motors. However, with a varied range of products there will be no common physical unit of capacity and so forecast demand will need to be converted into standard hours of manufacturing time.

If average weekly demand exceeds average weekly capacity then a decision must be taken on whether capacity should be increased. This decision is likely to be influenced by the following factors.

1 Long-term forecasts of changes in market size and market share
2 The expected return on the capital investment required
3 Possible future innovations in the product or the production process.

Activity	Weeks
Purchase raw materials	1 2
Manufacture intermediates	3 4
Manufacture base pigments	5
Standardise	6
Blend final product and test	7
Dispatch	8

Figure 16.5 Production stage chart for pigment manufacture

If it is decided that an increase in capacity cannot be justified then one or more of the following alternatives can be considered.

1 Increase the number of purchased or subcontracted items
2 Use overtime or shift working to increase effective capacity
3 Eliminate items with low profit margins from the product range releasing capacity for more profitable product lines.

Aggregate planning

The analysis described above should ensure a reasonable match between capacity and demand on an annual basis. In addition there will be the need to cope with variations in demand over the year. These may be due to seasonal variations, changing economic conditions or random fluctuations in orders from week to week. A company which has sufficient capacity to meet average demand will find that there are periods during the year when demand is appreciably above average. As a consequence either sales will be lost or delivery periods will become unacceptably long. On the other hand, if capacity is based on peak demand then the utilisation of labour and equipment will be low during periods of below average demand.

Aggregate planning is an attempt to schedule production over a six- to twelve-month period taking into account forecast variations in demand. The following methods of handling fluctuations in demand can be considered.

1 Vary the number of hours worked each week by the use of overtime or additional shifts during periods of peak demand

2 Vary the size of the workforce by recruiting casual workers during peak periods
3 Use spare capacity during periods of low demand to build up stocks of finished goods for use during periods of above average demand
4 Increase the amount of sub-contracted work during periods of high demand.

Each alternative will cause substantial additional costs to be incurred. The use of overtime or sub-contracting involves premium charges relative to the cost of manufacturing internally during normal working hours. Changes in the size of the workforce involve recruitment and lay-off costs. Stock building involves high stockholding and obsolescence costs. The optimum solution will be the combination of these alternatives which minimises total costs. A number of techniques for aggregate planning have been developed. The main approaches are outlined below.

The linear decision rule

This technique for obtaining a minimum-cost solution to the above problem was developed by Holt, Modigliani, Muth and Simon. The approach takes account of normal time and overtime labour rates, recruitment and lay-off costs, inventory holding, back ordering and machine set-up costs. These are used to derive two linear decision rules for computing the workforce levels and production rate for each period taking into account forecasts of sales for each period over a specified planning horizon.

This approach provides an optimum solution and is easy to apply once the two decision rules have been derived. However, the assumptions on cost structure may provide a poor approximation to reality. Also there are no restrictions on the size of the workforce, the hours of overtime worked or the number of units held in inventory, so the solution generated by this technique may be impractical.

Linear programming

The Simplex method of linear programming takes the same cost data as the linear decision rule approach and also generates a minimum cost solution giving workforce size and production rate period by period. An advantage over the linear decision rule method is that capacity constraints can be incorporated into the model. A major limitation of linear programming is that all constraints and cost functions must be linear. This will be unrealistic whenever economies of scale exist. A further limitation is that only a single objective can be optimised at a time whereas aggregate planning is usually concerned with satisfying a number of conflicting objectives simultaneously.

Goal programming is an extension of linear programming which to some extent overcomes the problem of being limited to a single objective. A set of management goals is specified and a solution is generated which is as close to this set of goals as possible.

Search decision rule

This is an iterative procedure which starts with an initial solution and determines the overall cost of this solution. The procedure then searches for an alternative solution with lower costs. This continues until a solution is reached for which further alteration would not yield significant cost reductions. Unlike the first two procedures this does not yield a mathematical optimum solution. In other words it yields a good but not necessarily minimum-cost solution. However it has the advantages of being less complicated and requiring less computation.

Management coefficients method

This is a method developed by Bowman in which management's past planning decisions are analysed statistically to determine the decision criteria which were used. A set of decision equations are then derived in which the numerical coefficients are based on this statistical analysis. These decision equations can then be used to prepare future schedules using the same criteria. This should result in an improvement in performance due to the criteria being applied more consistently.

Parametric production planning

This is a technique suggested by Jones which uses a search procedure to quantify four parameters associated with minimum cost in aggregate planning. The four parameters are then inserted into equations which are used to determine workforce size and production rate for each period. The method involves no constraints imposed by the mathematical structure of the model and the parameters and equations are specific to the company. While the method is non-optimising it is claimed to produce very good results.

A performance comparison of the alternative aggregate planning procedures

Lee and Khumawala carried out a comparative study of alternative aggregate planning procedures in a company manufacturing capital goods. The aggregate planning procedures evaluated were the linear decision rule, the search decision rule, the management coefficients method and parametric production planning. The application of these procedures was simulated and the profit performance achieved compared with the actual performance of the company. All of the planning methods yielded better profits than the company's own planning procedures. The greatest improvement (14 per cent) was achieved using the search decision rule.

Tactical planning

Once the aggregate plan has been prepared all of the key policy decisions will have been made. The next step is to prepare a detailed operating plan. This will involve a series of tactical decisions regarding;

1 the operations necessary for the manufacture of each product or order and their sequence
2 allocation of jobs to facilities
3 scheduling the start and finish times of each operation.

These tasks are more appropriately dealt with as part of production control.

FURTHER READING

Bowman, E. H., 'Consistency and Optimality in Managerial Decision Making', *Management Science* 9, January 1963. This article provides a detailed description of the management coefficients method of aggregate planning.

Buffa, E.S., *Modern Production Management*, 5th edition, Wiley, New York, 1977. An excellent and comprehensive coverage of the techniques of production management.

Constable, C. J., and New, C. C., *Operations Management*, Wiley, New York, 1976. A good general introduction to production management with particular emphasis on the strategic aspects.

Holt, C. C., Modigliani, F., and Muth, J. F., *Planning Production, Inventories and Workforce*, Prentice-Hall, Englewood Cliffs, 1960. Covers all aspects of aggregate planning with particular emphasis on the linear decision rule method.

Jones, C. H., 'Parametric Production Planning', *Management Science* 13, July 1967. This article describes the parametric production planning technique for aggregate planning.

Lee, W. B., and Khumawala, B. M., 'Simulation Testing of Aggregate Production Planning models in an Implementation Methodology', *Management Science* 20, Feb. 1974. This article describes the comparison of alternative aggregate planning techniques referred to in the text.

Skinner, W., 'Manufacturing—Missing Link in Corporate Strategy', *Harvard Business Review*, May–June 1974. This article discusses how top management can take a more active role in the formation of manufacturing strategy.

Taubert, W. H., 'Search Decision Rule for the Aggregate Scheduling Problem', *Management Science* 14, Feb. 1968. This article describes the search decision rule for aggregate planning.

Twiss, B. C., 'Developing and Implementing Strategy For Production', *Long Range Planning*, April 1974. This article provides a framework for the strategic planning of production.

Wheelwright, S. C. and Makridakis, S., *Forecasting Methods for Management*, Wiley, New York, 1973. A useful handbook for all managers involved in preparing or using forecasts.

17 Production control

Peter Jackson

Production control is concerned with producing goods in the right sequence in the least time at the lowest cost. As such it is a balancing act between contradictions. Good production control involves compromises and best fits rather than theoretical ideals. The main aspects are:

1 Loading and scheduling work
2 Provisioning material, parts and production aids
3 Monitoring and progressing work
4 Producing management information enabling the total system to be controlled.

DIFFERENCES BETWEEN SYSTEMS

Every company will have a different system depending on its products and production facilities. Some relevant factors are:

Complexity of the product

Single-operation plastic mouldings are much easier to control than components going through any combination of up to twenty operations. This is especially true if assembly of components is included.

Length of cycle time

If a job stays on a machine for a fortnight it is much easier to replan than if each operation takes only a few hours.

Repeatability of the work

Regular jobs will have predictable cycle times. The production facilities they require, such as tooling, will be known and available. One-off jobs are not so easy to control.

Forward notice available

Some companies know every job they will do for a year ahead and can plan accordingly. Others do not, or claim they do not, know a week ahead what orders will be required.

Dependence on outside suppliers and subcontractors

Where control is not completely within the company greater allowance must be made for slippage.

Seasonal nature of the workload

Where seasonal peak loads occur capacity utilisation will obviously vary.

Availability and quality of information on capacity and workload

Companies which have detailed time standards, process layouts and up-to-date capacities can load to a fuller degree and schedule to a tighter time-scale than those which have to rely on rough estimates.

Despite all these differences companies with a wide range of products and production facilities have similar problems and have developed similar solutions.

LOADING AND SCHEDULING WORK

Loading is filling available capacity with sufficient jobs in a given time period. Scheduling is determining the desired sequence of jobs. The two are interrelated and in some procedures may be indistinguishable. When work is correctly loaded and scheduled full use can be made of capacity, completion times can be predicted and met and urgent jobs can be given priority without upsetting the rest of the work.

Stages

Loading and scheduling will probably be done in several stages from the overall factory planning when a new order is received to the detailed plan for each machine in the period immediately before production. The mechanics are similar at each stage. When the order is accepted little detail may be known of the work load involved or of the machine capacity available in the proposed production period, yet some estimates must be made to enable delivery dates to be quoted. Such forward loading is done on an overall basis using broad measures.

As the time for producing the order draws near the drawings, parts lists and process paperwork will have been extracted enabling loads on each machine to be calculated. Also, nearer the production time available capacity can be more realistically assessed. This enables detailed short-term loading to be done.

Data required

Units

The basic need is a common unit in which both capacity and load can be expressed. The most common unit is time. Load can be measured by work study or estimation or historical information can be kept. The accuracy required of these time standards depends on the degree of repetition of the work. Often good estimates are sufficient provided they are on average right. Where times for individual components are used they must be multiplied by the batch size and an allowance for setting time included.

Capacity in terms of time is easily expressed in man- or machine-hours with suitable allowances for breakdowns, re-work and other contingencies.

Where times are not available a physical count may provide a suitable unit. Foundry output is often expressed in tonnes. A shoe factory may make so many pairs a day. A warehouse may process so many orders. Here the load is already defined, capacity is found from historical data.

A third measure of capacity and load is money. Orders are often considered in terms of their financial value and this may be a convenient way of loading a factory. An output of £10 000 per week may be a good measure of a factory's production. Again capacity is measured historically. Because of the nature of material and labour costs it is unusual to use money as a unit for detailed machine loading.

Load centre capacities

A load centre is the production unit to which jobs are allocated. It could be a factory, a section, a machine group or an individual machine or operator. With several stages of loading it could be all of these in turn. When it involves more than one machine either all work loaded to it should be capable of being done on any of its sub-units or the mix of work should on average match the mix of the sub-units.

Before breaking the load down to individual machines it should be considered whether the production control department are the best people to do this. The foreman or supervisor will have detailed knowledge of the capabilities of particular men and machines and be able to react to breakdowns and other immediate problems. It may, therefore, be realistic to load to machine groups leaving the final allocation to the man on the spot.

The capacity of the load centre is calculated in the appropriate units. Some capacity may be reserved for emergency work or special customers but this must be kept to a small proportion and revised regularly.

Processes

The sequence of operations, usually called the process layout, must be known if each operation is to be loaded separately.

Parts lists

Where assemblies are manufactured the parts list of each assembly and subassembly will be needed. The requirements for common parts need to be batched up. For some components it may be more economical to make for stock than make on a one for one basis for final assembly.

LOADING METHODS

There are two main methods: job sequence, in which each job is loaded in strict sequence against a time-scale, and control period where a list of jobs is planned for a defined time period but can be carried out in any sequence.

Job sequence loading

To load jobs in strict sequence against a time-scale requires some visual display such as a planning board. Such boards can be purchased ready made although a home-made version can often fit particular requirements better. The load centres are usually displayed along the left-hand edge with a time-scale along the bottom. Jobs are planned to load centres either by writing on the board with an erasable medium or inserting a card in a slot (see Figure 17.1).

This method is best used close to actual production for loading individual machines. It can only be used for forward planning where contracts cannot run simultaneously. An example of this would be forward planning ships on the slipways of a shipyard.

Machine	Hour beginning							
	08 00	09 00	10 00	11 00	12 30	13 30	14 30	15 30
Capstan lathe	1053	1053	1053	1154	1154	1154	1154	1154
Herbert lathe	1186	1186	1186	1186	1186	1701	1701	1701
Holbrook lathe	1188	1188	1188	1188	1188	1188	1790	1790
Jig borer	REPA	IR AN	D MAI	NTENA	NCE			
Universal miller	IDLE	IDLE	IDLE	IDLE	1185	1185	1185	1185
Horizontal miller	1081	1081	1081	1081	904	904	904	1225
Automatic—1	1300	1300	1300	1300	1300	1300	IDLE	IDLE
Automatic—2	IDLE	IDLE	IDLE	IDLE	IDLE	IDLE	IDLE	IDLE

***Figure 17.1** A job sequence loading chart*

This simple configuration is suitable for blackboard and chalk. The numbers in the squares are job numbers

Advantages of job sequence loading

1 Clear visual display of information
2 Full utilisation of capacity possible
3 Rapid throughput of jobs loaded on more than one load centre
4 Planning boards can be used for progressing.

Disadvantages of job sequence loading

1 Updating is difficult and time consuming
2 Only suitable for limited periods ahead because of the likelihood of the situation changing
3 Relies on precise measurement of load
4 Cannot cope with overall allowances for reduction of capacity. For example, 10 per cent allowance for breakdowns.

Control period loading

A list of jobs is produced for each load centre for a fixed period of time, the control period. The total load of these jobs equals the capacity of the centre. For example, a machine group of two lathes each worked 40 hours a week has a capacity of 80 hours if the chosen control period is a week. A list is produced of jobs for these machines up to a total of 80 hours. Any further work is loaded into the following week.

The list becomes the programme for that load centre for that period. Jobs can be done in any sequence on any machine in the centre, provided they are finished by the end of the control period.

Multi-operational jobs are programmed at one operation per control period resulting in all jobs going through at an equal pace. The completion time of each job can be predicted.

The choice of control period depends on the length of the jobs and the sophistication of the production control system. Setting a target of one operation per week may not be very ambitious but may compare favourably with what was achieved without a loading system. It is better to start with a long control period and shorten it when experience has been gained rather than start with an unrealistically short one.

Control period loading is used in long-term planning where the overall work load can be compared with the overall capacity; for example, accepting orders up to £10 000 value a month. It is also used for short-term planning on groups of machines. This allows supervision flexibility to allocate particular jobs to individual machines or operators.

Advantages of control period loading

1 Simple to operate
2 Not dependent on completion of every job. Late jobs can be caught up without upsetting the programme

3 Allows supervision discretion in allocating jobs to particular operators or machines
4 Enables forward load picture to be produced over a reasonable period.

Disadvantages of control period loading

1 Overall throughput time is slow compared to job sequence loading, although much quicker than if no planning is used at all
2 Work in progress is higher than for job sequence loading.

Forward and backward loading

Using either job sequence or control period loading it is usual to start at the present time and load jobs in the earliest available capacity, slowly building up a forward load picture. This is known as forward loading.

It is, however, possible to fix a completion date a number of weeks in advance and load backwards from this date thus arriving at a date when the job must start. This is called backward loading.

Assuming that delivery dates have been set realistically, backward loading ensures that jobs are not started needlessly early. If all jobs are loaded in this way capacity may well be exceeded as one of the main reasons for loading is to set achievable delivery dates. It may help to backward load a certain proportion of jobs, key ones whose delivery dates are important, and then fill in the remaining capacity by forward loading the less urgent jobs.

PROVISIONING

Provisioning is ensuring that everything required is available when production is scheduled to start. This includes drawings, tools and gauges as well as parts and material. Such aids can hold up production just as much as material shortages and lack of them is often harder to put right.

Make or buy

Preliminary decisions must be taken on whether the part is to be made in-house or bought out or part sub-contracted.

Factors affecting the decision are:

Available capacity

This may fluctuate changing the decision.

Available skills and technology

Outside firms may specialise in certain processes.

Volume required

Normally a firm would not make its own nuts and bolts but if it used millions then it would.

Available lead-times

Much tighter control can be exercised over internal manufacture.

Where external suppliers or sub-contractors are used it is vital to obtain commitment to delivery dates. Progressing is best done by personal visits. In any case it is wise to build in latitude in the lead-times of externally sourced parts. Rating of suppliers on delivery is obviously worth while but cannot guard against every contingency.

Quantities

Certain items will be made on a one-for-one basis according to sales demand with perhaps a small allowance for scrap or spares. A few items may be made continuously throughout the year. The majority of items are made in batches. The size of the batch can be determined in two ways. Economic batch sizes can be calculated to available standard formulae. Where a batch is manufactured internally the setting cost replaces the order cost in the formula.

An alternative is to make regular batches to return the stock to a desired level. These batches will vary in size but enable the factory to be programmed on a regular repetitive basis. For example, using the Pareto stock classification, A items might be made once a month, B items once a quarter and C items once a year.

In fact the mathematics of both methods are not dissimilar. If batches are made regularly the average stockholding is slightly higher than if economic batches are made when a re-order level is breached.

Kitting and pre-allocation

Before a job is issued to the shop floor it should be established that all things needed for its production are available. It should not be the job of a skilled operator to queue for drawings, tools and gauges before he starts work. Even less should he have to spend time searching on the section for missing items. All such production aids should be collected by stores staff before a job is issued. Where a job is repeated a card can be kept recording everything required for the job.

Where assemblies are produced kitting problems are more apparent. Often a set of parts will be collected for issue and shortages found. Either the job is issued incomplete or it is held in stores where it may tie up parts which could be used elsewhere. Such parts may be removed from the kit, further complicating the problem.

In such situations a paperwork exercise can be carried out where all the components are checked for availability though not physically collected. This dummy kitting or pre-allocation means that if it is not feasible to issue Job A because of shortages it may be possible to issue Job B using some of the components from Job A.

If parts lists and stock levels are kept on computer and are up to date such pre-allocation can be done automatically and rapidly with obvious advantages.

MONITORING AND PROGRESSING

The aims of monitoring and progressing are to:

1 Highlight jobs running late
2 Assist such jobs to catch up
3 Anticipate problems further down the production cycle that late jobs would cause
4 Enable customer enquiries to be answered.

The first principle is to progress by exception. Collecting a vast amount of information about jobs which are running to time may give people a feeling of achievement but does little real good.

The second principle is that information must be up to date. Elaborate computer runs analysing where jobs were three days ago may be ignored in favour of a physical search of the section.

Monitoring

The simplest way of monitoring the position of jobs is to utilise the work booking system. At the end of each operation the completed job card is used to update a master progress record which is held in the production control office. Problems may arise where booking is not done immediately at the completion of a job.

A similar system is to have a set of tear-off tickets attached to each job. As the job passed a control point the appropriate section of the ticket is detached and sent to update the master progress record.

Increasingly the completion of jobs is being recorded on data collection devices linked to computers. These can be on the shop floor beside the machines and can given an extremely rapid update of the production situation.

Progressing

When the current state has been monitored action has to be taken. As a job running late in its initial stages can cause problems all the way down the line progress meetings are often held for all those involved. Provided such meetings are kept short and involve more than marking up lists they can be valuable.

Progress men are often used firstly to monitor the state of jobs and secondly to urge priority jobs. Again if this is largely marking lists it could be done better by a good clerical booking system. Progress men oil the wheels by putting urgent jobs at the front of the queue and arranging special transport between operations. However, sometimes their work can be self cancelling. In one engineering works there were fourteen progress men to one hundred machinists. Each of the five foremen could have up to fourteen people requesting that their job be done first.

Urgent jobs

It is common for urgent jobs to be given some distinguishing mark, a red label or a star for example. The trouble is that such labels multiply until 80 per cent of the jobs have red stars. Then someone gives the really urgent jobs two red stars and so the system escalates. Fifty urgent jobs are a contradiction in terms.

A strict upper limit, ten for example, should be placed on the number of urgent jobs. If another is required an existing one should be dropped from the list. To do this the person deciding the priorities should be senior enough to resist sectional pressures and see the overall picture. A shop floor supervisor can often be approached by many different people in the management structure each asking for different jobs to be given priority.

Long-term solutions

Although it is sensible to give a few urgent jobs an extra push, if late and rush jobs are a large and constant problem then the overall situation needs to be looked at. Are delivery dates being realistically set? Is there sufficient capacity? Could the effort spend chasing rush jobs be better spent improving the throughput time?

It may be possible to chase one job through the factory with it hardly touching the ground. What is not seen is the trail of delays and increased costs on other jobs that this action causes. Many customers will ask for jobs sooner than they need them because they know only priority jobs will be chased and the rest left to drift through.

One solution to the problem of conflicting priorities is to have each progress man responsible for all the throughput of one section. When operations are completed in this section the jobs become the responsibility of the progress man in the next section and so on. This is in contrast to the usual system where a progress man is responsible for all stages of a particular range of jobs. Sometimes there is a need for both types of progress but the balance must be held.

Where two or more divisions of a company share a common resource (for example, a machine shop), conflicts over capacity and priorities will often happen. Where possible such facilities should be split. If this cannot be done the capacity may need to be expanded over what might be theoretically required to allow for interference between the user departments.

MANAGEMENT CONTROL INFORMATION

A production control department processes vast amounts of information, levels of stock, states of orders, capacities available and so on. It should, therefore, be the source of the overview of production that higher management needs. Too often management will concentrate on solving particular problems using their authority to get things done. This may solve the particular issue but create a whole set of other problems and delays. It is management's job to look at the total picture, making decisions about capacity and load, leaving the day-to-day problems to those paid to cope with them.

The production control department can help by supplying regular information on relevant totals. The particular figures will vary but might include:

Order book

Forecast sales
Total orders received
Total orders dispatched
Total orders on hand

Customer service

Current average delivery times
Delivery promise achievements
Number of complaints

Factory performance

Total production
Programme achievement
Arrears
Forward load versus capacity

Stocks

Raw material
Work in progress
Finished goods

For most of these figures it would be difficult to set an ideal level though it is always good to aim for a target. The important thing is the direction in which the figures are going, improving, worsening or staying the same.

It may be necessary to break the total figures down into separate product lines. The temptation to produce lists of individual jobs for higher management should be avoided.

PAPERWORK

Production control departments produce a mass of paperwork, schedules, lists, tickets, progress records, computer printout. Over the years new systems may have been introduced partly duplicating existing ones. Records may be kept which are no longer required. Individuals produce and maintain their own systems.

It is possible to have a department called production control which produces a large amount of paper yet influences what happens on the shop floor hardly at all. It is said that when the weight of a ship being built exceeds the weight of paperwork required to build it then it is ready for launching.

Different production systems will require different paperwork but a typical outline is shown below.

Advanced warning

When an order is first received a document is raised to notify departments concerned. It will contain basic details of the order and the provisional delivery date quoted. An example is shown in Figure 17.2.

The receiving departments, typically industrial engineering, stock control and production, will confirm whether the provisional date can be accepted.

Job paperwork

Each job needs:

1. A loading/progress document which stays in the production control department and is used first to schedule the job and then to record its progress. It may well be a card which can be slotted into a planning board.
2. An identification label which goes round with the job (job ticket).
3. Instructions for the people doing each stage of the job.
4. Material or parts requisitions.
5. Paperwork for booking each stage of the job. This may be in the form of cards which are returned to the production control office showing date, time, scrap and the operator's name.

Examples of production control paperwork are given in Figures 17.3 and 17.4.

Schedules

Lists of jobs will be made of work to be done on a section in a given period. These may be in sequence or highlight jobs with a higher priority. These lists will also be used to progress the work.

Methods

Various ready made paperwork systems are available but there may be limits on their flexibility. The main proprietary systems used are:

Stockcards

Where visible edge filing can give rapid access to a large number of records.

Line selection systems

Using special spirit duplicators, information from a master can be combined in different sequences to provide sets of job cards, material requisitions, master progress cards and other required paperwork.

Computer systems

Can be used to print production paperwork. Output does not have to be on conventional computer paper but can be on cards, labels and other forms.

Whatever method is used it should be simple and functional. Periodically paperwork systems should be reviewed and improved or discarded where necessary.

WORKS ORDER | Job Number

Customer	Send to (if different)

Date issued	Customer's order No. and date	Delivery date promised	Carriage by

Items to be supplied

Quantity	Drawing number	Description	Unit price	Total price

Special instructions

£	
+ VAT @ %	
Total	

Distribution

Catalogue items and specials			Specials only			
Stock control	Dispatch	Accounts	Chief engineer	Chief inspector	Works manager	Production control

Figure 17.2 Works order

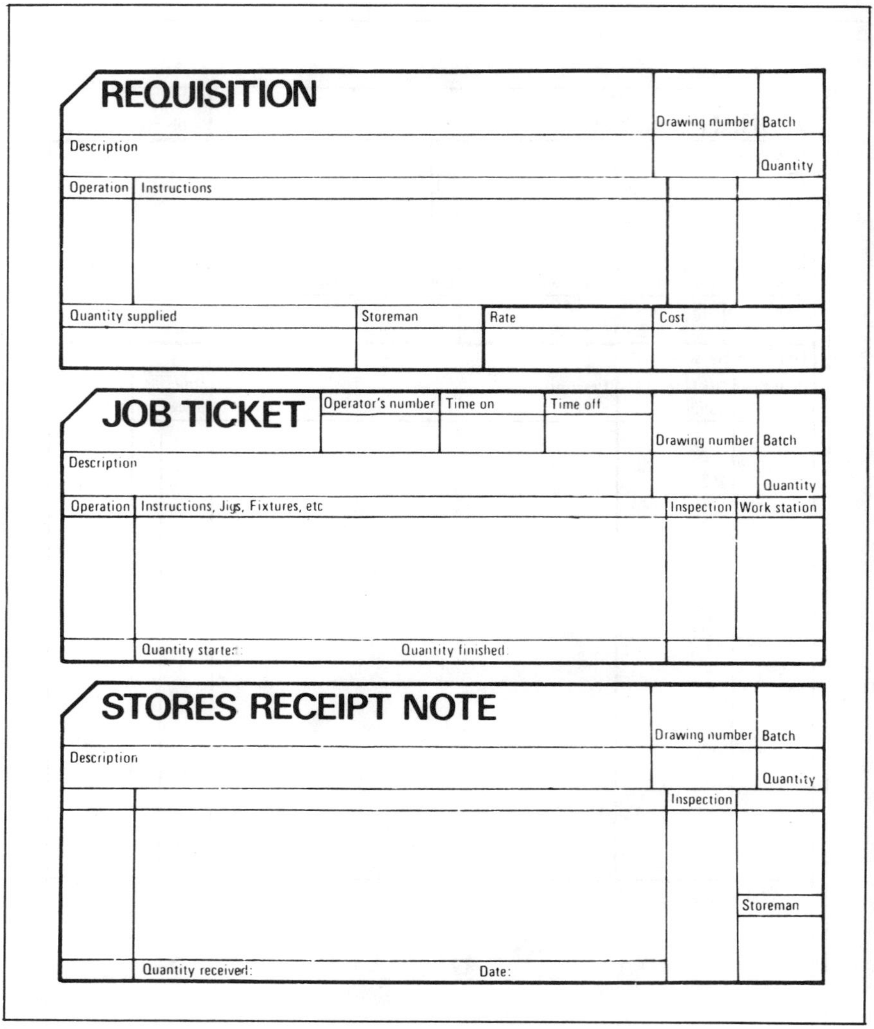

REQUISITION
Drawing number | Batch
Description
Quantity
Operation | Instructions
Quantity supplied | Storeman | Rate | Cost

JOB TICKET
Operator's number | Time on | Time off
Drawing number | Batch
Description
Quantity
Operation | Instructions, Jigs, Fixtures, etc | Inspection | Work station
Quantity started: Quantity finished:

STORES RECEIPT NOTE
Drawing number | Batch
Description
Quantity
Inspection
Storeman
Quantity received: Date:

Figure 17.3 Requisition, job ticket and stores receipt note

COMPUTERS

Computers have been applied to production control since the 1950s with varying degrees of success. With large mainframe computers at head office information was first punched on to cards and then fed into the machine when it was available from its other tasks and more importantly, when it was working. The result was that computers were good at showing what the production situation was a week last Friday.

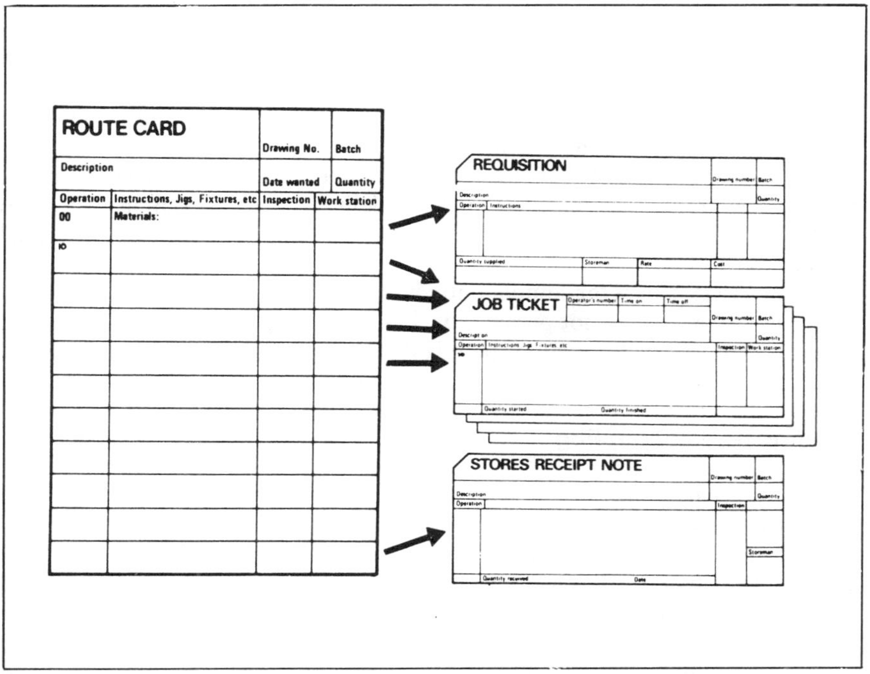

Figure 17.4 Production control and documentation package

With faster, smaller, more reliable and much cheaper computers it is possible to have one dedicated full time, at least in working hours, to production control. Remote terminals mean information can be input as it is generated on the shop floor or in the stores. Not only does this save time but it decreases copying errors. Output need no longer be thick piles of computer paper showing the current state of everything. Selective enquiries can be made via a terminal with the answer appearing at once.

Material requirements planning

The principal use of computers in production control is for material requirements planning (MRP). The forward order position is entered in terms of end products required per week. The computer checks these against finished stock and produces the net requirements. These are then broken down using the parts lists for each assembly. The requirements for each component for each week are totalled. These again are checked against existing stock and orders and the net requirements produced. These net requirements can be batched and turned into orders either manually or by computer. Lead-times can be included so that raw material is called for a number of weeks before the final assembly is due.

In complex situations assemblies may break down to sub-assemblies which break down to sub-sub-assemblies and so on. Up to as many as twelve such levels may be encountered before the basic parts or raw materials are reached. Using MRP the entire schedule of demand for each level can be produced in a few hours or less. Manually it would take weeks or months.

Conventionally the MRP file has been updated once or twice a week with all new orders, production achieved and stock delivered. It is becoming possible to feed in such changes as they happen giving a continuous updated material requirement plan.

Using MRP, orders for components and material are based on actual forward demand. Where this is not possible or feasible traditional stock control can be done on a computer. Predictions based on past usage and average lead-times are made. Reorder levels and batch sizes are calculated.

Loading and scheduling

Various packages are available for loading jobs on to machines. They are generally based on the critical path network approach.

The limitation of such packages is the sheer complexity of the task. To load even a few jobs on a limited number of machines can give several hundred possible combinations. With a realistic number of jobs and machines the possibility may be hundreds of thousands. Manually such loading can be done using a planning board. The human brain can produce a result that is adequate and takes most considerations into account. The computer can only try all possible combinations until it finds the one best solution. To shorten the process, jobs are assigned priorities and other simplifications are made. The result is still a lengthy computer run producing a result little better than a manual one. In a fast-changing production environment where machines break down, times overrun and priorities get altered the computer may not yet be the tool for sequential loading.

What the computer can do well is provide totals of loads on sections or machines so that advance warning is obtained of over or underloads.

Future development

In the future production control will be almost entirely computerised, even in small companies. The chief requirement is for comprehensive, accurate, up-to-date information. Data recorders linked to each machine and to the computer will be a large step towards this.

FURTHER READING

Burbridge, J.L., *Principles of Production Control*, Macdonald & Evans, London, 4th edition, 1978. A wide-ranging and practical book.

Lockyer, K.G., *Production Control in Practice*, 2nd edition, Pitman, London, 1975. A good introduction, particularly to the numerical side of production control.

New, C.C., *Managing Manufacturing Operations*, BIM Management Survey No. 35, 1976. A survey of practice in 186 plants giving a good basis for comparisons.
Walley, B.H., *Production Management Handbook*, Gower, 1980.

18 Quality control

David Desmond

There is no single definition of quality control which has universal acceptance. Certainly when Dr Walter Shewart (of Bell Telephone Laboratories) introduced the term in 1924, he was concerned with statistical methods for examining the quality of goods produced by an process for uniformity. His philosophy was that if uniformity could be established over a considerable period, then it was reasonable to infer that the quality produced was the best possible with the existing facilities.

Developments over the first thirty years were largely directed towards improving the technique through increased use of statistical methods. Later there was a reaction, and many people applied the term to any kind of procedure which had the object of supplying quality to the consumer's requirements. Much of this was merely old-fashioned inspection and the term 'quality control' became something of a gimmick. Even today it is not uncommon to hear that 'Quality control has let us down' when bad work has been produced – as if this had nothing to do with the department that actually produced the inferior goods.

PRINCIPLES

Quality control is considered here as a technique of scientific management, in the form envisaged by Dr Shewart. Thus it has the objective of making the best use of resources. It is first necessary to establish standards of quality from an analysis of existing records or by a special study. Then a suitable control has to be set up, usually based on a control chart, to ensure that the quality standard is maintained. In some cases the initial quality standard is not good enough to satisfy the technical or market requirements, in which case changed or additional operations must be introduced. These often take the form of complete inspection (sorting) but this should not reduce the need to maintain achievable quality standards. It is preferable to regard such complete inspection as a temporary expedient, and to carry out experiments to determine the optimum operating conditions so that better standards can be instituted.

Quality control is concerned with processes. It accepts variation in a process as being perfectly natural, as long as the results of the variation can be explained by statistical laws. Originally, Shewart was only concerned with manufacturing processes, but the technique can be extended to any process, such as a service (transport, dry cleaning), or performance (rate of working, absenteeism), or cost.

The method consists of making observations on a number of small samples collected from the process over a sufficient period of time so that all variation which would be expected naturally will have an opportunity to occur even if the appropriate technical control is maintained. These observations on each sample are then summarised in any convenient form and plotted in sequence on a simple chart in which the vertical axis shows the summarised measure and the horizontal axis gives the order of taking the samples. The pattern of these plotted points is scrutinised to see if it is consistent and stable and, if so, a pair of horizontal lines are drawn to contain all the plotted points.

These lines indicate the degree of scatter which will be obtained in the future if the quality remains the same. Control can be exercised by projecting the parallel lines into the future and continuing to plot the same summarised measure on the same chart. It may be confidently inferred that future quality is the same as the earlier quality if *all* the plotted points fall within the bounding lines.

There will be many occasions when the original pattern of plotted points does not satisfy the conditions of consistency and stability; this would indicate the presence of an unknown disturbing factor spoiling the uniformity of the process. Such a factor can be removed by suitable technical action but it will not be known at the time of plotting what action should have been taken. However an estimate of the achievable uniformity can be obtained by drawing the parallel lines so as to contain all the points which do produce a consistent and stable pattern. Procedures are available to examine whether any pattern is consistent and stable and, if not, provide an objective method of deciding which samples should be rejected.

A crude control will be obtained if a visual judgement is made of the plotted points and the parallel lines are drawn by eye. This will satisfy the statistical philosophy but the control will only be as good as the judgement. More objective results will be obtained by the use of mathematical procedures in deciding the acceptability of the pattern of plotted points and in computing the positions of the control lines. This will enable changes to be detected more rapidly and, more important, it will prevent unnecessary (detrimental) adjustments to the process when apparent changes are really due to the inherent variability in the process. Such mathematical procedures give rise to statistical methods and show which summary measures give the maximum information from a given amount of data. They provide an objective interpretation of the observed variation and, not only show whether a disturbing factor is present, but also provide an estimate of its effect on the quality being examined. Finally, they give a consistent method for drawing the control lines based on a known and acceptable risk.

ORGANISATION

Like every other management technique, quality control must be properly organised in a factory. It needs the active support of top management which must believe that this is in the best interests of the firm. It is a full-time job in itself and cannot be a mere appendage to another major function such as inspection or work study. It must carry sufficient status to attract the right kind of person. There will be no difficulty in arousing and maintaining interest once the programme gets under way.

The first step is the appointment of a statistical quality control (SQC) officer who can have any title which fits in with the staff structure. This is preferably an internal promotion of somebody who has an understanding of the firm's products and processes. He (or she) need not be an expert in the relevant technology but he should have an appreciation of it. Neither is it necessary for him to be highly skilled in mathematics or statistics. There are no computations which cannot be easily performed with the mini-calculators now readily available. He should gradually appreciate the statistical principles behind the procedures he has to use and ultimately he will be able to adapt them to use more efficient methods. He should be encouraged to attend one of the many short courses which deal with the simpler concepts and to get together with SQC officers from other firms (whose products may be very different but will be using the same fundamental principles to solve their quality problems).

It is important that the new section shows early successes. This can be ensured by careful selection of the processes to be subjected to SQC methods. No factory is working as well as possible all the time and in most cases nobody really knows the quality they are capable of producing! An initial analysis of recent records will indicate where substantial quality improvements can be made. If these are associated with less scrap or rectification, there will be obvious financial gains. It is easy enough to estimate what these potential savings are. The target should be to realise 50 per cent of the potential within a month and over 80 per cent permanently after three months.

It is less easy to estimate the increase in markets and consequent better utilisation of resources arising from improved quality. This is frequently much more important than the direct savings from scrap and rectification. It is the basis on which the future wellbeing of the firm is founded.

Experience shows that may SQC applications produce even greater quality improvements than can be expected from past records or from an initial study. Part of this might be due to underestimates of the initial quality standard because of the limited data available but there must be the same possibility of overestimates. Somehow, there is an evolution of better technology from the immediate feedback of information. The SQC programme should recognise this situation as soon as it occurs so that the improvement can be incorporated into the process.

A number of steps in quality management should be taken before any useful quality control application can be made. The areas that should be examined are listed in the checklist in Figure 18.1.

Workplace
- lighting
- heating
- ventilation
- space
- cleanliness
- freedom from accident hazards
- availability of materials
- disposal of products

Services
- power
- gas
- compressed air
- vacuum
- others

Material
- sufficient quantity
- correct specification
- required time

Plant
- capable of doing jobs
- jigs and fixtures
- maintained

Operator
- instructed how job is to be done
- knows what is required
- given facilities to do the job
- trained to use the facilities properly
- means to verify that he has done so
- understands he is responsible for quality

Product
- quality specified on a document
- means to measure quality made
- disposal of defectives
- disposal of acceptable work

Figure 18.1 Quality management checklist

REQUIREMENTS

Formal quality control requires sets of rules to:

1 Analyse data to determine whether the observed variation could occur without any disturbing factor
2 Estimate parameters which define the achievable quality to be taken as standard
3 Compute control limits within which the summarised measurements from future routine samples must fall if the standard quality is to be maintained.

These rules will differ according to the method of measurement, and detailed procedures are available to cope with all situations likely to arise in any factory. Full details of a simple recommended procedure are given later. This will show how to establish a preliminary quality standard for a process whose output is subject to the manufacture of random defectives. More elaborate procedures are available to provide more reliable quality standards from the same data (see Desmond, 1971).

The first group of rules applies to measurement by counting items or to occasions which do or do not possess some desirable attribute. This applies where quality is measured by the number of defectives in samples inspected visually or by Go Not-Go gauges. Exactly the same method can be used for the numbers of breakages in unit time, counts of absentees, numbers of occasions that a machine is not working during work-sampling surveys or numbers of defects per unit (such as scratches on chromium-plated lamps).

The second group applies to direct or inferred measurement on a continuous scale of some physical quantity such as diameter, length, weight, hardness, moisture, pH value, etc. Simple procedures can be very successful where the variation from unit to unit is largely associated with a single source but more complex methods will be required when several sources of variation operate simulataneously.

There are situations where either method of measurement can be used. For example, the diameter of a bolt may have a specification of 1.990–1.995 cm so any piece can be checked for compliance with a Go Not-Go gauge. But there is obviously more information in the knowledge that it has a diameter of 1.992 cm rather than merely knowing it is acceptable. One believes intuitively that the extra information obtained by direct measurement should give better control and this is found to be true. Nevertheless, the simplicity of the number defective control chart has led a majority of firms to adopt this method and the examples quoted herein are based on it.

USING CONTROL CHARTS

The *control chart* is the means by which the manufacturer is able to confirm that the quality standard is being maintained. The method consists of assessing the quality of a sample selected from the product that has just been made and comparing it with an established value – the *control limit*. The control limit is chosen so that if the process is producing standard quality then the quality of the selected sample would be outside the limit only on very rare occasions:

When the quality assessment of the sample comes within the control limit, it is accepted as verifying that standard quality is still being produced and the process is allowed to continue running without alteration. However, if the quality assessment reaches or exceeds the control limit, this is considered as sufficient evidence that standard quality is no longer being produced. Then, if normal operation of the process is known to produce standard quality, this is also evidence that technical operating conditions are no longer normal. They can be restored by appropriate technical action and it is essential that such action is taken immediately.

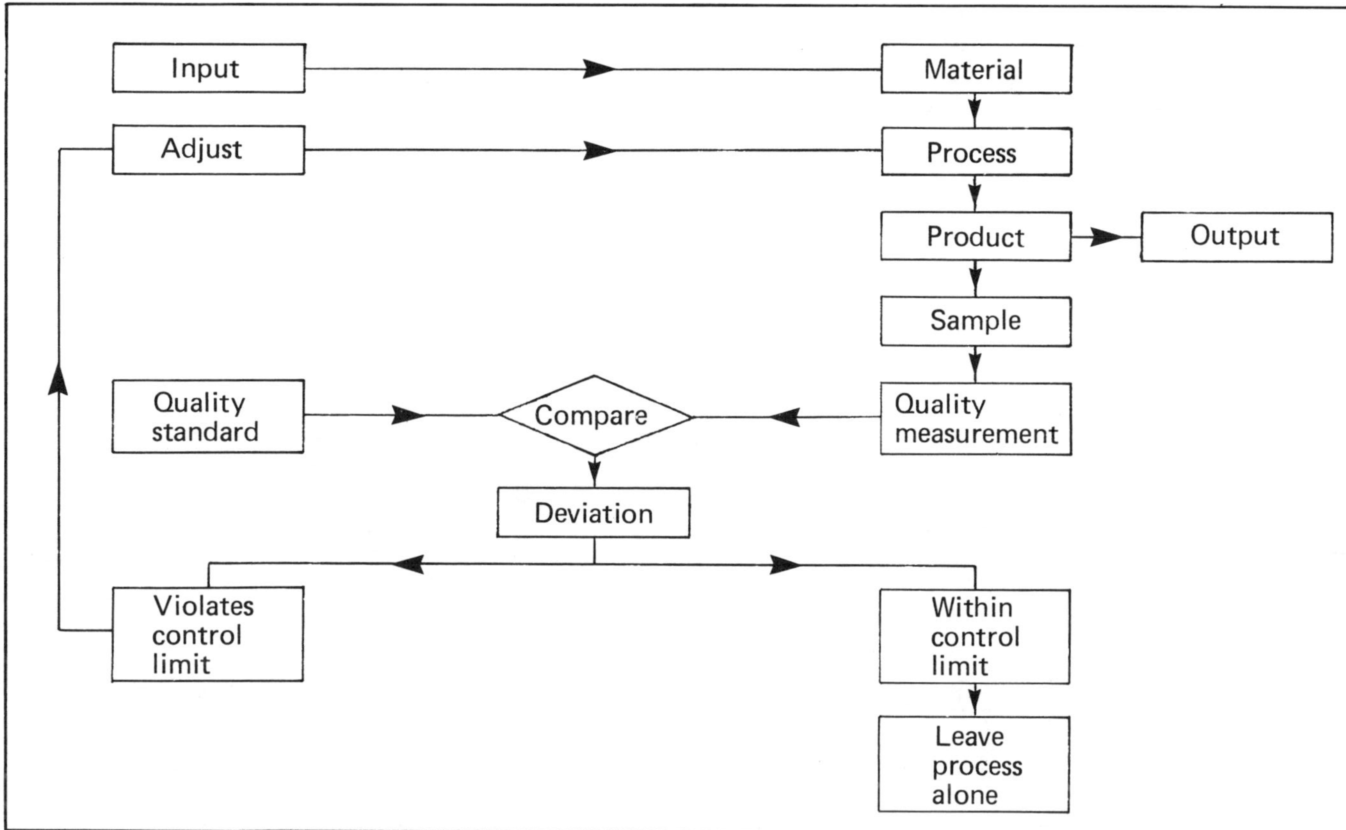

Figure 18.2 ***Quality control flow diagram***

The way in which the control chart works is very similar to that of any other closed-cycle control system. This is illustrated by the flow diagram in Figure 18.2. The random variation due to sampling is analogous to 'noise' and any real technical deviation will produce a signal which is distorted by the inherent noise. The control chart gives an efficient way of distinguishing between a genuine signal and the background noise.

A simple control chart

The principles of control charts will be illustrated by the number defective chart, of which an example is given in Figure 18.3. At regular intervals a sample of items is taken from the output of a process, each item is examined for compliance with technical requirements, and the number of defectives in the sample is plotted against the time and date of sampling. Any technical change such as a new batch of material is marked along the horizontal scale.

This example shows the standard as having one defective per sample. It can be seen that over the twenty samples plotted, the numbers of defectives vary between zero and three. The sample size is not shown but if it is large (twenty or more) with the established average of one per sample, then about one sample in twelve will have three or more defectives just by the chance selection of the items which constitute the sample. Thus three defectives must be expected quite frequently.

The occurrence of four defectives starts to raise some doubt but this must be expected about once in fifty-three samples. There should be sufficient confidence in the ability of the technical staff in maintaining normal operating conditions to be able to accept this as just an unlucky sample which will occur about once per week merely by chance. Thus, the process should be allowed to continue without adjustment (particularly as any alteration to a correctly operating process can only worsen the quality).

Next suppose that the sample contains five defectives. The decision now is whether technical control has been maintained while a one in 273 chance sample was obtained or operating conditions had truly and unexpectedly changed. Experience will show what decision should be taken. Obviously it will be influenced by the confidence placed in the technical staff.

There would not be much doubt if the sample should contain six defectives. This would represent a one in 1700 chance if the process was truly unchanged. This must shake the confidence in technical control, no matter how strongly it was held before the inspection of the sample.

The level of probability at which one rejects the assumption that the process is operating normally is decided in advance and will depend on the kind of process being examined and the procedure used. It will also depend on finding an acceptable compromise between adjusting the process too frequently when it is working at standard quality and failing to obtain an indication of a change that has truly occurred. A limit of one in 200 is recommended for most purposes. Thus there would be a control limit at five defectives in this example.

In practice, the sample size is not very important as long as there is only a small proportion of defectives (up to 10 per cent). This limiting case will

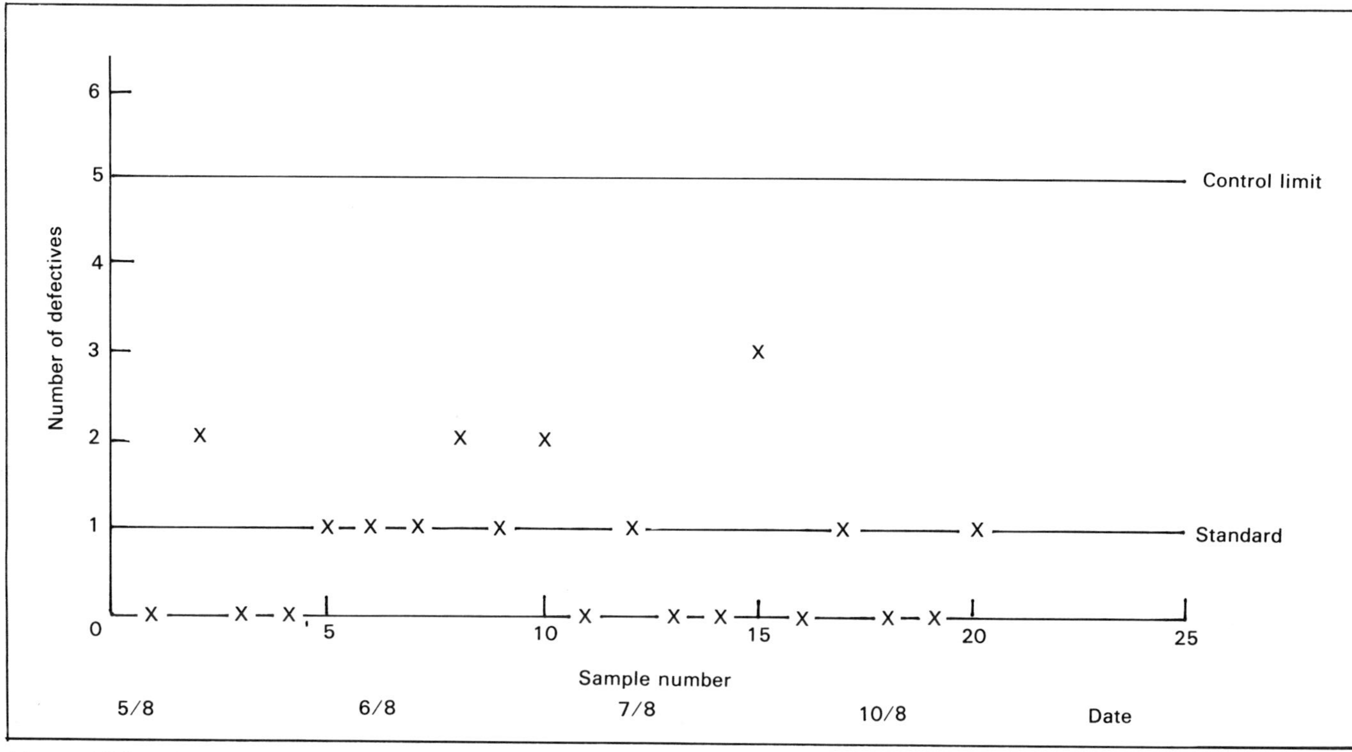

Figure 18.3 ***Number defective control chart***

correspond to samples of ten units and then four or more defectives will be found once in seventy-eight samples (instead of fifty-three). Similarly, five or more defectives will be found once in 611 samples (instead of 273). Despite these different figures, the choice of control limit will remain at five defectives. It is safe to use Figure 18.4 to read off the control limit in terms of average number of defectives per sample for all situations where the proportion of defectives is less than 10 per cent. The control limit is the value opposite the interval containing the expected number of defectives. Use the lower value in marginal cases; for example the control limit corresponding to 2.57 defectives per sample is 8.

This table can be used for a sequence of samples. For example, if the expected number is 1.2, and the control limit is 6, two consecutive samples will expect 2.4 with the control limit at 8 while three consecutive samples will expect 3.6 with the control limit at 10.

Expected Number of defectives per sample	Control limit 1 in 200	Expected number pf defectives per sample	Control limit 1 in 200
0.000		4.94	
	1		13
0.005		5.58	
	2		14
0.103		6.23	
	3		15
0.338		6.89	
	4		16
0.672		7.57	
	5		17
1.08		8.25	
	6		18
1.54		8.94	
	7		19
2.04		9.64	
	8		20
2.57		10.35	
	9		21
3.13		11.07	
	10		22
3.72		11.79	
	11		23
4.32		12.52	
	12		24
4.94		13.25	

Figure 18.4 ***Control limits for number defective charts***

This method can give a tighter control, thus the sequence 4 3 3 proves an out of control situation which none of these samples can do individually.

If much smaller samples are used with a higher proportion of defectives, then different decision rules should be adopted. Thus if the samples consist of only four items giving 25 per cent defectives to maintain the average at one defective per sample, a control limit of 5 would be meaningless. Even four defectives (the whole of the sample) would be obtained by chance once in 256 samples leading to a control limit of 4 (instead of 5). Although procedures can be designed to cope with this kind of situation, it is recommended that a technical investigation should be made if the quality standard is worse than 10 per cent defectives.

THE QUALITY STANDARD

Although it is possible to set up a control chart without prior knowledge of the quality that the process is capable of producing, such a chart cannot start with a realistic control limit. After fifty or so samples have been inspected, the data can be analysed for stability and then a provisional quality standard can be established. This would enable the appropriate control limit to be incorporated on the control chart and further routine sample results examined over the course of time. These should also be analysed at more or less regular intervals to determine the latest quality standard the process is producing.

These later analyses may indicate that the quality has improved under the influence of the control chart but usually such an improvement will be small and could be due to the chance of selection of the samples rather than any technical change. On the other hand, the later samples may indicate a deterioration in quality which was not corrected by the use of the control chart. Again this could be due to sampling fluctuations.

A PROCEDURE FOR ESTIMATING THE QUALITY STANDARD

This procedure is used in an initial study of a process when quality is measured by the counting of defectives in samples selected from the output. The samples must all contain the same number of items and must be selected to cover a sufficiently long period of time so that all normal variation has an opportunity to occur.

It is also used when routine inspection data are available for analysis which relate to equal numbers of products inspected in each period.

The object of the test is to verify that standard technical operating conditions were maintained throughout the period studied and, if so, the data will directly give a valid estimate of the standard quality which the process can produce.

What the procedure does

The test method consists of comparing the sample with the largest number of defectives against the average number per sample. The data are accepted as being homogeneous if this worst sample could occur, merely by chance, more frequently than once in 200 times when technical operating conditions remain constant.

Provided that 80 per cent or more of the data are homogeneous, then the procedure gives a valid estimate of the quality standard which the process is capable of producing.

Details

1 Count the number of samples to give the quantity k.
2 Count the number of items in each sample to give the quantity n.
3 Add all the defectives in the whole k samples to give a total of Σc.
4 Divide the total defectives by the number of samples. This quotient $= \Sigma c/k$ is represented by the symbol $\bar{c}$. Use this value of $\bar{c}$ as a first estimate of γ.
5 Read off the control limit in Figure 18.4 corresponding to this value of γ.
6 Compare all the individual numbers of defectives in the samples against this limit and accept the set of data as being homogeneous if none is as large as the limit. If condition 6 is satisfied, accept this first estimate of γ as the average number of defectives to be expected in similar samples in future and the corresponding value of $\pi = \gamma/n$ as being the standard proportion defective for the process.
7 If condition 6 is not satisfied, remove all the sample results which reach or exceed the limit and compute the average number of defectives per sample for the remaining samples as in step 4. Use this revised value of $\bar{c}$ as a better estimate of γ and read off the corresponding limit in Figure 18.4 as was done in step 5.
8 Compare all the individual numbers of defectives in these remaining samples against this revised limit and accept them as forming a set of homogeneous data if none is as large as this limit.
9 If condition 8 is satisfied, accept this revised estimate of γ as the average number of defectives to be expected in similar samples in future and the corresponding value of $\pi = \gamma/n$ as being the standard proportion defective for the process.
10 Repeat steps 7 to 9 if condition 8 is not satisfied and repeat again as often as necessary for it to be satisfied.

Note: If 20 per cent of the samples have to be discarded it implies that the process is very unstable. New data should be collected and analysed after suitable technical action has been taken to stabilise the process.

Example 1.

A set of 25 samples each containing 20 items is available for analysis. The observed numbers of defectives were:

01100 15043 01042 10013 30000

Then

$$k = 25, \qquad n = 20.$$

By addition

$$\Sigma c = 30$$

and

$$\bar{c} = 30/25 = 1.2$$

Control limit = 6, corresponding to γ = 1.2 (Figure 18.4)

Largest number of defectives in any sample = 5.

Accept data as homogeneous with standard proportion defective of π = 1.2/20 = 6.0 per cent.

Example 2.

A 9-head filling machine has one head completely out of adjustment while the other heads produce 1 per cent defectives. The initial study consists of 15 samples each containing 25 packs.

Case (a)
The samples were selected at random from a box containing all the packs produced in the previous half hour. The observed numbers of defectives were:

35122 33370 32416

Then

$$k = 15, \qquad n = 25.$$

By addition

$$\Sigma c = 45$$

and

$$c = 45/15 = 3.0$$

Control limit = 9, corresponding to γ = 3.0

Accept data as homogeneous with standard proportion defective of π = 3.0/25 = 12.0 per cent.

Note that this analysis is unable to detect any real difference from sample to sample.

Case (b)
The samples consist of successive packs direct from the machine so every sample has two or three packs filled by the faulty head.
The observed numbers of defectives were:

23433 43323 23532

These give

$$n = 25 \qquad k = 15 \qquad \Sigma c = 45$$

and the interpretation is exactly the same as for case (*a*). There is a suspicion that the samples are 'abnormally uniform' but this procedure is unable to detect this.

It should be noted that one completely faulty head will produce 11.1 per cent defectives overall quite apart from any made on the other heads. As the standard worked out at 12 per cent, one completely faulty head is a plausible explanation but one should not jump to conclusions. A more advanced procedure is able to demonstrate that case (*b*) did produce abnormally uniform samples, confirming the suspicion of a faulty head.

In general one should try to collect the samples so that any item can be identified with a definite source. Although this is practical for a nine-head machine, it would not be possible from each of the 200 spindles in a frame spinning jute.

FURTHER READING

Caplen, R. H., *A Practical Approach to Quality Control*, Business Books, London, 4th edition, 1982

Desmond, D., *Quality Control Workbook*, Gower, 1971

Juran, Joseph M., *Quality Control Handbook*, McGraw-Hill, New York, 3rd edition, 1974

19 Maintenance

E N White

The demands made upon the works department concerned with the maintenance of structures, buildings, services installations, plant and machinery, vehicles, equipment or instruments, grow with the increased dependence upon these assets in today's environment. Pressures on maintenance personnel increase as high-cost assets require efficient utilisation with minimum out-of-use periods. At the same time, widening applications of new technology require added knowledge and improved techniques of servicing and repair. Clearly the role of the maintenance manager is expanded in this environment and improved systems and practices are often needed to ensure the correct degree of asset care. The manager of the maintenance function is seen as a major contributor to the "assets management' programme of the organisation and, as maintenance costs are recurring costs, he has an important part to play in controlling life cycle costs.

TEROTECHNOLOGY

The terotechnology concept grew out of a working party study on maintenance practices (see *Report by the Working Party on Maintenance Engineering*, HMSO). The scope of terotechnology is illustrated by the definition: 'A combination of management, financial, engineering and other practices applied to physical assets in pursuit of economic life cycle costs.'

This indicates the thinking behind the concept, namely, that attention to maintenance management alone would not provide the complete answer to the problems arising in the maintenance sector (or otherwise attributed to maintenance). It clearly was necessary to look at other management functions having an influence on the performance and costs of physical assets: in other words, those functions which contribute to assets management.

The broad application of the terotechnology concept is further illustrated by the note to the definition, which states:

> Its practice is concerned with the specification and design for reliability and maintainability of plant, machinery, equipment, buildings and structures; with their installation, commissioning, maintenance, modification and replacement, and with feedback of information on design, performance and costs.

Thus the terotechnology concept is applied both to buildings and plant, and to all stages of their life cycles from design to eventual replacement or disposal. Finally, terotechnology includes the feedback of data to produce management information.

The terotechnology system (Figure 19.1) is generally shown as a combination of management systems and communication channels which provide support for maintenance. Typical contributions include:

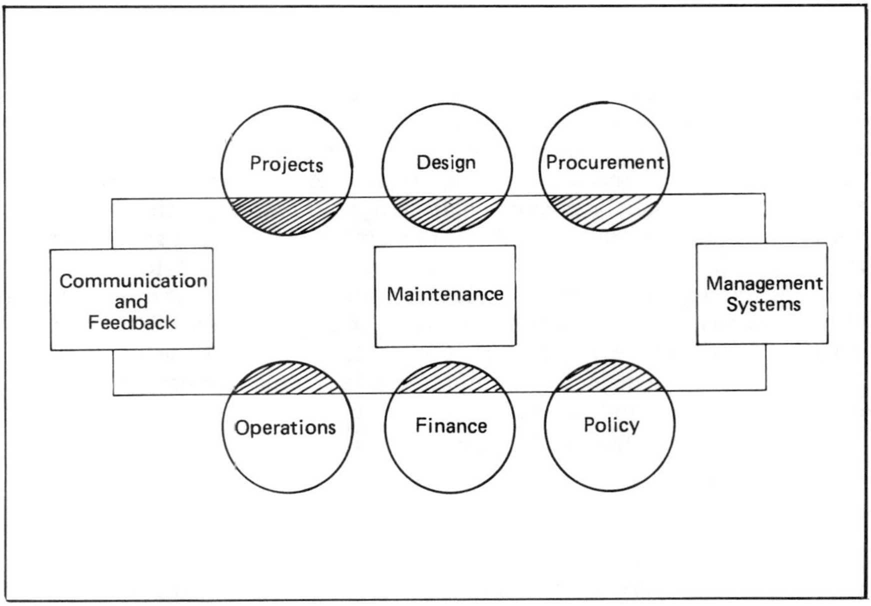

Figure 19.1 A terotechnology system

1 Design – assets designed for maintainability and reliability
2 Procurement – application of 'best buy' procurement techniques
3 Projects – provision of assets having operability and maintainability features
4 Operations – introduction of operating techniques which reduce downtime and improve care of assets
5 Finance – cost control, cost monitoring and feedback
6 Personnel – selection and training programmes for operating and maintenance personnel

Strategies for terotechnology (new assets)

Assets management is a cradle-to-grave strategy which commences with technoeconomic studies prior to an investment and proceeds through the implementation stages into the life cycle of use. During the period of use there will be operation and maintenance strategies, designed to give best use at least cost, and eventually a replacement or disposal strategy will be formulated based on technical and economic reviews.

Asset provisioning can be considered in three phases; preparation, decision and implementation. In the preparation phase it is important to consider historical data and feedback from operations and maintenance, and to attempt whole life predictions with life cycle costs. These and other data are considered during evaluation and decision, and it is important here to consider the views of operations and maintenance management. Finally, in the implementation phase the programme includes design, installation, commissioning and proving stages until the assets are handed over to the operations and maintenance personnel. Some important considerations in these phases are listed in Figure 19.2.

The utilisation phase requires the planned operation and planned maintenance of the asset with performance analyses and feedback of management information. Performance data should be recorded and used to benefit future designs and procurement decisions, and for frequent reviews of the whole life predictions. It is important also to apply controls to any modification programmes so that configuration control is maintained.

Finally there will be a review phase when all technical and economic factors are considered and the decision made to dispose of or replace the asset.

The terotechnology system demands that a number of 'trade-off' decisions be made. For example, the comparison between increased utilisation of a new asset and the attendant costs of operation and maintenance, especially if new technologies are incorporated, can be considered in a 'trade-off' against statistics for the assets to be replaced.

Strategies for terotechnology (existing assets)

Actions to implement terotechnology in the management of existing assets may be considered in two groups – actions within the maintenance function, and actions by other departments. Each of these groups further divides into actions which follow accepted practice, and actions based on analyses of feedback.

As an example, within the maintenance function, the applications of planning and control to maintenance work is probably the first reaction of many managers to a terotechnology programme. The principles are well documented, case histories exist and planned maintenance is accepted practice. However, at a later date, when the feedback inherent in a planned system is analysed, the control system may well be modified and condition-based maintenance introduced. It is the action based upon feedback which effects the most significant improvements. But it is often necessary to improve existing systems

Preparation phase
- Consideration of feedback (operations and maintenance)
- Planning (operating and maintenance policies)
- Technical forecasting
- Whole life planning
- Life cycle costing

Decision phase
- Direct participation by users (past and future)
- Preparation of procurement checklists, see Appendix 1
- Reviews of supplier profiles and quality ratings
- Specification of support systems, see Chapter 3
- Review of life plans and life cycle costs

Implementation phase
- Design (design records, design reviews, configuration control)
- Studies (maintainability, reliability, feedback from users)
- Project planning and control
- Support planning (information, training, spare parts)
- Information systems (disclosure of design data by manufacturers and suppliers)
- Preparation of documentation (manuals, specifications, training programmes)
- Maintenance planning (management systems and resources)
- Commissioning (testing, defect action, certification)
- Handover (operation, proving, final acceptance)

Utilisation phase
- Operation, maintenance, condition monitoring
- Technical and costs records
- Analysis of records
- Feedback to operations, maintenance, design, procurement
- Improvements and updating (configuration control)
- Reviews of life plans and life cycle costing

Review phase
- Technical and financial reviews
- Disposal or Replacement Decisions
- Feedback to benefit future projects

Figure 19.2 Terotechnology considerations in a life cycle

as a first step, so that meaningful analyses can be made as justification for further progress.

MAINTENANCE PLANNING AND CONTROL

Total maintenance planning embraces all activities necessary to plan, control and record all work done in keeping the assets to the acceptable standard. This includes preventive maintenance and corrective maintenance, planned overhaul, planned replacement, spares provisioning, workshop functions, repairs and renewals, plant history compilation, plant modification to facilitate maintenance, spare parts manufacture, preventive maintenance on spare parts, etc. In a fully controlled situation only the time spent on emergency work is 'unplanned' and this could well be less than 10 per cent of the available man-hours in the maintenance department. The three basic requirements of a planned maintenance system are:

1 A programme of maintenance activity for the buildings, plant and equipment
2 A means of ensuring that the programme is fulfilled
3 A method of recording and assessing results.

Figure 19.3 lists the basic elements of a planned maintenance system which is represented diagrammatically in Figure 19.4.

Assets register

A comprehensive register of all plant and buildings (or of that part of the plant and buildings which are the subject of the planning) is an essential base for the planning operation. Each asset must be positively identified in terms of:

1 Name and identity code
2 Description
3 Reference numbers - manufacturers, suppliers, etc.
4 Location - with provision for changes if item is interchangeable or mobile
5 Supplier's details.

The asset code can be numerical, or alpha-numerical and it usually replaces any existing plant numbering systems. Asset codes are given to buildings, plant, services installations and mobile plant, and are attached to the asset for identification purposes. The codes can be preceded by other letters or numbers if required for corporate purposes (investment analyses, depreciation calculations, etc.).

Asset codes can identify asset type (PU = pump), accounts codes (primary and secondary) and physical locations. Additional numbers can be added to link the basic asset codes to spare parts, special tools, work specifications, or to drawings and manuals filed in the maintenance library. The asset code must be used on all work cards, defect reports, materials requisitions and other documentation as the key to effective communication, feedback, and the compilation of history records.

Item	Description
1 Assets register	A complete inventory of the buildings and plant to be maintained
2 Maintenance schedule	Schedules for inspection, lubrication and preventive maintenance of the items in the register. The schedules may also include planned overhaul
3 Work specifications	Instruction cards or documents which identify exactly the tasks to be undertaken within the maintenance system
4 Maintenance control system	A 'trigger' system which initiates the activities on the maintenance programme at predetermined intervals as listed on the maintenance schedule
5 Resourcing schedule	A manpower allocation system to ensure that the resources are available to implement the maintenance requirements of the assets and that optimum use is made of labour
6 Maintenance records	A record of maintenance carried out and a system for reporting to management
7 Maintenance support organisation	The organisation of technical information, spare parts and tools, etc
8 Liaison with production	An effective system of agreeing with the user management when maintenance work can be done
9 Planned overhaul	Provisions for ensuring the planned overhaul of plant, either on a regular basis in accordance with the maintenance schedule or in response to condition monitoring
10 Costing system	Costing procedures to ensure adequate cost control and apportionment of costs in the maintenance department
11 Training	The necessary training of operatives and supervisors in the operation of the system

Figure 19.3 Components of a planned maintenance system

Maintenance schedules

Maintenance schedules list the requirements of each asset shown on the register in so far as routine maintenance is concerned. A typical schedule card indicates:

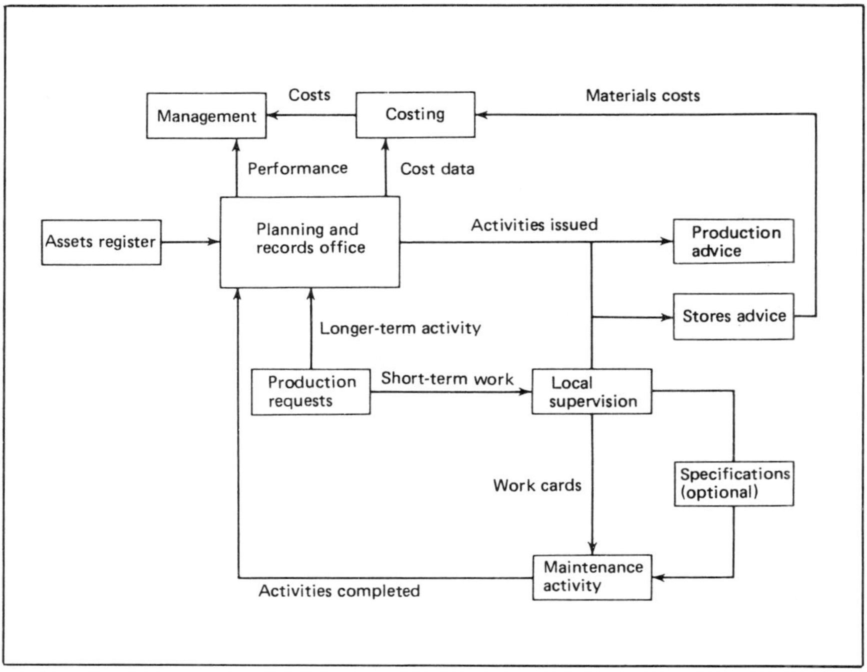

Figure 19.4 Typical maintenance control system

1 Grade of labour required
2 Frequency of the work to be done
3 Details of the work to be done
4 Estimated time for the execution of the work.

Where assets are identical or similar the schedules are repeated on additional cards so that a complete schedule exists for each asset. The preparation of the maintenance schedule is a skilled task. Not only must all necessary maintenance activities be identified and recorded, but the frequencies must be evaluated with availability for maintenance in mind as well as other more obvious factors including suppliers' suggestions.

Grouping work by slight adjustments of the frequencies can have a most beneficial effect on the operation of a maintenance programme.

Basic data can frequently be obtained from manufacturers' manuals but not all manuals have the necessary information, or have the information in the required form. The maintenance planning engineer must therefore use any available information as a basis but must interpret it in accordance with the local requirements and with his own knowledge and experience. (Obviously care must be taken within the guarantee period of new equipment to conform with any special instructions which form part of the supplier's guarantee.)

Maintenance controls

When the extent of the preventive maintenance activity is known, a suitable control system can be selected to 'trigger' activities at the required frequencies. Control systems range from a manually sorted card file, through automatic job-card sorter/printer devices to a system in which a computer printout represents the programme for the selected period.

If a computer-based system is used a study will be necessary, as with the introduction of any data-processing system, to determine the availability and the cost of programs, the cost of installation and the availability of computer time on any existing installation. When installing a computer-controlled system based on time from an existing computer it is necessary to safeguard the availability of that time before abandoning existing methods and accepting full computer dependence.

The functioning of a typical control system is illustrated by Figure 19.5. The 'trigger' system gives rise to the issue of the work card and materials; the detailed instructions (work specification) can be issued at the same time. At the completion of the scheduled work the documents are returned to the control office for recording and for any corrective work to be initiated.

Manpower resourcing schedule

Once the routine maintenance requirements have been determined for all items on the assets register, it will be necessary to table estimates of the man-hours needed from each grade of labour. Using these estimates, a phased schedule can be compiled by allocating the appropriate hours to the relevant dates for each planned activity. Such a chart will be made to show detailed requirements for a medium-term control period, with summaries added to extend the plan to two, three or even five years as a resource planning tool.

Manpower resourcing in the maintenance department only makes sense when full control and full support for the maintenance activity is provided. The routing of maintenance staff during work is important. Studies have shown that 15 per cent of the available working time can be devoted to obtaining instructions and making journeys to the work point in an industrial installation of average size. Full support in terms of test equipment, spare parts and technical manuals can reduce the number of journeys made to workshops or the stores.

Maintenance records

The operation of an effective maintenance records system provides the following information:

1 The percentage of planned work achieved in the period
2 The ratio of planned to unplanned work
3 Downtime for the period
4 Ratio of preventive work to corrective work

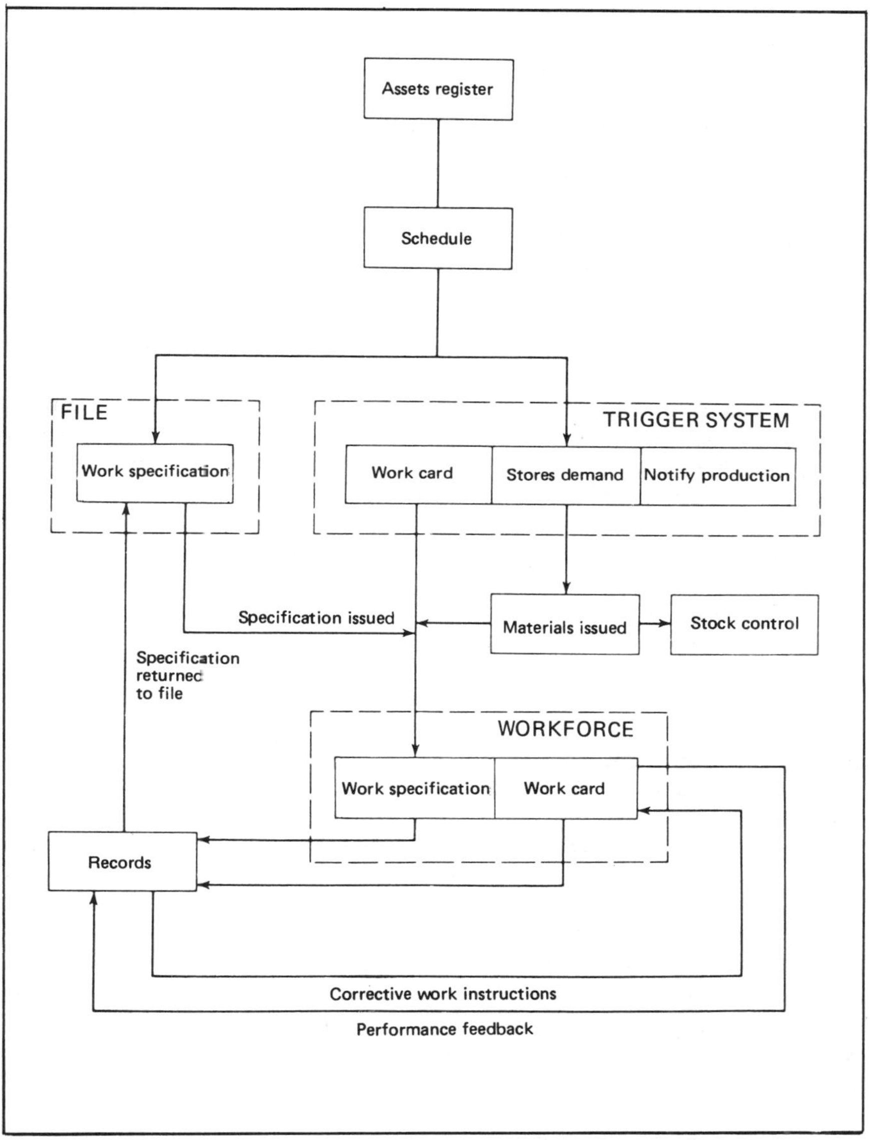

Figure 19.5 Maintenance control with trigger system

5 Maintenance requirement comparisons between individual assets, between types of asset, or between groups of assets
6 Indicators for reliability of the products of particular manufacture
7 Trends in spare parts consumption
8 Equipment failure patterns

9 Performance detail for personnel, by individual or by trade group
10 Materials used, for guidance on restocking policies
11 Indicators on possible standardisation policies.

Records are kept in many different ways, ranging from card files to computer data stores. The labour required for updating records or work done is a deterrent to many managers and can only be justified if use is made of the information. If a computer is used, lengthy printout sheets can be time consuming also. However the computer is a useful tool for providing summary information on a regular basis so that trends can be observed. Whatever system of records is used, detailed investigations have to be reserved for individual situations in which the cost is justified.

In a simple system a practical level of recording is obtained by writing on the actual work card as issued. Successive workers on the asset can refer to the working history and to their predecessors' comments. This can be useful in passing on the defect history or wear trends but can precondition the worker in his approach to the work, sometimes to bad effect. Other simple systems provide for the issue of new cards each time but for up to six or ten of the completed cards to be retained in the control office at any time to give a short history record. Thus with a two-monthly activity the continued retention of six cards would produce a one-year history. These systems do not provide detailed financial records, which would be provided on separate cards or as a function of the company accounts department.

Liaison with the user

Effective liaison between the operating managers or planners and the maintenance planners is essential to the operation of the maintenance programme. The extent of this liaison depends upon the method of operation, the worst situation occurring when continuous use is required. However, in continuous process plants the awareness of the requirement for liaison is generally such as to encourage efficient planning. The most difficult situations occure where the degree of use or the volume of production fluctuates and a peak period can coincide with an intended maintenance activity.

In an ideal working environment both long-term (annual) and short-term (monthly) plans are regularly reviewed. Short-term release of assets for maintenance purposes can substantially reduce the need for weekend working by maintenance staff. Among the disadvantages of weekend working are the supervision problems, non-availability of materials, spares, and other services at weekends, and possible personnel problems as the maintenance staff tend to become socially separated.

Another important aspect of liaison is the request for service originated by operatives. When standby maintenance staff are available, requests for assistance are frequently made verbally. Formal requests include details of the fault and of the particular item requiring attention together with a priority indication, advice as to whether operations have been halted and an indication of the maintenance trade needed. Cost code information is required for any work undertaken by the maintenance staff in response to requests by operatives. Depending upon the arrangements for cost codes this allows expenditure to be allocated to particular machines, to individual buildings or to operators stations.

Manpower allocation

In the operation of a planned maintenance system, staff of appropriate skills have to be allocated to various tasks in accordance with the requirements originated by the control office. The actual method of allocation may be a simple manual system or a computer program but this is one aspect of planning in which good local supervision often produces the best results.

A basic work programme must originate from the control system with a batch of work cards issued for the particular period. However, the issue of these cards to particular personnel is still, even in quite sophisticated systems, a matter for personnel control by the foreman/supervisor. There are many local factors which may affect the decision on sending Mr Smith or Mr Anderson on particular routes on a particular day. The system is satisfied if two men in a given labour grade are matched to a two man-day load, but with the foreman left to assign the two individuals between the jobs on the schedule.

Downtime analysis

The maintenance records must provide for an acceptable level of downtime analysis, either from the records themselves or in direct summary form from the maintenance requests (see Figure 19.6). Useful information produced in this way includes:

Date	Item	Fault	Downtime (hours)
1	Main panel	Fuse blown	0.1
2	Spreaders	Latches snapped, main arm	1.3
6	Mixers	Gearbox shaft broken (spare gearbox fitted)	0.25
10	Main press	Burst pipe (guard to be fitted)	0.3
11	Water sprays	Valve burnt out (revert to manual – no spare)	0.1
15	Water sprays	New valve fitted	0.4
16	Dryer burner	Faulty electrode (spare fitted, jets cleared)	1.20
19	Compressor	Bearing collapsed (spare fitted – re-order)	3.00
22	Product lift	No upward drive (contacts cleaned)	0.4
24	Main press	Burst pipe (repaired – guard fitted)	0.5

Figure 19.6 Record of downtime

1 An indication of downtime per building, per machine, or if necessary per operator
2 The time taken for fault diagnosis and repair on various types of fault, or on specific machines, or by various personnel
3 Indications of the causes of breakdown.

Among the useful points made clear by analysis 1 might be:

(*a*) The true ratio of downtime to use time (to answer rumours or inaccuracies being quoted against the maintenance department)
(*b*) The need for further investigation, by the operations or maintenance managements, of high downtime
(*c*) The relationships between operator performance and the downtime on individual assets.

Analysis 2 may help to define:

(*a*) High downtime areas where permanent standby repair staff or zone workshops might be beneficial
(*b*) Suppliers to be avoided on future procurements
(*c*) A requirement for specific training (e.g., electronic fault-finding) for maintenance workers
(*d*) The most efficient members of the maintenance staff for the various types of work (fault-diagnosis, repairs, renewals, etc.).

Analysis 3 will define:

(*a*) The spare parts and materials requirements for the various assets
(*b*) Any requirement for increased operator training
(*c*) Problems caused by variations in the product materials used in manufacturing processes.

It will be seen that downtime analysis is complementary to any cost-analysis work. However, downtime recording in detail is relatively expensive and, if economies are sought, may be applied only in certain areas rather than generally. The areas chosen may be high-risk areas containing plant which is vital to a high production figure, or may be areas of rising maintenance cost as defined by the normal cost summary, or areas in which large consequential losses could occur.

Costing

The maintenance control system must provide for accurate costing of work and materials for all maintenance activities. Work cards, materials requisitions, work instructions, maintenance requests, defect reports and time sheets must all carry significant codes to indicate cost allocations. The level of accounting practice adopted will determine the structure of the code system which may define costs in terms of:

1 Individual factories
2 Process lines

3 Individual machines
4 Separate buildings
5 Office units
6 Administration departments
7 Canteens and other special areas.

There is a wide variety of functional and physical hierarchies which may be adopted. The cost codes can conveniently be incorporated in the asset codes, so that costs to a particular asset are cross-referenced at once to the correct accounts.

COMPUTER-CONTROLLED SYSTEMS

A variety of computer systems have been developed for the assets registers, work control, manpower resourcing, stock control, maintenance accounts and, in some systems, analyses of feedback and costs. In general these are based on mainframe computers which, in industrial and commercial applications, are also employed for a variety of other purposes. This can give rise to delays, with the works department low in priority for computer time, especially when major financial programs are being run. The ideal computer system is interactive, dynamic and dedicated. 'Dedicated' means that it is always available to the maintenance department for logging vital information or for instant retrieval of data. These requirements can be met using a minicomputer or microcomputer within the maintenance department.

Computer applications in maintenance planning and control include:

1 Recording or updating asset records or asset movements
2 Managing lubrication activities and modifying the schedules if required by feedback
3 Acting upon inspection reports from lubrication operatives
4 Managing preventive and corrective maintenance activities and incorporating emergency maintenance when necessary
5 Acting upon feedback from maintenance activities
6 Resourcing for capital works programmes
7 Acting upon feedback from emergency maintenance
8 Managing spare parts stocks.

Other uses for the computer in the maintenance department can include:

1 Management of the works department stores
2 Planning and control of capital works programmes
3 Management of production tools, dies, moulds, etc.
4 Energy conservation through monitoring and control
5 Security and fire monitoring through remote sensors
6 Monitoring of automated processes or boiler plant
7 Co-ordination of condition monitoring inputs
8 Register of technical manuals and drawings
9 Register of defects and defect actions
10 Register of tests and quality documentation.

A fuller account of computer applications in maintenance management in given in *Computerised Management in the Maintenance Department*, M and E White Consultants Ltd.

CONDITION-BASED MAINTENANCE

Condition-based maintenance is maintenance work ordered as a result of the condition of an item as discovered during routine or continuous checking. Corrective maintenance ordered after the discovery of cracks in a wall or overheating noticed in a machine during a preventive maintenance check constitutes condition-based maintenance. Condition reports arise from human observations, checks and tests, or from fixed instrumentation or alarm systems grouped under the name 'condition monitoring'.

Benefits expected from a condition monitoring programme include:

1 Reduced expenditure on preventive maintenance
2 No unnecessary dismantling of plant items
3 Less (or less serious) breakdowns
4 Avoidance of consequential damage.

Levels of monitoring

Condition monitoring can be considered at four levels:

Level 1 Inspection monitoring based on the human senses, as in preventive maintenance schedules
Level 2 Assisted monitoring, using portable equipment
Level 3 Lubricant analysis and wear debris collection
Level 4 Fixed monitoring systems connected to alarm systems or data logging equipment.

The inspections at level 1 of the monitoring programme form part of the normal preventive maintenance schedules and are generally included in the daily and weekly activities. The inspectors are expected to use sight, hearing, touch and smell and to obtain a sensory impression of the condition of the asset. The senses may be assisted by magnifiers, viewing devices, temperature sensing strips or paints, stroboscopes, fixed instruments or indicators.

At level 2 the inspector is assisted by a range of portable test equipment to make a variety of measurements. Examples of the tests to be made and the types of equipment used are:

Measurements	*Equipment*
Speed and running time	Tachometers, counters
Electrical quantities	Test meters
Fits and tolerances	Proximity testers
Temperature	Thermography
Vibration wear	Vibration analyser or shock pulse tester

Movement	Frequency analysis
Deterioration of materials	Radiography; ultrasonics; dye penetration

This type of monitoring is applied to selected assets from the asset register for which a condition history file is built up. Quantities and characteristics are recorded and variations observed and interpreted.

Level 3 monitoring is confined to lubricated items and consists of checks on component wear together with checks on contamination of the lubricant. Wear of components is usually indicated by metal particles and debris in the lubricant. Contamination of the lubricant is detected by sampling and subsequent spectrometric analysis.

Fixed monitoring systems for level 4 monitoring range from simple remote alarm systems to comprehensive data gathering systems based on minicomputers or microprocessors. A wide variety of contact points, transducers, accelerometers, counters and other sensors are employed. Data can be transmitted directly to the display or can be electronically processed on a time-shared signal transmission system.

CAPITAL PROJECT MANAGEMENT

The stages in the life cycle of a new capital project are:

1 Conception – formulation of project idea
2 Approval – preliminary discussion and agreement on study
3 Formulation – study of various implementation methods
4 Evaluation – decision on implementation
5 Procurement – selection of suppliers
6 Design – development of concept
7 Construction – manufacture of hardware
8 Installation – construction and installation (often run concurrently)
9 Commissioning – often referred to as 'start-up'
10 Hand-over – buyer accepts responsibility
11 Proving – testing under normal conditions.

The handover is sometimes partial and proving is then necessary before final acceptance by the buyer.

If time and money is to be spent in a study of a project idea, approval is sought and budgetary provisions made. This study might entail consideration of:

1 Life-cycle costs, and return on investment for the existing installation (if applicable)
2 Predictions for these after the project has been implemented
3 Predictions after implementation by the various methods available
4 The development costs, operating costs, maintenance costs and possible problems arising if new technologies are introduced
5 The possibilities for achieving similar results (technical or financial) without introducing new techniques and non-standard plant.

The operating and maintenance aspects must be fully considered and the maintenance manager consulted. The effect on maintenance investments for a separate plant or an extension of an existing plant may include increases from the sources listed in Figure 19.7.

Typical operating costs for the maintenance department will include:

1 Salaries for the additional personnel
2 Other payments for the additional personnel
3 Spares and materials costs
4 Depreciation of buildings occupied by the maintenance staff
5 Overhead charges, insurances, etc.
6 Depreciation of workshop plant, tools, spares and equipment
7 Sub-contract costs.

In the first year of a new installation additional costs may include:

1 Excessive overtime working during familiarisation period
2 Increased use of vendor service engineers
3 High spares consumption caused by start-up problems and also some wastage
4 Further training requirements for maintenance staff.

In addition, low utilisation rates and increased downtime are sometimes features of first-year working.

The maintenance budget may be 7 to 10 per cent of the total investment in an industrial installation (although actual budgets vary enormously). The approximate allocations are:

Cost item	*Allowance*
Materials and subcontract	25 per cent
Personnel - total costs	40 per cent
Depreciation and overheads	25 per cent
Other items	10 per cent

The maintenance manager may request a number of studies by the project engineers. Typical studies are:

1 Study of supplier's proposals for assistance.

  (a) Should the proposals for training, etc., be accepted?
  (b) Should training and product support be subcontracted to specialist firms?
  (c) Are independent commissioning engineers to be used?
  (d) Is a servicing contract desirable?

2 Study of operating and maintenance requirements.

  (a) Will required utilisation be achieved?
  (b) What numbers and grades of manpower are necessary?

Item	Separate plant	Extension
Maintenance accommodation	New maintenance building or floor space allocation in new buildings	Possibly a zone workshop. Additional floor space if existing accommodation inadequate
Workshop plant, tools and access equipment	An appropriate proportion of the project costs based on existing knowledge	Equipment for zone workshop with an evaluation of use to be made of existing main workshop. Transport between zones
Staff requirements. Installation and commissioning	Manager or assistant manager and staff. Allocation of maintenance management and staff during installation phase to achieve familiarity with new plant	Supervisors and additional staff
Product support	The capital cost and charges arising from the documentation and training aspects	
Spares provisioning	A complete range of plant spares plus standard stocks of parts and materials	The recommended range of spares, less any adjustments for rationalisation
Staff training	Requirements for special staff training, above the machine training provided by the vendor, if new techniques are introduced	
Maintenance Consultancy	Development of maintenance policy, organisation of effective product support and introduction of maintenance planning	

Figure 19.7 Effect on maintenance investments

- (c) Have all services requirements been clarified?
- (d) Are all aspects of maintenance support provided for?

3 Study of maintenance planning and control systems.

- (a) Is planned maintenance provided for?
- (b) Which control method will be used?
- (c) Can this plant and others be combined to justify more sophisticated planning systems?
- (d) Will a maintenance consultant be appointed?

4 Study of spare parts requirements.

- (a) Are supplier's recommendations acceptable?
- (b) Will drawings be supplied for local spares manufacturer?
- (c) Is the spares investment at acceptable level?
- (d) Are original sources of spares known?
- (e) Are spares compatible with existing stocks?

5 Study of monitoring techniques.

- (a) Is vibration analysis or other condition monitoring included?
- (b) Is remote control or centralised surveillance desirable?
- (c) Are adequate alarms provided?
- (d) Are fault diagnosis methods provided for?

These and other studies set the pattern for subsequent maintenance of the plant at an acceptable utilisation factor.

The total involvement of the maintenance manager in new project work is essential if effective maintenance is to be a feature of future years. If effective maintenance planning and control methods are used in an existing maintenance department, the maintenance manager should be available for participation in new work programmes.

Figure 19.8 lists a number of factors contributing to efficiency which merit attention when a capital project is planned. Possibly the most important is item 3 – the inclusion of the support items within the penalty clauses.

It is the responsibility of the project planner, with assistance from the maintenance manager or chief engineer, to set the pattern for a controlled situation in the maintenance department. The introduction of planning methods, control systems and effective supporting organisations depends upon the disciplines imposed at procurement, first, upon the planner to know what is required and to provide for it, and second, upon the plant suppiers to meet their obligations. It is the responsibility of the project planner to discipline all concerned into a successful project. This may entail the appointment of a terotechnology consultant (see Figure 19.9). His duties would include:

1 Formulation stage – evaluation of maintenance aspects of various methods and development of monitoring and maintenance policies
2 Procurement stage – vetting of contracts for maintenance aspects
3 Design and construction – monitor maintainability aspects
4 Installation and commissioning – evaluate product support activity by

	Factor	Remedy
1	Insufficient attention to reliability and life maintenance predictions during research and development phase	Improved R and D management disciplines and design analysis
2	Procurement on lowest tender without regard to possible life maintenance costs	Increased technical vetting by maintenance manager during procurement
3	Procurement without specification of and enforcement of product support requirements to be met at time of installation	Includes spares, maintenance manuals, tools, training assistance, commissioning, etc.
4	Insufficient appreciation of role of maintenance by works managers, production managers, etc.	Maintenance appreciation courses for managers of associated departments
5	Failure to plan the maintenance operation and to budget accordingly	Information and training for project planners, and chief engineers
6	Ineffective communication in the maintenance hierarchy	See items 3 and 8
7	Inadequate training for maintenance staff beyond basic skills level	Maintenance training courses of wider scope (fault-finding and repair training, for example)
8	Insufficient management training for engineers required to manage maintenance departments	Training in communication, management by objectives, budgeting, control and planning, terotechnology and maintenance improvement techniques

Figure 19.8 Factors affecting maintenance efficiency adversely

vendors and enforce contract provisions. Develop planned maintenance system, plant records, and technical information system. Arrange training programmes

5 Post-commissioning – finalise technical information system, review planning system, update as necessary.

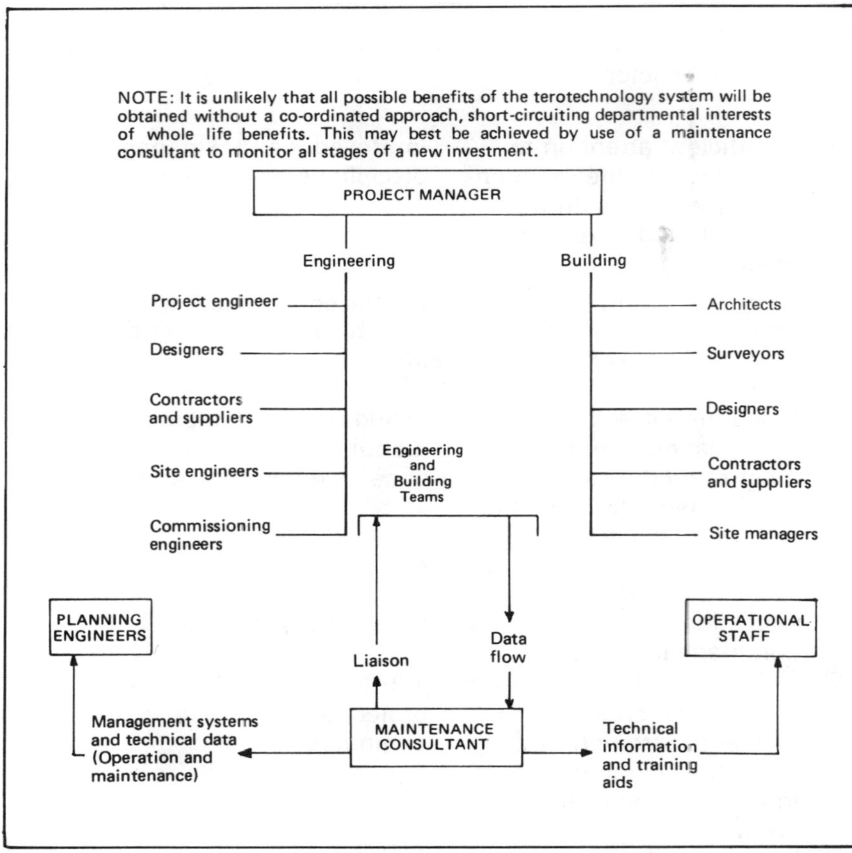

Figure 19.9 A maintenance consultant in a project team

FURTHER READING

Report by the Working Party on Maintenance Engineering, HMSO, London
The Terotechnology Handbook, HMSO, London
Logistics, M. & E. White Consultants Ltd, Winnersh, Wokingham, Berkshire
Computerised Management in the Maintenance Department, M. & E. White Consultants Ltd, Winnersh, Wokingham, Berkshire

PART FIVE

ADMINISTRATION

20 Company law

F W Rose

It is not always appreciated that a company registered under the Companies Acts 1948 to 1981 has a legal existence and personality quite separate and distinct from that of persons holding shares in the company. Many legal formalities must be complied with before such a company comes into existence. When formed the company has rights and liabilities in law which depend upon a careful analysis of the relevant statutory rules.

It may be necessary when an individual makes an agreement with a company to determine its precise power to contract, its financial position and future prospects. If the company is experiencing difficulties in trading profitably, the rights of the shareholders to control the company may be of vital importance.

This chapter explains some of the more important legal provisions. Use of technical language which would be unfamiliar to non-lawyers has been avoided.

FORMATION OF A PUBLIC LIMITED COMPANY

A private company is often formed to carry on a family business. Frequently there are only a handful of shareholders, usually members of the same family. A private company may trade successfully for several years, but further expansion will require additional capital which cannot be supplied by existing shareholders. A public company may be formed to take over and carry on the business; members of the private company will exchange their shares for shares in the new public company. The additional capital for such items as land, new buildings and machinery will be provided by issuing shares which the general public may purchase if they wish. About 2 per cent of all UK companies are public companies.

Registration

The company must be registered. This is effected by filing the following documents with the Registrar of Companies:

1 The memorandum of association

2 The articles of association
3 A statement of nominal capital
4 A list of persons to act as directors and secretary, together with their signatures as evidence of their consent to act as such.

These formalities are usually dealt with by a solicitor, accountant or a company formation firm specialising in this type of work. This person or body also files a declaration that the company has complied with all formalities necessary for registration. The Registrar then issues a Certificate of Incorporation which is conclusive evidence that the company has been properly incorporated.

In law the company now has an existence separate and distinct from that of the individual members who hold shares in the company. The company:

1 Can own property, and members have no rights in that property: their interest is in the shares they hold
2 Can make contracts with other individuals, companies or members
3 Will continue to exist irrespective of the death of an individual member, whose shareholding is then taken over by the person who succeeds to his property
4 Must act through the medium of human agents who will control its affairs, such as directors.

Public companies existing when the Companies Act 1980 came into force are given fifteen months to decide whether to remain as public companies by complying with the requirements of the 1980 Act, or to become private companies instead. A public company is subject to stringent rules designed to protect persons investing money in the company, for example, by prohibiting loans to directors from company funds.

The memorandum of association

This is the charter of the company embodying its constitution and powers. It must state:

1 The name of the company, indicating that it is a public limited company with 'Public limited company' as the last words of the name
2 The location of the registered office of the company
3 The objects to be carried out by the company
4 A declaration that the liability of members is limited
5 The share capital and its division into shares.

The objects clause

This states the company's main business objective. It is followed by a large number of ancillary clauses giving the company power to effect other objects incidental to the main purpose. Examples would include power to buy land, borrow money and purchase shares in other companies. In practice, the objects clause will be widely drawn to include almost every conceivable business objective, coupled with a declaration that they should be construed as main objectives and not subsidiary powers.

The original purpose of the objects clause was to delimit the company's powers so that capital subscribed by investors could be used only for the company's main and, presumably commercially sound, objective; not in some other subsidiary and risky enterprise in which the investor would not have chosen to place his capital.

The concept of limited liability

An investor who purchases shares must pay to the company the purchase price agreed upon. Usually shares must be fully paid for at the time when they are allotted to a shareholder by the company. If they are only partly paid for, then the shareholder is contingently liable to pay the sum still outstanding, even if the company is in liquidation. Once the shares have been fully paid for, the shareholder's liability is complete. He cannot be required to make further contributions, even if the company fails and is unable to settle debts owed to creditors who have supplied goods and services to the company.

Limited liability is one of the most important attractions of shareholding in a public company. After fully paying for his shares the investor has fixed the amount of money that he is prepared to place at risk. However disastrous the company's financial collapse, he cannot be called upon to pay more.

Articles of association

These govern the internal management of the company, regulating the rights of the members among themselves on such matters as:

1 Appointment and power of directors
2 Issue, transfer and forfeiture of shares
3 Rules regulating meetings of a company
4 Payment of dividends
5 Preparation of accounts and auditing
6 Alterations to the capital structure of the company
7 Rights of different classes of shareholders.

It is usual for a company to register its own special set of articles which make specific provisions on matters of internal management, particularly suited to the needs of that individual business.

The prospectus

The usual object of forming a public company is to raise money from the investing public to finance the company's policies of expansion. A company may apply for a stock exchange quotation so that shares can be easily bought and sold through the medium of stockbrokers and jobbers. The company will issue a prospectus which sets out:

1 The objects it will pursue

2 Reports by experts on property owned, its financial position and trading prospects for the future
3 The names of directors; if the board of directors includes well-known experts it may be an inducement to buy the shares
4 The details of the company's capital structure.

These details will enable the investor to determine whether he wishes to purchase shares.

CAPITAL AND SHARES

The authorised (or nominal) capital is the amount of money that the company is authorised by the memorandum of association to raise from the public, for example, £5 000 000. In practice the company may not require this amount immediately, but it can issue shares up to the limit specified at any time when it wishes to do so.

The issued capital is that part of the nominal capital which has been actually issued to the public for cash or other consideration, such as land or buildings, in return for an allotment of shares, for example, an issued capital of £2 500 000 out of the nominal capital of £5 000 000. If a subscriber is required to pay only half the amount due on his share allotment, then the capital actually received by the company (that is the paid-up capital) will be only £1 250 000 in the above example. The amount not yet paid up on the shares issued is referred to as uncalled capital and it may be declared by the company to be incapable of being required from a shareholder except in a winding-up of its affairs.

Certificate of entitlement to commence business

A public company may not commence business after incorporation or borrow money unless it has received a certificate to this effect. This will not be granted until the issued capital is at least equal to the authorised minimum permitted (at present £50 000). In addition at least one-quarter of the nominal value of each share, plus any premium payable as part of the purchase price, must have been paid up.

Serious loss of capital

As a result of adverse trading or other factors, a company may have lost much of the capital that it has raised to finance its operation. Where the net assets of a public company are half or less of the company's called-up capital, then the directors on becoming so aware must convene an extraordinary general meeting of members within the next twenty-eight days. The meeting itself must be held within fifty-six days of becoming aware of the position. There are no legal provisions requiring any specific type of action that the company must take to deal with the problem. The meeting will give shareholders the chance to consider the company's financial position before insolvency supervenes to stop further trading activities.

Payment for shares

The person allotted shares in a company may pay for them in money or 'money's worth', that is granting some form of benefit instead of cash. Payment in a form other than cash may result in the company not receiving the full value of the shares given in return, thus the law has been strengthened to prevent such abuses. A public company cannot accept an undertaking by an allottee of shares to do work or perform services for the company as consideration for an issue of shares. If there is a failure to observe this requirement, the allottee still remains liable to pay the required sum in cash.

A public company is permitted to allot shares in return for an 'undertaking' to transfer a non-cash asset, such as land, within five years from the date of allotment. The non-cash asset must be valued by an independent person qualified to act as a company auditor to ensure that the company is receiving proper value in return for its shares. These provisions are inapplicable where one company takes over or merges with another company and shares in the company being taken over are exchanged for shares in the company that has made the take over.

Increasing capital and pre-emption rights

When a company has issued all of its capital and received payment in full from shareholders, it may require further cash to finance an expansion of its operations. The company will usually be authorised by its articles to alter the capital clause in its memorandum and, if the members in general meeting so decide, an ordinary resolution may be passed to increase the share capital. Shares can then be issued to raise the additional capital. Suppose that prior to the issue of the new shares for cash, an existing shareholder, Jones, holds 60 per cent of the company's total shareholding. In effect he controls the company as a majority shareholder. The issue of new shares to other persons could take this away by reducing his percentage of the total number of shares now in issue. The Companies Act 1980 now provides that a company must not allot shares for cash unless an existing shareholder has been given the opportunity to buy the new shares in proportion to his existing holding. Thus, Jones could, if he so wished, buy 60 per cent of the new shares on offer and retain the same percentage interest in the company's capital. The company's articles, or members by special resolution in general meeting, may give power to directors to exclude or modify pre-emption rights from all share allotments for a maximum period of five years. This power can be revoked at any time by ordinary resolution of members or extended for a further period up to five years maximum.

Power over unissued shares

A takeover bid occurs when one company (Company A,) offers to buy or has already acquired a majority of the voting shares in another company (Company B). The directors of Company B may wish to resist the takeover as undesirable, or because they fear that they will be removed from office once the takeover has been achieved. In the past if Company B had not yet issued all of its authorised capital, the directors could have used a power, often granted to them by the articles, to issue new shares representing hitherto unissued capital to themselves and their supporters. This manoeuvre may have given the directors and supporters control of a majority of the voting shares and so thwart the takeover to which the other shareholders were agreeable.

Under the Companies Act 1980 directors may not exercise any power of the company to allot shares, or other securities such as debentures which can be converted into shares at the holder's option, unless authorised to do so by an ordinary resolution of members in general meeting or by the articles. The power so granted may be a general authority to allot, or limited to a specified amount. When such authority is granted it must state the maximum amount of securities that may be allotted, the date of expiry of the authority and its duration, which must not exceed five years. The authority may be renewed for a further period (maximum again five years) by members in general meeting. None the less members now control the directors' actions in this area, since any authority given may be varied or revoked at any time by ordinary resolution in general meeting.

MEMBERSHIP

A shareholder is a member of the company entitled to the following rights:

1 To attend meetings and vote on issues affecting company policy, including the appointment and removal of directors. He may requisition a meeting if he wishes to discuss any matter of concern provided that he alone, or in conjunction with his supporters has at least 10 per cent of the issued share capital carrying a right to vote, or some lesser proportion as prescribed by the articles
2 To receive an annual report and accounts giving details of the company's affairs
3 To share in the profits made in the form of a dividend declared by the directors
4 To share in the assets of the company if its affairs are wound up, provided any property remains when the rights of other creditors with prior claims have been met
5 To transfer his shares when he wishes by selling or giving them to another person
6 To present a petition to wind up the company or ask for an order controlling its affairs.

Different classes of shares

A company usually issues different classes of shares, each having its attractions for the investor.

Preference shareholders are entitled to the following payments in priority to ordinary shareholders:

1 A yearly dividend out of profits, at a fixed though moderate percentage of the capital invested, for example, 7 per cent. Unless the articles of association state otherwise, arrears of dividend not paid in a previous year when there were no profits are carried forward and must be paid in future years when sufficient profits are available
2 Repayments of the capital contributed to the company when it is wound up, if, as is usual, the articles so provide.

Ordinary shareholders are entitled to:

1 The remainder of profits available for distribution, which will secure a high rate of dividend if the company is successful. However, if a loss results in any trading year a dividend may not be paid at all
2 Return of capital contributed to the company when it is wound up, if sufficient assets remain to satisfy these claims.

The market value of shares will rise if the company trades successfully and the ordinary shareholder, in particular, may make a capital profit on selling his shares.

Ordinary shareholders bear the risk of substantial loss if the company fails; consequently, they have a right to vote at meetings and control the company's affairs to the exclusion of preference shareholders who are usually entitled to vote only if:

1 Their dividend is six months in arrear
2 Their rights as a class are affected by some issue under discussion at the meeting
3 On a resolution to wind up the company.

Acquisition and transfer of shares

When shares are first issued by a company an investor may make an offer to purchase them by submitting an application form. Allotment of shares by the company creates a binding contract with the investor. Shares may be issued at a premium; for example, 50p may have to be paid for a share with a nominal or face value of only 25p. This means that existing shares already issued have a market value of 50p, thus the real worth of a share is determined by reference to the market value, not the face or par value.

A share certificate will be issued by the company stating the name of the shareholder and the extent of his shareholding. The register of members, kept by the company, will record the shareholder's name and address and the number of shares held.

The shares of public companies are quoted on the Stock Exchange and the shareholder can determine the present value of his shares by referring to the Stock Exchange list which is published in leading newspapers. One of the main advantages of shareholding is the ability to sell quickly and realise the value of the shares.

Debentures

A company needing finance for a programme of expansion may be reluctant to raise the additional capital required by issuing more shares for two reasons:

1 The money will only be needed until the new equipment purchased earns sufficient profits to repay the capital borrowed: the company may not wish to raise capital on a permanent basis for such relatively short-term needs, since regular dividends must be paid
2 Once shares have been issued a company cannot buy them back when it has sufficient cash available, with the exception of redeemable preference shares (which may be issued for the same reasons as debentures).

The company borrows money from the lender and in return issues a debenture, redeemable at a fixed or determinable time or at the company's option. The debenture holder is entitled to:

1 A fixed rate of interest which must be paid even if it is paid out of capital, not profits
2 Repayment of the principal sum when due
3 A charge on the company's property. This means that if the company fails to repay the loan and interest when due, the debenture holders may satisfy their claims by disposing of the company's assets. These claims have priority over, and must be satisfied before, claims by all types of shareholders.

MEETINGS

The company is obliged to hold various types of meetings from time to time to transact business. An annual general meeting must be held every year to deal with:

1 Declaration of dividends
2 Consideration of the accounts and balance sheet and the report of directors and auditors
3 Appointment of directors
4 Appointment and fixing of the remuneration of auditors.

Members must be given twenty-one days' notice of the meeting.

An extraordinary general meeting may be called by directors if important business needs to be transacted which cannot await the next annual general meeting. Holders of one-tenth of the paid-up share capital with voting rights may requisition such a meeting, even against the directors' wishes. Members must be given fourteen days' notice of the meeting.

DIRECTORS

Every public company must have at least two directors and a secretary. A proportion of the directors, usually about one-third, retire at each annual general meeting, and the members may re-elect them or appoint others in their place. A director may be removed by an ordinary resolution passed by members, but the director may make representations on the issue showing why he should not be removed.

The directors must manage the company's affairs by taking decisions at board meetings, otherwise they may be personally liable for their actions.

A director may be required by the articles to hold a certain number of shares in the company which are called his qualification shares, otherwise he must vacate his office. This gives him a personal interest in furthering the fortunes of the company to the best of his ability.

The articles may provide for the payment of a fixed fee to a director, but his remuneration is often stated in a service contract which he makes with the company. His remuneration must be disclosed in the annual accounts. A director is not entitled to compensation for loss of office or on retirement, unless approved by the shareholders.

The powers of the company, as determined by the memorandum and articles, are usually delegated to the directors in so far as they are not exercised by the company in general meeting. Members in general meeting cannot interfere with the manner in which the directors exercise their powers, unless they alter the articles accordingly. The directors should communicate their policy to the shareholders from time to time. If directors exceed their powers the members may ratify their actions, provided the act is within the powers of the company.

Publicity concerning directors

The company must make available the following information about a director:

1 A register of directors and secretaries must be kept at the registered office and open for public inspection, specifying a director's name, address, nationality, business occupation and other directorships held, except directorships in wholly-owned subsidiaries
2 A register of directors' interest in the company's shares and debentures must be kept at the registered office or place where the register of members is kept. It must be open for public inspection. Such holdings by a spouse and minor children must be disclosed
3 Details of a director's service contract must be kept at the registered office, or place where the register of members is kept or at the company's principal place of business. It must be open for inspection by members
4 The names of directors must appear on business letters, trade catalogues, circulars and show cards.

Shadow directors and connected persons

The various statutory provisions that impose numerous legal obligations and duties on directors, also cover any person occupying the position of director whatever name is used to describe his office. 'Shadow' directors are also treated as if they were directors for some purposes. This concept covers persons giving directions to directors, who then are accustomed to follow them irrespective of any legal or other obligation to do so. Thus directors may manage a company in accordance with the policy dictated by the controlling shareholder. That shareholder becomes a 'shadow' director. A person giving professional advice, such as an accountant, does not thereby become a 'shadow' director. Persons 'connected' with a director may also have the same restrictions placed upon their activities as the director himself. A 'connected person' includes:

1 Director's current spouse and his children up to the age of eighteen
2 Trustees of a trust which has as one of its beneficiaries the director, his children, his current spouse or an 'associated' company
3 Partner of the director or a partner of the director's spouse, his children or his trustee
4 A company with which the director is 'associated' where the director and his connected persons hold one-fifth of the nominal value of the 'associated' company's equity share capital, or where the director, his connected persons and any company he controls hold one-fifth of the voting rights at a general meeting.

Disclosure of interest in contracts

A director may have a personal interest in a contract made by the company with some other body, such as a partnership in which the director is himself a partner, or another company in which he holds shares. The company is entitled to the unbiased advice of a director, unfettered by conflict between personal interest and duties owed to the company. Every director having an interest, direct or indirect, in the contract which the company is about to enter, must disclose that fact to the board of directors when the matter is discussed. Such disclosure permits the director to make a personal profit from the contract which the company enters into, but failure to disclose enables the company to rescind the agreement so made. These principles also apply to 'shadow' directors.

Where directors have wide powers of management the risk arises that a director may sell his own property to the company at an inflated price with the connivance of fellow directors, or purchase the company's property at an undervaluation. An 'arrangement', which covers transactions not strictly enforceable at law as a contract of sale, cannot permit a director or his connected person to acquire a non-cash asset from the company or its holding company above the 'requisite value' of over £50 000, or one-tenth of the value of the company assets if over £1000, whichever sum is smaller. Further, a director or his connected person cannot sell a non-cash asset over the 'requisite value' to the company or its holding company. Arrangements exceeding the requisite value are permitted, however, if approved by members in general meeting. The holding company must consent as well as the subsidiary company directly involved. Here the shareholders have the opportunity to assess the advisability of the arrangement and will give their consent only if the company's interests have been safeguarded.

Service contract for a director

A director may be dismissed by a majority vote in favour of his removal passed by members in general meeting. To protect himself financially the director may have an express, written contract of service with the company for a fixed period of time (for example, ten years). If removed from office before expiration of the period he may claim damages for salary, less tax, that he would have earned during the unexpired portion of his service contract. The sum involved may be considerable, thus dismissal can be an expensive luxury for the company. Under the Companies Act 1980 shareholders are given the opportunity of voting at general meetings on whether directors are to be given such long-term service contracts.

A service contract for less than five years' duration, or for over five years' duration but terminable by giving reasonable notice (which means in practice about six months' notice) may still be approved by the board or the managing director, depending upon the person or body to whom the requisite power has been delegated. The consent of the members in general meeting is required for a service contract over five years' duration if not terminable by notice, or only terminable in specified circumstances. In the absence of such consent the contract itself is valid, but the term on duration is void, and the contract may be terminated by giving reasonable notice.

These new provisions are designed to prevent abuses whereby directors negotiate such contracts on terms set by themselves immediately prior to an anticipated takeover bid or removal on a vote by members, so that on loss of office they recoup substantial sums as damages for breach of contract.

Loans to directors

There are strict limitations on companies making loans to directors. Their position as managers may permit abuses at the company's, and consequently the shareholders' expense, as by making loans on terms that are commercially unsound.

A company is prohibited from making a loan to its own or a holding company's director, or providing a guarantee, indemnity or security in connection with a loan by some other person to such a director. However, a company may provide funds for a director to meet, or avoid incurring expenditure he has or will incur for company purposes, or to enable him to perform properly his duties as a company officer. Members in general meeting must give their prior approval with knowledge of the purpose and amount of the loan, or retroactive approval before or at the next annual general meeting. In the absence of such approval the loan becomes repayable, and the resultant liability must be discharged, within six months of that meeting. Not more than £10 000 must be outstanding by way of loan at any one time to a particular director or his connected person from a 'relevant' company.

Moneylending companies

There are situations where a company may make a loan 'quasi loan', or guarantee such transactions, for the benefit of its director or his connected person. Such a transaction must be part of the company's ordinary business – an important limiting factor since not many companies lend money or guarantee loans as part of its ordinary business activities. Further, the amount involved must not be greater, nor the terms more favourable then those it is reasonable to expect a company to have offered to a person unconnected with the company and having the same financial standing as the director or his connected person. A 'relevant company' must not lend over £50 000, but there is no such limit imposed on a recognised bank if the transaction is on commercial terms and disclosed to shareholders. A 'quasi loan' catches arrangements whereby the company agrees to make, or makes without so agreeing, a payment to a third party on behalf of a director of its own or its holding company or his connected person, on the understanding that the sum will be repaid by the borrower to the company. For example, the company may allow a director to use a credit card in the company's name with the director agreeing to reimburse sums spent within a year of the company settling the credit transaction.

Credit transactions

A 'relevant company' must not enter into a credit transaction or provide a guarantee, indemnity or security in respect of credit transactions for its own or a holding company's director or his connected person. Thus a company cannot lease a car for use by a director with the car being returned to its owner at the end of the hiring period. There is the usual exception for company expenses and also where the total sums involved are not over £5000. Also permitted are transactions in the ordinary course of company business, as where a company in the car hire business leases a car to its own director for his private and personal use, if the value is not above and the terms more favourable than those offered to persons unconnected with the company with the same financial standing as the director or his connected person who is party to the credit transaction.

Indirect transactions

A company cannot acquire rights and liabilities by a transaction that would have been prohibited if it had been made directly by that company. Thus, if a third party makes a loan to a director, the company cannot agree to take over the third party's rights. It would be using its resources to give a director credit with the same ultimate results as if it had made a direct loan to him. Nor may a company induce a third party to enter into a transaction, which would have been prohibited if that company and its director had been party to it, in return for a promise to benefit that third party. For example, the company cannot induce a third party to make a loan, quasi loan or credit transaction for a director's benefit by promising to place substantial orders with that third party to purchase his goods. Provisions of expenses for a director are an exception to these situations.

PROVISION FOR EMPLOYEES

A company may make provision for its own employees, or former employees, or those of a subsidiary company, when that company or one of its subsidiaries ceases business or transfers its business to a new owner. This provision permits a redundancy payment to an employee losing his job above the maximum sum authorised under the Employment Protection (Consolidation) Act 1968. The proposed payment must be sanctioned by members in general meeting approving an ordinary resolution. The articles or memorandum may state that a resolution by the directors suffices, or give a greater element of control to members by requiring a special or extraordinary resolution in general meeting.

DIVIDENDS

Dividends are trading profits divided among members in proportion to the number of shares held. The directors are responsible for fixing the rate of dividend, with the sanction of the general meeting. Shareholders cannot demand a dividend if the directors refuse to declare one, even though the annual profits seem to warrant some payment. Profits do not have to be distributed as dividends, as the directors may think it wiser to use them to offset past losses, or to transfer them to reserve to meet future liabilities. Once a dividend has been declared, however, a shareholder may sue to recover the sum he is entitled to receive if payment is not made.

The dividend is declared as a percentage of the share's nominal value; for example, a 30 per cent dividend for each 50p share held. The market value of the shares will be probably higher than the par value, say £1.50, consequently the real return on capital for a recent purchaser will be a more modest 10 per cent. A preference shareholder's dividend is usually at a fixed percentage, but ordinary shareholders will receive a dividend varying annually as the level of profits changes.

Limited companies have always been subject to rules as to what property may be used to pay dividends to its members. The basic purpose of these rules has been to prevent a reduction of capital by returning to shareholders money which the company should retain to settle debts to its outside creditors.

All companies are prohibited from paying a cash dividend to members except out of profits available for that purpose. Fixed capital may be invested in the business with the intention of retaining it more or less permanently to produce income, such as in business premises and machinery. On a sale of such items the company may make either a profit or a loss. Revenue profit or loss is the result of the company purchasing or producing property with the express intention of selling it again in the hope that a gain will accrue. Profit is made up of those accumulated and realised profits from revenue or capital from the date of incorporation which have not been used by the company for any distribution or capitalisation, minus realised losses of revenue and capital from incorporation date not previously written off. The company must also take account of losses which are anticipated but not yet realised. What constitutes a profit or a loss is left to the commercial world, to be determined in accordance with normal accounting practices. The articles may restrict the meaning of profit available for distribution, but cannot make it wider to justify a payment not authorised by statute.

It is not possible to make a distribution from a capital profit that has not yet been realised. Thus an increase in the value of land held by the company cannot support a dividend payment until the land is actually sold and the profit realised. A company's profits and losses for one accounting period cannot be treated in isolation from those of other accounting periods, but as a part of a continuing process. A company making a revenue or realised capital profit in the current accounting period cannot pay a dividend before making good previously incurred capital and revenue losses. For example a loss made in the financial year 1980–81 must be made good out of the profits for the 1981–82 financial year before a dividend can be paid for the 1981–82 period.

INSIDER DEALING

An insider dealer is someone connected with a company such as a director, company secretary, auditor, employee or other person in a business or professional relationship with the company, who has acquired in confidence specific information; that is, unpublished price-sensitive information, materially affecting the value of that company's shares and debentures or the securities of a company in the same group. The insider dealer then buys or sells such securities on the Stock Exchange without disclosing this information, which is not generally known to those persons who deal in, or would like to deal in, the securities affected. Persons who receive unpublished sensitive information are prevented from dealing in securities to which the information relates.

An individual who has price-sensitive information and/or is prohibited from dealing in a company's securities must not counsel or procure another person to so act, knowing or reasonably believing that such dealing would occur.

FURTHER READING

Northey and Leigh, *Introduction to Company Law*, 2nd edition, Butterworths, London, 1981. Good coverage in a style that is easy to follow.

Smith, K., and Keenan D. J., *Company Law*, 4th edition, Pitman, London, 1981. Some excellent background material and a useful summary of case law.

Tolley's *Companies Act 1980* (1st edition), Tolley, Croydon, 1980. A clear exposition of complex new legislation.

21 Office services

R S Henderson

No firm can hope to operate effectively, and therefore profitably, unless it is properly supported by all the necessary services and facilities that go to make up a modern office. These range from the maintenance and cleaning of the building to the provision of stationery; from well-established security and emergency procedures to the handling and distribution of the post. The task of administering all these services is almost always a thankless one. If all goes smoothly the service is taken for granted; when it falls down, everyone looks for a scapegoat, who is invariably the unfortunate office manager.

The office manager – always underestimated, at least as far as the importance of his job is concerned – finds himself managing by complaint. He is responsible for a large number of diverse and individual systems which he probably has inherited from a predecessor, and which tend to operate much as they always have done. He hesitates to examine their workings too closely for fear of causing disruption, and indeed is probably too busy to do so thoroughly and methodically until he gets a complaint from above. He is then forced to react quickly and as a result may make ill-considered changes with potentially disastrous results and certainly unfavourable reactions from the operating staff.

ORGANISATION OF OFFICE SERVICES

In setting up an office services department, senior management should consider:

1 The person they charge with looking after the running of the building and its supporting services and facilities will probably have one of the largest budgets and workforces in their organisation. The department may not be a profit centre, but it has tremendous significance in terms of total operating cost
2 The quality of the service provided by this department impinges on all aspects of the business, including the profit centres. If that service is efficient, reliable and flexible it will be a positive aid towards profitability.

3 To maintain a high level of service the office manager must be able to predict future demands to be made upon his department. He will only be able to do so if he is kept informed and preferably forewarned of all policy changes and decisions which affect his areas of responsibility.

These three points lead to the clear conclusion that the role of office administrator should not be regarded as an inferior occupation. It should have a clearly defined place in the organisational structure with direct links to top management. Only in this way can channels of communication be maintained to ensure that the planning of office administration is based on full and accurate information.

The scope of office services

Figure 21.1 shows the potential range and scope of the services and facilities needed by a medium-sized company occupying its own office block. For smaller firms some of these items would be reduced in scope but the range of services and facilities applies to all. Even a company with only twenty or so office staff will undoubtedly need an element from each of the main headings. At this level it will probably be the company secretary or his equivalent who will be responsible, but the same principles will apply to their organisation and management as for a much larger firm.

Organisation structure

In Figure 21.1 the range of services has been grouped under ten headings. For administration and organisation purposes they could be brought together as indicated in Figure 21.2. There are obviously many variations on this theme and much will depend on the size of the company and the complexity of the administrative services needed. However, the aim should always be to avoid having every query finishing up on the office manager's desk. He should be a manager rather than a supervisor.

He should be able to plan for the future, to budget, to introduce new methods and systems, to improve existing ones; he should study trends in the development of new equipment with the aim of phasing it in as the opportunity arises; he should train and develop his staff, particularly the younger ones, to take on new responsibilities as the need occurs; and above all he should manage the administration of the office so that it runs smoothly, effectively and economically.

OFFICE LAYOUTS

This whole chapter is devoted to the provision of efficient services to the office operation and how these contribute to the smooth running of the company. An essential element of these office services and one that is often overlooked or neglected is the responsibility for the layout of the offices. All too often layouts of partitioning, and even of desks, are inherited from a previous occupier, with

Reprographics

Printing
Photocopying
Stationery issues
Microfilming

Telecommunications

Telephone exchange
Internal systems
Paging system
Public address
Telex, telecopier terminals

Security & Safety

Security guards
Fire precautions
Emergency procedures

Industrial and commercial espionage measures (e.g., shredding equipment and counter-surveillance measures)
Statutory requirements

Reception

Main reception
Commissionaires
Booking of meeting rooms
Travel arrangements

Post

Postal service
Messengers
Document movement

Central services

Typing
Secretarial
Filing
Word processing
Library

Staff welfare

Canteen
Refreshments
Social/recreation
First aid/medical
Rest room
Shop

Transport

Company cars/vans
Chauffeurs, drivers
Transport records
Car park allocations

Purchasing

Stationery
Equipment
Furniture
Leasing arrangements
Contract arrangements

Building maintenance

Building:	Cleaning, upkeep, repairs, redecoration, rubbish and waste disposal, external upkeep (e.g., grounds and car park).
Plant & equipment:	Maintenance contracts for heating/ventilation/air conditioning, lifts, window cleaning gear, day-to-day maintenance of plant, plumbing services, electric power and lighting, clocks etc.
Office equipment:	Typewriters, calculators, printing equipment, furniture, filing systems, etc.
Office layouts:	Planning layout revisions, alterations to lighting, partitioning, telephone and power points, furniture moves, etc.

Figure 21.1 The scope of office services

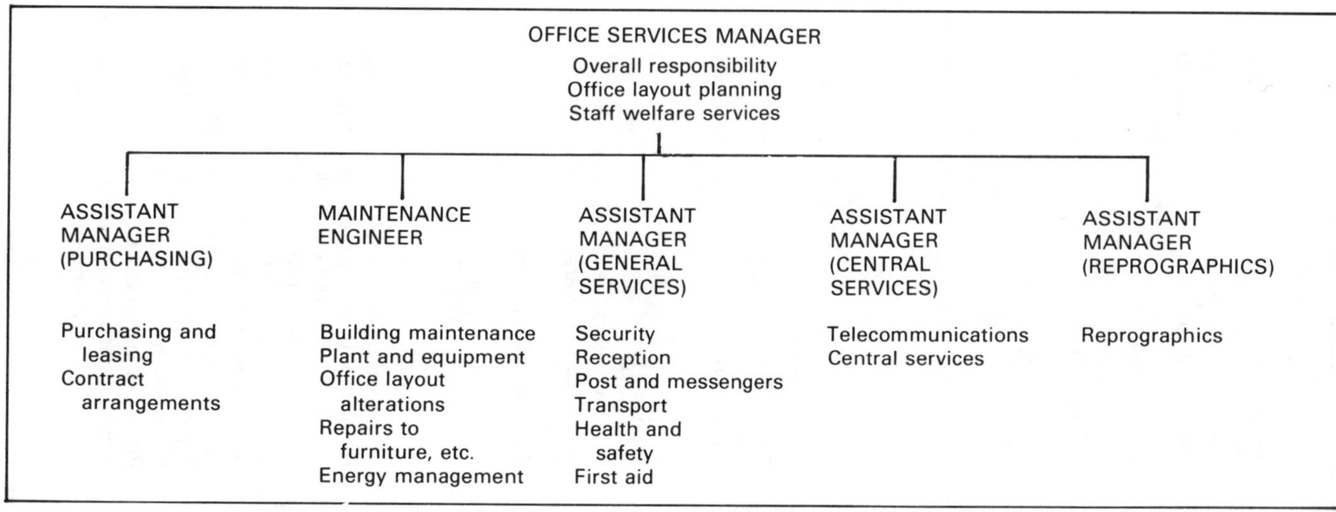

Figure 21.2 ***An office services departmental organisation***

This is just one of a large number of possible organisations which might be found in an office services department. Obviously the organisation must depend on the size of a company and the activities which it performs; the arrangement shown here might be found in a medium to large engineering company

cost dictating a minimum of alterations, and the new users having to adapt their work routines to suit. Even when the layouts suit requirements in all respects on initial occupation, very few organisations remain static for long. Very soon, growth and/or changes in operations and structure inevitably call for modifications. If these are not responded to there begins an, at first unremarked, deterioration in the working arrangements.

Piecemeal changes in shared or open offices, even of an apparently minor nature, can have a domino effect leading to overcrowding in some areas and wasted space in others. It is a fairly straightforward matter to establish a routine whereby the office manager is consulted and controls all layout changes. It is perhaps more difficult to make sure that he has the authority to make his proposals work. In any event, a major reorganisation or relocation exercise may overstretch his resources, and it would be unwise to treat this as part of the normal office services role. If an outside specialist is called in on these occasions, it should be to work with rather than instead of the office manager. The professional planning consultancy will need his advice and guidance and his detailed knowledge of the building at all stages if their schemes are to be effective and worth while.

The subject of office planning is worthy of a book in its own right, so it is impossible to give comprehensive advice here. However, the few guidelines reproduced below may be helpful to the hard-pressed office manager.

Office planning guidelines

1 Do not underestimate the importance of planning office layouts to meet individual functional needs
2 These needs change from time to time as new working methods are developed to meet changing market forces
3 Do not assume knowledge of how people perform their day-to-day tasks and how they relate to each other in a department or organisation
4 The first step is always to study requirements by formally interviewing both the management concerned and as many of their staff as practicable
5 Base the layouts plans on your analysis of needs. For example, private rooms, only for those with a high proportion of their time spent on confidential matters; more space in the open office for those who need some measure of privacy and freedom from distraction
6 Better to arrange informal groups of desks reflecting, perhaps, a team approach, than to adopt a schoolroom regime
7 Avoid rows of private offices along one side of the office floor with the open area on the other. This promotes the idea of 'them and us'. Try to site offices where they are needed and to create pools of related open space between them
8 Walkways and escape routes in open offices need not be straight, but should always be clearly demarked by items of furniture such as low screens and filing cabinets
9 Open planning does not necessarily save any space, but it is more adaptable to change. If properly done, it can result in pleasant working conditions for everyone.

REPROGRAPHICS

Reprographics is the business of reproducing the written word or picture. It is a vast and growing subject in itself. There is hardly an office without at least a simple photocopying machine of some kind, and sophisticated in-house printing facilities are commonplace. The reprographics function also includes the printing of plans and technical drawings and, especially in more recent years, microphotography (alternatively called microfilming or micrographics). Any but the very smallest reprographics department uses materials and bought out services at an expensive rate, takes up a lot of office space, and needs equipping with costly machinery. Effective supervision of the department is essential in order to keep operating costs down.

Photocopying

It is necessary to be aware of the abuse to which the simple photocopier can be subjected, from the illicit production of private copies to the bigger problem of wastage by taking more copies than are really needed. In the same way as the original Mr Colman is said to have made his fortune from the mustard left on the side of the plate, so must the paper and copier manufacturers be doing from the high volume of unnecessary copies.

The most effective way to control copy quantity – and quality – is to place every photocopier within a central reprographics department, staffed by one or more trained operators, and with copies only given against duly authorised requisitions. Under such supervision, the machines will prove more reliable, and print quality can be maintained at a good level.

In a large organisation, a centralised photocopying facility may not be convenient to all staff, where the ability to obtain a few copies quickly saves the time of senior people and helps to promote efficiency. The wastage inherent in allowing staff free access to unsupervised copiers can be more than offset by the time saved. One solution to cut down wastage at local copier stations is to lock the machines, and provide suitable staff with keys. Another, less cumbersome approach is to provide machines for local use capable of giving the cheapest possible copies consistent with readable quality and reliable performance. Copies for internal use do not have to be up to exhibition standard. Where high quality or large numbers are justified, then the central facility must be used.

Photocopier technology continues to develop rapidly. The basic principles come in several quite different categories, each with its own multiple variations. Plain paper copiers using xerography (an electrostatic process) produce cheap prints at the cost of high technology and, therefore, expensive machinery. Copiers using coated paper may be electrostatic, photographic or with an infrared or ultraviolet source of light. In addition to wide variations in the cost per print, each method produces different degrees of response to the colours in the original document; some copiers will not copy faint blue images and others are relatively insensitive to red.

Many factors need to be considered when choosing a copier for the first time. Will it take the size of paper needed (usually the choice is between B4, A4 or

A3)? Some machines can reduce the image if required, for example printing out an A4 copy from an A3 original. A flat bed copier is useful when books have to be copied (observe the copyright law!).

Apart from the number of copies which the machine can make in a minute (i.e., the copying speed) a more telling factor is the time needed to make the first copy. Some copiers take ten minutes or more to warm up, with the result that they are left switched on all day to consume and waste electrical power and to emit heat and noise into the office. Some form of automatic or semi-automatic document-feeding device is often justifiable as a time saver, and it may also be desirable to include a sorter than can collate multiple sets of copies into convenient stacks ready for binding or stapling. One or two copiers even do the stapling.

As with the purchase of all office equipment, it is prudent to seek out other users of similar equipment and find out whether they would recommend it. The supplier will usually be willing to give introductions to such referees, although he is unlikely to be very open about sites where major problems have occurred.

The total cost approach is essential when choosing copiers. The starting point is to determine the number of copies to be made each month at each copying station. This is bound to be a variable figure, depending on seasonal factors and the level of activity in the business generally. In addition to an estimated average usage per month (for annual budgeting) it is also necessary to estimate the maximum and minimum numbers. Knowledge of the maximum number of copies will eliminate some copiers at the outset because they would simply be too slow or too unreliable to cope with the workload predicted. Manufacturers often specify the maximum capability of their machines, although they sometimes tend to be optimistic.

The reason for estimating the minimum number of copies needed over slack periods is purely one of economics. It is important not to commit expenditure to a machine which is too big for its job, since to do so must result in the cost per copy at low levels being inflated through the high burden of machine rentals or depreciation costs.

In the total cost approach it is useful to draw a graph for every machine under consideration relating the monthly copy volume (x axis) with the total cost of those copies (y axis). This total cost should certainly include machine rentals (or depreciation), all materials such as paper, toner and consumable spares plus maintenance costs. It may also be possible to estimate operator costs, although this is not essential and may be too difficult. Where alternative tariffs are quoted for the same machine, one graph should be drawn for each option. The curves will indicate clearly penalties payable where copy volumes are low and fixed costs high, in addition to the more straightforward cost per copy at higher rates of usage. This is a practical application of marginal costing. Photocopier salesmen are persistent people, unwilling to take 'No' for an answer; they are however easily impressed and intimidated when faced with a carefully produced set of graphs that provide a good basis for negotiating discounts and reduced terms in the face of their business rivals.

Printing and duplicating

Although some large plain paper photocopiers are able to produce fairly cheap long duplicating runs, spirit duplicators or stencil machines can be considered where low cost is the only consideration, to the exclusion of high quality prints. If it is essential to maintain decent print quality, then offset litho printing commends itself.

In the offset process, an image is prepared on a printing plate by direct typing or by photography. The image is transferred to an intermediate surface in the machine (and reversed) and thence to the paper (reversed back again). Thus it is not necessary to work with a reverse print master. Copy quality is excellent, long runs are possible, and the process is cheap. A skilled operator is essential for best results.

Once an in-house printing facility has been set up it is inclined to grow. Machines for sorting, collating, punching, folding, stapling and binding may have to be acquired. Still more expense occurs when artwork and typesetting capabilities are taken on. As these facilities and their attendant staff proliferate, so may the volume of printing itself increase to take advantage of the 'cheap' service available. It becomes easy to modify forms and produce infinite variations on letterheads and other printed documents. The result can be a very expensive and unjustified operation, generating high volumes of unnecessary forms and scrap paper.

No firm should embark on an in-house printing installation without a very careful study of its requirements. When evaluating the cost performance of a proposed internal unit, it is easy to underestimate the cost of the space which the department will occupy - not only the rent and rates but also service charges, heating, lighting and a share of the upkeep costs of the building. Although a small department may be essential to some companies, it may be better to use a local printer, and ask him to stock stationery and forms for availability against call-off orders.

Plan printing

Printing of engineering drawings and plans is almost always carried out using the diazo process. Masters are drawn on translucent or transparent material, and in the printing process a coated material is exposed to ultraviolet light, passed through the original in close contact with the print, and the positive image is developed by ammonia. Such machines consume a considerable amount of electrical power - often in excess of 10 kW - and the heat and ammonia fumes produced have to be ducted off into a flue. The process is ideal for producing large-sized prints on paper, or on any other film or sensitised medium.

MICROFILMING

Any office manager responsible for providing office space is aware that document filing is usually very space consuming, and staff continually request more and more filing equipment. Indeed, it could be said that any company will eventually choke to death on its own paper files if the growth of such files is allowed to continue unchecked. Clever filing equipment, some of it mechanised, is available to minimise the space needed; this is achieved by transporting the documents within the system in such a way that waste space (e.g., roof voids) can be used. Other measures include the provision of storage space off site, in a warehouse or similar building, where files can be boxed and held available for occasional reference at (say) a day's notice.

A more drastic and usually sensible way to reduce filing bulk is to question the need to keep documents at all. Certainly, when a member of staff asks for an additional filing cabinet, he or she should be asked first to clear out unnecessary paper from the other cabinets and drawers in the office. Nevertheless, a considerable amount of information has to be stored within easy reach in most companies, and a cost-effective and convenient approach to the problem is to hold the documents on microfilm, which dramatically reduces the space needed for storage. Properly managed, access time to any required document can also be reduced, simply because the files are concentrated in a small area, and no walking is needed to retrieve items. Accurate and sensible indexing is the essential requirement for microfilm retrieval.

Microforms

There are several variations on the microfilming theme, each suitable for a particular office application.

16-mm film is used widely for the storage of complete files. The original documents can be any size up to foolscap. Longer documents can sometimes be filmed so that the image lies along the major axis of the film. By mounting the film in a cassette, and using viewing equipment with a suitable indexing device, rapid retrieval of the document required is possible. Approximately 1 500 A4 original documents can be held on a 100 ft (30 m) roll of film. The roll film method is only really suitable for files which will not be updated because the replacement of a document would entail cutting and splicing the film.

16-mm jacket fiche is a system based on the use of 16-mm roll film, but which allows editing, additions and revisions. Documents are filmed on to the roll, which is then processed and cut up into individual documents or groups of documents according to the file index. For example, one subject could be the name of an individual in a personnel records system. Using a special jig, the strips of film are inserted into transparent plastic sheets, which allow a grid of frames to be assembled. The sheets contain a series of horizontal channels to accommodate the film. Outdated information can be removed from the jacket fiche using tweezers. Additional or revised information is filmed and inserted in the appropriate place in the jacket. Retrieval is achieved with a special fiche viewer, using an index system that first identifies the particular jacket fiche, and then locates the frame on the sheet by a grid reference system.

Microfiche is similar in some respects to jacket fiche, but the degree of reduction is greater. Many more documents can be held on one fiche, which is a single piece of photographic film of a size suitable for filing in a card index tray.

Every frame is photographed on to the fiche sequentially to form a pattern of images in regular columns and rows. As with jacket fiche, any single frame can be identified by a grid system of co-ordinates but, since microfiche is a direct photographic image on film, it can only be updated by changing a whole fiche. Microfiche is applicable to whole books (since books do not get updated in general, and a whole book can be contained on only a very few microfiche sheets). The method is also used for catalogues and spare parts lists, the whole set of fiche being replaced when a new issue is required.

35-mm film allows larger documents, such as engineering drawings, to be microfilmed without the loss of definition which would result from any attempt to use 16mm. Drawings up to A0 size can be filmed successfully on 35 mm. *70-mm film* is used in limited applications where even greater definition is needed.

35-mm aperture cards are similar in appearance to data processing punched cards, but a rectangular aperture in the card carries a single 35-mm image frame. Usually, drawings are filmed on to a 35-mm roll, which is then cut up into individual frames for mounting into jackets cemented on the face of the aperture cards. Aperture cards can also be obtained in magazines, with the film already in place on each card. Exposure takes place in a special camera, which also develops and processes the image automatically. The advantage of aperture cards over unmounted roll film is in the ease of handling and retrieval made possible. In fact, provided care is taken not to damage the film, aperture cards can be punched and printed with the relevant drawing number and title, and mechanical sorting and automatic feeding to a printer become possible.

Quality control and techniques

With all microforms, quality control is essential at every step in the process. The exposure must be right, the original document must be well and evenly illuminated (sometimes from underneath using a glass table), the degree of reduction should be accurate in order to maintain the correct scale on reproduction, and of course the image must be in focus over the entire area. Developing, fixing and washing also require careful control to ensure that the film will keep without deterioration – especially important for archive microfilming. Good conditions can be obtained using automatic equipment which is electronically controlled. Otherwise, a reliable bureau should be employed. An incidental, but extremely important, extension of quality control and supervision is the care given to the original documents during the process to prevent damage or loss. Obviously such originals must be protected until the microfilm has been processed and the image quality checked.

Storage and copying

Ordinary photographic film, using a silver halide emulsion, is referred to as 'silver' microfilm for short, and this is the material with the longest storage life for archival purposes – say up to fifty years or more. The diazo process can be used to make cheap contact copies from roll film or from aperture cards or fiche. Such cheap copies are usually of very high quality, with adequate storage properties for normal use. For widespread publication of books, catalogues and the like in microfilm, diazo copies are ideal. In engineering offices, 'satellite' reference files of drawing aperture cards can be arranged in a number of locations to give local access to drawing information while the silver masters are locked away for security.

Viewing and printing

A wide range of commercial viewers, viewer-printers and printers is available. There are also projectors. Many of these viewers are fitted with a retrieval device, allowing a particular frame to be found easily on a roll film cassette or fiche. Printing methods include xerography on to plain paper, an electrolytic process, and a heat-developed image using photographically sensitised paper.

Computer output on microfilm (COM) is a system in which the need for a paper document is discarded. Instead, the data output from the computer is photographed directly on microfilm from a viewing screen. More modern techniques use lasers, and video discs will replace some microfilm techniques altogether, with information stored in digital form from which an image can be printed out or projected on a viewing screen. At this point the discussion leaves the realm of office services and becomes more a question of data processing.

TELEPHONES

Telephones are often said to be the life blood of a company, although they certainly can be the death of sustained concentration for the individual! Nevertheless, a well-run telephone service is important, particularly in the way calls are handled by the operator. The first impression a potential customer receives is often from that anonymous voice. If it is helpful and obliging, and above all seems interested in being so, the impression is going to be a favourable one. It will become part of the company's image and reflect their standing in their market.

There is, of course, much more to this than making sure the operators have good telephone manners. For example, the internal telephone directory must be kept meticulously up to date, or the image will very quickly be tarnished. They should also be involved enough in the company's business to be able to direct a vague enquiry about a new product, for example, to the person dealing with it. This applies just as much to the full-time operators of large PABX systems as to the maid-of-all-work who is combined receptionist, switchboard girl and part-time invoice clerk/typist.

Another aspect of telecommunications which the office manager has to be aware of is the need to establish and foster good relations with the local British Telecom engineers and sales staff. They can be remarkably helpful over an unexpected need to move telephone extensions or to cope with some other crisis. Certainly their advice and assistance can be invaluable in planning a move of any size, a new layout, or the introduction of new equipment.

The subject of telecommunication is, of course, a complex and rapidly developing one. It is neither appropriate nor necessary to deal here with all the possible ramifications which might come under the office manager's wing. There is a wide range of equipment available to meet most normal telephonic needs. With the end of British Telecom's monopoly this choice will inevitably become even wider. Similarly, as electronic systems become cheaper and more commonplace, so will the twin technologies of data processing and telecommunications become interdependent. Such developments are discussed more fully in the chapter on the electronic office (Chapter 23).

SECURITY AND SAFETY

Not so long ago security measures were aimed at preventing pilfering and occasionally thought was given to safeguarding confidential information. Now vandalism and even bombings necessitate turning buildings into fortresses and, once again, it is the office manager who is responsible for seeing that the drawbridge is raised. It is a manifestation of a rapidly changing society that buildings planned and designed only a few years ago for ease of access for goods and staff and the general public are now considered vulnerable and therefore ill-conceived.

As usual, technology leaps to the rescue and sophisticated services abound to cope with each new problem as it arises; protective film for windows, closed circuit TV systems to monitor the thieves' progress; anti-bugging devices to confound the electronic eavesdroppers – all these and many more are readily available to cope with specific security problems. The drawback is, however, that apart from the cost, they nearly all impose constraints and discipline on the law-abiding users of the building. It is important, therefore, to strike a balance between security risk and acceptable constraints. The office manager should assess the risks, and make his recommendations so that management can decide the appropriate level of security precautions necessary.

No avoidable risks should be countenanced, however, when it comes to fire precautions. These really fall under two headings – minimising the risk of fire breaking out and spreading, and the provision of safe means of escape from the building in the event of fire. In both instances close liaison with the local fire officer and strict compliance with his recommendations, however irksome, are essential. In renovating older premises these may well include having to shorten escape distances by the provision of protected corridors, or even the construction of an additional fire escape.

Whilst under the provisions of the Health and Safety at Work Act the employer has a legal obligation to ensure as far as is reasonably practical, the health, safety and welfare of all his employees, the office manager must relate the spirit of the law to the services for which he is responsible. For example, there are a number of very real hazards which can be created by the mis-use, or irregular maintenance of electrical services. Frayed or trailing cables, the use of multi-socket adaptors, damage to electric cabling caused by inadequate protection at outlets and changes to electrical heating systems without consideration of current loading are all common examples of dangerous practices. Similarly, with the increasing use of furniture systems it is essential that components are put together strictly in accordance with the manufacturer's instructions to avoid, for example, accidental tipping of screens carrying storage units.

BUILDING MAINTENANCE

Many aspects of building maintenance are worth touching on here in so far as they fall within the ambit of the office services manager.

There are, of course, the routine daily processes of cleaning and disposing of rubbish and waste and there is the contract maintenance of a wide range of items from typewriters to lifts. These, though, can be dealt with satisfactorily, once they have been set up, with only routine supervision and an occasional detailed check on performance. What is all too often overlooked, however, are the opportunities for preventive maintenance and planned replacement procedures.

For example, most office building leases have clauses requiring tenants to redecorate externally and, sometimes, internally on a regular basis. Apart from financial planning, or budgeting for what could be a major item of expenditure, it makes sense to plan ahead for the disruption that internal redecoration can cause. With forethought it can be done progressively, taking advantage of the inevitable changes of layout as they occur and which take place regularly in any dynamic organisation. This is far better than expensive out-of-hours working with attendant security problems, or having to shuffle people around to create working space for decorators.

Also on the preventive maintenance side, it pays to include an annual wet clean of all painted surfaces in the cleaning contracts. Here again, this can be done progressively and should show a considerable saving on the redecoration bill. The same principle applies to toilet installations, floor coverings, kitchen equipment and so on, where the work can be carried out by specialist contractors.

CENTRALISED SERVICES

Even a relatively small organisation will consider at some time or another the centralisation of typing and secretarial services. With the advent of the word processor there is now even wider scope for providing an efficient and comprehensive service. Here is yet another area which demands a proper study of the users' needs before investing in new technology. There is a wealth of information available through specialist magazines and so-called seminars, but most of it is devoted to describing what the equipment will do. Very little is said about how to analyse the need for word processing and how to match that need with an economic system. However, there are now plenty of companies with direct experience of using word-processing systems, from stand-alone machines to complex intercommunicating systems. Most of them are quite happy to pass on the benefit of this experience, not only concerning the equipment, but also their staff reactions to it, and this represents a valuable source of information.

As with all change, the new ideas and methods have to be introduced in a planned way. The operators themselves should be made to feel involved in the process and some care should be taken over the physical environment in which they will be working. The aim should be to make them feel that they are being brought together and provided with expensive computerised equipment, not with the aim of forming a typing factory, but to give them the opportunity to share the workload fairly between them and to help each other out as the need arises. It should be emphasised that there is no need for this centralised service to be restricted to typing only. With the right staff and the right telephone arrangements the group can provide a very efficient central secretarial service, handling messages, appointments, travel arrangements and so on for the whole company. The executive then should not feel deprived at the loss of his personal secretary; in fact he will get an even better service. The typists have their job horizons broadened and their working day is therefore much more varied and interesting.

Other contenders for centralisation are reprographics, stationery and filing as well, of course, as the more common services such as post and messengers, tea and coffee services, etc. In all instances centralisation should be approached with some care and a great deal of planning. It is no good setting up a photocopying service with fast, expensive equipment only to find people wanting to retain their individual machines because they need instant copies and cannot get them. Similarly, an elaborate stationery store which is only open for half an hour every fortnight will soon lead to the creation of individual mini-stores throughout the office.

A final note of warning concerns the continuing need to keep an eye on the future. In this rapidly changing world, all equipment is obsolescent virtually on the day it is installed, but awareness of this fact can help avoid costly errors.

FURTHER READING

Books

Company Administration Handbook, Gower, 5th edition, 1982

Denyer, J. C., *Office Administration,* Macdonald & Evans, Plymouth, 3rd edition, 1978

Journals

Business Equipment Digest
Business Systems and Equipment
Office Equipment News
What to Buy for Business

22 Managing information

R E Wiggins

A growing proportion of the populace is concerned with creating, processing and providing information as the developed world moves from being an industrial to an information society. Certainly the quantity of information available to individuals and organisations continues to increase. In the scientific and technical fields alone published literature has been estimated to double every ten years or so. What is more pertinent, however, is that the rate of increase far exceeds the fundamentally unchanging rate at which the information seeker can properly assimilate knowledge even in his or her area of specialisation. Since quality of information rarely increases with quantity, the problem is further compounded.

The means which should be available to organisations to minimise such problems are therefore central to the task of managing information. Particular emphasis needs to be given to exploiting sources of relevant information. Furthermore, in-house information services need to be developed where external services prove inadequate. In addition appropriate 'new technology' must be utilised, including that arising from the convergence of computing, word processing and telecommunications, and developments such as viewdata and teletext. Suitable organisational structures and staff are required to ensure, for example, that new information services and systems can be properly evaluated and implemented in the light of company requirements and broader national and international issues.

INFORMATION AND THE ORGANISATION

To be useful, information has to be communicated in the right quantity and form, and at the right time to those who have need of it. Communication processes and information flow are therefore important elements to be considered in a detailed investigation of information needs and of the ways and means of satisfying them. They are not, however, central to the present discussion.

Information types

Information can be categorised into data – facts, figures, tabular material – and text both of which may originate within or outside the organisation (see Figure 22.1). Clearly there is a spectrum of information between these extremes comprising both data and text in varying proportions.

	Internal	External
Data	Marketing Financial Engineering	Official statistics Handbooks Maths tables
Text	Reports Memos Letters	Journals Laws Books
Characteristics	Confidential and non-confidential Captive area Under own control	Confidential and non-confidential Amorphous mass Variable quality

Figure 22.1 Information types *(after Vander Noot, 1976)*

Activities and information needs

Internal data are generally handled by management information systems (MIS) concerned with, for example, the control and monitoring of the company's production activity. It is worth remembering, however, that an MIS does not necessarily have to be computerised. Those that are designed with mechanisation in mind must be based on sound premises because the failure of an MIS can often be traced back to the use of false assumptions at the design stage.

Although the need to consider total information resource management in an organisation is important, the main emphasis is on external information and internal text with the former category together with processed internal information being particularly important for strategic planning by senior management and executives. Information for planning and change is largely subjective and qualitative. Hence it is less amenable to computerisation than that used for operational control by lower levels of management. This is summarised in Figure 22.2.

Organisational activity	Information system
Operations	Activity-oriented Mainly internal data Often computer-based
Control	Information-oriented Mainly internal data Often computer-based
Planning	Information-oriented Mainly external data/text (often qualitative) Difficult to computerise
Change	Project-oriented Diverse information needs No standard approach

Figure 22.2 Information systems for different activities
The level of management seniority increases from top to bottom

INFORMATION - ITS ACQUISITION AND VALUE

The cost of acquisition should ideally always be related to the value of the information sought and acquired.

When searching for information there has at some stage to be a limit to the time, effort and money which the enquirer is prepared to spend. Once this limit is reached, the information is in effect deemed not to exist and, if still required, the knowledge has to be created by undertaking research or market surveys, for example.

Information can play a vital role here. Initiation of research has been shown to rise roughly in proportion to the increase in the level of technical information support received by the projects.

Where the knowledge does exist, but is not discovered, there is the danger of duplicating work already undertaken or of suffering expensive consequences due to ignorance. For example, it was estimated in 1962 that avoidable and unintentional duplication of UK research was associated with 9 per cent of projects, and could be costing the country nearly 2 per cent of its research and development budget, while the collapse of some concrete buildings in the UK in the 1970s was due to the use of high alumina cement, a material banned in France in 1947 for reasons well documented in 1958. All too often it takes such disasters to awaken an organisation's information consciousness. The remedy is to be wise before the event.

SOURCES OF INFORMATION

The information seeker has two basic sources available – other people and recorded knowledge. Direct interpersonal contact is often the quickest and best method of obtaining what is required. It has the advantage that the problem can be discussed and misunderstandings resolved. However, the enquirer who is impressed by the personality, standing or experience of the person consulted, may accept too readily, and without question, the answer provided. Thus it is often wise to check the result using other sources. This practice of confirming, or otherwise, the validity of information is particularly relevant where important and expensive decisions hang on the outcome.

Aside from people, there is the vast variety of recorded knowledge which is at least theoretically available to the information seeker in published literature and internal company reports. This indirect method of transferring information between its originator and user is necessary because it ensures continuity and permanency of knowledge independent of people and time.

The broad range of sources is categorised in Figure 22.3. It incorporates the previously mentioned elemental information types of data and text which may originate from within or outside the organisation. Clearly, not every information source can be unambiguously assigned to a single category. The classification does, nevertheless, provide a structure for a more detailed consideration of particular sources of information for the end-user.

Primary, secondary and tertiary sources

The first instance of recording a piece of information in traditional documentary form – or, as is increasingly happening, in machine-readable form for access via some form of computer terminal or screen – represents the primary source for that information.

The quantity of such material produced, both within and outside the organisation, long ago rendered it impossible for the user to find, let alone read, all information which might be relevant to his query. Hence numerous services have emerged to provide various secondary sources and aids to assist the enquirer. Paramount amongst these for published material has been the abstracting and indexing services, whose origin can be traced back to the nineteenth century in the field of scientific literature. Although science and technology still represent a major proportion of this industry, it has long since broadened its subject coverage to provide summaries of and references to published material in such fields as management, social science, and the press.

As might be imagined, these services are themselves producing more products than can be effectively handled. Technology is helping to ease the problem of access to information by enabling computer-stored data bases containing indexes, abstracts and even the full text of the originals to be searched online via a computer terminal. Nevertheless, such technology takes little heed of quality. Even the emergence of the so-called tertiary services, which aim at producing quality reviews and syntheses in key subject areas, are merely adding to the information overload felt by the end-user.

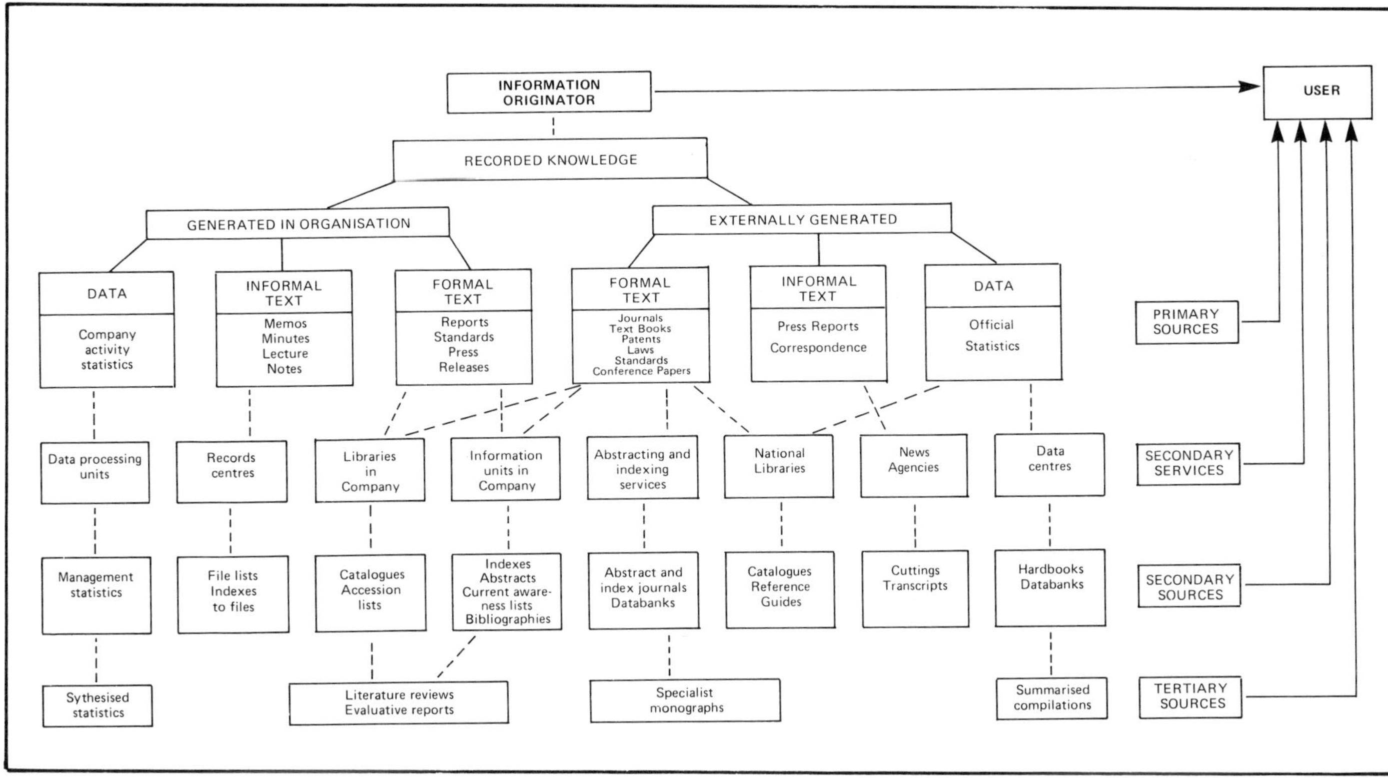

***Figure 22.3* Sources of information – a general outline**

A major factor in this lack of success is the occasionally piecemeal approach and blinkered outlook that some managements and information service providers assume towards the organisation of information, and its exploitation.

INFORMATION RESOURCE MANAGEMENT

In most companies the categories of information shown in Figure 22.1 are still held in different repositories, each of which is the responsibility of different parts of the organisation (see Figure 22.4). Co-ordination and co-operation between all these various units is often minimal. However, the advent of 'new technology' as exemplified by the microprocessor, and its exploitation in computing, telecommunications and office automation, has brought about a technologically possible convergence of those very parts of the company which often have responsibility for information repositories and services. As this convergence becomes a reality, the incompatabilities, overlap the gaps in information acquisition, processing and provision by libraries, data processing sections, registries and information units, for example, become all too clear. If nothing else, the microchip has made companies look long and hard at their information-handling activities.

The problem can be particularly acute for internally generated information since it is largely irreplaceable, and is rarely as well organised for retrieval as published material. This is largely due to the splits in organisational responsibility for internal information, and the fact that published material is an important, freely available resource exploited by a well-established industry which undertakes analysis, indexing, storage and dissemination for a profit (or at least not a loss).

A further complication is that much company information, and for that matter external information, does not reside in the traditional repositories. It is held by those concerned, for example, with corporate planning, investment, marketing or research and development. If a company does not take steps to organise all its captive information, and to integrate it with that which is generated externally, then no one else will.

	Internal	External
Data	Data-processing sections	Information units
Text	Registries Record units	Libraries

***Figure 22.4* Traditional repositories for information** *(after Vander Noot, 1976)*

Definition of an information resource system

The concept of an information resource system (IRS) needs closer definition. Such a definition does, however, depend largely on the type of environment in which the system resides and on the needs to be satisfied. Here the emphasis is on the business environment and the needs of a commercial organisation and its members, particularly management.

The information resource comprises not only internal and external data and text (recorded information), but also the expertise and knowledge of people inside and outside the organisation. The term 'system' is not to be construed simply as a computer-based facility (many effective and efficient information systems are purely manual). Rather it encompasses all the components (for example, people, recorded information, technological aids, users and originators of information) which interact and are concerned in some definable way with the creation, movement, storage, retrieval, manipulation and use of information for the benefit of the organisation and its members.

This approach makes use of systems thinking which is increasingly being used, as an effective means for tackling real-world problems that cannot be categorised into traditional subject discipline areas. In particular, it facilitates identifying the boundaries and components of the system to be examined. All too often, studies are commenced without prior thought as to the influence that changes in one part of an organisation will have on another. The systems approach may therefore be usefully applied to the analysis, design, implementation and operation of an organisation's information 'facilities'.

An information resource system exists to satisfy the needs of its users, and ultimately to further the objectives of the organisation. These objectives should be defined. If, however, they prove difficult to formulate directly, then a roundabout route using answers to such questions as what does the organisation do?, how does it do it? and why?, may suffice.

Determining the needs of users may prove equally difficult, not least because 'needs' are often confused with 'wants'. Furthermore, certain needs may never be articulated since the user often assumes that the system cannot satisfy them. Nevertheless, such needs must be established so that a specification for the IRS can be formulated.

The precise nature and content of the specification will vary from one application area to another. In general, however, an organisation's IRS should be designed to satisfy three requirements:

1 Aid the full range of management activities, from routine to planning and change
2 Match the changing pattern and structure of management at all levels
3 Produce information which meets the manager's needs and his capacity to use it.

The specification provides criteria against which the information resource system design is matched, and indicates the system components to be adopted, modified or disposed of. The need to encompass all types of relevant information in the system is likely to be a fundamental prerequisite. The mix of mechanised and manual activities has to be decided. In the design stage the aim must be to fit the IRS to the organisation and not vice versa. In this respect modern information technology is proving particularly beneficial because it enables increasingly sophisticated equipment to be decentralised and kept under local control, while still allowing any necessary centralised influence to be exercised remotely via communication networks.

Implementing the information resource system

Once the system is agreed, it has to be implemented. For complex systems involving a large number of people and the introduction of mechanisation the implementation phase requires particularly careful planning. As in the design stage, close collaboration between the system designers and users is vital. The critical interface areas between machine and human being must be identified together with the activities to be undertaken by each. Additional, superfluous and amended activities have to be identified and quantified, as do any changed levels of human effort for each discrete area of work relating to the IRS.

Following implementation, the IRS should be evaluated in terms of efficiency and effectiveness. Both these measures need to be applied if management is to be able properly to judge the worth of the venture. The ideal IRS will exhibit both high efficiency and high effectiveness; if there has to be a trade off between the two, it is effectiveness that must be given priority.

Managing the information resource system

The description of an IRS which has just been presented is, of course, generalised and idealised to a large degree. In practice, the IRS is rarely a tangible entity, but comprises a variety of discrete information systems, developed for a wide range of applications, together with other less well-defined and organised information resources. Some of these systems will be designed to satisfy specialised needs in specific departments or units of the organisation (for example, the collection and processing of data from research experiments). Others (such as a personnel records system) will have a more obvious, and direct influence across the whole of the company. The localised systems are likely to be most suitably managed, on a day-to-day basis, by relevant staff in the particular departments and units concerned. The pervasive systems will tend to be the responsibility of more senior management who have a greater company-wide role than their departmental colleagues. Given this scenario the question arises how best to manage the total IRS.

As well as the need to satisfy local requirements for information, and to delegate, as appropriate, day-to-day control of information systems, there is also the increasing need simultaneously to meet corporate-wide demands. These include the desire for ready access from any part of the organisation to information and information manipulating facilities (for example, word processing and data processing), located elsewhere, the aim being to minimise the need to replicate them locally. In addition, executives in corporate head offices wish to see consistent, reliable and timely information reaching them from all their business activities so that they can properly assess present performance, and plan for the future.

The need for a proper balance between these various demands argues for a small, central IRS management unit with emphasis on planning, policy making, co-ordinating, controlling and supervising the overall system. Although it may be involved in sponsoring projects to develop the IRS, it should not generally get involved in the provision or detailed running of specific information services and activities. Its chief responsibilities, in all likelihood, will be to monitor them so as to seek out areas for improvement such as filling information gaps and eliminating unnecessary duplication, and to lay down agreed standards, thereafter ensuring that they are adhered to. 'Standards' is an emotive word, but in this context must not be construed as being a restrictive, but rather a liberating factor. Thus it is sensible for a corporate telecommunication network design to conform to national, and international standards, otherwise remote communication may be difficult if not impossible.

Once the decision is taken to establish a central IRS management unit, a suitable person must be put in charge who will report to the executive level of the company and, if appropriate, be an actual board member. What qualifications, experience and type of person are required for this position? Certainly the previously mentioned convergence of technology in data processing, offices and communications, has been a major catalyst in causing individual managers from both inside and outside these areas to reconsider their roles. Some have felt threatened by such a development, although many have seen it as an opportunity for broadening their field of influence; examples include administrative managers, (computer) systems professionals, records managers and archivists, and librarians. A recent survey of information professionals in the USA showed that over a quarter of a million (17 per cent) were in some way managing information operations. Occupational titles included Comptroller, Database Manager, Director of Information Center, Library Director and Vice-President for Information.

What is important here, of course, is not the title which a person holds, but the experience, expertise and personality that he or she can bring to the job. As was done in the formative stages of establishing the IRS itself, a specification should be drawn up, but this time for the post of IRS manager. This being a novel venture for most organisations, there is as yet little experience on which to draw. Clearly an amalgam of the talents possessed by the managers noted above will form a significant element of the job specification, but there are certain dimensions to the task which are unlikely to be adequately covered in this way. A valuable contribution here arose from discussions between the Information Industry Association in the USA, and the US Federal Government concerning an occupational standard for an Information Resources Manager. The proposed standard recognises that the manager must be concerned with both technological aids and the usefulness of the information which they handle, must be the principal adviser to top and middle management on such aspects as plans, budgets, security of information, and the quality of information sources, and must above all be a resource manager. Both general and specialised experience is required, and in the latter instance it is suggested that this should ideally be drawn from at least two out of four clusters of occupations. These broadly comprise, first, library, archival, records and related areas; second, computers, telecommunications and office automation; third, statistics, operations research and finance; and, fourth, technical writing, editing and reprographics.

In the UK, the Institute for Information Scientists has developed and promulgated key criteria for information science which largely embrace these topics and include resource management as a main theme.

Staffing the information resource system

The constituent parts of the IRS, be they data processing units, record centres, libraries or information units, for example, must be adequately staffed in terms of numbers, experience and expertise. Where such staff have direct dealings with their clients, it is essential that they understand and speak 'the language' of their users' subject specialities, at least to a degree where communication and understanding do not impair the relationship. If clients do not have confidence in those there to assist them, the service will not fulfil its mission.

Unfortunately, it still happens that key collections of information or the establishment of a library service for example, are entrusted to staff ill-fitted for the role. They may have been unsuited to their present work and a position – any position – has to be found for them elsewhere, or it may be felt that a shy individual will be best employed in quiet backwaters in charge of the library. Users should not be surprised if they get the service they deserve, rather than that which they desire. Over the years, however, various professional bodies have evolved or been established to help ensure that adequately trained and educated people are available for such areas of activity. The courses include postgraduate qualifications and higher degrees which provide an information-type qualification on top of the first degree already possessed. It is therefore possible, for example, for a chemist to obtain an MSc in information science to prepare him for work as an information scientist in a research centre. Details of these professional bodies are noted at the end of this chapter.

Having given general consideration to the information resource system, attention will be directed to the particular area of information and library services.

INFORMATION AND LIBRARY SERVICES

The particular services offered, their position in the hierarchical structure and the titles they are given will vary from one organisation to another. Such decisions will mainly depend on the objectives set for the services, but should also take account of the support, both financial and moral, likely to be forthcoming from the management streams in which they may reside. It is not necessarily the case that the most appropriate management stream for a service unit will be that occupied by its main users. In order to operate effectively, the information and library service (ILS) needs the full back-up of, and preferably control over, its own administration and office services such as typing, reprographic facilities and filing.

In general, an ILS should encompass a records responsibility and be involved in acquiring, organising and exploiting external text and data (much of it published material), and internal text (records) for the benefit of the company. Internal data, as previously noted, should also be integrated in the IRS.

General ILS activities will be outlined together with an indication of the special requirements of functions such as engineering, research and development, marketing, planning and public relations. Figure 22.3 and the further reading section at the end of the chapter, provides a reference point for the matters described.

Acquisition

Relevant information, in whatever physical form, must be acquired from any suitable source, and will include:

External information:

- books, periodicals and other formally published material
- official publications of governments, etc.
- standards and specifications
- documents and reports which are not published formally and if classified will be available on a 'need-to-know' basis
- patents
- trade literature
- news media, papers, the press and transcripts
- audio-visual material

Internal information:

- internal reports
- laboratory notebooks
- standards and specifications
- project files
- meeting minutes
- other records containing non-ephemeral information
- expertise register
- audio-visual material

The ready availability of up-to-date standards, specifications, codes of practice and similar material is especially important for technical staff. Superseded standards should also be retained if, for example, they have been applied in the construction of existing plant.

Certain classified information will be available to a company if it has, say, a supply contract with the government. The ILS should be involved in obtaining and be responsible for safeguarding such material.

Patents are generally a sadly neglected source of knowledge. They often represent the only record outside a company of developments it has made. They are therefore an excellent way to monitor competitors' activities for the benefit of the corporate planning and research functions.

Accumulation of relevant trade literature is essential for technical and purchasing departments, and can be facilitated, although not wholly replaced, by subscription to suitable product literature agencies.

Information should be gathered from the various news media if, say, it is desired to monitor press coverage of one's company, keep an eye on competitors or acquire knowledge of political trends and government legislation to assist the public relations, marketing and planning functions.

Audio-visual material includes slides, films and video-tape, and is as worthy of acquisition as other information. It is an invaluable resource for company staff involved in meetings and exhibitions, for example.

The cost of acquiring all relevant information for retention within one's own company is clearly prohibitive. Exchange arrangements with other information providers can reduce costs, and the ILS should be a party to such agreements. In general, however, the aim should be to have on site just that primary information of high quality which needs to be at hand. Access to other external information is obtained in a more cost-effective and cost-efficient manner by buying-in selected secondary sources – published indexes, abstracting services, etc., by utilising external on-line data bases and by consulting other organisations, individuals and secondary services in response to specific enquiries, and generally as the needs arise.

The ability to select what is relevant relies heavily on the ILS staff maintaining regular contact with their users so that current and future needs are known.

The mode of acquisition of internal information will depend on the type of record involved. Discrete and substantive items such as reports, laboratory notebooks, and in-house standards are probably best copied, or removed from traditional files (leaving a reference as to where they are stored) so that they can be processed as other important material. Correspondence and like records, because of their physical nature, are more difficult to handle in this way, and may be left on file but referenced, or copied, say, on to microfilm. The aim in every instance is to ensure that the existence of substantive internal information is known so that it can be suitably referenced for use at some later date.

A vital information source is an expert. There may be much to gain by maintaining within the ILS a register of staff within one's organisation who, if they agree, could usefully be contacted should an enquiry arise in their fields of expertise.

While information acquisition is a vital activity, so is disposal. There have been various estimates made as to how quickly the published literature becomes obsolete in different disciplines. However, none of these results should be rigorously applied since the information needs of people, both as individuals and groups, differ and change with time. The company and the ILS should nevertheless strive to weed out that which is no longer required to support its activities. Due consideration must be given to retention of irreplaceable material, especially internal information, and to statutory and historical requirements. The latter may most suitably be given professional attention by an archivist. The aim is to ensure a consistent policy throughout the organisation towards the retention, organisation and disposal of information.

Organisation

Once acquired, the substantive information must have its description and location catalogued, and its relevant information content analysed and recorded by classification and indexing.

Descriptive cataloguing provides a record of the discrete pieces of information held, i.e., the available source material. To aid consistency in library applications, for example, the standard cataloguing rules of the Library Association are widely employed to produce the ubiquitous catalogue card giving details of author, title, publisher, etc. The principles should be adopted for any type and form of substantive information.

Information content analysis comprises the use of index terms, keywords, identifiers, etc. which will subsequently facilitate finding the source material via the information it contains. It embraces subject classification and indexing which differ in concept from one another.

Subject classification involves the conceptual, and often physical grouping together of items dealing with the same topic. One has in effect to determine to which subject 'pigeon hole' a piece of information is assigned. Despite the availability of regularly updated, and widely accepted standard classification schemes, such as the Universal Decimal Classification (UDC), the principles are difficult to apply consistently, as anyone will know who has tried to decide on which single file a piece of correspondence dealing a variety of topics, should be placed. The classification codes are typically used to determine the filing order for the information. More than one classification code can be applied to a document to reflect different subject viewpoints. In filing terms this is similar to copying one item on to the several different files with which it is concerned.

Internal records, such as correspondence files, pose special problems because of the sheer quantity often involved and the variability in their quality and worthiness for long-term retention. If possible files should be conceptually organised to fit in with the way the users of the files work. Thus project, case and company name files are likely to satisfy the needs of those concerned with research work, litigation and suppliers respectively. If simplicity and comprehensibility are attained in this way, staff are more likely to rely on and use the filing system. Although standard classification schemes (as noted earlier) may be applied in certain circumstances to provide file titles, and hence subject 'pigeon holes' for records, it is more likely that if a subject classification is required, it will need to be tailor made.

Subject classifications, then, direct one to the part of a collection most likely to include the information that is relevant to an enquiry.

Indexes, however, will indicate specific and likely relevant items of information within that collection. Indexes exist in many forms, and may be produced manually, or with the aid of computers, or by a combination of the two. They appear in books, in card indexes and provide conceptual access to computer-stored information. More will be said of computer applications later, particularly for large quantities of information.

It is not amiss, however, to consider first smaller, personal collections of information since it is often these that will grow and merge with one another to form the larger ones. For small information collections, card indexes may prove suitable when memory alone can no longer be relied upon. The edge-punched card is an example of an 'item entry' system in which a card exists for each item indexed, and contains the bibliographic reference together with all the index terms used and possibly a summary of the item. The peripheral holes are each assigned a specific index term and are punched out according to the terms applied for a particular item. The collection is searched by inserting needles through the holes representing the selected index terms. Relevant cards will fall out as the needles lift the cards (Figure 22.5).

The 'term entry' system is an alternative and its capacity for index terms is not so rigidly limited. Here each card represents an index term, and on each card reference is made to all the documents to which that term has been assigned in indexing. The reference is usually a document accession number. This can be written on a card in a column headed by the number which terminates the accession number (Figure 22.6), or in another system is indicated by the position of a hole punched in the body of the card (Figure 22.7). The terminal digit card system is searched by seeking a common number

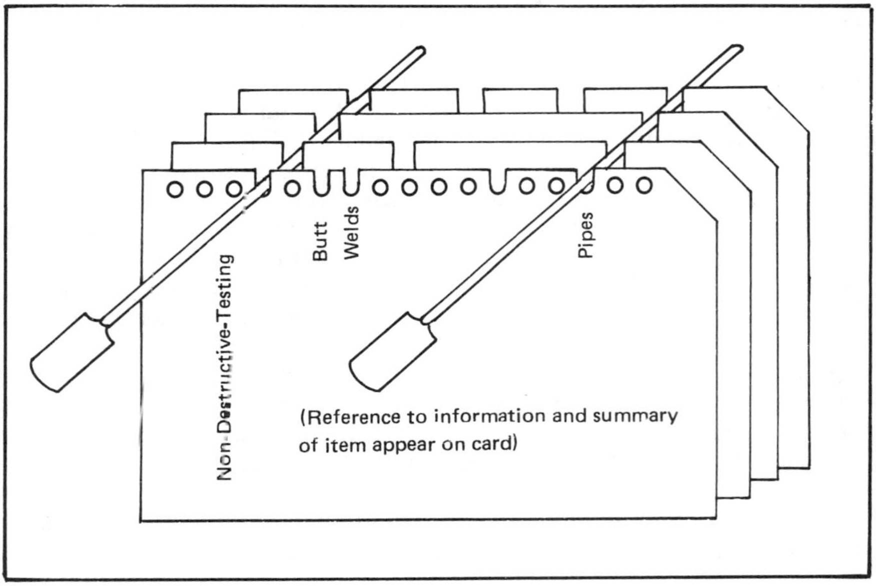

Figure 22.5 Item entry edge-punched card
Three cards relate to non-destructive-testing of pipes

on the selected terms cards, while the body punched cards are scanned by superimposing selected cards over a light source.

The concept of the 'term entry' system lies behind the way information is indexed and retrieved in most computer-based information retrieval systems as described later.

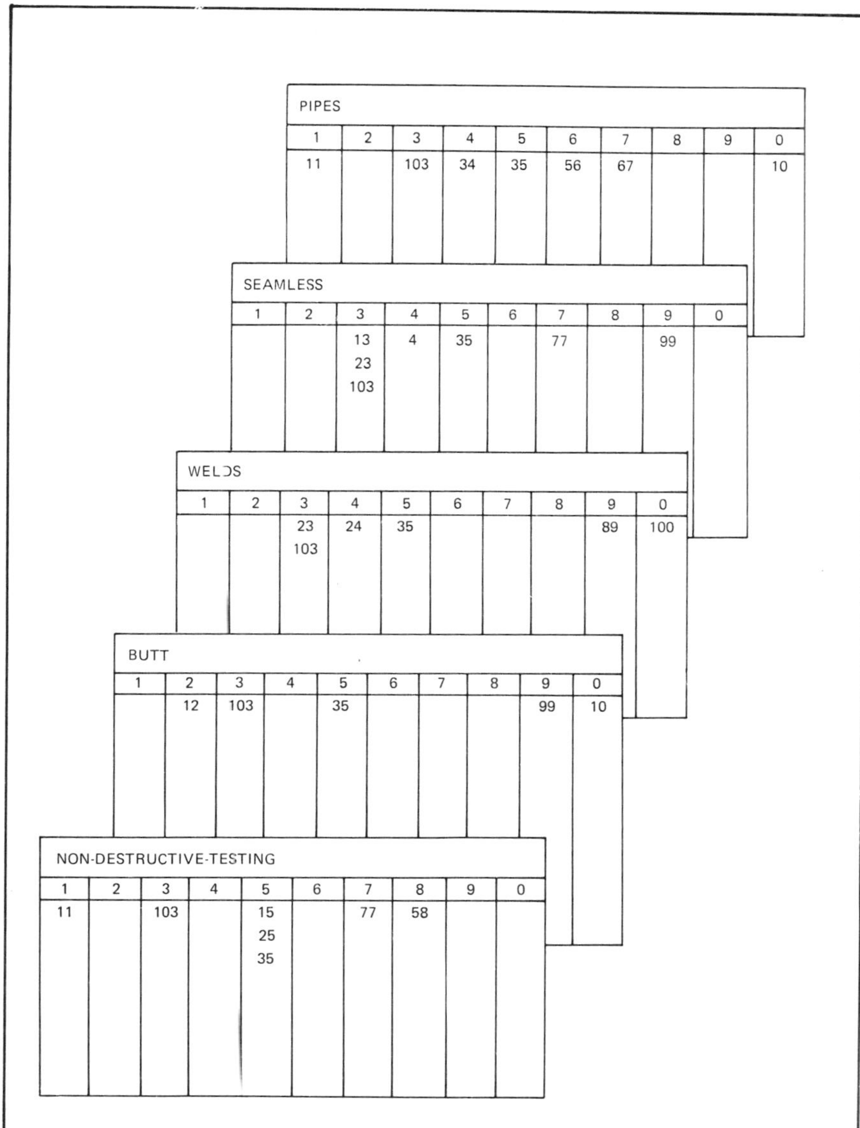

Figure 22.6 Terminal digit term entry cards
Document numbers 35 and 103 relate to all terms shown

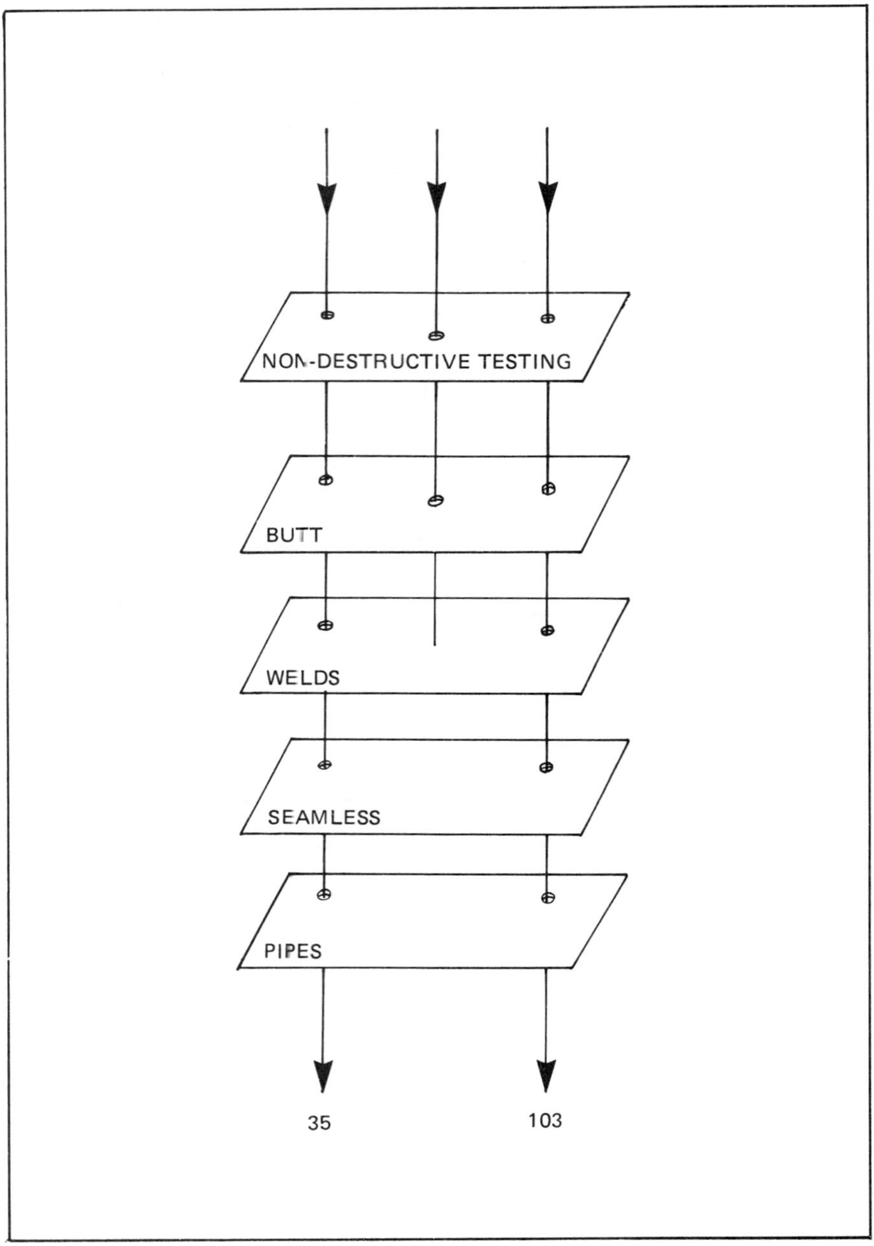

***Figure 22.7* Optical coincidence (Peek-a-boo) term entry cards**
Documents 35 and 103 relate to all terms shown

In choosing index terms, they may be 'natural language' terms selected, for example, from the original text, or those taken from a controlled vocabulary, or a combination of the two. The vocabulary, or so-called thesaurus, provides control, for example, over synonyms, code lists, semantic ambiguity (homographs and homonyms) and generic relationships (broader and more specific terms). As with subject classification schemes, it may be necessary to devise one's own thesaurus if the available published versions prove unacceptable. The intellectual effort and time required to create and maintain an extensive controlled vocabulary are considerable and are often underestimated. The process of information storage and retrieval as a whole should clearly be seen to benefit from such an approach before it is undertaken.

Utilisation

The ILS must exploit its information resources and know-how not only by just responding to enquiries received, but also by promulgating its services and disseminating its information products.

Enquiry answering includes dealing with requests for specific documents which may be supplied by purchase, lending from existing stock or borrowing from outside sources. The UK has a particularly well-developed public and special library network for tracing and inter-library lending of publications.

Specific information may be sought which can be answered quickly using standard reference works, a basic collection of which every ILS should have. These will include business and product directories, guides to statistical sources, guides to prominent business and political personalities, and general reference works, dictionaries, timetables, etc.

A more complex enquiry may necessitate a detailed and comprehensive search through a variety of primary and secondary sources. If such enquiries take time, or involve the use of specialised knowledge, an indexed record of them should be made to avoid having to repeat the work later.

For all enquiries, the real need behind the question should be ascertained by the ILS staff and expressed by the enquirer, since what is asked for may not be what is wanted.

Current awareness is an important dynamic aspect of an information service which will bring to the attention of its clients newly received information of possible relevance to their work. At one level there are the general blanket services such as library lists of newly accessioned material. Periodicals received by the ILS may be selected and seen on circulation by company staff. A variation is to distribute on request copies of the contents pages in place of or as well as the periodical circulation. It does, however, have the disadvantage for recipients that contents pages do not notify them of specific product information, or advertisements appearing in the publication.

A more selective service involves qualified ILS staff scanning through journals, conference proceedings, etc, to select items of relevance to the company for notification via a regularly issued bulletin. If the recipients do not have ready access to the original items, then the ILS staff may prepare abstracts of them which are included in the bulletin. If these summaries are made sufficiently informative, a reader may not need to see the original. However, the preparation of such abstracts, particularly in specialist subject fields, requires the time of skilled and experienced abstractors and is therefore expensive. An acceptable alternative may be to use abstracts which appear with the original; for example, author-prepared summaries.

Selective dissemination of information (SDI) is a personalised service which can effect still further savings in the time a recipient has to spend in scanning publications. It involves an individual, or possibly a small team working in the same field, expressing their particular interests in sufficient detail for the ILS staff to prepare an SDI profile containing the key search elements. These may be the name of a competitor, subject expert or journal coupled with subject key-words or phrases. An SDI service can be run manually by the ILS staff monitoring incoming information and comparing its content with the profiles. Notifications by phone, letter or photocopy, for example, will alert clients to the selected information. A manual service can only cater for a limited number of users, hence SDI only truly becomes a ubiquitous reality when the capacity of speed of a computer are harnessed to undertake the matching process.

Information product development goes beyond the regularly operating current awareness and SDI services. For an ILS to be truly effective it must be capable of anticipating, and not just reacting to new requirements. This will involve the production of specific and specialised products such as bibliographies, critical literature reviews and evaluative reports covering, for example, emerging fields of interest for corporate diversification, and competitors' activities in certain product and geographical areas. The ILS with its expertise in information storage and retrieval, and involvement with specialist users, is a likely centre for identifying and developing computerised data bases containing, say, items from its current awareness publications or the plant throughput statistics of competitors.

Examples of other areas where an information enhancement role can be exercised are:

- patents and licensing by monitoring and assessment
- press and public relations by issuing and assessing reactions to press releases
- standards and specifications monitoring and updating service for the company
- translation preparation and commissioning
- reporting procedure creation and administration
- board level services highly tuned to requirements
- extension of selected services outside the company to associated companies and the public.

Publicity and public relations

Publicising and marketing an ILS are just as important activities as the initial acquisition of information. All suitable means should be adopted including displays, talks by ILS staff, films and use of house journals. The ILS must be in regular contact with its existing and potential users to obtain feedback on its performance and to determine changing needs. In addition top management and line management must be kept aware of significant and regular information activities, and their support fostered in preparation for any development proposals.

TECHNOLOGICAL AIDS

Undoubtedly developments in computing, office automation and communications have greatly facilitated the storage, processing, retrieval and transmission of information. These developments have gained extensive publicity, and in some cases notoriety (viz. the microchip) and there is a danger that many are being oversold as the ultimate solution to the 'information problem'. In the end, information is created and used by people. Many of the problems inherent in the information-handling process are human ones which are not solvable technically as they relate to such factors as misinterpretation, ignorance, deficiency, overabundance, misdirection and incomprehensibility of information. So long as the human element is not forgotten, technology has much to offer.

Information retrieval

An information retrieval system is centred around a combination of hardware (the computer and associated equipment) and software (programs). The latter undertake and control the input, processing and retrieval of the stored full text or (more usually) indexed references to it. Depending on the software employed, the system will assist with the indexing by automatically selecting terms from the stored text, or from a stored controlled vocabulary (the thesaurus) or a combination of the two. During searching, the terms chosen to represent the query are entered via a terminal and matched by the computer against the stored index terms. One can typically search for number ranges (useful for dates), the beginning, end or central stem of a word (for example, all words beginning with 'plan'), combinations of words and alternative terms while at the same time exercising control over synonyms (for example, when searching for 'United Kingdom', the system can be designed to retrieve information indexed by 'UK'). In fact the presence or absence of any set of characters, including spaces, can be searched for given the appropriate software and design of data base (the machine-stored collection of information). The system displays intermediate results and the searcher can amend his strategy interactively until he is satisfied, at which time the final results are displayed or printed out. In addition to searching the data base in response to specific enquiries, the system is admirably suited to providing an SDI service as noted earlier. The interest profiles of users are stored in the computer which compares them with newly entered information. When a sufficiently close match is achieved, the client receives a suitable notification.

A variety of such software is available commercially for use within one's own company and details are maintained by Aslib (see the list of organisations given at the end of this chapter).

Increasingly the cheaper microcomputer end of the hardware market, in conjunction with developed software, is proving capable of satisfying basic demands for information handling and retrieval. In addition, developments in word processing are facilitating the creation and input of information into retrieval systems and are themselves offering increasingly improved retrieval facilities rivalling established products.

Electronic publishing and document delivery

The origins of electronic publishing lie in the publically available computer-stored bibliographic files (data bases) developed from the publishing activities of the major abstracting and indexing services in the USA. The number of such files available to Europe grew from 335 in 1975 to 654 in 1980 and contain around 150 million records (mainly references to published literature) over 80 per cent of which are accessible interactively and remotely from a suitable terminal. The number of data banks covering facts and figures has increased even more remarkably from 51 to 755 over the same period.

For bibliographic files, one generally only incurs a charge when the file is being accessed. A typical cost for access from Europe to one of the popular technical files held in the USA, is about £1 per minute, inclusive of telecommunication charges. An average search by a skilled user will take say fifteen minutes and therefore costs £15. For other services an annual charge may be made irrespective of usage.

Once relevant references are found from such a service, the documents must be acquired. Delays here can be considerable and much thought and effort is being put into electronic document delivery systems based, for example, on advanced facsimile equipment or the scanning and digitising of full text.

Many electronic publishing ventures are still based on paper products. Increasingly, though, publishers are moving some of their products wholly to electronic form or developing new ones well suited to electronic distribution. Public and syndicated electronic services linked by telecommunication or telephone networks to personal microcomputers which act as intelligent terminals are already in use.

The Prestel viewdata-type service of British Telecom and the Ceefax and Oracle teletext-type services of the two UK broadcasting authorities are examples of UK-developed electronic publishing services. Both use a modified television receiver. Prestel allows two-way communication when accessing several thousands of frames of business and leisure information placed on computers by a variety of information providers. Viewdata does not provide the highly interactive and sophisticated information retrieval facilities mentioned earlier since it is aimed more at the general and casual user. Furthermore the information is not so much indexed as classified, and the user is guided along a tree-like conceptual structure to the desired information. Unlike Prestel, the teletext services are free to use but only allow one-way communication to a more limited, but more rapidly updated, set of information frames. On

Prestel-type services, one can acquire private closed user groups with access to it open only to those nominated by the PCUG owner. The more recently developed 'gateway' facility allows a commercially acquired viewdata system, for example, to be linked to a company's computer for simple distribution of and easy access to information held on the computer. In this way viewdata technology can become an integral part of the company's computing and information services network.

Prestel technology has been marketed abroad and rival systems have since appeared overseas.

Storage

Apart from the use of electronic storage systems, information may be held on microfilm which continues to offer a highly competitive alternative to hardcopy particularly with the use of computer output microfilming (COM) techniques. Various systems exist and are being developed to mechanise the storage and retrieval of microforms, but many are limited in their capacity and require the user to have access to reading equipment and sets of the microforms which need updating. Video scanning and digitising of microform images and hard copy, for example offers the opportunity for remote access, transmission and updating of the information.

For many applications, storage systems must be able to combine text, graphics and photographic images if they are to have a major impact on the information handling activities of organisations. Video disc technology is one area of great potential and commercial applications are already being promulgated.

Putting it all together

Efficient and effective information storage and retrieval is not enough in itself. To be fully effective the system must be capable of producing a wide range of outputs such as printed products, either directly or by interfacing with other

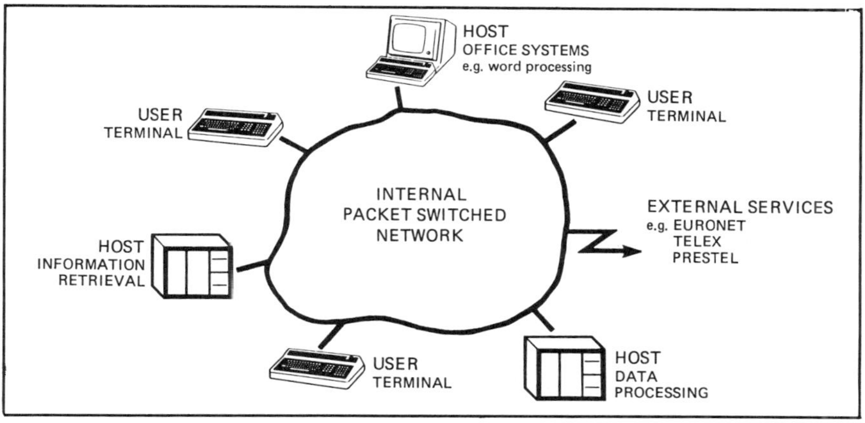

Figure 22.8 Integrated service network

systems. Word processing of the input, and computer typesetting, computer output microfilming and formatting of the output are examples of what are required to eliminate labour-intensive clerical operations and unnecessary multiple keyboarding of the same information. The system should be fully integratable with office systems, data processing and external services (Figure 22.8 on page 359). It will take some time to achieve this. Meanwhile systems introduced for specific applications should be designed as building blocks with this aim in mind.

FURTHER READING

This select list is arranged under the main headings used in the chapter itself. Titles of some journals which will enable readers to keep abreast of topics covered by this chapter are noted at the end of this list.

Information and the organisation

Allen, T.J., and Cohen, S. I., *Information Flow in Research and Development Laboratories*, Administrative Science Quarterly, vol. 14, 1969, pp. 12–20. A study of information flow including the role of technological gatekeepers as key figures in the transfer process.

Wood, C. C., *International Barriers to Information Flows*, Business Intelligence Program, SRI International, Croydon, England, March 1981. Considers transborder data flows (TBDF), the attempts to harmonise TBDF laws and the influence of these on company communications.

Information - its acquisition and value

Aguilar, F. J., *Scanning the Business Environment*, Macmillan Co., New York, 1967. A classic investigation of how top management, particularly in large chemical companies, gain relevant information about opportunities and threats. The kind of information required and methods of improving the scanning of the environment for information are covered.

Lamberton, D. M. (ed.), *Economics of Information and Knowledge*, Selected Readings, Penguin Books, Harmondsworth, 1971. A collection of eighteen previously published papers covering surveys, economic organisation, information and efficiency, information policy, international aspects and business planning.

Sources of information

It is, of course, impossible to provide a comprehensive list of sources. Those listed are only examples, and enquirers should consult their company library or information unit, or an appropriate external information source covering their field of interest. Membership of such organisations as Aslib and the British Institute of Management are well worth considering (see list of organisations at end of chapter).

Dare, G. A., and Bakewell, K. G. B., *The Manager's Guide to Getting the Answers*, Library Association, London, 1980. A basic information survival kit produced jointly by the British Institute of Management and the Library Association.

Hall, J. L., *On-line Bibliographic Data Bases*, 1979 Director, Aslib, London, 1979. A guide to computer-stored information which relates to published material and is available via a suitable computer terminal.

UNIDO Guides to Information Sources, Industrial Development Organisation, United Nations A series of guides, primarily aimed at developing countries, which covers both published sources and organisations and can provide a useful starting point in an information search. A complete list appeared in *UNIDO Newsletter*, no. 140, Dec. 1979.

Walford, A. J., *Walford's Concise Guide to Reference Material*, Library Association, London, 1981. Over 2 500 published reference works are noted which together cover most subject fields.

Information resource management

Arnold, D. V., *The Management of the Information Department*, Institute of Information Scientists Monograph, André Deutsch, London, 1976. Aimed primarily at those concerned with the management of small or large industrial information departments, and covers communication, management, planning and design, organisation, co-ordination, control and analysis.

Anthony, L. J., 'A National Information Policy for the United Kingdom', *Aslib Proceedings*, March 1981, pp. 73–82. Recent developments and possible future policy are described and discussed.

Atherton, P., *Handbook for Information Systems and Services*, United Nations Educational, Scientific and Cultural Organisation (UNESCO), Paris, 1977. Although aimed at the emerging managers and students of information systems and services in developing countries, it provides an excellent introduction to the topic, and covers policies and plans at the national and international levels, management aspects, organisation, national and international networks, procedures and methods, standardisation, facilities and equipment, education, training, professional associations and directories.

King, D. (ed.), *Key Papers in the Design and Evaluation of Information Systems*, Knowledge Industry Publications, White Plains, N.Y., 1978. A collection of twenty-six previously published papers covering evaluation methods, evaluation applications and system design.

Smith, D., *Systems Thinking in Library and Information Management*, Clive Bingley, London, 1980. Describes and discusses the relevance and value of the systems approach to information work. Numerous references are cited to allow the interested reader to delve further.

Townley, H. M., *Systems Analysis for Information Retrieval*, Institute of Information Scientists Monograph, André Deutsch, London, 1978. Covers the application of traditional systems analysis including preliminary ideas, the initial system study, storage, search strategies, conversion to the final design and implementation.

Vajda, E., *UNISIST Guide to Standards for Information Handling*, Pt 2, United Nations Educational, Scientific and Cultural Organisation (UNESCO), Paris, 1980. An invaluable guide for all kinds of users and producers of information. It covers the intellectual preparation of documents and subject analysis, production of documents, reproduction of documents, representation of information, editing of documents, preparation of bibliographic records, interchange of machine-readable bibliographic data, management of document collections and numeric data.

Information and library services

British Standards Society, *The Operation of a Company Standards Department*, British Standards Institution, London, 1979. Provides useful guidance on the setting-up and running of a company standards department, and indicates how it may be integrated with, or make use of expertise in, other company information handling operations, for example the library.

Rowley, J. E., and Turner, C. M. D., *The Dissemination of Information*, André Deutsch, London, 1978. Although intended for library and information science students, it provides a comprehensive, well-referenced source-book for those interested and concerned with the dynamic service aspects of information and library services.

Technological aids

Advisory Council for Applied Research and Development (ACARD), *Information Technology*, HMSO, London, 1980. A report of a working group established to consider the impact of information technology in the United Kingdom, and to make recommendations arising therefrom.

British Computer Society, *A glossary of Computing Terms for Introductory Courses*, British Computer Society, 1979. A reliable concise guide.

Cook, M., *Archives and the Computer*, Butterworths, London, 1980. Describes computer systems and their application to records management and archives.

Crawford, S. (ed.), 'Perspectives on Computer and Communications Technology', *Journal of the American Society for Information Science*, March 1981. Five state-of-the-art reviews covering computer technology, transmission of information, information storage and display, technology and communication in the future, and online systems in the communication process.

Rowley, J. E., *Mechanised in-house Information Systems*, Clive Bingley, London, 1979. A description of various systems, including information retrieval systems, and case studies.

Woolfe, R., *Videotex*, Heyden, London, 1980. A description of the various videotex systems (viewdata, teletext, etc.) and their potential for business.

Selected periodical titles

Annual Review of Information Science and Technology, Knowledge Industry Publications Inc.
Aslib Proceedings, Aslib.
Electronic Publishing Review, Learned Information.
IDP Report (Information and Data Base Publishing Report), Knowledge Industry Publications Inc.
Information and Management (the International Journal of Information Systems Applications), North Holland Publishing Co.
Journal of Documentation, Aslib.
Journal of Information Science, Institute of Information Scientists, North Holland Publishing Co.
Journal of Systems Management, Association of Systems Management, Cleveland, USA.
Journal of the American Society for Information Science, John Wiley & Sons.
Online Review, Learned Information.

Selected organisations

Aslib, 26 Boswell St, London WC1.
Promotes the establishment and development of special libraries and information services by means of research, publications, training, conferences, advisory and other services.

British Computer Society, 13 Mansfield St, London, W1.
The major professional and representative body of the computer profession.

British Institute of Management, Management House, Parker Street, London WC2B 5PT.
A professional institute and representational body to provide practical assistance and advice.

Business Archives Council, 185 Tower Bridge Rd, London SE1 2UF.
Provides advice and promotion relating to business records of historical interest.

Institute of Information Scientists, Harvest House, 62 London Road, Reading RG1 5AS.
Professional body for promoting high standards in special information work and for establishing qualifications in this field.

Library Association, 7 Ridgmount St, London WC1E 7AE.
Professional body concerned with librarianship, libraries and education for the profession.

23 Managing the electronic office

Ted Bennett and Garfield Collins

Until recent times, each aspect of office equipment development could be seen as a separate, clear-cut path of progress. Thus the typewriter was the forerunner of the word processor, early mechanical calculators gave way to powerful electronic computers, plugboard telephone exchanges were the start of a communications industry which now produces fully electronic exchanges, and the handling of stored information has progressed from large paper filing systems, through microfilm techniques to data stored in digital form on videodisc. Although their origins were completely separate, each avenue of development has ended with one common feature. In every case, the handling of information is entrusted to electronic circuits using microchip circuitry, with the information coded in digital form. With this convergence has come the possibility of automatic intercommunication between office machines – and between remote offices – which were until recently regarded as separate entities.

This chapter summarises the more important recent technological developments, and discusses their role in the electronically integrated 'office of the future'.

WORD PROCESSING

The preparation of documents by word processor is, in essence, an extension of the traditional secretarial tasks of typing/retyping documents of all kinds to produce a finished product. The basic method of performing those operations is by using text composing/editing/amending software resident in a digital computer with an associated keyboard, printer and display screen. The document is entered via the keyboard, as in a normal typing operation, with the text appearing on the screen as it is typed. The format of each document may be predefined, leaving the operator to type as fast as he/she feels comfortable, without having to worry about tabulations or other format rules. If any errors in spelling, punctuation, etc., are seen on the screen, they can be corrected easily.

The document may be amended, edited and even rearranged by moving sections of text from one part of the document to another. The final version is printed only when it is perfect.

Word processing equipment ranges from the personal microcomputer with a television screen and simple matrix printer, through a single screen/keyboard word processor with single-element printer, to a multi-station word processing installation using a comparatively large central computer, high volumes of disk storage and several printers. It is also possible to provide word processing facilities using a large mainframe computer offering time-sharing services and specialised software to support text manipulation; in this case it is not likely that letter quality printing will be widely available unless special arrangements are made. From being a simple replacement for the electric typewriter, word processors have developed so that they now offer, amongst others, the following facilities:

List processing, to produce, for instance, mailing lists
Sorting of information
Statistical/mathematical software packages
Text communication with other word processors or equipment
Spelling software, in various languages

Use of all the available options associated with up-to-date word processing equipment, far from deskilling the secretary's job, has produced a new job classification of word processing operator - exponents of which trade can demand, in general, higher salaries than traditional typists.

Printing facilities can be chosen to suit the exact requirements. For drafts and other documents where high print quality is not essential, a high-speed matrix printer can be used to give a legible, but inelegant typeface. For letter quality printing the options are multipass matrix printers, single element devices (golfball or daisywheel), or inkjoy or laser technology printing. These last two types use very expensive technology, and they are more likely to find use as a shared unit serving several work-stations.

The development of word processing has been rapid, and will continue. The software offered by the various suppliers will become more sophisticated including graphics and more advanced communications facilities as well as varied application programs. Eventually, as the cost of microcomputer technology decreases, the word processor of the future will perform many or all of the functions of the existing small business systems.

COMMUNICATIONS

Telephones

The most obvious basis for developing inter-office communications is the public telephone network. This is because the telephone system is already in place, serves all locations and handles large volumes of traffic. It is not necessarily the best communications medium for every office, but it should not be discarded out of hand. Of the two basic systems, analogue and digital, analogue transmission is only suitable for voice and alarm signal traffic. Thus all further discussion here refers to digital equipment.

Modern private automatic branch exchanges (PABX), controlled by a digital computer, offer a wide range of communication aids both within and between office buildings. It is possible, for example, to 'camp on' a call to an engaged number: this means that the caller can arrange for both handsets to ring when the line becomes free. Calls can be redirected automatically to follow a person around a building, simply by setting up redirection instructions from the base extension. Simultaneous connection of several extensions to give 'conference' facilities is another useful feature. The exchange can be programmed to dial external numbers which are frequently called by a shortened number – the so-called 'short code' facility. Because the exchange is controlled by a software program, changing extension numbers becomes a job which can be done by the subscriber. When office removals take place, there is no longer any need to worry about the appearance or non-appearance of engineers: a simple re-programming job allows all staff to retain their existing extension numbers.

For cost-conscious managers, call logging equipment can be attached to the PABX, providing a record of numbers dialled from each extension and the call durations – a good way of detecting abuse of the system. The level of service from every extension can be predetermined, so that at the lowest level no access to the outside servie is possible at all, at the intermediate level local public exchange calls can be made, and at the highest level of service complete access to the STD (subscriber trunk dialling) and IDD (international direct dialling) is allowed.

Further applications of digital automatic telephone exchanges will be examined later in this chapter.

Telex and facsimile

Another area of improvement is in the transmission of telex and facsimile documents. Telex is, of course, a very well-established method of sending information but it is also relative cumbersome and fraught with difficulty when time zone changes are involved. Telex switch equipment, using VDU consoles to prepare the message, electronic media to store the text, and digital computer techniques to control the transmission of the text, relieves many of the problems associated with the traditional telex methods. The introduction of teletex transmission standards and systems will also ease the successful transmission of messages across the world. Facsimile transmission of documents has its place in the office world, especially where a combination of speed and the need for an 'original' document is necessary. The development and widespread implementation of facilities to store the document images electronically and transmit them at the appropriate time will, as with the telex, improve the acceptability and use of facsimile devices, as will increases in transmission speed.

Text transmission between word processors

Combining the use of word processors and modern telephone techniques opens up another area of aid to the harassed office worker. This is the transmission of documents produced on one word processor, via the telephone system, to another word processor which could in theory be across the world although it is more likely to be a matter of metres away. This is the famed 'electronic mail' system although the term is misleading, implying as it does that every person has access to a word processing screen. This technique has great utility where it is feasible. This does mean that it is *only* possible to communicate with a compatible device; casual interchange of text will not be possible until all manufacturers comply with a single standard or set of standards for text interchange (or until the advent of a truly omni-function adaptor for word processor communications).

All-purpose communication system

The developing market in digital technology based telephone exchanges offers a potential for using these exchanges as message-switching devices for controlling a classical 'star' network for computer-type applications, allowing access to any 'extension' on the network, whether it be a telephone or a more sophisticated device. Such exchanges offer all the usual services associated with advanced telephone equipment as well as, for example, an electronic mail or 'message store and forward' service; they may also be used to provide links into the telex/teletex system.

When the exchange is used as a message-switching device, the particular mode of communication used is not material, the circuit being left open until one of the parties 'hangs up'. Other forms of local network rely on various methods of providing broadcast facilities for the propagation of messages. These may be electrical, radio link, or optical-fibre cables. Most current local area networks use transmission of addressed packets of data as their basic method. All rely on the recipient(s) recognising data which is addressed to them and processing it accordingly. There are several variants of such systems in use, all essentially incapable of communicating with each other.

With the evolution of international standards for information exchange it should become possible to communicate with any site anywhere either because the different suppliers will adopt the standard, or because there will be a series of adaptors available to interface with the standard protocols. Whichever option is chosen by a supplier, it is always wise to determine this method of complying with the standards, as there would be great loss of flexibility if there were no such compliance.

Choice of supplier will also be determined by technical factors such as line capacity which will be discussed later in the section relating to how to implement office automation projects.

DOCUMENT STORAGE AND DATA RETRIEVAL

The basic storage medium for word processing equipment is the 'floppy disk', a device allowing up to 2 million or so characters per exchangeable disk. This is not inconsiderable volume of storage when the sole requirement is the preparation and storage for reprinting of documents, some of which may be quite lengthy. The separate ('stand alone') word processor is not suitable for information retrieval, quite naturally, as this function is not normally part of the design considerations for this type of equipment.

The main requirements for storage and sensible retrieval of information are a screen/keyboard to access and display the information and a large volume of disk or other storage media together with powerful information retrieval software. The specific equipment requirements for text storage and retrieval will depend upon the environment and use to which the system is to be put and this will be discussed in detail in the section relating to project execution. Below we shall discuss in general terms what might be used for the purpose.

The major element is fixed disk storage, either in the form of the small, high-density 'Winchester' disk or the large, high-volume disks as are normally attached to mainframe/mini computers. The maximum storage volume available with these devices will depend, in real terms, upon the number of disk controllers with which the processor used can cope without any gross degradation of service. It will thus be obvious that the larger the processor used, in general, the higher the volume of disk storage which may be made available.

The software required to make effective use of the disk storage will increase in sophistication with the increase in storage volume. Access to text will, in the simplest cases, be via document name or reference. As the software becomes more complex, access will be via keywords with or without Boolean operations – this means that keywords may be specified in combination. The most sophisticated software offers 'full text' retrieval, or access on any field in any document stored, this may also include Boolean algebra facilities. At this most useful, and most complex software level, the processor used is either a large minicomputer or a dedicated computer which is often referred to as a 'database machine'. This latter device is used solely to maintain the disk files and to provide rapid access to the database.

Storage of text need not be restricted to disks. In some cases, especially for archive purposes, it is perfectly reasonable to store documents on magnetic tapes; access is slower but this need not be a problem. Other techniques for archiving may include storage on microfilm or videotape with microprocessor-controlled access via electronic cameras to give display on normal video screens.

For comparatively low-volume storage requirements, sophisticated electronic devices such as 'bubble memory' and holographic storage may be used. These give very rapid access to data, but are expensive in comparison to disks and are not really suitable, as yet, for large volume text storage and manipulation uses.

The main requirements of any document storage and retrieval system, of whatever level of complexity and sophistication are:

1 Physical reliability, especially for floppy disks, some of which are mechanically suspect
2 Consistent and reliable software operation; this need not be a function of the size of the supplier, but does tend to relate to the number of units sold.
3 Predictable response; it should be possible to know, within reason, how long it will take to retrieve a document when using a specific retrieval method
4 Coherent support for maintenance and recovery from failure. Some suppliers provide systems built from parts produced by several different manufacturers and provide their own software. This can lead to problems
5 'Suitable' software products. If it is predicted that a fairly sophisticated method of retrieval is to be used at some time, it must be possible to achieve this without major re-equipping to do it.

In general terms, the future requirement, up to say three to five years as a minimum, for storage and retrieval should be the guideline for selection of the hardware and software for the system. It may be that in the early stages of system use the system is over-sophisticated; this is preferable to major disruption when it becomes obvious that the initial system is inadequate.

A LOOK AHEAD

There are a number of developments of which a great deal is heard but of which little, so far, has been seen.

Voice response systems

Computer systems which recognise and respond to the spoken word, either with vocalised output or a more normal computer response, have been in existence for some time. As yet, the main applications of this technique have been for 'command' systems in process control and aircraft control. Here the system responds to spoken commands to initiate specific actions. The general purpose computer system which will pause and respond to normally spoken sentences in a natural language is still some way off. As and when such systems come, fully developed, to the market, a new era in office systems will begin, offering the elimination of current conventional input techniques for the small price of clear diction.

Video-disc storage

Video-disc storage devices are available now, in a prerecorded form, for reading via video screens in the same manner as the already accepted video cassettes. For office system use, a reliable and cheap method of recording the information on the discs is required. When this device is made available to the general user, the storage of massive amounts of information in small, cheap, replicable plastic discs will be possible. The availability of video discs will not alter the requirement for transient data storage devices such as magnetic disks, because the video-discs are not re-usable. Any information added to such a disc is permanent and, although it can be rendered unreadable, it cannot be erased and re-used in the same way as magnetic media.

Voice storage systems

With the advent of digital technology telephone systems has come the possibility of using digital computer techniques to store bit pattern representations of telephone messages for processing, or for onward transmission to another telephone handset. This is true message store and forward technique, giving great flexibility to a digital telephone system and allowing better communications within the office. The reproduction of such a stored message might be rather depersonalised, indeed it may not even be possible to recognise the sender of the message, but the message will be received.

Fibre optics technology

This technology is being developed rapidly and will give greatly enhanced transmission speeds to data transmission networks. This will be especially useful for local area networks in the office environment. The interface devices for fibre optics are more complex than for electronic technology, involving frequency division multiplexing techniques which are much more costly to develop and implement than the time division multiplexing techniques which are in common use.

IMPLEMENTING THE CHANGES

The introduction of any office automation, from a single word processor to a fully integrated system, can be a source of problems within an organisation. These problems will include:

1 Provision of space for the equipment, together with a suitable environment
2 Recruiting, training and establishing salary scales for staff to operate the equipment
3 Organising equipment systems, sometimes leading to quite radical changes in the office
4 Planning for the expansion of services as the equipment gains acceptance.

These and other problems will now be discussed in the context of carrying out a project to install office automation equipment of a non-specific type. The methods presented are applicable to any kind of office automation project, and to any type of equipment. Before actually starting, however, project planning is essential. Each stage of the project has to be identified and defined in terms of work to be done and the output expected in the shape of reports, plans, statistics and so forth. If possible, an estimate of the effort required for each stage should be attempted, in order to plan realistically. The separate stages will now be described.

Definition of project objectives

Objectives might include:

1 *Improvement of secretarial services:* faster document preparation, better quality of product, more efficient use of secretaries' time, increased throughput with the same staff
2 *Improved communications:* better voice, telex, facsimile and data processing communication facilities
3 *Replacement of paper files:* less storage space, easier and faster information retrieval, better security and easier transmission of documents
4 *Operational improvements:* more flexibility, more ability to cope with change, lower unit costs and wider availability of facilites.

Setting the project scope

The areas of the organisation to be studied must be determined, based upon the stated project objectives. Both the different types and levels of staff, as well as the physical areas within the organisation, must be specified and this must be communicated to those involved. If the reaction to the news is unfavourable, then attempts must be made to win over opinion, as the type of project under discussion is virtually impossible to implement successfully without active co-operation.

It is obvious that some project objectives, such as improvement of telephone facilities, will affect all areas of the organisation, whereas others may concern only specific parts. Studying a part of the organisation as an experiment, or proving ground for technology, is worth consideration as a way of gaining both experience and approval from the staff involved.

Studying the organisation

Whichever elements of the organisation are studied, the following are the actions from which a selection must be made depending upon the objectives of the project proper.

1 Produce a register of all the equipment currently installed; this must include:
   Word processors/typewriters
   Copying machines/printing facilities
   Facsimile and telex machines
   Computers – mainframe/mini/micro
   Telephones
   Microfilm equipment
   Viewdata sets/services.
   Both numbers and locations should be specified.
2 Survey secretarial staff to determine:
   Total workload, broken down by type of work – typing, filing, photocopying, dictation, etc.

The different kinds of documents typed: letters, proformas, telexes, reports, statistical typing, originals, retyping
The need for facilities not currently available

This survey should include both secretaries and typing pool staff.

3 Carry out a mail census, of 'normal' mail, telex, facsimile and any other forms of document transfer. The volumes moving between groups within the organisation, as well as between the organisation and its environment must be measured over a representative period, excluding holiday times and any other odd periods. The disposition of the mail should be noted, whether it is filed, read and destroyed, read and redistributed, passed on, etc.
4 If it is possible, a census of telephone usage should be taken. This will indicate the numbers of calls, successful and otherwise, both within and without the organisation and any facilities such as call-blocking and re-directing which might be required.
5 Audit the computer services available, to determine the information retrieval facilities offered and their likely expansion throughout the organisation. Note that in many organisations information retrieval system use is fragmented. As part of the information retrieval audit, any library and paper-based information services should also be studied.
6 Survey the staff involved in the study to determine how the installation of office automation equipment might improve their performance. It should be made clear that the object is not to automate the functions which the staff carry out, it is rather to remove bottlenecks in the performance of the mundane and release time for more productive effort.

Collating the information

When the survey is complete, a picture of the current information system of the organisation and of its needs for the future may be drawn up. At this stage no commitment to specific equipment should be made, despite any particular items already in place. Following the digesting of the information, the next stage may be embarked upon.

Developing the strategy

A strategy for the provision of the required facilities may now be developed. The strategy will indicate the systems which must be developed, the equipment and software which must be used to support the systems, the development timetable for the installation of the systems and the staff training required for effective operation. The systems to be developed will be of several types and might include:

Advanced telephone systems based upon digital technology private exchanges.
Shared facility word processing systems, either of a proprietary nature or constructed from a variety of suppliers' equipment linked with a local

communications network.
Powerful reprographics facilities based on laser technology printers; these may be linked to computer systems or word processing systems.
'Electronic mail', based either in word processing networks or digital telephone exchange equipment.
To connect a variety of word processing, computing, information retrieval and telex terminals, large volume magnetic storage and printing facilities.

The costs of all the elements of the strategy must be estimated, together with the effort involved in all stages of the strategy implementation.

Strategy implementation

The strategic plan will include a series of stages and will indicate which elements of the strategy should be implemented at each stage. Care should be taken that each stage is completed and accepted before the next stage is begun, so that the implementation proceeds in an orderly and controlled fashion.

Post-implementation review

When the implementation of the project is completed and all of the systems are operating, a review should be undertaken. Each of the systems implemented (for instance, a shared facility word processing system), should be audited and measured against the stated objectives of that system laid out at the beginning of the project. Depending upon the results of the comparison, it may be thought necessary to re-evaluate the original objectives, or to amend the implemented system to meet the original objectives.

THREE CASE STUDIES

To illustrate the practical achievement of office automation benefits in a reasonably straightforward manner, three different examples are given below.

Productivity improvement from word processing

A survey established the case for word processing in several offices within a commercial company. A common equipment range which suited the general requirement was selected. However, the system was installed first in one representative department. The work done in this department was analysed and figures for time taken for each type were obtained prior to the changeover.

After the new system was operating routinely, measurements of increase in productivity for each type of work were made.

The categories of work and productivity gains are given in Figure 23.1. Also shown are relative proportions of different types of work. Evaluation of work mixes in other departments were then made and these results applied to them. It was clear that some departments did not merit word processing as originally thought, whilst in others the productivity increase to be expected was greater.

Time saved (a)	Type of work	Proportion of total office work (b)	Weighted time saving (a) × (b)
25%	Reports	25%	6%
20%	Letters and memos	30%	6%
70%	Standardised letters	35%	25%
80%	Tabulations	10%	8%
	Totals	100%	45%

Figure 23.1 Productivity improvements from word processing

It all depended on the relative work mix.

The company gained benefits where they were genuinely available and avoided marginal cases. Throughout, compatible equipment was used which facilitated both staff training and the achievement of later links to mainframe computing.

Combined data processing/word processing/microform techniques

This second example illustrates the evolution of a successful real time sales ledger processing system into wider office automation techniques.

The ledger handles tens of thousands of customers and many million invoices annually. For audit reasons, copies of customer accounts need to be dumped regularly and stored for years. Also, signed copies of the invoices as proof of delivery need to be stored for many months. All this storage was in paper form, requiring a heavy print load, much storage space and significant staff time in retrieving documents.

The account records are now stored on microfiche produced from a magnetic tape at a computer bureau. The invoices are photographed internally on to microfilm. Fast access to any given record is achieved by using indexes maintained on the normal real time system and by auto searching of the microfilm. A common reader is used for both microform media.

Figure 23.2 illustrates this sytem and shows also a word processor connected on-line to the computer for production of high-quality automatically addressed debtor letters.

This company achieved major benefit from space and staff time saving by introducing this system in a single department and it affected the work of no other department. The only disadvantage could occur in the area of equipment compatibility. If different departments installed other makes of word processor and microform equipment, problems of the transferability of skill could arise.

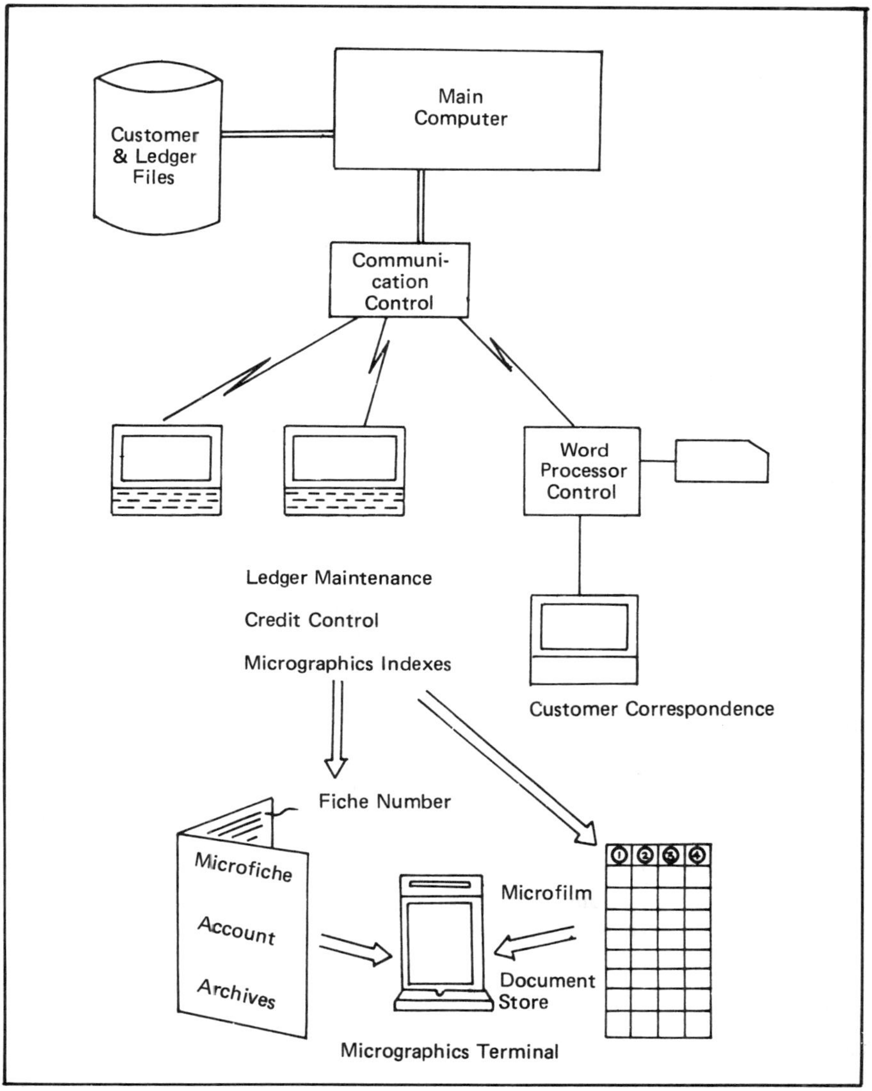

Figure 23.2 Example of an evolutionary approach to a combined word processing, data processing and microfilm system

Combined text and voice communications

The company concerned consisted of a head office with a number of major branches and had the following problems:

1 Difficulty of tracking staff within locations for telephone contact
2 High telephone line costs and frustrated calls through trunk line congestion
3 Considerable 'electronic mail' within UK and worldwide at all locations using telex with resulting:
   high cost of equipment and staff cost in establishing connection
   inconvenient input
   lack of consistent recording of messages
4 Need for timely status reports from branches to head office: for example for senior management meetings at 9.00 on Monday mornings a mixture of voice messages, dictation and telexes gave an unsatisfactory system requiring considerable activity in finalising and collating reports prior to the meetings.

A study of voice systems identified the need for linked electronic PABX systems to facilitate staff tracking and provide other benefits. Traffic analysis identified considerable savings (£200 000 a year) from use of tie lines between locations.

At the same time it was realised that simple text input terminals with limited text editing facilities could be installed in all locations. They were linked to a message switching computer which had a central telex link. Telex messages in convenient format could be input or received at any location.

This equipment was no more expensive than the telex devices it replaced. However, in addition a company-wide electronic mail system was possible. Messages were electronically pigeon-holed at the central message switch and retrieved as well. This provided the basis for a much more timely and convenient status reporting system.

Transmission costs for the electronic mail system were very cheap. Pairs of multiplexers enabled the text transmission to piggy back on the same lines as the voice network. The two systems used separate frequency channels within the line and were physically separate at each end.

The benefits to this company were major cost savings associated with a more integrated communications capability. Since they did not have to justify the electronic mail system other than on the grounds of replacing telex and an inadequate status reporting system, they could confidently install the new terminals in each location.

Growth in other uses of the electronic mail facility has threatened the capacity message switch, but this is a simple component which they foresee will be easy to enhance. The system is summarised in Figure 23.3.

FURTHER READING

Jarrett, Dennis, *The Electronic Office: a management guide to the office of the future,* Gower, 1982

Price, S. G., *Introducing the Electronic Office,* National Computing Centre, Manchester, 1979

Saphier, Michael, *Planning the New Office,* McGraw-Hill, New York, 1978

Urwick Nexos and Francis Kinsman Associates, *The Structure and Design of Tomorrow's Office,* Urwick Nexos Ltd, 1980

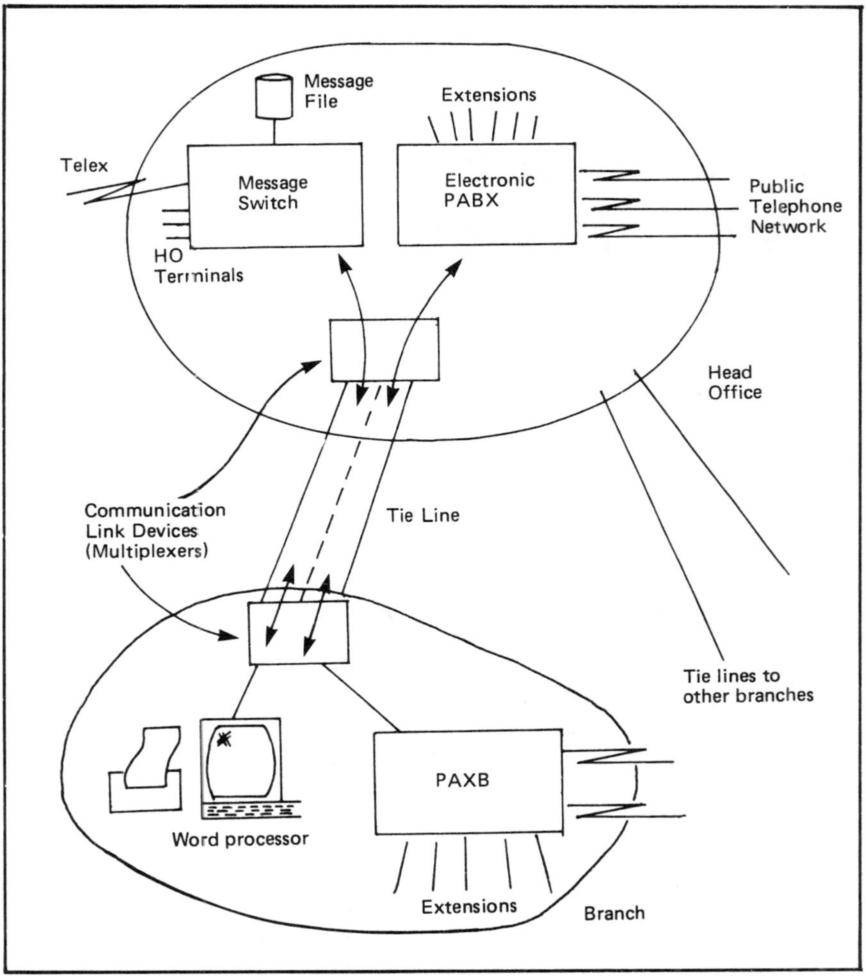

Figure 23.3 ***Combined text and voice communications***

24 Warehouse operation and management

Ken Firth

It cannot be said that warehousing has been a source of great inspiration to many who are in senior management positions in the UK. Too often the designing, building, running and controlling of warehousing systems have been left to individuals who have been passed over in their original speciality or those who are approaching retirement and have been given a supposedly less demanding job to do. Such lack of enthusiasm is unfortunate because standards of warehouse efficiency can have far-reaching effects upon customer relationships. A succession of missed delivery dates or failure to deliver a complete order influence a customer's thinking far more than the helpfulness of the salesman who originally obtained the order. Yet warehousing, as one of the least glamorous aspects of business systems, is often starved of resources in both physical and human terms.

Effective warehousing depends, like very other aspect of management, upon a clear understanding of what the system is expected to provide, a carefully outlined plan, and, above all, continuously supervised implementation with great attention to detail. The rewards can be considerable to small and large organisations alike, for although small systems cannot take advantage of economies of scale they often have a considerable edge in their ability to give personal service through effective managerial control.

MODERN WAREHOUSING

The seeds of modern warehousing operations were planted more than a hundred years ago with the arrival of crude but effective pallet handling equipment. Such equipment enabled human beings to move modular loads around manufacturing systems which would otherwise have been difficult to handle. It was not until the advent of a machine which could lift modular loads one above the other as well as undertaking horizontal movement – in the form of the early fork-lift truck – that the revolution in warehousing method took place. This started in the 1930s and accelerated very rapidly during the Second World

War when the United States Army recognised that such machinery could revolutionise their approach to logistics. The result was that warehouses ceased to be multi-storey affairs convenient to manhandling, and modern wide-span steel or concrete portal frame building predominated. Since that time there has been unremitting design effort to improve the lifting height capacity of fork-lift trucks and at the same time reduce operating aisle widths. The objective is to take maximum advantage of building cube in storage areas in the knowledge that building costs per cubic metre provided are substantially reduced between the heights of 6 to 15 metres for steel portal frame construction, thereby reducing the total systems cost. The term 'total systems cost' is important because in the context of the firm it is that cost which must be minimised – there are many circumstances where it is justifiable to increase warehousing operating costs *provided that greater savings are made elsewhere.*

The basis of modern warehousing is the principle of load unitisation, combined with the remaining principles of materials handling which are:

1 Utilisation of cube
2 Minimisation of movement
3 Flow effectiveness
4 Safety and security

all at lowest total systems cost.

LOAD UNITISATION

Although load unitisation is commonly associated with pallets and fork-lift trucks, there are many other forms of unit-load, large and small, which have an important place in warehousing and should not be overlooked – tote pans for small components is a typical example.

The underlying concept of load unitisation is the combining of like products together on some regularly dimensioned load board or in a container, so that they may be more easily handled by man or machine. Simple though this idea is, it is only too easy to make mistakes either through not recognising the problem involved or not being sufficiently stringent in applying the standards laid down.

Two main aspects have to be considered; on the one hand, the physical characteristics of the product including its protective packaging; and on the other, the most suitable kind of load board or container for the job in hand. When stacking products upon flat timber pallets it is preferable to have rectilinear packages or cases which are modular to the pallet dimension (to avoid loss of utilisation) and at the same time ensure that the packages will 'brick' together in layers (Figure 24.1) thereby ensuring good load stability. A package which is a perfect cube is undesirable because it cannot be bonded to its partners except by the use of strapping, stretch wrapping or other devices. Packages which overhang pallets are to be avoided because they offer scope for damage.

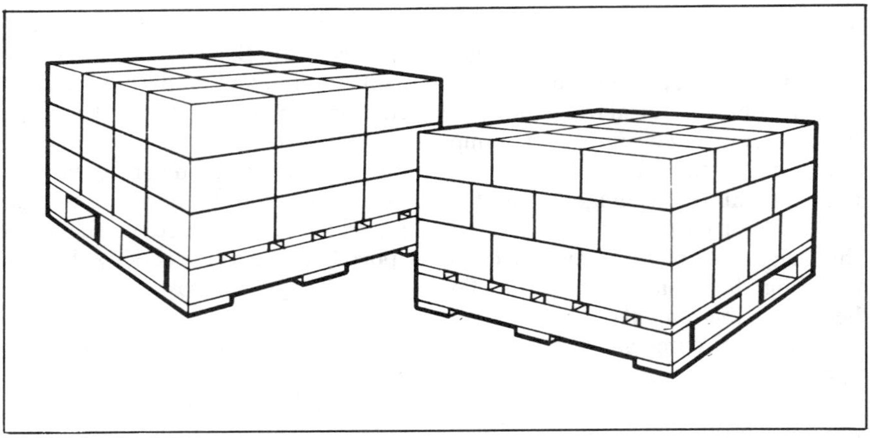

Figure 24.1 Cartons stacked on pallets
Here are two ways of stacking cartons on pallets. The wrong way (left-hand pallet) allows each pile of cartons to sway and topple. The right way prevents this, because the cartons are arranged in an interlocking pattern

In building up suitable pallet patterns it is usual to construct the largest feasible load because by so doing movement is reduced. The achieving of this objective is conditioned by many constraints, typical of which are the overturning moment of the load, crush loading of packages, the height available within the warehouse, the lifting heights of the fork-lift trucks available, and by the type of vehicle on which the pallet might be transported.

Arriving at the best answer is often a matter of compromise but where overturning or lack of stability is the problem there is a variety of devices, such as layer interleaving, strapping, stretch or shrink wrapping which help to overcome the difficulty. In cases where pallets and loads need to be stacked simply one on top of another, it is essential to perform stacking tests over a period of weeks to be certain that progressive stack collapse will not take place. Such factors as poor carton design or high humidity may well cause stacking problems which cannot immediately be detected.

Once a unit load has been properly formulated and agreed it should be recorded – if necessary the pallet stacking pattern can be printed upon the outer package so that anyone not familiar with the correct procedure can ensure uniformity.

In specifying a pallet board or other form of container it is fundamental to obtain a piece of equipment which will provide least cost over its *total life cycle*. The lowest available price is no criterion if the pallet has not been adequately designed and tested to carry its specified load, has poor resistance to damage and is difficult to repair. The attempts to achieve the ideal pallet have caused more contention than any other aspect of materials handling and a great lack of standardisation prevails. However, the International Standards Organisation (ISO) supported by the British Standards Institution (BSI) and other overseas organisations have slowly approached the problem of standardisation of through-transit pallets and dimensional and testing standards for the following sizes exist:

1200 mm × 800 mm (Europal)
1200 mm × 1000 mm (Grocery pallet)
1200 mm × 1200 mm (Oil drum pallet)
1200 mm × 1800 mm (Paper and furniture pallet)
(BS 2629 Parts I, II and III.)

The 1200 mm dimension is ideal for loading onto the side of flat vehicles in the UK, but less than convenient in box vehicles and ISO containers. A pallet size of 1100 mm × 1100 mm strongly advocated by the Japanese which fits perfectly into ISO containers has not been approved by ISO because it is not modular to 600 mm × 400 mm × 400 mm which is a specified ISO unit dimension.

Although there have been many attempts to depose timber as the most used material for the construction of pallets, no adequate substitute has emerged. In the manufacturing engineering industry and the motor car industry there has been widespread use of metal cage and box pallets because of their longevity under the arduous conditions in which they have to work and because of their ability to handle awkward shapes. Many experiments have been made with plastic pallets but their cost, which has escalated since the oil crisis, tends to restrict their use to applications where hygiene is a paramount consideration. The most used pallet in the UK is the 1200 mm × 1000 mm 4-way entry perimeter-based pallet built to BSI specification 2629. A typical life of a wooden pallet in the UK is said to be three to five years, but whether this is entirely due to fair wear and tear is a matter of some doubt. In recent years the company GKN/Chep has introduced a pallet pool exchange system which is worthy of consideration, particularly in the case of companies which have large pallet populations which have to be transported over great distances and where collection of empty pallets and their return is a costly and haphazard operation.

Loaded pallets should not normally be stacked one on top of another to a height greater than six times the minimum base dimension of the pallet and only then when the condition of the pallet and its environment have been carefully checked. For example, uneven floors can create stacking difficulties and lightly loaded pallets stacked outside can be affected by high winds. In adverse conditions the height of stack should be reduced to four times the minimum base dimension or less. There can, of course, be exception to such rules, but any change should be agreed with the appropriate safety representatives.

The care given to unit-load design must never be relaxed and what is certain is that as handling and storage sophistication increases, so must the attention to design. There are endless examples of mechanised equipment being damaged or rendered useless through permitting off-dimension or damaged pallets into the system.

Thus the establishment of the unit-load is the first step towards efficient warehouse operation and from this follows good utilisation of the cube, minimisation of movement, creating effective flow, all in keeping with high standards of safety and security at lowest total systems cost.

UTILISATION OF THE WAREHOUSE CUBE

The price of new warehousing can vary quite considerably due to a variety of factors, such as location, degree of refinement of the facilities, negotiating variations and the economic circumstances prevailing. At current prices it is commonplace to discover that the building and building services can account for as much as 40 per cent of the operating cost of the warehouse. Support for the conservation of warehouse space has long been given by UK fork-lift truck manufacturers who have always been at the forefront in the design of narrow aisle height lift trucks. Very narrow aisle equipment which will lift 1.5 tonne loads at heights of 12 metres is readily available for use in gangways only 1.5 metres wide. Whilst reducing gangway widths is an obvious approach to the reduction of space costs, increased lift height is less so. Although increased lift height means more expensive equipment, which is also more expensive to maintain, the disadvantage is offset by the fact that as single-storey warehouses increase in height up to about 15 metres their costs per cubic metre reduce because most of the cost is in the roof and floor. This fact can produce a favourable trade-off of building cost against equipment costs.

The efficient storage of palletised loads demands a careful analysis of the stockholding profile within the warehouse. That is to say stockholding data must be collected for each product stored and the products then ranked in order of quantity of pallets held. A ranking of products in order of throughput quantities should also be prepared. Although the determination of the method of storage is primarily dependent upon the quantities by stocks held, throughput must be taken into account when considering what handling equipment is most suitable. Once the stockholding analysis has been completed it is useful to make use of the simple flow diagram (Figure 24.2) to produce a list of alternatives which require consideration. It is important to remember when using the diagram that whilst all pallet profiles can be randomly stored by individual pallet, they are not all readily block stackable. The objective of using the flow chart is to eliminate looking at unnecessary alternatives.

Pallet block storage

The concept behind palletised block storage is that of stacking pallets one above the other and in rows of suitable depth. The rows of pallet stacks (identical product within each row) are assembled side by side to form a three-dimensional matrix (see Figure 24.3).

The operation of this simple idea can become very complicated in execution due to various constraints which can be placed upon the system and the warehouse manager may find that because of such constraints, his warehouse is badly utilised so that only 60 per cent of the pallet spaces provided can actually be occupied by physical stock.

This may be brought about by one or more of the following ways:

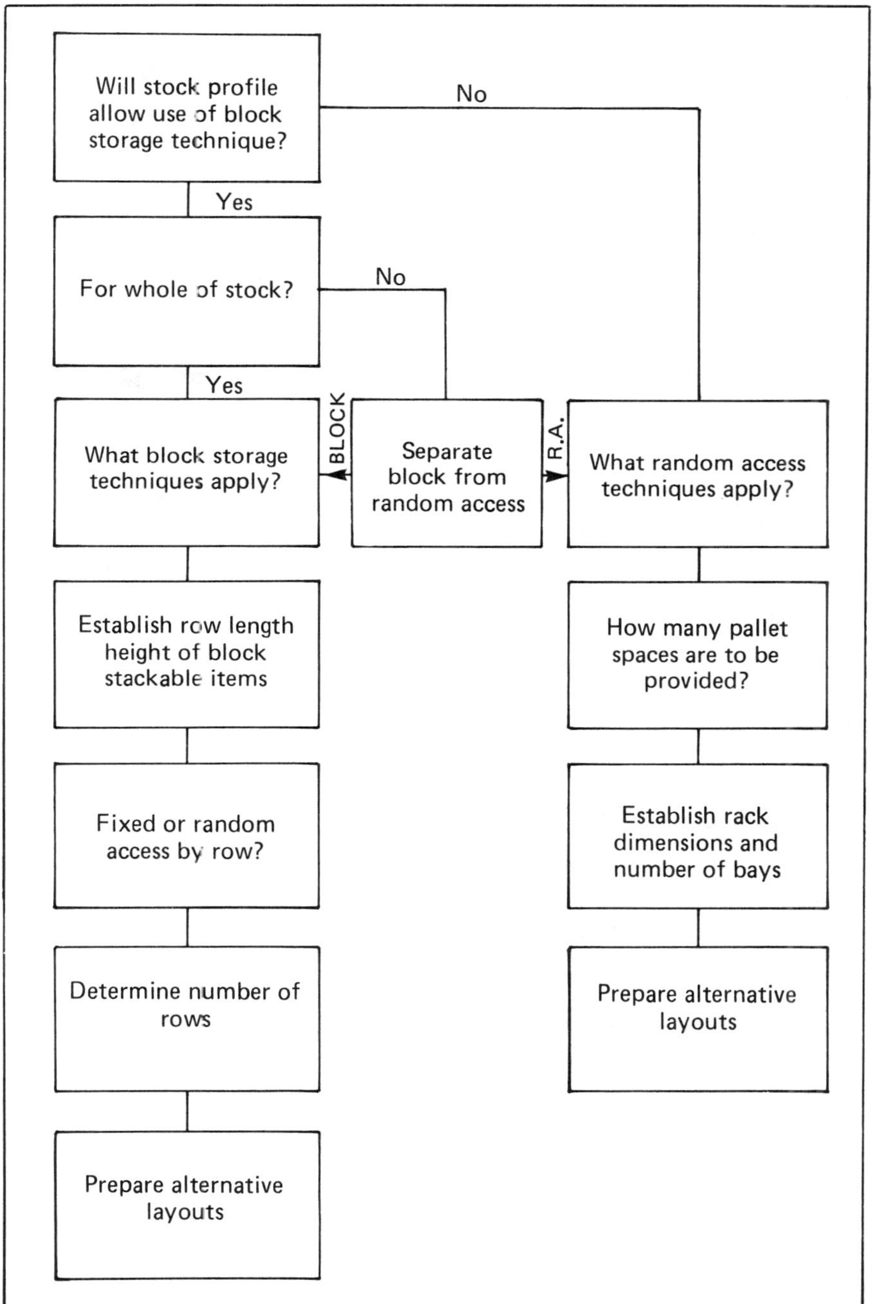

Figure 24.2 Simple flow diagram for palletised bulk storage design

Figure 24.3 Simple block stack

1 Insufficient stock per line item to form significant blocks of storage which leads to 'honeycombing' and loss of cube
2 The use of a fixed location system for products when there is a significant variation between maximum and minimum stocks. This problem may be solved by arranging rows of product randomly within the warehouse at the expense of a control system
3 Incorrect row length. At first glance the longer the row length the better the relationship between stack and gangways. Space utilisation is, however, a function of stock quantity and time of occupancy which the following simple calculation illustrates:

Twelve stacks of pallets are received into stock and the stockholding time is estimated at 24 days. The options on row length vary between 1 row of 12 stacks and 12 rows of 1 stack, but each row has the same area of gangway allocated to it.

For example, if we say that a stack occupies 2 m^2 and the gangway allocation per row is 3 m^2 the area required for a single 12 stack row will be 27 m^2. Moreover, the area will be unavailable for re-use until the last pallet is withdrawn after the 24th day has elapsed (unless double handling or poor stock rotation is accepted). The 'cost' incurred amounts to 24 × 27 m^2 = 648 m^2 days. A 2-row approach will mean that half the original space occupied will be free for use after 12 days and the space cost incurred will be only 540 m^2 days – a significant saving. The calculation for all the variants is as follows:

1 row	648 m^2 days
2 rows	540 m^2 days
3 rows	528 m^2 days
4 rows	540 m^2 days
6 rows	588 m^2 days
12 rows	780 m^2 days

In this instance a row length of 4 pallets is the most suitable choice. It is possible to conceive that this approach to row length can be considerably refined to optimise warehouse block storage layouts
4 Limitations upon stacking height. With simple block stacking i.e., pallets simply supported one on top of each other, the problem is usually that of overturning or crush-loading. This may be prevented by the use of 'drive-in' racking which has all the attributes of block storage whilst separating pallets vertically (Figure 24.4)
5 First in, first out rotation of stock can be a problem with simple and drive-in block storage systems – the best situation usually achievable is rotation by row. When stock is fast moving this does not present a significant problem, but where it is, the options of pallet live storage, or powered mobile storage offer a solution. Although in both cases the storage equipment cost is high, it usually represents a very small proportion of the total warehouse cost and there are many instances where the higher space utilisation provided by more sophisticated systems has resulted in a favourable trade-off against building costs

6 The orientation of block storage in relation to building dimension and the choice of direction of entry of forks into a four-way entry pallet can materially affect the number of pallet spaces available to the system and also the distances travelled by handling equipment. Care has to be taken that the advantage of increased storage does not interfere with flow or impede managerial control.

Figure 24.4 Drive-in racking

Palletised random access storage

Virtually every form of palletised random access storage is associated with a racking system and this means, almost by definition, some form of adjustable pallet racking. A random access system, as its name implies, enables individual access to every pallet, the disadvantage being that a record of what is held in each location has to be kept, on a first in, first out basis by product, and this can be prone to error. The other significant advantage of adjustable pallet racking is that it enables the utilisation of headroom in a building to levels beyond what is generally acceptable for simple block storage systems (provided the building headroom is available), but when used in conjunction with counterbalance or even reach fork-lift trucks can be wasteful of space due to the relatively poor aisle space to rack occupancy relationships. This disadvantage can be largely offset by the fact that the pallet space utilisation factor can be as high as 95 per cent and when this factor is coupled with a very narrow aisle system at heights above 6 metres can result in cube utilisations considerably superior to most block storage systems (see Figure 24.5). The significant exception is powered mobile storage which combines the attributes of both block and random access and can result in total cube utilisation factors in excess of 45 per cent.

The simplest way of overcoming the problem of error in placement and removal of stock is to operate a ticket system which indicates the co-ordinates of the pallet position but at the same time incorporates a random check digit which the operator has to record in placement or retrieval. If a mistake occurs this can be rapidly checked by the pallet location control clerk and the fault rectified before too much time has elapsed. The most recent development of stock location validation is the fitting of microprocessors complete with optical character readers, which enables the driver to scan the pallet ticket and pallet location to ensure a match. In the event of a mis-match, a warning signal is activated.

Damage to racking and products caused by fork-lift trucks for whatever reason is a cause of concern. The problem can be alleviated by proper training of fork-lift drivers and what is probably more important by adequate supervision once the training has been completed. It is wise to ensure that racks conform to an approved standard – that of the Storage Equipment Manufacturers Association is appropriate to the UK – and equally important that the racks are competently constructed and fixed to the floor. In the event of damage the section of the rack affected should be unloaded and remain so until the faulty component has been replaced. Efforts to straighten thin section members once distorted should be avoided.

High-bay pallet silos

The high-bay pallet silo (Figure 24.6) serviced by automatic storage and retrieval machines (stacker cranes), although by no means a new concept is arousing increased interest for storage and warehousing throughout the world, nowhere more so than in the USA and Japan at the present time. The reasons for this surge of interest are many but a common one is the economy of not having to move storage off an existing site as more and more companies become locked into urban sprawl with limited expansion potential. In addition, computing and control expertise has developed rapidly over the past ten years, both in the area of data and power transmission, which has greatly increased availability potential of such installations. It must be admitted that the cost justification in straightforward accounting terms can be difficult, but it is becoming increasingly apparent that this kind of equipment can offer

Figure 24.5 Very narrow aisle racking and truck

tremendous advantage in terms of speed and accuracy of operation, which in turn makes levels of service available previously unachievable with manually operated systems.

MINIMISING MOVEMENT

Movement, like warehouse space, is a costly resource whether it be attributable to man or machine. Whilst there are many techniques available to reduce movement time, both in a system and an equipment sense, all can be rendered virtually useless if adequate standards are not imposed. A guaranteed way of

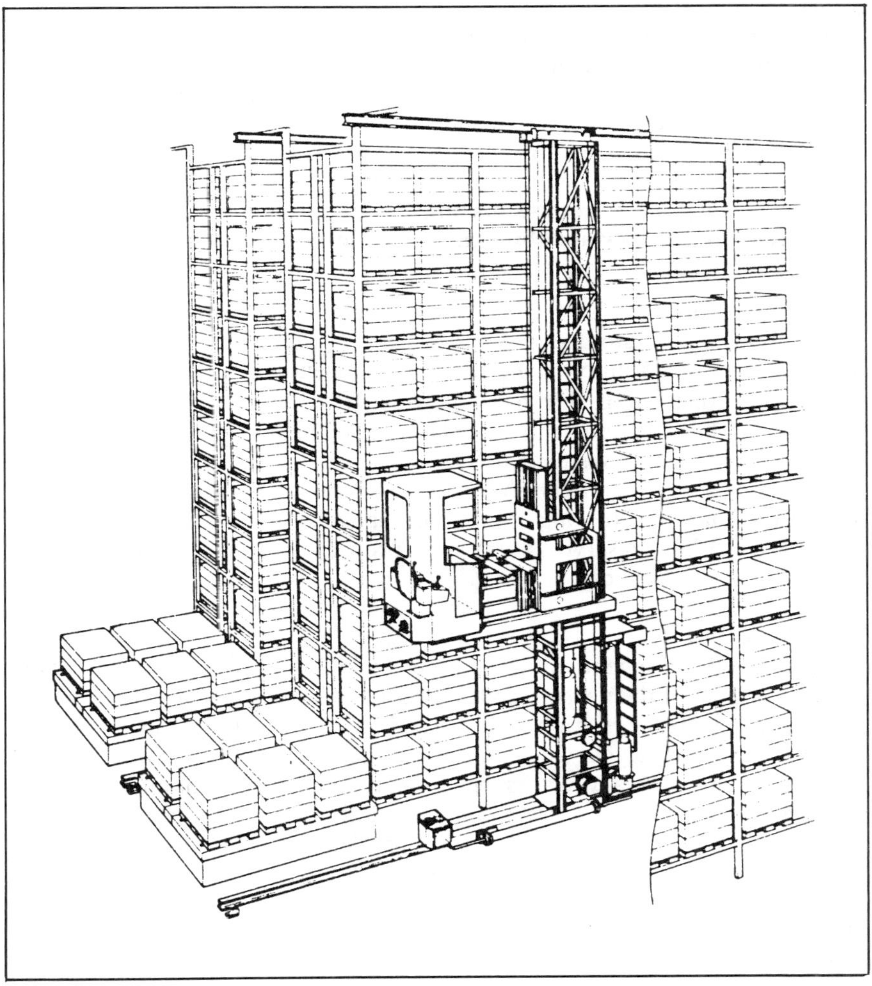

Figure 24.6 High-bay warehouse

ensuring continuing poor performance is to overman when setting up a new warehouse – this may be due to the absence of standards or over anxiety by management in their desire to have a smooth start. Another major failing on start up is to do so without adequate commissioning of equipment or sufficient staff training. Warehouse planning should ensure that a start-up commences slowly and, for preference, at a quiet time of the year. Synthetic time study data for a variety of materials handling tasks is available which can be used until properly measured work standards can be applied.

Order selection tends to be the function of warehousing which is the most intensive user of labour per unit of throughput, although in some applications where load modularisation and quality control is extensive goods receiving comes a close second.

An order-picking system (see Figure 24.7) should be organised in such a manner that a fully representative range of stock is presented in the smallest possible area conducive with safe operation, so that orders may be selected accurately at the service level demanded, avoiding unnecessary stockouts and without excessive movement from reserve to forward location. Because many of these requirements are not complementary to one another, the process is essentially one of compromise making use of the minimisation techniques appropriate to the stock and throughput profiles of the picking systems under study. The techniques available are:

Functional separation. This is the consideration of whether to keep order picking and reserve storage in separate parts of the warehouse or physically integrate the two. In simple terms the answer depends on the ratio of stock held in reserve to that required in order picking. If the difference is large there is scope for holding the reserve in a specialised stockholding area making use of a space efficient storage system, such as high-rack stacking or drive-in storage. Where there is a closer relationship say 3 to 1 or less, it may be more sensible to hold reserve pallets in racking immediately above the order-picking pallets (see Figure 24.8). Where reserve is a very small proportion, it may be feasible to pick from multi-level locations.

Popularity

An analysis of movement within an order-picking store usually demonstrates that 80 per cent of the visits to collect product are made to only 20 per cent of locations. Knowledge relating to these products makes it theoretically possible to arrange them in a layout which minimises the movement of the order pickers. However, there are many factors which can render the concept infeasible such as congestion, seasonal changes, promotions and cataloguing difficulties, which suggest that caution should be exercised in implementing the idea. Popularity is probably of greater significance when related to a fixed-location palletised bulk loading operation or when the popularity of products can be accurately monitored by computer, provided that in the latter case the stores movement involved does not result in confusion.

Batching orders

In instances where there is a large range of products covering a wide area and the average quantity picked per order is small, it is often feasible to group orders together to be picked upon a single circuit of the order-picking area. Inevitably, some sorting must be carried out either on circuit or at the end of the pick and the justification is that the cost of sorting is less than the cost of the time saved by reduction of movement around the system. The objective should be to maximise an order-picker's carrying capacity for a given picking circuit within the limits of the capability of his handling equipment. This means that if on

Figure 24.7 Second level order-picker

Figure 24.8 Base location order-picking system

average single orders satisfy this requirement a batching system is usually unnecessary. There are occasions where a batch pick of a day's work is brought to a forward area and sorted, the advantage being that this serves as an automatic checking device provided that balancing errors in sorting have not occurred.

Zoning

Some large warehousing systems, notably mail order, find it advantageous to divide their systems departmentally according to merchandise or by size and throughput of product. The procedure is to route orders only to the departments concerned with the specific items required on an order and bypass the rest. Order pickers are allocated to each department or zone and only pick in that restricted area, passing the order and goods to the next department featured on the picking list, until the full order has been picked. This not only reduces pedestrian movement but permits specialisation.

Randomisation of order-picking locations

By far the majority of order-picking systems in the UK are based upon fixed-location systems which allow the order picker to learn, relatively quickly and easily, the location of any product. Some wide-ranging systems with constant obsolescence and introduction of lines find it impossible to cope with fixed location because when a bin has been vacated by an obsolete product, it has to be replaced by another. This automatically randomises the locations, but does keep the picking face within reasonable dimensions. A consequence is that the location is first identified by its co-ordinates and secondly by its contents. Control of such systems has to be comprehensive because a product once lost is hard to find, additionally the administrative complexity is so great that computer control is almost mandatory.

Goods-to-picker techniques

It is not unknown for an order picker to have to walk more than ten miles a day to complete his or her work, which clearly may take up more than 50 per cent of the time available. Provide a system where the goods can be brought to the picker and that time is available to carry out a lot more picking (see Figure 24.9). With a few exceptions, the endeavours to achieve such savings in a case-picking environment have met with little success – the costs, under UK conditions, have been greater than using conventional techniques. On the other hand, the potential for using goods-to-picker techniques on small components applications appears considerable because these are often associated with high range and relatively small volumes and weights per line item. The control complexity required to implement an effective system should not be under-estimated.

It is important to remember that whilst one or more of the above techniques may be used to reduce movement in an order-picking system, their applicability can only be determined through a full understanding of the system's requirements.

PAPERWORK REDUCTION

Research into the control of order-picking systems has shown that up to 30 per cent of the time spent by an operative can be in handling paperwork. This can be brought about in a wide variety of ways, for example, looking up stock location records and stock cards, documentation that is difficult to read, products listed in a sequence which does not follow the picking run, etc. It is interesting to observe that the incidence of such problems is being greatly reduced by the introduction of the small computer into warehousing which operates in real-time on either a stand alone basis or as part of a distributed system. The speed and accuracy of a well-designed warehouse computer system rapidly repays the effort and expense involved and can do much to improve customer and staff relationships. It is little wonder that more and more companies are embarking upon such projects.

Figure 24.9 Horizontal carousel order-picking machine

RECEIVING AND DISPATCH

A surprising number of relatively well-planned warehousing operations have been let down to some extent by the inadequacy of their load/unload facilities. One possible reason is that the work involved, particularly in the receiving area, is dependent upon external factors which can be difficult to control. Much more attention is being paid to how products are being delivered into the warehousing system, how well they are modularised, whether the quantities delivered relate accurately to the order quantity, whether the delivery on time, early or late, and how easy is a consignment to identify. Lack of attention to these and many other factors has caused delays, congested loading docks and made unnecessary work, but above all inadequate communication has contributed to the confusion. More and more VDU terminals are being located directly at the receiving point. Their ability to identify rapidly whether a consignment is required, to state what level of quality control should be applied and to show where the product is to be located, contributes greatly to the smooth and accurate flow of product.

The other major factors are what area should be allocated to the function, how many loading bays are required, whether the loading bays should have raised docks or be at floor level, and whether the loading and unloading areas should share common facilities or be separated. Their determination is by analysis of the products and their load unitisation, the quantities throughput per unit of time, the kinds of transport entering and leaving the systems and other criteria such as the value of the product together with safety and environmental requirements. The increasing costs of transportation are forcing some companies to consider more carefully ways of means of turning around vehicles to maximise productivity, nowhere more so than in Japan, where much attention is being paid to the mass-loading of different types of road vehicle.

Figure 24.10 is a general view of a modern loading bay.

CONCLUSION

Much remains to be done to improve standards of warehouse operation and management but evidence exists that over the past ten years the business world has become increasingly aware of the importance of the subject and how its costs need to be controlled. This may be seen by looking at the organisational and managerial changes which have been taking place in specific companies and

Figure 24.10 General view of a modern loading bay

recognition that formalised training in the skills of distribution are a necessity. Slowly universities and other educational establishments are beginning to introduce courses which will enable future warehouse managers to establish status which equates with that of more fashionable disciplines. Perhaps by the year 2000 a new professional class will be fully established.

FURTHER READING

Burton, J.A., *Effective Warehousing*, Macdonald & Evans, Plymouth, 2nd edition, 1979

Gattorna, J. (ed.), *Handbook of Physical Distribution Management*, Gower, 3rd edition, 1983

PART SIX

HUMAN RESOURCE MANAGEMENT

25 Recruitment and selection

P T Humphrey

No matter what has been written or said about recruitment and selection, everyone believes that he is an expert in this field. It is probably the one area of personnel management where 'the professional' is inevitably challenged by 'the layman', whatever the circumstances. Nevertheless, it is one of those situations where often a manager or supervisor has to face up to the problem of becoming totally involved in the recruitment and selection process without quite knowing how to tackle what is in reality a complicated task, in spite of the apparent simplicity of the ultimate decision to be taken – 'to hire or not to hire'.

However, before going into detail a few basic points must be established and emphasised at the outset. Almost everyone in any organisation has at some stage or other the responsibility for requesting materials or finance in order to carry out their work effectively. These requests which can lead to heated discussions between superior and subordinate, or between peers, are essentially concerned with inanimate objects – 'vegetable, mineral or abstract'. But the request for a replacement as someone is leaving the organisation, or for more staff to carry out the work, will inevitably lead to consideration of the 'animal' category. The true relevance of this is the ability, apart from the right of this 'animal' category to hold and undoubtedly voice opinion and comment, constructive or destructive, about the way in which the recruitment and selection process is handled. This 'answering back' facility is acknowledged by all professional recruiters, who only ignore it at their peril. It is probably the one point which many managers do not appreciate, for while most managers are accustomed to dealing with human problems within their own job function, they are dealing with known people within a specific and generally accepted framework. People who apply for a job with a particular organisation are not subject to, nor do they hold, the corporate values, real or imaginary, which form part of the daily working lives of those already employed.

The second point which naturally follows on from the first is that the principle of 'do unto others as you would be done by' underpins the total recruitment and selection procedure. The applicant for a job, whatever the level, expects to receive the normal human courtesies not only in the face to face situation but also at all other points of contact during the decision making process. In spite of the obvious economic nature of employment, a great deal of attention must be placed on the underlying social processes.

Thirdly it is important not only to acknowledge but also to understand that the situation is not one sided as far as the decision taking process is concerned. The conclusion of a recruitment task does not occur with the decision 'we'll offer you the job', this is merely a unilateral decision. The conclusion in reality only comes when the applicant says 'thanks, I accept your offer'.

The final basic point to be made is that in any organisation there is at the same point in time both a buyer's market and a seller's market as far as jobs are concerned. It is important to distinguish between them, for while the same basic administrative approach is both necessary and applicable, the tactics to be adopted can differ widely. This is equally true of shop floor and boardroom situations alike. Bearing these points in mind the objective now is to provide managers at all levels no matter whether they are experienced or inexperienced, with positive guidelines to tackle the job effectively, and to gain, by the end of the day, a sense of personal satisfaction from a task well done.

BASIC PLANNING AND PROCEDURE

Everyone, without exception, will realise and readily acknowledge that all organisations including one's own family must have financial resources in order to function at all, and in order to utilise these financial resources correctly some systematic methods must be devised and implemented to account for income and expenditure. But not everyone is prepared to acknowledge that the same principle has to be adopted in relation to recruiting and terminating staff, in spite of the fact that no organisation can function without staff! The total cost of recruiting an employee of average skill can be assessed at approximately three to four times the weekly wage, and very much more for senior grades. So any organisation that does not set up an effective system for handling recruitment is likely to put at risk sums of money in the immediate short term which under normal circumstances would be referred to board level for approval.

Statistical information on the numbers already employed in the organisation categorised by status, department, works or site, and sub-divided in relation to occupational skills required, levels of work involved or merely by job titles, must be available in order to provide a reference point from which the whole procedure begins.

The subsequent steps are as follows:

1 Receiving requisition and/or authorisation for replacements or additional staff 2 Gathering information about the job 3 Checking against obvious internal sources 4 Advertising the vacancy – internally and externally 5 Processing of applications	Stage 1: Run up

6 Setting up the interview 7 Conducting the interview 8 Administering appropriate tests 9 Making the appointment	Stage 2: Face-to-face – the employment interview
10 Introducing the new employee to the organisation 11 Following up the progress of the new employee 12 Reviewing and evaluating the recruitment and selection process.	Stage 3: Follow through

Upon examination, even the most *ad hoc* example of recruitment reveals that the above procedure has been followed and that often the tactics/approach/mechanics vary in relation to the nature of the job to be filled. In many instances it is the level of the vacancy which is the determining factor. Therefore, where applicable, attention will be drawn to the different requirements in recruiting staff at the following levels:

1 Managerial, including supervisory
2 Clerical and technical
3 Operational.

STAGE ONE: THE RUN UP

Requisitions

The need for a sound method of producing the right statistical information, such as number employed, labour turnover and absenteeism, has already been made. However, even in cases where this information exists, many organisations are quite indifferent to the way in which requests for replacement or additional staff are made. In many respects the underlying attitudes which permitted this have been altered by the economic circumstances of the last decade. Closer scrutiny of labour costs is taking place and the requisition for staff at all levels has almost the same cachet now as the capital requisition.

What kind of information has to be included on a staff requisition form?

1 Name and location of originating department
2 Job title
3 Main job function
4 Salary or grade
5 Reason for requisition
  (*a*) Replacement
  (*b*) New appointment
  (*c*) Additional appointment
6 Required by: (date)
7 Signatures .... Department Head: Authorised Date

While it is appreciated that it does take a certain (minimal) amount of managerial time to complete such a requisition, nevertheless its value to the person responsible for recruitment is incalculable. The main advantage is that it leaves no room for doubt. No one has to rely on the recollection of what was said about the job during a lunch-time conversation which ranged from detailed shop talk through gossip to personal hair-letting down. Far too much valuable managerial time can be wasted in reference back by telephone or by personal visit to verify the position. Certainly the time of the recruiter can be spent to better effect in the next step of the process.

Job information

A great deal of confusion exists over the different terms used in this area. The term 'job description' means different things to different people, and indeed the context in which the term is used can alter its apparent meaning. Nevertheless an attempt has been made by the Department of Employment in its publication *Glossary of Training Terms* to standardise usage of such terms, e.g. 'A job description is a broad statement of the purpose, scope, duties and responsibilities of a particular job'. 'A job specification is a detailed statement of the physical and mental activities in a job'.

However, jobs must be viewed as part of a dynamic organisation, with the result (as so many management writers have said) that the job description presents at best only a point-in-time interpretation. Consequently many managers who inevitably feel 'pushed' in the everyday situation will question the necessity of having a job description at all. But there are simple operational reasons which can help in the argument to overcome such resistance. These are:

1 The job description acts as a basic means of communication between the manager and the recruiter as far as the position to be filled is concerned
2 It is an invaluable mechanism for discussing and finalising the tactical approach to the selection process
3 It can yield vital information for the candidates who have come to have a high level of expectation in terms of job information. This certainly has a useful 'plus effect' in promoting confidence about the organisation amongst the candidates
4 It ensures that there is an accepted factual basis from which information can be selected for advertising purposes
5 Finally it provides the reference point against which all decisions taken and judgements made can be evaluated.

Thus, time sensibly spent on this important preparatory work can yield significant dividends in preventing over-interviewing and indeed in ensuring that advertising and other expense is used to maximum effect.

The job description

What information, therefore, needs to be included in the job description? The following items are essential no matter what level of appointment is being considered:

1 Job title: This must be self explanatory wherever possible and certainly where either unusual technical terms or terms specific to the organisation are used, adequate explanation must be given
2 Name of department: As in (1)
3 Accountability: The job title of the person to whom the job holder is responsible
4 Main job function: A brief but lucid statement of the purpose of the job
5 Responsibilities for people and/or equipment. No need to detail every nut and bolt, but include categories and numbers of people to be supervised together with major items of equipment.

Additional items are required when considering managerial, supervisory or technical positions. These include:

6 Limits of authority – particularly in relation to spending money
7 Levels of contact – this is of special importance in a multi-divisional organisation and with working relationships outside the organisation.

Useful questions to keep in mind during this process of gathering information and writing the job description include:

1 Is the informant's statement accurate?
2 What degree of bias is contained in the statement?
3 Who can provide a second opinion?
4 Does the written description contain all the relevent facts?
5 Is it accurate?
6 Can the layman understand it? (In other words is it too simple, simple enough or too complicated?)

The job specification

The job description now has to be extended and interpreted specifically in relation to the physical and mental activities of the job, and the consequent demands to be made on the job holder.

While it might appear that there is considerable difference in requirements at the various levels of appointment, nevertheless, five basic categories of the job specification can be defined as follows:

1 Qualifications, knowledge appropriate to the job
2 Specific skills, abilities and aptitudes required
3 Experience required
4 Personal attributes
5 Physical attributes.

These categories can be qualified as appropriate for each selection by a scale of relevance – vital/desirable/of no consequence.

1 Qualifications

This category is the bane of every recruiter's life, for more heat can be generated over this than almost any other topic to do with recruitment. The stand point to take must be 'is it relevant?' Is a PhD really vital to do the job of sales manager in an electronics firm? It might be. On the other hand it is certainly not a vital qualification for the sales manager with a confectionery firm. A sense of reality must be maintained, for it is just as easy to be swayed by degrees and professional qualifications as it is by medals and decorations. Indeed the relevance of City and Guilds qualifications to the craftsman and technician, is probably more deserving of the recruiter's attention than has been the case in the past.

Instead of qualifications it is often more advisable to list areas of knowledge which are required, e.g. plastic injection moulding for a production manager, standard costing for a senior cost clerk, export procedures for a shipping clerk.

2 Specific skills, abilities and aptitudes

This category is not to be regarded as a rag-bag for glossy management 'in' phrases, which in the end result merely in directing attention away from the main purpose. Rather the intention is to define accurately (and quantify if at all possible) those factors which are regarded as necessary to achieving success in the job. For instance the skills required in negotiating with trade union officials, or the different skills required in the negotiation of commercial contracts with suppliers, must be stated in the appropriate specifications. Abilities to be considered can include the ability to sell 'an idea' or a product, or even the ability to see 'the wood for the trees'. Among the aptitudes those that readily spring to mind are verbal, numerical and mechanical, where great strides have been made in assessing and quantifying them among the population at large. All this must be geared to reality, and fanciful ideas of what might be required should be discounted. Simplicity really is the key note in this section.

3 Experience required

This is most important, and every attempt should be made to build up an accurate picture of the kind of previous experience required. In many situations accuracy in this respect can often lead to better advertisements, easier pre-selection and more searching interviews. What kind of detail then is necessary? Early 'formative years' experience – apprenticeships, studentships, exposure to more than one commercial or industrial situation, or maybe service in the Armed Forces or Merchant Navy.

First post of responsibility – chargehand, section leader – technical responsibility, e.g. in chemistry laboratory, secretary to a departmental manager, territory salesman. Subsequent responsibility requirements can then be added depending on the nature and level of the post being specified.

Indeed a relationship must be established between the foregoing and the environments in which the experience was gained. For instance with the post of foundry manager, experience of working with specified materials or in making a certain size of castings is very relevant. So also is information concerning the general standing of the companies or organisations in which the experience was gained.

The other most important aspect of the experience required is in relation to the major tasks of the job. This is just as important at operational as well as the other levels where, for example, garage fitters in general are not experienced in maintaining high-speed packing lines at peak performance. Another example can be taken from a supervisory situation which calls for experience in handling a large department of 600 employees. However, unless it is specified whether the employees are all males or all females, there is considerable scope for some fascinating misconceptions!

4 Personal attributes

More attention is being paid now to this category. The impact of the new individual on an existing work group and vice versa can be vital in many situations, particularly where incentives are based on group performance. Some attempt must be made to analyse the 'chemistry' of the situation – acceptability is probably the key word in this context.

However, on occasions it may well be absolutely necessary to specify what might appear to be unwelcome attributes. Abrasiveness is one such attribute which nevertheless can be vital in stimulating complacent teams at all levels. Preparedness to accept a challenge, to work under trying circumstances, or to subordinate one's own convictions in certain situations are other examples.

5 Physical attributes

These are probably more obvious, but it is often found that only lip service is being paid to the mental health aspects of the working situation. The question of stress and the individual's capacity to absorb stress is very important, especially at certain decision making levels; also where working hours, such as 12-hour shifts in noisy, dusty conditions, or train or aeroplane crews having to 'stop over', can have a serious effect on an individual's necessary domestic or social relationships.

These attributes must be specified accordingly and whenever possible professional advice must be obtained. The amateur doctor or psychologist can do untold harm, and such an occurrence must be avoided.

Having gone through all these steps in describing the job and obtaining the specification, a firm basis has been established. The recruiter can now proceed with great confidence to find 'Mr (or Ms) Right' for the post in question.

Internal sources

Many companies still have the tendency to overlook the bank of talent contained in their existing work forces despite the publicity of the last decade, aimed at management succession plans, or schemes for 'growing your own'. It is therefore very important to look inwards to try and identify potential internal candidates from all parts of the enterprise. In doing this the political pressures of the organisation will come into full play, and therefore it is essential to maintain a very independent stance throughout the exercise. This independence is sustained by the very nature of the factual information contained in the job description and the subsequent specification. Nevertheless if potential internal candidates are found, it is vital that they are subjected to the full selection process. This must not be regarded as an act of 'bloody mindedness' or 'bureaucracy', for its very purpose is to safeguard, for the organisation, the integrity of the process itself as well as of all those who play a part in it, especially the candidates.

Advertising

The job advertising market has developed since the 1950s from very small beginnings into a multi-million pound business, and inevitably it has given rise to various fads and fashions from time to time. Special job advertising agencies have been set up, and selection consultants, office staff bureaux and appointment registers have followed the trend by extending the range of services available. A great deal of material has been published on the subject and indeed many professional recruiters, depending on their own personal inclinations, are either disappointed or delighted if their daily postbag does not include at least one printed circular on job advertising.

The main purpose in advertising a job is to attract sufficient candidates of the right calibre to reply, thereby securing a reasonable field from which to choose the most appropriate person for that job. How does one tackle this attraction process?

1 Define the audience (i.e. the type of people to be reached)
2 Decide on the means and establish the cost of making the contact
3 Write the message
4 Monitor the results.

The audience

The level and nature of the position to be filled will largely define the audience both in terms of volume and geographical spread. At the operational level there is on most occasions a local audience which can be tapped, but from time to time instances do occur when special skills are being sought, and these are not available from the local audience. When this does happen, some preliminary investigation is called for, in order to establish the location of the required audience as well as the potential available. This also applies in the clerical and technical level, though there is a tendency for technical people to restrict their own availability by becoming too clearly identified with particular processes, even within the one organisation.

It is at managerial level that the audience becomes national in character. It is also pertinent to define the audience at this level in broad functional terms – e.g. accountants, engineers, buyers. In addition, consideration must be given to defining current salary levels from which potential candidates can be drawn.

The means

A great deal of detailed information from many sources is available to the recruiter on such matters as circulation of papers or publications of professional bodies, types of people who can be reached and the costs involved.

Decisions therefore have to be made on the worth of national coverage against local coverage, the amount of space required, and whether any apparent extraneous points, i.e. company image, or wider public relations exercise, need to be taken into account. While it seems natural to turn to press advertising, consideration must also be given to other methods. These can include:

1 TV or cinema advertisements
2 Posters in places where the appropriate audience is likely to congregate – newsagents, public halls, schools and colleges
3 Leaflet distributions, especially on housing estates
4 Word of mouth – with the inevitable discount for mis-statements
5 Notice boards outside the place of work
6 Notice boards inside the place of work
7 Department of Employment job centres
8 'Recruitment circus' i.e. using a caravan as a travelling recruitment centre, e.g., for the armed forces
9 Use of a pre-recorded message on tape or a disc which can be distributed.

However it must be stated that most of the above means are more appropriate when considerable numbers of people are required at the same time, especially when a new site is being manned or expansion is taking place. Eventually and inevitably cost must play its part in the final decision.

The message

Above all simplicity is the key note, together with the need to use technical terms on a restricted but meaningful basis. There is certainly an art in constructing the message, for a basic emotional appeal to the audience is necessary. However not only must one present this appeal, but also sufficient hard information. These two together must make the appropriate candidates reach for their writing pads, cause them to telephone, or make them sufficiently curious to make a personal visit. However the message must be tailored to suit the means chosen. Consideration must also be given to technical detail, especially size of print, headlining, number of words that can be used, for the message includes everything within the defined physical boundaries of the medium, whether it be words, white or black space, line drawings, or company symbols. Indeed from time to time it is necessary to consider whether or not it is important to write in English or another language. But advice on many of these details is readily available from the organisation which is going to publish the message.

The results

It is extremely useful to maintain a record of the response to advertisements whatever the means used. This enables the user to evaluate in financial terms the relevance of certain media in reaching the required audience. The main statistic is 'cost per reply' which can be refined in relation to numbers interviewed, candidates short listed and appointed from that particular source. A relatively simple form can be designed and maintained at negligible cost by a clerk or a secretary. The type of information required includes:

1 Appointment title
2 Media used
3 Size of advertisement
4 Cost
5 Number of replies
6 Cost per reply
7 Numbers interviewed
8 Numbers shortlisted
9 Numbers appointed.

It is quite surprising how useful this information can be, not only in relation to developing realistic advertising budgets but also in settling arguments and destroying preconceived ideas.

A final word on advertising: a great deal of free information and help are available; a telephone call or two will soon establish a connection, for agencies who place advertisements receive their commission from the publishers, not the originators of the advertisement.

Processing of applications

The greatest sin in recruitment is not so much to lose an application (which is bad enough) but to ignore it, to leave it unacknowledged. Most applicants are prepared for the occasional 'mislaying' of letters, but not one will tolerate being ignored. This again is in the realm of extending natural courtesies to the people who have been sufficiently interested to respond to the message.

Keeping track of applications over the selection period which can extend on occasions to several months demands a good administrative system, preferably one which dovetails with the sorting process. A suggested outline appears in Figure 25.1.

Most organisations revise their application forms from time to time, but it is important to remember that the form itself can be so designed to promote effective administration by allocating space for action signals at appropriate points.

There is a strong argument for having standard letters, provided that these are individually typed and addressed. The amount of time that can be saved is considerable, apart from the important question of maintaining cordial relations with the candidates. Admittedly a certain amount of time is taken up initially in constructing standard letters, but it then avoids the necessity for dictating individual replies. This is doubly relevent when 50 to 60 replies are received and demand equal attention. The major standard letters should cover:

1 Acknowledgements of receipt of application

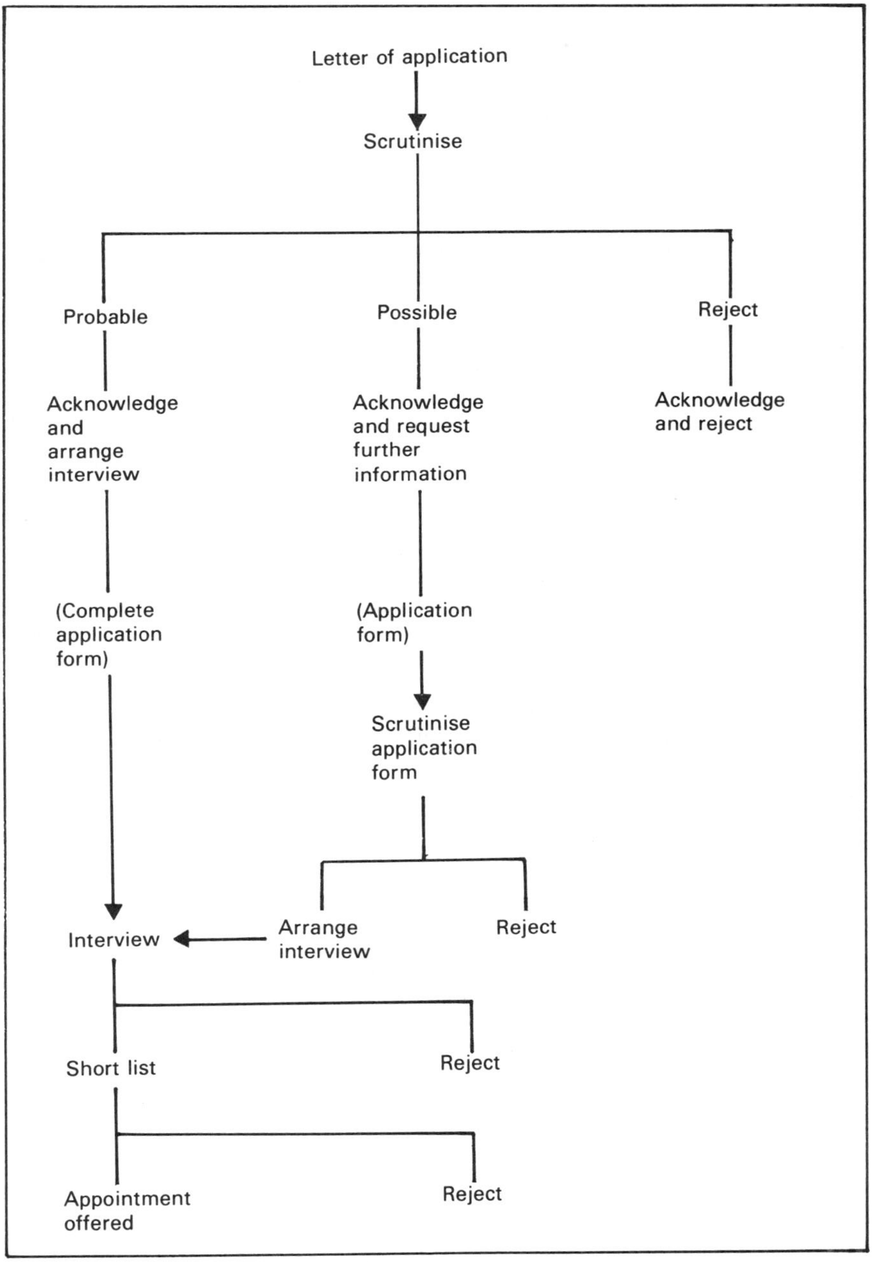

Figure 25.1 Processing of applications

2 Invitation to interview
3 Request for further information

A well-thought out and well-tried system will not only keep candidates and recruiter happy, but will also avoid the unwelcomed letter to the chairman from an aggrieved candidate, which will inevitably lead to an embarrassing post-mortem!

STAGE TWO: FACE-TO-FACE: THE EMPLOYMENT INTERVIEW

Up to now all work on which the recruiter has been engaged has been directed inwardly on the job to be filled and outwardly only in terms of the audience to be contacted. However, the next stage – 'face to face' – is the one where many managers feel quite exposed. Confrontation is a major part of any manager's job, but it tends to be in a specific commercial or operational context where individuals are aware of the institutional constraints which surround the meeting. The employment situation cannot be classified in the same way, and therefore a framework must be constructed and a number of ground rules established.

However, before discussing the framework in more detail some explanation is necessary in order to highlight the special nature of the employment interview as compared with other aspects of confrontation. First of all, for any situation to be described as an interview it must meet the following criteria:

1 It is a tool of the communication process
2 It is a vehicle for the transmission of information from one person to another
3 It focuses upon specific subject matter that is relevant to its situation, occasion and purpose;
4 It requires the participation of two people who interact freely with one another
5 It is initiated to achieve one or several objectives
6 It takes place in a particular physical and social setting
7 It occurs as part of a procedural sequence of events.

Having established the intrinsic nature of the interview, a further simple classification test can take place. It is for:

1 Information exchange: simple acquisition or dispersion, taking down details of a person's career history, obtaining information on attitudes – sampling for market research purposes or opinion surveys
2 Problem solving: aimed at resolving conflict; changing attitudes, altering behaviour patterns; career guidance
3 Decision making: objective demands agreement on a course of action, order giving, if necessary terminating employment, engagement interview.

It will be found that most confrontation situations can be easily classified into one category or other, but such is the subtlety of the employment interview that its various stages, not necessarily in sequence, can encompass all categories within the one situation. This is of tremendous importance, for quite often it is vital for the interviewer to identify these various categories during the actual interview in order to remain in control of the situation.

Further, it is also of value to understand the various levels or planes on which the interview takes place:

1 The primary level deals mainly with facts
2 The secondary level deals with both facts and judgements
3 The tertiary (or depth) level deals with motivation and attitudes.

This basic background will help to establish a framework for the interviewer, and from this position he will then be able to develop his own pattern and style to suit the interview situation which he will have to handle.

Setting up the interview

There are three equally important aspects to be taken into account when considering this task. They are the administrative back-up, the physical setting and the social setting.

Administrative back-up

Sufficient attention is not paid to the detailed arrangements that are a necessary preliminary to the actual interview. On the pure documentation side all relevant papers for each interviewee must be to hand – original letters or copies of all correspondence, application forms, the job description and specification, plus all other documents which contain information which the candidate might want or which the interviewer wishes to pass on to the candidate. While it is quite possible to go to extremes in providing such information, too often the reverse happens to the detriment of all concerned.

It is also vital to ensure that all people to be involved in the interview process are given adequate warning and briefing. This must include internal staff such as receptionists, security officers, secretaries or personnel clerks who have the very considerable responsibility for greeting those who may ultimately become employees of the same organisation.

The question of domestic arrangements should not be neglected either. Awkward situations can arise through lack of foresight or experience, in dealing with travel arrangements, overnight accommodation where necessary, and prompt reimbursement of travelling expenses.

All these considerations are not just chores, but contribute to the interview situation by setting the tone to the meeting. This is just as important to the craftsman or operative applicant as it is to potential general managers.

The physical setting

Privacy is a prime requirement, rather than the scale or type of furnishings, for nothing can be more disturbing or distracting to both the interviewer and interviewee than being knowingly overheard. While in a certain sense the interview has a social context, it is nevertheless a business meeting. Therefore the furnishing of the room has to be functional, especially if it is a room that has been specifically designated as an interview room. Should the interview take place in an office it may well be necessary to reflect upon such things as tidiness, positioning of chairs and desks, taking the internal telephone off the hook, and turning off loudspeakers. Privacy includes avoidance of interruptions as well!

Social setting

The tone of the interview is as important to the interviewer as to the interviewee. While conditions of physical discomfort can assist in setting the appropriate tone, nevertheless every effort must be made to establish rapport with the candidate. This can be summed up in the one word 'consideration'. If this ingredient is missing, then the chances are that the objective of the meeting will not be achieved unless a deliberate stress situation has been brought about for a specific purpose. It is a good tactic to try to establish cordial relationships with candidates by setting the necessary tone during the exchange of letters. It is also important to ensure that necessary courtesies are extended to candidates during any waiting period which may have to elapse before they are seen. Feelings of being isolated or ignored can so easily be aroused in candidates through inattention or lack of foresight as to what can happen during the waiting period. Once a candidate has been placed in this position, it does take a tremendous amount of effort and time to overcome these effects and bring the situation on to an even keel.

Conducting the interview

While of necessity the discussion so far has been about the employment interview, it is nevertheless most important to define the context of the particular interview in question. For example, five different contexts can be defined:

1 Preliminary interview which may well only be concerned with meeting a person in order to exchange information and form initial judgements
2 Background information – where the purposes could be merely to record all relevant detail about a person in preparation for another situation. One such example is assisting a candidate to complete an application form
3 Discussion situation where the main objective is to elaborate on information already available and to talk around potential or real problems
4 Stress interview, where the requirement is to put pressure on a candidate in order to achieve a certain objective. In reality if a candidate is subjected to pressure and stress and reacts favourably to it, the only valid conclusion is that the candidate is capable of coping with stress and pressure in that context only. It is highly dangerous to generalise from this particular situation and claim that the candidate is capable of withstanding pressure and stress in general. The way in which the candidate has handled the situation is probably of more significance and value than anything else
5 Group situation – where a candidate is facing a number of interviewers at

the same time. This can easily develop into an uncontrolled situation, where the only person to benefit will be the candidate – for he always acts on his own behalf, and therefore will be the only consistent factor in the situation.

These then are some of the different contexts in which an interviewer can find himself. When the context has been defined the interviewer has to decide on which level he wants to operate, and also he has to determine the style which he is going to adopt. The levels have been discussed earlier, but in terms of style there are fundamentally three choices: directed, non-directed and probing.

Directed

This involves direct questions which require definite answers. There are always circumstances within employment interview situations which demand the adoption of this style, but there are also occasions when this is the style necessary for the total interview. It is especially appropriate with school leavers, with applications who have complicated job histories and when there is a suggestion that 'facts' may be in dispute.

Non-directed

This means asking open questions which allow the respondent to choose an answer. This is the best way of searching out a person's real views on a particular matter, or to allow the person to project into a situation and develop a point of view. When using this approach it is useful to develop the technique of promoting. While each interviewer will develop his own pattern, the subtle prompt – 'and so, then what happened' – places a real burden on the respondent to continue with the story, or to reveal something which was not intended.

Probing

This style of interview covers and recovers the same ground by different questions. In many situations the interviewer needs to check on work done, or claimed to have done, or to check on apparent or real inconsistencies in the job history or even on attitudes displayed which may not be in character.

It is certainly true to say that these three styles are not mutually exclusive, nevertheless it is important that the interviewer should make a positive decision to adopt a certain style. But in addition the interviewer should develop an awareness and sensitivity to the interview situation which will assist him to change styles during the course of the interview without losing control.

However, practice makes perfect, and indeed a great deal of experience is required before the interviewer can intentionally change style, and purposely lose control and still achieve his objective.

A few words about control are necessary. In the majority of cases the interviewer starts off in control of the situation and if he is to achieve his ends, he must remain in control. However there are many occasions when the interviewee will try to assert himself and assume control. These attempts can be thwarted relatively simply by a rapid change of subject, offering the interviewee a cigarette (especially if he is already smoking one), or asking an innocuous question like the date of his wedding anniversary, or even why he is married or not married. The main element here is the buying of time to re-group one's thoughts and to recommence the questioning along the lines one wants to.

Every interview has its own sequence but there are five distinct aspects of the employment interview which must now be discussed:

1 Opening
2 Giving and receiving of information
3 Recording
4 Guiding
5 Closing.

Opening

In any sales training programme a great deal of attention is paid to developing a salesman's skill both in opening and closing a sales 'interview'. The same degree of attention must also be paid to the employment interview – opening and closing.

In opening the interviewer must attempt to put the interviewee at his ease, and also at the same time to win his confidence. Normal courtesies form a base from which to operate, and it is important to get the interviewe to speak about something in order merely to loosen his vocal chords – the squeaky hesitant voice or dominant aggressive tone must be eliminated at the outset before it forms an important part of the interchange between the parties. A useful opening 'gambit' is to outline the time limits for the interview, or to clear any domestic problems over travelling, or best of all to try to establish a common link with the interviewee which assists in forming a bond between the two people. This latter gambit must be free from any social or racial overtones. In addition the interviewer must be able to conceal any prejudice, particularly in relation to ethnic origin, forms of dress, regional speech, sex or physical appearance. Conversely he must not appear to be attracted by affinities – old school ties, the shapely form of a potential secretary, or someone who smokes the same brand of tobacco, or who plays a certain sport. Apparent objectivity is the keynote to establish at the outset.

Giving and receiving of information

The why, what, where, whom and how – this is the kernel of the interview situation. It is at this point that the quality of the preparatory work is tested. If this preparation has been reasonably thorough, then the interviewer will be able to answer most questions; however it is an invariable rule of the professional recruiter not to stretch the truth too much, and to openly admit that an answer cannot be provided if that is the case. An honest approach to difficult or unanswerable questions or problems will be accepted by the interviewee on most occasions.

While one must always give the candidate every opportunity to ask pertinent questions, the interviewer must make sure that he has enough time to check all relevant details of the candidate's background and work history.

Recording

In many situations a great deal of information about the candidate will have been recorded already – either in correspondence or on an application form. However, interviewers can never hope to remember the answers to all the questions put to the candidate; therefore it is necessary to have some policy and method for making notes during the interview. Most candidates will expect this, but it must be done in the least obtrusive way possible. A common document for all interview situations is useful, particularly one which allows the interviewer to complete a preliminary assessment after the candidate has departed. One such example is shown in Figure 25.2. Quite often it is suggested that a person cannot really do more than one thing at a time, but the proficient interviewer should be capable of asking questions, listening closely to the answers and taking notes at the same time. However there are times when something is missed, and in those situations the interviewer must be strong enough to ask the candidate to repeat his answer.

Guiding

This is part of the control process, nevertheless it is important to keep the discussion within bounds both of subject and time. It is really surprising how often candidates are allowed to ramble on on unimportant points, and this then leads to pressure on time, with an inevitable dropping of standards. It must be stressed that the interviewer is in the driving seat and therefore can and must guide the candidate and the discussion along the appropriate lines.

Closing

This is possibly one of the most difficult parts of the interview to handle effectively. The interviewer must be absolutely sure of what he has to do to end the interview. A lot obviously depends on the actual place of the interview in the selection procedure, but it is very easy to mishandle the situation and promote unnecessary uncertainty and suffering in the candidate. Above all a positive approach must be taken and the candidate made aware of the position; e.g. he will be receiving a letter to let him know the outcome within 10 days; or his name will be placed on the short list; or you are sorry but you will not be able to take his application any further; or will he be good enough to wait in reception while you contact the next interviewer.

The 'silent' interview

Before going on to what might logically be described as the next step – namely the assessment – a short pause is required to think upon what may be described as the 'silent' interview. During the actual interview, while the participants have been talking, a great deal of non-verbal interaction has taken place, and this takes place on two planes – the psychological and the physical. Some of the relevant points have already been touched upon, but it is necessary to draw the attention of all interviewers to the non-verbal aspects of the situation.

First the psychological aspect; each of the participants will bring in to the interview certain expectations – to sell himself well, to gain a good under-

Date:	Time:	Ref. Number:
Name:	Age:	Job:
Education, training and qualifications		*Impact*
		Appearance
Relevant experience		
		Personal

Figure 25.2 Interview notes

standing of the candidate, to show them just what a good chap he is, to demonstrate yet again that the candidate cannot put one across him.

There will also be individual prejudices and biases which will colour the situation. Irrational fears often promote feelings of inadequacy in candidates, while on the other hand interviewers are susceptible to 'halo' effects and stereotypes.

Next the physical aspect; apart from the actual interview surroundings which, depending on the colour scheme can convey a sense of lightness (pastel shades) or of depression (brown and battleship grey), the degree of comfort or austerity contributes in some measure to the quality of the interview. Physical proximity and position – chairs too near for comfort, especially with a fidgety person – can soon lead to a situation of unease without a single word being spoken. Gestures and postures provide a visual means of communication either emphasising or qualifying a verbal statement. Eye movements can also be important in establishing and maintaining contact, although most people tend to comment adversely on the person who is 'shifty-eyed'. This is very similar to the 'limp handshake' phenomenon. Voice expression conveys its own message which need not be connected with the words used. Especial care needs to be taken with the person who hesitates or stammers.

Awareness of these factors is most important for the person new to employment interviewing, for by being aware one can be on one's guard, and with experience gradually learn to cope with and interpret such phenomena.

Assessment

At the conclusion of each interview it is necessary to stop and think, and ideally to make an initial assessment of the candidate. This can be done quite quickly and effectively by using the outlines of the seven point plan as in Figure 25.3. The value of this initial assessment cannot be over-stressed, especially when there is a considerable time interval or delay between interviewing candidates and the final decision.

Name:	Age:	Job:

Impact and appearance	very good/good/acceptable/poor
Training and qualifications	very good/good/acceptable/poor
Other abilities	very good/good/acceptable/poor
Motivation	very good/good/acceptable/poor
Adjustment	very good/good/acceptable/poor
Experience	very good/good/acceptable/poor
Assessment (all factors)	very suitable/suitable/reserve/ unsuitable

Figure 25.3 ***Initial assessment and interview summary***
This list should be attached to the interview notes

The five-point plan developed by J. Munro Fraser from the initial seven-point plan devised by the National Institute of Industrial Psychology and A. Rodger draws the interviewer's attention to five separate points that need to be observed, discussed, and finally assessed. These points are:

First impressions (and physical make-up)
Qualifications (and expectations)
(Brains and) abilities
Motivation
Adjustment

The scale attached to each of these factors is rather crude, but nevertheless it provides a framework, and the basic simplicity of the five point plan is so attractive in this context that in these days of sophistication it does tend to be overlooked. But by this method the interviewer is able to summarise his thoughts, make an initial judgement (qualified if necessary in his notes) and then turn his attention to the next step of the selection procedure.

Administering appropriate tests

A great deal of space in management literature has been devoted to arguing the case for and against using tests of various kinds in the selection process. Although it does not generally appear under this sort of heading, the most common test applied is the medical one, whether it be a screening by a trained nurse before engaging operators for a food factory, or a full blown medical conducted at the medical centre of the Institute of Directors. The case for even this test can be argued both ways, although enacted legislation does tend to set some basic parameters. Nevertheless most companies or organisations have a reasonable defined policy and practice to follow, and therefore guidance is probably already available to the recruiter.

However, in non-medical areas questions inevitably arise over the value of using tests in the selection process. In many instances a case can be made for using appropriate tests, especially where there is already sufficient information available to establish the validity of the tests in that particular context. But a word of warning is necessary, for certain safeguards have been introduced by the National Foundation for Education Research in England and Wales, in conjunction with the British Psychological Association, into the administration of many tests in the United Kingdom. Where there are any possible problems over the use of tests in a selection or management development situation, reference to the above bodies, to a qualified person, to the test constructors or to an organisation such as Independent Assessment and Research Centre is a must.

What can tests test? Skills like manual dexterity, intelligence, aptitudes, abilities, interests, colour blindness and various aspects of the personality are some of the areas where additional and important information can be gained about candidates in order to make a full and final assessment about their suitability for the job in question.

Managerial level

This is an area where the impact of an individual personality can make a great deal of difference - both positive and negative. In terms of tests, therefore, thought must be given to the main personality characteristics which can contribute to successful performance, and to those which could be contra indicators, i.e. would detract from successful performance. Abilities, interests and aptitudes are important especially in making decisions about people who are starting out on a managerial career for the first time, and especially at this time when many people are likely to find themselves switching career paths once, twice, or even three times in their working life. Therefore in constructing a test package for a particular selection procedure leading to a managerial post, professional advice must be sought, and due weight given to professional opinions in the final assessment.

Clerical and technical

Here typing and shorthand skills are obvious, but in many routine clerical jobs tasks such as checking information against source documents are important. Tests of accuracy are available, and indeed, with the growth of mechanised accounting systems and computers, quite a number of tests of proven validity have been constructed and developed. Sometimes it is important to administer even simple arithmetic and verbal comprehension tests which can be constructed to suit the local situation, provided of course that the recruiter knows what he is trying to achieve.

Operational

Tests for would-be apprentices, dilutee craftsmen, plant operators and assemblers are available to those qualified to use them correctly and interpret the results properly. The test as to their acceptability is one which can only be resolved in each individual situation. But since a great deal of time is required in training those selected to do the job properly, the use of tests must often be justified on financial grounds.

While most tests give detailed instructions on procedure, test administration is nevertheless important, and the recruiter should make certain that he achieves as near to optimum conditions as possible for all test sessions. The correct physical conditions and the right psychological tone are essential to good test performance by the candidates, and if these conditions are not available then the test session can become a futile exercise in apparent sophistication. A guarantee as to the confidentiality of the result is highly important to candidates, and the approach to be encouraged is that of the medical profession in dealing with personal information of this nature.

Making the appointment

The moment of decision has arrived! Again it must be stressed that the decision to offer the position to one of the candidates is one-sided, and until the offer has been accepted, the recruitment task has not been completed.

At this stage the 'evidence' on all the candidates should be available for review and final assessment. In all probability, at least two people will be concerned in the final decision, and in most cases they should meet together to discuss the matter as fully as necessary. Sometimes one candidate stands out among all others, and consequently the decision comes easily. But on many occasions a 'debate' occurs with an informal cataloguing of the pros and cons, and inevitably some sort of compromise has to be made in relation to the 'ideal' job description and candidate specification prepared at the beginning of the recruitment and selection process. Indeed in filling some positions the selection decision is made, not by comparing candidate against candidate, but by assessing the only candidate in relation to the specification.

The important point here is to approach the decision making session in a systematic way, so that the reasons for the choice of one candidate and the rejection of the others become quite clear. No one should be afraid of stating and if necessary restating that a liking for a candidate has tipped the scales in his favour. As Robert Townsend says in *Up the Organization*, 'The important thing about hiring is the chemistry of the vibrations between boss and candidate; good, bad, or not there at all'. Any manager who denies this truism has already reached his level of incompetence.

Having made the decision, this must be conveyed in written form to the successful candidate. The formal offer of employment should always be qualified with the phrase 'subject to obtaining satisfactory references', unless of course references have already been obtained. No self respecting potential employee will accept and act upon a mere verbal offer, and until an acceptance letter has been received the process has not been completed. It is also useful at this stage to clear with the appointee any remaining matters relating to the conditions under which he will be employed.

STAGE THREE: THE FOLLOW-THROUGH

Introducing the new employee to the organisation

Any new employee will require a period of familiarisation before he can begin to perform his job properly. In many cases it is possible to set up a formal introductory course through which new employees learn about the policies and practices of the organisation. Sometimes it is possible to put a number of employees through the same course, while for others the introduction will have to be tailor-made. The major aim of induction, whether conducted on a formal basis or informally by the new employee's boss, is to integrate the newcomer as soon as possible. This is not an altruistic concept, but is based on sound economics, for the sooner a person is settled the sooner performance reaches standard.

Perhaps the best basis from which to start the induction process is the question: what does the newcomer want or need to know? A programme of induction must cover such matters as conditions of employment, departmental information, general health and safety. Remember also that new employees will find it difficult to assimilate a mass of information at one sitting, and a suitable time scale should therefore be devised.

For induction programmes at technical, supervisory or managerial level, a useful guide is to be found in the pamphlet *Induction – Acclimatizing People to Work* by W. R. Marks, published by the Institute of Personnel Management. However, the important principle to bear in mind is that the programme must be constructed around the requirements of the job to be done, and the time scale must also be realistic, for most newcomers just want to settle down and prove their worth.

Following up the progress of the new employee

This is of specific importance where a probationary period of employment (not more than 12 weeks) has to be served successfully before confirmation of the appointment takes place. In these cases a formal procedure has to be adopted in order to maintain adequate records and background information for the decision which has to be taken. If the review takes place on a weekly or monthly basis then the employee should be given some idea of what progress he or she is making. This need not be on a formal basis, for given good supervisors, the effect of an 'informal chat' can result in either a mending of the ways or a spurring to even better performance.

In general terms though, contact needs to be maintained with new employees until it becomes quite apparent that they have settled down and become part of the team. This contact between the recruiter, the new employee and his boss can be of considerable benefit in developing an awareness, in the recruiter, especially of the sorts of people who successfully survive the hesitation of the first week or month and become settled members of the company or organisation. In looking at labour turnover figures it is not surprising to note that in many instances most of the leavers quit within the first three months of being employed. There is therefore a real economic meaning and purpose to follow up after induction.

Reviewing and evaluating the recruitment and selection process

In basic terms most organisations check their recruitment and selection methods on the exception principle – the new recruit who doesn't fit in becomes the stick with which the recruiter is beaten about the head, no matter how many 'successes' can be listed! However it is possible to examine the actual methods by which the final decision is reached in a more objective way. Such questions must be asked: Are we advertising the vacancy properly? Are we attracting the right sort of candidates? Are we treating the candidates in the right way? Have we got the right system for obtaining the preliminary information about the job? Generally are the candidate specifications lucid enough? Are we getting the right sort of information about candidates from the tests we use? How long do new employees of various categories stay with us? Is this a result of over or under recruitment?

The answers to some of these questions will give an indication of what is going on in the selection process, and provide a reasonably sound base for further improvements.

In respect of the competence of the recruiter himself, it is to the advantage of the organisation itself to ensure that its 'gate-keepers' can discriminate (in the nicest possible sense) between those who should or should not be admitted. Apart from professional competence as an employment interviewer and a test administrator, the recruiter must be able to maintain the confidence of his peers and colleagues within the company, as well as enjoy the confidence of the candidates who come in front of him. Integrity is a vital word in this context both from a professional and personal point of view as far as the recruiter is concerned. Indeed all managers eventually build up a 'track-record' on their effectiveness in taking on the right people for the tasks in hand.

Finally it must be stated that most companies and organisations are now beginning to realise that the recruitment of the necessary human resources requires the same attention, effort, and concentration as purchasing essential raw materials, plant and supplies. In the last analysis it is people who, collectively or individually, make or break the company as a viable concern. The cost and effectiveness of the recruitment and selection process must be a major concern for top management, especially as the annual company report now contains the average numbers of people employed over the year and the amount of wages and salaries paid to them. In the last analysis, value for money is the unspoken question in the selection decision.

FURTHER READING

Higham, M., *The ABC of Interviewing*, IPM, London, 1979
Plumbley, P., *Recruitment and Selection*, 2nd edition, IPM, London, 1976
Ungerson, B. (ed.), *Recruitment Handbook*, 3rd edition, Gower, 1983

APPENDIX: THE IPM RECRUITMENT CODE *

In 1980, as a result of discussion through the columns of the *Financial Times*, the Institute of Personnel Management was prompted to publish the Recruitment Code. The Code was produced after much debate and heart searching amongst interested parties, recruiters and applicants alike. Its declared aim is 'to set down briefly and clearly guidance on those matters which most commonly cause resentment to recruiters and applicants. The faults are most often the result of inexperience or thoughtlessness, rarely the result of deliberate intent'.

The Recruitment Code sets out the obligations as follows:

Recruiters' obligations

1 Job advertisements will state clearly the form of reply desired (for example curriculum vitae, completed application form), and any preference for handwritten applications.
2 An acknowledgement or reply will be made promptly to each applicant by the employing organisation or its agent.
3 Candidates will be informed of the progress of the selection procedure, what this will be, the time likely to be involved and the policy regarding expenses.
4 Detailed personal information (for example religion, medical history, place of birth, family background, etc.), will not be called for unless and until it is relevant to the selection process.
5 Before applying for references, potential employers will secure the permission of the applicant.
6 Applications will be treated as confidential.

Applicants' obligations

1 Advertisements will be answered in the way requested (for example telephone for application form, provide brief details, send curriculum vitae, etc.).
2 Appointments and other arrangements will be kept, or the recruiter be informed promptly if the candidate discovers an agreed meeting cannot take place.
3 The recruiter will be informed as soon as a candidate decides not to proceed with the application.
4 Only accurate information will be given in applications and in reply to recruiters' questions.
5 Information given by a prospective employer will be treated as confidential, if so requested.

* Reproduced with kind permission from the Institute of Personnel Management, IPM House, Camp Road, Wimbledon, London SW19 4UW.

Sticking to the Code is a matter for personal choice, but nevertheless it is a valid and necessary statement of guidelines which deserve to be adopted by all engaged in the recruitment process. It has a particular value for those who become involved infrequently.

26 Salary management

Irene Innes

Companies employing up to fifty staff normally have an informal salary policy – and rightly so. However, when total staff exceed this number, anomalies begin to appear in the system and some form of framework is necessary. This is particularly so when rapid expansion is taking place.

Although there must be a co-ordinator, the responsibility for salary management is that of line management. What is needed therefore is a salary policy laying down administrative parameters within which discretion may be exercised and providing salary ranges based on simple job evaluation.

Involvement of line managers at this point is essential in order that they recognise the need for regularising salary management and make a positive contribution towards drawing up a salary policy.

EXAMPLE OF A SALARY POLICY STATEMENT

Introduction

The aim of this document is to set down the company's policy with regard to salary. It is the responsibility of all who apply it to explain it fully to their subordinates.

Aims

The aims of the company's policy are:

1 To recognise the value of all jobs relative to each other within the company and in comparison with similar jobs outside
2 To recognise the value of the individual to the company and to relate this to the salary range applicable to his or her job.

The foregoing is subject to government legislation, as appropriate.

Salary structure

The salary structure will be based on job evaluation. Each job will have a declared minimum and maximum salary range and it is the company's policy to pay at least the minimum for each job.

Job evaluation

It is the policy of the company to ensure that staff are fully involved in job evaluation, including representation on the job evaluation committee.

Job evaluation is a continuing process and once salary grades have been established, the committee will met regularly to deal with re-evaluating existing jobs as well as evaluating new jobs.

Initial salary

In determining an individual's salary on appointment, no differentiation is made on the grounds of sex. In addition, the following features are taken into account:

1 The value to the company of the relevant experience he or she brings
2 The individual's value in the outside market
3 The individual's value compared with existing staff who hold similar jobs.

Performance appraisal

An integral part of salary management is the regular appraisal of staff. This is the basis on which management counsels individuals in order that everyone has maximum opportunity to develop his or her own potential. In order that individuals utilise their abilities to the full, short and longer term objectives will be mutually agreed with management.

Salary reviews

It is the policy of the company to review quarterly the salaries of all staff under the age of eighteen years. At age eighteen years and over, all staff salaries will be reviewed annually. Performance increases, if any, will be paid effective from 1 April.

Promotion

When an individual is promoted to higher-grade work, his or her salary will be increased by 10 per cent or she will be paid the minimum for the new grade, whichever is the greater. If the individual fails to measure up to the needs of the new job, he or she will be made aware of his or her shortcomings and given an opportunity to improve and, failing this, to move to a more suitable job. If this results in moving to work of a lower grade there will be no salary decrease. Instead there will be a salary standstill until the rate for the new position equals that of the old.

Progression within salary range

Everyone will know the salary range for his or her job. Those who do their job particularly well will reach the maximum for their salary range within four years.

Long-serving staff who are already on their salary ceiling will be subject to a salary review every third year to a maximum of six years.

Grievance procedure

Anyone who feels that his or her salary indicates that an injustice has been done has the right to appeal first to his or her manager and then to the managing director whose decision will be final. The individual has a right to bring along a colleague to help support his or her appeal.

Communication

As important as the preparation of a salary policy is the need to communicate it to everyone concerned: indeed there is no reason why every staff member should not have a copy of the actual policy statement.

By far the best way of passing on information is for each departmental manager to call a briefing meeting with all his or her staff to explain what the policy covers and, more important, how it will affect each individual. Care should be taken that each employee's questions are answered sympathetically and honestly. Employees should also be fully aware of the company's intentions regarding possible salary anomalies.

JOB DESCRIPTIONS

In every company there are formal and informal arrangements about who reports to whom and how work is done. It is important, therefore, to establish and seek agreement on an organisation or accountability chart. Job titles can be very misleading and some renaming may be necessary. This in turn involves the writing of *job descriptions*.

A job description is a basic statement covering such features as:

Job title
Department
To whom responsible
Date
Tasks/areas of responsibility
Job titles of subordinates
Training and/or experience required for job.

The completed description must be agreed by both the job holder and his supervisor. (Where disagreements arise, the grievance procedure should be operated.)

A specimen job description follows.

Speciment job description

Position: Secretary to Chief Mechanical Engineer
Department: Project Engineering
Date:
Overall Aim: To provide a complete secretarial service to Chief Mechanical Engineer by organising the routine aspects of his work.

Daily tasks:

1 On receipt of mail, sort into order of priority, attach previous correspondence, if any, and type routine letters for signature
2 Take dictation from Chief Mechanical Engineer and deal also with urgent correspondence dictated by senior mechanical engineers
3 Against a tight timetable, type complicated statistical tables connected with department's project work
4 Deal with department's travel arrangements and prepare travel itineraries
5 Maintain simple time records concerning progress of experimental projects. Ensure that progress charts are kept up to date
6 Act as an assistant to Chief Mechanical Engineer by dealing with the more routine aspects of his work
7 Act as a 'shield' by dealing with callers personally and on the telephone.

Weekly tasks:

1 Prepare for accountant short summary of personal expenses incurred by department during previous week, and allocate to individual projects.

Monthly tasks:

1 Collect brief reports prepared by senior engineers on their respective projects and type draft of progress report for the Project Engineering Director.

Six-monthly tasks:

1 Transfer old files to basement and make out new files for next six months.

Annually:

1 Type statement of account showing income over expenditure on previous year's projects:

Minimum age:	Twenty-one years
Educational qualifications:	Five 'O' levels (including English Language) and secretarial college training
Experience:	Three years' practical office experience including one year in a similar firm
Induction:	Three months

Other information: The Chief Mechanical Engineer is frequently off site and the job holder is expected to deal with all routine problems arising during such absences

JOB EVALUATION

Many companies avoid installing job evaluation because they feel it is either too costly or too sophisticated. This need not be the case. Two methods should be considered as practicable:

1 Ranking
2 Job classification.

Ranking involves the study of each job description and placing it in order of importance. Note that it is the *job* which is being graded and *not* the person doing it. Here is a likely plan of attack:

1 Constitute a committee of, say, three people who have a good knowledge of all the jobs being covered
2 Select about 15–20 jobs as being a good representative sample of all the jobs being covered. These are the benchmark or key jobs and form the basis of job evaluation
3 Write job descriptions of the benchmarks
4 Separately rank those jobs in order of importance and seek agreement with other committee members
5 Design a job questionnaire (see Figure 26.1).
6 Brief all employees on how they should complete the questionnaires (see Specimen briefing notes below)
7 Ensure that all questionnaires are agreed by the respective supervisors
8 The committee finally slot in jobs according to benchmarks to reach an overall rank order.

Specimen briefing notes

Introduction

Job evaluation is a method of looking objectively at jobs and ranking them in order of importance. By comparing them one with another, each job will be placed in a salary grade relative to its worth. However, it must be stressed that it is the *job* which is being considered and *not* the individual.

A job evaluation committee has been formed under the chairmanship of Andrew Brown, the company secretary. The other members of the committee are Alan Garnett and Jill Pepperell.

The scheme

After a great deal of investigation, the committee has decided to use a classification or grading scheme, a copy of which is described later in this chapter.

Job title ____________________

Department ____________________

Responsible to ____________________

Agreed by ____________________ Date ________

1 What is the overall objective of the job?

2 Draw up a family tree showing the job in perspective

3 Give a concise description of the main areas of responsibility in the job. Take it area by area and stress the important features

Daily tasks

Weekly tasks

Monthly tasks

Quarterly tasks

Figure 26.1 Job questionnaire

1 *Overall objective.* One sentence will normally suffice here. It should be concise and give the reason for the job's existence in order that the committee has 'something to hang its cap on' before looking at the job in depth. For example:

> Process all orders ensuring that departmental computer data codes are included and that the VAT figure is correct

2 *Family tree.* A clearer picture of your job is given if you draw up a family tree of your department showing your job in relation to all other jobs

Half-yearly task
Annual tasks
4 Give the titles of the jobs which you *directly* supervise
5 Contacts – With what levels of people in other departments and/or outside the company do you have contact in order to carry out the job effectively? Is contact by telephone or in person? Comment on the reason for contact *Internal*
External
6 Comment on the qualifications and/or previous experience necessary to do the job effectively
7 Other information

Figure 26.1 (continued)

3 *Job description.* It is always difficult to write one's own job description: consider therefore that you are transferring to another department in the company and that you must prepare a note for your successor covering the main elements of the job. Describe the job as it is now and not how it should be. Do not be afraid to go into detail.

Write down the area headings first, such as correspondence, planning, queries, staff; and describe the responsibility involved under each heading. For example:

> Correspondence – on receipt of mail, decide what can be delegated to subordinates and retain non-routine letters. Where necessary give instructions regarding the handling of particular letters.

4 *Supervisory responsibility.* Supervisory responsibility can only be assessed fairly by examining carefully the job descriptions of those jobs under his or her

jurisdiction. By looking at the situation as a whole, the supervisory aspect should be accorded its proper degree of responsibility.

5 *Contacts.* The strength of the company lies in the service given to customers. This does not diminish the value of internal contacts. What is important is the level at which contact is normally made and the reason for contact in the first place.

6 *Qualifications and/or experience.* Comment should be made here regarding the minimum qualifications and/or experience which must be brought to the job *before* it can be done effectively. It may be possible to state an actual qualification or the job may simply call for 'an aptitude for figures'. Experience required must be quite specific. For example: six months' practical experience in credit control.

7 *Other information.* No questionnaire can possibly cover all aspects of a job and since it is important that every member of staff has the opportunity to comment on all areas of the job which are important, space is provided for this. For example:

> Large proportion of work is concerned with meeting tight time schedules

These comments should cover features which are an integral part of the job and not temporary difficulties.

Completion date for questionnaires. All questionnaires must be completed and returned to Jill Pepperell by Monday 29 January.

Completion date for job evaluation exercise. With the co-operation of everyone, the committee hopes to complete the evaluation exercise by 15 March.

Right of appeal. Any member of staff who feels his or her job has not been fairly evaluated has the right to appeal to the committee through his or her head of department. The individual can then expect to be invited, along with his or her head of department to discuss the job in detail with the members of the committee.

Paired comparisons

An extension of ranking – *paired or forced comparisons* – should be considered. Each job is compared with every other job and decision is made about which job is the more important. An example of a paired comparison is given in Figure 26.2).

A word of warning: fifty jobs is the maximum number that can be ranked manually.

Once this is done, a matrix is drawn up showing the jobs in rank order (see Figure 26.3).

Grading/classification

Grading/classification is a means whereby jobs are separated into

	Accounts clerk	Invoice typist	Receptionist/ telephonist	Wages clerk	Messenger	Costing clerk	Director's secretary	Shorthand typist	Stock clerk	Sales Clerk
Accounts clerk	X	1	0	0	2	0	0	0	1	0
Invoice typist	1	X	0	0	2	0	0	0	1	0
Receptionist/ telephonist	2	2	X	1	2	1	0	1	2	1
Wages clerk	2	2	1	X	2	1	0	1	2	1
Messenger	0	0	0	0	X	0	0	0	0	0
Costing clerk	2	2	1	1	2	X	0	1	2	1
Director's secretary	2	2	2	2	2	2	X	2	2	2
Shorthand typist	2	2	1	1	2	1	0	X	2	1
Stock clerk	1	1	0	0	2	0	0	0	X	0
Sales clerk	2	2	1	1	2	1	0	1	1	X

Figure 26.2 Ranking chart

Reading from the left, compare each job in turn with every other job shown along the top. If the job is more important, insert 2; if equally important, insert 1; if less important, insert 0. For example in this chart an accounts clerk is considered less important than a receptionist, more important than a messenger and the same as an invoice typist

natural/homogenous groups on a whole-job basis. This is achieved by:

1 Writing 15–20 benchmark job descriptions
2 Ranking them
3 Marking natural 'break points' between those jobs which have the same relative work
4 Defining in short paragraph form the common features of those jobs in each group
5 Writing job descriptions for the remaining jobs and matching them against the appropriate grade/classification definition.

Director's secretary	2	2	2	2	2	2	2	2	2
Receptionist/telephonist		2	2	2	2	1	1	1	1
Wages clerk		2	2	2	2	1	1	1	1
Costing clerk		2	2	2	2	1	1	1	1
Shorthand Typist		2	2	2	2	1	1	1	1
Sales clerk		2	2	2	2	1	1	1	1
Invoice typist							2	1	1
Stock clerk							2	1	1
Accounts clerk							2	1	1
Messenger									0

Figure 26.3 ***Job evaluation matrix***
Derived from the ranking chart shown in Figure 26.2

Example of a grading or classification scheme

Grade 1 Tasks are simple and conform to clearly laid down procedures. No training or experience required. Continually supervised. All written work and calculations are checked. Up to a few weeks' training required.

Grade 2 Tasks are subject to laid-down procedures but can involve a limited measure of initiative. Work subject to spot checks. Up to six months' training or experience required.

Grade 3 Tasks are carried out and decisions made in accordance with standard procedures, subject to infrequent supervision. Routine contact, external – and internal – up to own level to obtain and provide information. Probably minimum of two years' experience.

Grade 3 Tasks are carried out and decisions made in accordance with standard procedures, subject to infrequent supervision. Routine contact, externally and internally, up to own level to obtain and provide information. Probably minimum of two years' experience.

Grade 4 After specific direction, plans and arranges work within main work programme with little or no supervision. Only non-routine problems referred to superior. May have supervisory responsibility. Can have contact at higher level than own, externally and internally, to obtain and give information which may be of a confidential nature. Specialised knowledge may be required. Probably four to five years' experience.

Grade 5 After general direction, plans and arranges work with little or no supervision. Tasks can involve work of a non-routine nature requiring an original approach as to planning and method. Would normally have contact at a higher level than own, externally and internally, to obtain and give information which may be of a confidential nature. Can be required to make decisions as to daily action and direct work of subordinates. More than five years' experience required.

SALARY BANDS/GRADES

Five grades ought to suffice up to and including supervisory level. To have more will mean that differentials between grades will be reduced and staff will see little financial advantage in taking on more responsibility. Alternatively, the salaries co-ordinator will be faced with an excessive number of appeals for upgrading each time there is a slight increase in responsibility.

In general, jobs will tend to fall into broad groups but there are bound to be some jobs which will cause much soul-searching. The establishing of grades completed, the jobs on either side of the break point must be scrutinised carefully to ensure they are in the right group. In the event of appeals being raised, it is likely that they will spring from this grey area.

Salary ranges

Now comes the problem of allocating actual cash to each band or grade. A number of structures is possible, but a structure like that in Figure 26.4 is recommended for its flexibility.

As will be seen, the salary ceiling is roughly a 30–50 per cent addition on the base figure and the base for the next grade starts at approximately the midpoint of the previous grade. This means that on promotion an employee may move easily from one grade to another. It also recognises that an employee on his or her ceiling on a grade 3 job is worth more than one about to start on grade 4 work with less experience of the company's business.

Grade		
1	£3 500	£4 300
2	£3 900	£4 900
3	£4 400	£5 550
4	£5 000	£6 500
5	£6 000	£8 500

Figure 26.4 ***Salary structure***
Overlapping salary structure

SALARY SURVEYS

Although salary comparison is a continuing exercise, a particular effort must be made to obtain factual information when designing a new salary structure. This can be done in four ways:

1 By consulting national or local salary surveys
2 By telephoning your opposite number in other companies in the area and exchanging information
3 By sending to selected companies a job description from each grade, and asking for a comparison. (It is wise to telephone personally to inquire if the company is willing to take part.) This must be followed up by sending to the participants details of the survey but excluding actual company names
4 By inviting four or five opposite numbers in your area to form a Salary Comparison Club with the first meeting on your premises. An agreed agenda should be drawn up stating the jobs to be discussed in order that salary information is forthcoming.

Even at this point, the salary ranges cannot be thought conclusive until a thorough internal costing is completed.

USE OF GRAPHS

The use of graphs is invaluable when creating a new salary structure. Only when the situation is presented visually do anomalies stand out. Using a bar graph to study the number of people in each grade for instance a crude distribution curve will be obtained, i.e. the bulk of the jobs will likely be in the middle grades.

As an *aid* to determining what jobs should finally be in which grade it is helpful to do a scattergram. (See Figure 26.5.) Here is how it is done:

1 On a graph plot each job holder by basic salary and grade. This will give you the scatter on your current salary structure
2 Draw a (curved) line through the centre of the scatter so that there are roughly the same number of points above as below the line. This will give you the mid-point of each new salary range. (The technical description for the line is 'line of best fit')
3 The pure approach is to fix 15–25 per cent above and below the line the minimum and maximum salary figure for each new salary range
4 The jobs falling above and below the minimum and maximum are, of course, anomalous in the new structure.

DECIDING HOW MUCH TO PAY

You now have a) an external salary survey; and b) a formal salary structure which reflects accurately the *current* company position. It is likely these two aspects require reconciliation.

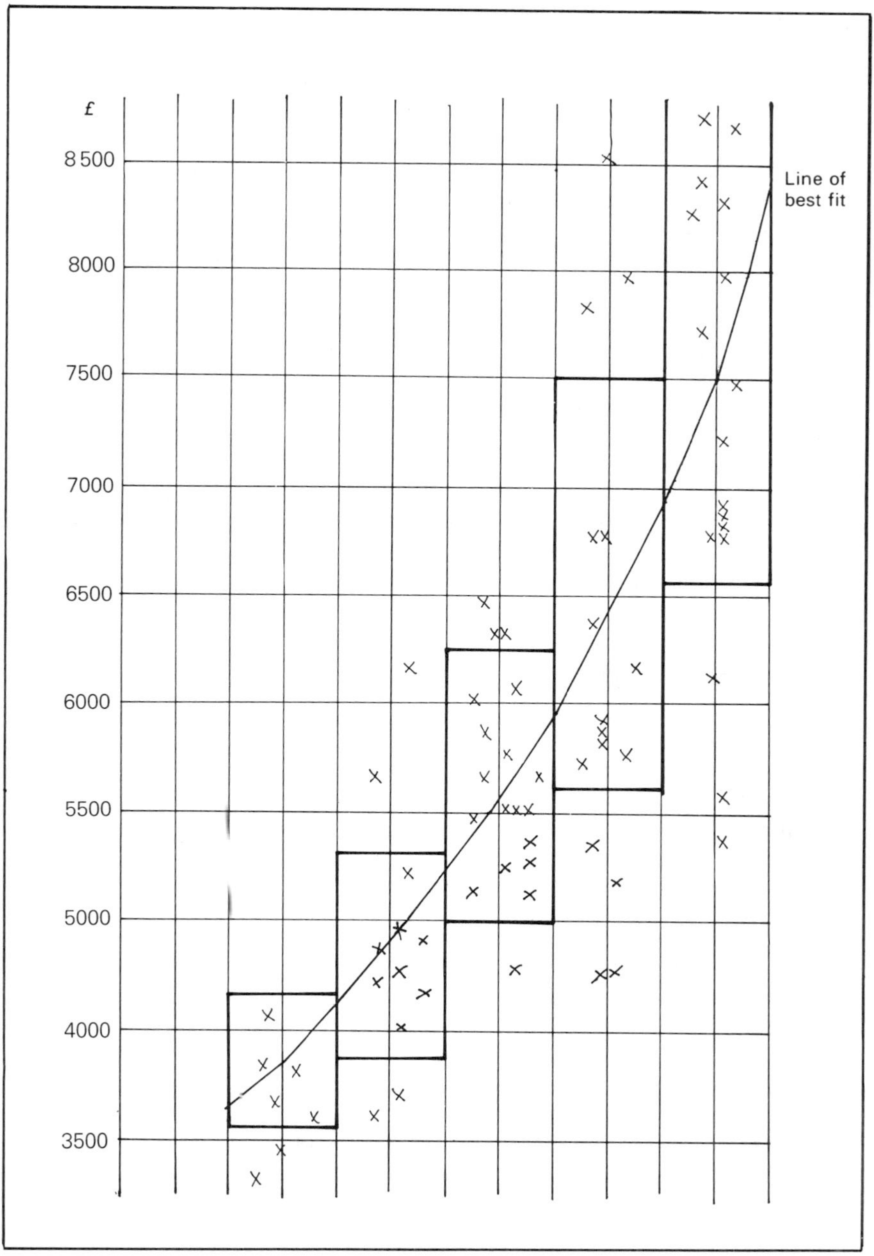

Figure 26.5 ***Comparison of old and new salary structures***

Three terms are used to describe your own position in the marketplace – lower quartile, median and upper quartile. In simple terms, let us say that you have surveyed eight different companies' rates for, say, a wages clerk. These rates are then placed in rank order. Starting from the bottom rate, rate two is the lower quartile, rate four is the median and rate six is the upper quartile. In a bigger sample, the median figure approximates to the average rate as well.

As a *general* rule, the company which chooses to be in the lower quartile tends to have a poorer calibre of staff and consequently more of them to cope with normal business pressures. The reverse is the case with the higher quartile company. Labour turnover is a costly factor not to be viewed lightly.

RATE FOR AGE

Few companies find it useful to retain a rate-for-age scale. It is the experience of a large number of organisations that the inflexibility of such a system, even with merit rating on top, can result in a rapid turnover among staff of high potential.

If however a rate-for-age scale is maintained, care must be exercised to ensure that, on the eighteenth birthday, recognition is made of both the increase in social security contributions and rail travel (if applicable). Otherwise young adults should be paid at least the minimum of the grade applicable to their job.

SALARY ANOMALIES

Once salary grades have been established, it will be found that the majority of staff will be on a salary within the new grade boundaries. However, there will probably be a number of staff who are either over or underpaid. Those underpaid should be brought up to at least the minimum for the grade. Apart from explaining the situation to those staff who are over the maximum for their job grade, the following should be considered:

1 Promotion to higher-grade work
2 Rearrangement of job content in order that some higher-grade work is included
3 Salary standstill until the new rate catches up with the old.

EMPLOYEE BENEFITS

When constructing a new salary structure, consideration must at the same time be given to the adequacy and cash values of existing employee benefits. When conducting a salary survey, therefore, employee benefits must also be taken into account.

Staff accept fringe benefits as a fact of life but different social groups within the company and indeed within the area will view different benefits with varying degrees of interest. Young people are more attracted to a company by the promise of a realistic salary than by the offer of a generous sick pay or pension scheme. Assisted house purchase, membership of a hospital scheme and profit sharing is likely to appeal to management.

In designing the salary structure, therefore, it is important to consider how much influence employee benefits need have on the salary ranges.

DEPARTMENTAL BUDGETS

Every department should have a budget and within this there should be an agreed figure for salaries. This should be decided one year in advance and should take into consideration staff retirements (with recruitment on a lower salary level), promotions and increases in staff complement. It should also take into account a figure to be set aside for salary increases. This can either be an arbitrarily agreed lump sum or, more usually, something like 3–4 per cent, excluding cost-of-living increases.

PERFORMANCE

An integral part of salary management is performance appraisal. Many companies regard appraisal as a management tool for deciding staff potential but it is much more than this. Appraisal is a two way exchange of concerns and aspirations. In the past too much stress has been placed on the assessment of ethereal areas such as initiative, co-operation and judgement and ignoring the *opportunity* individuals have had to display these tendencies. Much more can be gained from a six or twelve monthly counselling session aimed not only at furthering the objects of the company but also developing each individual's potential. If a target has not been achieved, it is far easier to discuss in plain man's terms why this was not accomplished than to comment, 'He's not a born leader – yet!'. But take care . . . It is easy to set targets and not to do a follow up on the due day. Be aware, therefore, that target setting is time consuming: take it seriously or leave it alone. A drop in morale is costly.

SALARY REVIEWS

A review does not necessarily mean that all staff receive a salary increase. Staff over the age of eighteen should have their salary reviewed annually: staff under eighteen should have their salary reviewed six-monthly or even quarterly.

The timing of reviews is important. A review coinciding with Christmas should be avoided if possible. The festive spirit can overcome the managers' commonsense! October and/or April are useful periods to consider. A salary review form is shown in Figure 26.6.

MANAGEMENT SALARIES

Salary management is based on job evaluation and this is difficult when a small number of managers is involved. Furthermore, their jobs will tend to expand considerably if the company is in course of rapid growth. Individual managers are therefore paid a figure which represents their individual worth to the

Salary review – 1 April 19XX											
Confidential								Department			
Name	Job title	Age at 31 March	Service at 31 March	Date of last performance increase	Amount	Present salary	Grade	Maximum salary	Proposed Increase	New salary	Remarks
Total											

Figure 26.6 Salary Review Form

company. It is unlikely they will have a salary ceiling unless the company's growth is fairly static.

Salary surveys are still necessary though best handled at director level.

Once a company employs fifty managers, including supervisors, then is the time to rationalise management salaries.

FURTHER READING

Bowey, Angela M. (ed.), *Handbook of Salary and Wage Systems,* 2nd edition, Gower, 1982

Lupton, T., and Bowey, Angela M., *Wages and Salaries*, 2nd edition, Gower, 1982

Vernon-Harcourt, A., *Rewarding Management,* Gower, annually.

27 Wage management

Irene Innes

The wage structure must be linked to what the company is trying to achieve. It is not unusual to find a company with a wage structure in direct conflict with the company's overall objectives. For example, a company may plan to produce a high-quality product while at the same time it may have a direct incentive geared to quantity. These questions must be asked:

Apart from profit, what are we in business for?
Where are we going during the next two to three years; in the next five to ten years?
How do we plan to get there?
What influence will these plans have on our wage structure?
How can the wage structure aid the company in meeting its objectives?

From this a business plan is built up, in simple terms, expressing the company's short- and long-term objectives and how these will affect specific areas. It may be, for example, that in two years' time a massive capital investment is planned. In terms of human resources this will probably affect the way work is organised, manning arrangements and job demands. Care must be taken, therefore, to ensure that the new wage structure will form a satisfactory springboard to cater for future developments. Consideration must also be given to the spin-off which will affect the whole company.

Management style

It is necessary to identify what the company's management style is. Is it predominantly autocratic, paternalistic, participative or *laissez-faire?* Incompatibilities arise if a wage structure is implemented in isolation of this major consideration. An autocratic management style for instance is in conflict with a Scanlon/Rucker plan. Since the pay structure expresses to employees how the company values them, a real attempt must be made to draw up a declared wage policy. A framework for a policy statement is given later in this chapter.

CHANGING A WAGE STRUCTURE

The desire to change a wage structure usually springs from an existing structure which management no longer controls. Common features are that the present structure suffers from wage drift, that it has numerous rates which are inequitable in terms of individual contribution and there has been a gradual build-up of 'special' allowances.

Most companies, when faced with the need to change their wage structure, begin by looking for alternative incentives. In reality this is prejudging the issue. The first step should be an initial investigation to ascertain the pressure points which exist in the present structure. Only by discovering the 'lumps and the bumps' in the present system will the way ahead seem clear. A discussion with the senior wages clerk will be an enlightening experience since that individual, more than anyone else, is fully aware of the inadequacies and inequities of the existing system.

Wage analysis

This should be based on a thorough examination of the gross pay earned department by department for, say, a 'typical' week at two points in the year. All special allowances should be examined and the totals expressed as a percentage of labour cost. Consideration should be given to the effectiveness of the incentive element.

Overtime

The number of hours overtime should be broken down and scrutinised to see what indicators exist. Excessive overtime working usually means an unrealistic basic hourly rate. What, for example, would be the result if overtime working were curbed? If overtime earnings were consolidated in the basic rate on the understanding that productivity was maintained, would the need for overtime working cease? And would this be socially acceptable in your locality?

Work study

One of the main reasons why a company decides to change its wage structure is because work study values have worked loose and wage drift has become a dominant feature. For example, is the pace of working closely related to that shown on the time sheets? Too often top management assumes that because performances are high on paper, all is well. If the company's present work study team cannot cope with the situation, the use of consultants should be considered. An alternative is to employ experienced work study personnel on a short-term contract.

Labour turnover

Annual figures should be produced and broken down by department. These figures are normally associated with the social aspects of employment but it is not by any means unknown for a definite correlation to be established between them and the method of payment. For example, it is possible that a very low labour turnover linked to a very high rate of absenteeism indicates that earnings may be unusually high for the area but working conditions are intolerable, leading to low morale: the employees cannot afford to leave. In other words, it is just as problematic to grossly overpay people as to underpay.

Age and sex

On a departmental basis, figures should be produced for both men and women grouping them by age, for example 16–18, 19–25, 26–40; 41–50, 51–60, 61–65, 65+. Men and women in particular age groups have different attitudes to work and how their pay packet should be made up. Additionally, they will have fairly specific ideas about what they are prepared to do to earn £*x* per week. It is doubtful, for example, whether a middle-aged male work force would be enthusiastic about the introduction for the first time of direct incentives.

Attitude survey

Ideally an attitude survey should be made to ascertain what needs have to be satisfied through a wage structure. What are the employees' attitudes towards the current pay structure and what are their deeper expectations? The pay structure to a large extent determines and reinforces attitudes. Two of the areas a survey ought to highlight are the reasons why employees work for a particular company and what motivates them. Every company has a reputation as an employer and if it has achieved, for example, a 'quick buck' image, it will attract a particular type of employee. Thought must therefore be given to the kind of image the company wants to have and how it plans to achieve it.

What motivates people in your geographical area? What kind of incentives are socially acceptable, for instance? The whole of the Midlands is almost incurably on direct incentives and a firm that works otherwise is viewed with suspicion. In a free bargaining situation, a company introduced a new incentive scheme which theoretically should have increased take-home pay – and the impact was nil! An investigation highlighted the fact that the social custom was for young people to lay their unopened pay packet on the kitchen table each pay day and to receive in turn a fixed amount of pocket money. A little unusual in the 1980s, perhaps, but knowledge of this factor would have saved the company much time and trouble.

The survey should be done by an outside specialist in order to gain the confidence of the work force.

Influence of production method

Insufficient consideration is normally given to the link between the technological aspects of production and how people are paid. It is obvious that this is important and yet many operatives in a machine-controlled situation are on direct incentives intended to make them work faster! Similarly, it is not unusual for a company specialising in one-offs to have a direct incentive scheme which entails on-the-spot bargaining between, say, a rate fixer and a shop steward for every unit produced: the result is a hardening industrial relation climate.

These questions should be asked:

1 Are runs short, long, one-offs?
2 How important is quality, quantity, accuracy, consistency?
3 Is the operation operator- or machine-controlled? And what happens *in practice?*
4 What are the capital investment plans for the next 3–5 years? Will these developments influence pay structure?
5 What are the market pressures? Are there seasonal fluctuations?
6 Can buffer stocks be kept or is the product perishable?
7 How much is lost through scrap? (If the material is reconstituted, cost this.)

JOB EVALUATION

Job evaluation is an essential exercise if a company is to be truly in control of its wage structure. Certainly it is the only answer to leapfrogging pay claims and escalating special allowances.

Job evaluation can be as difficult or as expensive as a company likes to make it. Ranking is quite satisfactory: the basis of job evaluation is ranking anyway and all other methods are, in simple terms, administrative systems which are in aid to maintaining the original rank order of the benchmarks. Points rating is the most commonly used system, however.

Nowadays it is normal for a joint management/union committee to introduce job evaluation though this depends to a large extent on the industrial relations climate. It is important, however, for the committee to be trained before embarking on the exercise.

At the other end of the industrial relations scale, however, is the multi-union situation, or long-established union militancy, or a combination of both. In such a situation, the unions should be consulted regarding their role but they will probably prefer to let management make all the decisions while they reserve the right to object on behalf of their respective members. In any case, such unions are probably accustomed to an autocratic management style and a large dose of participation is just as difficult for the unions to countenance as for line management. Obviously, union participation simplifies the situation but involvement does not guarantee instant success: there will still be appeals. What is important is that job evaluation is regarded as a quite separate situation from negotiating actual rates.

The Industrial Society's book *Job Evaluation* is useful.

LEGISLATION

Two Acts of Parliament are intended to safeguard, among other things, women's wage rates and how they are established:

Equal Pay Act, 1970
Sex Discrimination Act, 1975

In simple terms the legal framework provides for a right of appeal, depending on the case, to an Industrial Tribunal or to the Central Arbitration Committee, for a decision. To avoid such a situation, the following points should be observed:

1 Job evaluation should have been carried out
2 Each job grade should contain jobs carried out by either sex, e.g. there should not be a grade below 'labourer' grade comprising jobs filled entirely by women
3 The jobs in each grade should be 'the same or broadly similar' to each other.

COSTING

The basis of a carefully considered wage structure is sound costing. The company accountant, therefore, has an important role to play. Here are the major areas to be scrutinised for key indicators:

1 Budgeted labour cost for the coming year
2 Trend of total labour cost over the last five years
3 General breakdown of cost of the various wage components which contribute to the total labour cost for, say, the last two years
4 Earnings distribution for each department for 2 typical weeks
5 The unit cost of producing each selling line and the proportion of labour cost attributed
6 Cost of employee benefits. Frequently overlooked, these benefits are nonetheless part of the total labour cost
7 Cost of labour turnover. As a rule of thumb, a routine factory worker who leaves after, say, three months, has probably cost the company approximately £2000. This figure includes recruitment costs, interviewing time (allowance must be made for the average number of interviews to fill each job), initial training and a scale linked to the likely contribution an individual will make as his skill and know-how increases. A new employee does not begin to function as a member of a team until one or two weeks have elapsed
8 Cost of absenteeism. (Absenteeism is being used in a wider context than simply illness.) It is a useful pulse to take: if, say, absenteeism is running at a steady 20 per cent, possible causes are overmanning, overpaying or simply low morale. The cost of morale is not a balance sheet item but it is nonetheless an important hidden cost which must not be ignored.

FINANCING THE WAGE STRUCTURE

It is inflationary to set out to design and implement a new wage structure without first agreeing with the unions concerned that the increase in the wage bill must be found from within the company's resources. The actual cost of changing a wage structure is about 5 per cent of the wage bill, excluding cost-of-living for example. At first glance this figure will appear to be high: in effect a redistribution of cash and control is taking place with a short-term gain for the operatives involved and a medium-term gain for management. In a stable economy, no matter how sophisticated a company's techniques and know-how, it is possible to find savings to cover this cost. Of prime importance at the beginning of the exercise is agreement by management and unions on how the savings are to be achieved and shared.

Running concurrently with the initial investigation should be the operation of productivity groups or quality circles bent on finding savings. These groups, under the leadership of their supervisors, should comprise *operatives* meeting on a sectional or departmental basis during working hours or at the end of a shift (on overtime). Their remit should be a broad one where they may discuss every aspect of the organisation and planning of the work in their immediate working area.

While the structure of the groups will depend on the size of the section or department, the numbers meeting at any one time should not exceed eight to ten. A simple record of decisions made should be kept by each group for the sake of continuity and an effort made to communicate this within the group. Training will be necessary to help the groups to assess each problem and to make recommendations. Many companies underestimate the wealth of untapped potential which exists at shop floor level. However, companies which have attempted a similar exercise have discovered that operatives are quite capable of using simple problem solving and costing techniques (for example). Provided the groups understand in essence the services supplied by, say, the company's work study or production engineering specialists, the groups will ask for expert advice if the need arises.

DESIGNING THE WAGE STRUCTURE

Having established the realities of the existing structure, the next step is to design one which will meet the company's needs. The trend is for a company to have a two-tier wage structure: a basic hourly/job rate tier accounting for 80–85 per cent of the wage bill; an incentive tier (if any) accounting for 15–20 per cent.

Number of grades

The trend is to have four to six grades covering all factory personnel. The more straightforward the production process, the less reason for numerous grades. Without prejudicing the situation in the early stages of the investigation, there should be at least £7.50 per week differential between each grade. To have less will act as a disincentive to internal promotion. In effect this means reducing the number of grades to a point where the differential is a significant demonstration that work in a higher grade really is more important to the company. If the pay steps are too small, management will be faced with numerous requests for regrading jobs every time a fraction of responsibility or a grain of dirt is added to the job.

The decision regarding the break point for each grade is largely arbitrary. It will probably be a negotiating point. On the whole, jobs tend to fall into homogeneous groups but no matter where the break points are made, 'grey area' jobs on either side of the line will give rise to much tooth-sucking. It is from this area that job evaluation appeals usually spring.

As an aid to deciding where the break points might be, it is useful to produce some scattergrams showing how, for example, the results of job evaluation compare in relation to job holders' basic rates as well as gross pay (see Figure 27.1). The next step is to determine the 'line of best fit': in simple terms a line is drawn through the centre of the points already plotted. It is then possible to determine roughly what the pay steps might be. In practical terms this is a quite considerable exercise and it may be that a 30 per cent sample, say, of all jobs might suffice.

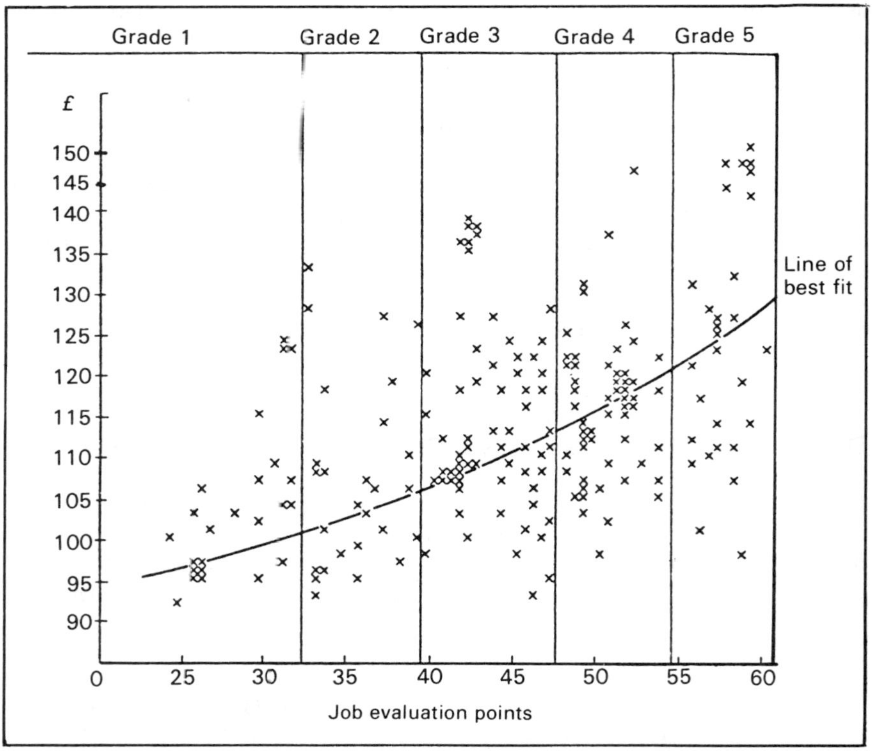

Figure 27.1 ***Scattergram of earnings (excluding overtime)***
Related to job evaluation points as well as to possible break even points between grades and new pay steps

Yet another statistical aid is the use of bar graphs. In most companies the bulk of the jobs will be in the middle two grades with roughly the same number in the bottom and top grades.

Deciding the basic rate

Traditionally, manual workers have been in a position where the ratio of basic rate to incentive was 2:1. However, this ratio now tends to be nearer 4:1 largely because companies moving towards single (staff) status are rightly challenging the concept that a manual worker's earnings should fluctuate with the company's production throughput.

The case for greater security of earnings should therefore be considered as a matter of course. If nothing else, a proportion of 2:1 is a prime cause of wage drift. Theoretically, a wage survey should be conducted with other firms but since the make-up of gross pay is so variable from company to company, it is difficult to establish any meaningful form of parity. A company must examine its own costing system in terms of budgeted labour cost and the relationship this bears to unit cost. In other words, management must decide how much of the budgeted labour cost should be attributed to basic rate and how much to incentive, if any. Since this is negotiable, management should also know in advance the influence on unit costs of different break points or alternative basic rates.

One company employing about 1 000 people avoided this problem by taking the budgeted labour cost for the coming year and giving to the unions concerned three different 'mixes' of total wage cost. This was broken down into 3, 5 and 7 grades complete with incentive calculated at 80, 90 and 100 BSI. (80 BSI is a good average rate of working.) The unions were told that they could produce another option still coming to the same total if they so desired. The company in question, while unused to this level of participation, had a history of good industrial relations. Obviously some unions will question the budgeted labour cost but this does not detract from the principle proposed.

Dealing with anomalies

Once the job evaluation exercise is completed and new basic rates determined, a scattergram will pinpoint those jobs which are likely to be over or underpaid in relation to the new rates. Provided the old structure was not completely out of control, the bulk of the jobs will be just about right and roughly the same number over as underpaid. The options open to management are:

For overpaid employees

1 Retrain the individuals concerned in order that they can take on work of a more responsible or skilful nature and therefore justify the new level of payment
2 Make the difference between the old rate and the new a personal allowance which would be eroded each time a new basic rate was agreed. In time the new rate would catch up with the old
3 As for 2, but the old rate – sometimes called a Red Circle Rate – is retained for ever and ever. This is not advised. In time this becomes a thorn in the side of other employees
4 Buy out anomalies by paying a lump sum comprising the difference

multiplied by a negotiated figure. This is a strong negotiating area. What must be considered is the percentage of employees involved and whether or not most of the differences will be swallowed up within twelve to eighteen months anyway.

For underpaid employees

There are no options here: the individual's pay must be brought into line.

INCENTIVE ELEMENT

The word 'incentive' is synonymous with the word 'effort' in the minds of many. But this is not so. An incentive is some form of financial encouragement recognising a particular contribution made by the work force. It is, in effect, a sum of money additional to the basic rate which a company pays to ensure that its most important production aspects are being optimised. For example, a capital-intensive company might have an incentive linked to machine utilisation; a company making diamond-tipped tools might put particular emphasis on a low scrap value while still maintaining quality. Nonetheless many companies insist that effort is the only factor to recognise despite the fact that automation is very much with us.

Thought must be given to the *cost* of maintaining any one incentive: how many work study personnel, bonus clerks, tally clerks and inspectors are required to maintain standards? Can it be done in a more simple, effective way? Need there be an incentive? Will people only work on a carrot and stick basis? Will you, the reader, only work on this basis or are you different? What contribution does first-line supervision make to motivating people? Will the system encourage or stifle the growth of tomorrow's supervisors?

The basic decisions to be made about the incentive element are whether or not it is going to be individual, group, department or company based or a combination of these. The other important feature is whether the incentive is to be based on a straight-line formula (the more units produced the more earned *ad infinitum*) or on a curve where rather less is earned proportionately the more units produced, sometimes with a cut-off point to limit production and thereby restrict bonus. Yet another approach is to have a cut-off point beyond which any bonus earned is placed in a common pool. This in turn is used to help finance basic rates when these are renegotiated.

Direct incentives

Definition. A method of payment whereby a bonus is paid in direct relation to effort.

Advantages

1 Appropriate where a high level of physical effort is necessary and it is difficult to supervise workers effectively
2 Can generate substantial motivation as payment occurs shortly after achievement

3 Flexibility in allocating added reward for added effort
4 Introduction can mean a reduction in labour
5 Can be useful in the short term to increase the pace of working as an interim step to moving on to a more sophisticated system.

Disadvantages

1 Management is not in control of production
2 Tendency to ignore avoidance of waste
3 Supervisors in time may earn less than their subordinates, skilled less than semi-skilled
4 People learn how to achieve earnings without undue effort, for example by qualifying for special allowances, avoiding promotion to non-lucrative jobs, embarking on slow-downs during 'testing' of new rates
5 Can ruin industrial relations
6 Mobility of labour becomes virtually impossible
7 Supervisors become good progress chasers but rarely good managers.

Measured daywork

Definition. Measured daywork is a stabilised direct incentive system where the incentive element is consolidated in the basic rate, thereby achieving a high, non-fluctuating weekly wage or salary.

It is based on sound training, sophisticated work measurement techniques and sound management. It is still payment by results except that the underlying philosophy is one of trust – that an individual will work at an agreed pace provided work is available for him or her. The most common types are:

High day rate, which is suitable in an assembly-line. Each new employee is fully trained before starting work on the factory floor. He or she will be expected to produce work of a specified standard and to maintain a fixed working pace of, say, 90 BSI. The aim is to achieve a controlled work flow: those individuals who have a naturally high pace of working would normally be transferred to indirect work. Those who have a naturally slow pace are subject to warnings and then either transferred to indirect work or dismissed, following reasonable warning.

Advantages

1 Simplified pay structure usually based on job evaluation
2 Considerable operating flexibility
3 Trust and responsibility given proper emphasis
4 Management is in control of production and uses work study standards as a condition of employment as well as for management information.

Disadvantages

1 Not always possible to elicit acceptable levels of performance without the 'pull' of a direct incentive
2 Sophisticated control techniques, such as daily computer data, are necessary

3 High calibre of supervision is essential
4 Disputes can be tougher than in direct incentive plants as employees can slow down without impairing earnings.

Philips premium pay plan is suitable where individuals can control the pace of work. The same principles as those for high day rate apply except, perhaps, the problem of disputes since PPP is based on individual effort.

The pay structure is a simple one, usually based on job evaluation, but unlike high day rate, it is graded in steps according to the pace of working (see Figure 27.2). Each individual contracts through his supervisor to work for a period of three months at a particular pace. If this pace is not maintained and the fault is not that of management, a warning is given. If the pace of working does not meet the agreed standard during the following three months, he or she is either retrained or moved back to a lower pay band. If he or she is unable to maintain an acceptable pace, he or she is liable to dismissal.

Group/departmental incentives

Definition. A method of payment whereby a bonus is paid either equally or proportionately to individuals within a group/department as a result of, say, output achieved over an agreed standard.

Advantages

1 It encourages team spirit
2 It breaks down demarcation lines
3 The group disciplines its 'slackers'
4 Job satisfaction is achieved through seeing the complete operation within the group area.

Disadvantages

1 Management is not in control of production
2 The bonus ceases in time to be an incentive and management might as well

SALARY AND WAGE ADMINISTRATION

GRADE	80 BSI £	90 BSI £	100 BSI £
I	113.00	122.00	131.00
II	104.00	112.00	120.00
III	95.50	102.50	109.50
IV	87.50	93.50	99.50
V	80.00	85.00	90.00

Figure 27.2 Example of a wage structure of the Philips Premium Pay Plan type

consolidate the rate
3 Individual effort is not rewarded

Plantwide incentives

There are three main types:

Factory throughput. Linked to, say, tons leaving the factory, the bonus is distributed either equally or proportionately according to skill. Basic concept is that workers become more closely associated with the company's aims.

Advantages

1 Improved atmosphere
2 Demarcation less pronounced
3 Employees are aware of the production targets the company plans to achieve.

Disadvantages

1 Individual effort is not recognised
2 Employees find it difficult to associate themselves directly with the bonus
3 To safeguard against bad weeks/months, companies sometimes maintain a bank, so that the bonus becomes an employee benefit
4 If a bad week/month is experienced it's always the fault of 'other' departments.

Scanlon plan. An alternative name is 'share of production plan'. The nub of the system is the formation of a joint management–union productivity committee which has *executive authority*. The bonus is based on productivity improvements and is usually calculated monthly.

Rucker plan. An alternative name is 'cost reduction plan'. The basic theory is that there is a constant relationship between wages and production or added value. A joint management–union productivity committee is formed but it has *advisory authority* only. Savings made by reducing costs are shared either equally or proportionately and are usually distributed on a monthly basis.

In a nutshell, Scanlon is strong on industrial relations and weak on mathematics and Rucker vice versa. In practice, the best of both methods is adopted. The share-out is usually about a third of total savings. The basic concept for both is that manual workers have very much more to offer to a company than simply effort.

Advantages of Scanlon/Rucker plans

1 Can encourage better use of resources and raw materials and thereby produce substantial savings
2 Focuses attention on co-operation and teamwork to reduce costs
3 Trust and responsibility given proper emphasis
4 People accept change more readily

5 Normally covers direct and indirect workers and can include staff directly linked with production
6 Work group has a stake in how well management performs – and has freedom to criticise poor decisions: it therefore keeps management on its toes.

Disadvantages of Scanlon/Rucker plans

1 Cannot in themselves create a willingness to co-operate or a management capable of exploiting cost reduction
2 Some groups have more control over results than others and some contribute more than they receive
3 Parochialism can result: good communication is essential
4 Success largely hinges on sophisticated cost control techniques over a long period – and deciding on the 'right' calculation for distribution of savings.

Profit-sharing

Definition. On the basis of company profits, employees either receive an annual cash bonus or actual company shares. Basic concept is participation.

Advantages

1 Thrives in non-union firms
2 From management's point of view, extra rewards are allocated only when they can be afforded
3 Improved teamwork and co-operation. However, to optimise this, management must communicate the economic facts of life
4 The system is self-adjusting although the method by which profits are calculated or the form in which the money is distributed may come under attack.

Disadvantages

1 Workers have little control over final profit achieved
2 An industrious worker does not necessarily achieve extra payment
3 Tendency to withhold part of the profit to be shared against less fortunate times, thus making it a handout or employee benefit
4 Many schemes do not pay sufficient money to make an impact on motivation.

Merit-rating

Definition. A method of payment based on management decisions about an individual's personal *qualities and aptitudes*. Basic concept is that management reserves the sole right to pay people individually.

Advantages

1 Supervisors regularly consider each subordinate's contribution
2 Method of payment is flexible
3 Employees feel they are being treated as individuals.

Disadvantages

1 Because it is usually a subjective assessment, it is difficult to discuss problem areas without an element of emotionalism – always supposing they are discussed at all
2 Economic pressures often result in the system being bent with everyone ending up at the top end
3 Supervisors find it easier to pay everyone the same so that it effectively becomes an employee benefit.

ADDED VALUE

It is a well-established fact that in a *stable economy* there is an almost constant relationship between labour costs and added value. It follows, therefore, that this provides a useful formula on which to calculate savings: these in turn can be used to fund annual wage increases on a plantwide basis.

For example, assume that unions and management agree (as a result of information provided by the company's auditors) that over the last five years labour cost has been 34 per cent of added value.

	£
Sales	100 000
Less raw materials, utilities and depreciation	55 000
Added value	45 000
Labour cost	15 300
Labour cost: Added value	34%

It is agreed that any savings made in labour costs beyond this reference point of 34 per cent will be shared equally between management and unions.

Assume that sales increase 20 per cent and that with no additional increases in basic cost the cost of providing raw materials is a further £11 000, and that labour costs increase by 10 per cent. The situation would appear thus:

	£
Sales	120 000
Less raw materials, utilities and depreciation	66 000
Added value	54 000
Labour cost	16 830
34% × £54 000	18 360
Saving in labour cost	1 530
Proportion contributed to plantwide increases	765

A total of 4.5 per cent on the total wage bill

It will be obvious that companies will be required to open their books if the operation of the added-value concept is to maintain credibility. Set against this is the fact that the more information which can be produced prior to negotiation, the less conflict there will be between management and unions.

Approximately half of all disputes leading to stoppages are caused by friction over wage rates. A removal in part, even, of some of the reasons behind these stoppages would give both management and unions more time to contribute to other important areas.

PRODUCTIVITY AGREEMENTS

A productivity agreement is a statement jointly agreed by management and unions on how work and people may be more effectively organised to mutual benefit. Two types of agreement are:

1 An agreement using the 'buying out' principle on the basis of *quid pro quo*. In effect, this type of agreement covers immediate wage increases in exchange for relaxation of rigid demarcation lines; elimination of tea breaks; forfeiture of mates; reduction in manning levels
2 An agreement which lays down a framework for allowing savings to be accumulated over six to twelve months. These savings are normally shared equally between management and shop floor employees.

In a nutshell, the difference between the two is 'jam today or jam tomorrow'. In selecting the right approach, a company must consider what will best match its industrial relations climate *and* its overall company objectives. It may be that its lack of operating flexibility demands a 'buying out' agreement in the short term but its longer-term objectives require phased steps towards a position where greater participation will fund wage increases as well as strengthen the company's future. But it must be *planned.*

In times of high unemployment, productivity agreements of the buying-out type are not popular with unions. In any case, it is narrow to assume that increased productivity can *only* be achieved through a reduced labour force: there are numerous options which are equally valid. For example, what would be the effect of better machine utilisation, improved work flow, reduction in scrap value, introduction of shift work? It is rather a question of selecting the right tools in order to make the best use of human resources.

Whatever form the agreement takes, it is, in effect, a *statement of intent* signed by both parties: what must not be overlooked is that it is not a once-and-for-all effort but a document calling for positive action throughout its term with regular progress reviews properly communicated. All too often companies negotiate excellent productivity agreements but fail to follow them through.

SINGLE STATUS

Employee or fringe benefits provide an element of security, a security which up until the last few years was the preserve of staff and management only. With the trend towards removing the differences in conditions between blue and white collar workers, unions are becoming increasingly aware of the value to their members of negotiating, for example, increased pensions. If the incentive element influences employee attitudes, how much more that of employee benefits? Sometimes overlooked, the Equal Pay Act requires equality in particular employee benefits as well as pay. If single status is the ultimate aim, a phasing operation must be planned in order that costs may be absorbed. The point being made is that employee benefits are part of the total labour cost and must be taken into account when looking at overall pay and conditions.

COMMUNICATION

An important area not stressed sufficiently is the need to communicate effectively. *The need to know* what is happening must be satisfied. Managers are often as starved of information as operatives! Will your present system cope? It is not the shop stewards' job to communicate management's intentions. Can your supervisors brief their subordinates face to face? What can you do to help them? Above all, every individual affected by the new pay structure must *understand* how it works. Could a simple booklet be produced? These are the main points concerning communication but since it is vital to the success of the whole project, readers are strongly advised to read the Industrial Society's booklet on 'Communication' in the *Notes for Managers* series.

SUPERVISORY STRUCTURE

Because many companies are attempting to move away from direct incentives, it is wise to comment on the need to investigate the existing supervisory structure and to consider the calibre, in effect, of first-line managers. Whatever management decides in terms of a new structure, first-line supervisors will be required to manage more effectively. Apart from training needs, the span of control must be examined. If a supervisor is to manage effectively, the most he can control and motivate is fifteen to twenty operatives. The successful implementation of a new wage structure hinges on how carefully this aspect is handled.

EXAMPLE OF A WAGE POLICY STATEMENT

It is the intention of management that this document be issued to every employee whom it concerns. It is the responsibility of first-line management to explain it fully to their subordinates. Should anyone feel that any aspect of this policy is not operating in practice, he should as a first step discuss this with his supervisor.

Aims

The aims of the policy are:

1 To recognise the value of all jobs in relation to each other within the company
2 To take account of wage rates paid by companies of similar size, product and philosophy
3 To ensure stable earnings
4 To enable individuals to reach their full earning potential as far as is reasonably practicable

5 To ensure employees share in the company's prosperity as a result of increasing efficiency.

Job evaluation

The basis of a sound wage structure is job evaluation. It is in the interest of both unions and management that this is carried out on a joint basis.

Job evaluation is a continuing process and therefore must be maintained if it is to retain its usefulness. To ensure that the scheme is still relevant, it will be reviewed jointly by unions and management at the end of its third operating year.

Wage structure

In designing the wage structure, the company aims to make the best use of its employees in order to achieve the company's short and longer-term business objectives. By achieving these objectives the company hopes to remain a leader in its field, thereby ensuring greater job security for all concerned.

Rate for the job

No one will be paid less than the recognised rate for the job. Equal pay is in force on the basis of 'equal pay for work of equal value'. While the company recognises the right of the unions' joint negotiating panel to negotiate on behalf of its members, management believes that first and foremost rates should be linked to the company's prosperity.

The company does not aim to pay the top rates in the area but rather to place the emphasis on good working conditions, security of employment and an atmosphere in which individuals may reach their full potential. Nonetheless the company aims to be in the top 15 per cent as far as total earnings are concerned. (Total earnings includes employee benefits.)

Number of grades

The number of grades will be as few as possible in order that differentials are of a sufficiently high level for real differences in responsibility and/or skill to be recognised.

Incentives

The company does not accept that its employees will work only on a carrot and stick basis: neither does it believe that its employees will give of their best if earnings fluctuate from week to week. This policy is reflected in the company's wage structure which is based on measured daywork.

Every employee should, wherever reasonably practicable, have the opportunity to reach maximum earnings for his grade. Provided work is available, employees are expected to work at a mutually agreed pace. Where work is not immediately available, employees will not lose financially but will be expected to move to alternative work in order to maintain production.

Where individual targets are not maintained, and management is not responsible, an employee must expect to be counselled, disciplined if necessary and, as a last resort, dismissed.

Work measurement

The basis of the wage structure is work measurement. The company aims to use the most advanced methods available. However, it does not intend to wrap these methods in a jargon not easily understood. All production managers (including first-line supervisors) and shop stewards will attend jointly sponsored appreciation courses in order that any disagreement over standards is discussed in full knowledge of how the system works.

Indirect workers

Indirect workers such as maintenance, cleaning and catering employees play an important support role in the overall production process. It is not possible to apply work measurement techniques to indirect jobs at an economic cost. An enhanced day rate will therefore be payable to employees in this category.

Minimum earnings

No employee will receive less than £120.00 for a 40-hour week. This ensures that lower-paid employees are paid a 'living wage', but employees in other grades must not expect that established differentials will necessarily be maintained.

Overtime

The wage structure is designed to ensure that excessive overtime is both unnecessary and unattractive. Overtime is a requirement which will only arise in very exceptional circumstances. Since it is management's responsibility to plan work effectively and determine manning requirements, 72 hours' notice will be given of the need for overtime working, except in very exceptional circumstances.

Promotion

The company operates a policy of internal promotion, wherever possible. When a promotion takes place, the individual will immediately take the 'rate for the job'. However, if the individual is on maximum earnings for his old grade, he will retain the old rate for three months until he has established himself in the new grade.

In exceptional cases where the individual fails to maintain a satisfactory level of performance, he will be transferred to lower-grade work. He will, however, retain the higher rate until the annual negotiation of wage rates when his personal rate will be eroded.

A similar policy operates for staff promotions.

Single status

It is company policy to remove progressively all differences in employee benefits for blue and white collar employees. To this end, the cost of such benefits will be included in overall labour costs. The ultimate aim is to move towards a 'package' concept negotiated annually.

Share of prosperity

The company believes that employees have a right to share in the company's prosperity. It also believes that increases in its labour bill should not be passed automatically to its customers. A special formula has therefore been agreed between management and unions whereby all savings made as a result of shopfloor participation will be divided on a 50/50 basis and used to finance increased wage costs.

Negotiating information

The company believes that only by providing its recognised unions with sound, factual information can a positive industrial relations climate be fostered. Agreed information will be issued quarterly to the joint negotiating panel.

CHECKLIST: CHANGING A WAGE STRUCTURE

The following checklist is intended to provide a starting point for discussion before installing a new wage structure. The list is by no means exhaustive but answering such questions should enable managers to decide the direction in which they plan to go in the short and longer term.

Company objectives

1 Apart from profit, what are you in business for?
2 Where are you going during the next two to three years; in the next five to ten years?
3 How do you plan to get there?
4 What influence will these plans have on your wage structure?
5 How can the wage structure aid the company in meeting its objectives?

Product

1 Are runs short, long, one-offs?
2 How important is quality, quantity, accuracy, consistency?
3 Is the process operator- or machine-controlled?
4 What are the capital investment plans for the next three to five years? Will these developments influence the pay policy?
5 What are the market pressures? Are there seasonal fluctuations?
6 Can buffer stocks be kept or is the product perishable?
7 How much is lost through scrap? (If the material is reconstituted, cost this.)

Work measurement

1 Are measurements loose, tight or a mixture of both?
2 Is pay related to effort? Is this what you want anyway?
3 To what extent are you subject to wage drift, that is, increasing labour costs with little or no increase in productivity?
4 Do your supervisors and shop stewards understand the principles of work measurement?
5 Have you enough industrial engineers to ensure that three separate studies are made before each standard is decided?
6 Are your existing studies sufficiently accurate to allow you to consider the introduction of synthetic ratings?
7 How about method study?
8 Will it be necessary to employ contract work-study personnel? Or experienced industrial engineers on a short-term contract?

Wage analysis

1 How many wage rates exist?
2 Where do national agreements fit in?
3 Is there a 20 per cent differential between supervisors' pay and the average gross pay (less overtime) of those they supervise?
4 What is the budgeted labour cost for the coming year? Does it include the cost of employee benefits?
5 What is the trend of *total* labour cost for the last five years?
6 How many elements make up gross pay? How many of these do you wish to consolidate? Or buy out?

7 What is the earnings distribution for each department for two, separate, typical weeks?
8 What trends are indicated from a breakdown of overtime worked?
9 What is the cost of producing each selling line and the proportion of labour cost attributed?
10 What is the cost of labour turnover?
11 What is the cost of absenteeism?

Job evaluation

1 What is the simplest possible method you could use which would satisfy the company's and the job holders' needs?
2 Should there be a joint job evaluation committee?
3 Should it be a full or part-time exercise?
4 To what extent can you involve the job holders?
5 Who should write the job description? The job holder, a job analyst or a member of the job evaluation committee?
6 How much information are you prepared to give to job holders about the scheme? Do you mean, for example, to tell each job holder the number of points allocated to his job? Could you give everyone concerned a copy of the scheme?
7 Will your existing appeals procedure match the needs of a job evaluation exercise?
8 Could you time and cost in advance the implementation of job evaluation?

Financing the wage structure

1 Can you finance from within the increased cost of the new wage structures?
2 Could you negotiate initially the share-out between company and employees of any savings made?
3 How can you communicate effectively the aims of the exercise?
4 What training will have to be undertaken?
5 How can you involve your supervisors in order that they make a major contribution to the exercise?

Social aspects

1 What is the age and sex distribution by job and department?
2 What motivates your employees? What are their aspirations? Would an attitude survey be useful?
3 What kind of image does your company have? Is it what you want?
4 What kind of incentives are people used to in your geographical locality? Would your proposals cut across the expectations of your employees? What can you do to engineer the change?
5 How do you rate your industrial relations? How can this exercise improve them?
6 What is the company's predominant management style? Will the new wage structure alter this in any way? How can you involve middle and senior

management in such a way that they become party to the proposals?

7 What plans have you regarding such things as security of employment and earnings; single status?
8 How important is a stable work force to the company? Is it company policy to promote from the shop floor? Will the new pay structure influence or detract from this?

Designing the wage structure

1 From scattergrams of the existing situation, what anomalies exist? How many of these can you hope to get rid of first time around?
2 Using the scattergrams, how many grades ought you to have in the short term? What are you aiming for in the long term?
3 How can you involve your company accountant in order that the exercise is properly costed?
4 Is an alternative incentive planned? Do you need incentives anyway? If you do, will they be individual, group or company based? Or a combination of these?
5 What effect will the incentive element have on your products, the way you plan work, the way you manage people, employee attitudes?
6 Could you work out three possibilities for, say, a 3, 5 or 7 grade structure complete with differentials and incentive element, if any, each coming to the total budgeted labour cost?
7 How competitive would these rates be locally?
8 What is your policy on equal pay?
9 What will your unions be expecting at the negotiating table?
10 What kind of productivity agreement do you need? To what extent can you make it a charter for the future?
11 How far can you go in giving information to your unions in order that negotiation may be constructive?
12 How will you handle pay anomalies?

Implementing a wage structure

1 How can you improve your methods of communication in order that everyone *understands* what is happening?
2 Do senior managers understand how the new pay structure might affect them? Marketing and sales, for example?
3 What training can you give to your supervisors in order that their status and respect is strengthened and not weakened by the demands of the new pay structure?
4 Is your supervisory structure adequate in relation to the needs of the new pay structure? Can you give your supervisors more scope for decision-making without reference to the next level? Is their span of control about right in view of the demands which will be put on them?

5 What training should you give to shop stewards in order that they are aware of the implications of the new structure?

FURTHER READING

ACAS, *Advisory Booklet No. 1 – Job Evaluation*, Advisory Conciliation and Arbitration Service, London, 1979

Bowey, Angela M. (ed.), *Handbook of Salary and Wage Systems*, 2nd edition, Gower, 1982

Lupton, T., and Bowey, Angela M., *Wages and Salaries*, 2nd edition, Gower, 1983

28 Working conditions

Patricia George

In recent years the moral responsibility of management to provide reasonable working conditions for their employees has, more and more, been taken over by legislation. No one would deny that the objectives of such legislation are well founded, but so much has been produced (with so many changes) that a concise summary will help to ensure that readers obey the letter, as well as the intent, of the law.

HEALTH AND SAFETY AT WORK ACT 1974

One of the main purposes of this Act is to provide a comprehensive and integrated system of law to deal with the health, safety and welfare of people at work. Based on the concept of a general duty of care, the Act has been drawn up in such a way that it can be changed, expanded and adapted to cope with risks and problems in industry for many years ahead. It has been described as the most significant statutory advance in this field since Shaftesbury's Factory Act of 1833. The Act applies to all people working in any capacity: employers, employees (except domestic servants in private employment), self-employed and to certain members of the public.

The basic obligations of all employers and all employees, which the Act deliberately couches in very general terms, are given below.

Basic obligations of employers

The employer must ensure, so far as is reasonably practicable, the health, safety and welfare at work of all his employees. This duty includes the provision of (and maintenance of, as appropriate):

1 A safe, healthy working environment with adequate facilities and arrangements for welfare at work
2 A safe, healthy place of work with safe means of access and egress
3 Safe, healthy plant and systems of work

4 Means, etc., to use, handle, store or transport articles and substances without risk to health or safety
5 Information, instruction, training and supervision necessary to ensure the health and safety of his employees
6 Written statement of his general policy for the health and safety of his employees, and the organisation and arrangements for carrying out that policy.

Employers must, in specified circumstances, allow their employees to appoint their own safety representatives, consult with them and, if so requested, set up safety committees.

Directors will be required to give information in their annual reports to shareholders on what their companies are doing in this field. The Companies Act 1967 was amended accordingly by *s*79 of the Health and Safety at Work Act on 1 April 1975.

Additionally employers have a duty to ensure the safety of persons other than employees who enter their premises and to ensure that their activities do not endanger anybody outside their employment.

Basic obligations of employees

Every employee has a duty to take reasonable care for the health and safety of himself and of others who may be affected. He must co-operate with his employer to enable the duties and requirements of the Act to be carried out.

Many processes or activities are now, or will be, governed by regulations or approved codes of practice. In general contravention of the appropriate regulation will be an offence. A person will not however be open to criminal proceedings for failing to observe a particular code of practice but in the event of criminal proceedings any relevant code of practice is admissible in evidence.

The Health and Safety Commission, Executive and Inspectorate

In general, the Commission is responsible to the Secretary of State for Employment for making whatever arrangements are appropriate for the general purposes of the new legislation. It has an information, education and advisory role and the power to carry out investigations and inquiries within the health and safety field.

The Health and Safety Executive, responsible to the Commission, is its operational arm and has been set up to carry out the Commission's functions under the Commission's direction. In its turn, the Executive is empowered to appoint inspectors to carry out its enforcement and advisory functions. Inspectors of factories, mines and quarries, nuclear installations, alkali and clean air and explosives have been transferred to the Executive for this purpose.

An inspector can enter an employer's premises at any reasonable time (at any time in a situation which in his opinion is, or may be, dangerous) to carry out his function.

Improvement and Prohibition Notices. An inspector will be able to issue Improvement and Prohibition Notices.
Improvement Notice. Requires the employer to remedy a contravention of Act or a regulation under it within a specified period.
Prohibition Notice. Requires the employer to stop (immediately if necessary) any activity which carries risk of serious personal injury.

There is a right of appeal to an industrial tribunal against these Notices. Improvement Notices will be held in abeyance pending the appeal but Prohibition Notices will remain in force unless the employer satisfies the tribunal to the contrary, by application prior to the hearing.

Employment Medical Advisory Service

In addition to having an advisory role, the Act:

1 Authorises a medical adviser to carry out a medical examination of any employee whose health is believed to be in danger because of his work, provided the employee himself consents
2 Requires an employer to inform the local careers office when recruiting a person aged less than eighteen to work in a factory, specifying the nature of the work he will be doing.

Disclosure of information

The Commission can serve a notice on any person to reveal information affecting health and safety.

An inspector can in appropriate circumstances inform the employees at a workplace of matters affecting their safety, health and welfare.

The Safety Representatives and Safety Committees Regulations 1977 require employers to make certain information available to safety representatives.

Enforcement of the Act

The Executive is required to make adequate arrangements for enforcement except where regulations made by the Secretary of State place the duty on local authorities or other bodies.

*Responsibility for fire prevention and fire precautions. S*78 amends the Fire Precautions Act 1971 so that the fire authorities and the Home Office can deal with general fire precautions (means of escape in case of fire, fire-alarm systems, fire-fighting equipment and so on) under the Act. The Commission and Executive will remain responsible for control over risks of fire associated with particular processes or the use of particular substances, and for all fire precautions in certain scheduled premises (which will include major hazard factories).

Offences. S33 lists the offences and the type of penalty which may be imposed for each: fines and/or imprisonment.

Action by management. Management should:

1 Prepare and issue a written safety policy statement
2 Set up an accident prevention programme
3 Provide training in safety policy and practice
4 Designate line and functional responsibilities for health, welfare and safety.

The main provisions of the Act came into force on 1 April 1975 and largely replace most of the existing law on safety and health in industry. Among the major Acts which will eventually be replaced or mainly replaced are the Factories Act 1961, and the Offices, Shops and Railway Premises Act 1963.

THE FACTORIES ACT

The Factories Act 1961 and the regulations made under it remain in force for the time being. The Act applies to all factories as defined in *s*175 of the Act, as well as to certain other premises, such as building sites, which are not factories in the normal sense of the word. For the purpose of the Act, a factory is defined as a place to which the employer has right of access or of control and where two or more persons are employed in manual labour, by way of trade or for the purpose of gain in any of the following operations:

1 Making any article or part of an article
2 Altering, repairing, ornamenting, finishing, cleaning, washing, breaking up or demolishing any article
3 Adapting an article for sale
4 The slaughtering of cattle, sheep, swine, goats, horses, asses or mules
5 The confinement of such animals while awaiting slaughter at other premises provided those premises are not maintained primarily for agricultural purposes and do not form part of the premises used for holding of a market in respect of such animals.

Furthermore, whether or not they fall within this general definition, *s*175(2) specifically applies the Act to the following groups of premises, provided that persons are employed in manual:

1 Packing articles, washing or filling bottles or containers incidental to the purposes of the factory
2 Sorting articles prior to work in a factory
3 Printing or bookbinding carried out as a trade or incidental to a business
4 Making up or packing of yarn or cloth
5 Laundering carried on as an ancillary to a business or public institution. (Ordinary commercial laundries are factories within the general definition quoted above.)
6 Constructing, reconstructing or repairing vehicles, locomotives, or other plant used for transport purposes, when ancillary to a transport, industrial or commercial undertaking (other than running repairs to locomotives)

7 Production of films. (It would be wise to assume that the production of recordings on videotape might be treated as coming within this definition, though the point could lead to much legal argument.)
8 Making or preparing articles for the building, fishing and engineering industries, the theatre and for films
9 Dry docks in which ships are constructed, repaired or broken up
10 Gas holders of over 5000 cubic feet.

Certain sections of the Act also apply to electrical stations and substations, warehouses, docks, wharves, ships and sites where building and civil engineering are carried on.

Premises that come under the definition of a factory but are used by public authorities or charitable institutions may still be subject to the Act even though they are not actually operated 'by way of trade or for the purpose of gain'. The same applies to factory premises occupied by the Crown or a local council.

A place sited within the factory precincts is not a part of that factory if it is used solely for a purpose different to the processes carried on in the factory, for example the office buildings in the factory may not be part of the factory.

The principal matters legislated for under the Factories Act are:

1 Cleanliness, overcrowding, temperature, ventilation, lighting, sanitary conveniences, washing facilities, drinking water, seating, and accommodation for clothing. (Provision of first-aid facilities came under the Act orginally but, with effect from 1 July 1982, is covered by The Health and Safety (First Aid) Regulations, 1981.)

Cleanliness

Dirt and refuse must be removed daily from floors and benches in workrooms and from staircases and passages. Workroom floors must be washed or otherwise cleaned at least once per week. All inside walls, partitions and ceilings must be periodically washed, painted, whitewashed or otherwise treated as prescribed by the Factories (Cleanliness of Walls and Ceilings) Regulations 1960, amended by S.I. 1974 No. 427. Factories must be kept free of effluvia from drains, sanitary conveniences, etc.

Overcrowding

Workrooms must not be so overcrowded as to be dangerous to health. The employer must allow at least 400 cubic feet (11.3m^3) of space for every person employed excluding any air space more than 14 feet (4.27m) from the floor.

Temperature

The temperature must be reasonable. If a substantial proportion of the work in a particular room is done sitting and does not involve serious physical effort, the temperature must be at least 15.5°C (60°F) after the first hour and at least one thermometer must be provided in every such workroom. However, Statutory Instrument 1980, No. 1013 restricts heating to a maximum temperature of 19°C (66.2°F), unless certain industrial processes require more heat.

Ventilation

Fresh air must be circulated to provide adequate ventilation, and measures taken to protect employees from inhalation of dust, fumes or impurities which may be injurious or offensive.

Lighting

Lighting, artificial or natural, must be sufficient and suitable.

Sanitary conveniences

The Statutory Rules and Orders 1938 No 611 as amended by S.I. 1974 No. 426 setting out the minimum requirements for factories can be obtained from the Stationery Office. The conveniences must be maintained, kept clean and effectively lit. The general scale is one convenience for every twenty-five men or twenty-five women but when employing more than a hundred this scale may be varied by the substitution of urinals for water or chemical closets.

Washing facilities

Must include a supply of clean, running hot and cold or warm water, soap and clean towels or other suitable means of cleaning or drying and be suitable and adequate for the number employed.

Drinking water

The employer must provide an adequate supply of drinking water, with an upward jet convenient for drinking or with suitable drinking vessels and facilities for rinsing them.

Seating

The employer must provide suitable seating where an employee (male or female) has reasonable opportunities for sitting without detriment to his/her work.

Accommodation for clothing

Adequate and suitable accommodation must be made for clothing not worn during working hours, with arrangements where practicable for drying such clothing. The risk of theft is an element which must be taken into account in deciding whether accommodation is suitable.

First aid

A box or cupboard containing first-aid requisites (one for every 150 employees or fraction of that number) must be provided in every factory. The First Aid Boxes in Factories Order 1959 stipulate the minimum contents. Such boxes must be in the charge of a responsible person. Where more than fifty persons are employed, there must be at least one person who has been trained in first aid. In addition a notice must be placed in every workroom stating the name of the person in charge of the box or cupboard provided in respect of that room.

On 1 July 1982 this section of the Factories Act was replaced by The Health and Safety (First Aid) Regulations 1981, and Code of Practice;

2 Safety: there must be:
Safe conditions of workplaces, including floors, stairs, passages and gangways, and the means of access to places where people have to work. The requirements for handrail and fencing are stipulated for means of access, for workplaces, and for openings in floors
Precautions against dangerous fumes, dust and other health and safety hazards, protection of eyes, restrictions on lifting heavy weights.
Fencing on dangerous machinery and parts of machinery which are in motion or use, restriction on cleaning machinery by persons under eighteen and women, training and supervision of young persons required to operate certain machines
Safe construction and safe operation of cranes, hoists and other plant with special hazards
3 Restrictions on the employment of women and young persons, including limitations on normal hours, overtime and holiday work
4 Statutory registers kept and statutory reports made, regarding (for example) accidents and industrial diseases, inspection of factories and other administrative matters.

In addition to the requirements of the Factories Act itself, many specific processes are subject to special regulations made by statutory instruments under the Act. These include detailed requirements for certain types of machinery, (e.g., woodworking machinery) and for certain types of industrial employment for example, building operations and works of engineering construction.

OFFICES, SHOPS AND RAILWAYS PREMISES ACT

The Offices, Shops and Railways Premises Act 1963 is in force for the time being. It extended to such premises some of the requirements formerly applied only to factories. *S*1 details what premises are covered but these can be briefly summarised as follows:
Office premises: A building which is used solely or principally for office purposes from filing to the preparation of material for publication. Premises used in connection with office premises, such as storerooms or canteens, are also subject to the Act even if they are not physically part of the office premises.
Shop premises: In addition to a shop of the ordinary kind, the term is defined to include any building or part of a building

> of which the sole purpose or principal use is the carrying out of retail trade, for example the sale to the public of food or drink for immediate consumption, retail sales by auction and the lending of books or

periodicals for the purpose of gain
occupied by a wholesale dealer or merchant who keeps goods there for sale
which members of the public visit to deliver goods for repair, etc, or to carry out repairs, etc, for themselves
used to sell solid fuel.

The Act does not apply to:

Offices in which the total number of man hours worked does not exceed twenty-one a week
Moveable office structures in which people work for less than six months
Permanent buildings in which persons work for less than six weeks.

The Offices, Shops and Railway Premises Act is mainly concerned with the following:

1 Physical working conditions:
Cleanliness, ventilation, lighting, drinking water, seating, accommodation for clothing.
Overcrowding: the employer must allow at least 40 square feet of floor space for each person normally employed in a room, or where the ceiling is lower than 10 feet, 400 cubic feet per person. Furniture, fittings, machinery and other such items should be ignored when measuring the size of the room.
Temperature: unless the room is used by the public and it is impracticable to do so, a reasonable temperature must be maintained. Where a substantial proportion of the work does not involve severe physical effort the temperature must not be less than 16°C (60.8°F) after the first hour but not less than 19°C (66.2°F). The employer must provide a thermometer on each floor in a conspicuous place for the use of the employees.
Sanitary conveniences and washing facilities: the Sanitary Conveniences Regulations 1964 and the Washing Facilities Regulations 1964 lay down the minimum requirements
2 Constructing, maintaining and keeping reasonably free from obstruction floors, stairs, passages and gangways
3 Restrictions on lifting heavy loads
4 Fencing dangerous machinery, restricting the cleaning of certain machines by persons under eighteen and training and supervising persons using certain prescribed machines which are registered as particularly dangerous;
5 Registration of offices and shops with the local council, obtaining a fire certificate from the fire authority, and other administrative matters
6 Eating facilities for those working in shops.

REGULATIONS

As noted earlier, many regulations have been made for special processes and industries. They are too numerous to quote here, and most apply only to a few specialised processes, but mention should be made of the regulations for safety representatives and safety committees, building operations, and canteens.

The Safety Representatives and Safety Committees Regulations 1977

These regulations provide for the appointment of safety representatives, describe their functions and give them the right to certain time off to carry out their tasks and for training. The representatives are also empowered to carry out inspections and have access to certain documents and information. The setting-up of safety committees is also prescribed if at least two safety representatives make such a request in writing.

Building operations

Regulations apply not only to the erection of new buildings but to the repair and maintenance of existing buildings, including redecorating, repointing and external cleaning of buildings. They thus affect firms, who without being engaged in the construction industry, employ their own teams of maintenance workers. The main requirements for such operations are contained in four sets of regulations:

The Construction (Working Places) Regulations 1966
The Construction (Lifting Operations) Regulations 1961
The Construction (General Provisions) Regulations 1961
The Construction (Health and Welfare) Regulations 1966
and Amendment 1974

Building Regulations

Part III of the Act, which will be the responsibility of the Secretaries of State for the Environment and for Scotland, extends the power to make building regulations governing the structure of buildings.

Canteens

Staff and works canteens are included under Food Hygiene (General) Regulations 1970, made under the Food and Drugs Act. These regulations include provisions for cleanliness (and personal cleanliness) and other precautions against the contamination of food. A canteen within the curtilage of a factory and used by employees working on the manufacturing process is also subject to the Factories Act. A staff canteen used by office workers, whether part of the office premises or not, is subject to the Offices, Shops and Railway Premises Act.

CODES OF PRACTICE

Regulations will, where appropriate, be supplemented by Codes of Practice. These will not be statutory requirements but nevertheless may be used in criminal proceedings as evidence that statutory requirements have been contravened.

A Code of Practice covering noise was published in 1972. It applies to all persons employed in industry who are exposed to noise and sets out recommended limits to noise exposure. The Health and Safety Commission have proposed a noise law to ensure that workers are not exposed to a noise level of 90 decibels or over, averaged throughout an 8-hour day. Codes of practice have also been issued on the appointment and time off for training of safety representatives, and on the establishment of safety committees. A Code on First Aid is to be published.

EMPLOYERS' LIABILITY

The Employers' Liability (Compulsory Insurance) Act 1969 prescribes that all employers must insure against liability for personal injury and disease sustained by their employees and arising out of, or in the course of, their employment. The Social Security Act 1975 does not exempt the employer from taking out this insurance.

FIRE PRECAUTIONS ACT 1971

There must be means of escape in case of fire, adequate in regard to the circumstances and number of people employed, and suitable fire-fighting equipment and systems must be available. Application must be made to the local authority for a certificate that these requirements have been met.

CHECKLIST OF NOTICES TO BE POSTED

In the following list of statutory notices which have to be displayed, where relevant, the numerical references are to the sections of the Factories Act (FA) and the Offices, Shops and Railway Premises Act (OSRPA) in which the requirement appears. An asterisk against an item indicates that the notice displayed has to be in a prescribed form, copies of which can be obtained from the Stationery Office.

1 *Prescribed abstract of the Factories Act (FA 138). The employer is required to show on this the addresses of the employment medical adviser and the district inspector
2 *Prescribed abstract (or a copy) of any statutory regulations made under the Factories Act and applicable to the premises (FA 139)
3 *Prescribed abstract of the Offices, Shops and Railways Premises Act, unless every employee affected has been given a copy of the prescribed booklet containing the same information (OSRPA 50)
4 *Notice in each factory workroom showing the maximum numbers of persons permitted to work in that room unless the factory inspector exercises his power to exempt a factory from this requirement (FA 2)
5 Notice showing the name of the person in charge of the first-aid box for the workroom or office (FA 61 and OSRPA 24). With effect from 1 July 1982, the Health and Safety (First Aid) Regulations 1981 and Code of Practice

replaced the first-aid sections of the Factories Act and the Offices, Shops and Railway Premises Act

6 *Notice of any exemption for or granted under the Offices, Shops and Railway Premises Act (OSRPA 46)
7 Notice showing the hours of work, times of meal breaks, etc, for women and persons under eighteen (FA 88, 90, 94 and 115)
8 *Cautionary placards required to be displayed under regulations for certain special processes (for example, chromium-plating and power-press regulations)
9 Placards showing the recommended treatment for electric shock, if electricity is used at voltages above 125v ac or 250v dc
10 Notice in sanitary conveniences used by persons handling food, requesting them to wash their hands (this is a requirement of the Food Hygiene Regulations 1960)
11 Notice showing the piecework rates payable for certain prescribed operations (FA 135 and orders made under the Act) unless every employee is given a written note of these rates
12 Fire regulations and drill
13 Certificate of insurance against liability to employees for injury or disease incurred whilst at work.

It is an offence for any person to deface or pull down a notice displayed under the Acts.

CHECKLIST OF NOTICES TO BE SENT TO FACTORY INSPECTOR OR OTHER AUTHORITY

The following notices must be sent to the district inspector of factories, unless otherwise stated. The numerical references are to the relevant sections of the Factories Act (FA) and the Offices, Shops and Railway Premises Act (OSRPA). An asterisk against an item shows that the notice must be sent on a prescribed form obtainable from the Stationery Office.

1 *Notice that premises are to be used as a factory (FA 137)
2 *Notice to local council that premises are to be used as offices or shops (if the offices are to be on factory premises, the notice must be sent to the factory inspector instead; if at a mine or quarry it must be sent to the inspector of mines and quarries) (OSRPA 49)
3 *Application to the fire authority for a fire certificate for a factory, office or shop (FA and OSRPA 29)
4 Notice to fire authority when material structural alterations are made to premises, or number of employees materially increased, after fire certificate has been granted (FA 41 and OSRPA 30)
5 Notice to the local careers officer of the Youth Employment Service when recruiting a person under eighteen (a requirement under the Health and Safety Act Part II) to work in a factory
6 Notice of any fatal accident or major injury to any person, whether or not an employee, and of any accident which, while not causing death or injury

is of the type specified in the Notification of Accidents and Dangerous Occurences Regulations 1980 should be notified to the Health and Safety Executive or other authority of it by the quickest possible means (usually by telephone) and confirmed by a written report within seven days

7 *Notice to factory inspector and also to employment medical adviser of any cases of industrial disease. These diseases are prescribed in *s*82 of the Factories Act and in various orders made under it

8 *Notice of intention to employ women or young persons on overtime (FA 90)

9 *Notice of intention to employ women or young persons at different times from those stated on routine notice posted in factory (FA 88)

10 *Notice of intention to take advantage of permitted exemptions to the legal hours for women and young persons allowed in certain industries (FA 99 to 112)

11 *Notice of intention to employ persons in an underground room, i.e. one with at least half of its height below ground level (FA 69)

12 *Biannual return to local council (in February and August) of any outworkers working on certain processes (FA 133 to 134)

13 *Intention to begin building operations or works of engineering construction expected to last for six weeks or more (FA 127).

The special regulations for certain processes also contain the requirement that the use of such processes shall be notified to the factory inspector.

CHECKLIST OF REGISTERS TO BE KEPT

All the following records and registers must be kept on the prescribed forms, published by the Stationery Office.

1 General factory register. This provides a record of young persons employed, periodical painting or limewashing of the factory, accidents and dangerous occurrences, cases of industrial disease, persons trained in first aid, testing of fire warning systems, and any exemption granted by the factory inspector concerning the hours worked by women and young persons (FA 140)

2 Certificates, etc, attached to general registers. Reports and certificates of various examinations and test of plant required by the Factories Act and regulations made under it are, in most cases, required to be entered in or attached to the general register. The fire certificate issued by the fire authority must also be attached to the general register

3 Accident book kept under the Social Security (Claims and Payments) Regulations. This book (from BI 510) must be kept by every factory and on all other premises where more than ten persons are employed. It is separate and distinct from the accident book which forms part of the general register and is provided so that an injured workman, or someone acting or him, may record details of any accident which might lead to a claim for National Insurance Benefits

4 Health registers. The regulations for certain special factory processes

require the medical examination of workers engaged in them; the results of these examinations must be recorded in the prescribed health register for the process

5 Register of overtime. This must be used to record overtime worked by women and by persons under eighteen (FA 90).

6 Record of hours worked by van boys, etc. This must be used to record the hours worked by young persons employed outside the factory on business connected with the factory, for example as van boys or messengers (FA 116).

ADVICE AND FURTHER INFORMATION

Advice on health and safety can be obtained from local offices of the Health and Safety Executive, which are represented by HM Inspectorate. A list of their addresses is given below.

Health and Safety Inspectorate addresses

Area	*Address*	*Local authorities within each area*
1 South West	Inter City House, Mitchell Lane, Bristol BS1 6AN Tel 0272 290681	Avon, Cornwall, Devon, Gloucestershire, Somerset, Isles of Scilly
2 South	Priestly House, Priestly Road, Basingstoke RG24 9NW Tel 0256 3181	Berkshire, Dorset, Hampshire, Isle of Wight, Wiltshire
3 South East	3 East Grinstead House London Road East Grinstead West Sussex RH19 1RR Tel 0342 26922	Kent, Surrey, East Sussex, West Sussex
4 Neasden (London N)	Chancel House, Neasden Lane, London NW10 2UD Tel 01-459 8855	Barnet, Brent, Camden, City of London, Enfield, Hammersmith, Harrow, Hillingdon, Hounslow, Kensington & Chelsea, City of Westminster
5 London N	Maritime House, 1 Linton Road, Barking, Essex 1G11 8HF Tel 01-594 5522	Barking, Hackney, Haringey, Havering, Islington, Newham, Redbridge, Tower Hamlets, Waltham Forest
6 London S	1 Long Lane, London SE1 4PG Tel 01-407 8911	Bexley, Bromley, Croydon, Greenwich, Kingston-upon-Thames, Lambeth, Lewisham, Merton, Richmond-upon-Thames, Southwark, Sutton, Wandsworth
7 East Anglia	39 Baddow Road, Chelmsford, Essex CM2 0HL Tel 0245 84661	Essex except the London Boroughs in Essex covered by Area 5; Norfolk, Suffolk
8 Northern Home Counties	14 Cardiff Road, Luton LU1 1PP Tel 0582 34121	Bedfordshire, Buckinghamshire, Cambridgeshire, Hertfordshire

9	East Midlands	Belgrave House, 1 Greyfriars, Northampton NN1 2LQ Tel 0604 21233	Leicestershire, Northamptonshire, Oxfordshire, Warwickshire
10	West Midlands	McLaren Building, 2 Masshouse Circus, Queensway, Birmingham B4 7NP Tel 021 236 5080	West Midlands
11	Wales	Brunel House, 2 Fitzalan Road, Cardiff CF2 1SH Tel 0222 497777	Clywd, Dyfed, Gwent, Gwynedd, Mid Glamorgan, Powys, South Glamorgan, West Glamorgan
12	Marches	The Marches House, The Midway, Newcastle-under-Lyme Staffs ST5 1DT Tel 0782 610181	Hereford and Worcester, Salop, Staffordshire
13	North Midlands	Birkbeck House, Trinity Square Nottingham NG1 4AU Tel 0602 470712	Derbyshire, Lincolnshire, Nottinghamshire
14	South Yorkshire	Sovereign House, 40 Silver Street, Sheffield S1 2ES Tel 0742 739081	Humberside, South Yorkshire
15	West & North Yorkshire	8 St Pauls Street, Leeds LS1 2LE Tel 0532 446191	North Yorkshire, West Yorkshire
16	Greater Manchester	Quay House, Quay Street, Manchester M3 3JB Tel 061-831 7111	Greater Manchester
17	Merseyside	The Triad, Stanley Road, Bootle L20 3PG Tel 051-922 7211	Cheshire, Merseyside
18	North West	Victoria House, Ormskirk Road, Preston PR1 1HH Tel 0772 59321	Cumbria, Lancashire
19	North East	Government Buildings, Kenton Bar, Newcastle-upon-Tyne NE1 2YX Tel 0632 869811	Cleveland, Durham, Northumberland, Tyne & Wear
20	Scotland East	Belford House, 59 Belford Road, Edinburgh EH4 3UE Tel 031-225 1313	Borders, Central, Fife, Grampian, Highland, Lothian, Tayside and the island areas of Orkney & Shetland
21	Scotland West	314 Vincent Street, Glasgow G3 8XG Tel 041-204 2646	Dumfries and Galloway, Strathclyde, and the Western Isles

Employers' organisations and trade associations can also provide guidance, as do the British Safety Council and the Royal Society for the Prevention of Accidents. Detailed information about the responsibilities of employers in regard to working conditions and liability to employees will be found in the following standard works.

FURTHER READING

Fife, I., and Machin, I. A., *Redgrave's Factories Acts,* Butterworth, London 1976, and Supplement 1979. Gives the full text of the Factories Act and regulations made under it, with legal references and explanatory notes.

Fife, I., and Machin, I. A., *Redgrave's Offices and Shops (together with Agricultural and Railway Safety),* Butterworth, London, 1973. A companion volume to the above, giving text and notes for the Offices, Shops and Railway Premises Act and the Agriculture (Safety Provisions) Act.

Goodman, M. J., (ed.), *Encyclopaedia of Health and Safety,* Sweet and Maxwell, London; and W. Green, Edinburgh. The annotated texts of the Factories Act, and the Health and Safety at Work Act, the Offices, Shops and Railway Premises Act (and other Acts), with the regulations made under them, bound in loose leaf form to accommodate periodical revised pages supplied under a follow-up service.

Munkman, J., *Employer's liability at Common Law,* Butterworth, London, 1979. A comprehensive work dealing with general common law obligations and the effect, in civil actions, of breaches of statutory duty.

The Stationery Office publishes the texts of all Acts and regulations, the prescribed forms, Codes of Practice, guidance notes and various advisory booklets. Details are given in the publications catalogue available from the Health and Safety Executive. A bi-monthly "Newsletter" is also available from the Health and Safety Executive and films can be hired or bought from the Central Film Library in London.

29 Industrial training

Derek Torrington

Those responsible for training in companies often regard their work as vulnerable. If times are hard, then training programmes are among the first to suffer cutback. It was partly to change this situation that we had the 1964 Industrial Training Act to boost the provision of training in companies. That intervention was only temporarily successful and the more rigorous circumstances of recent years have shifted governmental priorities in the UK towards provision for the unemployed, and companies are less constrained by the requirements of industrial training boards.

Company training budgets remain vulnerable because training is often regarded as an optional extra: 'without proper training we may not be here in five years, but without more productivity and cash in the bank we won't be here next week'. Sadly some training programmes are indeed expendable because they are not geared to real organisational needs and are of dubious effectiveness. The purpose of this chapter is to make a case for training and then to review some methods of putting it into practice.

THE NEED FOR TRAINING IN COMPANIES

The advantages of training range from more effective use of resources to considerations of the overall purpose of the enterprise.

Resources

The people in an organisation are its major resource. If they are not appropriately trained for the work they have to perform they will not do it as efficiently as they could and operations will not be as profitable as they might be. Some degree of investment in training can make the human resources at the disposal of the management more productive and more profitable.

Fragmentation of work

Specialisation is growing so that the work to be done within the undertaking is constantly being broken up into smaller parcels. New departments are set up to specialise in a particular aspect of the company's affairs, and each employs people to work in a specialised rather than in a general field. In the management ranks this produces the functional specialist who can do one or two things well, replacing the gifted amateur who could do many things with reasonable competence. This means that each employee needs training to undertake his duties, and this need is likely to become greater.

New skills and knowledge

One consequence of specialisation is obsolescence in skills and knowledge. Many people in the financial and administrative field, for example, have forced themselves through the traumatic experience of accepting electronic data processing in the last decade. This acceptance has made it necessary for them to take some training so that they understand the monsters that are spewing forth information at such an alarming rate. The arrival of the computer has rendered obsolete some of the established administrative skills. This effect of technological development is apparent in every part of commerical and industrial activity. Few if any people will still be practising at forty the skills they learned at twenty. The new skills have to be taught.

It is short-sighted, expensive and impractical merely to hire new people who happen to have picked up the new skills elsewhere. The challenge of retraining the adult has to be faced, both by the employer and by the individual concerned. With managerial staff especially, there is the even more demanding need constantly to develop new understanding of the environment in which the organisation is functioning. Changes in law, economic circumstances and in the community outside the organisation have great influence on affairs within the organisation, and knowledge of the environment is essential to managers.

On the job training

Some people counter this sort of argument by saying that training should take place outside the field of employment, and that the substantial proportion of the gross national product channelled into further education should take care of industrial training needs by training people in colleges and government training centres in the whole span of skills and areas of knowledge that are developing. Those who make this point would usually be surprised by the extent of what is done in this way, but still the training that is done off the job cannot be completed off the job. Just as a person learning to drive has to sit in the driving seat and drive along the street during his training, so the apprentice engineer, the trainee typist, laboratory technician, supervisor, personnel officer, sales manager and other industrial trainees all have to get their academic training in practical perspective, which is best done in the working situation.

Also much necessary training is in routines which are peculiar to one company, so that although a supervisor may learn much of great value on a supervisor's course at the local college it will be equally important for him to learn his own company's disciplinary procedures, and this can obviously come only from an agent of the employer.

Employee expectation

There is a standard of expectation which prospective employees have about what the company provides for its recruits. They will expect canteen facilities and locker rooms. Many will expect pension provision and sick pay. If these basic expectations are not met, they will not come and work for the company unless they have no choice, or unless they are likely to earn much more money than they would elsewhere. More and more employees are expecting to receive systematic training for the job when they join a new company rather than having to 'sit next to Nellie'. A well-run training scheme will be an aid to recruitment. Complete lack of training will be a disincentive to prospective recruits.

Social purpose

All administrators and managers have a view of the purpose of their enterprise that goes beyond mere survival and profitability. One of management's many objectives is that the company should be a place worth working in, and that the people working there can to some extent achieve personal fulfilment. Assuming that a company has a personnel policy which recognises its employees as people rather than simply resources, then the requirements for industrial training are the requirements of the people employed as well as the requirements of the employer.

ADMINISTERING THE TRAINING FUNCTION

The passing of the Industrial Training Act led to many companies taking the concept of specialisation too far, and training departments were set up where the managers reported directly to the managing director or to the general manager quite independently of the personnel department. The reason for this was usually the calibre of the incumbent personnel manager, or the alarm of the managing director at the prospect of being 'fined' by his industrial training board for not meeting their requirements. In the mid 1960s many personnel managers were limited in their thinking to aspects of employee welfare such as canteen, lavatories and record-keeping rather than taking the broader view of personnel which is common today. As a result this type of personnel manager was not considered the appropriate person to be responsible for training with its new levy sanction, and most of the bright, keen training officers who started emerging were not prepared to report to that type of company executive.

This produced a split in the personnel function. Fortunately this practice is now less common except in the largest organisations with substantial training requirements, but it is important to appreciate that personnel work is an amalgam of many activities including training, employment, payment, trade union recognition, discipline, grievances, the design of jobs and consultative arrangements. Each of these interlocks with the others and they have to be co-ordinated and administered under an overall personnel policy. One cannot be isolated from the rest without risks. Effective training depends on effective selection, improved industrial relations often require new training programmes and training innovations frequently influence the industrial relations environment. In considering how the training function is administered, it is therefore of primary importance to see it as part of personnel work.

The personnel function should not usually report to a line manager. If the responsibility for any aspect of personnel comes under, say, the production manager, then managers in marketing, R & D and other areas will regard it as a specifically production function – as may the production manager. It must be seen to be available to, and necessary for, all company functions. Furthermore the responsibility of the training specialist does not interfere with the line authority of the manager. The training officer provides a specialist service to all line managers in the organisation. His particular usefulness lies in his understanding of the requirement of the training board for the relevant industry, his expertise in the skills and the knowledge needed to administer a training programme, his awareness of how people learn, his knowledge of courses and potential visiting lectures. He has a general responsibility for the quality of training provided in the organisation, but the individual line manager remains responsible for the performance and competence of his own staff. The line manager needs to appreciate what the training function can do for him in developing that competence: he cannot wash his hands of the responsibility and 'leave it to personnel'. They can only provide him with some services that he has to understand and use.

Integration with other functions

Responsibility for specialist training services needs to be integrated with the whole of the personnel function, which must in turn be integrated with the management of the enterprise. Personnel and training are actively concerned with ensuring that the organisation meets its business objectives, not some parasitical unnecessary growth imposed by an outside agency.

Objectives

Corporate objectives need to be reappraised to consider the place of training within the total personnel activity. What are its objectives? How do these fit in with the existing business objectives? What targets have to be achieved? This procedure sounds obvious, but it is perhaps the aspect of training which is most often ignored, with the consequent vulnerability of the training arrangements.

Identification of training needs

The person responsible for training has first to establish what the training needs of the organisation are. He will consider two aspects of this. First he will investigate the operational efficiency of the organisation. Later he will look at the training needs of individual people, and the need of the organisation for people to be trained. In considering operational efficiency, he will seek to identify those jobs within the organisation that appear to be holding back to the achievement of proper levels of performance and where training may help to lift this level to one that is acceptable. He will take note of the various indicators which personnel people use to 'take the temperature' of working groups.

Absenteeism, labour turnover, punctuality, sickness, changes in output level, complaints and labour troubles can all be indicators of the state of morale in a department, and low morale may be caused by inadequate training. There may be data available from work study officers who feel that the work standards in a particular department are not satisfactory. Conversations with managers and supervisors will suggest other areas requiring attention. The training officer's own experience and training will suggest others, as will the officers of the industrial training boards.

The training officer will therefore collect a mass of information about the training needs that exist within the company, and can then begin to draw up proposals about what training should be done and in what order, the priority usually being determined by the likely pay-off. He may suggest, for example, that the training of typists could be altered to enable newly recruited school-leavers to reach an acceptable level of proficiency in half the time now considered as necessary, at a saving of £*x* a year, followed by specially designed programmes of operator training in selected departments to reduce the level of labour turnover and to boost output. He might suggest middle managers attending courses at a business school, or supervisors having a series of discussions on the implications of recent legislation. Whatever the particular proposals, he will draw these up and require them to be endorsed by his management colleagues or superiors, so that he has a mandate to start work.

Implementation of the training programme

When the training officer has received his mandate he will also be empowered to spend some money to implement his programme. This will be based on his prediction of how much he can produce in the way of operating economies. The expenditure will come broadly under two headings. First there will be expenditure on hardware and fees, which are outgoings that would not be incurred if the training were not done. Hardware can range from boxes of chalk to overhead projectors, teaching machines and fully equipped, soundproof lecture theatres. Fees will be either the fees payable for employees to attend courses, or payable to outside experts to come and take part in internal courses. The training officer, like any other executive submitting a budget for approval, is likely to ask for more than he needs under this heading, as he expects those who have to sanction his budget to cut it. It may be sensible for a newly established training function to start off with a minimum of equipment and to invest more heavily when experience has been gained. The reason for this is that most training programmes change fundamentally after a spell of running in and the benefits of experience. Heavy initial investment can result in an accumulation of expensive equipment that is unused, and a dearth of equipment that is needed but not available because the budget has been overspent.

The second category of expenditure is salaries and wages of trainees, where the administrator perhaps needs to scrutinise proposals closely. Employees away from work on training courses are still being paid. In the case of most managers and supervisors this adds nothing to the cost of their duties being carried out. Someone else will deputise for them in their absence, they will catch up with their work when they return, and that is that. In some other cases, however, there may be expenditure of either increasing the establishment for a department so that people absent for training can be covered, or arrangements for colleagues to work expensive overtime to make up the shortfall. The training is necessary, but this type of consideration needs to be thought of before the training begins so that the cost implications are fully appreciated.

As well as hardware, the training officer will need some space to run his schemes in. Some training will be done on the job or in a training section of the normal job environment, such as the apprentice bench in an engineering shop. Some training will be carried out away from the premises altogether, as when a young manager goes to the nearby polytechnic to take a management course. But there will be a need for some of the training programme to take place away from the job but on company premises. Typists are often trained in a small school within the company, and a number of short courses may be run to give managers or others an appreciation of a subject or to give training in certain skills that are needed.

Evaluation of training effectiveness

Finally in setting up a training function, there is a need for some means of evaluating the training, and this is one of the most nebulous and unsatisfactory aspects of the training job. The starting point is to compare the results achieved with the original objectives and, where possible, to measure the degree of improvement. This can be done in such areas as labour and material utilisation, or the reduction in the number of despatch errors being made in a warehouse. It can only be guessed in the more difficult areas such as the quality of supervision by a foreman before and after a training course. This often depends on a subjective assessment that may be influenced by the reactions of the trainee.

Another possible means of evaluation is to measure the benefits that are set as objectives at the beginning of the programme. It might be a drop in labour turnover and other measures of improved efficiency and employee morale. There may be fewer accidents or reduced levels of overtime. It is also important to attempt some evaluation of the intangibles, such as atmosphere in industrial relations, customer satisfaction, self-confidence among managers and so on. To some extent this can be done by the use of an outside adviser who can come along for a day to examine the situation relating to training within the organisation and then report upon it, rather like an auditor.

It is useful from a training point of view to carry out some form of performance appraisal regularly among employees. If this is done systematically over several years, the validity of training arrangements will be confirmed – or otherwise.

TRAINING FOR DIFFERENT CATEGORIES OF EMPLOYEE

Operators

The largest single grouping in the employed population is the operator on the shop floor who has no craft skills – the general worker. His job may require such a small amount of skill and knowledge that he needs no training other than a short period of 'being shown how' by his supervisor. There are, however, very few jobs which genuinely fall into this category. Most would be done better by more satisfied employees if they were preceded by a period of training, which covered induction to the organisation and the place of the job in the manufacturing process, as well as the mechanics of how it should be done.

As operator jobs in manufacturing are usually specific to each employer, the training needs to be set up and run within the company, as there is no outside body either with the understanding of the job or any alternative source of supply of trainees. The training officer will need to study the operations and to use a process of skills analysis to devise a programme of training to be carried out by an instructor instructing trainees. Seldom is the training load large enough to justify a full-time instructor, and it is usual for an experienced operator in each department to be trained in instruction so that he does all the instruction needed by new recruits. Another method is for the foreman to be trained so that he inducts and trains all those in his department. This may be the best method as long as the training job is not going to take up too much of his time.

Skills analysis can be learned at one of the many introductory courses for training officers run within the further education system. Alternatively there are short crash courses available. Instructors can be trained by one of the Training within Industry (TWI) courses provided by the Training Services Division of the Manpower Services Commission.

Clerical

Very little training is provided in clerical duties in most organisations, although the provision of training is spreading and companies find that it pays big dividends in cost savings and employee satisfaction. The practice of clerical training is similar to that for operator training, although there are certain more general occupational skills involved, so that the further education system is more helpful. Widely available is a course in office skills which is taken by young people on leaving school. They attend technical college for one day a week and learn simple office skills and routines to fit in with the working experience they are beginning to acquire. There are also many courses in shorthand and typing, although the demand for shorthand is declining and the school-leaver with reasonable GCE 'O' level achievement can take courses in business studies on day release.

Craft

One of the first areas to repay attention is the training of craft apprentices, as this is a long and expensive business. Some of the training boards gave the largest amount of their attention to this area in the first few years of their operation.

Apprentices are recruited at the age of sixteen on leaving school, and serve an apprenticeship of several years before being accepted as craftsmen at the end of their training, usually at the age of twenty-one or twenty-two. Most apprentices are young men, although young women do follow apprenticeships as well, but these are heavily concentrated in hairdressing. Many companies follow the customary practice of binding apprentices by indentures, under which the apprentice is obliged to stay with the employer until finishing his 'time' and the employer agrees to provide his training.

A major part of the apprentice's time is spent in further education at a local college, learning the theoretical background of his craft and some manual skills. While with the employer, he needs to practise the skills he is learning and to develop them by applying his knowledge and ability to a growing range of work. Traditionally this has been done by watching, helping and copying a craftsman at work. Gradually this method is being replaced by systematic and full-time training under an instructor in charge of a group of apprentices.

If an organisation is not big enough to warrant the services of a full-time instructor, it is often possible to join a group training scheme, in which a number of small and medium-sized companies pool resources to employ a training officer who organises the training of the apprentices in all the companies. In return, the individual company pays a relatively modest fee to the group scheme. Also, the individual apprentice has a better training as he probably moves from one firm to another in the group.

There are usually national agreements between employers and trade unions regarding the employment and training of apprentices.

Technician

A category in which the number of employees is growing is that of technician, who is one step up from a craftsman and is likely to be concerned more with design than with manufacture. In the field of engineering, the fitter is the craftsman and the draftsman is the technician, although there are many others classified as craftsmen and technicians respectively in that industry. To some extent the training needs are common, as the basic technology is the same, but the technician's training needs go further. He is likely to have better educational qualifications at the outset and his further education will go to a higher theoretical level. His practical training will tend to lie in conventional white collar rather than manual operations. It is usually carried out in close conjunction with a qualified man.

Technologist

It is difficult to distinguish between technicians and technologists and in many industries such a distinction cannot be drawn at all. A rough and ready identification would be by the word 'professional'. In engineering, for example, the technologist is the professional engineer who has achieved membership of one of the constituent bodies of the Council of Engineering Institutions. This requires a high level of academic qualification together with the appropriate working experience.

In this category will be the ex-technician who has taken the HNC/HND route through day release or evening courses, as well as the technical graduate who starts his working life in his early twenties. These are the people on whom the technical competence and progress of the organisation will depend. The HNC/D method of qualification has been replaced by the scheme of the Technical Education Council (TEC). Courses for technical graduates now have the interesting development of a small number of courses in selected universities that combine engineering and management studies, usually over four years of study.

The man who comes up through the ranks will need facilities to pursue his academic studies, either by day release or by sandwich course. His practical expertise will be acquired almost incidentally as long as he has reasonable opportunities for varied working experience, rather than being classified as a trainee who cannot be given a proper job because he has not finished his education.

The technical graduate who joins industry in his early twenties with academic qualifications of a high order but no practical experience usually needs some form of graduate apprenticeship while he spends a number of months acquiring the practical experience that is needed to go with his theoretical grounding.

Management

Training managers is a very different matter from training other categories of workers in industry. This is largely because a smaller proportion of the manager's job content can be isolated and taught. To be effective a manager needs to learn management techniques, such as various methods for the quantification of data so that decisions may be soundly based. He also needs knowledge in such areas as the behavioural sciences so that he can understand how employees may react in certain situations, and so that he may plan sensibly for the future. Beyond this, however, there is still a large area of training or development needed for the individual management trainee, so that he acquires the stature and confidence needed for the job of leadership, gains judgement and determination and develops good timing and a sensitive awareness in handling people.

Largely because of the difficulty and lack of definition in the task of management training, most large organisations separate this particular aspect of training and give the responsibility to management development officers within the training function. The body of knowledge and some of the skills can come from the educational system. In addition to the business schools, which cater for a small fraction of the total amount of management training, there are a number of polytechnics and universities with management departments running courses with recognition from some professional body. The most widely recognised management qualification available in the field of further education is the Diploma in Management Studies, run under the auspices of the Department of Education and Science. It is operated at a limited number of centres and provides a broadly based management education for the well-qualified entrant with limited practical experience. There are also courses run under the aegis of, for instance, the Institute of Personnel Management and the Institution of Industrial Managers which provide a broad management education with particular emphasis on the specialism that the professional body represents.

In conjunction with further education, the trainee manager will need controlled working experience and career development so that he can apply his developing skills and knowledge. He may also need careful coaching to help him develop qualities such as judgement and timing. All managers need constantly to bring themselves up to date with new techniques or with new knowledge. Thus, professional bodies like the British Institute of Management and many firms of professional consultants conduct admirable short courses, running for a few days or a few weeks, to update the experienced manager. Typical of these have been the endless variety of courses and conferences to brief managers on unfair dismissal legislation, safety and health, or negotiating skills.

Supervisory

Training of first-line supervisors is generally unsatisfactory in the United Kingdom, and the foreman has more than once been referred to as the forgotten man of British industry. Much of the problem lies in the uncertainty about the nature of the job. In the early years of this century the foreman was a man of considerable power and authority in a factory, with extensive discretion in decision-making, and was often a general manager in all but name. Since then we have seen the professionalisation of management and the development of shop steward authority. The professionalisation of management has spawned countless middle managers who have taken bits of the foreman's job away from him, like the production engineer and the training officer. The development of shop steward authority has largely done away with the foreman's role as representative of shop-floor feeling, and he is constantly bypassed as shop stewards negotiate with middle and senior managers at meetings he is not invited to attend.

As the position of first-line supervisor is so difficult to define, training for it presents obvious problems. The most useful approach is probably the in-company course which aims to inform foremen of the changes taking place around them and give them an understanding of company procedures together with an introduction to such vague but necessary subjects as leadership and human relations. An attempt to establish a course for foremen within the further education system has not received widespread support.

Administrative

The term 'administrative' covers an amorphous group of people who are lumped together because their work is neither clerical nor managerial. They are such people as cost accounts, computer programmers and systems analysts, salesmen and O & M staff.

For the cost accountant, training will usually be on the job as a cost clerk while he makes his way through the further education courses for cost and management accountants, perhaps after starting with an Ordinary National Diploma in Business Studies while he is making up his mind about the area in which he wishes to specialise.

The training of computer personnel operates at various levels. Most courses in management include some elements of computing, even if only at the appreciation level, and there are a number of degree courses in computation. Computer operators and data input personnel are still mainly trained by computer manufacturers or specialised private agencies.

Shop stewards

The final category is shop steward. It is the joint responsibility of management and trade unions to train shop stewards. The best courses for stewards are provided by the trade unions, and an introductory course for newly elected shop stewards is run at many educational centres under the auspices of the TUC. It is difficult for many employers to provide satisfactory courses of their own, as stewards are likely to be suspicious of them, but this field of training will no doubt develop.

TRAINING METHODS

Teaching someone to *do* something requires a different approach from teaching someone to *understand* something. This broad distinction between training in skill and training in knowledge has been refined by research in the training field to produce a division of all types of learning into five basic types.

Some learning involves theoretical subject matter, knowing how, why and when certain things happen. This is *comprehension*: examples are the laws of thermodynamics, the currency structure of the EEC, or the arguments justifying the recognition of trade unions. *Reflex* learning is involved when skilled movements or perceptual capacities have to be acquired, involving practice as well as knowing what to do. Speed is usually important and the trainee needs constant repetition to develop the appropriate synchronisation and co-ordination. Typing is one of the many jobs that requires reflex learning. *Attitude* development is concerned with enabling people to alter their attitudes and social skills. *Memory* training is concerned with learning how to cope with varied situations and *procedural* learning is very similar except that the drill to be followed does not have to be memorised, but located and understood. This categorisation produces the mnemonic CRAMP.

Learning for comprehension requires the whole subject to be treated as an entity and the lecture or training manual are appropriate methods. Attitude change is typically handled by group discussion, but reflex learning is best handled by part methods, which break the task down into sections, each of which can be studied and practised separately before putting together a complete performance. Memory and procedural learning may take place either by whole or part methods, although memorisation is usually done by parts.

FURTHER READING

Annett, J., *Task Analysis*, HMSO, London, 1971

Bass, B. M., and Vaughan, J. A., *Training in Industry*, Tavistock, London, 1968

Industrial Training Research Unit, *Choose an Effective Style: A Self-instructional Approach to the Teaching of Skills*, ITRU Publications, Cambridge, 1976

Kenney, J. P. J., Donnelly, E., and Reid, M., *Manpower Training and Development*, IPM, London, 1980

Stammers, R. B., and Patrick, J., *The Psychology of Training*, Methuen, London, 1975

Winfield, I., *Learning to Teach Practical Skills*, Kogan Page, London, 1979

30 Employee relations

Derek Torrington and J L Cookson

This chapter deals with regulating the working relationship between employer and the employees collectively. It is an unrealistic and oversimplified view of management that sees managers making decisions and issuing instructions for others to obey. The conception – shaping and implementation of executive action in organising – is a complex process that depends heavily on employee consent. This consent is ceded to managers by employees individually, as they decide to accept rather than decline an offer of employment, as they work with enthusiasm rather than apathy and direct their activities towards the objectives of organisational success that managers determine.

Consent is also, however, ceded to managers by the employees collectively who give, implicitly or explicitly, a mandate to managers to make decisions and issue orders. There are many ways in which managerial action can be frustrated by collective employee resistance which would be beyond the scope of employees individually. There are not only the extremes of industrial action, but co-operative or unco-operative working within the guidelines of union agreements, the degree of enthusiasm with which changes are accepted and implemented, the care with which safety routines are followed, flexibility of manning arrangements, and many more.

Whatever the level of national unemployment and economic gloom, and no matter how tightly collective agreements are worded, managers depend on the collective consent of employees to *allow* and *support* them in their duties. That consent can perhaps be required or even forced in some situations for a short time, but sustained and productive consent has to be won: it is won by managers who earn it through paying close attention to the working relationship.

TRADE UNION RECOGNITION

When a trade union has recruited a number of members in an organisation it will seek recognition from the employer in order to represent those members. What is recognition? It involves first of all that the employer singles out that trade union from others, so that the step of recognising by an employer means that, while he will have to take seriously the representations of one union, he will not usually have to deal with others as well for the same group of employees. There are exceptions to this, especially when the number of union members is low, but it is a normal component of recognition. The second aspect is that the employer has to allow the recognition to affect his behaviour by taking seriously what the union representatives say to him. This does not necessarily mean agreeing to their claims, but it does mean taking time to talk with them to seek accommodations. It is an important, irrevocable step away from all decisions lying unilaterally with management. There are three points to consider about recognition:

1 The timing of recognition – when to recognise
2 Identifying the people, or groups of people, whom the union should represent
3 Deciding which topics should fall within the scope of recognition – for what to recognise.

Reasons for recognition

Why should an employer recognise a union at all? Is there any advantage or is it simply an unfortunate yielding to pressure? The answer to that question depends on the wishes of the employees. If they collectively want trade union representation it is unlikely that they will co-operate with the employer who refuses it. They will want recognition partly because of their general experience and beliefs about working life and partly because of their particular experience with the individual employer where a recognition claim is brought. Manual employees tend to regard trade union representation as normal and necessary, managerial employees tend to regard it as abnormal and unnecessary, and administrative and clerical employees lie between these two extremes.

A more positive reason for recognition is the benefits which can flow to the employer from having representatives with whom to discuss plans and problems. It offers at least a useful method of communication and can be a way of contriving improved working relationships, hastening necessary change and developing trust in the motives and competence of the management.

When to recognise a union

The time at which to recognise a union is a fine judgement for managers to make. If it is too soon there will not be enough support among employees, who may feel that what should be *their* decision is being made for them. A union with only 5 per cent of the employees in membership has a small and potentially clique-like constituency, recognition of which might antagonise the majority. At the other extreme, the refusal to recognise a union which has 95 per cent of the employees in membership would be antagonising the majority of the labour force in a different way, possibly with more serious results.

In the days when unions could seek recognition by legal means if an employer refused, the Advisory Conciliation and Arbitration Service (ACAS) often recommended recognition when the proportion of union members was below 40 per cent. The factors influencing the decision of when to recognise are the degree and efficiency of union organisation, the number of representatives, the size of constituency and the degree of opposition. None the less the key indicator is obviously the number of union members. It may be useful to ballot the employees to determine their wishes, although the greatest stimulus for a management to recognise union *A* is often the fear that union *B* may start recruiting members. Only recognition by management can check that move towards multi-unionism.

Identifying the groups of people to be represented by a recognised union

Another judgement to be made is to define the group of employees to be represented by the union. If the group is too large its members do not have enough interests in common for representation to be feasible. If it is too small there may be other employees, outside the group, who claim the same treatments as the union members because the terms and conditions of employment are similar. The employer either concedes the same benefits and antagonises the union members who regard the others as 'riding on their backs' or refuses and antagonises the non-union members. The normal test is to consider what different groups of employees have in common.

Some of the more common boundaries are between manual and white collar workers, where members of the two groups are seldom represented by the same union or involved in the same procedures and agreements. Another boundary is manual skill, where union membership or *grade* of membership is often jealously guarded on behalf of those who have completed a craft apprenticeship or other preparation that is acknowledged to justify special representation. In some situations the Amalgamated Union of Engineering Workers may represent employees who are skilled as well as those who are semi-skilled and unskilled, but the grade of membership would be different and arrangements with the employer would recognise that difference. The same union, through its Technical and Supervisory Section, may well represent white collar employees in the same company, but that would be through a different section of the union, with different officials and different agreements.

More difficult boundaries are those connected with status in the organisational hierarchy. Should the supervisor and those he supervises be represented by the same body? In manufacturing industry it seems that he will usually be represented separately, to cope with the problem of the union member seeking representation against the management action of his supervisor, who is a member of the same union and entitled to the assistance of the same union official. In local government it is quite common for the Chief Officers in an authority and the most humble clerical personnel all to be members of the National and Local Government Officers Association.

What to recognise

A union can seek recognition on anything that might be covered in a contract of employment, but the employer may agree to recognition for only a limited range of topics. The basis is to recognise a union to represent the grievances of members. That excludes any consultation on payment, terms and conditions, working practices and the other potential ingredients of a recognition agreement. It may be that an employer will proceed progressively with recognition, so that the range of topics grows with familiarity in the negotiating relationship. It should be noted that the potential benefits for management from a recognition arrangement come only when recognition is on a wide basis. Also, if the employees are up in arms on an issue, it may be pedantic to refuse discussion because it is not covered by the recognition agreement.

The legal position on recognition

The fragmented structure of collective bargaining in the UK is partly attributed to the traditional abstentionist policy of the State, departed from only in statutes prescribing the structures of nationalised corporations. During the 1970s, however, both major political parties were agreed upon the necessity for statutory machinery to resolve recognition disputes. The purposes embodied in the recognition provisions for the Industrial Relations Act 1971 were largely frustrated by the policy of non-cooperation on the part of the labour movement.

The Employment Protection Act 1975, sections 11–16, represented an attempt by the State to steer a course between legalism and voluntarism in this area. These sections permitted a recognition issue to be referred by an independent union to ACAS for examination, inquiry and report. If an employer failed to comply with a recommendation by ACAS for recognition and conciliation failed to resolve the dispute, the union could present a claim for specified terms and conditions to the Central Arbitration Committee (CAC) for unilateral arbitration. Any terms and conditions awarded by the CAC would thereafter take effect as part of the contracts of the employees.

During their currency, these provisions were subjected to several criticisms:

1 The statutory processes culminating in unilateral arbitration could only be invoked by the union side
2 Inquiry procedures were protracted
3 ACAS's functions were capable of being seriously impaired by the absence of any requirement that employees should co-operate in enquiries, and by judicial review of ACAS's exercise of its powers
4 The ultimate sanction fell short of requiring an employer to recognise a union.

The response of the Conservative Government elected in 1979 to these criticisms (in the Employment Act 1980) was to repeal sections 11–16, returning to voluntarism in union recognition.

The closed shop

In some ways the logical development of union recognition is the 'closed shop' which is an agreement whereby *all* employees in a particular category should be members of the recognised union, as a condition of employment.

Perhaps nowhere is 'the dilemma between the function of the law to protect the individual and its function to help adjust power relations in Society' (Kahn-Freund) more clearly demonstrated than in the debates which have raged since 1970 over the issue of the closed shop in British industrial relations and the extent to which the State should extend or restrict its operation. At the level of public policy, the issue is whether, given the ostensible commitment of the political parties to the system of collective bargaining, it is appropriate to provide individuals with a statutory right of disassociation and if so, in what circumstances.

The provisions of the Industrial Relations Act 1971 heavily influenced by doctrines of individual rights which paid little heed to the realities of collective labour relations, aimed to outlaw the closed shop notwithstanding a pledge of support for the principle of collective bargaining. In the event, established closed shop arrangements remained largely unaffected by the 1971 statutory measures, and it came as no surprise that the incoming Labour Government of 1974 should remove the right of disassociation from the statute book, thereby re-legalising the closed shop through providing limited statutory protection for religious objectors. Undoubtedly, statutory support for union membership agreements during the period 1974–1980 reinforced the willingness of employers (based upon administrative convenience) to conclude such agreements to the extent that approximately one-fifth of British employees and two-fifths of trade union members are covered by some form of closed shop arrangement.

The Employment Act 1980 is calculated, if not to render closed shops unlawful, at least to limit their objectives and restrict their future development. The 1980 Act significantly narrows the circumstances in which employees may be dismissed fairly for not being a union member. It is now unfair to dismiss an employee:

1 Where the employee genuinely objects on grounds of conscience or other deeply held personal conviction to being a member of any trade union whatsoever or of a particular union
2 Where the employee was a member of the class of employees covered by the closed shop agreement before it took effect and has not subsequently been a member of a union which is party to such agreement
3 Where the closed shop was introduced on or after 15 August 1980 and has not been approved by a secret ballot of affected employees showing that at least 80 per cent of those entitled to vote supported the agreement.

Employers may also require a union or other person to be joined as a party in unfair dismissal proceedings where the employer claims that the dismissal was the result of pressure exerted by such union or person calling or threatening industrial action because of the complainant's non-membership of the union.

The 'joined' party may be ordered to contribute towards the compensation awarded if the complaint of unfair dismissal is upheld.

A further significant feature of the Employment Act 1980 is the restoration of statutory recourse to law for individuals who, in relation to employment subject to a union membership agreement, are unreasonably excluded or expelled from membership of a specified union.

Further statutory reform of the closed shop laws is embodied in the Employment (Trade Union Immunities) Act, 1982. Given the practical importance of the closed shop in British industrial relations and the doubts, based upon the experience of 1971–74, concerning the extent to which long-standing practices can be eradicated by law, the Conservative Government's intention is not to outlaw closed shops altogether but to impose further restrictions upon their operation. The Act makes the following provisions:

1 Increased compensation for unfair dismissal for refusal to join a union
2 A dismissed employee may 'join', as a party to tribunal proceedings, the union that has contributed to the dismissal by exerting pressure on the employer. An award may be against, and be recoverable directly from, that union
3 Periodic ballots at five yearly intervals to ascertain current support for continuance of existing closed shops. It is unfair to dismiss an employee refusing to join a union not receiving the support of 80 per cent of those covered or 85 per cent of those voting
4 Compensation may be payable by the Secretary of State to victims of closed shop agreements who were dismissed under legislation passed by the last Labour government and who would have been protected as existing non-union members or conscientious objectors if the EA 1980 closed shop provisions had been in force
5 It is unfair to dismiss an employee for not being a union member in a closed shop which took effect before 15 August 1980, unless in the five years preceding dismissal it had been supported in a ballot by 80 per cent of the employees covered or 85 per cent of those voting
6 The definition of a lawful trade dispute, on which the immunities from civil actions rest, is restricted to disputes between workers and their own employer if wholly or mainly related to the subjects of a 'trade dispute', as listed in TULRA *s*29
7 Control of the exertion of pressure on a contractor, by the person engaging his services, to employ only union labour, since this requirement can involve conscription into unions of disinterested employees. The Act stipulates that:
   (a) any clause in a contract will be void if it requires the employment only of persons who are members of a union, or persons who are not members
   (b) it is unlawful to discriminate, in inviting tenders, or making contracts, to require that those employed to perform that contract should be trade union members, or alternatively should not be members

   (c) immunity is removed for industrial action which interferes with performance of a contract primarily on the grounds that those employed to do so are, or are not, union members

8 The trade union itself, as a body, is liable in tort and may be sued for both injunctions and damages in respect of:

   (a) unlawful acts not committed in contemplation or furtherance of a trade dispute
   (b) secondary picketing, indiscriminate secondary action and industrial action to compel union membership
   (c) tortious wrongs of union officials committed on behalf of the union itself, on the principle of vicarious liability.

Further pressure for new closed shop legislation will stem from the decision by the European Commission (August 1981) that the United Kingdom was in breach of Article 11 of the European Convention of Human Rights and Fundamental Freedoms in failing to guarantee three former employees of British Rail a right to dissociate from membership of the appropriate railway union.

ARRANGEMENTS WITH TRADE UNIONS

Within the framework of a recognition agreement, which may or may not have closed shop features, there are a number of arrangements which may help to put management/union relationships on a satisfactory footing.

Collective procedures

Procedures provide a structure within which the parties can engage each other in discussion, problem solving and negotiation at the same time as exercising some degree of control over each other. Some actions are laid down to be followed and others to be avoided, so that it is commonplace for a procedure to state than an employee with a grievance about his employment must seek redress *first* from his immediate superior. It is also typical for a procedure to state that industrial action will only be resorted to when procedural steps are exhausted and that changes in payment or other major terms and conditions of employment will not be made without prior consultation.

The essence of a procedure is to predetermine how matters shall be handled, so that everyone knows what the next step is if they cannot solve a problem or reach agreement. There is a similarity to legal procedure, with its clear path from court to higher court, but it is an area of industrial relations activity that remains free from law. It is quite possible for employer and union to make legally binding agreement, but it remains most unusual.

The most common procedures cover discipline and grievance. The law relating to the contract of employment assumes that there will be a grievance procedure and the law on unfair dismissal assumes that there will be a procedure for discipline, so these are becoming almost universal, although the degree of sophistication is seldom great. The next most common are procedures for negotiation and consultation, which only exist when employer and union have reached the stage of recognition that embraces more than terms and conditions of employment. There is also a frequent link with a procedure operated by an employers' association on a regional or national basis. Procedures are likely to bring clarity, fairness and consistency to employee relations, but they have limited effectiveness in altering the custom and practice of the workplace and they can make change difficult.

Rights of employee representatives

An inevitable consequence of recognising trade unions is the need for union representatives to have some facilities.

Conventional industrial relations wisdom holds that the conduct of collective labour relations is improved by ensuring that employee representatives are informed and enjoy those facilities which they require to perform their functions. Thus, it has been an aim of public policy in recent years to strengthen the quality of workplace representation.

Under section 27 of the Employment Protection Consolidation Act 1978 officials (including shop stewards) of independent, recognised unions have a right to take time off from work with pay to a reasonable extent and subject to reasonable conditions, in order to carry out their duties concerned with industrial relations between the employer (or associated employer) and the employees or for the purpose of undergoing training relevant to those duties. Such training must be approved either by the TUC or the official's own union. For safety representatives, an analogous right is provided by the Safety Representatives and Safety Committee's Regulations.

Disputes concerning whether these rights have been denied are ultimately determined by Industrial Tribunals, which may seek guidance from the recommendations of the ACAS Code of Practice 3, *Time Off for Trade Union Duties and Activities* (1978). This jurisdiction forced tribunals to the heart of workplace industrial relations in so far as disputes concerning time off require close consideration of both the structures of collective bargaining and of the functions which it is appropriate for shop stewards to perform.

The Code of Practice (para 13) gives examples of union officials' duties, though the list is not intended to be exhaustive:

1 Collective bargaining with the appropriate level of management
2 Informing constituents about negotiations or consultations with management
3 Meetings with other key officials or with full-time union officers on matters which are concerned with industrial relations
4 Interviews with and on behalf of constituents on grievance and discipline matters
5 Appearing on behalf of constituents before an official body such as an industrial tribunal
6 Explanations to new employees, whom he or she will represent, of the role

of the union in the workplace industrial relations structure.

The code offers no guidance, however, upon whether, in the case of multi-site organisations, time off with pay should be afforded to allow stewards from one site to consult with those from another. This has been the central issue in much of the case law to date. Tribunals have usually applied a restrictive interpretation of the statutory provisions, though more recently, the Employment Appeal Tribunal (Good v. GEC Elliott Process Automation Ltd) rejected the contention that an official's duties can only be those which fall within the area of recognition.

Disclosure of information

During the 1970s, public policy supported the view that disclosure of information by employers to employees and their representatives is conducive to sound industrial relations and improves the processes of bargaining.

The Employment Protection Act 1975 substantially re-enacts the disclosure provision of the Industrial Relations Act (never activated) by imposing a duty upon an employer to disclose (on request) to representatives of an independent, recognised union information relating to his undertaking or that of an associated employer without which the representatives would be materially impeded in their conduct of bargaining and which it would be good practice to disclose.

ACAS was required to produce a Code of Practice for the guidance of the parties. The Code on Disclosure, published in 1977, represents a disappointing gloss on the statutory provisions. Noting that the relevance of information is determined by the particular structure within which collective bargaining takes place, ACAS rejects the possibility of formulating a list of items which is universally relevant and disclosable. Instead, it provides examples of items of information which could be relevant in particular situations. These cover pay and benefits; conditions of service; manpower, performance; and finance. The central recommendation of the Code is that the parties should reach voluntary agreements on what information is to be disclosed, when and in what form. The scope of the statutory duty to disclose is restricted by the provision of certain safeguards for the employer, who is not required to disclose information communicated in confidence or which relates to an individual unless consent is given or, most importantly, which would cause substantial injury to the employer's undertaking.

Upon complaints of failure to disclose, the Central Arbitration Committee is empowered to declare what information an employer should disclose and by what date. As formerly with recognition claims, the ultimate sanction for failure to comply with such declaration is for terms and conditions to be determined by unilateral arbitration.

The Employment Protection Act provisions on disclosure are less stringent than the obligation of US employers to 'bargain in good faith' under which certain information is presumptively relevant and disclosable. Nor do they make provisions for disclosure to individual employees.

CAC hearings to date reveal little consistency in current disclosure practice as between sectors of British industry. It is, however, possible that the disclosure laws could, in the long term, contribute to more professional bargaining and alter both the structure and scope of the bargaining process.

Picketing

UK picketing laws have been the subject of public controversy. Given the variety of criticisms directed from so many different quarters, it is hard to understand how the Donovan Commission concluded that the law on picketing was satisfactory. Statutory changes were introduced in 1971 and 1974; litigation arising out of picketing received prominent coverage by the media; and the subject was a prime target of further legislative change via the Employment Act 1980. The main aims of the Act's picketing sections are to curb secondary picketing such as by miners at power stations, mass picketing as at Grunwick; and the phenomenon of the 'flying picket' used in the building industry dispute of 1972. Additionally, the Act increases the scope of legal remedies available to employers who suffer as a result of unlawful picketing.

Section 15 of the Trade Union and Labour Relations Act 1974 (as amended by section 16 of the Employment Act 1980) renders it

> lawful for one or more persons in contemplation or furtherance of a trade dispute to stand at or near *his own place of work* or if he is an official of a trade union, at or near the place of work of a member of that union whom he is accompanying . . . for the purpose only of peacefully . . persuading any person to work or abstain from working.

Special provisions apply to mobile workers and to employees who have been dismissed during a strike. Generally speaking, therefore, it is unlawful for workers to picket, albeit peacefully, at premises other than those at which they work. Picketing which is accompanied by violent, intimidating or obstructive behaviour also exceeds the lawful limits of section 15. In respect of such unlawful picketing, employers may seek legal redress via an application for an injunction. It should also be noted that lawful picketing is confined to attendance 'at or near' a worker's place of work, not inside, which constitutes trespass.

The Code of Practice (1980) makes reference to picketing with excessive numbers and suggests that, as a general rule, the purposes of peaceful communication and persuasion can reasonably be achieved by six pickets or fewer at an entrance to a workplace. Since the Code must be considered by a court during legal proceedings, this suggestion may crucially affect the outcome of an employer's injunction application. Evidence that more than six pickets were present may be construed as indicating unlawful purpose.

Hitherto, the legal remedies (injunction and/or action for damages) available to employers in respect of industrial action have been statutorily restricted via civil immunities conferred upon the organisers of such action. An extremely important feature of the Employment Act 1980 is that for the first time, such immunities (under TULR Act 1974, section 13), are linked to the legality of picketing. Where picketing exceeds the limits set by section 15, the immunity from civil liability no longer applies so far as the organisers of the action are concerned, though trade union funds remain protected. In this way, the opportunity for employers, customers and suppliers to exercise legal remedies is significantly increased.

In applying for an injunction to remove an unlawful picket, the employer must name the organisers (usually a full-time union official or shop steward) and submit evidence by affidavit that the picket was unlawful and that damage has been sustained. If granted, the injunction will ordinarily apply to both the named organisers and to others acting on their instructions or on their behalf. Employers may experience difficulty in identifying the organiser(s) of an unlawful picket. Identification, however, remains the responsibility of the employer, not that of the police, and a suggestion that the police be required to assist employers in this context appears unlikely to be implemented legislatively.

STATE AGENCIES

Several state agencies are charged with a duty to advise employers on aspects of industrial relations practice. On specific matters there is the Equal Opportunities Commission and the Commission for Racial Equality or the Race Relations Advisory Service of the Department of Employment. The main agencies are ACAS and CAC.

Advisory, Conciliation and Arbitration Service (ACAS)

ACAS is a body run by a council that has both employer and union members, and there are offices in most large UK cities. An employer can obtain from them advice on the full range of employment practice, from how to draw up a contract of employment to the administration of job evaluation. This advice is also available to unions and members of the public.

Conciliation is provided in an attempt to solve problems between employers and employees, or ex-employees by informal discussion with one or both parties. The most widespread call on this service has been in the many cases of dismissed employees seeking compensation, but it is also available to assist with collective issues, such as pay claims or other disputes.

When agreement between employer and union cannot be reached by the parties themselves, or after conciliation, ACAS can offer the services of a single arbitrator or a panel. In these situations, the arbitrator decides the matter for the parties after hearing evidence from both sides.

Central Arbitration Committee (CAC)

The statutory framework governing the processes of conciliation and arbitration was established by the Conciliation Act 1896 and extended by the

Industrial Courts Act 1919. These statutes were largely repealed by the Employment Protection Act 1975. Following the creation of ACAS and to give final effect to the aim of establishing an independent (and therefore, more acceptable), conciliation and arbitration agency, the Central Arbitration Committee replaced the Industrial Arbitration Board as a permanent, arbitral body maintained at State expense but expressly protected from ministerial direction.

Its composition is tri-partite with legal chairmen plus representatives of employers and employees, all appointed by the Secretary of State after consultation with ACAS. It may sit publicly or privately and, since its creation, it has proved to be a more regional body than its predecessor; approximately 80 per cent of its hearings have been outside London. The Committee has developed its own procedural rules having the overriding aim of achieving informality and flexibility – an aim further encouraged by the fact that there exists no direct right of appeal against its awards. In line with tradition, the Committee's awards are usually not legally enforceable. Its principal statutory functions include:

1 Adjudicating on claims under the Fair Wages Resolution 1946
2 Amending discriminatory agreements and pay structures under the Equal Pay Act 1970
3 Determining complaints from independent unions of employers' failure to disclose information under the Employment Protection Act 1975.

The Committee's philosophy is innovative and clearly expressed in its First Annual Report 1976:

> The Committee is not a court . . . its proceedings and hearings are structured so as to achieve . . . informality. The aim is to encourage the approach by way of problem-solving rather than by emphasising the aspects of conflict and verdict. Above all, there is a commitment to the principles of sound industrial relations and workable solutions.

Thus, the Committee attempts to locate both problems and solutions in an industrial relations context. The 'general considerations' section preceding the 'award' is used by the Committee to try to assist the parties in resolving industrial relations difficulties from which the issue in the terms of reference has arisen.

FURTHER READING

Advisory, Conciliation and Arbitration Service, *Industrial Relations Handbook*, HMSO, London, 1980

Brown, W. (ed.), *The Changing Contours of British Industrial Relations*, Blackwell, Oxford, 1981

Farnham, D., and Pimlott, J., *Understanding Industrial Relations*, Cassell, London, 1979

Muir, J., *Industrial Relations Procedures and Agreements*, Gower, 1981

Payne, D., *Employment Law Manual*, Gower, updated regularly

31 Redundancy and redeployment

Peter Mumford and Tom Carew

The Employment Protection (Consolidation) Act 1978 defines redundancy as occurring when an employer ceases to carry on the business for which the employee was engaged in the place where he was employed, or has insufficient work of the type which the employee was engaged to do.

When an actual redundancy situation has to be administered and decisions made about the treatment of individuals which will affect their own immediate future (and perhaps their long-term employment prospects), as well as the success and profitability of the organisation, then the many variations in interpretation and the implications of this apparently clear-cut definition becomes apparent.

Redundancy is a complex situation involving moral, social, legal, financial and operational issues such as the right of a man to his job, the needs of the organisation, the worth of one individual as opposed to another, the role of the employer and his responsibilities to his employees, the community, the owners and short-term expediency opposed to long-term needs.

To the majority of organisations, the people employed are its most valuable asset. On purely financial grounds their recruitment, training and bank of experience represent a very considerable investment per head. Like any other asset, therefore, they should not be lightly disposed of or neglected. On both moral and social grounds, they are thinking, feeling, individual human beings.

REDUNDANCY POLICY

Need for a policy

The greatest safeguard and security the employees can have is an efficient, profitable organisation, in which forward thinking and planning are of prime importance, so that the necessary action can be taken quickly to take advantage of changing circumstances, rather than have circumstances manage the organisation. A vital part of this forward thinking is the plan to regulate and control the manpower to meet the overall corporate objectives.

The most sophisticated forecasting techniques cannot, of course, cover every eventuality and there may be circumstances so outside the organisation's control that rapid reductions in the manpower requirements are inevitable. Effective planning of resources may also mean that it will be necessary to change the manpower requirements to such an extent that the redundancies are the best way of effecting these changes.

To meet these requirements, an effective plan is needed for dealing with redundancy as an integral part of the organisation's manpower policies.

The best time for formulating the redundancy provisions of the manpower plan is when the organisation is recruiting hard; when the emotional issues are least likely to obscure judgement.

Content of a policy

In drawing up redundancy policies and plans, decisions will have to be taken on:

1 The objectives of the policy
2 The different types of redundancy situations
those forced on the organisation by reductions in business or other outside factors; and those designed to benefit the organisation by, for instance, taking advantage of technological change
3 Avoiding redundancy
4 Reducing the impact of redundancy
5 Transfers and retraining
6 Voluntary redundancy
7 Selection methods to be used
8 Consultation
9 Notice of redundancy
10 Compensation
11 Pension rights
12 Re-engagement.

In all these areas, both the human aspect and the legal requirements have to be taken into account in order that positive plans and procedures can be agreed.

Some general social and company considerations

If the short-term efficiency of the labour force were the only consideration, it would probably be desirable to use a redundancy as an opportunity of getting rid of the unwanted, the troublemakers, the least able, the least adaptable and the least hard-working.

If management had allowed any significant number of these categories to continue in employment until the need for redundancy occurred, it is likely that the policies and practices of the organisation would be such that getting rid of them at this late stage would have little effect.

Equally, management must consider the social implications of their actions, both upon individuals and the community in general.

So far as individuals are concerned, the chief consideration must be the degree of hardship they will suffer, which will be affected immediately by their commitments and family responsibilities and, in the longer term, their age, fitness and chances of finding alternative employment.

Sympathy for individuals must not be allowed to prevent management ensuring that the organisation has a properly trained and balanced labour force to give it the best possible chance of meeting its objectives in the future.

In a community where there is a shortage of various categories of labour, the release of suitable staff by one organisation would obviously be welcomed.

Where there is already unemployment and redundancy, where one organisation is a major or sole employer then redundancies will have far-reaching consequences on the community and individuals.

Where the redundancy is foreseeable, as part of changes which will benefit the organisation, consideration should be given to the possibility of timing, either by speeding up or delaying the dismissals to suit the circumstances in the community.

Detailed forecasting and planning starts from the corporate plan which will show the long-term growth pattern, changes in methods and products which will affect the requirements for skills of different types, the grades and perhaps the ages of staff needed in the future.

In many organisations, this plan may exist only in a most rudimentary form so that the discussion with senior executives, in order to formulate their views, will be a valuable exercise in itself. Once this process has been started, it proves far less difficult to build up an overall picture than is usually imagined. Like all other techniques, forecasting improves the more it is practised.

1 Objectives

The purpose of all personnel policy is to assist management to achieve the organisation's objectives more efficiently. Within this broad purpose, the objectives of a redundancy scheme are to reduce labour costs and protect the interests of individuals affected by it.

These objectives should be quantified when an actual redundancy occurs, so that precise and specific reductions can be made and the success of these plans measured. It is important not to sacrifice long-term profits for short-term savings. It would, for instance, be relatively easy to reduce costs by dismissing all the short service staff and create later difficulty as a result of shortages of certain skills and an ageing labour force.

2 Types of redundancy

Where the redundancy is forced on the organisation by outside factors, action usually has to be taken quickly and it is difficult to increase costs by over-generous compensation. The legal minimum payment may be the right amount.

In cases where the organisation will benefit from new equipment or methods, it is reasonable that all should benefit from these savings and the levels of compensation can be higher.

3 Avoiding redundancy

Adequate forecasting of future demand and changes, together with high efficiency, are the most effective ways of avoiding redundancy. If the staff requirements are known in advance, recruitment, training and retirement programmes can be used in conjunction with one another to constrain the manpower resources to the required levels.

A high level of efficiency will ensure profitability with reserves for tiding over difficult periods, together with the avoidance of surplus staff.

If, however, redundancy becomes inevitable it is still possible to reduce the effect of it.

4 Reducing the impact of redundancy

Methods which can be used include:

1 Selling surplus capacity even at marginal cost in order to retrain skilled staff
2 Bringing subcontracted work into the organisation's own workshops
3 Building up stocks against future needs to avoid losing markets to foreign competition
4 Stopping overtime so as to share out the work available: retraining of staff may be necessary
5 Restricting recruitment and filling vacancies by internal transfer and retraining wherever this is possible
6 Dismissing employees who have been allowed to work on past normal retirement age
7 Retraining staff to give greater flexibility and increased efficiency in future
8 Offering early retirement.

5 Transfers and retraining

The numbers to be dismissed can often be reduced, or a valuable man retained in the organisation, by transferring staff from one department to another or even to another company in a group.

Providing the work offered and the conditions are not significantly worse than the employee's present job and the work is within the employee's capacity, then he will not, in law, be considered to be redundant even if he refuses the transfer.

However, should another worker be dismissed as a result of the transfer, then he will be considered to have been made redundant and entitled to compensation.

The offer of alternative work or transfer should be made to the employee, before his notice expires, in writing, specifying the work and the conditions. Providing the transfer takes place within four weeks of the end of the original job, the employee's service will be considered to be continuous.

If the employee is offered a different type of work, he is entitled to a trial period of four weeks.

A long period to cover necessary retraining may be agreed between employer and employee. Details of such an agreement must be written.

Where they may be differences in earnings due to the operation of bonus schemes or other factors, it is usual to allow a period of make-up pay until the employee has had an opportunity to adjust to the new conditions.

It would also be reasonable to give assistance with removal expenses if the transfer would involve moving house. In the case of experienced workers, the cost of this would probably be less than the total of compensation, plus recruitment and training costs of a new employee.

Retraining to allow staff to acquire skills which are still required by the organisation can be remarkably successful if it is carried out systematically and sympathetically. The experience of many organisations has shown that most people can acquire new skills rapidly and effectively. In many cases, grants are available to reduce costs which will generally be less than the costs of compensation to long-service employees.

There will also be benefits of improved morale and greater flexibility of staff.

6 Voluntary redundancy

It is obviously advantageous in terms of morale and goodwill if people can be encouraged to leave voluntarily. There are two broad categories:

1 Those eligible for early retirement
2 Other age groups.

Both are dependent on generous compensatory packages and are therefore initially expensive, but co-operation by staff and unions, avoidance of disputes, maintenance of good relations and the meeting of social obligations to long-service staff have been seen by many organisations to justify this.

In early retirement the usual approach is to offer an enhancement of the service contribution towards pension rights. Thus a male employee of 58 with 25 years service might be given 7 years enhancement, allowing him to retire with the pension he would be entitled to at age 65, i.e. $^{32}/_{60}$ of his current salary.

For staff more than 10 years away from retirement age, usually a cash sum sufficient to encourage them to leave voluntarily is required. Sums representing up to three or four years basic pay have been offered by many large organisations for this purpose. The attractiveness of the package will often depend on the possibility of obtaining other work in the locality.

Some schemes for voluntary redundancy have been too attractive, leaving the organisation short of staff, short of skills or an unbalanced age mix. Very careful planning for these factors is required before setting up a blanket scheme. A safer approach is to give selected individuals the opportunity to volunteer.

Repayment from the Redundancy Fund may be claimed only if it can be seen that the individuals leave because there is no more work for them.

7 Selection of workers to be made redundant

The most controversial and difficult aspect of any redundancy is the method for selecting those who are to be dismissed.

The simple solution is last-in first-out (LIFO), based purely on the length of service. This is favoured by many unions, is easy to operate, understandable and allows people to know fairly accurately where they stand. Because compensation is geared to length of service, it is also cheaper for the organisation.

If all employees were of equal worth and if all sections of the organisation were equally affected, then this policy could satisfy most needs. In most redundancies, and particularly in those caused by technological or product changes, it is unlikely that all departments or all grades of staff will need to be reduced by the same amount, and even in those departments whose overall numbers have to be reduced, there will be certain key jobs for which skilled workers are in short supply and whom it would be quite wrong to dismiss.

Additionally, there will be problems created by hardship cases, the registered disabled, those under training for skills required in the future and the future age structure of the company.

The effect of a number of even small-scale redundancies can be to bias the age structure significantly upwards which may create difficulties in, say, five years' time.

From the broader social point of view, there is also a danger of creating a category of worker who will always be first out and who, through no fault of their own, will never be able to build up any service to qualify them for redundancy payments.

An ideal selection method would strike the balance between the requirements of the organisation and the social needs of individuals. Both the present and future needs of the organisation in terms of skills, flexibility, potential, age range and replacement costs of individuals should be considered, together with the individual's circumstances. These include his commitments and responsibilities, likely difficulties in obtaining new work, age and length of service.

Selection that departs from agreed procedure or established custom will be considered unfair unless there are very good reasons for non-conformity.

It is essential to avoid the risk of charges of discrimination on grounds of union membership, sex or race being brought against the organisation because of the selection methods used.

Where LIFO is used, jobs should be categorised within departments so that selection can be made within a group of skills, rather than across the whole department which may include skills which are still required. Key personnel, whose absence could affect the output of other sections, should not be dismissed purely because of seniority considerations.

8 Consultation

Management must obviously make the decision about the need for redundancy and the scale of it but the more employees are consulted about the way in which it is to be handled and they are to be treated, the easier it will be to design a scheme which meets all needs.

The recognised trade union for the group of employees to which the affected personnel belong (whether or not they are individually trade union members), must be consulted as early as possible to allow the trade union representative to suggest alternative action, retraining, etc.

If more than 10 employees are likely to be made redundant during one month, this consultation should start at least 60 days before the dismissals take place. If more than 100 people are to be made redundant over a period of 90 days, then the consultation has to start 90 days before the dismissal date. Trade union representatives have to be given the following information:

1 The reasons for the proposed redundancies;
2 The numbers and description of jobs affected;
3 The total number employed of these descriptions at the establishment;
4 The proposed selection method;
5 The proposed methods and timing for the dismissals.

Although most unions are committed to the principle of a man having a right to his job, which means no dismissal unless there is no alternative job available, full-time union officials are realists and accept that some redundancy is inevitable. They also accept that the LIFO principle must be applied only within the grades of the jobs affected. Where it can be shown that there are substantial differences in the skill and worth of one individual over another, they will generally accept the organisation's need in preference to rigid adherence to seniority.

If there is no union representative in the organisation, staff committees or representatives can act in the same capacity as a trade union.

9 Notice of redundancy

For employees who are to be dismissed, the Act specifies minimum periods of notice according to their lengths of service (see Figure 31.1). Where necessary, payment may be given in lieu of notice.

In cases where the change can be foreseen longer in advance, it is reasonable to give longer notice of intention. However, such announcements may precipitate a rush of key workers to secure the first place in the queue for scarce jobs in other organisations.

A system of premium payments may be used to encourage staff to work out their notices. They also lose their entitlement to redundancy payments under the Act if they do not obtain their employer's permission to leave before the

Length of continuous service (years)	Minimum period of notice (weeks)
4 weeks	1
2	2
3	3
4	4
5	5
6	6
7	7
8	8
9	9
10	10
11	11
12	12

Figure 31.1 Formal notice required

expiry of their notice. Even so, a severe unemployment situation locally can make it more attractive for individuals to secure the long-term advantage of another job rather than a once-only cash payment.

It is usually best to restrict formal notice to the requirements set out above, but to give notice of intention as part of the normal consultation procedures. This will help to maintain good faith with employees and prevent the spread of rumour and loss of confidence.

10 Compensation

Lump-sum payments are made to employees dismissed through redundancy on a scale according to age and length of service as shown in Figure 31.2. These lump-sum payments to the employee are tax-free (within limits) and do not affect his entitlement to unemployment benefit or earnings-related supplements. The payments are made by the employer who then claims partial repayment from the Redundancy Fund.

Where redundancy is due to insolvency and the employer is unable to make these payments, they are made direct to the employee by the Department of Employment.

Many employers consider that these payments represent a minimum and supplement them by scales of their own, usually related to length of service. A simple way of doing this is to add a fixed percentage to the statutory payment. Only the statutory scale of payment is eligible for rebate.

It is much easier to justify more generous treatment where the redundancy is due to circumstances from which the company will benefit and there is,

Employee's age	*Payment for each complete year of service*
18–22	½ week's pay
22–41	1 week's pay (max. 20 weeks at £130 per week)
41–64 (men) 41–59 (women)	1½ week's pay (max. 30 weeks)

Service under the age of 18 does not count for this purpose.

For men of 64–65 years, and women of 59–60, the entitlement is reduced by one-twelfth for every month over 64 or 59.

Full details are set out in leaflet RPL2.

Figure 31.2 Redundancy pay

therefore, merit in making additional payments in these circumstances only. Certainly in the extremes of redundancy where the organisation is insolvent, only the redundancy scheme scale can be applicable.

An alternative method of supplementing payments is to make weekly and monthly payments – again on a scale according to service – until the employee has either used his entitlement or obtains alternative employment. To avoid reducing entitlement to unemployment benefit, these payments must be limited to one-third of normal earnings.

11 Pension rights

The Social Security Act 1973 requires that occupational pensions of redundant employees, aged 26 and over who have completed at least five years' service must be preserved. The possible methods include:

1 Benefits already earned may be preserved to normal retiring age
2 Transfer of benefits to another scheme
3 Payment of reduced benefit before normal retiring age
4 Payment of increased benefit after normal retiring age
5 Repayment of members' contributions made before 6 April 1975.

A proportion of pension may be offset against redundancy payments, as outlined in leaflet RPL1.

Full details of possible pension arrangements are set out in memorandum 18 of the Occupational Pensions Board. This Board exists mainly to advise on preservation aspects of pensions.

In spite of these regulations, however, very substantial erosion of pension expectations, especially for senior executives, can take place as a result of redundancy. For an individual of 45 with 20 years of pensionable service, it has been calculated that loss of credit for service and inflation would result in a loss of value to the pension exceeding £20 000 per £10 000 of salary. Figure 31.3 shows pension damage: this table has been calculated for a pension scheme providing $^1/_{60}$ of final average salary for each year of service.

Pension damage arises because the new employer can rarely accept responsibility for revaluing an executive's accrued pension from earlier employment in line with salary increases in the future. Usually the rules of a pension scheme give early leavers an entitlement to deferred benefits, frozen according to salary at the time of redundancy. The loss is scarcely alleviated by a transfer payment (if this can be arranged) because these are usually sufficient to secure only a much reduced past service credit in a new employer's scheme.

To ensure adequate compensation for loss of benefits of this order, the effects on each scheme and individual need to be reviewed by pension specialists or actuaries.

12 Re-engagement

Should circumstances change more rapidly than anticipated, it may be possible to re-engage those dismissed; the fairest way being to re-engage in reverse order to dismissal.

Before re-engagement takes place, the question of service must be clarified. If payments under the redundancy payments scheme have been made, then clearly service under the re-engagement can count only from this date and similarly, if payments against pension rights have been made, then pensionable service must restart from the date of re-engagement.

Provided no payments have been made, it is usual to count service for pension purposes as continuous if the period between dismissal and re-engagement does not exceed one year. Thereafter, it is preferable to regard any re-engagement as a completely new period of service for all purposes.

Cases of hardship

Cases of special difficulty can be assisted by *ex gratia* payments or other more favourable compensations. To avoid charges of favouritism, a small committee of a senior executive, a staff or union representative, and the personnel manager or welfare officer can be formed for this purpose. The committee may be given a special budget, or terms of reference within which they make recommendations. It is essential that decisions be made rapidly.

Date of leaving

If a redundant worker finds another job he may be released before expiry of his notice (without affecting his entitlement to redundancy payments) provided he gives written notice and this is accepted by the employer. Wherever possible, arrangements should be made to release the employee in time to take up his new employment.

(1) Age of employee at withdrawal	(2) Pensionable service completed at withdrawal	(3) Value of loss of pension position per £10 000 pa salary	(4) Salary increase (as percentage of old salary to compensate for (3))
30	5	5 250	1-½
	10		
35	5	5 250	2
	10	11 500	4
40	5	5 500	2
	10	11 750	4-½
	15	17 500	7
45	5	5 500	3
	10	11 000	5-½
	15	16 500	8
	20	22 000	11
50	5	5 000	3-½
	10	10 000	6-½
	15	15 000	10
	20	20 000	13
	25	25 000	17
55	5	4 250	4
	10	8 250	8
	15	12 000	12
	20	16 500	16
	25	20 750	20
	30	25 000	24
60	5	2 750	5
	10	5 500	10
	15	8 250	16
	20	11 000	21
	25	13 750	26
	30	16 500	32
	35	19 500	37

Figure 31.3 ***Scale of pension damage***
Source: Shucksmith & Co., Actuarial Estimates
Courtesy of Times Newspapers Limited

Time for interviews

Under the Employment Protection Act redundant full time employees with two or more years' service, or employees working between 8 and 16 hours per week with 5 years' service, are entitled to reasonable time off with pay to look for another job or to arrange for training for a new job. 'Reasonable' is not defined since individual requirements may vary so much.

The TUC in their publication 'Job Security' cite two full days as a common entitlement, but this may seem inadequate in a period of 12 weeks' notice. Excessive demands from individuals are obviously to be discouraged.

TRIBUNALS

An employee declared redundant may appeal to an industrial tribunal if he considers he has been unfairly dismissed on the following grounds:

1 The dismissal is for reasons not covered by the definition of the Employment Protection Act
2 The means of selection are unfair because:
   (*a*) they concern membership, or non-membership, of a trade union
   (*b*) the accepted or agreed selection procedures have been disregarded
   (*c*) the warning given was inadequate, or efforts have not been made to find alternative employment within the organisation
   (*d*) there has been discrimination based on the race or sex of the employee
   (*e*) any other reason which the employee considers unfair.

To avoid such claims, it is essential that shortage of suitable work, however caused, is the only reason for redundancy; selection procedures are agreed and followed, and that each employee is given written notice of dismissal.

This formal notice should state the reason, the period of notice and termination date, the appeals procedure. Copies of such notice may then be used in evidence at any subsequent tribunal appeal by the employee.

If they agree that dismissal is unfair, the tribunal may make an order for reinstatement in the employee's old job, re-engagement in another job or payment of compensation. Maximum compensation is currently £8000.

If an employer is considered not to have met the requirements of prior consultation, a tribunal may make an order to postpone the dismissals or make a protective award requiring payment of normal wages for a specified period. The maximum protective award may not exceed the period specified for consultation (28, 60 or 90 days as appropriate).

Approaches to an industrial tribunal are made using:

Form IT1 for employees seeking decisions on their entitlement to compensation and the amount due
Form IT17 for employers seeking a decision on their entitlement to rebate against redundancy payments
Form IT18 in all other cases

for complaints arising in England or Wales to:

The Secretary
Central Office of Industrial Tribunals
93 Ebury Bridge Road
London, SW1

or for those arising in Scotland:

The Secretary
Central Office of Industrial Tribunals (Scotland)
St Andrew House
141 West Nile Street
Glasgow

The proceedings of tribunals are held informally, but applicants and witnesses may be required to give evidence on oath. They may be represented by lawyers, trade union or employers' association officials.

Details of the procedures are given in leaflets:

ITL1 for employees
ITL2 for respondents
ITL7 for employers appealing against failure to pay rebate

REBATES FROM THE REDUNDANCY FUND

Claims for rebates must be made to the Department of Employment within six months of the payment to the employee. Rebate may be reduced if the necessary notification is not given.

The notification is made on form RP1 which requires the following information for each employee: sex, national insurance number, income.tax reference number, date of birth, date of engagement, expected date of dismissal, amount of a week's pay.

It should be noted that the department may call for the production of records to check the claims or may ask permission for an officer to carry out the required checks on the employers' premises.

STANDARD PROCEDURES

Although every instance of redundancy is likely to be different in detail, drawing up a standard procedure will help to ensure that, if a redundancy becomes necessary, it can be dealt with rapidly and efficiently, so that administrative failures will not intensify an already emotional and critical situation.

Many of the procedures suggested have value and relevance to the organisation in general, quite apart from their value in the avoidance and administration of redundancy. They should be included in a redundancy agreement to demonstrate to staff that all possible efforts are being made to protect their interests and secure the well-being of the organisation.

Topics which should be covered in a redundancy procedure include:

1* Manpower planning as a positive part of the overall corporate plan
2* Consultation machinery
3* Categories of redundancy involving varying treatment
4* Means of avoiding redundancy, such as not subcontracting work, restric-

tion of recruitment, restriction of overtime working, voluntary retirement, retiring staff over retirement age, laying off part-time workers

5* Transfer arrangements
6* Training
7* Method of categorising jobs and workers
8* Selection procedures to be used
9* Notification procedure – for staff and Department of Employment
10* Formal notice including arrangement for amendments
11* Compensation
12* Welfare and assistance to dismissed employees
13* Assistance in finding new jobs
14* Pension arrangements
15* Terms for re-engagement
16* Publicity
17* Calculations of payments due and notification of amounts to staff concerned
18* Formal dismissal procedures
19 Claims for rebate from Department of Employment
20 Appeals:
  (*a*) By the organisation
  (*b*) *By individuals
21 Records
22 Evaluation after redundancy has occurred in order to improve;

Once the basic procedures have been drawn up, they should be discussed with staff representatives through the normal consultation machinery.

Items marked * in this list, or extracts from them, should then be used to formulate an agreement with the staff. Details of the administrative procedures are not necessary in such an agreement. In the case of item 1, for instance, it is sufficient to give an undertaking that forward planning and forecasting of manpower requirements will be carried out in order to constrain the availability and supply of staff as near to the requirement as possible.

EMPLOYMENT SERVICES AND AGENCIES

The Manpower Services Commission is responsible for providing a wide range of services to industry and individuals including:

Advice on manpower planning and forecasting methods
Assistance and advice in documentation for redundancy
Guidance on alternative employment available for dismissed employees
Temporary employment subsidies
Guidance on assistance and service available to help those dismissed
Advice on retraining facilities
Advice on appeals and industrial tribunals.

All these services are available in a redundancy situation, the advance warning called for by the Act providing time for them to be alerted and brought into use.

Where large numbers of staff are to be dismissed, an employment office can be set up on the organisation's premises.

Initial contact with the services should be made to the local Department of Employment office. The larger offices have specialist departments for dealing with all aspects of redundancy.

The following leaflets are available:

RPL1 Offsetting pensions against redundancy payments
RPL2 Ready reckoner for payments
RPL4 Service calendar
RPL5 Calculation of a week's pay for employees on shift and rota work
RPL6 Summary of information for employees

REDEPLOYMENT

Company schemes to assist redundant employees

Whilst there is no legal requirement on organisations to assist redundant staff beyond giving time off for job hunting, the traumatic effects of large scale redundancies, high levels of unemployment and increasing recognition of social obligations have encouraged many organisations to give much greater assistance than this.

The attitude of society towards unemployed people is changing rapidly in four respects:

1 The severance payments are becoming more generous; derisory ones are becoming less frequent. The figure quoted most often for a middle manager in mid-career after about five years' service with a company is around six months' pay
2 There are moves to change the law to counteract the pension damage suffered by mobile executives. Some employers are including pension damage in the calculation of severance payments
3 Those who are out of work are not the untouchables they used to be
4 Redeployment services have emerged from the purely advisory service amateur status into a proven executive marketing service. Recognising this, employers are starting to incorporate this service into the overall severance packages.

In addition to direct benefits to the redundant employees, there is a major spin off in improving morale for the retained staff.

There are three main areas where assistance can usefully be given by an organisation:

1 Helping the employees to clarify their future needs
2 Financial arrangements
3 Assistance with finding a new job.

The priorities of each of these will vary according to the circumstances of the individual involved; thus, if early retirement has been used to effect redundancy, the order of priority would probably be 2, 1, 3, whereas for a middle level executive in his early forties 1, 3, 2 might be appropriate.

The effect of being made redundant will vary from one individual to another; for one it may be a golden opportunity to acquire sufficient capital to retire or to start his own business. For the next, it represents disaster, the scrap heap, the stigma of rejection, loss of self confidence. Therefore, the needs of each one will be different, and there is no point in offering a standard package irrespective of need.

A preliminary interview with each individual is needed to establish their specific requirements from the services which it has been decided to make available.

Individual needs

Firstly, it is essential to help the individual determine exactly what he wants to do. In many cases people may not have given any thought at all to the problem and, in most cases, their ideas will be constrained within fairly narrow limits. In fact, the range of choice open to individuals can be very wide indeed.

A skilful counselling interview may enable many people to see redundancy as an opportunity rather than a disaster, and certainly should form the first step in the build up of confidence which will enable those who have been so affected to cope with their problems.

It cannot be over-emphasised that counselling to assist people to solve their own problems, rather than the provision of a shoulder to cry on or someone who will tell them what to do, is essential if individuals are to be helped to stand on their own feet again.

Choice of objectives

The range is infinite, embracing complete retirement, partial retirement, starting up a business or joining an established business (for example by buying a directorship), emigrating, undergoing training or education, seeking a different type of work, seeking a similar job, accepting unemployment as a positive rather than a negative move.

Financial arrangements

If the employee decides on retirement, then his needs are probably to use his compensation to supplement his pension. The individual starting up a business may need a capital sum to invest, a supplement to his income or a single premium contribution to an insurance/pension package. Those taking a training or education course, would probably need a supplement to whatever grant is obtainable.

Any advice given must take into account the individual's existing financial arrangements, other income or pension, mortgage, capital, his financial needs, health, age and commitments. Additionally, the effect of the various arrangements on his tax structure must be evaluated. The range of options available is so wide, and the advantages to be gained from optimum money management so high, that expert advice should invariably be sought.

Fair severance payments

Employers, executives and staff are all subject to the unpredictable vagaries of a market economy. This must be accepted, but there needs to be a fairer system to level out the compensatory payments received by individuals which are seldom a reflection of the merit of an individual or of his needs.

If the severance payments are to be treated as compensation to pay for the period of unemployment, then some yardstick for estimating this time is required.

Figure 31.4 sets out to quantify most of the factors which affect the time taken to obtain a new job.

Other employment

For the majority, whose prime requirement is a new job, much can be done by counselling and guidance to increase firstly confidence, and then the marketing of the skills of those made redundant.

Many people constrain their search for employment by looking only for jobs similar to those they are losing. Identifying the skills which they have acquired and used as a result of their experience will invariably widen the choice of jobs available to them. They can then be assisted in marketing their skills through skilful presentation, practice in letter writing, interviewing etc. The response rate to individual applications may be as low as 1–2 per cent so that secretarial assistance will be of considerable value.

Few people realise that seeking a job is hard, demanding work, requiring a disciplined, planned approach which must in itself be tackled like a full time job. Among the benefits of any scheme providing assistance with job seeking will be the inculcation of the necessary disciplines and commitment to this task.

Training

Training may form an essential element in the search for new employment. Skills training will consist of bringing existing skills up to date, adding a complementary skill (for example a language) or, on a longer term, acquiring completely new skills or knowledge or obtaining formal qualifications to match existing skills and experience. Career counselling should ensure that skills and qualifications are those for which there is a demand, or which will improve the market value of existing assets.

Many will require training in self-marketing. A typical four-day course would cover the following:

1 Marketing – (who are you, what can you do, who wants you, how to contact them)

Assumptions	The average executive	The average executive who is not naturally good at job hunting	The average executive benefiting from redeployment services
That short list selection interviews will be generated at the rate of.........	1 every 2 weeks	1 every 3 weeks	2 every 3 weeks
That on average there will be 6 people on the short list making their chances of selection likely to be.........	1 every 6 interviews	1 every 9 interviews	1 every 4 interviews

From these assumptions the following mathematical probabilities can be calculated

80% will have earned selection within.........	20 weeks	40 weeks	10 weeks
Through no fault of their own, just as a matter of chance, 5% will still be unemployed after	35 weeks	70 weeks	20 weeks

Initial delay

Add start-up time before first interviews are generated.........	5 weeks	7 weeks	3 weeks

Age Factors

Per year over 45 years	Add 1 week
Per year over 50 years	Add 2 weeks
Per year under 35 years	Deduct 1 week

Administrative factors

Delay by employers between final selection and arrival of offer	2 weeks
Delay between offer and taking up appointment	2 weeks
Delay before arrival of first pay cheque	4 weeks

Other Factors

Staying in employment during job search	Add 30%
High severance payments exceeding one year's	Add 10% per months salary
For every 100 000 over 1.5 million unemployed	Add 5%

Salary Factors

Per £1000 over £15 000 p.a.	Add 1 week
Per £1000 under £10 000 p.a.	Deduct 1 week

Figure 31.4 Factors affecting the time taken to find a new job (Percy Coutts & Co)

2 Career history and letter writing, telephone skills
3 Interview training (using closed circuit television)
4 Individual counselling

Unless the organisation has the necessary expertise to provide this training, it should be left to specialists such as career counsellors or training institutions.

The 'TOPS' programmes provided by the Manpower Services Commission at colleges and other centres, are particularly appropriate for redundant staff who generally qualify for subsistence grant whilst attending.

Job search

The need is to supplement the general services provided by the Department of Employment with services geared to the requirements of particular grades, such as senior executives and specialist staff. Even in cases of large scale redundancy, where the Department of Employment will open employment offices on the organisation's premises, a great deal can be achieved by a task force approach by the organisation's own marketing staff or specialist recruitment agencies to unearth every possible employment opportunity.

This should be coupled with guidance to staff on the approach they should take and the type of job best suited to them. Individuals will frequently have to choose between waiting until the right job appears, with the risk of rejection because of a long period of unemployment, or taking any job to give continuity of employment.

A 'job shop' set up on the employer's premises and manned by sales staff can provide redundant staff with a wide range of vacancies. The key to success is the training of staff to run the job shop, their enthusiasm, and the employer's commitment to maintaining it.

Specialist agencies

Because of the expertise and resources needed to conduct a full scale redeployment operation, may organisations rely entirely on outside agencies. Such agencies should be capable of providing the following services:

- Training courses to teach the skills of self-marketing
- Career history writing of a similar standard to creative writers in media firms
- Market researchers
- Office services: mailshot facilities, word processors and secretarial support
- Experienced counsellors and the availability of a professional vocational psychologist with experience in executive careers
- Interview coaching with closed circuit television facilities
- Promotional facilities in direct contact with the executive search and recruitment organisations.

These services should be continually available until the employee has obtained his next appointment.

Firms operating in this field who have been established for more than three years are:

Chusid
Forty Plus
Interexec
Minster
Percy Coutts & Co Ltd
Sanders & Sydney.

Financial advice can be provided by:

Douglas Deakin Young
Cockman & Copeman.

Benefits to the organisation

By involving the public relations element of the company, the negative reputation of being a company with redundancies can be turned into a positive reputation, by highlighting the image of a company which cares for its staff. Much good publicity can thereby be generated. This will help to obtain vacancies for the job shop, and will eventually attract higher quality applicants when recruiting resumes.

A company which is unprepared and has no positive redeployment policy will have managers who are reluctant to take a commercially correct decision to reduce staff because they feel they will be seriously damaging the careers of colleagues.

The adverse publicity associated with major redundancy programmes can add to the business problems of the company. A well-designed redeployment operation covering the weekly and hourly paid staff will show the employer as being forward-thinking, considerate and businesslike. This must be good publicity.

The internal morale of a company which sends off its surplus staff with positive job search support must be better than that of a company which wields the axe rapidly and ruthlessly.

FURTHER READING

Carew, T., *Get up and Go Job Search*, Percy Coutts & Co.
Daniel, W. W., *Whatever Happened to the Workers at Woolwich?* Economic Planning, London, 1972
Dobson, John, 'Planning a Voluntary Redundancy Scheme', *Works Management*, April 1975, pp 52–3
Employment Protection (Consolidation) Act 1978, chapter 44, HMSO, 1979
Gill, H. S., 'Handling Redundancy and How to Maintain Morale' *Personnel Management*, vol. 7, No. 3, March 1975, pp 34–7
Golzen, S., and Plumbley, P., *Changing Your Job*, Kogan Page, 1981
Golzen, S., *Working for Yourself*, Kogan Page, 1981

Guidelines for the Redundant Manager, 2nd edition, British Institute of Management, 1981

A Short Guide to the Preservation of Occupational Pension Benefits, Occupational Pensions Board, London

Kemp, F. et al, *Focus on Redundancy*, Kogan Page, 1980

Lubbock, Bill, *Finding Another Top Job*, Institute of Personnel Management, 1975

Mumford, P. A., *Redundancy and Security of Employment*, Gower, 1975

O'Brien, R., 'Points of Procedure', *Personnel Management,* August 1972, pp 23-5

PART SEVEN

THE SKILLS OF MANAGEMENT

32 Management self-development

Michael Williams

It is widely believed that management development = management training = 'send him on a course'. This view assumes that management development is 'done' by someone to someone else – applied, in other words, like an external treatment.

Management development planned in this spirit rarely involves the person who requires development in either the diagnosis of the problem or the formulation of the prescription and follow-up. Thus he tends to find himself playing a largely passive role in important activities concerned (as the case may be) with:

his growth as a person
his development for future promotion or transfer
improving his current performance or increasing his contribution as a manager
helping him make the transition from specialist to managerial role
developing his skills in specific areas.

Traditional forms of management training, moreover, are more likely to be 'off the peg' than tailor-made, and may not always be the most suitable for the individual in question.

Perhaps most serious of all is the constant failure to recognise that ultimately the company, a boss, or the management development manager is not responsible for the development of the organisation's managers. The managers themselves are. The boss's responsibility is to encourage, support and 'facilitate' the process of his subordinates' self-development and therefore is principally one of helping them to help themselves to develop and become more effective.

At its most fundamental, management development means self-development – that is, a conscious response on the part of the individual to deal with what *he* recognises as his development needs. Real development takes place when the individual sees, for himself, the need to modify his behaviour, change his attitudes, develop new skills, improve his performance, or prepare himself for a different role. The rationale that 'only the learner will learn' is recognised in some organisations and by a growing number of management development specialists, tutors and trainers.

Because many of the barriers to self-development that exist in companies and within boss-subordinate relationships are self-imposed and psychological, the process needs stimulation, guidance and sensitive managing. The next level up in the management hierarchy often serves as the best excuse for not getting things done and provides a frequent let-out for the individual who chooses to deny his responsibility for his own development:

> 'I'm employed by the company; it's up to my boss to decide what my development needs are. I don't know which way my career is going to go.'

Such self-imposed constraints are not strategies for success. They need to be recognised by managers as recipes for mediocrity. The evidence that such self-protective behaviour is prevalent at managerial and supervisory levels usually takes the form of:

- scepticism and a general 'don't want to know' attitude
- unwillingness to take ownership of problems
- reluctance to exercise initiative and authority
- opting out and buck-passing
- failure to take necessary risks leading to a record of lost opportunities
- forfeiture of influence as a 'power-source' within the organisation.

The true basis of self-development – namely that the individual takes responsibility for his own learning – may be quite alien to some managers. Traditionally much education (schools, further education and training) has put the emphasis on teaching rather than on learning. That approach tends to create inappropriately high levels of student passivity towards developing new attitudes and behaviours ('It's up to *them* to teach *me*').

To some people the idea of taking responsibility for their own learning is even seen as threatening, because it involves a personal shift from a largely uncommitted or passively receptive state to one which demands the individual's commitment and action.

Others may be so disillusioned with their particular lot or with the company in general that they are demotivated and demoralised to the extent that they cease to care about self-development altogether. To people in such negative states of mind the process is likely to be seen at best as 'pie in the sky'.

More probably it will be viewed with suspicion as a management confidence trick, personnel department propaganda or (by the real cynics) as a 'do-it-yourself hangman's kit'.

Some managers may take a tougher, more calculative view and expect to see direct links between any effort on their part in self-development and the company's reward system.

Finally there will always be managers (usually senior executives) who assume inviolability. They claim, with or without coyness, that they have already 'arrived' and that 'this sort of thing is all right for other people'.

SELF-DEVELOPMENT IN THEORY AND PRACTICE

There are two aspects of the human personality which are relevant to the understanding of self-development. These are:

1 The 'self image' (the 'me as I see myself') by which each individual identifies himself, his personal values, beliefs, knowledge, wants, needs and fears as well as his physical presence
2 The 'ego ideal' (which amounts to the individual's 'me as I would really like to be'). In essence this consists of the attainable 'plus-me' which exists in every individual in addition to the hopes, dreams and wishes which may make up the idealised or fantasy self.

Personal growth (which by definition is largely determined by self-development) is the linking route from the self-image to the ego ideal. This is illustrated in Figure 32.1.

Practical self-development in management, necessarily, is concerned with attainable realities – what have been termed the 'plus me', rather than simply with the individual's fantasy world. The 'plus me' represents the difference between what the individual currently does, how effectively he operates, what contributions he makes in his present role and what that person is realistically capable of doing and being, within *self-selected periods of time.* The concept of the 'plus me', therefore, is related to a series of progressively emerging horizons — rather than to some ultimate limit which he or others have put on his potential. The horizons become more readily discernible as the individual consciously links his current behaviour and performance to what he feels are, for him, *requisite* standards, levels or modes of behaviour and which he judges are within his identifiable capacity. In practical terms the 'plus me' can be related to and reinforced by what Hodgson and Myers refer to as the 'plus job'. This is an attainable, realistic and viable role in which there are opportunities for increased satisfaction for the individual, coupled with increased contribution to the organisation in which he operates.

Identifying the 'plus me' and the 'plus job' involves the individual manager working through a series of key questions, preferably with his boss and (where available) a management development specialist. From the responses are built up pictures of how the individual wants to grow as a person and how his job, or role, might be realistically developed to cater for and capitalise on that person's growth. The next stage is to evolve appropriate action plans, principally within the scope of the manager's work environment. Exercises are given later in this chapter which illustrate the processes and show how more diagnostic information can be obtained in order for the prescriptive action plans to be evolved for individual managers and for managerial teams. The crucial following activities are monitoring, review and follow-through, without which there would only be action plans – not action.

SELF-DEVELOPMENT: DISCLOSURE AND FEEDBACK

The self-diagnosis described above represents a systematic analysis of a

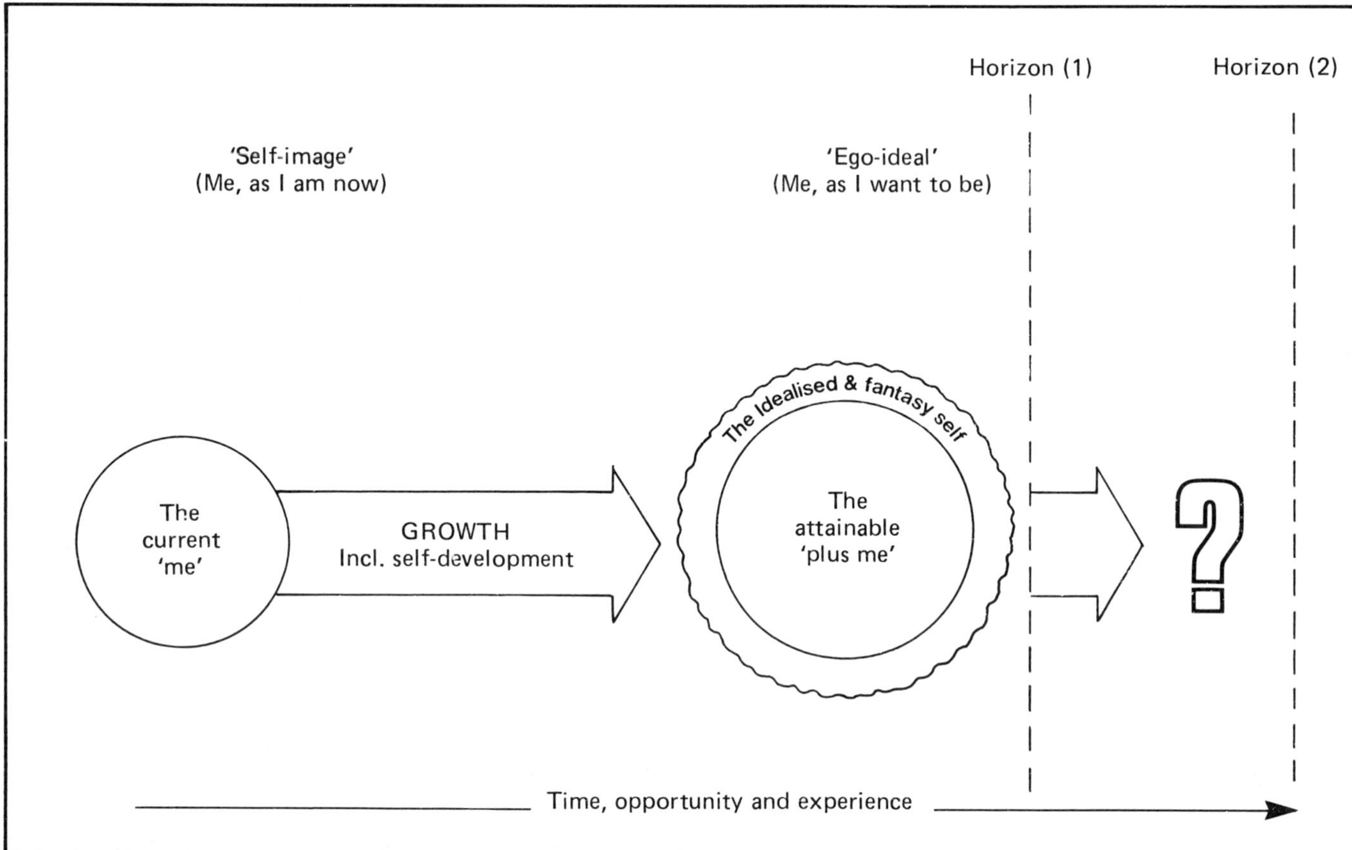

Figure 32.1 Personal growth

manager's performance, especially his behaviour in role and, therefore, his *management style*. The evidence of his immediate boss, his boss's superior, his peers and his subordinates represents crucial feedback to help him identify his real training and development needs for himself.

Informal performance reviews by his boss, periodic discussions with colleagues whose opinions and judgement he values, together with the data available to him from formal appraisal interviews all help him to place himself in relation to the demands of his job. Similarly, discussions with effective and experienced management development or training managers should provide valuable feedback and insights into how others see him and his contribution.

The process of feedback, however, is often best enhanced by *disclosure*, that is by disclosing expectations, needs or concerns which invite response and discussion. By specifically asking for information about personal effectiveness, management style, role as a colleague or boss, or contributions as a subordinate, a manager can build up a picture of both confirmatory and contradictory evidence about his perceived competence in his job. For example, he can turn what is so often the rather sterile ritual of the annual appraisal into a fruitful discussion by taking the initiative himself and encouraging his boss to ask the right questions. By using a simple self-appraisal instrument which more or less parallels the questions and areas of analysis of the company appraisal form he can prepare himself (and his reviewer) for a worthwhile and relevant diagnosis of his real performance improvement or development needs. One of the hallmarks of the really effective manager or specialist is his capacity to 'manage upwards'.

Influencing superiors is not the same as falling into the trap of self-weakening by *delegating* authority and responsibility upwards. Rather, it means letting a boss know exactly what you need from him, in order to do your own job more effectively. Equally, it means finding out from him where he needs you to change your behaviour in some way. The process is about helping a superior to act as a necessary and appropriately supportive source of organisational authority in order to open doors or give sanction to requisite innovation. Some managers may well feel vulnerable when the significance of their epaulets is drawn to their attention by a subordiante who is saying, in effect – 'Come on, you're the boss, so act like one and give me the authority to go and do what we need to get done'.

Generally most major or far-reaching changes require management at at least three levels within the organisation, as Figure 32.2 illustrates. First, there is the level at which the innovation or change is to be implemented. Immediately above that is the superior who may have to go out on a limb in order to give the necessary 'go-ahead' – hence the sense of vulnerability at this level. Then, above him is the 'umbrella' often necessary to provide senior managerial or organisational cover for the venture, even though all the evidence suggests that the change will result in necessary performance improvement.

Much of the art of the process lies in the extent to which both joint and mutually exclusive areas of accountability are identified and spelled out. In this way, mutual perceptions and expectations about obstacles to effective results and about opportunities that should or should not be exploited can be clarified.

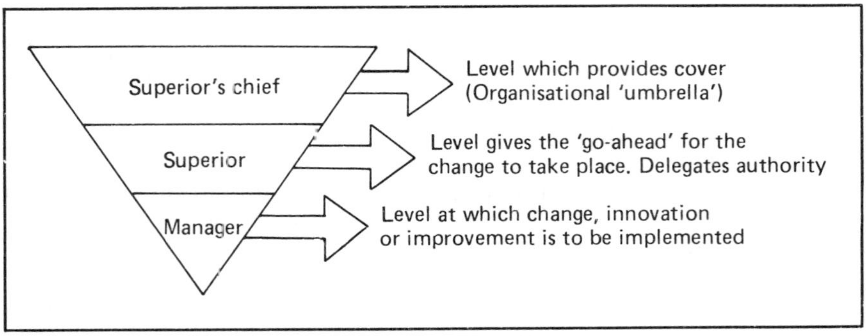

Figure 32.2 ***Hierarchical support needed for change to be implemented.*** *This diagram shows the levels of support required to implement and sustain far-reaching change and improvement*

Such disclosure and feedback need to be 'core' features of any boss-subordinate relationship in management, as a matter of course not just during periods of innovation and change. As an essential part of the personal (and hopefully mutual) stocktake which is what the annual performance appraisal should be, then at least the following questions need to be raised and worked through from the subordinate's point of view:

1. 'These are what I see as my current priorities'
2. 'This is what I believe(d) you (my boss) expect(ed) from me' or 'This is what I believe is/was expected of me in my job'
3. 'These are the results I believe I have achieved'
4. 'This is what I feel I have done well'
5. 'This is where I see I need to improve'
6. 'This is where/how I need you (my boss) to act on my behalf (or to give me support) in order for me to do my job more effectively'
7. 'These are areas where I see our relationship as
   - Good
   - Less than satisfactory
8. 'What do you need me to do differently in order for you to
   - act more effectively as my boss?
   - do your own job more effectively?'
9. 'I see these as my main training development needs'
10. 'What training or development do you feel I need?'

THE 'FLY-ON-THE-WALL'

A process which provides detailed minute-by-minute data about a manager's role and performance over several short periods of time is that of direct observation, accompanied by feedback and discussion. The purpose of the observation is to identify, record and review what a manager actually *does* in the course of several working days. Observation takes the form of a 'fly-on-the-wall' technique, which involves the observer sitting in with the manager so that the latter's every work activity can be recorded under appropriate headings and subsequently fed back to him for review and analysis. As a tool for learning, self-development and performance improvement it is invaluable, given an observer who is a credible, competent and sensitive individual in whom the manager being observed has confidence. The observer therefore may be a management development or training manager, external consultant, colleague, superior, or in some cases a subordinate.

The process can be structured to suit the situation, status and role of the manager being observed and the relationship between the observer and the observed. A case study later in this chapter illustrates a structured observation over a period of several hours. The subject in this case was a typical middle manager at work. His activities have been recorded in detail, in this format, in order to provide him with accurate data about:

1 How he spends his time in a variety of management situations, covering a range of managerial activities. In particular, where he needs to create periods of uninterrupted time for himself.
2 Where he could or should delegate and make greater use of other people – especially his secretary
3 In which situations and with which people he needs to control his 'boundaries' more effectively by developing more assertive approaches
4 How he could acquire vital information from other functions in a more timely way, with less effort
5 Where he needs to develop a more effective 'eyes and ears', or 'field intelligence' service through other people to reduce the amount of time he personally spends seeking information.

The amount of time required and frequency of observation for a 'fly-on-the-wall' exercise will vary, dependant upon –

1 The purpose and intended outcomes of the observations
2 The role and nature of the activities of the manager under observation
3 Whether or not remedial work is to begin after the first session or commence once all observation is at an end and diagnostic feedback has been completed.

Generally the process takes place in four or five phases, which are described below.

Phase 1: Initial discussion and decision to mount the exercise

This includes:

1 Agreement of the 'contract' between the observer and his client about mutual expectations and intended outcomes (N.B. the client may well not be the person to be observed; it could be his immediate superior, or other more senior executive)
2 Ice-breaking and establishment of relationship between observer and observed

3 Agreement on whether to hold observation sessions on set dates, or turn up on a random basis
4 Confirmation of what are and are not legitimate activities for observation.

Phase 2: Observation

This phase may consist of any number of sessions but, typically, four or five half-days over a period of two weeks represents the minimum necessary. During those sessions the observer is virtually 'glued' to the manager so that he may record the latter's activities and *reactions* in adequate detail. Normally the observer will use a log with appropriate headings under which he can detail what he sees happening (or not happening, since part of the observer's role during later stages will be to talk through significant omissions in the observed manager's behaviour). A typical log is illustrated in the case study later in this chapter (see Figure 32.3). Codes used are also explained in the case study. Others may be added as necessary. This is largely a matter of matching the tool to the task and evolving a relevant shorthand vocabulary which is convenient and quick to use.

Phase 3: The feedback stage

At this stage copies of the log are given to the manager. This may be done either at the end of each observation session, when his memory is fresh, or as a complete 'package' at the end of the exercise.

To stimulate review and analysis and to help the manager draw out the necessary learning points the observer usually works through a series of relevant questions, typified by the following:

1 How far do the observations match your understanding of what happened?
2 Are there any surprises in the data contained in the log?
3 Does time actually spent on some activities fit your recollections of the time you believed you spent?
4 What can you learn about the way you analyse situations, make decisions and take action?
5 When are you most effective? Which situations do you handle well?
6 When are you least effective? Which situations could you handle better?
7 What could and should you be delegating?
8 How well do you plan against contingencies and cope with events that you could not plan for?
9 How effective are you in obtaining the information you need to do your job?
10 How well do you warn others of impending difficulties, or actions likely to affect them?
11 What exactly do you need to do differently in order to be more effective at your job?

12 From all the above data what skills do you need to improve in order to be more effective and how best can you develop them?

Phase 4: The action plan stage

Both the data presented and the manager's response to that feedback provide the basis for his personal development action plans. Where appropriate the action plans may well be discussed with the manager's superior and a specialist from the personnel department or an external consultant. The plans need to be implemented and followed through to ensure that the requisite changes in operation, management style and personal development *are* taking place.

Phase 5

As a variation on a theme, a team workshop consisting of all the managers who have been through a 'fly-on-the-wall' exercise may be run to confirm development needs and action plans to meet the needs. Each manager (who is well known to the others) presents the essence of his feedback and the lessons drawn from it, together with his action plans for treatment. These are added to, modified and ratified by his colleagues or team mates on the basis of their knowledge of him. They are then implemented by the team on a mutually supportive basis which ensures a high level of monitoring, review and follow-through.

SELF-DEVELOPMENT – CASE STUDY IN ACTIVITY ANALYSIS

John Walton is a transport manager. In this exercise the procedure is described by which over three hours of his working day were recorded on an activity log in order to obtain an impression of his typical work pattern. The activity key looks fairly complicated, but it becomes relatively simple when considered under the four right-hand columns, as described below.

Format of the activity log

A proforma is used to record the activities, with the layout shown in Figure 32.3. A shorthand key is used to speed up the entry process and condense data into the limited space available on the form. In this example, the shorthand codes used were as follows:

Time start/ finish	Activity or event	Situation (sit)	Category (cat)	Behaviour (beh)	Who else involved

Figure 32.3 Format for activity log

Under 'sit' (the situation in which the individual was observed)

AW working alone
TI taking an incoming telephone call
TO making an outgoing telephone call
D discussion with one other person
MI meeting – informal
MF meeting – formal
O outside own office

The above can be used in combination, and might have been supplemented by:

WSP with superior

WSB with subordinate
WSBS with more than one subordinate
AD dictating to secretary
AT working alone – thinking

Under 'cat' (the category of managerial activity observed) the codes used were:

PA establishing causes of problems
SA clarifying situations or problems
GD giving data/information
BV briefing verbally
XCA checking data for relevance and accuracy
SDI seeking data/information
E evaluating or reviewing progress
O organising
OGI organising and giving instructions
RH requesting and requiring help

Other possibilities which might have been used under this heading are:

DA making decisions (choosing between alternatives)
P planning
PP protecting the plan (contingency planning)
CO controlling
S social chat
A arbitrating

The following codes were applied under the 'beh' column, where the behaviour of the observed individual was recorded

PA positive/assertive
LA listening attentively
Q questioning
D disagreeing
X confused
U constructive
C composed (when under stress)

To these codes might have been added:

UN uncertain/indecisive
CR critical
DI dominant
DG domineering
E emotional
DF defensive
SWO switched off
DY switched on (dynamo)
GA playing psychological games
AG aggression
H humour
NU nurturing/building

Codes under 'who else'

are simply the initials of others involved in the observed situation

Activity log for Mr John Walton

The activity log compiled for John Walton is shown complete in Figure 32.4. The impression gained is that the period of observation involved activities and work patterns which were typical of John Walton's normal work load and working style. Assuming this to be so, then what emerges as a representative picture is the following:

1 About 5 per cent of his time is free to work alone (thinking and planning time)
2 95 per cent of his time is spent face-to-face with someone, or on the telephone
3 50 per cent of his time is spent seeking information and clarifying situations
4 30 per cent of his time is spent giving instructions or briefing
5 The remainder is spent in arranging/organising transport, solving problems, etc.

Some questions raised by the analysis

Given that the above *is* typical of John's working day then some questions that need to be asked are:

1 How could JW create more thinking and planning time for himself?
2 How much of the time he personally spends chasing up data and information could be reduced by
   - using other information sources (production planning and control)
   - delegating to his subordinates the task of securing much of the information
   - the introduction of an up-to-the-hour information service to JW from production (or production planning and control)?
3 How much more, generally could and should he use his subordinates and push responsibility for solving problems back down to them?
4 The very nature of a transport manager's role, especially when combined with that of chief despatcher, is fraught with fire-fighting problems. Being at the 'end of the line' inevitably means collecting everyone else's rubbish, to some extent.
   BUT, there is much that JW's immediate superior could do to reduce the pressure on John by
   - sitting down with him and analysing the what, how, when and who of JW's work
   - assuming a higher profile and more assertive stance in managing the boundaries between finishing and transport/despatch.

   Ultimately, of course, many of the decision to delegate or not delegate rest with John himself.

Manager observed: John Walton
Position : Transport manager
Date(s) observed : 3 August 19XX
Times observed : 11.09am-12.30pm and 1.45pm-3.45pm

Time on/off	Subject/activity/event	sit	cat	beh	who else?
11.09		AW	PA	PA	
11.10	Arthur collects notes on transport routes	D	SA	LS	ART
11.11	Graphic statistics – analysing what, where and when	D	SA	Q	BRI
11.12	Cehcking details/facts/figures with supervisor	D	SA	Q	
			PA	PA	BRI
11.13	J. goes out to collect outwork book, disagrees on section III; agrees on sections I and II	D	SA	D	BRI
			GDI	PA	BRI
			BV	Q	BRI
	J. seeking reliable accurate information		BV	X	BRI
	(given contradictory 'facts')			Q	
11.18			SA	U	
11.19	Telephone call to Transport Haulage Company	TO	SDI	PA	
	– seeking information on lorries and drivers		SDI	Q	
11.26	– ? work completion notes to clerk	D	E	PA	CLE
11.27	Recommences work with BRI	D	BV	PA	BRI
11.28	Query work in progress	AW	O	PA	NEV
11.28	Telephone call	TI	SDI	PA	
11.28	Second telephone rings (J. also takes this one over from secretary)	TI	SA	PA	
11.29	First call finished and first 'phone rings again	TI	SDI	PA	Visitor
11.31	Organising people to do things, including	D	SA	PA/Q	Secret
11.35	gathering information	D	OGI	PA	MIK
		D	OGI	PA	DON
11.38	Given more wrong data	MO	SA	X	TER
	(goes out to TER next door)				
	Checks paperwork with loader (loader unhelpful)	MO	SDI	PA	LOA
11.39	Wrong feedback – visitor gets data/information	D	SA	XQ	DON
	mixed up	D	SDI	Q	
11.40	Talks to driver	D	GI	PA	Driver
		D	SA	PA	
11.40	Clarifying delivery situation on goods	D	SA	PA/Q	MIK
11.42	Discussion with driver – gives more information	D	GI	PA	Driver
11.46	Reaffirms delivery date on goods	D	SA	PA	MIK
11.47	MIK returns regarding possible shortages	D	E	Q/PA	MIK
11.47	Checks numbers of 'look in'	MO	GI	Q	TER
11.52	Checks/queries tonight's deliveries	D	GI	LS	PAC
11.55	Gives routes/delivery runs and quantities	D	SA	PA	BRI
12.00	Request for transport	TO	RH	PA	
			XCA	Q	
12.05	Availability of drivers' mates for twilight shift	TO	SI	Q	RON
			DA	PA	
12.07	Call for information (no-one there)	TO	RH	Q	
12.09	Request to J. for transport and driver	TI	GDI	PA	ANON
	J. goes out to talk to driver	MO	SDI	Q	Driver
12.13	Request for situation report	TI	GDI	PA	RAY
			DA	PA	

Figure 32.4 Activity log compiled for John Walton, Transport Manager
Entries would, in practice, be hand-written

Time on/off	Subject/activity/event	sit	cat	beh	who else?
12.14	Checks up on transport availability	TO	SDI	Q	VIC
		D	SA	PA	TER
	Do we have a car? Do we have a driver?		SA	Q	
12.19	Spare driver?	D	SA	Q	MIK
12.19		TO	SA	Q	CLI
12.20	Situation report	D	E	PA	MIK
12.21	No driver	TO	GDI	PA	
12.22	Briefing caller	TI	BV	PA	RAY
			GDI	PA	WIL
12.23	Situation report	D	BV	PA	MIK
		TI	DA	PA	PAU
		D	SA	PA	WIL
		TO	GDI	PA	CLE
12.25					
12.28					
LUNCH					
1.49	Planning procedures	D	GDI	PA	CLE
1.51	Making up loads for tomorrow	AW	DA	PA	CLE
2.06	Phone call	TI		PA	?
2.11	Clarifying schedule	D	PA	PA	MIK
2.12	Taking message	TI	A	PA	DIC
2.14	Phone (wrong number)	TI	A	PA	?
2.15	Call TER	TO		PA	out
2.17	TER calls back	TI	XCA	Q	TER
2.22	Goods (southern deliveries)	TI	SDI	Q	PAT
2.24	Meeting	MI	SDI	Q	NOR
			GI	PA	
2.28	Goods (midlands deliveries)	TO	SA	Q	PAT
2.30	Parcel arrives – goods components				PET
2.31	Makes out rail notes	MIO	DSI	PAQ	
2.32	Clarifying/explaining procedures	TI	E/BV	PA	CLI
	+ action: sorts out detail		O/DA	QPA	JON
2.42	Parking ticket from driver	M	XCA	QPA	Driver
2.42	Clock card	D	GI	PA	PAC
2.44		D	GI	PA	Driver
2.50	Calls for notes	D	SA	X	Driver
2.57	Writing	D	SA	PA	CLE
2.57	Sorts out midlands/north deliveries	D	E/ GDI	C	ART
3.09	Delivery of two reels of cable	D	SDI	Q	Driver
3.10	Electricians call	TI	BV	QPA	RAY
3.15	Ring for transport	TO	SA	PA	PAU
3.22	Needs information for PAT for goods (southern)	D	DA	PA	Visitor
3.24	Despatch priorities: goods (southern)	D	SA	PA	DER
3.28	Phone call	TI	SA	PA	DON
	Another call holding		SA	Q	ADR
	OBSERVER REJOINS PERSONNEL DEPARTMENT				

Figure 32.4 (continued)

5 Finally, there is the question of organisation. Is the structure of work done and current reporting relationships appropriate or is there a need to rethink and reorganise the whole question or ordering and using transport both at incoming and outgoing stages? This is obviously a far wider issue but inevitably the organisation structure is a major determinant of work loads, work patterns and comparative efficiency/inefficiency of managerial time.

ACHIEVEMENT OBJECTIVES AS A MEANS FOR SELF-DEVELOPMENT

Used either as a natural consequence of discussions at the end of a 'fly-on-the-wall' exercise or as an alternative approach, specific achievement objectives can lend structure, direction and impetus to a manager's self-development. Based on a diagnosis of needs, set within the context of a manager's role and agreed with his boss, achievement objectives represent yardsticks of attainment against which the manager can measure his performance and development.

Obviously the practice of setting objectives takes various forms in business. These range from formalised management by objectives (MBO) schemes to informal (but specific) targets set between bosses and their subordinates or within a work group set up to resolve a particular problem. The very process of management is about moving from a current situation (X) to a requisite state of affairs (Y) – usually within a set time limit. Typically managers work to the basic criteria as part of their day-to-day role, namely: quantity (how many and how much); quality (how well done or in what manner); cost (how much in financial terms); deadline (by when started/completed).

At the most senior levels philosophy, policies and strategies are normally based upon certain corporate goals – even though they may be sometimes more implicit than explicit. Normally corporate objectives are then translated appropriately at different levels down the line so that, necessarily, there will be a mandatory aspect to manager's objectives as well as a discretionary one.

In setting and agreeing personal achievement objectives as a means of stimulating self-development and improving managers' effectiveness, the diagram in Figure 32.5 illustrates the basic scope open to bosses and their

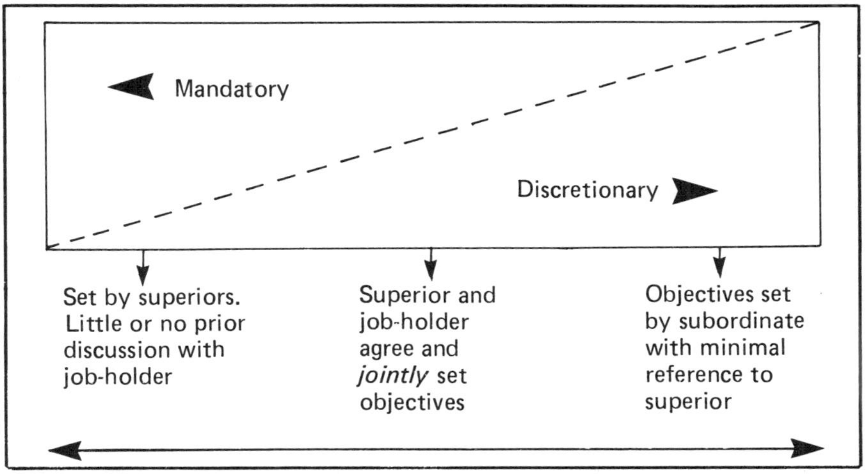

Figure 32.5 ***The extent to which objective setting between superiors and subordinates may be mandatory or discretionary***
Some objectives will be mandatory themselves by their very nature (budget targets for instance) but how they are to be achieved may be largely discretionary within the boss-subordinate relationship

subordinates. That scope can be refined by a structure which enables managers to select, define and sharpen objectives in a disciplined way that more closely relates the performance of individuals to the goals of others.

First, it is helpful to determine what objectives are and what they are not. Management objectives:

are	*are not*
required results	activities
achievements	effort
accountabilities	duties
what is required	how it must be done
'musts'	'shoulds'

Secondly, there are different types of management objective. The principal categories are those which reflect the results to be achieved, under the following headings:

1 targets: to meet a deadline, programme of activities or product launch
2 improvements: for example, to increase profitability levels, productivity rates or quality standards
3 resolution of specific problems: examples are the removal of obstacles or constraints in order to correct deviations and restore previous conditions
4 innovation and change: this would include introducing and implementing something new which represented a departure from previous practice
5 control: aimed at ensuring or maintaining a given set conditions
6 personal or team development: principally aimed at acquiring the behavioural knowledge and levels of skill needed to operate more completely.

Undoubtedly some areas of activity are easier to measure than others in terms of results. It is usually possible to apply at least one specific, quantified objective. This is particularly the case where the type of objective has been determined ('target', 'improvement', 'problem solving', 'innovation' and so on). Even in areas of activity such as research and development or operational research, where the final outcomes might be very difficult to predict realistically, it is still possible to set quantified objectives. This can be done by making the objectives of the form 'submit and present an interim report at the progress review meeting on 13 May and show all findings to date' (for example).

Objectives need to be realistic, attainable, accurate and expressed in clear language if they are to appear credible and relevant as a self-development exercise. They must not be couched in vague terms. For example:

1 'Reduce the use of consumable materials on numbers 1 and 2 lines to budget level by the end of December, and by a further 10 per cent by the end of March' NOT 'Cut down drastically on consumables'
2 'Submit proposals by the end of the month for reducing steel procurement costs by at least 12 per cent. Method: by the use of alternative transport arrangements from the mills' NOT 'Investigate methods for reducing steel procurement costs'
3 'Revise your own and your subordinates' job descriptions by mid-January,

clarifying the principal accountabilities for each person. Progressively ensure that only agreed principal accountabilities are retained and that all other work is delegated and reallocated to section heads by 31 January' NOT 'Delegate as much work as possible to subordinates'.

In some organisations people of high potential may be deliberately moved into the 'fast line' in terms of career progression by being appointed to specially designed 'development posts'. Although they usually carry out necessary functions the real purpose of their move is to groom them for a more senior, longer term position. In most organisations this probably does not happen and only selected tasks and objectives may be available for the jobholder's development. Where this is the case the opportunities for self-development could well lie outside the mainstream of the role in the areas of:

- Short-term tasks and objectives
- Priority objectives
- Innovation and change programmes
- Trouble shooting and problem solving

Figure 32.6 represents the typical structure of many managerial jobs where objectives are divided between main-stream and short-term goals.

SOME VEHICLES FOR SELF-DEVELOPMENT

Once the task and personal objectives have been agreed, there is the question of work opportunities through which to achieve those objectives and ensure the process of development. A crucial factor in the process is the extent to which the manager's boss facilitates his subordinate's self-development by:

- providing the necessary 'trigger' and encouragement
- sustaining and restimulating it
- capitalising on it to the advantage of both the individual and the organisation
- pressing on the appropriate 'nerves' when unnecessary obstacles get in the way

Learning is fundamental to self-development and most people in managerial roles tend to learn as the result of *experience*. However, that experience needs to be analysed, discussed and worked through in order to draw the appropriate lessons from it.

Learning by experience, within a management job, is likely to involve the 'learner' in at least:

- *doing* – followed by analysis and review
- experimenting with new or different experiences and activities
- questioning and testing out existing knowledge, custom and practice, prejudices, values and beliefs
- experiencing (and reviewing) both success and failure
- examples and models (other managers) against which the learner can compare, assess and, if necessary, modify his own management style
- study and reflection, in order to put experience into perspective and context.

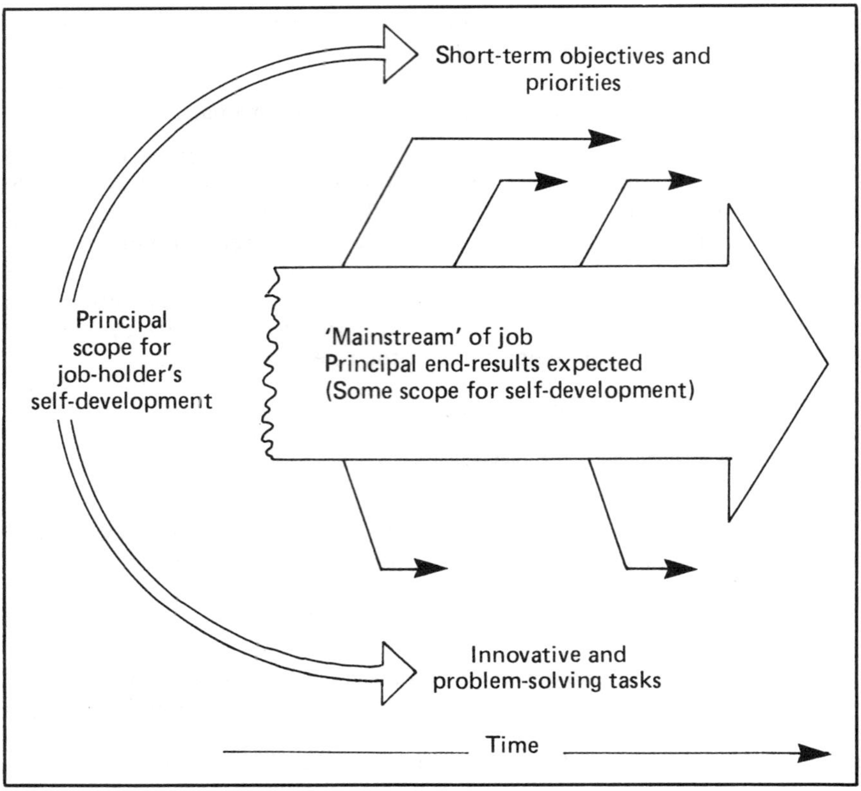

Figure 32.6 Scope for self-development within managerial jobs

Well-tried learning vehicles which provide opportunity for experiential learning and self-development include the following:

1 Keeping a work diary which is reviewed daily or, at least weekly, by the learner with his boss and/or a management development specialist
2 Setting up projects which are *relevant* and *realistic* and which have *real pay-off* for the company, the department and/or the individual. Such projects often carry far more weight when there is major representation to be made by the trainee to the chief executive or a senior panel, so that a sense of occasion is attached to the experience and it is seen to be important.
3 Cross-functional assignments involving multi-disciplinary teams of subordinates working together (for example marketing, product planning and engineering or production, industrial engineering and finance) where end results rely on co-operative, co-ordinated effort
4 Presentations on key issues – or contributions to key issues – to top management

5 Team development workshops in which members review:
   - 'our key objectives and priorities'
   - 'obstacles to achieving them'
   - 'my personal contribution to the team's goals'
   - 'our strengths and weaknesses as a team and as team members'
   - 'our action plan for the next 12 months'
6 'Bespoke' tutorials for individuals or groups using external professionals who test thinking and action plans by inputs of expertise, rigorous questioning and a wider perception
7 'Action learning', involving co-operation with managers from other companies and organisations, in the identification and resolution of each other's operational problems
8 Participation in junior 'boards', working parties, 'think tanks' or research teams, with or without senior executives involved, but where the outcomes are deemed to be important and relevant
9 Deputising for the boss:
   - by representing him at meetings, or on committees
   - visiting important external contacts, on his behalf
   - acting in his capacity for days/weeks/months at a time as appropriate.
10 Setting-up and running an entirely new product, department, function or small subsidiary company
11 Lecturing on personal accountability or a field of expertise to:
   - internal courses and seminars
   - professional courses run by universities, polytechnics or local colleges
   - educational programmes run by national, local or professional bodies
12 Planned reading, regularly reviewed and discussed with the trainee by one or more of the following acting in a mentor role:
   - his immediate superior
   - his superior's chief
   - appropriate in-company specialists, managers or supervisors
   - external professionals.

   Planned reading also involves keeping up-to-date by regularly choosing different areas of developing technology, important disciplines or relevant current events and systematically scanning the appropriate professional journals.

These, then, represent some of the learning opportunities that are available to enable a manager's self-development to take place at little or no cost to the company and with minimal interference with the day-to-day job that he is there to do.

The term 'self-development' means exactly what it says. The real drive to make it happen must come from within the individual himself, but his superiors can do much to ensure an encouraging supportive climate in which self-development can thrive and become regenerative.

SOURCES AND RESOURCES

Some organisations and bodies concerned with self-development

Organisation	*Contacts*
Anglian Regional Management Centre High Street, Stratford, London E15 2JB 01-590 7722	I. Cunningham
Association of Teachers of Management Polytechnic of Central London, 35 Marylebone Road, London NW1 5LS 01-486 5811	M. Greatorex
Centre for the Study of Management Learning, University of Lancaster, Gillow House, Lancaster LA1 4YX Lancaster 65201	J. Burgoyne R. Boot
Hodgson Myers Assoc. 103 Walton Street, Oxford, OX2 6EB Oxford 52353	A. M. Hodgson
The Open University, Walton Hill, Milton Keynes, Milton Keynes 74066	B. Lund
Polytechnic of Central London School of Management Studies 35 Marylebone Road, London NW1 5LS 01-486 5811	J. Bowden
Sheffield City Polytechnic Pond Street, Sheffield S1 1WB Sheffield 738621	M. Pedler T. Boydell
Michael Williams & Partners 27 Ferndale Park, Pedmore, Stourbridge, West Midlands DY9 0RB Hagley 884405	M. Williams

FURTHER READING

Austin, B., *Time and the Essence – A Manager's Workbook for Using Time Effectively*, British Institute of Management, 1979
Boydell, T. and Pedler M. (eds.), *Management Self-Development*, Gower, 1981
Hague, H., *Helping Managers to Help Themselves*, Context Training
Humble, J. W., *Management by Objectives*, Gower, 1975
Jaap, T., *The Steps to Self-Development*, Human Resource Associates
Mumford, A., *Real Learning – Making Experience Pay*, McGraw-Hill, 1980
Pedler, M., Burgoyne, J. and Boydell, T., *A Manager's Guide to Self-Development*, McGraw-Hill, 1978
Revans, R. W., *Action Learning*, Blond & Briggs, 1981
Toye, J., *Training for Versatility (Self Organised Learning)*, Industrial Training Unit (Cambridge)
Williams, M. R., *Coaching and Counselling*, The Leadership Trust (Symonds Yat)

33 Career planning

Michael Williams

At its simplest, career progression depends upon the interaction of two factors, or 'forces' – *personal ambition* and *organisation needs*. Figure 33.1 illustrates how these two forces act as the main determinants in the development of the individual's career path through his working life.

The more junior he is, the more will personal needs and ambition tend to be the predominant factor in the growth and direction of his career. By the time he has reached senior or top levels in the management hierarchy, the organisation's needs will usually be exerting the major influence over his career progression.

In up to thirty years in a managerial career the individual may have, typically, five or six different posts. It is unlikely that he will spend similar amounts of time in each. Generally, he may spend as little as one or two years in his earlier roles while in each of his final two posts he may spend seven, ten or more years, as Figure 33.2 shows.

The career 'plateau' apparent in this illustration may be due to many factors, both personal and organisational, but it might also be due to the onset of 'middlescence' and mid-career stagnation from which the individual never really recovers. The problem of 'died at forty, retires at sixty-five' is a common one and results in far too many career casualties, especially if there is an inadequate 'social support system' within the organisation to provide timely career counselling. Figure 33.3 shows the effects of the process on the career path of such a manager.

For many managers the mid-life period during the forties and early fifties may be something of a crucial personal 'stocktake'. It is for many a time of re-decisions, as well as decisions about career development, personal life and how the two can more satisfactorily co-exist. Fundamental reorganisation or technical change is also likely to have a significant impact upon the individual's career progression and, presupposing that the manager is prepared to respond to the organisation's needs, the picture of his career path may look like that shown in Figure 33.4. Similarly the shift from a predominantly technical role to

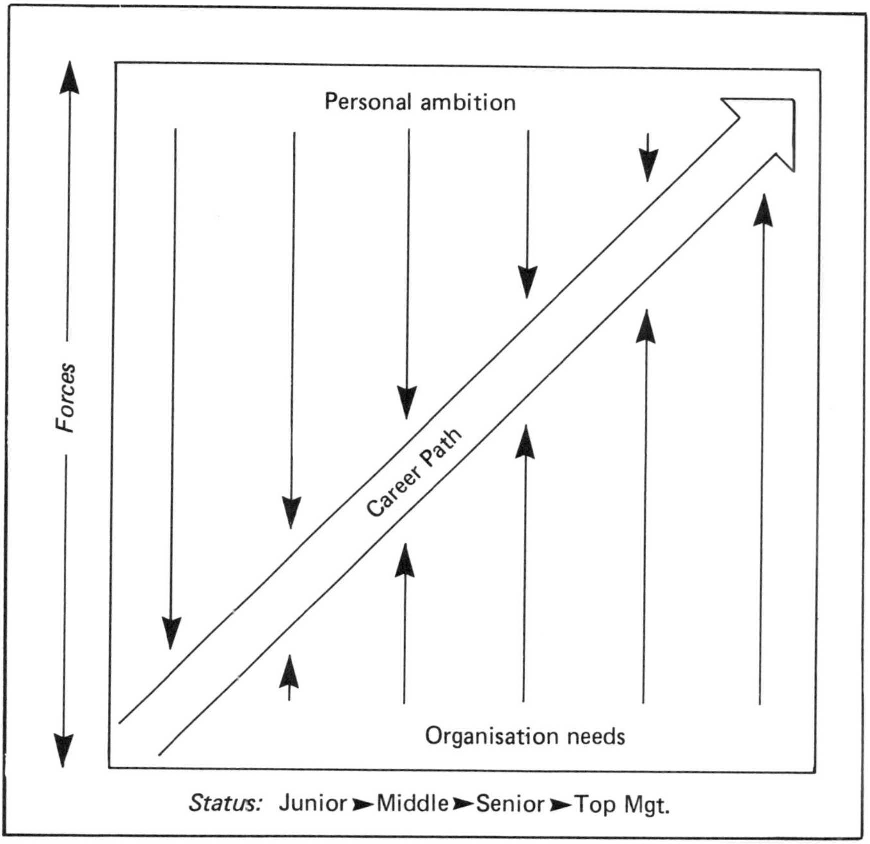

Figure 33.1 The influence of personal ambition and organisation needs on career development

largely managerial responsibilities which often comes with career progression to more senior levels will create learning demands upon the individual, as Figures 33.5 and 33.6 show. Whether the manager's career is largely one of transition from technical to managerial roles or a linear progression through the management hierarchy, the shift in the *type* of skills he will need to develop is depicted in Figure 33.7.

In the longer term, self-development needs to be related to the individual's career plans based upon where he or she wants to get to, within self-determined time scales.

The process begins when an individual starts by asking himself a whole series of personal questions such as:

1 What do I want from my career?
2 What don't I want from it?
3 What do I do well and what do I enjoy doing?

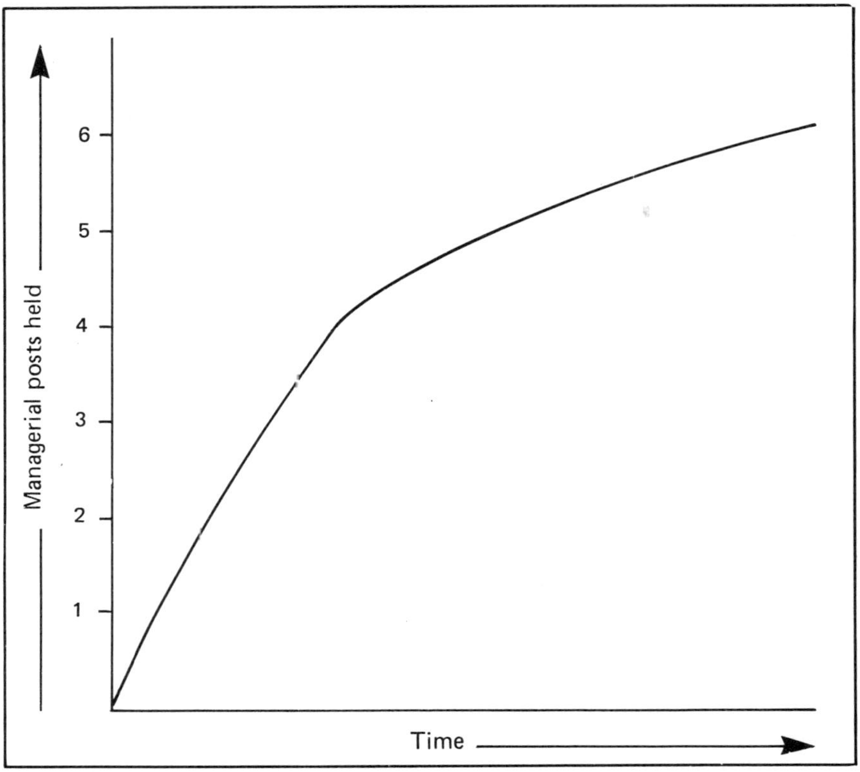

Figure 33.2 Typical managerial career progression

4 What do I want to be doing in two, five or ten years' time? Can I actually visualise the sort of job I want to be doing then?
5 What do I need to do better, or differently, to be more effective in my present job?
6 What do I need to do in order to prepare and develop myself for the jobs I believe I want to do in the future?
7 Where do I go to get the best possible help, guidance and advice about my career?

IDENTIFYING THE 'PLUS-ME' AND 'PLUS-JOB'

A first step to the process of deciding the right career path and self-development strategy might well take the form of a detailed personal 'stocktaking'. This involves identifying the 'plus-me' and 'plus-job' referred to in the previous chapter. The 'plus-me' exercise in Figure 33.8 invites you to make an assessment of you as you currently see yourself, and then to rate yourself (along the same dimensions) against the demands of effective performance in your current job. Simply use 'G' for good, 'S' to denote

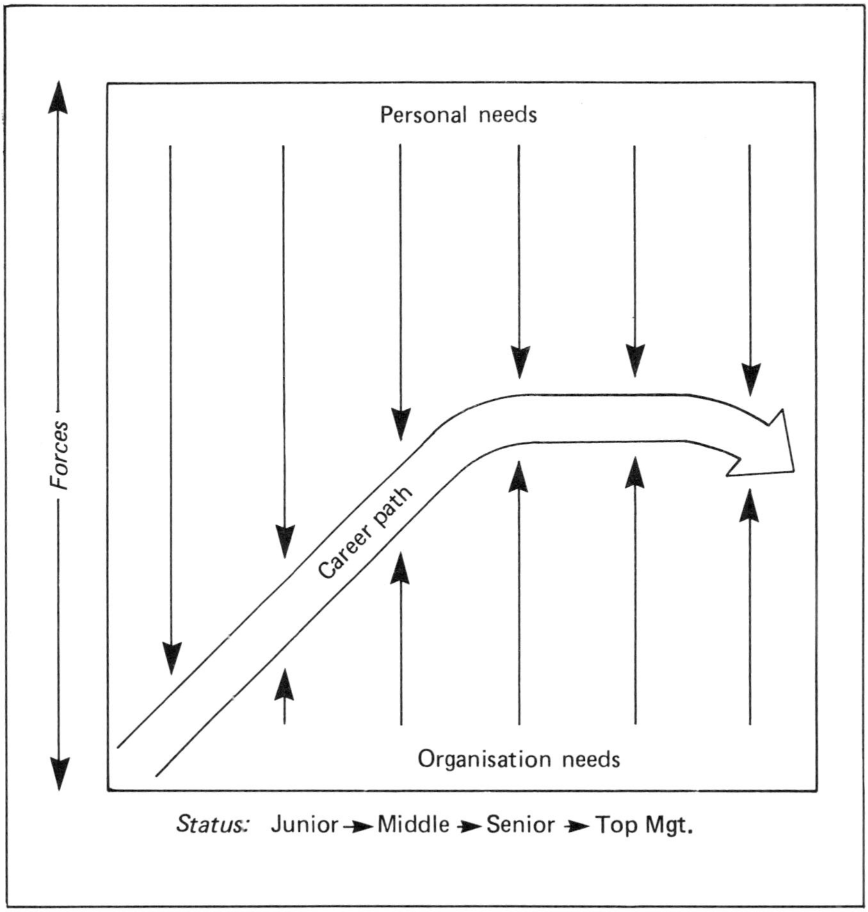

Figure 33.3 Impact of 'middlescence' on career path
This phenomenon appears to be complicated by a 'chicken and egg' argument about which comes first – the so-called 'mid-life crisis' or 'mid-career' crisis. The two are, however, often related.

'satisfied' with your performance or 'I' to indicate that improvement is needed.

When you have completed the 'As I am now' column, cover up your scores before filling in the right-hand column. When both columns have been completed, examine the results.

- What are your priorities for development action?
- Is there any pattern in your improvement needs – for instance, a lack of confidence – which inhibits your effectiveness?
- Are there any marked 'I' that you really cannot improve? How will you handle that?
- What about those marked 'G' – how will you build on those strengths and

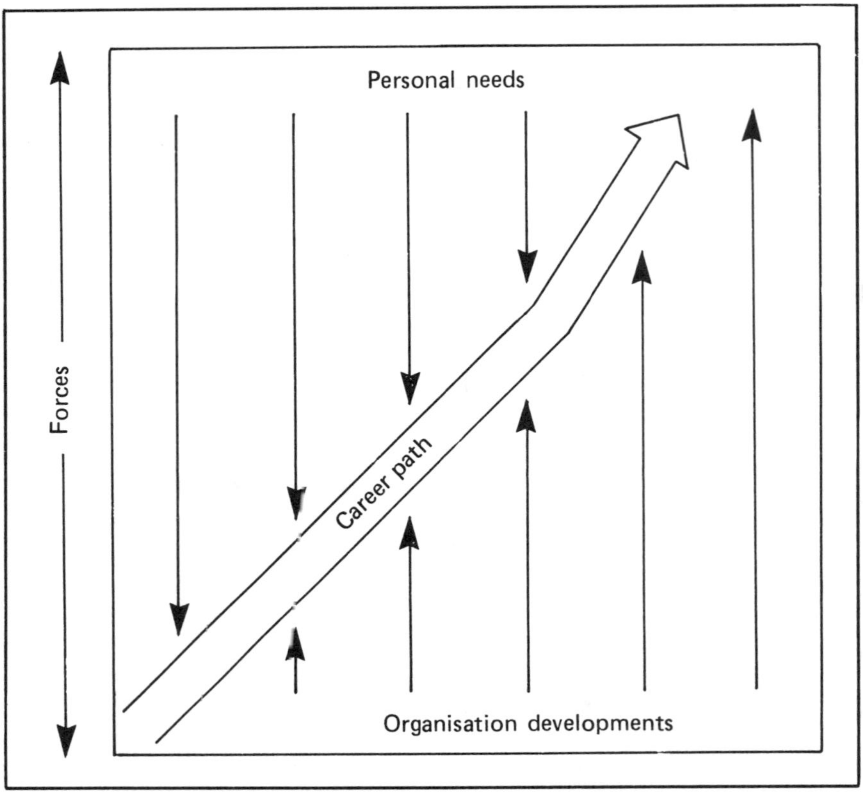

Figure 33.4 Influence of technological or major organisation developments upon career path

capitalise on them?
- What patterns emerge in your strengths? For instance are there any significant links between the 'G' scores? What clues do the patterns give you about your potential?
- What changes do you need to make to your job and work relationships to capitalise on the 'G' scores?
- What other key strengths do you have that make up your 'plus-me' and how do you intend to build on them?

The next part of the process is to consider your present role and the *attainable* 'plus-job' which may exist within it.

The 'plus-job' may not be your whole job, but the parts of it which match your strengths and which offer scope both for personal growth and increased contribution to your work group and your organisation. The 'plus-job' *consists of those activities that fulfil you and motivate you personally and professionally.*

Typically, the process takes the form illustrated in Figure 33.9.

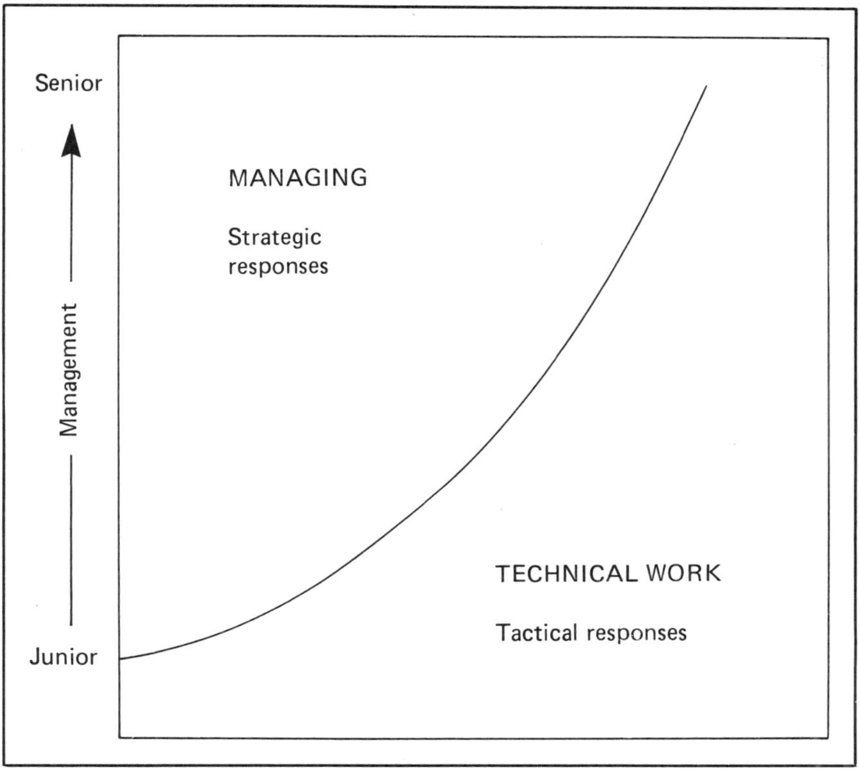

Figure 33.5 ***Shift in the nature of primary work***
Generally the more junior levels of management (especially in technical functions) are characterised by a considerable technical work content. This diminishes significantly with promotion, (although the manager may still cling to his original technical love)

1 Begin by listing those aspects of your work which are attainable within the overall scope of your current work which you identify as 'plus' features
2 Then against each of these features identify those strengths and positive attributes which you possess and which *strengthen* the plus aspects of your job. In other words, where do you excel, or have strengths, in the areas that motivate you?
5 Next, identify 'plus' features which you consider to be attainable in your present job, but which are not yet present
4 Against each of these potential plus features write what *action* you should take to make it feasible
5 Now, write down any personal strengths you possess, related to what you see as your 'plus-job'. Especially consider those which are not fully used at

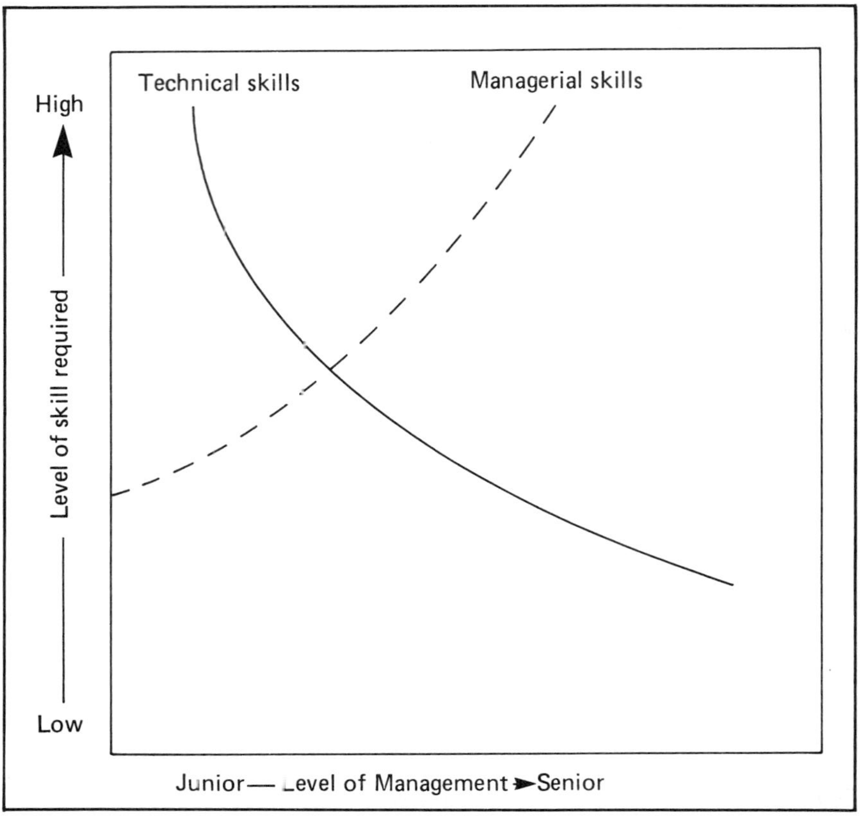

Figure 33.6 **Changing patterns of skills required to match primary work shift**

present and which you are therefore not developing as effectively as you could

6 Next, prepare an action plan for developing your attainable 'plus-job' and your strengths for discussion with your boss

7 Discuss it, implement what you can and follow through.

Particularly in the context of self-development and personal career planning, ' improvement' begins with 'I'. Other people are necessary to help the process, but only the individual himself has the ultimate responsibility for his development and growth.

CAREER TRANSITIONS

A considerable amount of research has gone into studies of the impact of major career changes upon executives and managers and most indicate that such transitions are usually accompanied by high stress and anxiety gaining the first

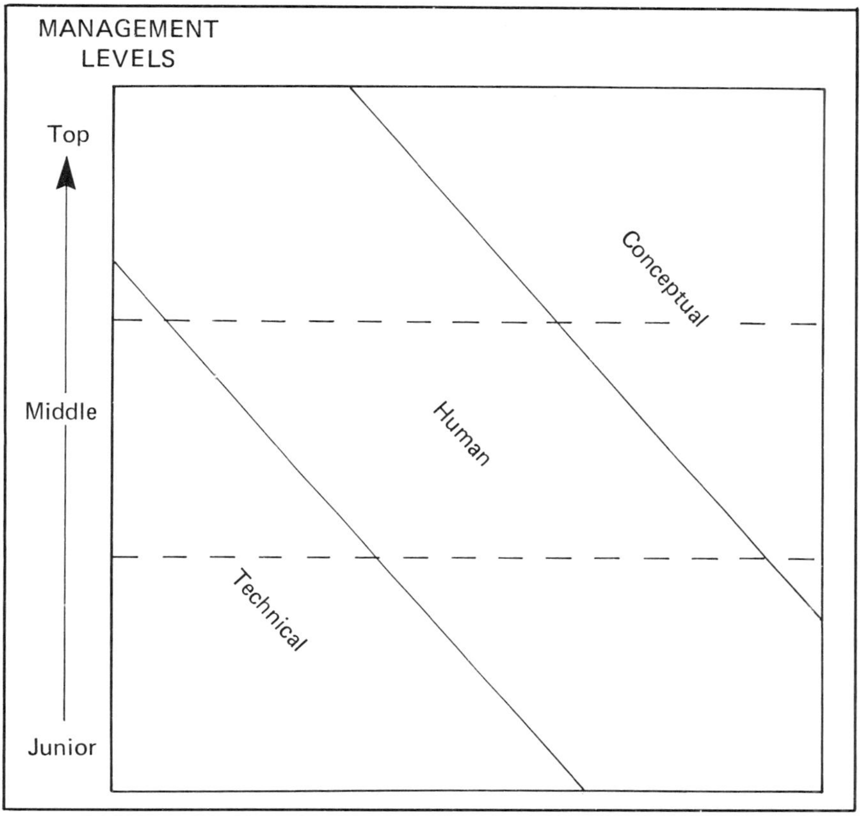

Figure 33.7 Evolving needs for different skills in 'linear' career progression
This figure shows the changing skills needed as the individual moves vertically through the hierarchy from supervisory or junior levels to the most senior executive posts

real job, obtaining significant promotion, feeling trapped in a routine 'prison', depression following redundancy, or apprehension about impending retirement are typical transition stresses.

At best, they are periods of considerable vulnerability where the individual may be unsure of

- what is expected of him in terms of skill, knowledge and performance
- whether he can cope with and come through the transition successfully
- what the ground rules, or guidelines (formal, or informal) are, which dictate how he should behave
- which are the key relationships he needs to make and use – especially who to turn to as the real source of support, help and guidance.

By definition, a crucial career transition occurs, through promotion, job stagnation, or job loss where the individual needs to *change* his

My Behaviour	As I am now	Demanded for success in my current job
1 Securing commitment from others		
2 Managing conflict.		
Giving praise and appreciation to others		
4 Getting enough praise and appreciation from others		
5 Defining problems accurately and realistically		
6 Exercising judgement in technical decisions		
7 Exercising judgement in managerial decisions		
8 Being sufficiently tough when I need to be		
9 Saying what I do, or don't, want from others		
10 Being assertive (*not* aggresive) when feeling insecure or threatened		
11 Listening effectively		
12 Confronting others who violate my basic rights		
13 Owning my own problems – and their solutions		
14 Asking for help when I need it		
15 Allowing others to manipulate me against my will		
16 Capacity to put my role and contribution into proper organisational context		
17 Giving unpopular instructions face-to-face		
18 Expressing myself when I need to in front of a group or audience		
19 Thinking before I speak		

Figure 33.8 The 'plus-me' exercise

20 Remaining in control of myself when under real pressure, face-to-face 21 Analysing situations thoroughly before acting 22 Giving encouragement 23 Giving others credit for their ideas 24 Taking risks in my decisions and actions 25 Collaborating with others		

Figure 33.8 (continued)

- beliefs, assumptions and perceptions about roles, jobs and possibly work itself
- relationships with superiors, peers and/or subordinates.

Both changes usually involve breaking new ground where a cycle of stages normally follows, including

exploration
↓
testing and probation
↓
building and consolidation
↓
re-charging and maintenance

These four phases of career progression relate, to some extent, to the stages of development identified by Dalton, Thompson and Price in *Organisation Dynamics* (issue No. 19, 1977):

Apprentice ⟶ Colleague ⟶ Mentor ⟶ and Sponsor

Both concepts suggest a series of transitions which 'peak-out' at some stage which, typically, is then followed by a significant change in role, influence and relationships.

However, *before* the peak is reached, there is usually – especially in managerial and technological career progression – a crucial move, often around the age of 35, which may have far-reaching consequences for the rate of climb to the peak, the level of the peak itself and possibly subsequent stages (see Figure 33.10).

Evidence from both surveys and writings about career progression suggest that many managers did not prepare for the crucial move as they subsequently feel they should have done. Equally, many feel that they were not helped by

'Plus' Features of Job	Personal Strengths
1 Dealing with large groups face-to-face	1.1 Confidence to get up and talk to people in groups 1.2 Ability to 'sway a crowd' 1.3 Keep cool under pressure
2 Taking significant decisions	2.1 Job knowledge 2.2 Innovative thinker
etc.	etc.

Figure 33.9 The plus job

their superiors, as much as they could have been, to understand and cope with the transition surrounding the crucial move in their careers. Role conflict and identity strains are two frequently cited problems facing managers and executives at this stage. Role conflict emerges because of the pressures imposed by the promotion upon the manager's domestic life, wider interests or clash with his previous life style at work. Identity strain often manifests itself in the form of confusion about

- how to relate to key figures in the organisation
- how to preserve 'territorial' rights and boundaries
- what to do about in-company 'politics' and what roles or stances to adopt
- what image to maintain and project and who to use as a model for management style

Neither role conflict nor identity strain is confined to the most crucial career change in the early- or mid-thirties. Such crises may occur at any stage in a manager's career, but particularly may re-emerge in a 'post-plateau' period, when the individual may find himself demoted, overtaken by far younger people, or made redundant. What is more, these two phenomena are likely to be aggravated, or considerably added to, by other stresses if they occur during post-plateau 'middlescence'.

For example, general anxiety and depression – the two 'common colds' of psychology – may well be at their most severe during the middle years, or mid-career crisis and may, additionally, give rise to: over-protective (but counter-productive) behaviour; increased resistance to change; loss of incentive and motivation; low morale; loss of tendency to innovate and take risks; increased suspicion of others' motives; withdrawal, self-imposed constraints and 'self-pity' cliques; or loss of perspective and sense of reality.

Any, or all of these, are likely to lead to a reduction in personal effectiveness, at a time when the individual's impact and contribution are of prime importance.

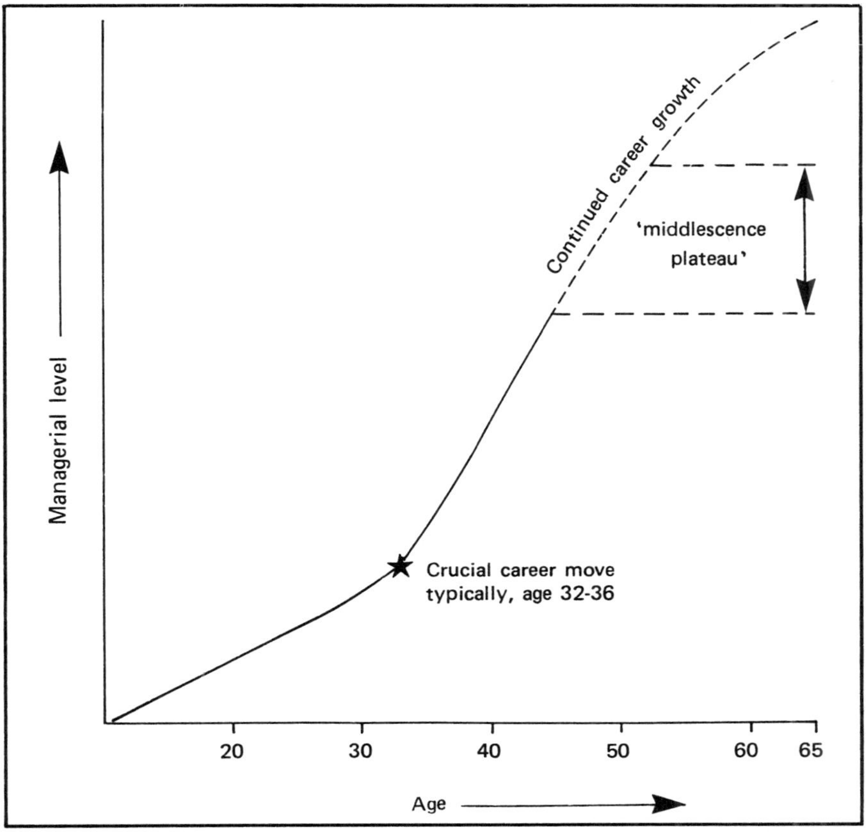

Figure 33.10 The crucial career move

WHAT CAN THE INDIVIDUAL MANAGER DO ABOUT CAREER PROGRESSION?

A fundamental need in career planning is *information* – whether the individual is:

- at a crucial stage in shaping his career
- about to lose his job
- conscious of being 'boxed-in', or on a plateau
- taking stock and considering the next stage
- close to retirement.

Another crucial need is likely to be for support, in the form of 'sounding boards' to test out perceptions, perspectives and options. The difficulty, here, is that of finding objective and valid views – or even other people's experiences which are closely related to one's own – and, therefore, an appropriate basis for comparison. Obviously vocational guidance specialists exist – both in private practice and in many city offices of the Department of Employment. Additionally several universities have conducted surveys into career planning, though much of the research is associated with mid-career crisis, redundancy and pre-retirement planning, rather than with the crucial 32–35 transitions. There are also books on the subject, which are worth reading, *selectively*, in order to pick up ideas about career planning and the crucial importance of preparing oneself systematically for job and role changes. Some of these texts are listed at the end of this chapter but one worth mentioning at this stage as a practical guide for women in management is *Managerial Woman* by Hennig and Jardim, published by Pocket Books of New York. Men normally have a wide range of executive 'models' provided by other male managers, executives and directors whose styles they can imitate, refine or avoid, as the case may be. By contrast, women still have comparatively few female success stories in the management world to provide suitable models.

Whether there is a proliferation or scarcity of managerial models, the problem remains of what to avoid and in which fields to ensure timely action is taken.

Probably the fastest disappearing years in any executive's life are those that take place between 35 and 40. Too often, managers find themselves living out their working lives and planning – or, rather *reacting* – on a day-to-day basis with little long-term thinking about their work, jobs, skill development, or managerial *style*. Specialists, particularly, are prone to career myopia and their preoccupation with their technological specialism, their pursuit of perfection or refinement of detail tends to inhibit long-term planning *away* from technology and into general management. If these patterns are well established, the chances are that the elusive years between 35 and 40 come and go with no energy having been put into conscious long-term career planning or development. The sudden awareness of one's own mortality – the true onset of 'middlescence' – usually coincides with the realisation that it is now too late to look forward to real advancement; and many managers drift into the mid-years plateau to escape into a niche, rut or sinecure and, eventually, retirement.

The effective counter is systematic long-term career planning at the early stages of managerial life. This involves identifying the many cues that signal a manager's need to

- acquire new knowledge and skills
- develop understanding of the managerial and business world in breadth, as well as technical depth
- experience leadership and managerial roles, where there is both accountability and the exercise of *authority*
- become increasingly aware of his own behaviour and the impact other people have upon his operational effectiveness
- recognise the supreme importance in management of self-confidence, which becomes more and more put to the test as the manager moves away from technology into line roles and general management.

Part of the process of career planning is to be aware of the personal 'horizons', referred to in the last chapter, rather than to try to assess 'ultimate potential'. Horizons, based upon the time spans of two or three years, within a context of a five- or ten-year planning period, provide the manager with realistic time scales within which to work out the experience, learning, training and development necessary to make the planned moves a reality. Finally, it is vital to accept that, come the point of transition, there will inevitably be the moving out of the 'womb' of familar roles, relationships and organisation into new fields where unfamiliar issues and problems must be confronted.

The tendency at such stages is to turn inwards, inhibited by anxiety and the wish to remain with the present, familiar world. It is, in fact, by turning *outwards*, to other people, that an objective view of the transition is to be had. By seeing how other people cope, by asking questions admitting to ignorance, the manager can acquire much of the necessary knowledge about his new role, *on the job*. The important thing is to get to know how the organisation *works*, who can provide what help, support and information and to recognise, as quickly as possible, the strengths and weaknesses of different executives' management styles in critical, but constructive and analytical, terms. In career planning - especially the development of realistic and flexible management styles - the manager's most powerful asset is an enquiring mind and a refusal to accept that the present way of doing things is necessarily the best. Too often, management practices become organisational sanctities, hallowed by little more than the passage of time - and that is no guarantee of effectiveness, especially in today's rapidly changing world.

FURTHER READING

Dalton, G., Thompson, P. H. and Price, R. L., 'The Four Stages of Professional Careers - A New Look at Performance by Professionals' *Organizational Dynamics*, 19 (1977)

Robertson, John P., *You and Your Next Job*, London, British Institute of Management, 1982

Sofer, C., *Men in Mid-Career: A Study of British Managers and Technical Specialists*, The University Press, Cambridge, England, 1970

Weiss, R. S., 'Transition States and Other Stressful Situations, Their Nature and Programs for Their Management', *in* G. Caplan and M. Killilea, eds., *Support Systems and Mutual Help: Multi-disciplinary Exploration*, Grune and Stratton, New York, 1976, pp 213–232

34 Personal organisation

A N Welsh

It has been suggested that the better manager is the better organised manager, who makes the best use of his time and best use of the time of his staff. However, just as there is no such thing as a born manager, so the effectiveness of a good manager cannot really be taught. *Effectiveness has to be learned* and the suggestions in this chapter are only some pointers as to how you can look at your work, develop a personal approach, and make the best use of your time.

THE NEED FOR PERSONAL ORGANISATION

When I had my first managerial job, I naturally found it very exciting and very demanding. I would come in on or before time, and to digress, a good manager should sometimes come in before time and perhaps stay after time. All sorts of things happen outside normal working hours: some people who get their work wrong or do not complete it within the day will stay behind or come back later to finish off, others will use company facilities for private purposes. However, I would come in on or before time and work furiously throughout the day, and by the end I had never completed all that had to be done and my head was full of all that was happening. In particular, I was concerned by matters affecting the well-being of others, and also attacks on my department's activities or my own standards of performance.

When I arrived home my head was buzzing and I would wake up in the middle of the night remembering things I had forgotten to do or thinking of new ideas. I had the choice then of lying awake during the rest of the night remembering whatever it was, or going to sleep again and forgetting the matter. At least I did not decide to hold a meeting about the situation!

CREATING A LIST

I listed all the jobs which I had to do, all the work in my in-tray and the functions which I had to supervise. I kept a diary, and a brought-forward file.

The latter in my case was a concertina file with slots for the days 1–31 and for the remaining months of the year. I would pop into the brought-forward file any correspondence, assessments, buying orders and the like which I wanted to review at a future date; these items were brought into the list as they 'came up'. Having made the first rough list, I then sorted it into order of importance and urgency. At the end of each day I used to go through the list and cross off what I had done and also any items which had ceased to be relevant. I would add to the list new jobs or problems which had arisen and then I would note which jobs I planned to do the following day.

In the morning there was my list telling me what I had to do that day. Obviously unexpected matters arose – in an operational situation one can almost budget for the unexpected – but by and large I worked through the list each day.

Communications

One of the standing items on the list, apart from going through the dairy and brought forward file, was to see *all my subordinates.* I kept at hand a list of all subordinates and made a point of seeing each one even if only to say 'hello', every day. It could be, of course, that you are often away, or that you have too many staff to see. Perhaps in the first case you should consider whether you are away too much to do your job properly; in the second case either you may have too many people directly under you or should delegate some of the communication process to subordinates. Communications is the name of this game: people require *regular contact* and in particular from their boss, and they will often say things, or you will be able to sense a problem which they would be diffident about bringing to your office.

Incidentally, what does your office look like to a subordinate? Can he come and talk to you, or are you involved most of the time in meetings, discussions or telephone calls? Communications can only exist on face-to-face basis, and they are of prime importance at every level. Many managers with considerable responsibilities in large organisations do not know the names or faces of their top management and directors. An even greater proportion never see, or are seen by, their top management in any operational situation from year to year end. *No amount of personnel work can make people think you care about them if they never see you.*

Personal planning

The first list of work is much more difficult to produce than the subsequent amendments, and to help you produce it there is a checklist of questions in Figure 34.1. These are general and analytical questions to be used in any review of your responsibilities, but they would assist in preparing the first list. When, you may ask, would there ever be time to do this, and is it possible with everyone rampaging around and the telephone constantly ringing?

Well, do you intend to spend the rest of your life in a managerial pigsty, and are you seriously going to say you are too busy to do your job? Half an hour's

1 What are the objectives of my department or function?
2 Am I satisfied that I feel these can be achieved – that I have a plan(s) for this?
3 In what ways can my department or area be improved?
4 Is the work in my area altering in nature, quantity or quality?
5 Can the work be done in a better way?
6 Have I the right equipment and facilities?
7 Have I the right number of staff?
8 Am I happy that all my subordinates are correctly placed and loaded?
9 Are my staff doing what I want them to do?
10 Do any of my staff need further training or experience? Have I a training plan?
11 What are staffing trends?
12 Are my staff happy? Do I spend enough time with them?
13 Have I a trained deputy?
14 Am I satisfied personally? Have I defined my personal objectives?
15 Is my authority defined and adequate?
16 Is my relationship with my senior management satisfactory?
17 Where is my next promotion coming from?
18 Am I doing too much routine or administrative clerical work?
19 Have I enough time for thinking?

Figure 34.1 Checklist for reviewing your function

planning can save hours – even days – of misdirected effort; the crisis anticipated proves to be no panic, and you should find in the normal situation that if you pursue this type of personal planning for a few months, you will get right 'ahead of the game' and that you can start looking for additional responsibilities.

Decide now on a specific half hour in the coming week to go through the list. Ask someone else to take the telephone calls and say you do not want to be disturbed (unless it is the Chairman!). Some of the questions will require further investigation, but whenever you reach an unsatifactory answer, answer the question: 'What am I going to do about it?'

THE CONSTRAINT OF TIME

Managing is conducted within a large number of constraints. What is your biggest constraint? Is it capital, working finance, material resources, machinery, property or is it people? People can be a big limiting factor, but you can always train them. Are you limited by the presence of other aspects? Many factors can constrain you, but *the biggest restriction of all is your own time*. You never have enough of it. There are only twenty-four hours in a day, seven days in a week, 52 weeks in the year and so many years in your career. You cannot produce more time; it keeps slipping away. Yesterday can never come back.

We would say, therefore, that we do not have as much time as we need, but would this be equally true for everybody, or would it apply in particular to you? Time can be replaced. Certain tasks can be performed by machinery and certain office work can be done by computers. Some tasks can be delegated to other people, although this is really a transfer of time. However, *the manager cannot delegate his management work* to a machine and seldom can he share it with anyone else. There is no substitute for time as far as he is concerned. Everything he does takes time. All business, all activity, all work uses time and takes place in time.

However, we do not manage our time naturally - as a whole we take it for granted. Now we could talk for a long time about this problem, and we could say that the unhurried, unheroic manager with a clear desk, and a reliable organised office is the efficient or effective manager, but what do you do about it?

Step 1

First of all, accept that, other thing being equal, *the best and happiest manager* is the one who *makes the best use of his time.* If you do not accept this, then this chapter was not written for you, but if you feel that you can make better use of time, and that if you do so you will be a better manager, then please read on.

Step 2

The second step comprises finding out what you are doing now. A simple method of doing this is to list various activities which you perform, and record for a week or a fortnight how long you are spending on them. This can be done by using a simple daily diary sheet; the diary sheets are analysed into what is called a work distribution chart at the end of the period. The work distribution chart will show quite clearly what you are doing and what proportion of your time you are spending on your various activities.

A specimen managers' activity list, with the activities given for example only, is as follows:

1 Visiting customers
2 Visiting suppliers
3 Queries from staff over technical matters
4 Customer complaints
5 Planning and control work
6 Training
7 Supervision
8 Reading mail
9 Chasing overdue accounts
10 Checking stocks and reordering
11 Management meetings
12 Recruiting
13 Staff problems
14 Personal.

Simple form for the diary sheet and work distribution chart are shown in Figures 34.2 and 34.3.

The work of a manager is variable, particularly as regards the subject involved. Completing a work distribution chart will not give a 100 per cent accurate picture of what the manager does or should do, but it will give a representative view of the proportions of his time spent on various activities, e.g., queries; accounts queries may relate to different transactions, but they will still be accounts queries. Once the work distribution chart has been completed, one can then move on to the next step.

Step 3

The third step is the analysis of the work distribution chart. A number of questions need to be asked at this stage.

WASTED TIME

1 What would happen if I did not do this kind of activity?

Date:

Time	*Activity*	*Inter-ruptions*	*Phone calls*	*1. Ines-sential*	*2. Some-body else could do*	*3. Wasting others' time*	*Notes*
8.30 *8.45* *9.00* *9.15* *9.30* *9.45* *10.00* " " " " 5.30 5.45 6.00 Evening	Enter number against time whenever activity changes	Enter a '1' for each, e.g., I, 11	As for interruptions. Note incidence and quantity. Analyse if too many.	Record impressions, if any, at the time	Record impressions, if any, at the time.	Record impressions, if any, at the time.	Note anything unusual or 'special'.

Figure 34.2* *Specimen manager's diary sheet

Activity no.	Activity title	Daily times										Total time	% of total	Comments and action
		1	2	3	4	5	1	2	3	4	5			
														(You can also do this kind of analysis with your staff.)
														These are taken to the nearest quarter hour.
											(No)	(No)		If phone calls and interruptions occur which are separate from the activity being recorded – multiply by 3 minutes; if the totals exceed 15% of the day, then analyse them. Possibly something is wrong.

Figure 34.3 Manager's work distribution chart

2 Am I spending too long on it?
3 Am I doing it ineffectively – for example, am I getting it properly set up and spending enough time on it? Short periods of supervision are of limited value with persons engaged on complex work
4 Am I failing to do any task which would contribute to the business because of the lack of time?

Supervision

A manager should be able to spend time with his staff – encouraging, training, supervising and just getting to know them and keeping in touch. The time required for this varies with the staff and the complexity of the work, but a rough quick figure is an average of forty minutes per person per day. This includes normal management duties, reports and 'personnel' work. It does not include 'checking' as distinct from normal supervision and training.

Checking

Checking should be considered carefully. Twenty or thirty years ago commercial convention looked for a high degree of literal accuracy and salary costs were lower in proportion to other expenses than they are now. There is a satisfaction in getting everything 'right', but we should first consider what the customer really needs. Checking is expensive and frustrating: it is no longer a motivating factor (if it ever was) for staff to have all their work checked.

Your work distribution chart will show how much of your time is spent checking, but you should consider whether the cost of checking is justified by the errors discovered and how much these matter. If the errors do matter you may have to continue to check, but you can consider whether random checks, occasional and unexpected, will serve as well where generally quality standards and methods are the main concern.

List of jobs

In the end you will finish with a list of jobs which you want to do and which you have to do, and a subsidiary list of jobs which you feel you should not be doing but perhaps you still have to do for one reason or another. (We are, of course, well aware that you cannot get rid of all inessential tasks, but you can reduce them.) You will *rank the list of jobs in order of importance* to the business, and estimate what general proportion of your time and energy should be spent on each.

You will have considered where time is being wasted on unnecessary work, and where time could be saved by better personal organisation and work methods. You should move to the next heading in your analysis of the work distribution chart.

DELEGATION

Ask yourself which of your activities could be done by somebody else to an adequate standard, or as well as you, or even better. The manager is paid to do his work, but if there are others at lower salaries who can do part of it and have the time, then is it better for the manager to be fully occupied or for the junior staff?

Another factor which comes out of this analysis is that the more senior people become, the larger becomes the proportion of their time spent on moving about and travelling, and you should think about this.

There will be certain customers who are very important, and who are accustomed to dealing with you personally; it may well be that you can introduce them to someone else who can deal with the routine parts of the account but, of course, you will remember to watch what is happening to the account from time to time subsequent to this arrangement. This would apply also to 'important jobs' and to important senior managers!

The present managing directors of several major companies in the United Kingdom were in very humble positions only a few years ago; in fact, consider where you yourself were five years ago, and now you are performing much more important work. Quite possibly within your area you have the managers or senior managers of the future, and you should keep a look out for them and give them a 'chance' as soon as you can. Not only will this be good for them, but it will also free you. Think about how to develop the business and to perform your other managerial tasks.

One thing which is very irksome to staff is to see people senior to them performing activities at greater salaries which they could perfectly well do themselves. In one major British company staff are asked the question 'What does your supervisor do that you could do yourself?' Could you ask this question of your staff, and would they know how to answer it? It is worth considering that they may have views on this subject themselves.

SUBORDINATES' TIME

A manager becomes a manager by promotion or appointment. He learns to be a manager by observing other managers, who themselves have been taught by observation, and by being shown, and from what is called the 'hard way'. There are certain training courses, but they are normally very short, and as a result most managers devise their style and system of management from their own experience. Often this is very good, but once personal inclinations creep in, funny things start to happen.

You should ask yourself the following question: 'Is there anything I do which wastes subordinates' time without contributing to their effectiveness?' You can begin to answer this question from your analysis of the work distribution chart, and you may even be able to ask it of the subordinates themselves.

Waiting around

For instance, how much time do your staff spend waiting for answers from you, items to be checked or approved, action to be taken, or for you to be available? Consider whether in your area you ever have two or more people involved in work which should be done by one person only. Normally it is more satisfying and efficient for a job which can be done by one person to be done by one person and not split between two or three. Staff learn from observing you (or colleagues), but sometimes you may be playing to an audience unnecessarily (and distracting the others).

Remember when you were a member of staff or a worker. Did your manager or foreman ever waste any of your time while you waited for him when he was late, when he had to check your work, while he had to get around to this or that but was (or allowed himself to be) interrupted by a variety of other matters? Did this frustrate you as well as waste your time? Staff are paid less than managers, but with overheads the difference is not as great as it once was. Are you working too hard; are you paying the proverbial dog then doing the barking yourself?

Crises

One thing which wastes time, particularly of subordinates, is a crisis. In many organisations crises occur regularly, and there are so many things which are unforeseen that one could almost describe crises as a routine situation. However, a recurrent crisis is a symptom of slovenliness. Certain crises such as making up the returns, the budget figures, sales figures, payroll, the peak season, are all known in advance. If the manager uses sensible planning and scheduling techniques he may well be able to provide for these, in which case they will become routine occurrences and not crises.

Panic action is expensive. People rushing off to make special deliveries, special visits to the post office, special trips out to acquire stationery, other things that are needed, people dropping things in the middle of picking up others and so on, all lead to ineffective use of time and also mistakes.

IMPROVEMENTS

The question here is, how can you use your time more effectively? The first thing to consider is your attention span. Are you a person who works best by sitting down quietly and for extended periods looking at a particular problem, or do you keep things running around in your mind? What are your best methods of working, and with whom and when?

Discretionary time

You need to have a certain amount of 'discretionary time', i.e., time at your free disposal, time available for important matters, perhaps the things you are paid for, and this must be kept in usable chunks. Not many managers feel they have much discretionary time, even after cutting out any wasted time, but they can generally set aside an hour or so each week. The question arises as to how much discretionary time is desirable. This is rather like maintenance on a car; you do not buy a car in order to service it, but if you do not carry out a certain amount of maintenance on the car it will not perform satisfactorily.

Your function

The same applies to your function. You need from time to time to review the total operation of your area and to go through the check list given previously; you need to make sure you see the staff regularly and review their situation. On a daily basis you may want to keep a list of the tasks which you have to do, and the problems with deadlines and priorities, and perhaps revise these either last thing at night or first thing in the morning. Also you may well want to use a brought-forward file or diary system so that you are automatically reminded of things that need to be done in the future. How long this should take is like the service on the car, except that it is you rather than the garage that must make the diagnosis and the decisions.

Suggestions

Simple suggestions for using your time more effectively are to concentrate on one thing at a time; deal with first things first, and one at a time. Allow enough time for what you are doing – nothing ever goes completely right and one thing you can always expect is the unexpected. Do not hurry, do not try and do several things at once. Do not assume that everything that was important yesterday is important today. Ask yourself the question 'If we had not already started on this activity would we start it now?' It is just as difficult and just as risky to do something small as something which is big, so allocate your time to the most important parts of the business.

When you have analysed your work distribution chart comparing the proportions of time spent on the various activities with their importance in terms of obtaining income, business and profit or other advantage for the company, you will most certainly find that you are spending a lot of your time on small irritating matters. Consider whether some of these can be allowed to slide without damage to the business, and whether things would be improved by concentrating on the main managerial requirements of the organisation.

FURTHER READING

Drucker, Peter F., *The Effective Executive*, Heinemann, London, 1967
Welsh, A. N., *The Skills of Management*, Gower, 1980

35 Negotiating

Bill Scott

This chapter is in three parts. The first describes a style of negotiating designed to produce the greatest area of agreement in the joint interest of both parties. This is a pattern of negotiating in which the parties work together, creatively, *Towards Agreement*. The second pattern is one in which each party is concerned more with its own advantage than with the joint advantage. Goodwill and agreement are still important, but the overriding consideration is that which is *To Independent Advantage*. Third, when goodwill is not important, negotiations can sometimes deteriorate into a pattern of *Fighting*.

NEGOTIATING TOWARDS AGREEMENT

When the parties are concerned to work together creatively Towards Agreement the key activities are exploration of one another's position, and creative recognition of what is in their joint interests.

Those phases of exploration and creativity, however, hinge on having first created a suitable climate and on having some procedure which helps the parties to work together. There is no cause for heavy use of negotiating tactics but there is a need for effective preparation.

The sequence in this section will therefore be:

Creating the climate
Opening procedure
Sequence in negotiations
Exploration
Creativity
Subsequent phases
Preparation

Creating the climate

Negotiators usually operate best when the climate is brisk and businesslike. When negotiating Towards Agreement, they need a climate which is also cordial and co-operative.

The pace of a negotiation, be it brisk or lethargic, is set very early. Within seconds of the parties coming together, during the rituals of meeting and greeting, a pace is established which is durable. It should be a brisk pace – briskness established by the pace at which the parties are moving about and by the speed at which they are communicating.

The cordial character is established in an ice-breaking phase. As the parties first meet and interact with one another, they need to adjust and to build their regard before getting into possibly controversial areas. The ice-breaking, therefore, needs to be a period in which they focus on neutral topics – the football, the weather, the journey and so on.

The ice-breaking is an essential preliminary, so important that it deserves possibly 5 per cent of the prospective negotiating time: a couple of minutes even at the outset of short negotiations; a preliminary dinner and evening out before protracted negotiations.

The brisk and cordial character is thus very soon established. The development of the businesslike and co-operative characteristics comes as the parties sit down and move towards business. Timing and the form of first remarks at the negotiating table should provide the 'business-like': timing, by an immediate statement so that there is no long gap as members get seated; and the form of the opening remarks focusing on business, Towards Agreement.

The co-operative character can be set too at this early stage. This depends on effectiveness in handling the opening procedure.

Opening procedure

There is nothing more likely to produce a co-operative atmosphere than the immediate question, on sitting down: 'Well gentlemen, can we first agree on procedure?'

Note that the word 'agree' is used at the outset. Note that the question is one which will almost certainly produce the answer 'Yes'. Note that the two parties both establish the 'agree' mood from the outset.

There are four procedural items which should be explored and agreed in this opening stage: the four Ps.

1 Pace
2 Purpose
3 Plan
4 Personalities.

The *pace* is the speed at which the parties need to move together. There needs to be harmony on this pace if parties are to work together effectively. There will not be such harmony if one believes that there is a whole afternoon available whereas the other has another engagement in half an hour.

The *purpose* is the reason why the parties are meeting. If one party thinks that the meeting is purely exploratory, while the other believes the purpose is to achieve a final settlement, then the parties are going to be working at cross-purposes.

Even when the purpose has been established in preliminary communication, it is still important at the outset to refresh the consciousness of that purpose. And to take the chance to emphasise that both parties *agree* on that purpose.

The *plan* should be in the form of a short agenda – some four main stages through which the meeting should move.

These first three Ps – Pace, Purpose and Plan – should be agreed at the outset of every negotiation.

The fourth P in the opening procedural stage is Personalities: the introduction of members who do not know one another, their backgrounds, what they can contribute to the meeting. Skilfully used, this opening procedure has great advantages:

1. The meeting can proceed with both parties recognising joint objectives and a joint means of moving forward.
2. The plan gives a framework for control of the remainder of the meeting.
3. The mood of agreement can be quickly stated and established.
4. The groundwork is set for a smooth and co-operative entry into the later stages of the negotiation.

There is a consistent sequence in these later stages of any negotiation. The sequence is:

1. Exploration
2. Creativity
3. Shaping the deal
4. Bidding
5. Bargaining
6. Settling
7. Ratifying.

These phases are – or should be – found in any negotiation, even though they may sometimes become mixed and muddled. The importance of each phase varies a lot, however.

In negotiating Towards Agreement, the key phases are those of exploration and creativity.

Exploration

When two parties come together, each has its own distinctive view of the aims and possibilities for the negotiation. If the parties want to work together to bake the biggest possible cake, it is imperative that each should

- *(a)* recognise what both see in the same way,
- *(b)* recognise and respect what others see in a different way, and
- *(c)* be clear about the way in which their own interests are distinctive.

From such recognition can spring the creative spark of what is then most in their joint interests.

To achieve that recognition each party should independently make a broad statement of its own position, and give opportunity for the others to seek clarification. Then get a comparable 'broad picture' of the other party's position, and clarify that.

Each opening statement needs to cover:

Our understanding. The broad area within which we believe the negotiation will take place.
Our interests. What we would like to achieve through the negotiation.
Our priorities. What are the most important aspects for us.
Our contribution. The way in which we can help to our joint advantage.
Our attitudes. The consequence of our previous dealing with the other party; their reputation as it has come to us; any special hopes or fears which we may have for collaboration.

Characteristic of the opening statement are the following points:

1 The opening statements of each party should be independent. Each should state its own position, and not attempt at this stage to state the joint interests of the two parties
2 They should not attempt to put assumptions about the position or interests of the other party. (The giving of this assumption serves only to irritate, to confuse and to introduce disharmony.)
3 The statements should be general, not detailed, not yet quantitative
4 The statements should be brief. Each should give the other party an opportunity to come into the discussion quickly, both so that the parties can quickly interact and so that others do not get a sense of being overwhelmed by either the duration or the complexity of an opening statement. Keep it short.

As one party makes its opening statement, the other party needs to listen, clarify and summarise.

Listen

Do not waste energy by thinking up counter-arguments.

Clarify

If in any doubt, question to get clear what he is trying to say. But note: question for clarification. Do not question for justification - that forces the other negotiator on to the defensive and runs counter to the creative climate being sought.

Summarise

Feed back the key points of what you understand him to be saying, so that he can check.

Having got clear the view of one party then comes the time for the other party to offer its own opening statement, and for first party's corresponding response

– listen, clarify, summarise.

For really creative negotiations, there is a need for these opening exchanges to be carried through frankly in an environment of mutual trust and respect. For these reasons great attention has been paid to creating a positive climate and to underlining agreement and preparing minds in the opening process.

Skilled negotiators are skilled at giving and getting information.

Skilled negotiators are also conscious that some other parties will seek to exploit them. They therefore look out for danger signals which would suggest a need to change strategy.

If in the ice-breaking, the other party insists on probing about business matters ('How's trade? cash-flow? quality?') beware. Probably he is simply an unskilled negotiator, but possibly he is aggressive, seeking information that he can later use aggressively. If he is highly assertive in the phase of proposing and agreeing procedure – then again we must beware. An amber light is flashing.

If he is excessively anxious that we should be the first to make an opening statement, or in challenging that opening statement: then a further amber light is shown – indeed, this is virtually a red light.

Given a succession of amber lights, or just one red light, then the skilled negotiator will be prepared to change his strategy. He should seek a recess, even though it is still an early stage of the negotiation, reconsider the other party's behaviour and decide whether he needs to change to either of the strategies in later sections of this chapter.

But skilled negotiators practising this characteristic style of negotiating towards agreement can normally produce a positive response.

There is thus a great need for negotiators to develop the skills of creating a co-operative climate, of agreeing procedure, and of openness in the exploratory phase.

Creativity

Agreement-oriented negotiators now have a unique opportunity to achieve something to joint advantage, something bigger than either party could get when negotiating to independent advantage. This is the moment to be seeking together to bake the biggest possible cake.

To achieve that creativity they need first to be imaginative. Later they must impose the forces of reality, but the most productive of ideas may not be seen unless the parties are prepared to range as far as the borderline between reality and fantasy. Be imaginative.

Scandinavian negotiators have a special phrase to launch into this phase. Having summarised the respective positions of the parties as discussed in their opening statements, they say 'All right then – what are the creative possibilities?'

In looking for those creative possibilities there are a few guidelines:

1 The pattern of generating the ideas must be broad in its sweep, and interdependent.
2 It must be broad because immediately the parties focus on one suggestion

(either criticising or exploring in depth), their minds cannot revert to broad and imaginative thinking.

3 It must be interdependent, not only to sustain the co-operation between them, but also because each fresh suggestion can kindle a new spark in the imagination of the other. The parties have great potential to be creative together.

This process of recognising creative possibilities should generate a number of different ideas. There then comes the need to form a bridge between the world in which the parties have been thinking imaginatively, and the world of reality in which their performance must be measured by business criteria. They must decide which of their imaginative ideas offer realistic possibilities. They must then assess and agree on the action needed to turn possibility to mutual advantage.

Subsequent stages

The critical periods of negotiations towards agreement are the exploratory and creative phases. From them springs the recognition of mutual interest. There is, of course, need for the later realities to be foreseen, for agreement on the commercial conditions, and for the establishment of realistic plans to implement decisions. Given however the creative atmosphere, then views and possibilities for these commercial and planning discussions can be developed in a similarly open atmosphere.

The approach – 'Let us now explore together' – can be sustained through these later stages without the need to get into the tough bidding and bargaining encountered (and to be further discussed) in the context of other strategies.

However, before starting any negotiation, each party must arrive at the negotiating table well prepared.

Preparation

For any form of negotiation, the negotiator must have done his homework beforehand. He must know the facts, the figures, the arguments.

He needs also to have prepared in two other respects. First, preparing for the procedure. He should think through the Pace, Purpose and Plan which he will suggest for the meeting. And having thought them through, it is advisable to jot down the headlines of pace, purpose and plan on a postcard, to serve as a reminder during the meeting.

Second, he needs to have prepared his opening statement: his understanding of the matter for discussion, his interests, priorities, contribution, attitudes; and again, to jot the headlines on a postcard.

It is important, when negotiating Towards Agreement, not to over prepare. The negotiator who has built a detailed framework of prices, deliveries and so on in his preparations is so mentally committed to those preparations that he obscures the possibilities for being creative in any wider sense.

To summarise, when their strategy is negotiating Towards Agreement, the parties must first create a climate which is brisk, businesslike, cordial and co-operative. They must then establish and agree on a procedure helping them to work together effectively. From the opening procedural discussion they move into important exploratory and creative phases, and thereafter should be able to sustain the high co-operation already established. This must be founded on effective preparation by each party before the event.

NEGOTIATING TO INDEPENDENT ADVANTAGE

Different skills are needed when the negotiator is concerned with gaining special advantage for his party. In some ways these skills mirror those needed when negotiating Towards Agreement; in other ways, new and different skills are needed.

In particular bidding and bargaining become the crux of the negotiation. Early moves set the framework; and a different form of preparation is needed. The sequence of this section will therefore be:

1 Opening moves.
2 Bidding
3 Bargaining
4 Preparation

Opening moves

The negotiator working 'to independent advantage' must approach the negotiation with a difference of attitude. No longer is his concern to work creatively together with the other party. Rather it is to establish the best deal in the interests of his own side.

Assuming however that the deal will need the other party's co-operation to be implemented, or that there will in due course be a need to negotiate some other deal with the same party, it is important that goodwill should be sustained. Aggressive tactics and power struggles should be avoided.

The negotiator's attitude should not be that he will work towards the other party's disadvantage. His attitude must be to find the best way to divide the cake to give satisfaction to both parties. If he likes icing more than fruit, and the other party likes fruit more than icing – there is no problem. Both sides can 'win'. The skilled negotiator thus works towards influencing the other party to value the fruit more than the icing.

The opening moves will again establish the climate for the meeting. Because of the concern for sustaining goodwill it is again important that the climate should be brisk, businesslike, cordial and co-operative; and it is again important that procedure should be agreed at the outset.

Exploration now takes a different form. It becomes necessary quickly to identify the shape of the deal, rather than to look creatively for some new shape. In this process, both parties become more concerned with 'what our party wants'.

The response to the other party needs to be one of probing, to find out which issues or which ingredients are important to the others. Are they, for example, more concerned about price than delivery, quality, terms of settlement?

It is important in these exploratory stages to keep the dialogue on a broad front. If the move to discussion of a particular item (such as price) is taken too soon or too deeply, it is likely to lead to a premature conflict and also to erode some of the most effective possibilities for later bargaining.

Bidding

Negotiating to independent advantage, the guideline to bidding is to start with that which is the highest defensible. (For buyers, the corresponding phrase is of course 'lowest defensible offer'.)

The opening bid needs to be 'the highest' because:

1 The opening bid sets a limit beyond which the party cannot aspire. Having once made it, no higher bid can reasonably be put at a later stage
2 The first bid influences others in their valuation of our offer
3 A high bid gives scope for manoeuvre during the later bargaining phases. It gives something in reserve with which to trade
4 The opening bid has a real influence on the final settlement level. The higher the level of aspiration, the greater the prospective achievement.

The opening bid needs to be high. At the same time it must be defensible. Putting foward a bid which cannot be defended does positive damage to the negotiating process. It is found to be offensive by the other party; and if it cannot be defended when challenged in subsequent bargaining, there is soon a loss of face, a loss of credibility, a forced retreat.

The content of the bid of course usually needs to cover a range of issues. The components of the opening bid in a commercial negotiation will not simply be price, but a combination of price, delivery, payment terms, quality specification and a dozen other items.

The 'highest defensible bid' is not an absolute figure, it is a figure which is relevant to the particular circumstances. It is specifically a figure which relates to the way in which others are operating. If they are pressing to their independent advantage, then we must open with a high bid; but if faced with a lot of competition, the bid must be tailored to the level at which it will at least enable us to be invited to continue the negotiations. If we have established cordial relationships with others, possibly over a long period of time, then we shall know the style in which they will operate and the degree of co-operation we can expect – we know the level at which it is prudent for us to make our bid.

On each individual item the opening bid needs to be the highest defensible. We are certain, when negotiating to independent advantage, to be pushed by others to compromise on one or two issues. We cannot be sure which until the bargaining process is under way; we must aspire high on all issues and keep room to manoeuvre.

The manner in which the bid is stated is important. It should be put firmly – without reservations, without hesitations – so that it may carry the conviction of a conscientious negotiating party.

It should be put clearly so that the other party recognises precisely what is being asked. The creation of a visual aid, i.e., taking a sheet of paper and writing figures on it, within the sight of the other party, whilst one is stating the bid – this is powerful reinforcement.

It should be put without apology or comment. There is no need to apologise for anything that can be defended. There is no need to comment since the other party can be expected to raise questions on matters which concern it. And voluntary comment (before others ask for it) simply makes them aware of concern about issues which they might never have considered.

Those then are three guidelines to the way in which a bid should be presented: firmly, clearly, without comment.

In responding to bids by the other party there is a need to distinguish between clarification and justification.

The competent negotiator first ensures that he knows what the other party is bidding. Precisely. He asks any questions which are needed to ensure that he gets the picture clear. He makes sure, in the process, that the other party recognises that these are questions for clarification and not demands to justify. And once satisfied, he summarises his understanding of the other party's bid, as a check on the effectiveness of communication between them.

First party should at this stage deflect questions which demand that he justifies his position. He has put a bid, and he has a perfect right to know what other is prepared to offer in return.

Bargaining

The first two steps in the bargaining process should be:

1 Get it clear
2 Assess the situation.

It is vital to establish a clear picture of other party's requirements at the outset. We should have got a clear picture of *what* he is bidding already. Now we need to know *why*.

The need is increasingly to build an understanding of what will give him satisfaction and of how to trade to advantage whilst giving him that satisfaction.

We must discover what for him are essentials and what else is desirable but not essential, and what aspects of his bid are really of fringe interest only – where he could readily give.

To achieve this clarity, the guidelines are:

1 Check every item of his bid. Enquire why. Ask how important the item is and how much flexibility he could introduce
2 Never speculate on his opinions or on his motives. A speculation only irritates. Moreover it is often misconceived – it is out of our frame of reference, not his, and confuses the negotiations between the pair of us. Never put words into his mouth
3 Note his answers without comment. Reserve our position. Avoid deep diving or premature diving into any issue. Keep it on a broad front.

Assuming significant differences between the parties there are now three options for the negotiator;

1 He can accept
2 He can reject
3 He can carry on negotiating.

If he decides to carry on negotiating then he must be prepared for the next round. His options at this stage are:

1 To make a new offer
2 To seek a new offer from the other party
3 To change the shape of the deal (vary the quantity or the quality or the use of third parties), or
4 Embark on give-and-take bargaining.

The steps for preparing for that give-and-take are:

1 Issue identification – list the issues in the package
2 Prepare the bargaining position:
   (*a*) an essential conditions list – those issues on which it is impossible to concede anything.
   (*b*) a concessions list – those issues on which concession is conceivable. For each such issue, a progression stepped from that minimum which could be offered (against counter-concessions from the other party) in the next round of bargaining, to that ultimate limit which might be forced in successive rounds.

During the bargaining stages, each successive negotiation meeting should be opened with a new round of climate formation and with agreement on procedure. Each round should be concluded with the establishment of some means of resolving outstanding difficulties.

In between, the negotiations should be conducted laterally rather than vertically. That is to say, the aim should be to reach agreement in principle on a broad front, then to tackle more detailed negotiations, still on a broad front. A sequence of several successive moves across the broad front; not a succession of narrow penetrations.

When the time comes for compromise, neither party will readily 'lose face'. Neither party will readily concede on one issue without having some corresponding concession on another. It is thus important to solve difficulties on a broad front or, at the least, two at a time; not simply one at a time.

For example, when the parties have been exploring a difference between them in price and when they are reaching the stage of preparednes to make concessions, it is helpful to both parties if one of them interjects a comment such as 'Well, just before we finish that discussion on price, could we at the same time tie in this question about (e.g., the shipping risk) and who is to be responsible for that?'

And so sustaining goodwill and sustaining efforts to keep a co-operative climate even through tough bargaining – the negotiation should move towards settlement To Independent Advantage.

Preparation

As ever, preparation is of critical importance, and the general pattern of preparation should repeat that previously described.

With one important difference. This is the need to be more specific during preparation processes. Whereas in creative negotiations it is important to keep one's preparations general and to preserve flexibility, in more divisive negotiations the negotiator needs to be protected from exploitation. He needs to have considered his bids at an early stage. There is this constant dichotomy between the need for flexibility and the need for precise preparations. The one is the enemy of the other. The choice should reflect the strategic situation which will be referred to at the end of this chapter.

To summarise: bidding and bargaining are the key phases in negotiating to independent advantage. It is a type of negotiation needing distinctive attitudes and skills. Bidding and bargaining become more important than exploration. Climate formation and procedural development remain important. So does preparation though it takes a slightly different form.

FIGHTING

Warfare is not a commendable form of negotiation. Nevertheless, negotiators do become involved in confrontations in which the aim has to be to 'win' – or, at any rate, to ensure that they do not 'lose' at the hands of an aggressive party.

This section will review:

- the use of fighting methods
- the pattern of a fighting negotiation
- fighting tactics
- counter-measures

The use of fighting methods

The fighter's aim is to win and to make the other party the loser.

This is a dangerous attitude to negotiations. It puts goodwill at risk; it obscures the possibility of creative co-operation; it naturally provokes the other party to fight back, causing delay and putting at risk the fighter's chances of success. Even when the fighter batters an 'opponent' into submission, he is not likely to find the deal implemented energetically.

The means which the fighter uses are powerful. Both by his personal behaviour and by the negotiating tactics which he uses, he seeks to reinforce the power of his position. His methods include:

- a constant search for gain at every opportunity
- at each successive stage in the process of negotiating, he wants fresh advantage
- any withdrawals must be deliberate, tactical withdrawals, designed only to promote greater advance
- power-methods; high in terms of the pace, size and forcefulness of

demands, low in readiness to listen or to yield
task-centred. Concern for his special advantage. Not concerned with other party's pride or dignity nor with their feelings. Forcing them to 'accept or else'.

The pattern of a fighting negotiation

The central concern of the fighting negotiator is to win. This winning takes place in the fighting phase of the negotiation – a special version of the bargaining phase. A special version at which he is expert and best able to use his personal characteristics. Quickly he leads the negotiation to the point at which his form of bargaining becomes the dominant activity.

This leaves little time or interest for the early stages of negotiating; little time to get on the same wavelength as other party, or to agree on a plan; little time to explore mutual interests. Even issue identification is hastened and the negotiation quickly becomes focused on his first chosen issue.

The pattern of the negotiation is then 'vertical', deep diving on the first selected issue. He aspires high and pushes until he 'wins' on that and each successive issue.

Fighting tactics

He knows a lot of tactics and manoeuvres, and regularly uses a number. He has his own repertoire, and admires (and tries to emulate) tactics which have been used 'against' him by other negotiators. Here are some of them:

1 *Probing from the start*
The fighter enters the negotiating room, shakes hands and wishes us 'Good morning' and immediately starts probing. Probing about our business situation, probing about the product or service in which he is interested, probing even about one's personal situation.
The advantages he seeks are in getting information, in building a picture about other party and especially in recognising weaknesses and vulnerabilities. Additionally, he establishes a power position – a pattern of aggressive leadership.

2 *Get/give*
He is concerned to get something before he will give anything. To get a small concession before he will give a small concession. To get a big concession before he will give a big concession. To get information before he will give information. To get the other party's bid before he will give his own bid. To get the power of being the first to make an opening statement.
Get/give tactics used by skilled negotiators can have positive commercial advantages in the short term. They may well gain ground during the early stages of a negotiation; but in the long run, they lead to delay and deadlock (neither party being willing always to give before it gets).

3 *Showing emotion* (anger, for example)
Loud and emotional statements, possibly banging the table: the form of

eye-contact, posture, gesture and voice, all displaying emotions.

4 *Good guy/bad guy*

This is a tactic for use by a team of two negotiators. One takes the role of the 'bad guy'; being aggressive, making excessive demands, dominating, un-co-operative. He holds the stage for a long time whilst his colleague remains quiet. When he has softened up the 'opposition' with his tactics, the 'good guy' takes over the lead role, constructively offering solutions, quietly trying to reach a mutual understanding.

The tactic parallels the archetypal method by which prisoners of war are cross-examined; the prisoner first ruthlessly interrogated by a tough investigator, then offered the sympathy of a different personality to whom – with luck – he would open up.

5 *Poker-faced*

Giving away nothing by expression, tone, posture or gesture. An important part of the fighting negotiator's armoury.

6 *Managing the minutes*

Taking responsibility at the end of each session for production of the record. Slanting interpretations of what has been agreed, always to his advantage. Readiness to include the odd item 'which ought to have been agreed' even if there was insufficient time to include it in the discussion – provided, of course, that the odd item is favourable.

7 *Getting upstairs*

When unable to come to an agreement with the other negotiator, taking steps to contact his boss, or boss's boss's boss.

8 *PR*

Many fights are conducted by negotiators acting on behalf of other groupings. For example, the union negotiator representing the workforce; the government negotiator representing his country. It is here important for the group which is represented to be kept informed and influenced so that they continue to give their backing to the negotiator. His ability at public relations is thus an important part of the fighter's armoury.

9 *Forcing moves*

There are, of course, yet other moves which some negotiators use. Bribery, sex, blackmail, bugging. Most negotiators would see such devices as rankly unethical; but people negotiating very important deals are at risk and need to be on their guard.

Counter-measures

Counters to those who fight are in two forms: long-term and short-term measures.

In the long term, where there is expectation of repeated rounds of negotiations, for example, in labour negotiations, there is a need for the development of attitudes, skills and relationships.

This development takes place best when the parties can come together at a place remote from their normal battlefield, and at a time during the off-season for fighting. Especially fruitful is the practice, which has been well developed in

Scandinavia, of holding joint working seminars for two or three days. The product of such seminars is not only the development of relationships but the planning of subsequent joint activities.

That is a long-term approach. In the short term, measures to counter the fighter fall into three categories:

1 Head him off
2 Control the battlefield
3 Cope with his tactics.

The most satisfying way of coping with him is of course to head off the fight before it develops. If this is to be achieved it must be done in the critical opening seconds and minutes:

deflect his opening questions
preserve a neutral ice-breaking period
do not be drawn by his probing questions
do not let him assert leadership
do not let him dominate the early moments – what is being talked about, when to stand and when to sit, the seating arrangements

We are able to control the skirmishing if we can somehow control the battlefield. In negotiating terms, this 'control of the battlefield' is control of the procedures of negotiating. Guidelines are:

1 Seek for form and plan for the proceedings
2 Seek for opening discussion of purpose, plan and pace
3 Keep bringing him back to the agreed plan
4 Keep things fluid. Use the 'broad front' approach
5 Seek for compromise. He will be impervious either to searches for creative resolution of differences, or to sensitive attempts to influence him. His metier is that of compromise. If his position is that he is asking £120 and ours is that it is only worth £100, then settlement is likely to be at the compromise point of £110. Bargain slowly until you get him down to at most £110.

Above all, keep control of the process – keep control of what is being negotiated and in which sequence – keep to the plan. It will irritate him. He much prefers to be able to run free, but do not worry. A caged fighter cannot do as much damage as one on the loose. To cope with some of the fighter's tactics: When he is using the 'get/give' tactic, we must not give too easily, for if we give before we get, he will regard this as a sign of weakness. He will want to get yet more and will change the tactic into 'get/get/give' and soon will be aspiring even higher to 'get/get/get'.

We must not give in. We must trade scrap of information for scrap of information, scrap of readiness for scrap of readiness, scrap of concession for scrap of concession.

The only counter to displays of anger is to suspend negotiations, either temporarily or permanently. The human brain is such that emotions (such as anger) are handled in one part of it, rational thinking in another part. Once the brain becomes focused on emotive thinking, then the rational part is cut off. The angry party cannot receive rational messages and it is no use other party trying to instil them. So the counter is to suspend operations.

It does not matter if first party's anger is simply a display rather than real anger. Second party has no way of being sure about the matter. First party has behaved in ways which are not acceptable and second party should immediately suspend.

The 'good guy/bad guy' tactic is difficult to recognise and difficult to counter. But, of course, if it has been recognised in one round of negotiating then the negotiator will be alert for it during later rounds and must hope either to be able to ignore the bad guy or to separate the two 'opponents'.

The counter to 'getting upstairs' is to state strong objection to the tactic and then to arrange for our own boss to come in and make it clear that theirs was a losing tactic.

Formality is, inevitably, a device used to try to bring order to such negotiations. However, the fighting negotiator becomes expert in framing and fighting for a rule-book which is to his advantage. He is expert not only in drafting and amending rules but in interpreting and manipulating them. The effective negotiator from the other side therefore is forced to build his own corresponding expertise.

Preparation is, as ever, of critical importance for effectiveness in negotiating. When faced with a fight it is imperative to be well prepared procedurally and imperative also to have precise objectives, targets and prepared concession lists. There is special need to prepare options ('scenarios' in the current jargon), alternative approaches which could enable both parties to move forward whilst minimising loss of face.

The counter to his competence at public relations is to develop equal competence and to ensure that the relevant public is suitably influenced.

In meeting with a fighting 'opponent' then, the negotiator is operating in a world of power. He needs skill to control the battlefield and to prevent his being exploited.

But that is a short term approach. The longer term interest demands that he should work for some joint development of attitudes, skills and relationships with the other party.

SUMMARY

This chapter has been concerned with three distinct forms of negotiation. First, with negotiations in which two parties seek to move forward co-operatively to create the best possible deal in their joint interests. Second, with patterns of negotiation in which both parties aim to preserve goodwill whilst at the same time trying to maximise their independent advantage. Third and finally, with fights in which continuing goodwill is not treated as being important.

The choice amongst these approaches to negotiating will depend on a number of strategic issues:

1 The extent to which the parties will need to come together again from time to time
2 The respective strength of the parties in the market place
3 The character and quality of their negotiators
4 The time-scale and the importance of the prospective deal.

These strategic issues are considered at greater length in the last two books given in the further reading list which follows.

FURTHER READING

Karrass, C. L., *Give and Take*, World Publishing Co., 1974. A good treatment of the tactics used by American negotiators.

Marsh, P. D. V., *Contract Negotiation Handbook*, Gower, 1971. Excellent treatment of negotiating strategy of general interest. Preceded by a mathematical/economic analysis of bidding - also excellent, but demanding a reader with mathematical talents.

Scott, Bill, *The Skills of Negotiating*, Gower, 1981. A highly readable expansion of his ideas by the author of this chapter of the handbook.

36 Effective communication

Gordon Bell

As a director, a manager or an aspiring manager you will be interested in facts. A survey of over 5000 men and women such as yourself revealed the following data:

1. On average, they had each received about fifteen years of formal education
2. Approximately a third of them gained degrees, diplomas or other paper qualifications
3. Only one in twenty-three felt that their subsequent achievements in life matched their abilities, qualifications or early ambitions
4. Fewer than one in twenty had taken the trouble to equip themselves with skills such as effective speaking, clear writing, handling meetings.

From the chairman of the largest industrial group to supervisors and staff, everybody uses words. Every business man and woman writes letters, reports, memoranda, orders. Reasonable people will agree that words are a vital tool in industry. The higher we go up the ladder of management the more important words become.

Many business meetings produce nothing but frustration and expense. The average executive spends a third of his working life talking at interviews, conferences and committees (to say nothing of the time and hassle involved in arranging them and getting there). How much of this talk is productive? How many business men are either confident or competent when making a presentation or delivering a speech?

The nub of effective management is communications. Time and effort that you invest in developing your own skills as a communicator must produce dividends. In this chapter we shall discuss three aspects of communications:

1. Speaking
2. Report writing
3. Meetings.

SPEAKING

Speaking is for other people. This fact about effective speaking is so obvious and so simple that many overlook it. An audience always evaluates a speaker subjectively. What did they get from the talk? The answer to this question measures the speaker.

A manager needs to command attention at conferences and other meetings: he must be able to make oral presentations to his board and to professional organisations; to brief his staff, to persuade, to convince. Particularly if he is a specialist, he must be able to clarify specialised concepts so that others, not necessarily qualified, can share his thoughts. Even the most brilliant man is useless until his ideas can be shared by others who can use them.

A successful speaker is a man who gives his audience a success.* Many managers, both male and female, suffer from the delusion that speaking in public is the same as a theatrical performance, or something suitable only for extroverts. This delusion often serves as a defence. The plain truth is that they fear exposure of their limitations as speakers. This state of affairs is deplorable. If a man has something worth saying, he should not only say it but also learn how to say it with full effect. 'Why should the devil have all the best tunes?' asked General Booth. It is also pertinent to ask, 'Why should the image-makers and the tricksters have a monopoly of effective speech?'

Let us examine the fear, sometimes amounting to terror, that afflicts otherwise intelligent men when they are asked to speak. What causes this fear? The unpopular but accurate answer is vanity – too great a concern with 'How am I going to do?' and not enough concern with 'How are they – the audience – going to do?' This truth is a hard one to face yet it applies at both ends of the scale. Vanity causes the glib, arrogant, loud-mouthed, no-nerves-at-all-I-can talk-at-the-drop-of-a-hat chap to subject his audience to a flood of waffle: it also causes the timid to worry about themselves at the expense of their hearers. If you face this fact now you can save yourself a lot of trouble.

A successful speaker is a man who gives his audience a success. The speaker's success stems from the audience reaction. If his audience reacts in the desired manner, the speaker has been effective. There is no other criterion.

Newton's third law of motion says, roughly, 'To every action there is an equal and opposite reaction'. A given stimulus creates the same response if conditions remain constant. Herein lies one of the most important points that a speaker must consider. An audience is never a constant factor. There is no such thing as a production-line human being. Everyone is unique. People in an audience vary in social levels, technical knowledge, prejudices, age, sex. Even the same people gathered together at different times or under different conditions can change an audience.

Effective speaking is a human relationship, not something that one person does alone and in isolation. A speaker wishing to get the desired reaction

*A note for women readers: I apologise for using words like 'man', 'his', 'him' throughout. Of course women are included in the thinking behind this chapter.

must obviously begin with a study of his audience. Unfortunately, many speakers begin with themselves and end in disaster.

So, the first point that a would-be speaker must think about is his attitude to his audience. His thinking must be positive and outward – not so much 'What subject am I going to talk about?' as 'How can I create a powerful relationship with my audience using the subject as both the generator and the cement which binds that relationship?'

Can you imagine anyone erecting Tower Bridge or building a locomotive who would begin by laying the first brick or polishing the whistle? A rational man starts with a purpose and a plan. So does a professional speaker – and you, whether you realise it or not, are a professional speaker, a professional report- and letter-writer and a professional meeting man. If you analyse your job as a manager you will find that you do little else but talk and write and discuss. Given equal knowledge of his business, a man who knows how to speak, how to write and when to listen always has the advantage over one who does not.

Preparing an effective talk

Many speakers complain that they have no time to prepare properly. If you know your subject you can prepare a talk in one hour. The method we shall discuss now is the one-hour method. There are three stages, roughly twenty minutes each. (When you have ample time, say, three weeks or six, simply extend each stage accordingly.)

Stage 1: Subject matter – gathering

Arm yourself with plenty of large sheets of paper and write down at great speed *every* idea on your subject that enters your mind. Make no attempt to think these ideas through. Get them down in rapid notes, symbols or any other shorthand form that will enable you to recognise them when you arrive at Stage 2 – the plotting stage. Work at speed. Your aim during Stage 1 is quantity; to amass hundreds of facts about your subject, various opinions, prejudices, misunderstandings, possible visual aids, thoughts about the audience, the occasion – anything which in any way may bear on your proposed talk. Note direct facts, oblique, tangential and even remotely relevant facts. Set down page after page of rough notes.

During Stage 1 it is most important that you concentrate and work non-stop at great speed. If time allows, do this several times until you have at least ten times more material than your final talk demands. Fix nothing, solidify nothing. Bear in mind that what might be old stuff, obvious to you, might well be new or in need of explanation to your hearers. So get it all down. Note everything. A thought unnoted often disappears for ever.

Give yourself all the options. Review the whole subject. This review jogs your memory, gives you flexibility, acts as a solid background for your talk and can prove particularly helpful if you are required to answer these questions. Instead of having to excavate facts from the deep recesses of your mind, you have them near the surface, fresh and ready for use.

Quantity. Now you have raw stuff to work on, stacks of it.

Stage 2: Purpose and people

Establish your precise purpose. What reaction do you wish to induce in your hearers? What job has the talk to perform? Write down your purpose; rewrite it several times until you express, exactly, in a few cogent words, the effect you wish to achieve. Know what you are doing, explicitly. Be thorough about this. Do nothing else until you have got your objective clear.

Now that you have ample subject matter and a vividly clear purpose, you must ponder on the real material for your talk – the people who will listen to you. Examine every link they have or might have with your subject because they will be completely uninterested until what you say has something to do with them. Obvious, isn't it? What is their technical level, their social, financial level; what are their needs in connection with you and your subject? Study the people until you can see their view of your subject. You can only put your view across in relation to theirs. If you do not know anything about your audience, you would be well advised to find out at once. A discussion with the organisers, even a telephone call, can prove useful. Get to know your audience and integrate them into your presentation *now*; it will be too late when you are on your feet talking.

So, purpose and people. These two essential elements for an effective talk rarely receive enough thoughts or attention.

Stop here, please.

You must go no farther until you have checked that you have the driving force of a clear purpose working for you. You must go no farther until you have developed a real interest in your audience and their needs. These two factors should already be allies helping you to establish a partnership with your audience.

Purpose. People. Theme. Main points.

After your talk, what message will your hearers carry away with them? What big points supported your thesis? No audience will remember everything that you said. Decide at this stage in your preparation what basic theme you wish them to remember. As with your purpose, write down your theme and work on it until it becomes simple, straightforward and crystal clear. Next, separate the one, two or three really important points from the lesser points. Which are the really big points that you want them to have working in their minds? If you do not establish them clearly now, they will not stand out prominently enough in your delivered talk. Your job as a speaker is to clarify the subject for your audience. You cannot do this unless you first clarify it for yourself.

Now build your talk on the foundation of your purpose, your people, your theme and your main points.

A few reminders. A successful speaker knows his subject and is enthusiastic about it.

He makes certain that he is well prepared.

He has considered his audience and believes that the subject is important to them.

Bad speakers are usually people who think about themselves too much.

Pertinent questions to be answered at the end of Stage 2:

1 What exactly is my subject?
2 Why am I speaking about it to this audience and what do I know about them?
3 What are the most important things I must tell them?
4 Have I picked out the main points which must be highlighted?
5 Have I arranged these points so that this particular audience will fully understand them and be involved in them?
6 Have I made sure that there is a glowing, dominant theme?
7 What will the audience gain from this talk?

Stage 3 – Delivering the goods

The audience must at once be made confident that the speaker knows what he is doing. They must find his first thoughts intensely interesting. This, of course, rules out the usual dreary openings, for instance, where the speaker talks about himself and his worries as a speaker.

The three-sentence technique can secure a telling impact on opening:

Sentence 1. You make any vivid, unexpected, off-beat, truly interesting remark you like (always of course bearing in mind your audience).

Sentence 2. You link, skilfully, sentence 1 to your subject and make clear exactly what your subject is.

Sentence 3. You *involve* the audience in both your opening remarks and your subject.

It is essential that you economise and discipline yourself to use only three sentences for this effect. There must be no woolly edges around these three sentences, no 'hums' and 'hahs', no interpolated oddments, no clutter. You are seeking a clean, crisp, immediate communion, a direct response. Experiment until you have got a really good beginning. Excite, Link, Involve. Do not be satisfied with the first openings you think of: try at least six ways before you decide.

Avoid the word 'I' for at least one minute. Substitute 'you', 'your', or group words describing the audience, such as engineers, Scotsmen, managers. Be as specific as you can. Talk about them and their links with the subject. Get the focus firmly on to them and away from yourself.

As soon as your impact has been achieved and the audience knows what your broad subject is, define your limits so that they will not waste their attention on parts of the subject outside the scope of your talk. Tell them where you intend to take them within your subject, sometimes even which aspects you intend to leave out. From the start concentrate their mental energy on the relevant aspects. Give them clear signposts, briefly.

Now, you have a dynamic purpose in your mind; you and your audience know where you are going. They have been intrigued by your opening remarks and are ready for the statement of your basic theme, ready for the development of your first main point supporting that theme – and they are eager to find out how and where they fit in with what you have to say.

The elements are prepared for you – the catalyst – to do your work.

There are no dull subjects. Everything under the sun teems with interest. From even such beginnings as a dirty ashtry or the Industrial Training Act a lively mind could create a fascinating talk. How are you going to tell your story, how give your facts their full value as facts plus that life which also gives them interest? The key to power in story-telling is to bind everything you say to people and things – the concrete rather than the abstract. You might well be talking about some entirely abstract technical concept. Human beings and physical, tangible things judiciously woven into your presentation will vitalise even the unlikeliest subject for a potent talk. Also, wherever you can, link your examples directly to your listeners. An earthquake killing thousands in China could leave your audience unmoved: but a gas explosion in Clay Street, Manchester will engender great interest – especially to those of your audience who live in Clay Street, Manchester.

Facts are sacred and must not be tampered with. Concrete examples emphasise facts and make facts stick in the mind. The closer the examples are to the experience and the environment of the audience the more surely your points will find their target.

Contrary to a common opinion, facts do not always speak for themselves. They need good men to speak for them. No fact of life need be colourless or less interesting than fiction. You must adroitly develop the story of each fact, giving it a good beginning, a lively motif, substance, excitement, strong, close-to-home examples and a language suitable for your hearers.

Words worry people. They say 'I have plenty of ideas but I haven't the vocabulary to express them'. This assertion is based on a fallacy. Words (or some other set of symbols such as mathematical formulae) are essential to clear thought. If you are fumbling for words, you have not clarified the thought.

Technical language and jargon incur much scorn and contempt; but they have their uses as a shorthand for the initiated. On the other hand, to use such esoteric stuff to show how clever you are or because you lack consideration for your hearers is unpardonable. Use you audience's language or explain your own. Otherwise you will waste your breath and, what is worse, waste their time.

Speaking style

A hypnotist wishing to put someone to sleep employs a subdued, monotonous voice and single soporific thought repeated and repeated and repeated until the patient gives up and slumbers. To arouse the patient he makes some sharp noise and brings his own voice to life by using a complete change of tone. The patient wakes up.

Human voices possess an immense range of volume, tone, pace, attack. Why be monotonous? Why be dull? Why mutter and bawl like a bull? Why not work out beforehand how you can give variety and the appropriate vocal clues to each part of your talk? Think in terms of main headlines and paragraphs and make sure that each new idea comes to the audience with a change in vocal approach. Particularly when introducing a fresh point, give your voice a lift. Watch sentence length; see to it that a few crisp short ones intervene between a series of protracted sentences. Watch the ends of sentences: a rising pitch holds more interest than a dying fall.

It is an odd fact of speaking technique that absolute silence for a few seconds – under control – can be the most effective part of a speech. Try to find, perhaps, two such moments when you can hold your audience to your thoughts during your calculated pauses.

The human voice is only one of the channels through which ideas can flow. Sound, sight, touch, smell, taste all provide means of conveying to other people. A good speaker gives his audience a chance to use as many of their senses as the occasion permits. With a little ingenuity you can give their ears a rest and switch channels. One obvious way of doing this is to show them the point, to demonstrate it. The term 'visual aids' does not mean only blackboard – chalk-and-talk stuff – or flipcharts or films or overhead projectors; solid-physical, three-dimensional objects have much more effect. If it is practicable show them the actual thing you are talking about. Let them handle it, smell it, taste it. Use your zest, imagination and enthusiasm to create a worthwhile experience for your audience. You can develop a reputation as a first-class speaker if you work at it and stop worrying about yourself. They will say you simply have a flair for this sort of thing, a gift. You must not mind that. A judicious use of the five senses will help you. However prosaic your subject, give it vigour, colour – life.

Please arm yourself with a pencil and a sheet of paper because we are going to create a graph. I would appreciate your comments in it and your physical co-operation. To begin with, here are the axes (Figure 36.1). Please read the notes, draw the axes exactly. Then proceed to Figure 36.2

Commentary

The shading at the foot of Figure 36.2 represents the grey sludge area at the beginning of so many talks, during what the poor speaker calls 'warming up'. The monologue here tells how unaccustomed the speaker is and what a trying ordeal he is experiencing in facing such a difficult, awesome set of people. In general, the self-centred blockhead isolates himself and destroys the goodwill of the audience by focusing in the wrong direction. No wonder he is nervous. No wonder the audience already begin to doubt whether they should have come.

Eliminate the sludge area altogether. Instead, get some vigour, elevation and impact into your beginning. Hoist the value-and-interest line clean through the sludge up to *X*, which marks your impact at opening.

Signposts help your hearers to concentrate on the special aspects of the subject that you intend to cover. Define your limits, briefly.

Now drive towards your first main point (*a*). You have it clear. You have already worked out how to make your facts come to life, how to link your vivid example both to the facts and to your audience. Follow your line, the theme, and support that theme with facts. Develop your message.

Summaries are a matter for your judgement. At least you must make certain that each main point holds fast in the minds of your audience before you tackle the next point.

Signposting internal to the talk, again, is a matter for you to decide. Will

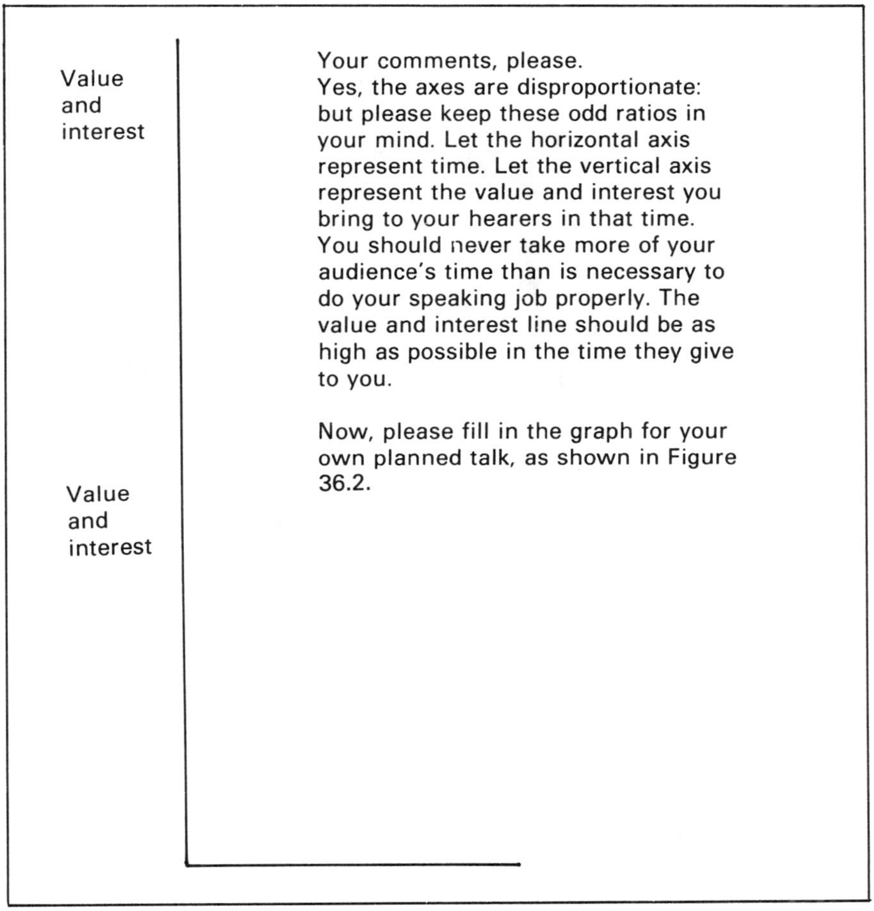

***Figure 36.1* Axes for graph of value and interest against time**
Use the proportions shown here to prepare the graph described in the text

summaries and signposting help the audience? If so, use them.

When you reach the climax of your talk, when you ram home your message you must remind your audience of the main facts which support your theme. Summarise crisply: remind them how the matter of your talk affects them and do have a powerful line at the end. (Make a really sharp, hard, strong point and sit down on it!)

Speaking for special occasions: case presentation

Persuasive speaking, getting people to say 'Yes'.

Please engrave this sentence into your mind: Nothing induces agreement

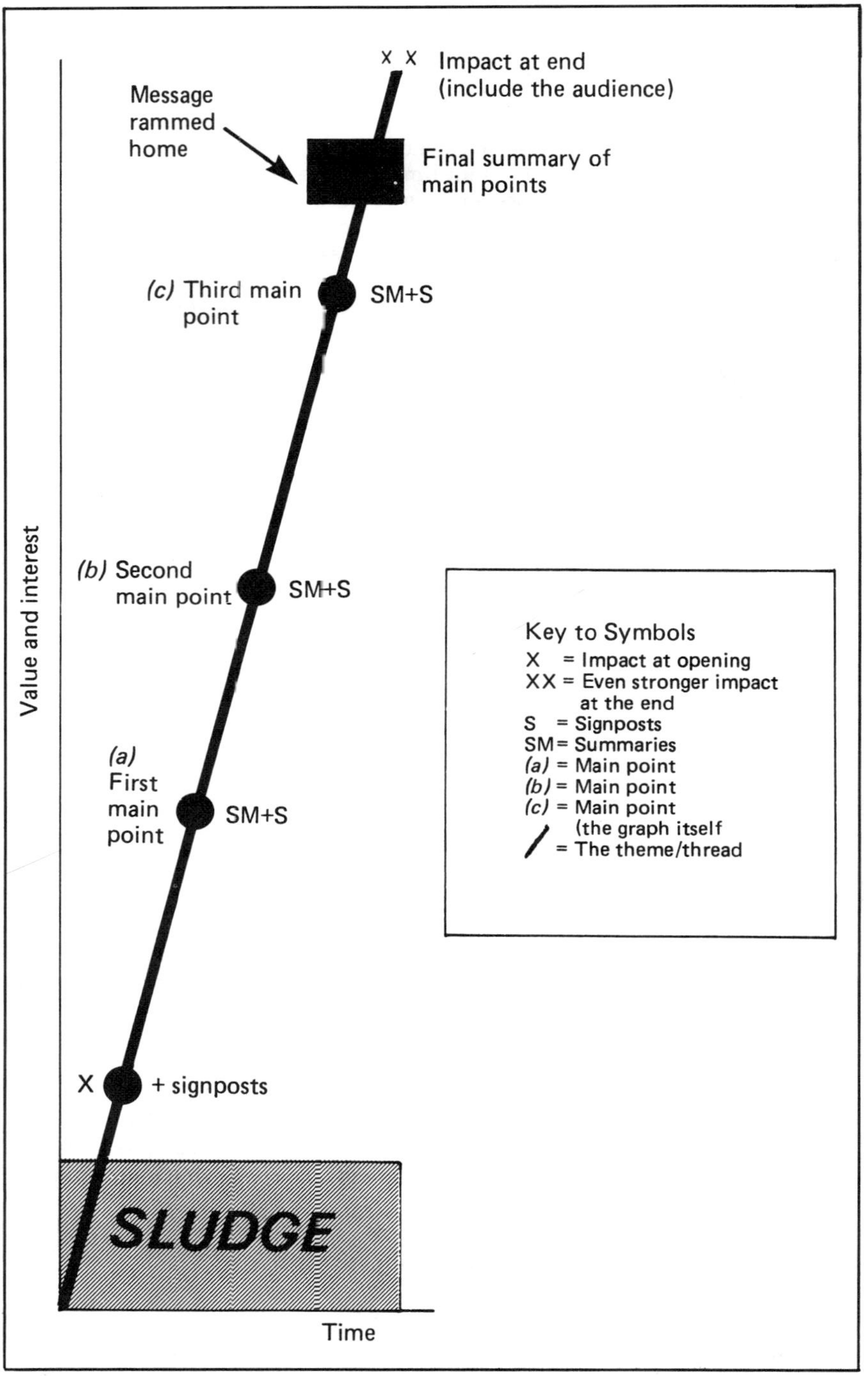

Figure 36.2 Graph of value and interest against time

faster than self-interest – the other fellow's self-interest.

Many business men have to recommend changes that will cost money. In most companies there is a procedure for this. The proposer has first to prepare a document setting out his proposal in detail. This goes through normal channels and may sometimes be agreed to or rejected as it stands. More frequently the proposer will be asked to appear before some board or committee to explain his proposal and to answer questions about it.

The written part of a proposal is a persuasive report and should be written with that in mind. The oral presentation is part speech, part meeting and part interview.

In preparing such a presentation, the proposer should ask himself these questions:

1 Do you know exactly what you want?
2 Do you really believe in your case?
3 Have you got all the facts that support your case and have you checked them?
4 What are the strongest arguments for your case?
5 What are the benefits for your listeners?
6 Why must the present situation be changed?
7 What is their problem?
8 Who else is affected? (Unions, other divisions, etc.)
9 What are the arguments against your plan?
10 What are the alternatives to your plan?
11 Do your benefits clearly outweigh these arguments and alternatives?
12 To whom are you presenting your plan? Have you done any lobbying? Do you need to?
13 Do you know who your probable allies and opponents are?
14 Have you discussed the finances with the experts?
15 Have you prepared hand-outs of any complicated figures?
16 It was a good idea when you first thought of it. Is it still – from their point of view?
17 Have you prepared a really effective presentation? (Time plus the value and interest ratio are particularly important in case presentation.)
18 How will you sum up and end?
19 Are you ready for questions?
20 Have you emphasised the benefits they (your listeners) will gain? Remember: nothing induces agreement faster than self-interest – the other fellow's self-interest.

The board is probably only interested in this question: 'Have they a problem and does your proposal solve it for them?' Ask yourself: 'Will your proposal satisfy their need, their greed, their self-esteem – or all three?'

Social speaking

Social speaking has one simple purpose: to give pleasure. What will make your audience purr? What will cause them to cry 'Hear! Hear!'? What will make them laugh? What will make them proud that they belong to this club, this company, this band of people brought together with a common cause? What sentiment will bring a lump into their throats? What will make them say afterwards 'Oh, I did enjoy that'?

Deliver the answers to these questions and they will be glad that you spoke, especially as you delivered with obvious affection for them, and warm appreciation of their values and you did so without going on and on and on. Work out a good line to end your speech and do not separate it by too long a time from your first-class opening line. Give them pleasure and enjoy the pleasure of their company.

One-to-one talking

An encounter across a desk can often make or break a manager. Failure follows almost inevitably if you present your ideas at the wrong time or if you insist on pushing a proposal from your own point of view.

By all means be relaxed but before you go in to win your point, or before the other fellow calls on you, do your homework. Get your purpose clear, have your facts ready. Know his problems in relation to your suggestion and start the discussion on the basis of his problems. Until you have established his problems and have shown that you understand them and are in sympathy with them, you must not try to sell him anything. You want him to react, to say 'Yes'. He will not react in your favour if your spend your time putting yourself across. Try it the other way round. Put him and his problems in the forefront. If what you have to sell solves his problems, he'll agree.

Some thoughts

Make contact with people. Use you eyes. Look at them. Include them in what you say. This is simply good manners. Take the trouble to prepare properly to ensure that you give them value in exchange for the time they are giving you. Develop a respect, even an affection for your audience. Remember that, however expert you may be, every man and woman there is superior to you in some way and could teach you something.

Speaking is probably the oldest form of human communication. It is certainly the most natural to modern man but, unless other minds can process and use what is said, speaking is just a useless shifting of wind.

There are few things more exhilarating than an audience reacting with interest, excitement and the sheer pleasure of enjoying a first-class speaker. Deserve such a reaction and your world will be that much better for having you around.

REPORT WRITING

John Logie Baird's discovery of the principles of television was useless. Einstein helped nobody with his thinking on relativity nor did Fleming with penicillin until they made their facts and theories known to other people.

Knowledge locked away in the recesses of a single mind has little value until other minds receive the key and gain access to it. Many specialists believe that their work stops when they have uncovered the facts. A question was asked of them. They worked on it, investigated it thoroughly and found the answer. And that, they say, is the end of their job. But is it?

Why do industrial concerns employ scientists, accountants and other specialists? The answer to that question is simple. Industrial concerns employ specialists in order to get from them information, and expert guidance towards profitable action. Yet although specialists study and sweat for 5, 10, 15, 20 years, a lifetime, to equip themselves as experts they rarely study the techniques of passing their hard-gained information to other people. And their readers do the sweating.

A report is a working document that helps the other man to do his job. A record may well form the basis for a report but it is not a report. Samuel Pepys' diary recorded his times, brilliantly, but scholars had to delve to extract the meat. Nobody expects to have to delve into a modern business report; readers expect you to present the meat ready for digestion. A long report is not necessarily better than a short one, if only because fewer people will bother to read it. On the other hand, if you are writing for qualified people who want to know not only the conclusions and recommendations but also the detailed results and the methods used to obtain them, your report must contain such facts in full.

A report is not a detective story. Agatha Christie could take a set of facts and cloak them so skilfully that few readers can get the crucial point until the final page. The facts are all there if only one has the nous to spot them. There should be no mystery about a report. The facts should be clear and the development logical so that the conclusions and recommendations follow them naturally.

There are five main considerations in thinking about reports:

1 Circulation and distribution
2 Physical layout
3 Numerical information
4 Visual aids
5 Language.

Circulation and distribution

All communications are a struggle for other people's interest and attention. The furniture in any busy man's office always includes a yawning wastepaper basket. If you have put this busy man on your circulation list for reasons of self-advertisement or because his name happened to be on a routine list, unedited for years, beware!

Before you begin to shape your report, please take the trouble to sort out the people whom it will help in their jobs. Nobody else should have it.

Many a report suffers from a false start. The managers who asked for it did not bother to discuss with the writer either the purpose of the report or the intended readership. Or the writer just said 'Yes' and ploughed on blindly into a document which did not meet the real requirements. Such a report will fail or at least have to be rewritten. Both the senior man and the writer contributed to the failure and caused the extra labour, the frustration, perhaps the anger ensuing from a job badly done.

So, before you write a syllable, establish who is going to use your report and what they have a right to expect from you. What is the purpose of the report from their point of view.

In many companies, the circulation is tacked on to the completed report as an afterthought. This deplorable custom should be opposed vigorously. Additions to the circulation list should be exceptional; better still, they should have been considered and meshed into the writer's reckoning from the start.

All this does not mean, however, that the facts should be coloured or slanted to affect the truth; no specialist worth his salt would wish to gain a point by distortion or trickery. His credibility would quickly disappear if he did, and rightly so.

Above all, your reader must find your report useful and the facts presented in such a way that he can absorb them easily and accurately. You cannot use suitable language, suitable layout or even select the material properly unless you know whom you are talking to and what he wants from the report. Consider your reader from the beginning. You cannot expect to do this unless you fix the circulation list at the outset. A report looks so forlorn in the wastepaper basket or even put aside – to be read 'later'. Do not plague people with reports they do not require for their own work. People have enough to do. All they want from you is help. Your useful reports will receive a welcome at the right time, at the right place and from the right man.

Physical layout

Your company has probably issued instructions on how its reports should be laid out. Such instructions were not written to while away an idle hour and it is the duty of every report writer to study them. The research department requires for its reports a different approach from the sales or public relations departments. Monsieur Ritz, the hotelier, made a fortune by following the precept 'the customer is always right'. The layout of a report depends almost entirely on how the readers like it. There are no rules, just a few principles. Your reader must be able to find his way about the report. If he is accustomed to a summary on the first page, that is where you put it. If he prefers all the graphs, tables, charts and detailed figures in appendices, put them there.

Reports should look as if they expect a welcome and want to be read. The ninety-third copy from a worn-out duplicator lacks inspiration and deserves neglect. The general appearance of a report must be appropriate to the contents and its purpose.

First appearance

The cover should immediately indicate the type of report that is inside: glossy for the chairman's annual report and other such public relations stuff; perhaps blue for research, green for personnel, or whatever the company's standard practice demands. The title and security classification must, obviously, be prominent before a page is turned.

The busy man's page

The first page must include the date of the report, the title, the author's name and that of the issuing authority and a reference/file number. Some readers also like a short circulation list on the title page – it is often useful to know who else has the report – and a very brief synopsis. This busy man's page should tell the busy man the object of the report and the reason why the work was done. It should give him a well-pruned summary of the investigation, the *main* results, the *main* conclusions and the *main* recommendations for action. He should get the guts of the report in fewer than 200 words, if possible on one page.

Any report longer than six pages should have a table of contents, clearly indicating where readers can find the special bits of the report that are all they intend to read. (Do not flatter yourself that everyone will read the whole of your tome.) Even avid readers will want to know where things are. A table of contents, reflecting a logical layout with clear, expressive headings, immediately creates an impression of order, thought and consideration.

So, you have already given your reader:

A cover that immediately tells him the style, title and security classification of the report.
A title page that tells who wrote it, when it was written, who authorised it and, sometimes, who else has the information.
A synopsis – the main elements of the report in a nutshell.
A table of contents that tells him where he can find all the details he wants.

Many of your readers, especially top management and laymen, will go no further into a report. They have all they need – a general appreciation of your work and enough information for discussion or appropriate action at their level. It is advisable to avoid technical language at this stage.

Your fellow specialists will now wish to dig into the report. They will expect an introduction which informs, or reminds, them of the circumstances which prompted your work. They will want to know how you set about your investigation, what methods, what tests, what equipment you used. They will expect a complete validation of your results and figures and to know what standards of accuracy you worked to. They will expect you to separate facts from opinions. The headlines for the main body of the work could read:

1 Introduction
2 Experimental details
3 Results
4 Discussion
5 Full summary
6 Recommendations
7 Appendices

This format cannot fit all circumstances and must be adjusted to suit the needs of your readers and the purpose of the report.

Please acknowledge the work of other people who have helped you, if only in a bibliography.

Information by numbers

Numbers form the backbone of most reports. Measurements of time, frequencies, distances, etc., are fundamental in presenting facts. Few readers need all the numbers; all readers need the significant numbers and wish them to be displayed significantly. Do not bury them or wall them up behind the background data. When you are planning your report, establish the vital numbers early on so that you can give them due prominence when writing.

Your reader will want to know your tolerances and to what degree of accuracy your figures are presented. Do not bother him with five decimal places if the approximate whole number will suffice for him. The main body of the report will flow more easily if the script is uncluttered by a mass of figures. Many thoughtful writers quote only those figures that make the point and then guide those people who may be interested in greater detail to an appendix which contains more complicated items such as mathematical formulae.

With numbers, significance is all – or nearly all.

Visual aids

If you were a sales director, how would you prefer to have the sales figures from May to October presented – as in (a), (b), (c) or (d) of Figure 36.6?

Sometimes readers would rather see the point than have it related to them. Please consider this.

Language in reports

'Tests showed that the handle gets too hot'

or:

'The results of a period of *ad hoc* experimentation supplemented by both statistical analysis and consideration of empirical factors thought to be universally viable in the context of the areas in which utilisation could be expected to approach a maximum indicated that the thermal conductivity of that portion of the equipment designed for prehensile digital contact was such as to present a surface whose temperatures would markedly exceed the generally accepted threshold of sensory discomfort.' Et cetera, et cetera, et cetera.

Why do so many technicians, trained in logic and precision, write such twaddle? Is it because they are suspicious of the arts, afraid that what they do might lose 'mystique' or is it that they cannot bother to bring logic and precision into their use of language? Many a brilliant young man, on reaching middle age, wonders what went wrong with his career. Let him re-read some of his reports. The answers could be found in them.

We have no space here to discuss grammar and the techniques of clear English, but you should learn a few basic points of control in your writing. You can then leave the rest to your genuine wish to help people to understand you. For instance, most readers will want to recognise, without much effort, two things about each of your sentences:

(*a*) The grammatical subject – whom or what you are talking of
(*b*) What happens – the action.

Let us look at (*a*) first. Concrete words such as 'polecat', 'sewing-machine', 'policeman' give your reader an exact image of what is in your mind. Abstract words and phrases leave room for doubt.

So prefer concrete words as subjects of your sentences.

Now (*b*). Your reader will readily understand the what-happens part of your sentence if you convey the action as simply as you can with power verbs, preferably active. Let us clarify this. Please examine these four sentences:

1 Oil lubricates bearings.
The subject of the sentence, 'oil', is concrete, tangible, clear.
The subject does the deed of the verb so the sentence is active.

(a)

The sales for May were 20 of type 1, 32 of type 2, 38 of type 3; for June, 28 of type 1, 30 of type 2, 36 of type 3; for July, 40 of type 1, 30 of type 2, 28 of type 3; for August, 26 of type 1, 18 of type 2, 28 of type 3; for September, 26 of type 1, 18 of type 2, 30 of type 3; and for October, 44 of type 1, 20 of type 2 and 28 of type 3

(b)

Sales figures for May to September

	Type 1	Type 2	Type 3
May	20	32	38
June	28	30	36
July	40	30	28
August	26	18	28
September	26	18	30
October	44	20	28

Figure 36.3 ***Four ways of displaying a set of numerical results***
This shows how careful thought can result in a more effective display

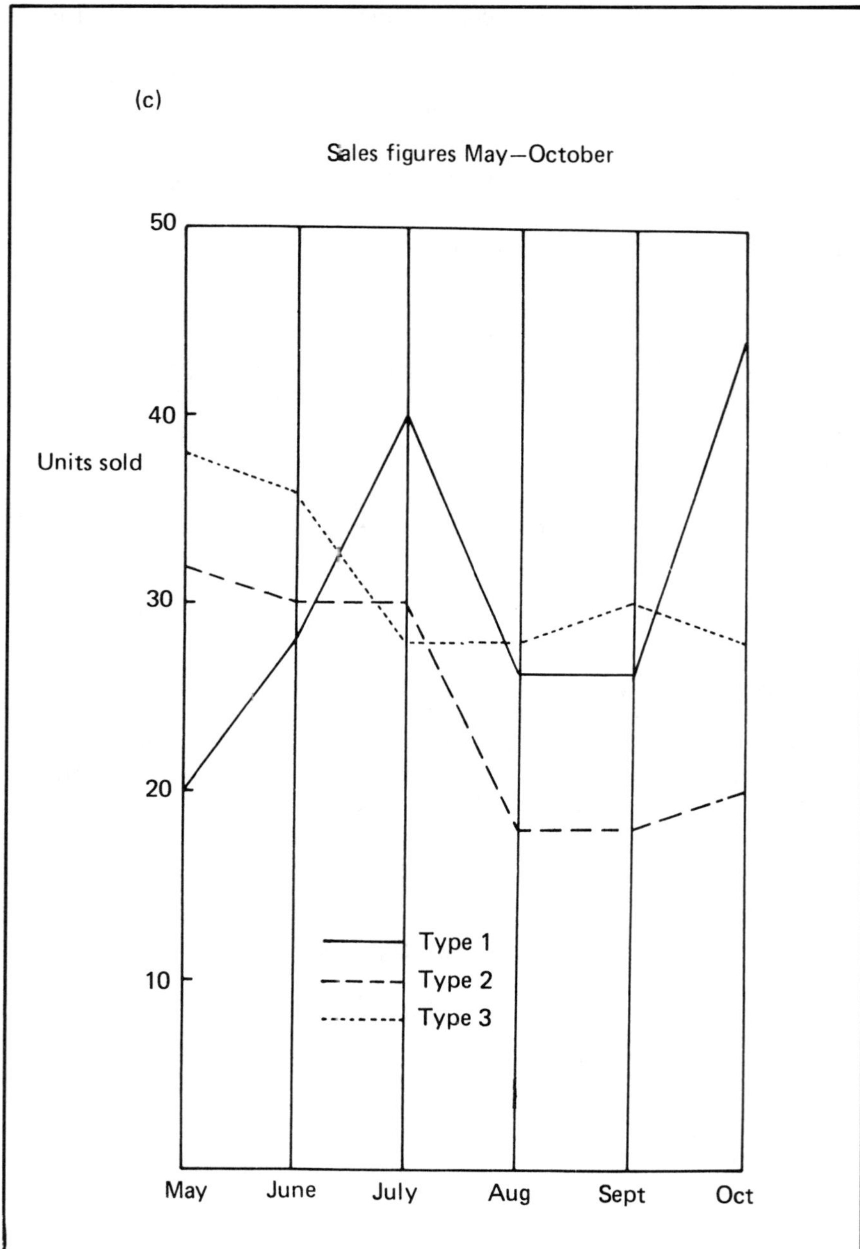

Figure 36.3 (continued)

(d)

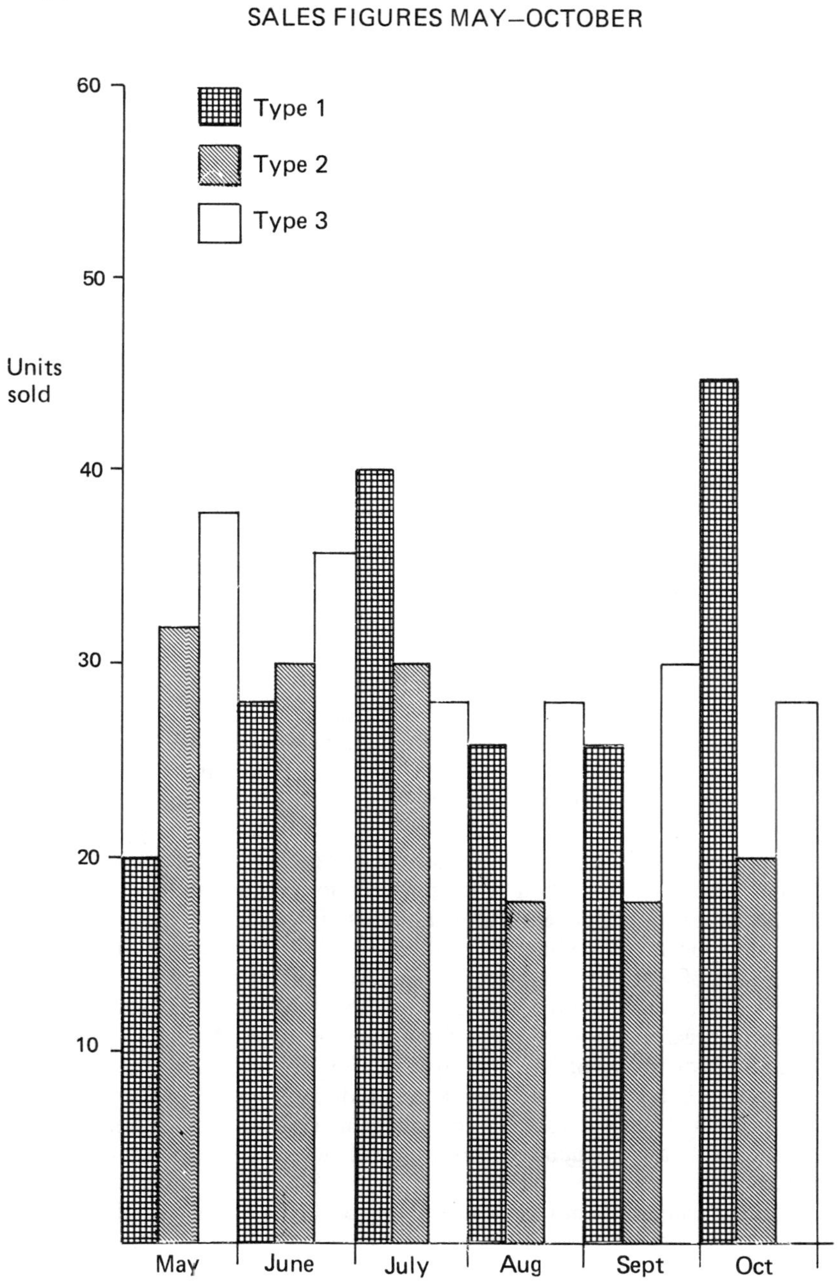

Figure 62.3 (continued)

2 Bearings are lubricated by oil.
The subject, 'bearings', is concrete.
The subject does not do the deed of the verb:
it gets done to, so the sentence is passive.
3 The lubrication of bearings is carried out by the use of oil
The subject, 'lubrication of bearings', is an abstract phrase.
The subject does not do the deed of the verb:
it gets done to, so the sentence is both abstract and passive.

Structure 3 often leads to:
4 In so far as the process of lubrication with respect to bearings is concerned, this is carried out by the use of an application of oil.

Exaggerated as it is, sentence 4 shows the beginnings of the decay that attacks so many specialists from about the age of twenty-eight. In any large organisation roughly one-third of the people over the age of twenty-eight are dead. They have accumulated sufficient cliché phrases and routine attitudes to lean on until their pensions turn up. There seems to be no reason for them to think any more. It is enough just to react according to the rule book and the jargon – 'We are in receipt of your favour of the 19th instant to hand, and it must be pointed out that in view of the fact that . . . ' 'The conceptual philosophy of commonality and standardisation at this point in time could be said to have, perhaps, groundings in feasibility which, with the basic assumption that . . . ' ' . . . the viability of these parameters, shiftwise . . . '. All non-think stuff, torture for the reader and highly dangerous for the writer.

Danger? What danger? We live in a sea of words. What is wrong with drifting along in the fashionable waters, swallowing the stuff and regurgitating it into the faces of our fellows? Why not? It's easier than thinking.

What happens to a muscle that gets no exercise? It becomes flabby. What happens to a machine that lies idle for years? It becomes rusty and useless. What happens to a brain that does nothing but gather verbal cobwebs? Adult thinking is impossible without a language or some other set of symbols that label the elements we develop into thoughts. If words, for instance, are the bricks and mortar with which we build the wall of thought does it not follow that the sort of words we habitually use is the sort of thinker we are? Near-enough words, that'll-do words, other people's tired old clichés provide neither keep-fit exercise nor nourishment for an active mind. A factory girl whose eight-hour day consists of fitting component A into component B and endlessly repeating the dreary process to feed some production line would go mad if she thought about it very much. So she works mechanically and dreams of her boyfriend or being a duchess. But this will not do for expensively trained managers.

Technical language has the advantage of being clearly defined. Used properly, it assists constructive thought and communication among those who understand it. Abused, or flaunted because you want to imply that you are superior to people outside 'the club', it can cause trouble – for you as much as for your victims. The English language provides one of the most precise, subtle, flexible and vigorous aids to clear thought and effective reports. No manager can claim to be more than half-baked if he does not learn how to control it.

Report writing check list

Before drafting a report ask yourself:

1 Have I insisted on a thorough briefing from whoever requested the report and discussed with him in detail: *(a)* that there is a need for the report, *(b)* the exact purpose of the report, *(c)* who is going to read the report, *(d)* the exact scope of the report?
2 Have I collected all the information I may need?
3 Have I selected from this the information the readers need?

When drafting a report, ask yourself:

1 Does the layout comply with any company standard and does it make things easy for the reader?
2 Is there a 'busy man's page' and does it contain the right information for him?
3 Does the report look good and can it be reproduced using the equipment available?
4 Is everybody who 'needs to know' on the circulation list?
5 Have I arranged for library copies and spare copies?
6 Is the circulation too wide?
7 Does the report need a security classification?
8 Have I used sufficient active verbs and concrete nouns?
9 Have I used short sentences and simple construction?
10 Are any technical or scientific words likely to be unknown to the readers?
11 Have I avoided padding and waffle-words?
12 Will the reader easily understand what I have written?
13 Have I avoided slant and bias?
14 Have I clearly stated conclusions and recommendations?
15 Have I used sufficient visual aids?
16 Are the visual aids in the right place, clearly labelled and cross-referenced?
17 Have I shown scales, dimensions and magnifications on my visual aids?
18 Are the tables and charts displayed in the best way?
19 Have I shown the units? Are units consistent and do they comply with British or other accepted standards?
20 Will the visual aids still be clear and easy to follow when reproduced by the available process?
21 Should I invite someone else to read the draft and discuss it with me?

A report is a working document that helps the other man to do his job. A manager who learns to write effective reports adds value to himself and his work.

MEETINGS

Believe it or not, some companies use up more cash at meetings than they spend on the raw materials with which they make their products. Much of this cash goes straight down the drain. Before you dismiss this thought as whimsical, consider the cost of meetings - air and rail fares, cars, hotel bills, salaries and expenses, conference and boardroom rents, rates, cleaning, postage of reports and other documents, typing and more money for many more items. Any large organisation spends millions of pounds each year so that people can discuss, decide and, one hopes, energise some profitable action. The waste is colossal.

Money is important - only a fool would deny that - but much more important is human life. Ineffective meetings not only waste money but they also devalue people's time and shrink the people concerned with them. Human relationships can be soured by bad meetings. A wise man takes the trouble to find out how meetings work and how to make them work for him and his associates.

A definition of business meetings might be 'two or more people getting together for a specific business purpose'.

The meeting itself forms only one link in a chain of events. If the other links lack strength the meeting can become merely the place where the chain breaks. Ninety per cent of an effective meeting happens before the meeting starts. Forging the before-the-meeting link requires thought, horse-sense and skill. If you intend to call a meeting, be completely clear about its intended purpose. What specific business should the meeting achieve? Is it to decide on action, to brief people, to inform, to persuade? What in specific terms - no vague abstractions - is the business purpose of the meeting? You must then face what might be a deflating question: is a meeting necessary at all? Must you deprive people of their time and put the company to expense? Can the business be done - the decision made, for instance - in some other way - a few telephone calls or half a dozen letters? Why are you proposing to call the meeting? Why?

So you decide that your meeting is a necessity; the business cannot be accomplished without a combination of other minds, interest and experience. Which people can provide you with such a combination? Nobody else should be invited. You want to get some business done. Avoid the hangers-on and the strange creatures who go to meetings just to get out of their own offices for a while. If your business is to get a decision and action, beware of the second-string man who cannot give a firm yes or no. He has to report back to his boss. Then there will have to be another meeting for his boss or even his boss's boss. Invite and accept only the people who can do the job properly. Do not forget, as so often happens, to invite the man who will have to take any action you decide upon. If your meeting decides to change the production line you cannot expect joyous co-operation from the production manager who was elsewhere when you decided how to run his department.

When and where the meeting takes place depends on the urgency of the business and the convenience of the people concerned. Be considerate about this. Merely the fact that you operate from Plymouth does not necessarily mean that your Glasgow and Ipswich colleagues will agree that your office is the perfect location. Must you start your meeting at 0900, which means an overnight trip for everyone except you? Timing, the date and the hour, can show you to be a thoughtful organiser.

If your colleagues have to examine reports, plans, figures or must equip themselves in other ways in preparation for the meeting, give them a fair chance to do so. Also make it clear to them precisely what the business of the meeting will be and that you expect them to come prepared. A meeting which has to be recalled because the relevant facts are missing reflects no credit on the convenor or the members. More meetings fail because the preparation has been neglected or skimped than for any other reason. No one should go to a meeting ill-prepared. Even if the meeting happens to be a quick get-together, and at short notice, a few minutes' thought beforehand will increase your value as a meeting-man. At least one man, you, will be able to talk sense.

The businesslike chairman will see to it that he or his secretary arranges a suitable conference room. He will indicate when the meeting is likely to finish; he will arrange breaks for the creature comforts of the conferers, and for telephone messages to be collected, outside the conference room – no interruptions will be allowed except for desperately urgent calls. He will plan an approximate timetable for the agenda so that timeworthy items get their due. Documents and, if required, suitable equipment for presentations must be available. Name cards help people to know who's who; make them bold – and do have them spelled correctly. There are of course a hundred and one other details, any of which might be important. A meeting succeeds in direct ratio to its intelligent preparation.

The formal rules for running meetings become more important when the gathering is a large one. For most business meetings, formal rules matter little. It is the spirit in which people attend the meetings that produces a good or bad meeting.

No real progress can be made without agreement. The object of meetings is to produce agreement. Even if, after disagreement, action results because of fear or force of personality, the action will only be half-hearted and possibly poorly performed. The chairman of a meeting must always be striving for agreement, not surrender.

Preparation for the meeting

The Chairman

Decide whether the meeting is really necessary. (Especially important with routine meetings which often occur even when there is nothing to be discussed or decided.)

Decide on the purpose of the meeting.

Decide on the subject or subjects.

Decide on the place and time.

Decide who is going to attend the meeting. Only those with something to contribute or who need to know exactly what was said and by whom should be present. Other people can get any necessary information from the minutes. The chairman should ensure that those attending are of sufficient standing, that they really represent their departments, and have the authority to commit them to action.

Decide on the agenda and roughly how much time to allow for each item. It is imperative that items are stated in concrete terms. Abstractions will inevitably result in rambling discussion that leads nowhere. One or two simple items first will get the meeting off to a good start. Even if the meeting is summoned hurriedly by telephone, members should be told what they are going to discuss. This is the agenda.

Study the subjects. The chairman must be sufficiently familiar with the subjects being discussed to be able to keep the discussion on the right lines.

Study the people attending. He must know the personal alignments that will help or hinder the meeting; who will not talk even though he has valuable contributions to make, and who will talk even though he has not.

The secretary

Responsible for all the mechanics of the meeting.

Must obtain for the chairman any points for the agenda and names of those attending.

Must obtain suitable accommodation, arrange for paper, etc., arrange for refreshments to be available when the chairman wants them, and arrange to disconnect the telephone.

Must circulate the agenda in good time.

Must prepare all the papers the chairman may require.

Members

Must study the subjects to be discussed and, if necessary, departmental opinions and agreements.

Must study the chairman and his idiosyncrasies.

Must study the other members.

Must work out how they are going to sell their ideas. (Refer back to Speaking for special occasions – case presentation – pages 595–7.)

Conduct of the meeting

The chairman

The meeting must start on time, even if there are absentees. If the chairman is absent the next most suitable person should start it for him. If the speaker on the first point is absent, switch the agenda.

Start briskly, laying down the purpose, the time available, and any other conditions that will help to control the meeting. A chairman cannot demand respect: he can only earn it – usually by giving it to others.

The chairman must watch the time. If he sees that he is getting behind time and wants to extend the meeting he must warn the members early, so that they can make any necessary arrangements or get a move on.

The chairman must keep feeding back to the members the state of the discussion, to ensure that everyone understands the situation. This is particularly important at the end of each item. This will also enable the secretary to take an immediate, accurate record of the decisions reached, who is to take action and by what date, without any risk of error.

The chairman must try to be impartial and only produce his own opinions late in the discussion, if at all. Otherwise he will inhibit proper discussion.

The chairman may have to keep reminding members of the subject and aim in order to keep them to the point.

The chairman must ensure that everyone has the opportunity to express his opinion, at the same time preventing any individual from taking up an excessive amount of time. A member with very strong views that he is determined to express should be given his head, unopposed, the chairman, at least, giving all his attention to what is being said. The chairman should try to extract the relevant points from what may be a confused discourse and ensure that they are properly considered by the meeting.

The chairman must summarise, clarify and emphasise the action arising from the meeting, name specifically who is to be responsible for taking action and record who should do what in precise terms.

The meeting should finish at the stated time unless the members have agreed to go on late.

The chairman and the secretary should leave the room immediately after the meeting is over, otherwise another meeting might ensue.

The members

Disagree without being disagreeable. A member must be clear in his mind what points he wants to get across and do it with the aim of convincing the other members that he is right. At the same time, he should have a sufficiently open mind to be able to change his opinion if someone else produces better arguments or ideas.

Avoid distracting personalities.

The secretary

During the meeting the secretary must take copious notes unless he can be sure that the chairman will provide him with the minutes as the meeting goes along. It is therefore impracticable for a member to act as secretary and do both jobs adequately.

Chairmanship - reminders

Before

Ensure that there is a clear, worthwhile purpose.
Check who will be attending.
Check on the points to be discussed.
Ensure that the secretary has organised everything.

During

Introduce the meeting and purpose.
Define the limits of the subject and time available.
Control the members. Ensure that all have a fair say and none dominate.
Keep the meeting to the point. Be quick to spot when people are wandering.
Feed back. Ensure that everyone is keeping up with discussions and understands the points that are coming out of the discussions.

Summing-up. Make sure that everyone knows the conclusions reached and especially who is to take action. Be impartial. Earn respect.

After the meeting

As quickly as possible after the meeting the secretary should write up the minutes, either for rapid circulation or to go on the files. The minutes should be kept as short as is practicable.

The essential parts of the minutes are the decisions, agreed action and who is to take it and when. These must stand out.

At an appropriate time after the meeting someone, probably the secretary, should check that members are getting on with action they undertook or were instructed to take.

The chairman must have at the front of his mind all the time, and occasionally remind members, that the object of the meeting is to benefit the whole organisation and not any section or individual. He should strive to ensure that profitable action will result from the meeting.

Anybody can talk, anybody can write, anybody can hold a meeting, but only he who can also obtain the desired responses ranks as a good communicator. A computer memory and its processing unit contain great quantities of facts; but the computer is simply a speedy automaton, subject to its program. The human memory and its processing unit contain facts, experiences, feelings, prejudices, social attitudes, business needs, expediency, cussedness, warmth, love, hatred and the breath of God.

Programming a computer to obtain a useful print-out – the response – demands skill and knowledge. How much more demanding is the need for a manager to acquire the knowledge and the skills for better human relationships. At least you can make a start by speaking more effectively, writing reports that help and by making your meetings successful.

FURTHER READING

Eyre, E. C., *Effective Communication Made Simple*, W. H. Allen, London, 1979

Jay, Anthony, *Effective Presentation: the Communication of Ideas by Words and Visual Aids*, Management Publications Ltd., London, 1970

Maude, Barry, *Practical Communication for Managers*, Longman, London, 1974

Wells, Gordon, *How to Communicate*, McGraw-Hill, Maidenhead, 1978

Williams, Beryl, *Communicating Effectively: A Manager's Guide to Getting Through to People*, Thorsons, Wellingborough, 1977

Index

Advertising 141–54
agency relationship 153
and market research 146–7
as marketing activity 143–4
campaign 150–51
concentration 150
domination 150–51
repetition 151
codes of practice 153
defined 143
developing image and subjective values 147–8
ethics 153
evaluation of 138
media planning 152–3
objectives and techniques 144–5, 148–9
strategic framework 151–2
tactics 145–6
unique selling proposition 149–50
Advertising Standards Authority
Code of Advertising Practice Committee 153
Advisory, Conciliation and Arbitration Service (ACAS) 494, 502, 503
Code of Practice 3, *Time Off for Trade Union Duties and Activities* 499–500
Code on information disclosure 500
Agricultural Mortgage Corporation 27
Alexander the Great 4
Allen, Louis 7
Annual accounts 32–51
directors' report 40–42
minimum contents 40–42
example and analysis of imaginary company's accounts 43–8
inflation accounting 48–51
judging company from 42
organisation of information for 42
requirements of Companies Acts 32–5
growth of information required 34–5
standard presentation 35–40
balance sheet 37–40
directors' emoluments 35–6
items requiring disclosure 40
profit and loss account 35, 36
taxation items 37–8
statutory accounts 34
Ansoff, H.I. 8
Aslib 363
Association of Market Survey Organisations (AMSO) 125
Atkin, Bryan 167, 173

Babcock and Wilcox Corporation
strategic planning problems 251
Babylonian Code of Hammurabi 4
Badger, Stephen 17
Baily, Peter 225, 233
Bank of England 18, 30
Barnard, Chester 5
The Functions of the Executive 6

Bass, B. 9
Beer, Stafford 10
Bell, Gordon 588
Bell Telephone Laboratories 276
Bennett, Ted 364
BOC Ltd 175
Bonds
  Eurobonds 25
  foreign-currency 25
Boulton, Watt Co. 4
Bowman, E.H. 258
British Airways
  Concorde trip to World Cup promotion scheme 161
British Computer Society 363
British Institute of Management 363, 489
British Market Research Bureau 125
British Psychological Association 418
British Rail
  and closed shop case 498
British Safety Council 478
British Standards Institution 380
  BS5179 on quality 231
British Telecom 335, 336
  Prestel service 358, 359
Budgetary control 52–68
  benefits 52
  budget centres 53–4
  budget defined 53
  compiling a budget 54–60
    balance sheet 59–60
  capital expenditure 57
    cash budget 59
    operating and service department budgets 57
    personnel budget 56–7
    production budget 55–6
    production costs budget 55
    profit and loss account 58–9
    sales budget 51
  controlling the plan 60–61
    timing of feedback 61
  disadvantages 52
  fixed budgeting 62
  flexible budgets 61–3
  installing the system 64–7
    budget committees 66–7
    budget manual 66
    budget period 65–6
    information codes 67–8
  use of computers 63–4
  zero-base budgeting 64
Building Regulations 1976 473
Bureau of Commercial Research 125
Burns, T. and Stalker, C.M. 13
Business Archives Council 363
Buyers
  factors influencing 182–3
  imperfect knowledge of market 183

Capital 17–18
  managing working, *see* Managing working capital
  structure 30–31
  venture 18
Career planning 548–60
  career transitions 554–5, 557–9
    crucial move 557–8
  effects of primary work shift 555–6
  evolving different skills in 'linear' career progression 557
  identifying 'plus-me' and 'plus-job' 550–54
    'plus-job' 557
    'plus-me' exercise 556–7
  impact of 'middlescence' on career 551
  influence of technological or organisation developments 552
  personal ambition and organisation needs 548, 549
  taking action 559–61
  typical career progression 548, 550
Carew, Tom 504
Ceefax teletext service 358
Central Arbitration Committee 446, 495 500, 501, 502–3
Chivers Jelly
  success of free goldfish promotion 159
Chusid 523
Cigarette cards 160
Cockman & Copeman 523
Collins, Garfield 364
Commission for Racial Equality 502
Commonwealth Development Finance Company 27
Communication, *see* Effective communication
Companies Acts
  accounting requirements 32–5
  of 1948 23, 32, 311

of 1967 32, 41
of 1973 32
of 1976 32, 40, 466
of 1980 32, 312, 315, 316, 321
of 1981 32
Companies House 32
Company law 311–24
capital and shares 314–16
certificate of entitlement to commence business 314
increasing capital and pre-emption rights 315
payment for shares 315
power over unissued shares 315–16
question of serious loss of capital 314
company directors 318–23
credit transactions 322
disclosure of interest in contracts 320
indirect transactions 322–3
loans to 321
moneylending companies and 324
publicity concerning 319
service contract for a director 321
shadow directors and connected persons 319–20
dividends 325–6
formation of public limited company 311–14
articles of association 313
Certificate of Incorporation 312
concept of limited liability 313
memorandum of association 312–13
prospectus 313–14
registration 312–13
insider dealing 324
meetings 318
membership of company 316–18
acquisition and transfer of shares 317
debentures 318
different classes of shares 316–17
rights of shareholder 316
provision for employees 323
Conciliation Act 1896 502
Construction Regulations
General Provisions 1961 473
Health and Welfare 1966 473
Lifting Operations 1961 473
Working Places 1966 473
Cookson, J.L. 492
Corey, E.R.
on procurement strategies 226, 227
Corporations
targets other than profits 174–5
Cost accounting 82–108
absorption costing 87–8, 107
versus direct costing 103–4
checklist 105–6
collection of cost data 86, 106
types of production and 86, 106
marginal costing 98–103, 107
determining total product contribution 101–2
margin of safety 102
value of 103
versus absorption costing 103–4
nature of 82–6, 106
types of cost 82–3
overheads
absorption of 90–92, 93, 107
apportionment 88–90, 93, 107
budgets for 97
fixed and variable rates 94, 96–7, 107
over and under recovery 92–4, 95
reasons for absorbing 97–8
standard costing 104–5, 107
Costs
fixed 176
overhead 176
role in pricing 175–9
absorption cost pricing 176–7, 177–8
variable cost pricing 177, 178–9
variable 176
Council of Engineering Institutions 488
Coutts (Percy) & Co. 521, 523
Crawford, Sir William 150
Cybernetics 10

Daily Star, The
bingo promotion scheme 161
Dalton. G., Thompson, P.H. and Price, R.L.
on career progression 558
Department of Education and Science
Diploma in Management Studies 489
Department of Employment 522, 560
Glossary of Training Terms 402

leaflets on redundancy 518
Race Relations Advisory Service 502
Redundancy Fund 516
Department of Industry 27
Department of Trade 32, 207
Desmond, David 276, 280
Diebold, J. 10
Distribution channels 118, 199–208
agents, brokers and merchants 206
commodity market 205–6
franchising 205
mail order 206
party plan selling 205–6
control of distribution 118–19
exporting 206–7
industrial distribution 207
planning 199–200
retail trades 201–5
cash and carry 203–4
chains 202
co-operative societies 203
department stores 202
discount stores 204
door-to-door selling 204–5
garages 205
hypermarkets 203
independent retailers 201
mobile retailers 204
multiple stores 202
supermarkets 203
van selling 204
voluntary groups 201
wholesaler 200
Drucker, Peter 7

Effective communication 588–612
meetings 608–12
chairman's role 609–10, 610–11
conduct of 610–11
members' role 610, 611
minutes 612
preparation 609–10
reminders for chairman 611–12
secretary's role 610, 611, 612
report writing 598–607
check list 607
circulation and distribution 599–600
first appearance of report 600–601
language 602–3, 606–7
physical layout 600
preliminary pages 601–2
presentation of numbers and measurements 602
visual aids 602, 603–5
speaking 589–98
case presentation 595, 597
graphs of value and interest against time 56
one-to-one 598
preparing effective talk 590–93
social 597–8
style 593–4
Electronics office management, *see* Managing electronic office
Employee relations 492–503
arrangements with trade unions 498–502
collective procedures 498–9
disclosure of information 500–501
picketing 501–2
rights of employee representation 499–500
Code of Practice 499
on picketing 501
state advisory agencies 502–3
trade union recognition 492–8
area of 495
closed shop 496–8
identifying groups to be represented 494
legal position 495
reasons for 493
when to recognise 493–4
Employers Liability, (Compulsory Insurance) Act 1969 474
Employment Act 1980 495, 496, 501, 502
Employment Appeal Tribunal 500
Employment Protection Act 1975 495, 500, 503, 514, 515
Employment Protection (Consolidation) Acts
of 1968 323
of 1978 499, 504
Employment (Trade Union Immunities) Act 1982 497
Equal Opportunities Commission 502
Equal Pay Act 1970 446, 503
Equity Capital for Industry 27
Eurodollars 24
European Convention of Human Rights and Fundamental Freedoms 498

Export Credit Guarantee Department (ECGD) 28–9

Factories Act 1961 468–71, 473–6
Factories (Cleanliness of Walls and Ceilings) Regulations 1960 469
Factory Act 1833 465
Fair Wages Resolution 1946 503
Farmer, Prof. D.H. 227
Fayol, Henri 7
  Administration Industrielle et Génerale 5
  principles of management 5
Fiedler, F. 9
Finance Act
  of 1965 33
Finance for Industry 18, 27
Finance, sources of, *see* Sources of finance
Financial gearing 31, 78–80
Financial Times 423
Fire Precautions Act 1971 467, 474
Firth, Ken 378
Follett, Mary Parker 5
  management research 6
Ford Motor Co. 157
Forty Plus 523
Fraser, J. Munro
  five-point interview assessment plan 418

Gabor, A. 169
  on pricing 175
Gallup Co. 125
George, Patricia 465
Golden Wonder promotion
  related to World Wildlife Fund 162
Good *v.* Elliott Process Automation Ltd 500
Gouldner, A.W. 8

Health and Safety at Work Act 1974 336, 475
Health and Safety Executive 466–7, 476
  Inspectorate's addresses 477–8
Health and Safety (First Aid) Regulations 1981 469, 471, 474
Heinz, H.J.
  presents free badges at Chicago Exposition 159
Heinz (H.J.) Co.
  charity-based promotions 162
Henderson, R.S. 325
Hennig and Jardim
  Managerial Woman 560
Herzberg, F.J. 8
Hobson, Jack 132
Holt, C.C., Modigliani, F., Muth, J. F. and Simon 257
Humphrey, P.T. 399

Independent Assessment and Research Centre 418
Independent Broadcasting Authority 153
Industrial and Commercial Finance Corporation 18
Industrial Arbitration Board 503
Industrial Courts Act 1919 503
Industrial Relations Act 1971 495, 496, 500
Industrial Relations Code of Practice 490
Industrial Society
  'Communication' (*Notes for Managers* series) 457
  Job Evaluation 445
Industrial training 480–91
  administering 482–6
    evaluation of effectiveness 485–6
    identification of needs 484
    implementation of programme 484–5
    integration with other functions 483
    objectives 483
  different categories of employee and 486–90
    administrative 490
    clerical 486–7
    craft apprentices 487
    management 488–9
    operators 486
    shop stewards 490
    supervisory 489–90
    technician 487–8
    technologist 488
  methods 490–91
  need for 480–82
    employee expectation 482

fragmentation of work and 481
new skills and knowledge 481
on the job 481–2
people as resources 480
social purpose 482
Industrial Training Act 1964 480, 482
Industrial tribunals 446, 499, 516–17
Information Industry Association, US 347
Information management, *see* Managing information
Innes, Irene 425, 442
Institute of Cost and Management Accountants
definition of cost centre 54
Institute of Industrial Managers 489
Institute of Information Scientists 348, 363
Institute of Personnel Management 421, 489
Recruitment Code 423–4
Interexec 1023
International Chamber of Commerce
Code of Advertising Practice 153
International Standards Organisation (ISO)
standardisation of pallets 380–81
Interviews 410–20
conducting 412–18
assessment 417–18
closing 415
directed interview 413
giving and receiving information 414
guiding 415
non-directed interview 413
opening 414
probing 413–14
recording 415, 416
'silent' 415–17
defined 410
planes of 411
setting up 412–13
administrative back-up 412
physical setting 412–13
social setting 413

Jackson, Peter 260
Jay, Antony
Management and Machiavelli 7
Jones, C.H. 258

Kelvin, Dr
Advertising and the Human Memory 146
Kodak Corporation 180
Kotler, P. 8

Lawrence, P.R. and Lorsch, J.W. 9
Leaper, Alan R. 52
Lee, W.B. and Khumawala, B.M. 259
Levitt, T. 8
Library Association 363
Likert, Rensis 9
Lupton, T. 8

McClelland, D.C. 8
McDonald, Colin 124
Mace Group 201
Machiavelli 4
Maintenance 289–308
capital project management 303–7
factors adversely affecting efficiency 307
computer-controlled systems 301–2
condition-based 302–3
levels of monitoring 302–3
planning and control 293–301
assets register 292
costing 300–301
downtime analysis 299–300
liaison with user 298–9
maintenance controls 296, 297
maintenance schedules 294–5
manpower allocation 299
manpower resourcing schedule 296
records 296–8
terotechnology 289–93
duties of consultant 306–7, 308
strategies for (existing assets) 291, 293
strategies for (new assets) 291, 292
Management principles 3–14
beginnings of 4–5
'classical' 6, 7
modern 10–13
different forms of management and organisation 12
importance of innovation 11–12

knowledge the key resource 11
motivational role of management 12
organisation as complex system 10
organisation as open system 11
science and art in management 12–13
small is beautiful 12
technical and social sub-systems 11
post-war theory 7–10
pre-war writers on 5–7
recent factors affecting 6–7
'scientific' 4
Management self-development 527–47
achievement objectives as means for 541–3
activity analysis ('fly-on-the-wall') 532–5
action plan stage 535
feedback 434–5
general lessons 535
initial discussion and inception 533–4
observation 534
case study in activity analysis 536–40
format of activity log 536–8, 539–40
questions raised by analysis 538, 540
disclosure and feedback 529, 531–2
need for heirarchical support 532
organisations concerned with 536–7
theory and practice 529
personal growth 529, 530
vehicles for 533–5
Managing electronic office 364–77
combined data processing/word processing/microform techniques (case study) 374–5
combined text and voice communications (case study) 376–7
communications 365–7
all-purpose system 367
telephones 366
telex and facsimile 366
text transmission between word processors 367
document storage and data retrieval 368–9
disks 368, 369
fibre optics technology 370
implementing changes 370–73
collecting information 372
defining objectives 371
developing strategy 372–3
implementing strategy 373
post-implementation review 373
setting project scope 371–2
studying the organisation 371
video-disc storage 369–70
voice storage systems 370
word processing 364–5
productivity improvement from (case study) 373–4
Managing information 339–63
indexing 352–5
'term entry' system 352–4
use of card indexes 352
information and library services 348–57
acquisition of information 349–51
organisation 351–5
publicity and PR for 356–7
utilisation 355–6
information and the organisation 339–41
activities and information needs 340–41
information types 340
information – its acquisition and value 341
information sources 342–4
primary, secondary and tertiary 342, 344
integrated service network 359–60
resource management 344–8
definition of information resource system (IRS) 345–6
implementing IRS 346
managing IRS 346–8
staffing IRS 348
technological aids 357–60
electronic publishing and document delivery 358–9
information retrieval 357–8
storage 359
Managing sales force 209–22
controlling sales operation 220–22
concept of control 220
descriptive standards 221
diagnostic standards 221
setting standards of performance 220–21
taking corrective action 222

variance production and analysis 221–2
motivating sales force 217–20
direct incentives 219
improving status 219–20
incentives and disincentives 217–18
payment by results 218
providing job satisfaction 219
providing security 219
question of remuneration 218
understanding nature of motivation 217
organising sales force 213–14
deciding number of salesmen needed 214
matching sales effort to customer requirements 214
understanding changes in buyer/seller relationships 213–14
planning sales operation 210–14
choosing methods of sale 213
deciding markets 212
deciding what is to be sold 211–12
developing sales plan 211
evaluating cost of selling 213
forecasting sales 211
setting objectives 211
training sales team 315–17
concept of customer orientation 316
field training 316–17
induction training 315–16
sales meetings 317
Managing working capital 69–81
liquidity 69–75
cash discount 74–5
cash flow 75
creditors 73–4
debtors 70, 73–4
stock and 71
profitability 76–81
gearing 79–81
solvency 81
working capital defined 70
Manpower Services Commission, Training Services Division
services 517–18
'TOPS' programme 522
Training within Industry (TWI) courses 486
Mapes, J. 247
March, J.G. and Simon, H.A. 9
Market Research 118, 124–41
advertising and 146–7
analysis, interpretation and use 139–41
defined 124
growth of 125
methods 130–39
consumer sample surveys 133–5
experimental design 137–9
panels 136
qualitative research 139
retail audits 131–3, 136
occasions for 125–7
description of market 126–7
helping company take action 126, 127
monitoring market changes 126, 127
pricing and 185
product testing 137–8
reasons for 128–30
sampling, *see* separate entry
test marketing 138–9
Market Research Society 125
Marketing 188
Marketing overseas, *see* Overseas marketing
Marketing planning 111–23
advertising and 143–4
avoiding bias towards own company 115–16
communicating profit responsibility 121–2
contingency planning 116–17
control of distribution 118–19
definition of total market 117–18
determining company objectives 113
developing plan 115
marketing as investment in company resources 120–21
monitoring plan 119–20
new product development programme 112–13
profit, the first operating expense 114
standards for measuring performance 112
Marketing research 112, 118
Marks, W.R.
Induction – Acclimatising People to Work 421
Marlboro Cigarettes
sales promotion lighter scheme 158–9
Maslow, A.8

Masquerade (novel)
buried jewel promotion 161
Mass Observation 127
Mayo, Elton
research on management 5–6
Mencius 4
Metal Box Co.
pricing policy 170
Minister 523
Mintzberg, H. 9
Moses 4
Mumford, Peter 504

National and Local Government Officers Association (NALGO) 494
National Foundation for Education Research 418
National Institute of Industrial Psychology 418
National Research Development Corporation 27
Negotiating 572–87
choosing approach to 586–7
fighting 582–6
counter-measures 584–6
methods 582–3
pattern of fighting negotiation 583
tactics 583–9
to independent advantage 578–82
bargaining 580–81
bidding 579–80
opening moves 578–9
preparation 582
towards agreement 572–8
creating climate 573
creativity 576–7
exploration 574–6
opening procedure 573–4
preparation 577–8
New, C.C. 247
Nielsen (A.C.) Co. 125
retail audit 131
Nightingale, M.J.H. 19
Noot, Vander 340, 344
Notification of Accidents and Dangerous Occurrences Regulations 476

Occupational Pensions Board 512
Office services 325–38
building maintenance 337
centralisation 337–8
microfilming 332–5
computer output on microfilm (COM) 335
microforms 333–4
quality control and techniques 334
storage and copying 334–5
viewing and printing 335
office layouts 326–9
planning guidelines 329
organisation 325–6, 328
scope 326, 327
structure 326
reprographics 330–32
photocopying 330–31
plan printing 332
printing and duplicating 332
security and safety 336
telephones 335–6
Offices, Shops and Railway Premises Act 1963 468, 471–2, 473, 474, 475
Olympic Games
promotions related to 162
Oracle teletext service 358
Ovaltine Co.
sales promotion LP 158
Overseas marketing
financial considerations 28–9
Owen, Robert 4
Oxenfeldt, A.R.
on pricing 171

Packard, Vance 147
Parkinson, C. Northcote
Parkinson's Law 7
Pennsylvania University
Wharton School 4
Personal organisation 562–72
creating a list 562–4
communications 563
personal planning 563–4
dealing with time constraints 564–8
diary sheets 565, 566, 568
work distribution chart 565, 566, 568
delegation 569
discretionary time 570
improving use of time 570–71
need for 562
reducing time wasted 568–9
listing jobs in importance 569

on checking 568
on supervision 568
reviewing one's function 571
saving subordinates' time 569–70
on crises 570
on waiting around 569–70
Petersen, Christian 155
Philips Premium Pay Plan 452
Pigors, P. and Myers, C.A. 8
Planning for production 247–59
forecasting demand 252–4
make or buy decision 254–5
preparing operating plan 254
aggregate planning 256–8
production management task 247–8
strategic level decisions 248–9
planning and control systems 249
plant location and layout 249
product range and design 248
selection of methods, plant and equipment 248
strategic planning 250–52
organisation and management 252
tactical level decisions 249–50
labour control 250
maintenance 249
production, stock and quality control 249
Plato 4
Republic 4
Polaroid Corporation 180
Price Commission 170
on BOC Ltd 175
on UG Glass Containers' profits 173–4
Pricing 167–98
aids to 184–5
market research 185
models and computer simulations 184–5
devising strategy and tactics 186–91
energy strategies 186–9
penetration strategies 186–8, 190
reviewing strategy 189–90
skimming strategies 186, 190
tactical considerations 190–91
discounts and discounting 191–5
types of discount 191, 192–5
economic theory and 168–9
'breakeven' concept 168–9
concept of elasticity 168
policies and techniques 171–84
competition and pricing 179–81
distribution structure 184
profit targets and other corporate objectives 173–5
question of buyer's attitudes 181–3
'right' price 173, 197
role of costs 175–9, 197
policy defined 170
relation of new product planning to 195–6, 197
relation of product lines to 196
strategy 170–71
tactics 171
Procurement policy 225–32
input management 227–8
materials management 228–30
purchasing and quality assurance 230–32
strategies 226–7
Production control 260–75
computer use 272–4
loading and scheduling 274
materials requirements planning 273–4
differences between company systems 260–61
loading and scheduling work 261–3
data required 262–3
stages 261
loading methods 264–6
control period 265–6
forward and backward 266
job sequence 264–5
management control information 268–9
monitoring and progressing 267–8
aims of 267
long-term solutions 268
urgent jobs 268
paperwork 269–72
advanced warning 271
job paperwork 271, 272
schedules 271
systems 271
works order 270
provisioning 265–6
knitting and pre-allocation 266
make or buy 265–6
quantities 266
Profit 173

Purchasing procedures 233–44
  completion stage 242–4
  contract stage 240–42
  initiation 234–7
    purchase requisitions 235, 236
  small order procedures 242
  supplier selection 237–40
    vendor rating 239–40

Quality control 276–88
  organisation 278–9
    checklist 279
    requirements 279–80
    statistical quality control (SQC) officer 278
  principles 276–7
  quality standard 285
    estimating procedure 285–8
  using control charts 280–82
    number defective chart 282, 283, 284
    simple chart 282–5

Recruitment and selection 399–424
  basic planning and procedure 400–401
  stage one: run up 401–10
    considering internal sources 405–6
    job advertising 406–8
    job information 402–5
    processing applications 408–10
    staff requisitions 402–3
  stage two: employment interview 410–20. *See also* separate entry, Interviews
    administering tests 418–19
    conducting 412–18
    making the appointment after 419–20
    setting up 411–12
  stage three: follow-through 420–22
    following up new employee's progress 421
    introducing new employee to organisation 420–21
    reviewing recruitment process 421–2
Redundancy and redeployment 504–24
  cases of hardship 513
  date of leaving 513
  employment services and agencies 517–18
  giving time off for job hunting 514–15
  industrial tribunals and 515–16
  rebates from Redundancy Fund 516
  redeployment 518–23
    benefits to organisation of sound policy 523
    choice of objectives 519
    company schemes to assist 518–19
    factors in finding new job 521
    fair severance payments 520
    financial arrangements 519–20
    individual needs 519
    job search 522
    other employments 520
    specialist agencies 522–4
    training 520, 522
  redundancy policy 504–15
    avoiding redundancy 507
    compensation 511–12
    consultation 510
    content 505
    general social and company considerations 505
    need for 502–3
    notice of redundancy 510–11
    objectives 506
    pension rights 512–13, 514
    reducing impact of redundancy 507
    re-engagement 515
    selecting workers for redundancy 509–10
    transfers and training 507–8
    types of redundancy 506–7
    voluntary redundancy 508–9
  standard procedures 516–17
Reeves, Rosser 150
Registrar of Companies 32, 40, 311, 312
  form of accounts to be filed with 34, 35
Report by the Working Party on Maintenance Engineering (HMSO) 289
Research Services 125
Rice, A.K. 9
Ridley, W.P. 32
Rodger, A. 418
Rothman's Cigarettes
  promotion linked to Olympic Games 162

Royal Society for the Prevention of Accidents 478

Sadler, Philip 3
Safety Representatives and Safety Committees Regulations 1977 467, 473, 499
Salary management 425–41
  departmental budgets 439
  deciding how much to pay 436, 438
  employee benefits 438–9
  job descriptions 427–9
  job evaluation 429–35
    grading/classification 432–5
    paired comparisons 432, 433, 434
    specimen briefing notes 431–2
  job questionnaire 429–30
  management salaries 439, 441
  performance appraisal 439
  rate for age 438
  salary anomalies 438
  salary bands/grades 435
    salary ranges 435
  salary policy statement (example) 425–7
    communication of 427
  salary reviews 439, 440
  salary surveys 437
  use of graphs 437
    scattergram 437, 438
Sales force management, *see* Managing sales force
Sales promotion 155–66
  bargain-based 156–62
    coupons 157
    price cutting 156–7
    rebate schemes 157–8
    self-liquidating offers 158–9
  charity-linked 161–2
  defined 155–6
  gift-based 159–60
    free item with product 159–60
    free product 159
    trading stamps 160
    use of picture cards 160
  international 165
  media of 162–4
    direct mail 163–4
    field personnel 163
    pack 163
    point-of-sale material 163
    presentation material 164
    telephone 164
  principles behind 156
  prize-based 160–61
  researching and evaluating 165
  special targets 164–5
Sampling 128–30
  clustering 129
  concept of standard error 128–9
  normal distribution 129
  stratification 129, 130
Sanders & Sydney 523
Scanlon/Rucker incentive plans 442, 453–4
'Scientific management' 4
Scott, Bill 572
Sex Discrimination Act 1975 446
Shares 316–17
  See also Sources of finance
Shewart, Dr Walter 276
Shucksmith & Co. 514
Simons, Leon 69
Social Security Acts
  of 1973 510
  of 1975 474
Social Security (Claims and Payments) Regulations 476
Socrates 4
Sources of finance 17–31
  going public 19–20
  long-term, for listed companies 20–25
    convertible and warrant stocks 24
    debentures and loan stocks 23–4
    foreign-currency bond 24–5
    ordinary shares 20, 23
    preference shares 23
  long-term, for unlisted companies 18–19
  methods of issue with listing 25–7
    offer for sale 25
    open offer 26
    placing 26
    rights issue 25–6
    underwriting 26–7
  reasons for capital requirement 17
  supplementing cash flow 27–30
    export finance 28–9
    long-term facilities 27
    medium-term facilities 28
    short-term facilities 29–30
  type of capital required 18

Spillard, Peter
  Sales Promotion – Its Place in Marketing Strategy 154
Stapleton, John 111
Steward, Rosemary 9
Stock Exchange 26
  listing on 19, 317
  United Securities Market 20
  Unlisted Securities Market 19
Stocks, *see* Sources of finance
Storage Equipment Manufacturers Association 387
Sun, The
  bingo promotion scheme 161
Sunday Express 162

Tavistock Institute 9
Taylor, F.W. 4, 8
  Principles of Scientific Management 4–5
Technical Education Council (TEC) 488
Terotechnology 289–93
Thompson (J. Walter) Co. 125
Timex Co.
  success of watch sales in US 126–7
Torrington, Derek P. 480, 492
Townsend, Robert
  Up the Organisation 7, 420
Trade Union and Labour Relations Act (TULRA) 1974 497, 501, 502
Trades Union Congress (TUC) 499
  course for shop stewards 490
  'Job Security' 515
Trist, E.L. *et al* 9

UG Glass Containers Ltd 173
Unilever
  SPD organisation 201
Universal Decimal Classification (UDC) 351
Urwick, Lyndall F. 5, 7
  'classical' principles of management 6
  Elements of Administration, The 6

VG group 201

Wage management 442–64
  added value 455–6
  changing a wage structure 443–5
    age and sex considerations 444
    influence of production method 444–5
    labour turnover 444
    need for attitude survey 444
    overtime 443
    wage analysis 443
    work study 443
  checklist 460–63
  costing wage structure 446
  designing wage structure 447–50
    dealing with anomalies 449–50
    deciding basic rate 449
    number of grades 447–8
  financing wage structure 446–7
  incentive element 450–55
    direct incentives 450–57
    group/departmental incentives 452–3
    measured daywork 451–2
    merit-rating 454–5
    plantwide incentives 453–4
    profit-sharing 454
  job evaluation 445
  legislation affecting 445–6
  management style 442
  need for good communication 457
  productivity agreements 456
  single status 456–7
  supervisory structure 457
  wage policy statement (example) 457–60
Walker, C.R. and Guest, R.H. 8
Warehouse operation and management 378–96
  load unitisation 379–81
    pallets 381
    stacking cartons on pallets 379, 380
  minimising movement 389–94
    batching orders 390–92
    goods-to-picker techniques 393–4
    order pickers' 390
    randomisation of order-picking locations 393
    zoning 392
  modern loading bay 395
  modern warehousing 378–9
    fork-lift truck 378, 379
  paperwork reduction 393
  receiving and dispatch 394–5

utilisation of warehouse cube 382–9
high-bay pallet silos 387–9
pallet block storage 382–6
palletised random access storage 387, 388
Weiner, Norbert 10
Welsh, A.N. 562
Western Electric Co.
Mayo's studies at Hawthorne Works of 6
Wheatley, Jack 199
White, E.N. 289
White, M. and E., Consultants Ltd
Computerised Management in the Maintenance Department 302
Whitney, Eli 6
Wiggins, R.E. 339
Williams, Michael 527, 548
Wilson, A.
on pricing 171, 175, 190–91
Wilson, M.T. 209
Wilson, R.M.S. 82
Woodward, Joan 9
Working conditions 465–79
codes of practice 473–4
employers' liability 474
Factories Act 1961 468–71, 473–6
matters legislated for 469–71
premises covered by 468–9
Fire Precautions Act 1971 474
Health and Safety at Work Act 1974 465–8, 475
basic obligations of employees 466
basic obligations of employers 465–6
Commission, Executive and Inspectorate 466–7, 476, 477
disclosure of information under 467
Employment Medical Advisory Service 467
enforcement 467–8
notices
to be posted 474–5
to be sent to factory inspector or other authority 475–6
Offices, Shops and Railway Premises Act 1963 471–2, 474
scope 472
registers to be kept 476–7
accident book 476
general factory 476
health 476–7
hours worked by young persons 477
overtime 477
regulations concerning 472–3
building 473
canteens 473
safety 473
World Wildlife Fund 162

Xerox Corporation 180

Young, Douglas Deakin 523